GOOD  HOUSEKEEPING

# Cookbook for Calorie Watchers

GOOD HOUSEKEEPING

# Cookbook for
# Calorie Watchers

## Plus Recipes for 7 Special Diets

BY HAZEL P. SCHOENBERG

Good Housekeeping    New York

*to Dorothy Marsh, who lovingly taught me the GH way*

GOOD HOUSEKEEPING BOOKS

Editor MINA WHITE MULVEY
Art Director WILLIAM LEFT
Art Consultant JOHN ENGLISH
Senior Editor PATRICIA DEMPSEY
Copy Editor JUANITA G. CHAUDHRY
Assistant to Art Director LYNN THOMPSON

*FOR* GOOD HOUSEKEEPING MAGAZINE

Editor WADE H. NICHOLS
Executive Editor JOHN B. DANBY
Managing Editor BENSON SRERE
Art Director BERNARD SPRINGSTEEL
Director, The Institute WILLIE MAE ROGERS

Photographs by James Viles

# CONTENTS

# How to Use
# This Book

This cookbook for calorie watchers has been planned
to answer your very special needs. It will, first of all,
enable you to eat your favorite foods, yet still lose
weight. It offers you a wide choice of diet plans and
tells you how to choose the one that is right for you.

But since we are well aware of your additional responsibilities as
a wife and mother, this book also shows you how to plan appetizing, nutritious meals for the whole family while still keeping
to your own slimming program. And as another bonus, it teaches
you how to cope with any of a number of special diets that may
have been prescribed, for medical reasons, for a family member.

No single reducing diet is right for everyone. But all good diets
do have a common theme. They produce weight loss at a safe,
moderate pace. They offer variety, so that the pleasures of eating
aren't sacrificed. And they teach new eating habits that keep you
from falling back into weight-gaining patterns once your goal is
obtained.

Nutritional safety is all-important for a good diet program. The
weight loss a crash diet produces may be paid for with a long-
term loss of health. Always get your doctor's approval before
beginning a diet with the object of losing more than ten pounds.
Taking into account your health, age, weight and normal activity, he will recommend the proper calorie level to be main-
tained. Usually this works out to around 1200 calories for a
woman, 1800 for a man—about two-thirds the intake of nondieters.
At this level, most people lose at the rate of one to two pounds a
week.

They lose, that is, if they stay on their diet. The trouble is that
many diets, including the fad variety, are so monotonous that it
takes a saint to stick to them. There is nothing more boring than
a diet that is limited to only a few foods—one, for example, that
forbids you bread for a sandwich or catchup for a hamburger.
That may seem extreme, but these and similar restrictions are a
common feature of many fad diets.

In contrast, the diets in this book all include foods from each
of the Basic-Four food groups essential for good health, and the
recipes—over 600 of them—provide such a variety of taste-pleasing

dishes that there will be little temptation to indulge in calorie-laden substitutes. All the recipes are the product of the Good Housekeeping Institute's kitchens, and have been evaluated for flavor, appearance and reliability. Then, for each, the caloric content has been calculated.

To make matters simple for the cook who must provide for a family member's special needs, at the end of each recipe, instructions for adapting it to fit the most important therapeutic diets are given, wherever possible. In addition, beginning on page 242, general information and 173 more recipes are provided for these special diets.

Diet plans and recipes are not all that is needed for successful weight reduction. Psychological factors are important too, as is a basic understanding of what is involved in losing weight. In this book you will find the fruit of Good Housekeeping's long experience in answering the questions of those with weight problems and in providing them with the necessary support to undertake a successful weight-reduction program. Exercises to help use up calories and to tighten too-long-relaxed muscles provide additional help toward a more shapely future. Finally, the Appendix includes a complete calorie chart, as well as charts showing the iron, sodium, protein, fat and carbohydrate content of a number of selected foods.

# A Doctor Talks Sense About Diet

BY DR. WALTER E. O'DONNELL

A well-known specialist in internal medicine, Dr. O'Donnell has helped thousands of women shed extra pounds, to the benefit of both their health and their looks. Drawing on his sympathetic understanding of their problems, he puts the problem of losing weight into a humane and sensible perspective.

Almost everybody agrees that being fat is bad for you. Fat people generally don't live as long as those of normal weight, and they look, feel and act older than their years in the meantime. Let's say you're in your twenties, thirties, or forties—younger women usually haven't begun to care, older ones have given up. You're in the doctor's office for a "checkup" because you always feel tired. Or you want to start on a weight-reduction program. So now settle back and lend an ear as we take it step by step.

*Step One: Let's get a few things straight*

*You Can Lose.* Most would-be weight losers are licked before they start—consciously or not, they are willing to go through the motions of a weight-reduction program, but mostly to prove the futility of the whole thing ("At least I tried."). Psychologically or emotionally, maybe some people *won't* lose. But that's a different thing.

*Calories Do Count.* It's really very simple, a matter of a person's intake versus output. If the number of calories you take in averages more than the number of calories your body uses, you will gain weight. If calories-in average less than calories-out, you will lose weight. If there is a balance between need and expenditure, your weight will remain unchanged. Nothing very complicated about that, but many patients refuse to accept it.

*There's No Quick Way.* There's no lack of "crash diets" or two-week tickets to a "slender, youthful figure." But if you are lugging around twenty to forty extra pounds, you'd better count on having to stick to the strict part of your diet for two to six months. Then you must find your ideal calorie intake and settle down for the long haul.

*There's No Easy Way.* There's no way to "sugarcoat" an effective diet. It's strong medicine, and there's no sense in denying it. "Take pounds off the easy way" is an invitation to frustration and failure.

*There's No New Way.* So-called "revolutionary" diets, exciting "research breakthroughs" and weight loss programs "based on an entirely new principle" are nonsensical come-ons.

*Dieting Is Not a Part-Time Thing.* It's not something you can set aside on birthdays or holidays or when you go out to eat. It's a full-time, twenty-four-hours-a-day, seven-days-a-week thing. Sorry to sound so uncompromising, but you *do* want to lose, don't you?

*All Men (and Women) Are Not Created Equal—Biologically, That Is.* "Well, if it's calories like you say, how about my friend Gladys. She can eat *anything* and *everything*, and she's as skinny as a rail!" exclaims a patient defiantly. You might as well face the fact now—if you haven't already—that there *are* people like that. It isn't fair, I suppose, and we don't understand why it should be so. But it is. Just don't use it as a reason why *you* can't lose weight. Losing may be harder for you, but you can do it.

*No Pill or Shot Will Take Off Weight.* People usually ask me, "What can I *take* to lose weight?" (They seldom say "What can I *do?*") I always tell them bluntly, "There's no medication that will take an ounce of flesh off you. There *are* pills and capsules that will help you control your appetite and combat the 'all-gone' feeling that goes with dieting. But that's all they can do."

*It's Up to You.* Friends can kid you, families can urge you and doctors can advise and help you—but in the final analysis it's up to you. Dieting is a lonely business and that's only one reason why so few stick to it. Let's move on to Step Two.

---

# Step Two:
# Now answer
# a few questions

## What Did You Weigh When You Got Married?

This question usually brings color to the cheeks of women and embarrassed smiles to the faces of men. It reminds them that they weren't born fat, and it often provides some kind of mark to shoot at. (See page 321 for height-weight charts.)

## What Does Your Family Look Like?

Patients leap at this question because it seems to provide an out. "Oh, weight runs in my family," they exclaim excitedly. "My father weighs two hundred and thirty pounds, and my mother— And you should see my sisters!" I admit that the family glands *could* be the cause of all this avoirdupois. But I point out that the more likely cause is the family appetite—seconds on desserts also "run in families."

## What Do You Look Like?

This calls for a degree of candor and self-inspection that many women can't muster. Go look in a full-length mirror. I don't know of any more effective instrument of motivation. Especially if you undress and coldly appraise yourself, front, side *and* rear. Next step: Look at some old pictures of yourself taken in your thin days. I would say compare these with some recent photos, but if you run true to form there isn't a single post-inflation picture of you (especially a full-length one) in the house. Right? Then get a snapshot taken for comparison sake.

## Why Do You Eat So Much?

This is, of course, a loaded question, the sort of when-did-you-stop-beating-your-wife query which provokes patients into spasms of self-righteous denial. They launch into a pitiful description of the few non-caloric morsels which made up their breakfast. They forget or don't mention the fact that weight-conscious people invariably starve themselves during the day or two before their doctor's appointment. Also passed over is the fact that very few obese people ever eat any breakfast to speak of.

When they see my face, they may retreat a bit. "Well," they say brightly—and hopefully—"I guess it's not that I eat so much. I just eat the wrong things." This is progress on two counts: They have admitted the fact that it's eating that has made them fat, and they have accepted the idea of calorie counting.

## What Are Your Eating Habits?

Most overweight patients eat little or no breakfast. It's a point of pride with them and usually the jumping-off place for their tale of mystification as to why the scales are groaning under their weight. They lose sight of the fact that the no-breakfast ritual merely sets the stage for all-day nibbling or, when coupled with a skimpy lunch, a really ravenous assault on a calorie-laden evening meal.

For most women the calorie crisis begins about midmorning. The older children have been packed off to school. Hubby has made his dash for the train or the highway. The baby has been put down for a nap. The stimulation of meeting deadlines wears off. Now the eating begins in earnest. Then comes lunch or "Just a sandwich," not mentioning the milk shake and dessert, either one of which may contain as many (or more) calories as the sandwich. Then there's a pick-me-up in midafternoon ("something to give me a little energy—I get so tired"). The pattern has infinite variations. One woman loves to cook, and, in the course of practicing her art, tastes everything. It's so automatic she hardly knows she's doing it—but her waistline shows it. A young mother eats "a little something with the kids" at five or six o'clock and then, in effect, has a second meal with her commuter husband at 7 P.M. "just to keep him company." But the time when calorie consumption per minute per overweight individual appears to reach its peak is between 7 and 11 P.M.—prime TV (and snack) time.

## Why Do You Want To Lose Weight?

Would-be weight losers have usually been overweight for months or years. Why the big push to lose just now? The answers are always interesting and often provide an index of how successful the dieter is likely to be. A tubby woman in her forties comes

steaming into the office. It seems she was at a party the night before and was mistaken for her husband's mother! Or was introduced through an error as Mrs. Hempstead —"who's sixty if she's a day." Class reunions also have a remarkable effect in resurrecting lost will power. A woman may shrug off her children's remarks, smile away her husband's reproaches and rationalize her own excuses. But when it comes to facing a jury of her peers who will coldly appraise "how Mary looks" five, ten or twenty years since graduation, that's a different story. It can make a girl lie awake nights—even lose her appetite!

## Do You Really Want To Lose Weight?

When I ask patients this question, they exclaim, "What? Why of course I do! Would I be here if I didn't?" Then I confront them with the hard question: How badly do they want to lose? Badly enough to face weeks, even months, of self-denial and self-discipline? Badly enough to be merely merry while all the others are eating and drinking too? Badly enough to endure those lonely seesaw battles in which you're sure *nothing* is so important as having that cake or candy? If you can't answer yes, better turn back now. Otherwise, you won't lose weight, but you will gain a guilt complex.

---

## Step Three: Next go see your doctor

Many overweight people skip this step. Of course, it *is* possible to lose weight without your doctor's supervision. Nevertheless, consulting a doctor is still a good idea. Even more important from my point of view, it's a test of your sincerity. If you're willing to spend the time, trouble and money, your chances of success already take a leap forward.

*The Checkup.* A basic medical examination is the same for the obese patient as for anyone else. It includes a good history of the patient's family background and health, a thorough physical examination and a few laboratory tests. The special questions the doctor asks himself in the case of the obese patient are: (1) Is this the usual story of too many calories? Or is this one of those rare cases in which there are glandular or other factors at work? (2) Is it safe to prescribe appetite-suppressing drugs or other medication to this patient? Or does the presence of coronary disease, etc., make this hazardous? (3) Are there any special precautions which should be observed in the diet prescribed or the rate at which this patient is encouraged to lose? For example, does she have diabetes or other problems which might make unduly restrictive diets or too-rapid loss unwise?

*Diets.* Don't expect any magic diets. There aren't any. It's calories that count—remember? My main reliance is on reeducating the patient through the use of the calorie diary. More about this shortly.

*Drugs.* Most physicians will give pills to curb the appetite or calm the nerves of would-be weight losers. But that's all. In truth, there's nothing else to give. The most potent agents must be supplied by the patient—motivation, willpower, determination.

*Follow-up.* Better than anyone else, the physician can play the dual role of benevolent enforcer and objective observer. He will feel free to say things that nobody else would dare to, and is unlikely to be taken in by implausible self-justifications. My advice is: Go see your doctor at not longer than two-week intervals.

## Step Four: Now the diet

I have one not-too-successful weight loser who paraphrases Mark Twain's comment on smoking: "Oh, going on a diet is easy; I've done it hundreds of times." And so it is. It's sticking to the diet that's hard.

*Take the Long View.* Once you've made your decision, stick to it. Don't redecide at every encounter with food or drink. If you do, there's bound to be at least one time when your willpower will be at low ebb. Result: A decision in favor of "just-this-once-won't-hurt." That first exception to the rule makes every subsequent one just that much easier, and pretty soon your diet will be a memory.

*Keep a Calorie Diary.* Now comes the most fascinating insight into the psychology of overweight people. At the doctor's—or anybody else's—merest hint, they will buy and take twenty-five dollars' worth of pills weekly, lay out hundreds of dollars for an exercise machine, struggle through hours of complicated gymnastics in solitary misery or in classes, and travel all over in search of dietetic foods. But will they keep a calorie diary? Something that costs them almost nothing, takes only a few minutes a day—and practically ensures the success of their diet? No.

"It's very simple," I say. "All it takes is a little book with calorie values, a notebook and a pencil—and about five minutes of your time each day. Remember, I'm going to ask to see it next time." Two weeks later I ask for the calorie diary—and get only excuses. Patients, I find, don't like to be their own policemen. Keeping a calorie diary reduces a weight-program to cold hard figures that make it almost impossible to deceive oneself. But faithfully keeping a calorie diary increases a patient's chances of losing weight about tenfold, in my experience. (Use the calorie guide on pages 325–341 to make counting easier.)

## How Many Calories?

There is no precise answer to this question because people vary in their ability to tolerate diets. Assuming the dieter is basically healthy and will remain under medical supervision, it really comes down to this: Should she try to lose fast or slowly?

Ideally, a slow, deliberate approach is best. Those who lose pounds this way are more likely to keep them off. Realistically, people are people and they want to see results or they'll soon quit. Most of my patients therefore go on an 800-calorie-per-day program.*

---

* Dr. O'Donnell keeps close tabs on his patients. For dieters not under medical supervision, the Good Housekeeping Bureau recommends a minimum of 1200 calories per day.—ED.

I let them make up that total out of almost anything, within reason, they want. If they follow orders and keep a diary, I get a chance to see what they are eating and can put a diet back in balance if it gets too wild.

I aim for a loss of about two pounds per week or a little less than ten pounds per calendar month. Motivation stays pretty well nourished at this rate of loss, I find.

At this point many a despairing patient wails, "You mean I've got to eat like *this* for the rest of my life! It's not worth it!" Which brings us to the distinction between a *weight-losing* diet and a *weight-mainte-nance* diet. I hasten to emphasize the fact that the beginning dieter is getting less food than she really needs so that she will lose weight. As soon as she has gotten down to a good figure, she can gradually increase her calorie allowance to a no gain, no-loss level. This is obviously considerably above the skimpy rations of her diet.

### Exercise?

I have nothing against exercise, but it's hard to imagine a more inefficient way to lose weight. But as a means of streamlining and redistributing body tissue after weight loss or as a means of diversion (to keep you away from the table), exercise is great. (See pages 54–64.)

*Eating Techniques.* Sometimes a poor loser with a long string of diet flops in the past will finally succeed because somebody thought to emphasize such reminders as: Eat slowly and savor each bite; chew your food well; don't eat while nervous or tense; divide your daily allowance into small frequent meals; after eating, get up from the table immediately and busy yourself doing something; line up projects to do and places to go in the evening so you won't just salivate in front of the television set; and, of course, don't keep *any* snack items in the house (for more suggestions, see page 34).

*Gimmicks.* Many a diet has been snatched from oblivion by the use of an imaginative gimmick. One rotund housewife had copies made of her most embarrassing photograph and posted these on her kitchen cabinets and on the refrigerator door—as a stern re-minder of what she is fighting for. A bet that will cost her dearly (or pay off hand-somely) is the way another dieter kept her-self honest. And, of course, one of the time-honored ways to lick any problem is to or-ganize; get together a group of fellow weight watchers in a sort of personal anti-calorie crusade. Like Alcoholics Anony-mous and similar emotionally linked groups, such an approach can be very effective. Whether organized formally in the manner of TOPS (Take Off Pounds Safely) or Weight Watchers, Inc., or loosely as an off-shoot of the bridge or bowling club, it ex-ploits the in-union-there-is-strength (and willpower) and misery-loves-company streak present in all of us.

---

## Step Five:
## Don't kid yourself

I've already mentioned this business of kid-ding yourself—or rationalization, to put it on a loftier plane. Underlying it is the very human desire to find a face-saving way to get out of doing what we know we should do. It's probably overstating the case to say that weight losers harbor a subconscious desire to fail. Most simply want to be exempted from having to try. There are infinite variations on the theme, but here are a few of the ones I hear over and over.
• "I gave up smoking and I just couldn't control my appetite."
• "We were invited out and I just couldn't hurt Mary's feelings by refusing food."
• "We went on vacation and there wasn't much to do but eat and sleep."
• "I got sick and you know you have to keep your strength up."
• "I lost twenty pounds and nobody even noticed it. It's not worth it."

The examples could go on and on. They all have three things in common: They are all partially true; they all could be resolved with just a little foresight or willpower; and they are all substitutes for the real reason for failure.

Now you know my recommended five steps toward becoming a good loser. Will you let them work for you?

# Choosing a Diet

There are good diets, bad diets and diets so disastrous that if followed for any length of time they can ruin your health and destroy your looks. To choose a diet that's right for you, you should have an understanding of the rules of good nutrition, as well as insight into your own emotional makeup.

Despite efforts by the country's leading nutritionists to demonstrate both the folly and hazards of fad diets, their popularity continues to grow. An estimated one out of three Americans are overweight to some degree, and nearly all, at one time or another, have tried to lose excess pounds by following "miracle" reducing plans.

Although miracle diets differ in the kinds and amounts of food recommended, they have one thing in common which endears them to weight-conscious Americans: they all promise a swift, easy, painless method of weight reduction.

If followed according to directions, fad diets often work—that is, they do result in weight loss. But the loss is hardly ever permanent, because the diets seldom provide directions for maintaining it through good eating habits. Within a few months the weight is regained and the dieter is not a bit better off than when he started.

## THE FOLLY OF FAD DIETS

A more serious drawback to fad diets is that they can be dangerous to health, particularly if followed for too long a period. Leading nutritionists agree that there is no way to take off excess pounds safely and keep them off except by counting calories—and by following the basic rules of good nutrition. This, of course, requires discipline, strong motivation and temporary discomfort.

Calorically, foods are divided into three categories: protein, carbohydrate and fat. Along with minerals, vitamins and water, these make up the nutrients essential for proper functioning of the body. Between 40 and 45 percent of the calories in the normal American diet come from fats, the same from carbohydrates. The remainder—10 to 20 percent—are derived from protein sources. These ratios vary from individual to individual and from day to day. Fats and carbohydrates can occasionally be as low as 30 percent or as high as 65 percent without damaging a person's health.

---

But fad diets, by their nature, are consistently out of nutritional balance. By far the most common type is the diet that is high in protein and low in carbohydrate. If it emphasizes meat, as most do, then it is also high in fat. Normally, carbohydrates supply half of the body's energy needs. The general theory behind a diet that restricts foods with a high carbohydrate content, primarily sugar and starches, without reducing the total number of calories, is that the body will be forced to use its own adipose (fatty) tissue for energy. Initial weight reduction on these high-protein regimes is due to a loss of water. If the diet is continued, any subsequent loss is probably due to decreased caloric intake, because the dieter gets bored with so limited a choice of food and stops eating as much. Even filet mignon, day after day, becomes monotonous.

There are also medical objections to a high-protein, low-carbohydrate diet, particularly if followed for any length of time. For one thing, protein foods must be broken down by the kidneys before they are excreted. When more protein is eaten than is normally required, the overloading puts an extra strain on the kidneys.

The liver also has to do more work. Glucose, a common blood sugar needed for brain and muscle functions, is obtained from carbohydrates. When carbohydrate intake is restricted, certain body tissues (primarily the liver) have to work overtime to manufacture it from protein.

A lack of carbohydrate can lead to a condition called ketosis, since carbohydrate is needed for fat to be oxidized (burnt up). The absence of sufficient carbohydrates leads to the buildup of ketones (compounds formed by the oxidation process). In ketosis the dieter's metabolism begins to resemble that of a diabetic. In essence, sugar is not metabolized properly.

Perhaps the most immediate danger to health from high-protein diets, however, is the increase in blood cholesterol which may result from eating too much animal fat in meat. Many researchers believe that arteriosclerosis, a thickening of the arterial walls which can lead to heart attacks, is associated with a rise in the blood's cholesterol level. Many physicians emphasize that, even in a normal diet, half the total fat intake should come from vegetable sources.

The five diets that follow are all high in protein, low in carbohydrates. All have attracted avid followers during the past decade.

Yet all are nutritionally unsound, particularly for people with existing kidney or heart disease or liver trouble.

| | |
|---|---|
| *The Doctor's Quick Weight-Loss Diet* | This is commonly called the Stillman Diet after its creator, Dr. Irwin Maxwell Stillman, a Brooklyn, N.Y., internist. Dr. Stillman has also advocated a low-protein diet, but his original diet consisted primarily of lean meats, poultry, fish, seafood, eggs, skimmed milk, cheese—all you can eat—and eight glasses of water a day. With no discernible source of carbohydrate, this diet could be dangerous for a person in poor health. |
| *Calories Don't Count* | This is an example of a fad diet that not only didn't work, but which resulted in a successful Federal court action against its originator, Dr. Herman Taller, a New York City obstetrician. Published in 1960, this high-protein, high-fat diet featured unlimited quantities of meat (including such high fat items as bacon and sausage), poultry and fish. The plan eliminated sugars and starches. Only vegetables containing minute amounts of carbohydrates were recommended. Dr. Taller stipulated that the dieter also take one safflower-oil capsule daily because he claimed "unsaturated fats . . . soften your body fat and help it out of your system." Taller was convicted in 1967 of mail fraud and violation of the Food, Drug and Cosmetic Act. |
| *The Air Force Diet* | Also called the Fat Pilots Diet, this variation of the eat-all-the-protein-you-want approach has no connection with the U.S. Air Force. It is also called the Low-Carbohydrate Diet because the main rule is restricting carbohydrate intake to 60 grams per day. A normal diet contains 300 to 400 grams. The Food and Nutrition Board of the National Academy of Sciences–National Research Council (NASNRC) suggests that the minimum daily requirement for an adult is 100 grams. The basic ingredients of the Air Force Diet are meat and poultry with moderate amounts of vegetables, cheese and eggs. Fish is to be eaten sparingly. The promised weight loss is seven to fourteen pounds a month. |
| *The Mayo Diet* | This high-protein plan has been circulated on a person-to-person basis for many years. It has never had any connection with the famed clinic in Rochester, Minn. Basically, it is a combination of eggs, grapefruit and meat with a few vegetables and fruits. It specifies the dieter eat only what is assigned for each meal with no snacking in between. The diet promises a quick weight loss of 20 pounds if followed for two weeks, but cautions the dieter not to continue longer than that. |
| *The Drinking Man's Diet* | Although the Drinking Man's Diet is basically the very same one that Dr. Taller used in *Calories Don't Count,* millions of |

people who did not want to give up alcoholic beverages tried it. Many failed to lose weight, because although alcohol has a low nutritive value, it is high in calories. The diet defeats its own purpose; a martini has as many calories as a lean lamb chop!

A diet high in carbohydrate and low in protein also creates nutritional imbalance. These diets usually emphasize a grain, such as rice, and limit protein intake to about 20 grams a day, far below the recommended daily allowance of 55 grams for women. Protein, found in every living cell, is needed for growth and to build and repair worn-out tissues. During the digestive process, protein is broken down into smaller units called amino acids, which are required by various tissues. When there is too little protein intake, the body suffers from negative nitrogen balance. This simply means that the body loses more protein than it takes in, and that the body's own protein stores in the form of muscle tissues have to be used to make up for it. But excess weight is usually fat tissue, and this is what you want to lose—not lean muscle tissue.

*High-carbohydrate low-protein diets*

Also inadequate in the amount of protein required daily, the Banana and Skim Milk Diet periodically attracts dieters who are drawn to extremes. Its title describes its basic ingredients; it calls for one quart of skim milk and six bananas each day for a week. The diet is inadequate in practically all nutrients.

*The Banana and Skim Milk Diet*

Originally used to treat hypertension (high blood pressure), the Famous Rice Diet consists of rice, fruit and fruit juice. It also restricts coffee and tea to three cups daily and eliminates salt (needed by most people for proper water balance). Essentially a crash diet, it is supposed to be practiced for at least three days but not more than six. It provides an insufficient amount of protein—about 20 grams per day.

*The Famous Rice Diet*

Supposedly a Zen Buddhist diet, the Macrobiotic Diet regime has been adopted recently by young people seeking spiritual awakening. At first, rice is coupled with fruit, vegetables and chicken. Then, as a higher stage of enlightenment is reached, the diet is limited to only rice. This diet can be extremely dangerous, because those who follow it mistakenly believe that brown rice contains healing qualities that guarantee freedom from age, tension and illness. A few years ago one young woman starved herself to death on this diet.

*The Macrobiotic Diet*

Usually used for several days to begin a diet, total fasting from solid food has been extended by some people to a week or even ten days. The idea was popularized after reports of high weight loss

*Starvation Diets*

in obese people who were hospitalized under a doctor's care during the starvation period. But active people who attempt this often run into difficulties functioning on a day-to-day level. Although fasting does take weight off, it doesn't solve the reducing problem. After the fast is over, the dieter continues to eat the same way as before.

*Six diets that really work*

The best way to lose weight successfully—and keep it off—is by developing good eating habits. Eat balanced meals, choosing foods daily from the Basic-Four Groups (see page 37). The recommended servings in each group provide 1200 to 1400 calories daily. For women on a reducing schedule, 1200 calories a day is suggested; for men, 1800. Weight loss should average one to two pounds a week. Since it is not practical to fit a woman's full iron requirement (18 milligrams daily) within the 1200-calorie limit, ask your physician to recommend an iron supplement. Men won't need this supplement, and the diets will otherwise meet nutrient needs. A hint for all dieters: Use only whole-grain or enriched breads, crackers, rice or pastas.

Any of the six diets that follow on pages 13 through 29 meet the Basic-Four requirements, yet each has a special theme to make dieting easier. Need a diet for the entire family, or one that really drives home the principles of good meal planning? Use the Basic-Four Reducing Diet. Hate rabbit food and tiny portions? Try the Meat-and-Potatoes Diet. Nibble constantly? The Six-Meals-a-Day Reducing Diet was meant for you. "Need" cocktails and snacks? Follow the Eat-for-a-Treat Diet. Do you like the metered-calorie formula drinks. Use them as part of the planned Magic-Formula-Plus Diet. Are you an on-again-off-again dieter? Plan to diet only four days a week on the Wisconsin Diet.

# MEAT-AND-POTATOES REDUCING DIET

If you want a reducing diet that offers hearty fare for your healthy appetite, this diet plan lets you have generous servings of meat, hefty sandwiches, hearty main-dish casseroles. For women, a sensible 1200 calories a day is recommended; men can have 1800 calories (including two snacks). For boys and girls 7 to 12 and teenage girls, use the basic 1200-calorie diet and add two glasses of skimmed milk. For teenage boys, use "for men" portions, adding two glasses of skimmed milk.

Choose a meal plan from each category every day.

## BREAKFAST

(300 calories for women, 400 for men)

1. **Juice, eggs, toast, milk**
   4-ounce glass orange or grapefruit juice
   1 soft- or hard-cooked, poached or scrambled (no added fat) egg
   1 slice toast, lightly buttered or jellied*
   8-ounce glass skimmed milk
   Coffee or tea**
   **For men:** Add extra slice toast

2. **Juice, cereal and fruit, milk**
   4-ounce glass orange or grapefruit juice
   1 cup ready-to-eat or ¾ cup cooked cereal with 1 teaspoon sugar and ½ sliced banana or ½ cup fresh or unsweetened frozen strawberries
   8-ounce glass skimmed milk
   **For men:** Have 8-ounce glass juice and extra half serving of cereal

3. **Fruit, pancakes, milk**
   ½ cup fresh or unsweetened canned orange or grapefruit sections or fruit cocktail
   2 4-inch pancakes (made from mix using skimmed milk) with 1 tablespoon maple-flavored syrup
   8-ounce glass skimmed milk
   **For men:** Have 3 pancakes

## LUNCH

(450 calories for women, 500 for men)

1. **Soup, sandwich, salad, milk**
   1 cup soup: beef, chicken or turkey noodle; tomato; onion; vegetable beef or vegetarian vegetable

* Use whole-grain or enriched breads and crackers wherever possible.
** Have coffee or tea with any meal. Use no more than 1 teaspoon sugar; save part of milk to use as "cream."

Sandwich on bread, toast or large roll with low-calorie mayonnaise and lettuce, filled with 2 slices lean beef, chicken, turkey or ham or ¼ cup flaked tuna or salmon
Large tossed salad with low-calorie dressing or celery, carrot and pickle sticks
8-ounce glass skimmed milk
**For men:** Add extra slice of meat to sandwich

2. **Soup, main-dish salad, bread, milk**
   1 cup soup: beef or chicken bouillon or consommé
   ½ cup egg, tuna, salmon, shrimp, or crab salad prepared with low-calorie mayonnaise and lettuce, celery and tomatoes as garnish
   1 slice bread or toast, lightly buttered
   **For men:** Have ¾ cup salad

3. **Cottage cheese or yogurt, bread, fruit**
   8-ounce container creamed cottage cheese or vanilla yogurt
   1 cup fresh fruit cocktail or dietetic-packed canned fruit
   8 saltine squares or Melba rounds (each lightly buttered)
   **For men:** Add large tossed salad with low-calorie dressing

4. **Omelet, toast, milk**
   2-egg plain, onion or mushroom omelet (skimp on butter to make omelet)
   2 slices toast or 1 toasted English muffin or 1 large roll (do not butter)
   8-ounce glass skimmed milk
   **For men:** Butter bread or roll

5. **Hamburger on roll or toast, salad, milk**
   1 4-ounce hamburger served on hamburger or hard roll, or on toast with catchup, mustard, lettuce and tomato or onion, as desired

Small serving coleslaw or tossed salad with low-calorie dressing

8-ounce glass skimmed milk

**For men:** Add small apple, peach or tangerine

6. **Frankfurter on roll, sauerkraut, fruit, milk**

    1 grilled or boiled frankfurter with mustard, catchup, or relish as desired, on toasted frankfurter roll

    ¾ cup sauerkraut

    1 serving fruit from list at right, below

    8-ounce glass skimmed milk

    **For men:** add ¾ cup tomato, noodle or vegetable beef soup

## DINNER

(450 calories for women, 600 for men)

1. **Meat, vegetable, salad, potatoes or bread, fruit**

    ¼ pound (weigh uncooked) lean beef, veal, lamb, pork or liver—panbroiled, or braised in tomato juice or water

    2 servings vegetables from list at right, below—one cooked and one as salad with low-calorie dressing

    ½ cup mashed or baked potato or 1 slice bread, 1 small roll, muffin or biscuit (all lightly buttered)

    1 serving fruit from list at right, below

    **For men:** Have ⅓ pound meat

2. **Fish, potatoes or pasta, vegetable, salad, fruit**

    ⅓ pound (weigh uncooked) cod, flounder, haddock, halibut, sole or any seafood, brushed with a little oil and broiled or poached in chicken bouillon or white wine

    ¾ cup rice, noodles or diced potatoes or 1 small baked potato (all lightly buttered)

    2 servings vegetables from list at right, below—one cooked and one as salad with low-calorie dressing

    1 serving fruit from list at right, below

    **For men:** Have ½ pound fish or seafood; add 1 slice lightly buttered bread or extra serving potatoes

3. **Chicken, potatoes or pasta, salad, dessert, fruit as snack**

    1 chicken breast (about ⅓ pound), broiled, baked or braised with pineapple juice, bouillon or white wine

    1 serving vegetable from list at right, below—cooked or as salad with low-calorie dressing

½ cup rice, noodles or diced potatoes or 1 small baked potato (all lightly buttered)

1 serving any dessert with up to 150 calories from pages 210 to 241

1 serving fruit from list below as snack

**For men:** Have 1 whole chicken breast (about ¾ pound)

4. **Casserole, vegetable, potatoes or pasta, salad, fruit**

    1 serving any 200 to 250 calorie main dish from pages 81 to 171

    2 servings vegetables from list below— one cooked and one as salad with low-calorie dressing

    ½ cup mashed or boiled potatoes (no butter), rice or pasta

    1 serving fruit from list below

    **For men:** Have 1½ servings main dish

## SNACKS FOR MEN ONLY:

Have any two of the following:

1 toasted buttered English muffin

15 potato chips

25 to 30 peanuts

½ cup pudding (made with skimmed milk)

12-ounce bottle carbonated beverage

12-ounce bottle beer

1 small cocktail

1 10" by 3" wedge watermelon

5 saltines spread with 1 tablespoon peanut butter

1 plain doughnut

1½ slices buttered toast

2 medium apples, peaches or oranges

1 medium slice angel food or sponge cake

½ cup ice milk or sherbet

2 homemade chocolate chip or other small cookies

3 large graham crackers

3 chocolate wafers dipped in 1 cup skimmed milk

8 small pretzels

## FRUIT AND VEGETABLE CHOICES

**Vegetables:** Asparagus, broccoli, Brussels sprouts, cabbage, carrots, cauliflower, celery, green beans, greens, Italian beans, okra, sauerkraut, spinach or tomatoes

**Fruits:** 1 small fresh peach or apple; ½ fresh pear or banana; 2 fresh apricots or plums; 1 cup fresh grapes, cherries, berries or melon cubes; ½ cup dietetic-packed canned or frozen fruit.

## SIX-MEALS-A-DAY REDUCING DIET

Dieting on six meals a day is a marvelously appealing idea to most women, especially to those who are confirmed nibblers. For men, although the plan might not be feasible during the week, it does make sense as a weekend diet. A man might follow one of the other 1800-calorie diets for the five working days and then "splurge" on the weekend with the Six-Meals-a-Day Diet.

This reducing plan allows for three regular meals a day plus three sizable snacks. It is a model of flexibility. The easy-to-fix menu ideas are divided into six mealtime sections: breakfast, midmorning, lunch, midafternoon, dinner and midevening. You choose one item from each group each day, from the foods that suit your preferences and schedule. A woman can switch any lunch with any dinner (each is 300 calories), or vary the order of the 150-calorie meals (breakfast and three snacks).

The diet is planned, of course, to provide the nutrients you need. (See note on iron, page 12.) And eating many small meals throughout the day will quell hunger pangs, keep your blood-sugar and energy levels primed for action.

## BREAKFAST—150 CALORIES

½ cup fruit juice (orange, pineapple, grapefruit, frozen grape or apple); 1 slice lightly buttered white, rye or whole wheat toast

½ cup unsweetened orange or grapefruit sections; ⅓ cup cottage cheese

½ cup fruit juice (see list above); 1 cup puffed rice or wheat with ½ cup skimmed milk

1 cup beef, chicken or vegetable bouillon; 1 slice (1 ounce) Cheddar, Swiss, etc., cheese; 4 saltine squares

1 cup puffed or flaked cereal; ½ cup fruit juice (see list above) as "milk"

1 hard-cooked or poached egg; 1 slice lightly buttered toast

BUTTERMILK PANCAKE COINS (see recipe, page 207) with 2 tablespoons applesauce

## MIDMORNING—150 CALORIES

2 graham crackers; 1 cup skimmed milk or buttermilk

4 small round crackers; 1 tablespoon peanut butter

1 small banana; ⅓ cup cottage cheese

fruit juice (see list under breakfast); 1 lightly buttered muffin

1 slice (1 ounce) lean boiled ham; 1 slice toast and lettuce

1 slice lightly buttered raisin toast; ½ cup orange juice

1 thinly sliced hard-cooked egg; 4 saltine squares

## LUNCH—300 CALORIES

roast-beef sandwich (2 slices bread, 1 ounce lean roast beef, low-calorie mayonnaise and lettuce); 1 cup skimmed milk or buttermilk; carrot and celery sticks

1 serving (¾ cup) beef-noodle soup; 2 saltine squares; ½ cup cottage cheese; ½ cup drained canned apricot halves

½ cup shrimp, tuna, crab or lobster salad (use low-calorie French dressing); tomato, celery, or lettuce; 1 small lightly buttered hard roll or 1 slice toast; 1 cup skimmed milk or buttermilk

OYSTER STEW (recipe, page 105); 10 oyster crackers; tossed salad with low-calorie dressing; ½ cup drained peach slices

bacon, lettuce and tomato sandwich (2 slices toast, 2 strips crisp bacon, lettuce, tomato, 1 tablespoon low-calorie mayonnaise); ½ cup skimmed milk or buttermilk

8 ounces (1 container) fruited yogurt; 2 saltine squares or 2 Melba rounds or ½ slice bread

1 cup (made with skimmed milk) cream of tomato or New England clam chowder soup; 2 scrambled eggs; 1 slice unbuttered toast

## MIDAFTERNOON—150 CALORIES

1 serving cream of chicken, mushroom or celery soup prepared with skimmed milk; 2 rye crackers

1 cup fresh strawberries, raspberries or blueberries; ¼ cup low-calorie sour cream made by blending cottage cheese until smooth

1 lightly buttered plain or blueberry muffin; ½ cup skimmed milk or buttermilk

2 saltine squares; 1 slice (1 ounce) Cheddar, Swiss, etc., cheese

1 8-ounce container plain yogurt

⅓ cantaloupe filled with ⅓ cup vanilla ice milk

1 slice American, Cheddar or Swiss cheese; 1 small apple or orange

## DINNER—300 CALORIES

½ cup tomato juice; two broiled, lean loin lamb chops; ½ cup broccoli; ½ cup carrots; lettuce wedge with 1 tablespoon low-calorie Thousand Island dressing

2 grilled frankfurters (catchup or mustard to taste); ½ cup sauerkraut

HERB'S FAVORITE FLOUNDER (recipe, page 92); ½ cup mashed summer squash; ½ cup mixed vegetables; ½ cup applesauce

beef consommé; 4 ounces (raw weight) pan-broiled chicken or beef livers; ½ cup peas; thinly sliced cauliflowerets with 1 tablespoon low-calorie dressing

BACON-STUFFED BURGERS (recipe, page 142); 6 asparagus spears; tomato and cucumber salad and 1 tablespoon low-calorie French dressing

CHICKEN KABOBS ITALIANO (recipe, page 130); ⅓ cup rice; tossed salad with low-calorie dressing

3 ounces (cooked) lean roast beef; ONIONS WITH A ZEST (recipe, page 182); ½ cup green beans; relish tray of carrots, celery, pickle slices

## MIDEVENING—150 CALORIES

12 medium 3-ring pretzels; black coffee or tea

2 small homemade chocolate chip or sandwich-type cookies; black coffee or tea

1½ cups popcorn with 2 teaspoons butter or margarine, salt to taste

12 potato chips; black coffee or tea

SHERBET SHAKE (recipe, page 70)

½ cup ice milk

watermelon—1 slice, 6 inches in diameter and 1½ inches thick

## BREAKFAST—200 CALORIES

½ cup fruit juice (orange, pineapple, grapefruit, frozen grape or apple); 1½ slices lightly buttered white, rye or whole-wheat toast

½ cup unsweetened orange or grapefruit sections; ¾ cup cottage cheese

½ cup fruit juice (see list above); 1 cup puffed rice or wheat with 1 teaspoon sugar; ½ cup skimmed milk

1 cup beef, chicken or vegetable bouillon; 1½ slices (1½ ounces) Cheddar, Swiss, etc., cheese; 4 saltines

½ cup fruit juice (see list above); 1 soft- or hard-cooked or poached egg; 1 slice lightly buttered toast or bread

½ cup unsweetened orange or grapefruit sections; BUTTERMILK PANCAKE COINS (see recipe, page 207) with 2 tablespoons applesauce

½ cup fruit juice (see list above); ¾ cup cooked farina or oatmeal with 1 teaspoon sugar; ½ cup skimmed milk

## MIDMORNING—200 CALORIES

4 saltine squares; 1 slice (1 ounce) Cheddar, Swiss, etc., cheese

5 graham crackers; 1 cup skimmed milk or buttermilk

4 small round crackers; 2 tablespoons peanut butter

1 large banana; ½ cup cottage cheese

fruit juice (see list under breakfast); 1 lightly buttered English muffin

2 slices (2 ounces) lean boiled ham; 1 slice lightly buttered toast; lettuce

1½ slices lightly buttered raisin toast; ½ cup orange juice

## LUNCH—400 CALORIES

roast-beef sandwich (2 slices bread, 2 ounces lean roast beef, low-calorie mayonnaise and lettuce); 1 cup skimmed milk or buttermilk; carrot and celery sticks; ½ cup dietetic-pack or fresh pears

1 serving (¾ cup) beef-noodle soup; 3 saltine squares; ½ cup cottage cheese; ½ cup drained canned apricot halves; 1 cup skimmed milk or buttermilk

1 cup shrimp, tuna, crab or lobster salad (use low-calorie French dressing); tomato, celery or lettuce; 1 small lightly buttered hard roll; 1 cup skimmed milk or buttermilk

OYSTER STEW (see recipe, page 105); 20 oyster crackers; tossed salad with low-calorie dressing; 1 cup canned peach slices, drained

bacon, lettuce and tomato sandwich (2 slices toast, 2 strips crisp bacon, lettuce, tomato, 1 tablespoon low-calorie mayonnaise); 1 cup skimmed milk or buttermilk; 1 small apple

8 ounces (1 container) fruited yogurt; 1 lightly buttered medium roll

1 serving (¾ cup) tomato or Manhattan clam-chowder soup; 2 scrambled eggs; 1 slice lightly buttered toast; 1 cup skimmed milk or buttermilk

## MIDAFTERNOON—200 CALORIES

1½ cup serving cream-of-chicken, mushroom or celery soup prepared with skimmed milk; 2 rye crackers

1 cup fresh strawberries, raspberries or blueberries; ½ cup low-calorie sour cream made by blending cottage cheese until smooth

1 lightly buttered plain or blueberry muffin; 1 cup skimmed milk or buttermilk

1 8-ounce container coffee or vanilla yogurt

watermelon—1 slice, 6 inches in diameter and 2-inches thick

2 thinly sliced hard-cooked eggs; 3 saltine squares

½ cantaloupe filled with ⅔ cup vanilla ice milk

## DINNER—600 CALORIES

½ cup tomato juice; 2 broiled lean loin lamb chops; ¾ cup chopped broccoli; ¾ cup carrots; 1 slice

lightly buttered rye bread; lettuce wedge with 1 tablespoon Thousand Island dressing; ½ cup canned peaches, drained

2 grilled frankfurters (catchup or mustard to taste) on frankfurter rolls; ⅔ cup sauerkraut; ½ cup fruited gelatin

HERB'S FAVORITE FLOUNDER (see recipe, page 92); ½ cup mashed potatoes; ½ cup mixed vegetables; tossed salad with 1 tablespoon French dressing; ¾ cup applesauce

beef consommé; 6 ounces (raw weight) panbroiled chicken or beef livers; ½ cup peas; thinly sliced cauliflowerets with 1 tablespoon Italian dressing; small bunch fresh grapes

BACON-STUFFED BURGERS (see recipe, page 142); 6 asparagus spears; tomato and cucumber salad with 1 tablespoon French dressing; ½ cup bananas in orange juice

CHICKEN KABOBS ITALIANO (see recipe, page 130); ¾ cup rice; tossed salad with 1 tablespoon French dressing

4 ounces (cooked) lean roast beef; ONIONS WITH A ZEST (see recipe, page 182); ½ cup green beans; relish tray of carrots, celery and pickle slices; thin slice sponge cake

## MIDEVENING—200 CALORIES

1 large jellied doughnut; black coffee or tea

15 medium 3-ring pretzels; black coffee or tea

3 small homemade chocolate chip or sandwich-type cookies; black coffee or tea

2 cups popcorn with 1 tablespoon butter or margarine and salt to taste (try garlic salt for an interesting change)

20 medium potato chips; black coffee or tea

1 small Danish pastry; black coffee or tea

⅔ cup ice milk (any flavor)

# BASIC-FOUR REDUCING DIET

The Basic-Four Reducing Diet provides 1200 calories a day for women and 1800 for men—the most practical (easiest to maintain) calorie levels for long-term reducing. There are literally hundreds of everyday foods to choose from, so you can fit the diet to your budget and special food preferences of your family.

Listed on the next page are your food choices, each with its recommended portion. Also, there is a list of diet "extras"—those foods which often make meals (and snacks) more appetizing.

Your Diet Plan, below, lists total servings allowed from each group each day. The menu outline with it suggests a practical way to distribute the servings among three meals. This is, of course, simply a guide, not a rigid menu plan. As long as you include the number of servings listed for each group in Your Diet Plan, you will get all you need nutritionally (see note on iron, page 12) and also reduce. Before you start, check the Suggested Menus and the Helpful Tips opposite.

## YOUR DIET PLAN

| FOOD GROUPS | WOMEN | MEN |
|---|---|---|
| **For the day** | **Calories: 1200** | **1800** |
| | servings | |
| meat and protein-rich foods | 2 | 3 |
| fruits and vegetables | | |
|    fruits | 3 | 5 |
|    vegetables | 2 to 4 | 2 to 4 |
| breads, cereals, pastas, some vegetables | 4 | 6 |
| milk and milk products | 2 | 2 |
| extras | 3 | 6 |
| **For each meal:** | | |
| BREAKFAST | | |
| fruit | 1 | 1 |
| bread, cereals, etc. | 1 | 2 |
| meat and protein-rich foods | * | * |
| milk and milk products | 1 | 1 |
| extras | 1 | 2 |
| LUNCH OR SUPPER | | |
| meat and protein-rich foods | 1* | 1* |
| vegetables | 1 to 2 | 1 to 2 |
| breads, cereals, etc. | 2 | 2 |
| fruit | 1 | 2 |
| milk and milk products | 1 | 1 |
| extras | 1 | 2 |
| DINNER | | |
| meat and protein-rich foods | 1 | 2 |
| vegetables | 1 to 2 | 1 to 2 |
| bread, cereals, etc. | 1 | 2 |
| fruit | 1 | 2 |
| extras | 1 | 2 |

At each meal, if you wish: coffee or tea with little or no sugar, with milk rather than cream.

* If one egg is eaten at breakfast, decrease luncheon serving of meat by one-third.

## SUGGESTED MENUS

*(portion sizes may be adjusted
for either men or women)*

### 1

**Breakfast:** Orange juice, cornflakes with sugar, skimmed milk
**Lunch:** Hamburger on toasted roll with pickle relish, coleslaw, apple, buttermilk
**Dinner:** Baked fish fillets with lemon sauce, greens, broiled tomatoes, buttered muffin, cinnamon-topped pineapple chunks

### 2

**Breakfast:** Half grapefruit, poached egg, toast with cream cheese, skimmed milk
**Lunch:** Grilled ham sandwich, tossed salad with low-calorie dressing, fresh-fruit cup, skimmed milk
**Dinner:** Pot roast of beef with gravy (see note in Helpful Tips), oven-roasted potatoes, Brussels sprouts, apricots and a cookie

### 3

**Breakfast:** Fresh-fruit cup with cottage cheese, ½ buttered toasted English muffin
**Lunch:** Tuna salad, pickle and celery slices, buttered hard roll, pears, skimmed milk
**Dinner:** Roast leg of lamb with natural gravy, herbed rice, Italian beans, peach halves on lettuce with blue-cheese dressing, for salad and dessert

### 4

**Breakfast:** Pineapple-grapefruit juice, oatmeal with sugar, skimmed milk
**Lunch:** Chili con carne, tossed salad with low-calorie French dressing, bananas with sour cream, skimmed mik
**Dinner:** Roast chicken with gravy (see note in Helpful Tips), mashed potatoes, chopped spinach, cucumbers in oil-and-vinegar dressing, canned peaches

### 5

**Breakfast:** Orange juice, puffed wheat with sugar, ½ cup skimmed milk
**Lunch:** Chicken-salad sandwich, celery sticks, tangerine, skimmed milk
**Dinner:** Grilled quick steaks, red cabbage, corn, tossed salad, low-calorie dressing, chocolate pudding (see last suggestion under Helpful Tips)

## HELPFUL TIPS

• Roast, broil or braise meat. Panbroiling is fine, but don't add fat unless you count it toward "extras."
• Trim extra fat from meats before you cook them.
• Four ounces of raw meat (without bone) will yield about 3 ounces of cooked meat.
• For gravies, slightly thicken canned chicken or beef broth with cornstarch. Season to taste with garlic, onion or celery salt or other herbs and spices.
• Have milk at any meal or as a snack—it's not essential to have it at breakfast or lunch.
• "Extras" can be saved from one meal to another, but remember to keep tabs on the total for the day.
• You can count all cheeses (except cream cheese) as a serving of either Meat and Protein-Rich Foods or Milk and Milk Products in order to gain the necessary number of servings daily in each category.
• Make puddings with skimmed milk. Count a ½-cup serving as ½ cup milk and an "extra."

## MEAT AND PROTEIN-RICH FOODS

**Cheese**
cottage,* farmer's, pot or ricotta, ½ cup
American, Cheddar, Edam, Swiss, etc.,†
   3 ounces
**Eggs (3 medium)**
**Fish and shellfish**
cooked bass,* bluefish, cod,* flounder,*
   haddock,* halibut, herring (plain), lobster,* mackerel, ocean perch, sole,*
   swordfish, trout, etc., 3 ounces
medium shrimp, 6
medium clams or oysters,* 10
crab,* salmon or tuna, ¾ cup flaked,
   drained
**Meat**
cooked beef, game meats,* lamb, liver
   (all kinds),* pork, rabbit* or veal,* 3
   ounces
boiled ham or lean luncheon meat,† 3
   ounces
frankfurters,† 3 small
**Peanut butter (⅓ cup†)**
**Poultry**
cooked chicken,* Cornish hens, duck,†
   goose† or turkey, 3 ounces

* Comparatively low in calories; use them often.
† Comparatively high in calories; use them sparingly.

## BREADS, CEREALS, PASTAS, SOME VEGETABLES

**Breads**
rye, white and whole-wheat,
    1 slice
matzoh, 1 piece*
raisin, 1 slice*
**Cereals**
flaked or puffed ready-to-eat,
    ¾ cup
cooked, ½ cup
**Crackers**
graham, 2 small
oyster, ½ cup
round, 5 2-inch
rye, 3 double crackers
saltines, 4 2-inch
soda, 3 small
**Pastas**
cooked macaroni, spaghetti,
    ½ cup
cooked egg noodles, ½ cup
**Quick breads**
biscuits, 1 average*
corn bread, 1½-inch cube*
English muffins, ½ muffin
griddlecakes, 1 4-inch cake*
muffins, 1 average*
waffles, 1 4-inch waffle*
**Rice**
cooked white, ½ cup
cooked wild, ½ cup
**Rolls**
large hamburger, hot dog,
    etc., ½ roll
**Vegetables**
beans, baked, ¼ cup
beans, cooked dried, ⅓ cup
beets, 1 cup
carrots, 1 cup
corn, ⅓ cup
onions, raw, 1 cup
peas, green, 1 cup
potatoes, white, baked, 1
    small
potatoes, white, mashed, ½
    cup
potatoes, sweet, baked, ¼
    cup
rutabagas, 1 cup
turnips, 1 cup
winter squash, 1 cup
* Count as I serving of Bread
and 1 serving of Extras.

## FRUITS AND VEGETABLES

**Fruits, fresh or dietetic-pack canned or frozen***

apple, 1 small
apple juice, ⅓ cup
applesauce, ½ cup
apricots, 2 medium
banana, ½ small
berries, ⅔ to 1 cup
cantaloupe, ¼ small
cherries, 10 large
dates, 2 small
figs, fresh, 2 large
grapefruit, ½ small
grapefruit juice, ½ cup
grape juice, ¼ cup
grapes, 12 medium
honeydew, ⅛ small
mango, ½ small
orange, 1 small
orange juice, ½ cup
papaya, ⅓ medium
peach, 1 medium
pear, 1 small
pineapple, cubed, ½ cup
pineapple juice, ⅓ cup
plums or prunes, 2 medium
raisins, 2 tablespoons
tangerine, 1 large
tangerine juice, ½ cup
watermelon, cubed, 1 cup
* If desired, occasionally substitute 1 serving regular, canned
or frozen fruit for 2 servings of
raw or dietetic-pack fruit.

**Vegetables—use them freely on diet, served unbuttered or with low-calorie dressing**

| | |
|---|---|
| asparagus | lettuce |
| broccoli | mushrooms |
| Brussels | okra |
|   sprouts | peppers |
| cabbage | radishes |
| cauliflower | romaine |
| celery | sauerkraut |
| cucumbers | spinach |
| endive | summer |
| escarole |   squash |
| green beans | tomato juice |
| greens | tomatoes |
| Italian beans | wax beans |
| kale | zucchini |

## MILK AND MILK PRODUCTS

Buttermilk, 1 cup
Cheese, American, Cheddar,
    etc., 1 ounce
Cottage cheese (creamed),
    ½ cup
Evaporated skimmed milk
    (undiluted), ½ cup
Nonfat dry milk powder,
    ⅓ cup
Skimmed milk, 1 cup
Yogurt, plain, 1 cup

## THE EXTRAS

almonds, 5 medium
butter, 1 teaspoon
cookies, 1 small
cream, heavy, 1 tablespoon
cream, light, 2 tablespoons
cream, sour, 2 tablespoons
cream cheese, 1 tablespoon
fudge, 1 tiny square
gumdrops, 4 small
hard candy, 2 medium
jam, scant tablespoon
jelly, scant tablespoon
margarine, 1 teaspoon
olives, 5 small
peanuts, 6 to 8
pecans, 5 medium
pickles, 3 dill
plain popcorn, ⅔ cup
potato chips, 3 medium
pretzels, 10 sticks
salad dressing, 2 teaspoons
sponge cake, 1 very thin slice
sugar, 1 tablespoon
syrups, scant tablespoon

This diet is designed for anyone who is too busy to fix three diet meals a day. By making use of those wonderfully convenient metered-calorie formulas, which take no time at all to prepare, it easily adapts to a hectic schedule. Keep both canned and powdered mixes in your favorite flavors on hand to add more variety to the diet. If you prefer, substitute instant breakfast made up with skimmed milk for the formulas. On the diet, you have one metered-formula meal a day—in our opinion, the best way to make use of these handy diet formulas. The remaining calories of your daily total of 1200 (1800 for men) are divided among your other two meals and snacks. The diet outlines for breakfast, lunch and dinner that follow (three for men, three for women) suggest how to apportion calories for the most satisfying meals depending upon when you prefer to have your formula.

# HERS: 1200 CALORIES FOR THREE MEALS AND SNACKS

| Formula for Breakfast | Formula for Lunch | Formula for Dinner |
|---|---|---|
| BREAKFAST: 225 calories<br>1 serving Formula plus<br>Coffee (black) or tea (with lemon)<br><br>LUNCH: 325 calories<br>Tuna- or egg-salad sandwich (2 slices bread, ¼ cup tuna or 1 chopped egg, low-calorie salad dressing and lettuce)<br>Tossed salad, low-calorie dressing<br>1 fresh pear, peach, apple or small banana<br>OR<br>Grilled frankfurter on toasted roll (mustard and/or catchup)<br>Lettuce-and-tomato salad (low-calorie dressing)<br>4-ounce glass skimmed milk or buttermilk<br><br>DINNER: 500 calories<br>3 ounces roast beef (with natural gravy)<br>½ cup lightly buttered herbed rice<br>Lightly buttered chopped spinach<br>½ cup tapioca pudding (made with skimmed milk)<br>OR<br>4 ounces roast leg of lamb (1 tablespoon mint jelly)<br>½ cup lightly buttered peas<br>Lightly buttered stewed tomatoes<br>Thin slice angel-food cake<br><br>SNACK: 150 calories—see Snackers' Guide, page 26 | BREAKFAST: 275 calories<br>4-ounce glass pineapple juice<br>1 cup cornflakes<br>1 teaspoon sugar<br>8-ounce glass skimmed milk<br><br>LUNCH: 225 calories<br>1 serving Formula plus<br>Coffee, tea or bouillon (try bouillon as a change of pace)<br><br>DINNER: 550 calories<br>1 4-ounce grilled roundburger (catchup, onions)<br>1 small baked potato (1 tablespoon sour cream or 1 teaspoon butter)<br>Lightly buttered Italian beans<br>½ cup fruited gelatin (1 tablespoon dessert topping)<br>OR<br>Hot herbed vegetable juice<br>4 ounces pan-broiled quick steak<br>½ cup lightly buttered noodles<br>Lightly buttered Chinese cabbage<br>½ cup chocolate pudding (made with skimmed milk) (1 tablespoon dessert topping)<br><br>SNACKS: 150 calories—see Snackers' Guide, page 26 | BREAKFAST: 315 calories<br>4-ounce glass orange or grapefruit juice<br>1 soft-cooked or poached egg on 1 slice lightly buttered toast<br>8-ounce glass skimmed milk<br><br>LUNCH: 375 calories<br>1 cup chicken-noodle soup<br>4 ounces pan-fried flounder, halibut or sole<br>½ cup lightly buttered carrot coins<br>Lightly buttered small hard roll<br>1 small apple or ½ banana<br>OR<br>¾ cup tomato soup<br>Swiss-cheese sandwich on rye toast (1 slice cheese, rye toast, lots of lettuce)<br>Cucumber slices in vinegar<br>½ cup fresh fruit cup<br><br>DINNER: 360 calories<br>1 serving Formula plus<br>A large salad of:<br>1 cup salad greens, carrots, celery, tomatoes, etc., 1 ounce cubed cheese, meat or poultry and low-calorie dressing, as desired<br><br>SNACKS: 150 calories—see Snackers' Guide, page 26 |

# HIS: 1800 CALORIES FOR THREE MEALS AND SNACKS

| Formula for Breakfast | Formula for Lunch | Formula for Dinner |
|---|---|---|
| BREAKFAST: 325 calories<br>1 serving Formula plus<br>1 slice lightly buttered toast<br>Coffee (black) or tea (with lemon)<br><br>LUNCH: 600 calories<br>Tuna- or egg-salad sandwich (2 slices bread, ¼ cup tuna or 1 chopped egg, 2 tablespoons salad dressing, lettuce)<br>1 fresh pear, peach, apple or small banana<br>8-ounce glass whole milk<br>OR<br>2 grilled frankfurters on 2 toasted rolls (mustard and/or catchup<br>Lettuce-and-tomato salad (low-calorie dressing)<br>8-ounce glass skimmed milk or buttermilk<br><br>DINNER: 675 calories<br>4 ounces roast beef (small serving gravy)<br>¾ cup lightly buttered herbed rice<br>Lightly buttered chopped spinach<br>½ cup tapioca pudding<br>OR<br>4 ounces roast leg of lamb (1 tablespoon mint jelly)<br>½ cup lightly buttered peas<br>Lightly buttered stewed tomatoes<br>1 lightly buttered large hard roll<br>Thin slice angel-food cake<br><br>SNACKS: 200 calories—see Snackers' Guide, page 26 | BREAKFAST: 400 calories<br>6-ounce glass pineapple juice<br>1 cup cornflakes with 1 teaspoon sugar<br>1 slice lightly buttered toast<br>8-ounce glass skimmed milk<br><br>LUNCH: 400 calories<br>1 serving Formula plus<br>1 slice lightly buttered bread or a small roll<br>½ cup fresh fruit cup<br><br>DINNER: 700 calories<br>2 3-ounce grilled roundburgers (catchup, onion)<br>1 medium baked potato (3 tablespoons sour cream or 1 tablespoon butter)<br>Lightly buttered Italian beans<br>½ cup fruited gelatin (1 tablespoon dessert topping)<br>OR<br>Hot herbed vegetable juice<br>6 ounces pan-broiled quick steak<br>½ cup lightly buttered noodles<br>Lightly buttered Chinese cabbage<br>½ cup chocolate pudding (made with skimmed milk) (1 tablespoon dessert topping)<br><br>SNACKS: 300 calories—see Snackers' Guide, page 26 | BREAKFAST: 500 calories<br>8-ounce glass orange or grapefruit juice<br>2 soft-cooked or poached eggs on 1½ slices lightly buttered toast<br>8-ounce glass skimmed milk<br><br>LUNCH: 540 calories<br>1 cup chicken-noodle soup<br>6-ounce serving pan-fried flounder, halibut or sole<br>½ cup lightly buttered carrot coins<br>Lightly buttered medium hard roll<br>1 small apple or ½ banana<br>OR<br>¾ cup tomato soup<br>Swiss-cheese sandwich on rye toast (2 slices cheese, rye toast, lots of lettuce)<br>Cucumber slices in vinegar<br>1 cup fresh fruit cup<br><br>DINNER: 460 calories<br>1 serving Formula plus<br>A large salad of:<br>1 cup salad greens, carrots, celery, tomatoes, etc.,<br>1 ounce cubed cheese, meat or poultry and 2 tablespoons French, Italian or Russian dressing<br><br>SNACKS: 300 calories—see Snackers' Guide, page 26 |

## EAT-FOR-A-TREAT DIET

If desserts and snacks are your dieting downfall, this diet may be the one for you. With it, you can have the choicest treats and *still* lose up to two pounds a week! Follow the daily menu patterns that allow 1000 calories for women, 1400 for men. Then choose treats totaling up to 200 calories (women) or 400 calories (men). The Snackers' Guide gives you just an idea of the possibilities, listing some of the traditional low-calorie snacks as well as rich once-in-a-while ones we all crave from time to time (or every day). Also included to help you fill the snacking quota: a dozen 200-calorie snacks—all permissible. And don't overlook the diet-defying recipes starting on page 65.

|  |  |
|---|---|
| FOR HER:<br>1000 CALORIES<br>PLUS 200 CALORIES<br>OF SNACKS | FOR HIM:<br>1400 CALORIES<br>PLUS 400 CALORIES<br>OF SNACKS |

## BREAKFAST

½ cup citrus fruit or juice
AND
1 egg and 1 slice lightly buttered toast*
OR
1 cup cooked or 1½ cups ready-to-eat cereal
AND
½ glass skimmed milk
**Any Meal:** coffee or tea, black or with milk and up to 1 teaspoon sugar

1 cup fruit or juice
AND
2 eggs plus 1 slice toast*
OR
1 cup cooked or 1½ cups ready-to-eat cereal
AND
½ glass skimmed milk
AND
see left

## LUNCH OR SUPPER

2 ounces **lean** meat or 1 medium serving poultry or fish; 1 serving these vegetables: asparagus, broccoli, Brussels sprouts, cabbage, carrots, cauliflower, celery, green beans, sauerkraut, spinach or tomatoes. (Serve hot, unbuttered, or as salads, using low-calorie dressing); 1 serving of the following: ½ cup potatoes, rice or noodles, 1 slice bread, or 1 small roll
OR
1 sandwich; 1 sliced egg or 1 slice poultry, lean beef or ham; 2 slices bread; low-calorie dressing; greens
AND
2 fresh apricots or plums; or 1 cup grapes, cherries, berries or melon; or 1 fresh pear, peach or apple (or water- or juice-pack canned fruit)
AND
½ glass skimmed milk

3-ounce serving meat or large serving poultry or fish; see left for vegetable servings

OR
same as left, but use 2 sliced eggs or 2 slices meat

AND
see left

AND
1 glass skimmed milk

## DINNER

3 ounces **lean** meat or a medium serving fish or poultry; 1 serving each vegetables and "starchy" foods—see lunch list
OR
1 serving low-calorie main dish from recipes, pages 81ff.; 1 serving vegetables—see lunch list
AND
½ cup gelatin dessert or pudding made with skimmed milk; or 1 thin slice angel-food or sponge cake; or 1 serving fruit from lunch list
AND
1 glass skimmed milk

4 ounces meat or generous serving fish or poultry; see lunch list for vegetable servings

OR
same as left plus ½ slice lightly buttered bread

AND
see left

AND
see left

### PLUS THE SNACKS

200 calories for snacks

400 calories for snacks

* Use only enriched breads, rice and pasta at all meals.

## SNACKERS' GUIDE

| CANDY, NIBBLERS, NUTS | |
|---|---|
| almonds (12) | 85 |
| Brazil nuts (2) | 55 |
| candy bar, average | 295 |
| caramel, plain (1) | 40 |
| cheese (1 oz.) | |
| American | 105 |
| Camembert | 85 |
| Cheddar, process | 115 |
| cream | 105 |
| Parmesan | 50 |
| Roquefort or blue | 105 |
| Swiss | 105 |
| chewing gum (1 stick) | 10 |
| chocolate cremes (1) | 50 |
| chocolate mint patty | 35 |
| chocolate (1 oz.) | |
| semisweet | 145 |
| sweet | 145 |
| chocolate syrup (1 tbsp.) | 50 |
| coconut (¼ cup) | 110 |
| dates, pitted (¼ cup) | 125 |
| fondant (1 oz.) | 105 |
| fudge (1" square) | 75 |
| gum drops (1 small) | 10 |
| hard candy (1 large) | 35 |
| marshmallows (1 average) | 25 |
| milk chocolate (1 oz.) | 145 |
| peanut brittle (1 oz.) | 120 |
| peanuts (8 to 10) | 55 |
| pecans (9 medium) | 70 |
| pickles | |
| dill (1 medium) | 10 |
| sour (1 large) | 15 |
| sweet (1 small) | 20 |
| popcorn, plain (1 cup) | 40 |
| potato chips (10) | 115 |
| pretzels (5 3⅛"-long sticks) | 10 |
| pumpkin seeds | |
| shelled (1 tbsp.) | 60 |
| unshelled (¼ cup) | 60 |
| sunflower seeds | |
| shelled (1 tbsp.) | 45 |
| unshelled (¼ cup) | 45 |
| walnuts (1 tbsp.) | 50 |

**BEVERAGES\***

| | |
|---|---|
| apple juice | 120 |
| bouillon | 5 |
| buttermilk | 90 |
| chocolate milk drink | 190 |
| cider | 120 |
| cocoa | 245 |
| cola drinks (6-oz. bottle) | 70 |
| cranberry juice | 160 |
| ginger ale | 85 |
| grape juice | 170 |
| grapefruit juice | 100 |
| lemonade | 110 |
| milk, whole | 160 |
| skimmed | 90 |
| orange juice | 110 |
| prune juice | 200 |
| tomato juice | 50 |

**RAW VEGETABLES, ½- to 1-CUP SERVINGS 20 CALORIES EACH**

cabbage (Chinese, green, red, Savoy, etc), cauliflower, celery, chicory, cucumbers, endive, escarole, lettuce (Bibb, Boston, iceberg, etc.), mushrooms, okra, green pepper, radishes, romaine, spinach, tomatoes, watercress

**BREADS, CRACKERS OR PASTRIES**

| | |
|---|---|
| bagel (1 large) | 165 |
| biscuits (1 medium) | 90 |
| bread (1 slice) | |
| Boston brown | 100 |
| cracked wheat | 65 |

| | |
|---|---|
| Melba toast | 15 |
| rye | 60 |
| white | 70 |
| whole wheat | 65 |
| crackers | |
| graham (4 small) | 110 |
| oyster (10 crackers) | 45 |
| round (1 average) | 15 |
| saltine (2" square) | 10 |
| soda (2½" square) | 25 |
| whole rye (1) | 20 |
| Danish pastry (1) | 275 |
| doughnut, plain (1) | 125 |
| jelly (1) | 185 |
| English muffin (1) | 145 |
| French toast (1 slice) | 140 |
| griddle cake (4") | 110 |
| hot cross bun (1) | 185 |
| matzoh (1 plain) | 120 |
| muffins (2½" diameter) | |
| blueberry | 140 |
| bran | 100 |
| corn | 125 |
| plain | 120 |
| popover (1 medium) | 120 |
| rolls, plain | |
| 1 small | 85 |
| 1 medium | 115 |
| 1 large | 175 |
| waffle (7" square) | 205 |
| zwieback (1) | 30 |

**CAKES, COOKIES, PIES**

| | |
|---|---|
| cakes | |
| angel-food (2" wedge) | 110 |
| chiffon (1/16) | 215 |
| cupcake, unfrosted | 90 |
| fruitcake (1/30 of 8" loaf) | 55 |
| poundcake (½" slice) | 140 |
| sponge cake (1/12) | 195 |
| cookies | |
| brownies (2" square) | 85 |

| | |
|---|---|
| chocolate chip | 50 |
| fig bar (1 square) | 50 |
| gingersnap (1 small) | 30 |
| oatmeal (1 large) | 65 |
| sugar (1 large) | 80 |
| sugar wafer (1 small) | 25 |
| pies (1/7 of 9" pie) | |
| coconut custard | 285 |
| lemon meringue | 305 |
| pumpkin | 275 |

**FRUITS\***
**75-CALORIE SERVINGS**

4 small apricots or plums
1 small banana or pear
1 medium apple or orange
2 small peaches or tangerines
¾ cup blackberries, blueberries, cherries or grapes
1 cup pineapple chunks, red raspberries, or sliced strawberries
3 tbsps. raisins
2 cups cubed cantaloupe or watermelon

**OTHER DESSERTS**

| | |
|---|---|
| apple brown betty (½-cup serving) | 175 |
| baked apple (1) | 130 |
| coffee cake (2" x 3") | 250 |
| frozen desserts (½ cup) | |
| frozen custard | 125 |
| ice cream | 165 |
| ice milk | 100 |
| sherbet | 130 |
| gelatin dessert (½ cup) | 70 |
| puddings (½ cup) | |
| butterscotch | 140 |
| chocolate | 175 |
| custard (baked) | 150 |
| junket | 50 |
| rice (¾ cup) | 225 |

\* 8-oz. glass

\* Fresh, water- or juice-pack canned, or unsweetened frozen fruits

## 12 SNACKS OF 200 CALORIES EACH FOR EAT-FOR-A-TREAT DIET

- ¾ cup sherbet or ½ cup ice cream (any flavor)
- 3 cups coffee or tea, each with 1 tablespoon light cream and 2 teaspoons sugar
- 2-inch wedge angel-food or sponge cake with ¾-cup serving fresh, unsweetened or water-pack canned fruit
- 1 cup puffed or flaked cereal with 8-ounce glass skimmed milk and 1 teaspoon sugar
- 1 slice lightly buttered bread or toast and ½ cup cottage cheese
- ½ cup pudding made with skimmed milk and 1 fresh peach, pear, apple or small banana
- 1½ ounces cheese and three 2-inch-square saltines
- 1 cup canned vegetable, noodle, minestrone or tomato soup and ¾ cup oyster crackers
- 1 buttered and jellied English muffin, large muffin or crescent roll
- 1 fresh pear, peach, apple or small banana and 1 cup oyster crackers
- 1 soft- or hard-cooked egg and 1 slice lightly buttered and jellied toast
- 1 serving any 150-calorie dessert from low-calorie dessert recipes (pages 210–241) plus coffee with sugar and light cream

# WISCONSIN DIET

Is dieting every day much too painful even to *think* about? Consider this plan! You diet Mondays and Tuesdays, Thursdays and Fridays, on 1200 calories for women, 1800 for men. On Wednesdays and over those weekends when dieting is difficult, merely hold the calorie line with a maintenance diet—2000 calories for women (1850 if you're over 40), 2800 calories for men (2600 for those over 45). As you'll see, maintenance days allow you enough calories for surprisingly hearty fare. You'll lose only one pound a week, but at that rate it will take less than three months to lose 10 pounds! Given here: a week of sample menus for inspiration. Figures in parentheses indicate portions for men. See the Basic-Four Diet for more menu ideas.

## A WEEK OF DIET MENUS TO GUIDE YOU

### MONDAY—A LOW-CALORIE DAY
**1200 CALORIES (HERS)    1800 (HIS)**

#### BREAKFAST
| | |
|---|---|
| 4-ounce glass orange juice | (6-ounce glass) |
| 2 poached eggs | (same) |
| ½ toasted English muffin | (whole muffin) |
| Coffee (black) or tea | (with lemon)* |

#### LUNCH
| | |
|---|---|
| 1 cup beef bouillon | (same) |
| Cheese sandwich on rye | (same, but |
| (1 slice cheese, 1 tea- | 2 slices cheese, |
| spoon dressing, 2 slices | 1 tablespoon |
| bread and a generous | dressing) |
| amount of lettuce) | |
| ½ cup raspberry sherbet | (¾ cup sherbet) |

#### DINNER
| | |
|---|---|
| 4 1-ounce meatballs | (6 meatballs) |
| (made with round of | |
| beef) | |
| ⅓ cup each: okra, corn | (½ cup each) |
| Kosher pickle sticks | (same) |
| 1 fresh pear | (same) |
| 4-ounce glass buttermilk | (8-ounce glass) |

### TUESDAY—A LOW-CALORIE DAY
**1200 CALORIES (HERS)    1800 (HIS)**

#### BREAKFAST
| | |
|---|---|
| 4-ounce glass grapefruit juice | (8-ounce glass) |
| ¾ cup hot oatmeal | (1 cup cereal) |
| 1 tablespoon each: honey, raisins | (same) |
| 4-ounce glass skimmed milk | (8-ounce glass) |

#### LUNCH
| | |
|---|---|
| Chicken-salad platter | (same, but |
| (½ cup cubed chicken, | ¾ cup chicken) |
| 2 tablespoons salad | |
| dressing, seasonings | |
| and lettuce) | |
| 1 slice whole-wheat bread | (same) |
| Crisp Chinese celery sticks | (same) |
| 2 whole apricots (fresh | (same) |
| or dietetic-pack canned) | |
| 4-ounce glass skimmed milk | (8 ounces whole milk) |

#### DINNER
| | |
|---|---|
| 2 pan-broiled frankfurters | (3 frankfurters) |
| (catchup or mustard) | |
| 1 lightly buttered large hard roll | |
| ½ cup peas | (¾ cup) |
| ½ cup fresh pineapple | (¾ cup pineapple) |
| chunks (tossed with ½ | |
| cup yogurt) | |
| 4-ounce glass skimmed milk | (whole milk) |

* Any meal; Hold-the-Line days, light on milk, sugar if desired.

### WEDNESDAY—A HOLD-THE-LINE DAY
**2000 CALORIES (HERS)    2800 (HIS)**

#### BREAKFAST
| | |
|---|---|
| 4-ounce glass orange juice | (same) |
| 2 slices French toast | (3 slices) |
| (1 tablespoon maple syrup) | (2 tablespoons syrup) |

#### LUNCH
| | |
|---|---|
| Glass tomato juice | (same) |
| Medium hamburger | (2 hamburgers) |
| (on toasted roll) | (on two rolls) |
| Carrot and celery sticks | (same) |
| ½ cup rice pudding | (1 cup serving) |

#### DINNER
| | |
|---|---|
| 1 cup minestrone soup | (same) |
| 1 cup macaroni and cheese | (1½ cups) |
| Large cucumber/tomato | (same) |
| salad (1 tablespoon | (same) |
| Italian dressing) | |
| ½ cantaloupe | (same) |

#### SNACKS
| | |
|---|---|
| 200 calories for snacks* | (200 calories for snacks*) |

### THURSDAY—A LOW-CALORIE DAY
**1200 CALORIES (HERS)    1800 (HIS)**

#### BREAKFAST
| | |
|---|---|
| 4-ounce glass tomato juice | (8-ounce glass) |
| (Worcestershire and | |
| lemon juice) | |
| 1-egg fluffy onion omelet | (2-egg omelet) |
| 1 slice jellied toast | (1½ slices) |
| 4-ounce glass skimmed milk | (8 ounces whole milk) |

#### LUNCH
| | |
|---|---|
| 3 ounces pan-broiled minute | (5 ounces) |
| steak (served on toast) | |
| ½ cup each: zucchini, carrots | (same) |
| Medium tossed salad | (same) |
| (low-calorie dressing) | |
| ½ cup rennet custard | (same) |
| pudding (made with | |
| skimmed milk) | |

#### DINNER
| | |
|---|---|
| Boned chicken breast, small | (same) |
| (sautéed and seasoned) | |
| ½ cup noodles | (same) |
| (with poppy seeds) | |
| ½ cup stewed celery | (¾ cup) |
| One small biscuit | (2 biscuits) |
| (unbuttered) | (lightly buttered) |
| One small apple | (same) |
| 8-ounce glass skimmed milk | (8 ounces whole milk) |

* See page 26 for snack suggestions.

### FRIDAY—A LOW-CALORIE DAY
**1200 CALORIES (HERS)    1800 (HIS)**

#### BREAKFAST
4-ounce glass pineapple    (6-ounce glass)
  juice
1 cup ready-to-eat oat cereal (same)
  (2 teaspoons sugar)    (same)
8-ounce glass skimmed milk (whole milk)

#### LUNCH
Fruit-salad bowl
  (½ cup cottage cheese,    (same, but 1 cup
  1 cup mixed fresh fruit,    cottage cheese,
  lettuce cup)    1½ cups fruit)
3 slices Melba toast    (4 slices)

#### DINNER
4 ounces pan-fried halibut    (6 ounces)
½ cup each: tomatoes,    (¾ cup each)
  peas
1 medium hard roll    (same)
  (unbuttered)
Tossed salad    (same)
  (low-calorie dressing)    (same)
½ cup orange sections    (1 cup sections)
8-ounce glass skimmed milk (same)

---

### SATURDAY—A HOLD-THE-LINE DAY
**2000 CALORIES (HERS)    2800 (HIS)**

#### BREAKFAST
4-ounce glass grapefruit    (same)
  juice
2 4-inch waffles (2    (3 waffles)
  tablespoons maple syrup) (3 tablespoons syrup)
4-ounce glass milk    (same)

#### LUNCH
Shrimp creole    (1½ servings)
  (½ cup serving on rice)
Tossed salad (1 tablespoon    (same)
  cheese dressing)    (2 tablespoons)
½ cup baked custard    (same)

#### DINNER
1 medium serving meat loaf (2 servings)
½ cup each: chopped broc-    (same)
  coli, mashed potatoes
Lettuce, shredded (with    (same)
  chili sauce)    (same)
1½ inch wedge angel-food    (same)
  cake (topped with rasp-    (same)
  berry sauce)
8-ounce glass whole milk    (same)

#### SNACKS
200 calories for snacks*    (200 calories for
      snacks*)

* See page 26 for snack suggestions.

### SUNDAY—A HOLD-THE-LINE DAY
**2000 CALORIES (HERS)    2800 (HIS)**

#### BREAKFAST
8-ounce glass tomato juice    (same)
1 fried egg    (2 fried eggs)
1 slice rye toast    (2 slices toast)
  (lightly buttered)
8-ounce glass whole milk    (same)

#### LUNCH
1 cup cream of tomato soup (same)
Bacon, lettuce and tomato    (2 sandwiches)
  sandwich
  (2 strips crisp bacon, 1
  tablespoon dressing, 2
  slices bread, lettuce and
  tomato)
Chilled fruit cocktail    (same)

#### DINNER
Broiled steak (about    (same)
  5 ounces boned meat)
½ cup sautéed mushrooms    (same)
½ cup buttered spinach    (same)
Small baked potato (2 table- (medium potato)
  spoons sour cream)    (3 tablespoons)
Tiny brownie    (2 brownies)

#### SNACKS
200 calories for snacks*    (200 calories for
      snacks*)

* See page 26 for snack suggestions.

## THE MOST COMMONLY ASKED QUESTIONS ABOUT DIETING

Over the years, the Good Housekeeping Institute has received thousands of inquiries about all aspects of dieting. Here is a sampling of questions most frequently asked about low-calorie diets.

Q. *How can I estimate the number of calories I need daily?*
A. Multiply your desirable weight (obtained from the height-weight charts on pages 323–324) by eighteen for a man and by sixteen for a woman. This is approximately the number of calories used daily by a moderately active adult. You may need about a fourth more calories if you are *very* active; a fourth less if you are less active. If you are over fifty-five, subtract another 300 calories for women and 400 calories for men.

Q. *Is overeating the only major cause of overweight?*
A. It's by far the dominant one. Obesity can be caused by any one or a combination of inherited, emotional or environmental factors. This largest class includes obesity due to overeating, inactivity, or a combination of the two. The other, much smaller, group involves some abnormality in the metabolism. (Remember, it's easier to blame metabolism than lack of willpower! )

Q. *Is hunger different from appetite?*
A. Yes. True hunger is a sensation that signifies the body's actual need for food. It may be a gnawing in the stomach, definite pain or faintness—feelings that are not only unpleasant but agonizing. Appetite is simply a healthy, normal desire for food. Although largely controlled by habit, it can be stimulated by the sight or smell of attractive food.

Q. *How can it be true that worry and nervous tension make some people lose weight, while others gain?*
A. People react in different ways to mental stress. In some, worry or fear creates what almost amounts to an aversion to food, which often is reflected physically by a "lump in the throat" that makes it seem impossible to swallow. Such people will, of course, lose weight. Others, however, find actual relief from their cares through eating, and may find particular pleasure in extremely rich foods which are associated with their childhood memories. These are the ones who gain.

Q. *Is it true that some foods "burn up" faster than others?*
A. The rate at which food is digested or absorbed in no way affects its calorie value. If total caloric intake exceeds your expenditure of energy, you'll gain weight. But foods do differ in satiety value—that is, how full they make you feel. It's important that you feel satisfied during a reducing diet. Include lots of protein and some fat, two nutrients with "staying power." (Remember, though, that fat is the most concentrated source of calories, so it should be used in moderation.) To supply bulk, supplement protein and fat-rich foods with plenty of salads, vegetables and fruits.

Q. *When I lose weight, what happens to fat? How does the body get rid of it?*
A. When you take in too much fuel (calories), the body converts it into fatty deposits (those bulges you hate to see showing). If you need more fuel than your food is giving at any particular time, the body burns or uses up the excess fat that has been stored in "fatter" times. When you lose weight, the body is forced to use this stored fuel. The burned fuel becomes energy, carbon dioxide which you breathe out, and water eliminated in perspiration and urine.

Q. *Is it true that people over forty should cut down on the calories and protein in their diet?*
A. Men and women over forty tend to eat less than they once did (a natural compensation for a slower metabolic rate, perhaps less activity). This is good, since those in this age bracket *should* cut calories—by a regulated diet, if necessary. They should *not*, however, reduce their daily intake of protein—at least two servings of meat, fish or poultry, and two glasses of milk, should be included in meals each day.

Q. *When I diet, I can lose several pounds the first week or so, but then I always hit a plateau and get discouraged. What's wrong?*

A. A number of things can prevent weight loss, even on a diet that is followed faithfully. You should know, first of all, that a change in the rate of loss is common. Try to accept the plateau as a natural thing. Wait a week or so and you'll start losing again. Changes in the natural water balance of the body will slow the rate of loss temporarily. It is quite usual to lose several pounds of water in the first weeks. Losing fat—the important part of a diet—comes more slowly. If you've been dieting for some time now, are you counting calories as carefully as you did at first? Many dieters fail to count all the foods they eat during a day, or underestimate the size of servings. Get out your scales and measuring cups and start checking serving sizes more carefully. Calculate calories in your homemade dishes; don't just take average values from a calorie chart.

Q. *Can it possibly be true that it takes only an extra 100 calories a day to gain 10 pounds in one year?*

A. If you eat 100 extra calories every day, you'll gain 1 pound every 35 days—or over 10 pounds in one year. But look at the other side! If you eat 100 fewer calories every day, you'll *lose* 1 pound every 35 days. Actually, most of us eat according to the a-little-bit-more-today, a-little-bit-less-tomorrow pattern, and so maintain our present weight without calorie counting.

Q. *I thought the quickest way to lose weight was to eliminate liquids and salt from the diet. Why do you always recommend lots of liquids and allow salt on your reducing diets?*

A. For long-lasting weight reduction, you must lose *fatty* tissue, not water. Everyone has to have a generous amount of water daily to preserve the body's water balance and thus maintain health. The average adult needs 2½ quarts of water each day from the natural water in foods plus beverages. Any

limitation of water intake should be only under strict medical supervision. It is true that salt intake helps to regulate the amount of water in the tissues. By cutting down on salt (sodium, to be precise), a few pounds of water will be excreted. But remember you want to lose fat, not water. Low-calorie diets are restricted at best. To eliminate salt and make food less palatable is asking too much of the average dieter.

Q. *Can anything besides retention of fluids cause a gain in weight of 3 to 4 pounds in two days, when elimination is normal? Is fluid retention a danger signal?*

A. To answer the first part of your question, we know of no other explanation for such a rapid gain. About 3500 extra calories are required to produce a gain of 1 pound. This means that 10,500 extra calories must be eaten to gain 3 pounds and 14,000 to gain 4 pounds. For example, an individual who has a maintenance calorie requirement of 2000 per day would have to eat from 7250 to 9000 calories per day to gain 3 or 4 pounds in two days. Eating this large an amount of food is just about a practical impossibility.

Retention of fluid is not always a danger signal. Normally, the amount of fluid held in the body tissues is regulated largely by the salt content of the diet. A liberal salt-user will retain more fluid, which the body needs under these conditions to maintain a proper balance.

The sharp drop in weight which may occur during the first days of a reducing diet is often due to fluid loss, especially if the diet emphasizes foods which are low in sodium and restricts use of salt both in cooking and at the table. Also, a temporary rise in weight due to fluid retention often precedes menstruation. Any continuing increase of weight in an individual who is not overeating or overusing salt should be brought to a physician's attention.

Q. *Won't I lose weight if I just eat two regular meals each day and half a grapefruit for lunch?*

A. You may lose some weight this way, depending, of course, on how much you eat for your "regular" meals. But this isn't a wise way to diet. For one thing, if you rely on only half a grapefruit to get you from breakfast to dinner-time, you're sure to nibble to keep hunger pangs down, and snacks can quickly add up to the calories you tried to omit by having a half-grapefruit lunch. You're better off in the long run, so far as successful dieting goes, to plan three well-balanced low-calorie meals instead of two "regular" ones with grapefruit in between. If you eat 500 to 700 calories less than you're eating now, spread over three meals a day, you'll probably lose 1 to 1½ pounds a week—and enjoy your meals in the process. And you'll be establishing a regular eating pattern, which will stand you in good stead when it comes to maintaining your "new" weight.

Q. *In your diet plans you list as interchangeable a fresh, medium-size peach, pear, apple and small banana. According to my calorie chart, a peach contains 46 calories; a pear, 95; an apple, 76; a small banana, 79. How can they be substituted for one another?*
A. You're talking about a precise figuring of calories that often isn't practical on an average reducing diet. It's better to allow a dieter a wide choice of foods within a total daily calorie amount. That is why the calorie values for the four fruits you mentioned are averaged to an interchangeable 75 calories in menu calculations. On the assumption that a dieter will eat all four fruits equally often, the higher-calorie pear will balance out the low-calorie peach.

Q. *What are the calories for salt, pepper, herbs, spices, extracts, baking powder, baking soda, etc.?*
A. Since the calories in these items are miniscule, they wouldn't alter calorie totals enough to warrant including them in the average chart, or in your calorie count.

Q. *Are "starchy" and "carbohydrate" synonymous?*
A. No, they're not. All starches are carbohydrates, but not all carbohydrates are starch. Carbohydrate is a general term (like protein, fat, vitamin and mineral) which identifies one class of food components. Several types of carbohydrates include fruit sugars, "regular" sugar, and the more complex starches, dextrins and cellulose.

Q. *Does honey have fewer calories than sugar? Can I substitute it for sugar in recipes?*
A. One cup of honey has 990 calories; a cup of granulated sugar has 770. If you'd like to substitute honey for sugar occasionally, you can do it successfully in recipes for puddings or fruit-pie fillings, or as a sweetener for fruit and beverages. For each cup of sugar in a recipe, use ¾ to 1 cup of honey and decrease the liquid in the recipe by ¼ cup.

Q. *Is it true that safflower oil has no calories? Are there any other calorie-free oils?*
A. The answer to both questions is an emphatic No. Safflower oil, like all oils, supplies 125 calories per tablespoon and is normally utilized by the body in the same way as other fats. Fats and oils should not be eliminated from reducing diets—they play an important role in contributing essential fatty acids. They have high satiety value. But they must be used with discretion, so you don't go overboard on total calories.

Q. *Does using a Teflon-coated skillet really help cut down the need to add fat for frying?*
A. In practically all cases, foods can be pan-broiled with no sticking. Obviously, the Teflon or other nonstick skillets are a great asset to those who must cook low-calorie dishes. They perform well for all cooking jobs. The newer ones don't scratch easily or require special cleaning tools.

Q. *Does food cooked in a skillet or pan with no fat added have more calories than food that is broiled?*
A. No, not significantly.

Q. *I have heard that bananas are good for a reducing diet because they're high in protein and low in carbohydrate and sodium. Is this true?*

A. By all means have bananas as part of the fruit allowed on your diet. Bananas are relatively low in calories, as are most fruits. But there's no particular reason to choose bananas over other fruits unless you happen to like them a lot. Many other fruits—watermelon, grapes, etc.—are lower in calories. Bananas are not high in protein; their protein content is negligible. They are low in sodium, but not low in carbohydrate, the main source of calories in fruit. When deciding which fruits to include in your diet, however, check the total calorie content, not just the amount of carbohydrate.

Q. *Do the packaged nonfat dry milks have all the same nutrients as regular liquid skimmed milk and whole milk? How do they compare in terms of calories?*
A. The nonfat dry milks contain all the protein, carbohydrate and minerals that are in regular skimmed and whole milk. Fat and fat-soluble vitamins (A and E) have been removed from this dry skimmed milk, but the rest of the vitamin content remains similar to whole milk. Most liquid skimmed milks and many nonfat dry milks now on the market have been refortified with vitamins A and D. Unmodified liquid skimmed milk and nonfat dry milk have essentially the same vitamin content. Modified skimmed milks have extra nonfat milk solids added to give more "body." Brands vary, but most contain 130 to 140 calories per glass. Dry milk reliquefied according to directions contains 90 calories per glass. But many homemakers make their own modified skimmed milk by adding extra dry milk. The flavor is better, the drink richer in nutrients.

Q. *There seem to be so many different kinds of margarine. Can you tell me what the difference is among them and how each should be used? And how do they differ in calories?*
A. *Regular margarine* is a mixture of partially hydrogenated vegetable fats and oils that has been churned with milk, colored, and fortified with vitamins A and D to give a butter-like consistency and flavor. The hydrogenation process changes liquid (polyunsaturated) fats into solid (saturated) fats. Regular margarine, which comes in sticks, can be used in recipes that call for butter or margarine.

*Special margarines* are processed so that they contain more polyunsaturated fat than regular margarines. In the ingredients list on these margarine packages, liquid oil (corn, safflower, etc.) is listed first. These margarines are recommended for diets rich in polyunsaturated fats. Stick margarines of this type can be used as you would regular margarines. Soft (tub) margarines in this special-margarine category can be used like other soft margarines (see below).

*Soft margarines* have been specially processed to be spreadable at refrigerator temperatures. They come in tubs, rather than as sticks. Many, but not all, of the soft margarines are also special margarines. They can be used successfully in most recipes. For baking, it is safer to use recipes developed especially for soft margarines.

*Whipped margarines* are regular margarines that have been whipped with air to increase their volume by about 50 percent. They usually come in pound packages, six sticks to a package. On a weight basis (pound for pound), they are the equivalent of regular margarine. On a volume basis (tablespoon for tablespoon), however, they're not comparable to regular margarine because of the incorporated air. They can be used in cooking and baking on an equal weight basis, but not on a volume basis.

*Imitation margarines* do not contain as much fat as is required by Federal regulations for regular margarines—they have about half the fat and calories of regular margarines. Because they contain less fat and more water than regular margarine, they should not be used for making baked goods.

Almost all the different types of margarines come both salted and unsalted. If a recipe specifies unsalted (sweet) margarine, by all means use it.

Q. *Why do the figures in various calorie books differ so much?*
A. Differences in a food's age, maturity,

variety, water content and the season it was grown can cause variations of as much as 10 percent. In a food such as bologna, depending on the proportions of fat, meat and starchy filler in a particular brand, the difference can go as high as 100 percent. In homemade baked goods and prepared dishes—apple dumplings, spaghetti sauce, etc. —the only way to get even a workable approximation is to calculate the calories yourself by adding the number in the individual ingredients and dividing by the number of servings. One word of advice: When calorie books differ, take the highest figure or at least an average figure. If you always take the lowest one, you'll only be cheating yourself.

Q. *Can alcohol be used by the body like food to supply calories? Does all the alcohol evaporate when wine, beer, etc. is used in cooking, and if so, does this eliminate all the calories?*
A. The body can and does use the calories from alcohol. A gram of pure alcohol provides about seven calories. In "hard" liquors, this amounts to 100 to 125 calories per 1½ ounce jigger, depending on the proof of the liquor.

The alcohol in wines and liquors does evaporate in cooking and boiling, and the calorie count is significantly reduced. In a dry wine, the number of calories is essentially lowered to zero. A sweet wine, however, contains sugar. When you cook with this, you lose the alcohol, but you're left with the sugar content, which does not boil off. The amount of sugar and, therefore, the remaining calorie content vary from one sweet wine to another.

Q. *How much difference does it make in calories when you drain syrup from canned fruit? Does the drained fruit have the same number of calories as fresh?*
A. Canned fruit absorbs a significant amount of sugar, so it's higher in calories than fresh even when drained. The degree of difference depends on the concentration of the syrup—light, medium, heavy, extra heavy—and the type of fruit. Draining does eliminate the calories you would get if you served some syrup with the fruit. This can mean 25 to 100 calories per serving.

Q. *Do the dietetic chocolate candies made with artificial sweetener contain fewer calories than regular chocolate candy?*
A. Regular chocolate candy has about 145 calories per ounce. "Dietetic" chocolate, sweetened with nonnutritive sweetener, has between 100 and 150 calories per ounce. In many cases, the "dietetic" chocolates contain dilutants (often nonfat dry-milk solids) to decrease the fat and calorie content. These chocolates usually list the caloric value on the label as calories per 100 grams. When you check to see whether their caloric savings are really worthwhile, remember that regular chocolate candy ranges from 475 to 530 calories per 100 grams.

## DIETING IS A STATE OF MIND

1. Pick a good diet plan. Make sure you select one that not only is well-balanced but includes foods you like. There's no need to eliminate high-calorie favorites if you know how to fit them in.
2. Set formal goals. Make a chart, like the one at right, on graph paper. On the left, starting at the bottom, enter your desired weight, then mark off each pound until your current weight is reached. Along the base line, fill in the number of weeks it should take to reach your goal. Expect a

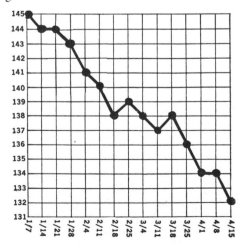

jagged chart: weight loss is never smooth from week to week. So don't get discouraged.

3. Throw out all fattening treats (or give them away). The fewer temptations you have around, the easier it is to resist "just one."

4. Keep busy. If you tend to nibble while you watch television, occupy your hands with knitting or crossword puzzles.

5. Perk up the table and diet fare with a colorful centerpiece, tangy relishes.

6. Take small bites and eat slowly. You will think you are eating more and your stomach will have more time to signal when you are full.

7. Avoid lunch and dinner invitations for the first few weeks.

8. Trade secrets with a dieting friend. While you wouldn't bore non-dieters with your dieting woes, it is helpful to talk to a kindred spirit. For more moral support, have tea or broth with her daily.

9. Mark milestones. When you have lost 5 or 10 pounds, get a new girdle to make yourself more shapely.

10. Have snapshots taken to show how you look in a tight dress or a bathing suit.

11. Make or buy a new dress or get out an old favorite that is a size or two too small. It will give you incentive to reach your goal.

12. Stamp out boredom. Plan a whole list of odd jobs. Do one every time you want a snack.

13. Study overweight people on the bus or street. Vow you'll never have hips, thighs or arms that heavy.

14. Walk away from the refrigerator when hunger pangs strike. A restful walk or casual bicycle ride will take you far from snack foods.

15. Schedule a fifteen-minute exercise session for the same time daily, preferably before you eat.

16. Get eight hours' sleep. You will have more willpower if you are well rested.

17. Weigh yourself at the same time of day, only once or twice a week so you can see a definite change each time.

## TIPS ON LOW-CALORIE COOKING

1. Panbroil meats in a skillet with a non-stick finish so you won't have to add fat.

2. Serve the hearty vegetables. Beets, carrots, peas, onions, winter squash and turnips have only 40 calories each per ½-cup serving.

3. For a hot cereal that is ready in a minute in pre-measured portions, try instant cream of wheat or oatmeal.

4. Trim all fat from pork chops and they will have the same calories as lean beef. Panbroil or braise with beef bouillon.

5. By draining the oil from canned tuna, you will cut its calories by one-third. Or use broth- or water-packed tuna, which has less than half the calories of oil-packed.

6. For cream sauces and sautéing foods, use half the usual amount of fat and substitute skimmed for whole milk.

7. For drinking, puddings, sauces, etc., use reliquefied nonfat dry milk in place of higher-calorie whole milk.

8. Bouillon makes a fine clear gravy for meats and has practically no calories.

9. Season with herbs or spices instead of butter or margarine. Rosemary, thyme, poultry seasoning and sage all add marvelous flavor but no calories to main courses, vegetables and pastas.

10. Start meals with filling, low-calorie appetizers: clear broths or soups, spiced fruit or vegetable juices.

11. Buy frozen unsweetened berries, loose in plastic bags, so you can take out only the amount needed. (They thaw to form their own syrup.) Buy frozen vegetables that way too.

12. When buying canned fruits, try pineapple packed in juice (not syrup) or unsweetened applesauce. Or drain heavy syrup from sugar-pack fruits and replace with unsweetened fruit juice.

13. Beware of hot breads. They contain more calories per serving than regular bread.

# Planning Meals

A homemaker has many different needs to meet in preparing food. But with a Basic-Four Food Chart as her guide, she can easily plan meals that will tempt the appetites and insure the well-being of every member of the family, from baby to grandparent.

As the keeper of the family diet, the homemaker has a responsibility to plan and prepare attractive, nutritionally balanced meals for a variety of age groups. She must not only keep in mind her own dietary needs, particularly during pregnancy, but develop healthy eating habits in her children while they're small, see that growing teens get necessary extra vitamins, keep an eye on her husband's waistline, and perhaps battle older family members' declining appetites. When you consider this diversity of dietary needs, it is truly amazing that a simple outline, The Basic-Four Food Guide, can be used to plan meals that provide for each and every one.

*The Basic-Four* The Basic-Four refers to a classification of foods into four major categories: Milk and Dairy Products; Meat, Fish and Poultry; Fruits and Vegetables; Bread and Cereals. To make sure that you are serving well-balanced meals that provide all the necessary nutrients, plan your daily menus to include at least the number of servings shown in each category. In most cases you will be serving more than the minimum, since most family members will need more than the 1200 to 1400 calories supplied by the basic outline. Complete your menus with extra servings from the basic food groups plus supplemental foods like butter and sugar. Use the Keep-Trim Guide on pages 38 and 39 to keep a continuing eye on calories by selecting relatively low-calorie foods from each group. The menus on pages 40 and 41 give a week of easy-to-fix meal ideas.

# THE BASIC-FOUR FOOD GROUPS

| THE FOOD GROUPS | THE SERVING SIZES | THE NUTRIENTS THEY SUPPLY |
|---|---|---|
| **Meat and protein-rich foods:** 2 servings of meats, fish, poultry, eggs or cheese. Occasionally dried beans, peas, nuts, etc., may be substituted for the meats. | one serving equals: 3 ounces lean, cooked meat, fish or poultry 3 eggs 3 slices (ounces) cheese 1 to 1½ cups cooked beans ⅓ cup peanut butter | Meats provide protein, iron, niacin and the other B vitamins. |
| **Fruits and vegetables:** 4 servings of fruits and vegetables. Be certain to include one serving of citrus fruit or tomatoes and one of dark-green or leafy vegetables daily. | one serving equals: ½ cup canned or cooked fruit 1 fresh peach, pear, etc. 1 cup fresh berries or cherries ½ cup cooked vegetables 1 cup uncooked leafy vegetables | Fruits and vegetables supply vitamins A and C plus the other vitamins, minerals and roughage. |
| **Breads, cereals and pasta:** 4 servings of enriched or whole-grain cereals and breads. | one serving equals: 1 slice bread 1 small biscuit, muffin or roll ½ cup potatoes, pastas or rice ¾ to 1 cup flaked or puffed cereals ½ cup cooked cereals | Cereals and breads are important sources of the B vitamins and they contribute supplemental amounts of protein and iron. |
| **Milk and milk products:** 2 servings of milk and other dairy foods for adults; 3 to 4 servings for children; 4 or more servings for teens. | one serving equals: 8-ounce glass of skimmed or whole milk 1 ounce (1 slice) cheese ½-cup cottage cheese | Milk contributes significant amounts of calcium, protein and riboflavin as well as vitamins A and D and the B vitamins. |

| | All You Can Eat, Anytime You Like | Great Big Servings (even seconds) |
|---|---|---|
| **MEAT AND PROTEIN-RICH FOODS** | | |
| **FRUITS AND VEGETABLES** | tomato or vegetable juices vegetables (unbuttered): asparagus, broccoli, cabbage, cauliflower, celery, cucumbers, endive, escarole, green beans, greens, Italian beans, kale, kohlrabi, lettuce, mushrooms, okra, peppers, radishes, romaine, sauerkraut, spinach, summer squash, tomatoes and wax beans | fruit or fruit juices (fresh, unsweetened frozen, or dietetic pack): apples, berries, cherries, grapefruit, grapes, melons, oranges, peaches, pineapple and tangerines soups—except cream soups and chowders vegetables (unbuttered): Brussels sprouts, carrots, green peas, onions and rutabagas |
| **BREADS AND CEREALS** | | Melba toast rye wafers |
| **MILK AND MILK PRODUCTS** | | skimmed milk: regular or reliquefied dry milk, evaporated skimmed milk, modified skimmed milk or buttermilk yogurt: plain |
| **SUPPLEMENTAL FOODS** | coffee or tea—little sugar and no cream consommé or bouillon gelatin desserts—artificially sweetened only salad dressings—low-calorie only seasoners, relishes: catchup, chili sauce, etc. soft-drinks—artificially-sweetened only; plain soda water | olives: ripe or stuffed |

THE BASIC FOUR FOOD GROUPS

| Generous Portions | Average Amounts | Take It Easy On These |
|---|---|---|
| cheese: cottage, farmer, pot and ricotta<br>eggs: baked, coddled, poached, soft- or hard-cooked<br>fish and shellfish (except breaded or fried): bass, cod, flounder, haddock, ocean perch, sardines (drained), shellfish (any kind), tuna (well drained or water or broth packs) and white-fish<br>poultry (except breaded or fried): chicken, Cornish hens and turkey | cheese: any not in Generous Portions<br>eggs: fried, scrambled and omelets<br>fish (except breaded or fried): bluefish, halibut, mackerel, salmon and swordfish<br>meats (except breaded, fried): lean, well-trimmed cuts of beef, ham, lamb, pork and veal<br>crisp bacon, canned meats, cold cuts, corned beef, frankfurters, rabbit and variety meats (liver, etc.)<br>poultry: duckling and goose | fried and breaded meats, fish and poultry<br>untrimmed or fatty meats |
| fruits (fresh or dietetic pack): bananas and pears<br>fruit drinks and nectars<br>fruit juices: grape, prune and cranberry<br>vegetables (unbuttered): beets, corn, limas, parsnips, pumpkin and winter squash | fruits: regular canned, dried, sweetened frozen or stewed | fried and breaded vegetables |
| | bread, crackers or rolls: any type cereals: ready-to-eat and cooked<br>dried beans: peas, lentils or limas<br>macaroni, spaghetti, noodles, etc.<br>pancakes and waffles<br>potatoes: white or sweet<br>quick breads: biscuits, muffins, etc.<br>rice: plain or seasoned | pies and pastries<br>pizza<br>snack foods: chips, pretzels and similar items |
| milk: regular whole and evaporated<br>yogurt: flavored | cream soups and chowders<br>custard: baked and sauce<br>milk drinks<br>puddings: regular or instant | eggnog<br>ice cream and frozen custard<br>malted milk drinks |
| gelatin desserts: regular (plain or fruited) and fruit whips<br>popcorn, unbuttered | angel food or sponge cake<br>candy: hard, jelly beans and marshmallows<br>honey and molasses<br>jams, jellies, marmalades, etc.<br>salad dressings: regular<br>sherbets, ices, ice milks<br>soft drinks: regular<br>syrups: maple, corn, etc. | butter or margarine<br>cakes: not in Average Amounts<br>candy: not in Average Amounts<br>cookies<br>creams: light, heavy, commercial sour<br>nuts and nut butters<br>sauces and gravies—rich ones |

# A WEEK OF MENUS FOR THE FAMILY

Each day's menus contain all the Basic-Four foods. By adjusting the serving sizes, you can serve these meals to the whole family without exceeding anyone's calorie quota. (One normal serving equals 3 ounces cooked meat, ½ cup fruits and vegetables, 1 slice bread and 1 8-ounce glass milk.)

## 1

BREAKFAST
pineapple juice
cornflakes with sugar
rye toast
milk

LUNCH
split pea soup with croutons
chicken- or tuna-filled omelet
zucchini coins
peach slices
buttermilk

DINNER
sautéed minute or veal steaks (with onion
gravy)
Italian green beans
Farmland Pepper Hash (see recipe page
200)
homemade cornbread
fresh fruit compote

## 2

BREAKFAST
orange juice
pancakes or waffles (with applesauce and
cinnamon)
cocoa

LUNCH
panbroiled hamburger
enriched rice with parsley
sliced radishes (with French dressing)
fruited gelatin
milk

DINNER
Broiled Mackerel Platter (see recipe, page
81) (with broccoli and tomatoes)
pear half with cottage cheese (on lettuce)
enriched hard rolls
angel-food cake (glazed with chocolate
syrup)
milk

## 3

BREAKFAST
orange sections
puffed rice with brown sugar
oatmeal-bread toast
milk

LUNCH
beef bouillon
Swiss cheese sandwich on rye
tomato wedges and cucumber slices
raspberry sherbet

DINNER
roast pork
Green Beans Italian (see recipe, page
191)
corn niblets
lettuce wedges (with French dressing)
broiled grapefruit halves
milk

## 4

BREAKFAST
tomato juice (with Worcestershire and
lemon)
baked eggs on toast
bacon
milk

LUNCH
fruit-salad bowl (with fresh or canned
fruit, cottage cheese and sherbet)
Crisp Crusts (see recipe, page 207)

DINNER
Lamb-and-Carrot Meatballs (see recipe,
page 157)
sautéed green-pepper strips
curried enriched rice
strawberries and sour cream (fresh or
frozen berries)

## 5

**BREAKFAST**
grapefuit sections
oatmeal with honey and raisins
milk

**LUNCH**
corned-beef hash and poached eggs (on toast)
canned baby carrots
banana slices and vanilla wafers
milk

**DINNER**
vegetable soup (with enriched saltines)
London broil
baked potato (with yogurt and chives)
Herbed Tomato Salad (see recipe, page 195)
pineapple chunks

## 6

**BREAKFAST**
tangerine slices
fluffy onion omelet
whole-wheat toast slices
milk

**LUNCH**
chicken livers and mushrooms (broiled on skewers)
enriched noodles

lettuce wedges (with French dressing)
canned fruit cocktail (drain syrup, then add orange juice)
milk

**DINNER**
Skillet Pineapple Chicken (see recipe, page 113)
peas and onion slices
buttered parslied potatoes
baked cup custard

## 7

**BREAKFAST**
orange juice
toasted English muffin
Canadian bacon
milk

**LUNCH**
tuna-salad platter
celery and carrot strips
enriched refrigerated biscuits (with jam and jelly)
fresh grapes or apples
milk

**DINNER**
meatloaf with mushroom gravy
mashed potatoes
spinach with nutmeg
Blueberry Cottage Pudding (see recipe, page 220)

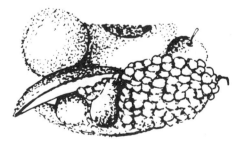

# DIET DURING PREGNANCY

Meal planning during pregnancy is no more complicated than at any other time, despite all the old wives' tales. Meals should be chosen from the Basic-Four food groups, plus an extra two glasses of milk each day to provide the additional protein and calcium needed by the developing baby. (The Basic-Four already calls for two glasses of milk; the extra two make up the one-quart requirement for pregnant women.)

The questions and answers that follow cover all the essential points a pregnant woman needs to know about her diet.

*Q. Does diet during pregnancy really make a difference in the baby's and mother's health?*
A. There is no question that it does. Nutritionists have found that mothers with the best diets have fewer difficulties during pregnancy, fewer premature births and healthier babies. During pregnancy the mother must supply the food necessary for her own body plus the nutrients needed by the developing baby. Quite literally she eats for both.

*Q. What foods should the mother-to-be eat?*
A. The Basic-Four Food Groups chart on page 37 gives the fundamentals for meal planning, but remember to include an extra two glasses of milk each day. The menu suggestions on pages 40–41 provide about 1800 calories; add two glasses of skimmed milk and they'll contain the 2000 recommended during the first three months of pregnancy. Go over this diet with your doctor; he may change it to fit your special requirements.

*Q. Is a quart of milk a day still the cornerstone of a pregnancy diet?*
A. Yes, it is. You need abundant amounts of calcium and riboflavin (a B vitamin) as well as protein, and milk is an excellent source of all three. If weight is a problem, cut the calories in half by using skimmed milk or nonfat dry milk. Practically all fresh liquid skimmed milks are fortified with Vitamins A and D; also keep an eye out for the new fortified nonfat dried milks on the market. Also consider evaporated milk or evaporated skimmed milk. Use them in custards, in place of egg in meat loaf, and cream sauces, etc. One-half cup undiluted evaporated milk is the equivalent to 1 cup of regular milk.

*Q. How about the filled milks, imitation milks, and coffee lighteners as a substitute for regular milk?*
A. We don't recommend them. Filled milk is basically skimmed milk with another fat substituted for the butterfat, but it is sometimes difficult to tell it from imitation milk. Imitation milk is a synthetic; many brands do not contain as much protein, calcium or vitamins as regular milk. Coffee lighteners are also poor substitutes; some brands are actually recommended for low-calcium diets.

*Q. Is the calcium and protein found in the cream part of milk?*
A. No, it's the skimmed milk part that is rich in these nutrients. The butterfat (cream) does "carry" Vitamins A and D, but most commercial skimmed milks have been refortified with these vitamins.

*Q. What if you don't like milk or are allergic to it?*
A. If it is a case of dislike, use milk to prepare puddings or creamed soups. Yogurt, cottage cheese, or hard cheeses are also fine substitutes for milk. Allergies are another problem. If your doctor approves, try goat's milk. It is available in most large cities and in dried form. Otherwise, your physician will probably recommend calcium in tablet or capsule form. And you will need to eat extra servings of other protein-rich foods to compensate for the protein in the milk.

Q. *Why is so much emphasis placed on meat, fish, and poultry in the pregnancy diet outline?*
A. Protein is the answer again. These foods plus milk and eggs are the best source of high-quality protein. Each day a pregnant woman needs about 80 grams of protein as compared with 55 grams for the average woman. In terms of food, a quart of milk and 6 ounces of cooked meat plus the added protein found in bread, potatoes, and cereals provides approximately 80 grams of protein.

Q. *Are there any other ways of getting protein?*
A. Yes, there are. Protein comes from both animal and vegetable sources. The rich animal sources are listed above, but dried beans, peas, and lentils as well as breads, cereals, and nuts are also good sources. However, the protein from animal sources can be utilized more completely by the body. Therefore, physicians recommend that at least half the protein in the diet come from animal sources. If you have bean-based main dishes, include cheese or meat in the dish. Or use milk or cheese in the same meal.

Q. *Is a Vitamin D supplement necessary?*
A. No, it is not. Assuming you have the quart of milk a day, you will be getting all the Vitamin D you need. In fact, Vitamin D as a supplement is now discouraged in pregnancy diets and vitamin supplements are now generally limited to 400 I.U. in one day's dosage.

Q. *How about Vitamin A?*
A. The daily quart of milk, butter or margarine, one egg, and a serving of yellow or dark-green leafy vegetables plus the lesser amounts found in other foods will provide the recommended amount of Vitamin A in the diet.

Q. *How much Vitamin C is recommended?*
A. During pregnancy, the recommended allowance is increased to 60 milligrams a day. A 4-ounce serving of orange or grapefruit juice plus the recommended amounts of other fruits and vegetables will easily provide this amount.

Q. *What about the B vitamins—thiamine (B₁), riboflavin (B₂), niacin, B₆, B₁₂?*
A. These vitamins are supplied in many foods—milk, meat, fish and poultry, whole-grain or enriched breads and cereals and many vegetables.

Q. *Is additional iron needed in a pregnancy diet?*
A. Generous amounts of iron (18 milligrams a day) are needed by all young women. Actual needs are not increased during pregnancy, since loss through menstrual flow is eliminated. The basic recommended diet will provide all the needed iron, providing a conscious effort is made to eat iron-rich foods daily and include one serving of liver weekly. If liver is not a favorite, try some of the more subtle forms like chopped chicken liver or liver mixed with beef to make hamburger or meat loaf. In addition to liver, eat other iron-rich foods—oysters, clams, dark-green leafy vegetables, eggs, dried peas or beans, dried fruits, and even mushrooms.

Q. *Should salt be used?*
A. You definitely should not go on a salt-free (low-sodium) diet unless your physician recommends it. However, many physicians do recommend going easy on salt during pregnancy—this means simply salting foods less at the table and avoiding the very concentrated sources of salt like potato chips and pickles. If you find swelling of the fingers, eyelids, or ankles, consult your physician immediately. During the last months of pregnancy, swelling of the ankles often occurs because of pressure of the growing baby. But let your doctor decide if this swelling is a problem which should be treated.

Q. *What about iodized salt?*
A. Iodine is important in the maternal diet and should have continued use during pregnancy. Use iodized salt unless your physician forbids it.

Q. *Should tea, coffee, and alcohol be avoided?*

A. Tea and coffee are allowed in moderation. Consult your physician about alcoholic beverages. But remember that alcohol provides "empty" calories and may unduly stimulate the appetite.

Q. *How much water should be drunk daily?*

A. The recommended amount of total liquid is six to eight glasses during the first half of pregnancy. The natural water found in food plus four to six glasses of water, soda, coffee, etc. will provide adequate amounts of liquid. This may be decreased during the later stages of your pregnancy, but your physician must be the one to decide.

Q. *What about smoking?*

A. Some medical research has found that the more the prospective mother smokes, the higher the incidence of premature births, toxemia, etc. Therefore, most physicians now strongly recommend that heavy smokers cut the number of cigarettes down during pregnancy or, if possible, stop smoking.

Q. *Do those passions for pickles, chilis, ice cream, watermelon, and other exotic foods that pregnant women are famous for mean that their diet is deficient in some way?*

A. Nutritionists have not found any relationship between these passions (technically called pica) and actual nutrient needs. Many physicians now feel it is caused by a combination of folklore suggesting the thought and a subconscious desire for sympathy.

Q. *Are there any foods to be avoided during pregnancy?*

A. None other than those foods that habitually disagree with the woman because of difficulty in digestion or, perhaps, an allergy.

Q. *How much weight should a pregnant woman gain?*

A. If her weight was normal at the beginning of pregnancy, her physician will probably recommend a total gain of 15 to 25 pounds. This allows for the baby's weight, the fluid that surrounds him, the placenta and enlarged uterus, and a small weight gain by the mother.

Q. *What if she was underweight before pregnancy?*

A. The doctor should decide, but most would recommend that she try to bring her weight to normal and then gain the additional 15 to 25 pounds.

Q. *What if she was overweight before pregnancy?*

A. Again the doctor must be the one to prescribe a diet, but it is possible to get all the needed nutrients during pregnancy and still not gain weight.

Q. *If weight gain turns out to be too rapid, should a pregnant woman go on a reducing diet?*

A. Only if it is recommended by her physician. If this excessive gain occurs over weeks or months, he will probably recommend using skimmed milk, lean cuts of meat and fish and poultry, and avoiding cakes, pastries, etc. to cut down on calories. If the weight gain is sudden—in a day or two—the physician should be contacted immediately. This type of weight gain is due to water retention and might indicate the beginning of toxemia.

Q. *Don't many women lose weight during the early months?*

A. Yes, they do. Morning sickness can lead to a general distaste for food. Eat too little and you will lose weight.

Q. *Can anything be done about morning sickness?*

A. Yes. As a first step, keep crackers by the bed and have one or two before getting up. Cut down on smoking. Move slowly when first getting up. If these precautions don't reduce the symptoms, ask your physician for help—there are a number of methods nowadays, that can help control morning sickness.

## MEALS FOR YOUNG CHILDREN

From the time a child is born until he is twelve months of age, his diet is controlled by the pediatrician. Follow the doctor's advice— he knows your child's needs. But after this medical supervision is relaxed, you may be unsure about just what to do.

Use the meal plan on page 46 and the ideas that follow as guidelines. The family budget and food preferences will determine variations. Remember that children need the same type of food as adults; only the amounts differ. Everyone needs meat, fish, poultry, eggs and cheese; fruits and vegetables; whole-grain or enriched cereals, breads and pastas; and milk and milk products. If your child has special problems, such as an allergy, your doctor will suggest substitutions for these basic groups.

Appetites do vary from child to child and time to time. As his rate of growth slows after the first year, the child will actually eat less, in proportion to his size, than he did as an infant.

• When the child is not hungry, don't force him to eat. Let him wait for the next meal. Forcing food can cause weight problems.

• Choose snacks from the basic foods. Save sweets for dessert.

• Keep portions small and make seconds available.

• Introduce each new food in small quantities and don't make a fuss if the child won't eat it. Try it again in a few weeks.

• Serve in miniature: milk in small glasses or cups; quarter slices of bread and toast; carrots cut into baby-bite-size pieces.

• Encourage the child to feed himself. And accept the spilled food and egg on the bib—it's all part of learning.

• When the child has several teeth, start him on foods that require chewing. If he is limited to pureed food, he may later be slow to accept solid food.

• Allow time to play quietly before meals.

• Avoid distractions during the meal.

• Prepare comfortable seating in a high chair, and keep adjusting the arrangements as the child grows.

• Silverware suited to the child's use should be small enough to handle, yet enough like the adult type so transition comes easily.

• Meals should be served attractively and, of course, in such a way as to encourage good table manners within the child's understanding.

• Give the child water to drink when he wakes up in the morning and, if constipation is a problem, prune juice or other fruit juice just before breakfast. Limiting liquids at supper and before bedtime make it easier for the child to remain dry through the night.

• Use milk in cream soups, puddings, cocoa, and other foods as well as for drinking. If getting enough milk into the child is a real problem, add nonfat dry-milk powder to mashed potatoes or cooked cereals. Make up double-strength nonfat dry milk to be used in puddings and soups.

## FOOD FOR CHILDREN ONE TO FIVE

| Food | Include Each Day | Average Serving for Each Age | | |
|---|---|---|---|---|
| | | 1 year | 2 to 3 years | 4 to 5 years |
| Meat, fish, poultry, cottage cheese | 1 to 4 level tablespoons | 1 tablespoon | 2 to 3 tablespoons | 4 tablespoons (about 2 ounces) |
| Eggs | 1 egg | 1 egg | 1 egg | 1 egg |
| Cooked vegetables (mostly green or yellow) | 1 to 2 servings | 2 tablespoons | 3 tablespoons | 3 to 4 tablespoons |
| Potatoes (white or sweet) | 1 serving | 2 tablespoons | 3 tablespoons | 4 tablespoons |
| Raw vegetables | 1 serving | a small serving such as ¼ medium carrot | | |
| Fruit (include one serving citrus fruit or tomato juice daily) | 2 servings | ¼ cup or ½ cup citrus juice | ⅓ to ½ cup | ⅓ to ½ cup |
| Enriched or whole-grain bread | 1½ to 3 slices | ½ to 1 slice | 1 slice | 1 to 1½ slices |
| Enriched or whole-grain cereal or pasta | 1 serving | ¼ cup | ⅓ cup | ½ cup |
| Milk | 3 to 4 cups | ½ to 1 cup | ½ to 1 cup | 1 cup |
| Butter or margarine as a spread on bread or on vegetables | | | | |

## MEALS FOR CHILDREN SIX TO TWELVE

During these years, emphasis should be put upon broadening the child's likes and interest in food. Serve as wide a variety of food as possible; encourage the child to accept suitable invitations to meals away from home so that he can see how other families eat. Emphasize good table manners, within the framework of pleasant, relaxed meals. While eating should be pleasant and fun, it should not be a reward for "being good." Good eating habits (and mental attitudes) formed during these years will last a lifetime. By the age of six, children need as many calories as an adult woman. Since they still eat relatively small meals with between-meal snacks, their food intake isn't always obvious. The Basic-Four Guide is particularly helpful in planning meals for this age group.

If a child is mildly overweight, there is no need to put him on a formal diet. Such a child is usually less active than others in his age group. Encourage him to get out and play more actively. If his lack of activity appears to stem from shyness or a sense of awkwardness, discuss the problem with his teacher. She'll be able to work on it during school hours. Adjust the child's caloric level by substituting skimmed milk for whole; replacing candy, cookies and other sweets with low-calorie snacks; and cutting down on servings.

If overweight has become severe, the child should be taken for a physical examination. Follow the doctor's advice on diet, and encourage the child to play actively. Since so many parents of overweight children are heavy themselves, they should also consider their own diet. "Do as I say, not as I do" never works, and is particularly inadvisable when dealing with today's keenly aware, well-informed youngsters.

## MEALS FOR TEENS

Teens are always hungry. Just to supply a seventeen-year-old young man with enough to eat can play havoc with the family food budget. If he is active in sports, he'll need up to 4000 calories a day, twice what his mother eats and half again his father's food needs. For the seventeen-year-old girl, the difference is smaller—2300 to 2400 calories for a moderately active girl as compared with her mother's 1900 to 2000 calories and 2600 to 2800 for her father.

This actual need for more food should make it easy to assure good nutrition for teens. Studies show, however, that teens (particularly girls) are among the most poorly fed people in this country. These girls will be mothers in a few years. By that time it is important that they should have established sensible eating habits and developed strong, healthy bodies that will enable them to respond easily to the stresses and strains of pregnancy.

To plan meals for teens, start with the Basic-Four Chart on page 37, plus two extra cups of milk. This basic diet will provide 1500 to 1700 calories each day. Boys need twice that amount simply to maintain their weight. Girls need approximately 600 additional calories. These are usually made up by additional servings and by this age group's favorite food—snacks. Following are suggestions for making sure that the snacks your teenager gets carry their weight nutritionally.

| | |
|---|---|
| *Snacks are the fun part of eating* | • Keep the ingredients for tasty sandwiches on hand. Rolls and lettuce, peanut butter and jelly or raisins, luncheon meats, roast beef or poultry to slice, cheeses of all kinds tempt teens to eat properly.<br>• A bowl of fresh fruit and nuts makes good eating as well as a decorative centerpiece.<br>• Don't keep potato chips, snack crackers, sodas, candy or other "empty calorie" food in the house and it won't be missed.<br>• The stick "candies" developed for the space program are now available to everyone. They taste like candy but are rich in protein and other nutrients.<br>• Have foods like carrots, cauliflower, cucumbers and tomatoes washed and ready to eat in the refrigerator.<br>• Keep whole-grain or enriched crackers on hand.<br>• Try buttermilk; cottage cheese; Swiss, Edam or other types of hard cheese; chocolate milk; cocoa (made with milk) or canned milkshakes as a different way of serving milk.<br>• Make up cocoa with an extra tablespoon or two of nonfat dry-milk powder in addition to the regular milk used.<br>• Add extra cheese to homemade or frozen pizza.<br>• Make milkshakes in an electric blender by blending ½ pint ice cream, 1 cup cold milk, 1⅓ cups nonfat dry-milk powder and 1 teaspoon to a tablespoon of flavoring like chocolate syrup, instant coffee powder, maple syrup or fruit jams (makes 2 servings). |
| *Eating breakfast* | Often it is difficult to get teens to take time out for breakfast. They may say they dislike it, or that they are too rushed to eat. Try getting the family started 20 minutes earlier to avoid the rush atmosphere. Then proceed to make breakfast as pleasant and delicious an experience as possible.<br><br>The basic breakfast pattern consists of fruit (preferably one rich in vitamin C like a citrus fruit) or tomato juice, enriched or |

whole-grain bread or cereal and a protein-rich food like eggs, meat or milk. Remember that hot cereals now come in instant form. Let the teen make his own portion, or prepare it the moment before breakfast. Or try frozen "TV" breakfasts, ready to eat twenty minutes after they are placed in the oven. And then there are the liquid "instant" breakfasts, which can be drunk even on the run.

For the breakfast non-conformist, try some of these "un-break-fast" foods:

1. Cottage cheese on fruit, cinnamon toast
2. Scrambled-egg sandwich with catchup on a hard roll; a tangerine to eat section by section
3. Juice, buttered enriched saltines and "fortified" cocoa (see opposite page)
4. Juice and a slice or two of frozen pizza, topped with extra cheese and warmed for 10 to 15 minutes in 400°F. oven.

Finally, *don't* insist that teens always have breakfast at home. Often a trip on the school bus does unsettle the stomach. Maybe the answer is breakfast in a luncheonette, but *do* insist that the meal be a good one—not coke and a doughnut.

---

Being underweight is as frustrating as being fat. Here are some suggestions to give teens who want to put on pounds.

• Be patient. It takes as much time to gain weight as it does to lose it. To gain one pound, you have to eat 3500 more calories than your body uses.

• Start with a hearty breakfast. It's been at least nine hours since the last meal and your body is ready for a meal.

• Plan on six meals a day. Lots of little meals seem less filling than only three large ones.

• Eat a variety of foods. It's the best way to get all the needed nutrients. "Fattening" foods like milkshakes may have more calories, but they are also usually more filling.

• Eat favorite foods. It's human nature to eat more of the things you enjoy.

• Make meals pleasant. A calm atmosphere and plenty of time to eat makes it easier to enjoy the extra food needed.

• Eat with a friend. Afternoon snacks are more fun if you can share them with someone. And it's much more difficult to "forget" to eat if you have made a formal date for a snack.

• Don't fill up on low-calorie liquids. The stomach needs room for food. Start with the main dish rather than soup. Drink the soda after the sandwich. Eat the pretzels, then quench thirst with a glass of milk.

• Get plenty of of exercise. Fresh air and exercise are nature's pepper-uppers.

*The woes of being underweight*

• Get plenty of sleep. Being rested and relaxed helps the body use food more efficiently and makes life (and eating) more fun.

## The woes of being overweight

Because the body's caloric needs during the teen years are so great, it's easier to lose weight than it ever will be again. Here are some suggestions to give teens who want to shed pounds.

• Pick a diet plan (like any of the six on pages 13 to 29) that fits in most closely with your current eating habits, but add an extra two glasses of skimmed milk or buttermilk. This will bring the calories up to 1400 for girls and 2000 for boys—more sensible levels for teen dieters. Don't expect to lose more than two pounds a week. But if you stick to the 1400 or 2000 calorie level, you can expect to *maintain* this rate of loss.

• Start with a good breakfast; have a reasonable lunch and a smaller dinner than usual; and then try not to eat after 8 o'clock. Keep yourself busy so that there's less temptation to snack. When you do go out with the gang, pick snacks wisely. Have sherbet, not ice cream; cole slaw, not french fries, with your hamburger; soda or lemonade, not a milkshake. Even cheat judiciously: Have two slices of pizza, not four; plain pizza, not with extra cheese; an ice-cream soda, not a milkshake; a slice of poundcake, not pie à la mode. Keep a good calorie guide handy. (Check the difference in the numbers of calories in the items just mentioned— you'll be surprised.)

• Last but not least, get more exercise. Walk, don't ride to school. Go out for a sport, and really *work* in gym class instead of hiding in a corner. Do calisthenics at home. (See page 54.)

## Complexion care for teens

As the endocrine and hormone systems develop during the teen years, they often get out of balance and complexion problems result. Careful skin care is necessary to minimize these problems, particularly acne and blackheads. Here are tips for teens with troublesome skin.

Most skin problems in teens are due to excessively oily skin. To remove excess oils, wash your face several times a day with soap and hot water; pat (don't rub) dry. Powder or other makeup tends to clog the pores and will aggravate pimples or blackheads. (However, blushers, which are applied more lightly and less extensively, may be used to add color.)

To remove blackheads, heat the skin with a hot damp cloth, then press out (don't pinch) the blackhead. If it doesn't come out easily, don't force it. Pinching the skin can spread the infection. If the skin condition is serious, see a physician. (Dermatologists are specialists in skin problems.) Medication can often do wonders where do-it-yourself remedies are futile and possibly harmful.

It has been found that acne is not *caused* by eating a specific food or group of foods—though in some cases a particular food might *aggravate* the condition and should be dropped from the diet temporarily. Follow your physician's advice. He may recommend that some of these foods be minimized in the diet: sugars and syrups; fats, particularly in fried foods, rich sauces, pastries; iodine-rich foods such as iodized salt and seafood; nuts and chocolate.

## MEALS FOR THE YOUNG FAMILY

Young men usually begin to gain weight when they start to sample their bride's first devoted culinary efforts. It's a new wife's responsibility to temper her cooking ambitions with discretion right from the start. She should heed the experts' warnings about the dangers of too many calories and too-rich foods. The typical American diet now provides 40 to 45 percent of the calories from fat. Although it has not been proven conclusively, there is good evidence that this high-fat diet is one of the prime factors contributing to heart disease.

The American Heart Association now recommends that the entire family reduce the total amount of fat in their diet and substitute polyunsaturated fats (soft and liquid fats in salad oils, special margarines, and so on) for the saturated (usually solid fats) from both animal and vegetable sources. The AHA also recommends that everyone go easy on cholesterol-rich foods such as egg yolks and shellfish, and avoid large amounts of sugar in beverages and desserts.

It is the young housewife's task to be aware of recommendations like these and to implement them in her meal planning. Although authorities do not agree on the scientific relationship of diet to disease, they do agree that a calorie surplus leads inevitably to overweight, which is a major factor not only in heart disease but in diabetes, high blood pressure, arthritis and many other debilitating diseases.

A young wife's success in instilling good eating habits in her family can assure them of longer and healthier lives.

## MEALS FOR MATURE ADULTS

Caloric requirements decrease with age. By sixty-five, a moderately active man needs only 2400 calories a day; a moderately active woman, 1700. By the standards of a teenager, this is a perpetual reducing diet. Luckily the appetite also decreases with age, so it is less of a struggle to maintain a reasonable weight. As part of the general cutback in calories, fats in the diet should be limited. Emphasize use of lean meat or fish and poultry; cut down on butter or margarine and high-calorie desserts; use skimmed milk or buttermilk. Any of the low-calorie recipes in this book will meet these requirements.

Nutritional needs in terms of protein, vitamins and minerals don't shift with age. But there is a tendency to eat less protein, often because meat is difficult to chew when the teeth are faulty. If there are health problems requiring a therapeutic diet, eating habits must be shifted. The special diet recipes and general information (pages 242–318) in this book cover, among others, the four therapeutic diets most often needed by this age group—low-fat, low-cholesterol; low-sodium; low-purine; and gallbladder diets.

In the later years, families are smaller, and there is less inspiration to cook. The first big adjustment is to get used to planning, buying and preparing foods for one or two and not four or five. Once that adjustment has been made, it soon becomes evident that in an age of freezers, instant mixes and convenience-food products, it is comparatively easy to cook attractive, nutritious, filling meals on a smaller scale. In any case, the following suggestions should prove helpful:

• Prepare in quantity and freeze. For example: Buy hamburger in 1-pound lots; divide into patties; wrap individually and freeze. Let thaw overnight in refrigerator and the meat will be ready to cook the next day. Or cook while still frozen, but allow at least double the cooking time.

• The same principle can be applied to casserole dishes. Prepare for four to six servings; divide into individual 1-cup to 1-pint servings; freeze. Thaw before rewarming for best results. Most dishes are hot after 30 minutes in a 350°F. oven. Remember to undercook main dishes slightly if they are to be frozen, since the food will be further cooked when it is reheated.

• Try commercial frozen main dishes—lasagna, cheese rarebit, Swiss steak, and so on. Keep a supply of favorites on hand.

• Use products that are frozen individually rather than in chunks, making it easier to separate just the amount needed: e.g., frozen veal steaks, minute steaks, shrimp, fish steaks, frozen vegetables in plastic bags.

• Buy bread in half-pound loaves and freeze what you don't immediately need. It will keep up to three months. Also, look for refrigerated biscuits packed five to a can. They must be cooked all at once, but warm extras for a second meal. There are also frozen brown-and-serve rolls. Rewrap unheated rolls tightly after opening the package and the remainder will stay fresh for later meals.

• Avail yourself of the myriad of individually packaged products on supermarket shelves. Although they may seem less economical than larger sizes, remember that you save nothing on food you throw away. Try *tuna and salmon* in 3-ounce cans (individual servings); *ready-to-eat and instant cooked cereals* in individual serving packets; *fruit juices* in one-serving 6-ounce cans; *single-*

*layer cake mixes; instant breakfast* in ready-to-serve single portions; *fresh fruit* (what could be more portion-controlled than a banana, apple or orange?). Also, buy butter by the half- or quarter-pound; eggs by the half-dozen; chicken in parts; small jars of instant coffee. (Flavor deteriorates if coffee is kept too long.)
• Take advantage of other convenience foods. For example, *sauce and gravy mixes* can be made up a quarter at a time. Just measure total mix, stir well, then use only one quarter; adjust other ingredients proportionately. Prepare according to directions. Do the same thing with *dried-soup mixes* or with *gelatin-dessert mix.* (Remember to seal leftovers carefully—the mixes lump if exposed to air.) *Dry coffee lighteners* keep indefinitely on the pantry shelf. The frozen lighteners last several weeks in the refrigerator and can be used on cereals as well as in beverages. *Refrigerator cookies* can be baked a few at a time or as you need them. *Pasteurized process cheese* can be spread on toast or used as "instant" sauce for vegetables or meat. *Instant nonfat dry milk* can be used as is in cooking, reliquefied as needed—even one glass at a time—for drinking.
• Buy some small equipment: 7-inch skillets, ½- to 1-quart saucepans, 1-quart casseroles, a small coffeemaker. If you broil food often, purchase a counter-top broiler. It's easier to clean than an oven broiler.

# Shaping Up with Exercise

Regular exercise is essential for good posture, suppleness, strength and vitality. Those are reasons enough to include it in a slimming program. But it also has more direct benefits, in terms of shaping you up while it helps trim you down.

*The role of exercise*

Whether it takes the form of calisthenics or walking, bowling, cycling or swimming, exercise should be done regularly and vigorously for best results. Walk a mile in twenty minutes; swim, don't float; bowl alone, not in a group of six; and exercise at least three times a week *in addition* to your regular activities.

Is exercise an efficient way to lose weight? The answer is obvious in the chart below, which gives the number of calories used up by some common exercises. An hour of vigorous walking uses fewer than 300 calories—not enough to get rid of a tenth of a pound. On the other hand, if you keep it up for a year, you could lose 10 pounds. So, on a long term basis, exercise *can* be effective.

Moreover, a reducing diet is most effective when combined with exercise. As the fat melts away, firm up the muscles with spot exercises. Physical-fitness expert Nicholas Kounovsky has developed sets of exercises anyone can follow. Illustrated on the following pages, they include Plan I for general muscle tone; Plan II, spot exercises for hips, waistline, etc.; Plan III for the practiced exerciser who wants to keep trim. Finally there are exercises specifically recommended for teenagers, new mothers and middle-aged adults.

### CALORIES USED UP BY ACTIVITIES

| Exercise | Calories Used Up per minute | Minutes to Use Up 100 Calories |
|---|---|---|
| Bicycling, fast | 8.9 | 11 |
| Bicycling, slow | 2.9 | 34 |
| Dancing, slow | 4.4 | 23 |
| Ping-pong | 5.1 | 20 |
| Running | 8.1 | 12 |
| Skating | 4.1 | 24 |
| Swimming, rapid | 9.2 | 11 |
| Walking, slow | 2.3 | 43 |
| Walking, rapid | 3.9 | 25 |
| Reclining | .1 | 100 |

## TIPS ON DOING EXERCISES

• Check with your doctor before starting an exercise program.
• Read and carefully follow directions for exercises. Be sure to breathe as suggested.
• Never force yourself. If an exercise cannot be completed without straining, do part of it and gradually work into the rest.
• Start by doing each exercise three times; work up to six. If an exercise specifies an alternate leg, do each leg six times.
• Wait at least an hour and a half after eating before you exercise. Remember, too, if you can exercise at the same time each day, it's more likely to become a habit.

The Kounovsky method of teaching physical fitness emphasizes six factors: endurance, suppleness, equilibrium, strength, speed and coordination. Plan I is a series of simple yet challenging exercises to develop these factors. Start gently at first, improve gradually. Work up from three to six times for each exercise. Be sure to read the Tips on Doing Exercises above, before you start.

## PLAN I: BASIC DAILY EXERCISES FOR EVERYONE

**FOR ENDURANCE**
(the body's ability to resist fatigue):

1. Assume a squatting position with fingertips braced on floor, weight on toes, head straight. Exhale.

2. Straighten up and raise left knee, bending arms over head with palms together. Inhale. Resume original position and alternate knees.

## FOR COORDINATION
(the body's ability to move smoothly and accurately):

1. With weight on right leg, simultaneously lift left leg and raise right arm out to side, left arm straight up.

2. Lunge on left leg to side, reversing arm positions as you do so. Breathe normally throughout. Alternate legs.

## FOR STRENGTH
(the body's muscular force)

1. From a full standing position, with fingers clasped behind neck and back held straight, bend knees so weight is on toes. Inhale.

2. Straighten up. Raise left knee and try to touch right elbow with it. Exhale. Go back to first position and alternate legs.

## FOR EQUILIBRIUM
(the ability to maintain balance):

1. Balance on toes of right foot for ten seconds, without moving that foot. Do same on left foot.

2. With eyes closed, balance for ten seconds on right foot, bending at waist with left leg extended. Breathe normally. Alternate legs.

## FOR SUPPLENESS
(limberness and flexibility of joints):

1. From a standing position, lunge sideways with left leg. Flex arms over head to right. Inhale.

2. Bend from waist and try to touch left toes. Exhale. Repeat exercise, starting with right lunge. Stretch fully as possible.

## FOR SPEED
(the rapidity of bodily movements):

1. Legs apart and straight, bend torso forward, with arms outstretched to sides. Keep head straight.

2. Swiftly twist trunk from side to side, touching floor with one hand while other arm points upward. Inhale and exhale slowly while twisting.

# PLAN II: EXERCISES FOR SPECIFIC PARTS OF THE BODY

After you've mastered the exercises in Plan I, you can begin to concentrate on particular areas: waistline, chest, arms, legs, abdomen, hips or thighs. These exercises are more difficult and it is wise to go slowly. Be sure to incorporate what you have learned from Plan I. For example, if you feel you need more suppleness, you should accentuate bending movements. As in Plan I, start by doing the exercise three times and gradually work up to six.

## EXERCISES FOR THE WAISTLINE

1. From a sitting position, bend knees, balance on hips, stretching arms forward, parallel to knees. Exhale.

2. Still balanced on hips, straighten legs and raise arms above head as high as possible. Inhale.

1. Lie on back with with fingers clasped behind head, left knee bent and parallel to floor. Inhale.

2. Sit up and try to touch left knee with right elbow. Exhale. Repeat with right knee, left elbow.

1. Lying on back, raise legs until vertical. With right elbow on floor, press left palm into right. Inhale.

2. Slowly lower legs to right side. Exhale. Do several times on right side; repeat for left side.

## FOR CHEST,
## ABDOMEN, ARMS, LEGS

The pace at which you exercise is an individual matter. Extremely lively and tense people should do exercises slowly and in a relaxed manner (the way a cat stretches, for instance). There should be an awareness of the entire self. On the other hand, if a person is tired and sluggish, the pace should be brisk and have a definite rhythm. Try background music to establish a mood and set the pace you want.

1. From a standing position with legs apart, bend forward until palms are flat on the floor. . . . .

2. Move hands farther out . . .

3. "Walk" forward with hands. . . .

4. Up on toes to go sideways. . . .

5. And stretch as far as possible (be careful not to overestimate your range). Breathe regularly throughout.

**FOR POSTURE (BACK,
HIPS, THIGHS, NECK,
UPPER ARMS AND
SHOULDER GIRDLE)**

1. Lie in prone position.
   Extend right arm out,
   with bent left arm
   back, right knee
   bent and up. Exhale.

2. Raise shoulders,
   right arm and left
   leg as high as pos-
   sible. Keep left arm
   bent back for sup-
   port. Inhale. Repeat
   with opposite leg
   and arm.

1. Start in standing
   position. Bend body
   from waist. With
   arms outstretched,
   head down, exhale.

2. Straighten back and
   raise head. Bend
   arms at elbows,
   placing hands be-
   hind neck. Inhale.

**FOR HIPS,
THIGHS AND
LOWER BACK**

1. Assume a kneeling
   position with hands
   flat on floor and
   head up. Exhale.

2. Slowly extend right
   leg to side, as
   straight as possible.
   Inhale. Return to
   position; extend left
   leg.

1. Start in kneeling
   position. Slowly ex-
   tend left leg back
   and up, so weight is
   on hands, right knee
   and foot. Keep head
   up. Exhale.

2. Pressing with right
   foot, straighten right
   leg to raise body,
   keeping left leg high.
   Pull shoulders back.
   Inhale when up. Re-
   peat with right leg
   up.

1. From standing position, place left foot forward, right leg back.

2. Wiggle hips from side to side. Repeat, changing legs.

1. Start in standing position. With feet together and knees bent, leap from side to side.

2. Keep arms out-stretched as you alternate leaps from side to side, six times each.

1. From crouch, bend left leg, extend right one to side.

2. Lift hips, shift legs from side to side, keeping weight on hands.

# PLAN III: SPECIAL EXERCISES FOR VITALITY AND VIGOR

This is your graduate course in exercising! After you have mastered the exercises in Plan I and those in Plan II that are applicable to any particular figure problems, add as many of these exercises as you have time for. They take a bit more practice, but, as in the case of all the exercises given, it is best to start slowly and improve gradually. Breathing should be according to intensity, but as steady as possible.

These exercises will help you gain the control that leads to graceful and assured movements. As you become more proficient at them, you will discover a paradox: The more control there is, the greater the freedom of movement.

Start from standing position. With feet together and keeping knees loosely bent, lightly jump forward (far left) and back (left). Do six times each.

Start in crouch position on toes with knees bent. Exhale. Swing legs out so body is to side. Raise right arm. Inhale. Alternate sides. (This is a difficult exercise.)

## EXERCISES FOR SPECIFIC GROUPS

Three groups—teen-agers, new mothers and middle-aged adults (although this group can mean anyone between the ages of twenty and eighty, depending on physical shape)—have particular problems that often can be helped by doing specific exercises. Following are the exercises from the three plans given in this section which should be emphasized if you fall into one of the groups.

### TEENAGERS

**Problem:**

The basic problems teen-agers have is a difficulty in coping with their rapidly maturing bodies, which results in awkwardness of movement.

**Exercises:**

Plan I, with particular emphasis on the exercises for COORDINATION.
Plan II, with particular emphasis on exercises for POSTURE, as well as individual problem areas.
Any of Plan III.

### NEW MOTHERS

**Problem:**

A new mother is naturally anxious to get back to the size dress she wore before pregnancy. But she usually must get rid of flabby inches in the region of the abdomen and waistline.

**Exercises:**

Two groups from Plan II, those for the WAISTLINE and the ABDOMEN. The latter exercise is also good for firming the pectoral muscles.

### MIDDLE-AGED ADULTS

**Problem:**

Decreased physical activity can result in flabbiness, stiffness, weariness, slowness, awkwardness, even lack of balance.

**Exercises:**

All of Plan I.
Plan II, with particular emphasis on exercises for the WAISTLINE.
Plan III: as many exercises as can be done comfortably. Progress slowly.

# Recipes
## for Calorie Watchers

The low-calorie recipes in this section cover everything from soup to dessert, plus hors d'oeuvres and snacks. Use them as part of a formal reducing diet (the Meat-and-Potatoes and Eat-for-a-Treat Diets on pages 13–14 and 24–27 both make special allowances for these recipes) or simply to keep trim by skimming away extra calories painlessly.

Almost all these recipes can also be used for family members with special diet problems—a need to cut down on cholesterol or sodium, for example, or to eat more iron. The changes necessary to adapt a recipe to special uses are listed at the end of each. Also check the section on Special Diets, pages 242–318; it contains general information, cooking hints and additional recipes.

All the recipes have been prepared, tasted, rechecked and tasted again in the Good Housekeeping Institute kitchens. To assure success, follow the instructions precisely and use exactly the amount of ingredients specified. This is essential in low-calorie recipes—an extra dab of butter here and a tablespoon of sugar there can add hundreds of calories to a recipe.

Calories per serving (rounded to the nearest 5 calories) are given for each recipe. They are determined by carefully dividing the yield into equal servings. You can use the same method to check the calories in other dishes. To do so, jot down the ingredients and amounts specified; then, using a calorie guide, determine the number of calories in each ingredient. Add the calories to get the recipe total; divide this total by the number of servings. Here's an example from page 218:

CUSTARD RICE PUDDING (6½-cup servings)

| | |
|---|---|
| 1 cup hot cooked rice | 205 calories |
| 2 eggs | 160 |
| ⅓ cup granulated sugar | 255 |
| ¼ cup raisins | 105 |
| spices* | —— |
| 2 cups skimmed milk | 180 |
| | 905 total calories |
| | 150 calories per serving |

* Salt, vanilla and cinnamon contain too few calories to be included in total.

A calorie guide is provided on pages 325 to 341. You might also send for the following booklets from the U.S. Government Printing Office, Superintendent of Documents, Washington, D.C. 20402:

*Nutritive Value of Foods* (Home and Garden Bulletin Number 72). Available for 25 cents, this booklet gives calories and other nutrient values for various foods in common serving sizes.

*Composition of Foods: Raw, Processed, Prepared.* Available for $1.50, this booklet lists nutrient, calorie, protein, fat, carbohydrate, vitamin and mineral values for a pound of food as purchased and for 100 grams of the same food as prepared.

# APPETIZERS AND SNACKS

## HOT CRABMEAT PIE (80 calories per serving)

**2 3-ounce packages Neufchâtel cheese**
**1 6½- to 7½-ounce can King crab, flaked, well drained**
**2 tablespoons instant minced onion**
**1 tablespoon milk**
**½ teaspoon prepared horse-radish**
**¼ teaspoon salt**
**dash pepper**
**¼ cup sliced blanched almonds**

About 30 minutes before serving: Preheat oven to 375° F. In medium bowl, thoroughly mix all ingredients but almonds. Spoon mixture into 8-inch pie plate; sprinkle with almonds. Bake 15 to 20 minutes. Cut into 10 wedges.

**Diabetic diet:** Exchanges per serving = 1 meat and 1 fat.

## EASY SWEET-AND-SOUR MEATBALLS (35 calories per meatball)

**⅓ cup packed dark brown sugar**
**¼ cup lemon juice**
**1 tablespoon catchup**
**¾ pound ground round steak**
**1 egg**
**¼ cup dry bread crumbs**
**¼ teaspoon salt**
**dash pepper**

About 30 minutes before serving: In medium saucepan, combine ½ cup water, brown sugar, lemon juice and catchup; heat to boiling. Meanwhile, in medium bowl, combine round steak and remaining ingredients. Shape into about 30 small meatballs; add to boiling sauce. Cook, covered, over low heat, for about 15 minutes. Keep warm in chafing dish; serve with toothpicks. Makes about 30 appetizers.

**Low-fat, low-cholesterol diet:** Prepare as directed but use only white of the egg. 1 gram fat per meatball.
**High-iron diet:** .5 milligram iron per meatball.

## CONFETTI COCKTAIL (105 calories per serving)

**1½ cups sauterne**
**2 teaspoons salt**
**2 pounds sea scallops, cut into quarters**
**1 4-ounce can pimentos**
**1 large green pepper, diced**
**⅓ cup diced celery**
**¼ cup chopped scallions**
**⅓ cup lemon juice**
**¼ teaspoon white pepper**
**lettuce leaves**
**lemon slices for garnish**

Early in day or day before: In sauterne, 1 cup water and salt, simmer scallops, covered, 5 minutes; drain. In bowl, combine scallops, ¼ cup diced pimentos, ⅓ cup diced green pepper, celery, scallions, lemon juice and pepper; cover; refrigerate, tossing occasionally.

About 15 minutes before serving: Cut rest of pimentos and pepper into strips. In compote or flat serving dish, arrange scallop mixture on bed of lettuce leaves; garnish with pimento, pepper strips and lemon slices. Spoon juice from scallops over them. Makes 8 first-course servings.

**Diabetic diet:** Exchanges per serving = 2 meat and 1 "A" vegetable.
**Egg-, gluten-, milk- and wheat-free diet:** Prepare as directed.
**High-iron diet:** 2 milligrams iron per serving.

## TANGY GARLIC DIP FOR RAW VEGETABLES (195 calories per cup of dip)

**1 8-ounce container plain yogurt**
**1 envelope (.7 ounces) garlic salad-dressing mix**
**cherry tomatoes, cucumber sticks, sliced raw turnips, mushroom slices, carrot sticks or celery strips**

About 2 hours before serving: In small bowl, blend yogurt and dressing mix. Refrigerate until serving time. Use as a dip for your choice of vegetables. Makes 1 cup.

**Low-fat, low-cholesterol diet:** Negligible fat per serving.

## VEGETABLE DIP (350 calories per cup)

**1 cup low-calorie (imitation) mayonnaise**
**2 teaspoons tarragon vinegar**
**½ teaspoon salt**
**½ teaspoon curry**
**⅛ teaspoon thyme leaves**
**dash pepper**
**2 teaspoons chili sauce**
**2 teaspoons chopped chives**
**2 tablespoons grated onion**
**raw cauliflowerets**
**4- to 6-inch celery sticks**
**4- to 6-inch carrot sticks**

About 30 minutes before serving: In small bowl, mix first 9 ingredients; refrigerate. At serving time, spoon mayonnaise mixture into small bowl; set in center of plate, surrounded by cauliflowerets, celery and carrot sticks. Makes about 1 cup.

**Low-fat, low-cholesterol diet:** Less than 1 gram fat per "dip."

## COOL CUCUMBER DIP (300 calories per recipe)

**3 medium cucumbers**
**1 8-ounce container creamed cottage cheese, sieved**
**1 tablespoon skimmed milk or reliquefied nonfat dry milk**
**1 tablespoon minced pimento**
**dash cayenne**
**2 teaspoons salt**
**½ teaspoon pepper**

About 30 minutes before serving: For dip, pare, then finely chop 1 cucumber, draining well on paper towels. In medium bowl, blend cucumber well with remaining ingredients. Cut unpared cucumbers into sticks about 4 inches long and ½-inch wide. Spoon dip into pretty bowl; set on plate, surrounded by cucumber sticks, for dunking. Makes about 1½ cups.

**Egg- and gluten-free diet:** Prepare as directed.
**Low-fat, low-cholesterol diet:** Less than 1 gram fat per "dip."

## PIQUANT DIP FOR SHRIMP (20 calories for each dipped shrimp)

**1 8-ounce container creamed cottage cheese**
**½ cup chili sauce**
**½ green pepper, chopped**
**1 teaspoon Worcestershire**
**2 drops red food color**
**dash cayenne**
**2 7-ounce packages frozen shelled and deveined shrimp**
**parsley for garnish**
**lemon slices, radish buds, carrot curls or pimento strips**

About 3 hours before serving: In electric-blender container at low speed, blend cottage cheese, chili sauce, green pepper, Worcestershire, red food color and cayenne. Refrigerate, covered, until serving time.

Cook shrimp as label directs; drain; refrigerate until serving time.

To serve: Stir cheese mixture; put into small serving bowl. Decorate bowl with nest of parsley; fill with chilled shrimp. Surround with lemon slices, radish buds, carrot curls or pimento strips. Makes 40 to 50 shrimp or nibblers for 8 to 10.

**Low-fat diet:** Negligible fat per dipped shrimp. Omit recipe from low-cholesterol diet.

## SPICED PINEAPPLE PICKUPS (about 5 calories per "pickup")

2 16-ounce cans pineapple
   chunks
¾ cup vinegar
dash salt
6 to 8 whole cloves
2 2-inch sticks cinnamon

Day before: Drain pineapple chunks, reserving ¾ cup syrup. In medium saucepan, mix reserved syrup and remaining ingredients; cover; simmer 10 minutes. Stir in pineapple chunks; refrigerate.

To serve: Drain syrup and spices from pineapple. Serve chunks in bowl with toothpicks as pickups.

**Egg-, gluten-, milk- and wheat-free diet:** Prepare as directed.
**Low-fat, low-cholesterol diet:** Negligible fat per serving.
**Low-sodium diet:** Prepare as directed but omit salt. Negligible sodium per serving.

## MARINATED CARROT STICKS (30 calories per serving)

6 medium carrots
1 garlic clove, halved
½ cup wine vinegar
1 teaspoon dried mint leaves
   (optional)

About 3 hours before serving: Scrape carrots and cut each crosswise, then lengthwise, to make 4 pieces. Cook in salted boiling water until just tender-crisp—10 to 15 minutes. In shallow dish, mix garlic, vinegar, mint leaves and carrot sticks. Cover, refrigerate, and marinate 2 to 4 hours. Drain carrots. Makes 4 servings.

**Diabetic diet:** Exchanges per serving = 1 "B" vegetable.
**Egg-, gluten-, milk- and wheat-free diet:** Prepare as directed.
**Low-fat, low-cholesterol diet:** Negligible fat per serving.
**Low-purine diet:** Prepare as directed.
**Low-sodium diet:** 15 milligrams sodium per serving.

## SESAME-TOPPED STUFFED CELERY (40 calories per stick)

¼ cup sesame seed
1 8-ounce container creamed
   cottage cheese*
¼ teaspoon onion salt
3 large green celery stalks,
   washed and trimmed

About 30 minutes before serving: Preheat oven to 350° F. In small baking pan, toast sesame 5 to 10 minutes, or until golden brown; cool.

Meanwhile, in electric-blender container, at low speed, blend cottage cheese and onion salt until smooth. (Or sieve cottage cheese and onion salt until smooth.)

Use mixture to fill celery stalks; sprinkle with toasted sesame. Cut each stalk into three even lengths. Refrigerate until serving time. Makes 9 servings.

* Use a brand with a relatively soft curd—it blends better.

**Diabetic diet:** Exchanges per stick = 1 "A" vegetable and ½ meat.
**Egg-, gluten- and wheat-free diet:** Prepare as directed.
**Low-purine diet:** Prepare as directed.

## SPICY GLAZED FRUIT (150 calories per serving)

1 large banana
3 tablespoons brown sugar
3 tablespoons butter or margarine, softened
⅛ teaspoon ground cloves
⅛ teaspoon salt
1 16-ounce can cling-peach
   halves, drained
1 15½-ounce can pineapple
   rings, drained

About 20 minutes before serving: Preheat broiler if manufacturer directs. Slice banana diagonally. Combine sugar, butter or margarine, cloves and salt; spread on top of bananas, peaches and pineapple. Place peaches and pineapple on broiler rack; broil 3 or 4 minutes. Add banana slices, and broil until tinged with brown. Makes 6 servings.

**Egg-, gluten-, milk- and wheat-free diet:** Prepare as directed but use milk-free margarine on milk-free diet.
**Low-fat, low-cholesterol diet:** Prepare as directed but use margarine instead of butter. 5 grams fat per serving.
**Low-purine diet:** Prepare as directed.
**Low-sodium diet:** Prepare as directed but use unsalted butter or margarine; omit salt. 5 milligrams sodium per serving.

## ORANGE-PINEAPPLE FROST (150 calories per serving)

**4 cups orange juice**
**2 cups pineapple juice**
**⅔ cup fresh lime juice**
**1 pint lemon or orange sherbet**

Early in day: Mix orange juice with pineapple and lime juice. Refrigerate, covered.

To serve: Fill 6 iced-tea glasses with juices; add a ball of sherbet to each. Makes 6 servings.

**Low-fat, low-cholesterol diet:** Negligible fat per serving.
**Low-fat, bland (gall bladder) diet:** Prepare as directed.
**Low-purine diet:** Prepare as directed.
**Low-sodium diet:** 5 milligrams sodium per serving.

## WATERMELON COOLER (40 calories per serving)

**6 thin lime slices**
**1 14- to 16-pound watermelon**
**cheesecloth**
**3 to 4 8-ounce bottles lemon-lime soda**
**granulated sugar**
**fresh lemon juice**
**mint sprigs for garnish**

Day before: Place lime slices in bottom of 1½ pint mixing bowl; add enough cold water to just cover; freeze until solid. Add more cold water to fill bowl; freeze.

About 30 minutes before serving: Using sharp knife, with a single lengthwise cut, slice across watermelon about one-fourth down from top. Place a double layer of cheesecloth on top of a large bowl. Using a large spoon, scoop out a few pieces of meat from larger section of watermelon onto cheesecloth, being careful to leave ½ inch of meat around the rind to form shell. Bring corners of cheesecloth together; then, holding it over bowl, squeeze out as much juice as possible. Discard pulp and seeds. Repeat this scooping and squeezing until all meat from both sections of watermelon has been turned into juice—10 to 14 cups in all. Discard smaller watermelon shell.

Using small paring knife, cut a sawtooth pattern around rim of larger watermelon shell. Also slice a piece of rind from bottom so that melon stands level. Skim air bubbles from surface of juice. Then, using measuring cup, fill watermelon shell, using 1 cup lemon-lime soda for every 4 cups of watermelon juice. For every 5 cups of this liquid, add about 3 teaspoons sugar and 1 teaspoon lemon juice, or to your taste; skim off any bubbles, if necessary. Now remove lime-decorated ice from bowl and place lime-side up, in watermelon shell. Serve garnished with mint sprigs. Makes about 20 servings.

**Diabetic diet:** Prepare as directed but substitute low-calorie sugar-free lemon-lime soda for regular; omit sugar. Exchanges per serving = 1 "free."
**Egg-, gluten-, milk- and wheat-free diet:** Prepare as directed.
**Low-fat, low-cholesterol diet:** Negligible fat per serving.
**Low-purine diet:** Prepare as directed. Omit recipe if carbonated beverages are forbidden on diet.
**Low-sodium diet:** Negligible sodium per serving.

## BLUSHING BUTTERMILK (70 calories per serving)

**½ cup icy-cold tomato juice**
**½ cup cold buttermilk**
**lemon juice (optional)**

To serve: Mix tomato juice and buttermilk; stir in dash of lemon juice, if desired. Makes 1 serving.

**Bland diet:** Prepare as directed.
**Diabetic diet:** Exchanges per serving = 1 "A" vegetable and ½ skimmed milk.
**Egg-, gluten- and wheat-free diet:** Prepare as directed.
**Low-fat, low-cholesterol diet:** Negligible fat per serving.
**Low-fat, bland (gall bladder) diet:** Prepare as directed.
**Low-purine diet:** Prepare as directed.
**Low-residue diet:** Prepare as directed.

## CAFÉ AU CRÈME (25 calories per serving)

½ cup evaporated milk
¼ teaspoon vanilla extract
1½ tablespoons confectioners'
sugar
½ teaspoon cinnamon
2 cups hot coffee
nutmeg

About 30 minutes before serving: In ice-cube tray, freeze evaporated milk, just until ice crystals form ½ inch in from edge of tray. In small bowl, combine frozen milk, vanilla, sugar and cinnamon; with electric mixer, at medium speed, beat until thick. Fill each of 8 demitasse cups one-fourth full with milk mixture; fill cups with hot coffee. Sprinkle each with nutmeg. Makes 8 servings.

**Egg-, gluten- and wheat-free diet:** Prepare as directed.

## MULLED APPLE JUICE (60 calories per serving)

1 quart (4 cups) apple juice
1½ teaspoons whole cloves
5 small cinnamon sticks
5 whole allspice

Day before or just before serving: In medium saucepan, heat apple juice to boiling. Tie remaining ingredients in cheese-cloth bag; add bag to juice; boil 5 minutes. Remove spice bag; serve hot. Makes eight ½ cup servings.

**Diabetic diet:** Exchanges per serving = 1 fruit.
**Egg-, gluten-, milk- and wheat-free diet:** Prepare as directed.
**Low-fat, low-cholesterol diet:** Negligible fat per serving.
**Low-purine diet:** Prepare as directed.
**Low-sodium diet:** Negligible sodium per serving.

## SHERBET SHAKE (140 calories per serving)

½ cup orange sherbet
2 cups skimmed milk or reliquefied nonfat dry milk

A few minutes before serving: In electric-blender container, at low speed, blend sherbet and milk until smooth. Divide between 2 large glasses.

**Bland diet:** Prepare as directed.
**Egg-, gluten-, and wheat-free diet:** Prepare as directed but use gluten-free sherbet on gluten-free diet.
**Low-fat, low-cholesterol diet:** Negligible fat per serving.
**Low-fat, bland (gall bladder) diet:** Prepare as directed.
**Low-purine diet:** Prepare as directed.
**Low-residue diet:** Prepare as directed.

## PINEAPPLE BANANA SHAKE (105 calories per serving)

1½ cups buttermilk
½ cup drained pineapple
chunks
½ medium banana
nutmeg for garnish

Just before serving: In electric-blender container, at high speed, blend first 3 ingredients until smooth. Serve sprinkled with nutmeg. Makes 2 servings.

**Bland diet:** Prepare as directed but substitute canned peaches for pineapple; omit nutmeg.
**Diabetic diet:** Prepare as directed but use pineapple packed in **juice.** Exchanges per serving = 1 skim milk and 1 fruit.
**Egg-, gluten- and wheat-free diet:** Prepare as directed.
**Low-fat, low-cholesterol diet:** Negligible fat per serving.
**Low-fat, bland (gall bladder) diet:** Prepare as directed for bland diet.
**Low-purine diet:** Prepare as directed.
**Low-residue diet:** Prepare as directed for bland diet.

## NIBBLER TRAY OF LOW-CALORIE GOODIES

Shrimp and Apple Ball. Spear cooked shelled shrimp with toothpicks and stick into large apple. Serve with chili sauce for dipping. Use Shrimp and Apple Ball as centerpiece and surround with:

Curried Ripe Olives. To low-calorie Italian dressing, add curry to taste. Pour over drained ripe olives. Refrigerate for several hours, stirring occasionally; then drain and serve as snacks.

Herbed Tuna. Break water-packed tuna into large chunks and marinate in low-calorie French dressing. Garnish with snipped parsley and chopped chives.

Topped Cucumber Slices. Top cucumber slices with Neufchâtel cheese and pimento strips.

Ham Rolls. Roll thin slices of cooked ham, salami or other sliced cold meats around cooked asparagus spears or slices of apple, melon, celery, cucumber or chicken.

Stuffed Celery Stalks. Fill small celery stalks with cottage cheeese seasoned with onion salt. Sprinkle with poppy seeds.

Swiss-Cheese-Pepper Squares. Toss together short, thin strips of Swiss cheese and green pepper, low-calorie (imitation) mayonnaise, salt, pepper. Trim crusts from pumpernickel-bread slices; cut into quarters. Top with Swiss-cheese mixture.

## KEEP-TRIM SANDWICH SUGGESTIONS

To make sandwiches that are lower in calories, keep these tips in mind: Use thinly sliced bread, or buy unsliced bread and slice it very thin. Don't spread the bread with anything before adding a filling; instead, choose fillings moist enough to hold bread slices together, and spread on only a thin layer. Lettuce will make sandwich fuller without adding calories; but pack lettuce separately if sandwich is to be carried to be eaten later. Season keep-trim sandwiches generously—a thin, tasty sandwich is much more satisfying than a thick, tasteless one. Pack fresh fruit, vegetable nibblers and a beverage with sandwich to round out lunch. And for a change of pace in sandwiches, try these:

COMBINE Roquefort and Neufchâtel* cheeses with a bit of minced onion or a dash of onion juice and some chopped canned mushrooms. Try it on dark bread.

TRY a combination of crumbled bacon and chopped sweet gherkins, moistening with cottage cheese "sour cream."†

MIX a bit of leftover cooked chicken with a few chopped ripe olives and just enough low-calorie mayonnaise‡ to moisten. Great on raisin bread.

SPARK tuna with minced celery, chopped onions, salt and a bit of cottage cheese "sour cream."† Spread on thin, thin, slices of date-nut bread.

CHOPPED canned shrimp and chopped apple make a nice salad, mixed with a bit of low-calorie mayonnaise‡ and curry. It's especially good on dark bread.

NEUFCHÂTEL cheese* and orange marmalade on raisin bread is a tasty quickie.

SPREAD rye or pumpernickel bread with apple butter; add thin ham slices for a flavor switch.

MIX cottage cheese with drained canned crushed pineapple and a bit of onion salt for a Hawaiian-style filling. Serve it on raisin or dark bread.

CHOP up leftover sautéed chicken livers with a few stuffed olives. It's very good on rye or pumpernickel bread.

FOR a man-size sandwich with girl-size calories, place a slice or two of ham or beef between rye or pumpernickel along with some coleslaw made with low-calorie mayonnaise.‡ (Pack coleslaw separately to carry.)

THINLY sliced green pepper and ham or beef slices on dark or white bread make a delicious sandwich.

---

* Neufchâtel cheese has 32 percent fewer calories than cream cheese.
† Cottage cheese, blended smooth in electric blender with a bit of water or milk, makes a tasty, lower-calorie alternate for sour cream.

‡ Salad dressing has about two-thirds the calories of regular mayonnaise. Low-calorie (imitation) mayonnaise has about one-fifth the calories of regular mayonnaise.

## SOUPS

### POTATO SOUP LACED WITH LIME (125 calories per serving)

1 10½-ounce can condensed
　cream-of-potato soup
1 soup-can skimmed milk or re-
　liquefied nonfat dry milk
1 lime

About 15 minutes before serving: Prepare soup as label directs but use skimmed milk. Cut lime in half. Squeeze juice from one half and stir into soup; slice remaining half for garnish. Makes 3 servings of a scant cup each.

**Diabetic diet:** Exchanges per serving = ½ bread and ½ milk.
**Low-fat diet:** 2 grams fat per serving. Omit recipe from low-cholesterol diet.
**Low-purine diet:** Prepare as directed.

### POTATO SOUP WITH OREGANO (125 calories per serving)

1 10¼-ounce can frozen con-
　densed cream-of-potato soup
1 soup-can skimmed milk or re-
　liquefied nonfat dry milk
¼ teaspoon oregano leaves

About 15 minutes before serving: Prepare soup as label directs but use skimmed milk and add oregano. Serve hot or cold. Makes three ¾-cup servings.

**Diabetic diet:** Exchanges per serving = ½ milk and ½ bread.
**Low-fat diet:** 2 grams fat per serving. Omit recipe from low-cholesterol diet.
**Low-purine diet:** Prepare as directed.

### APPETIZER SOUP (75 calories per serving)

2 beef-bouillon cubes
2 chicken-bouillon cubes
1 19-ounce can tomatoes
1 medium onion, chopped
½ cup thinly sliced carrots
2 stalks celery, cut into ½-inch
　slices
3 whole peppercorns
½ teaspoon sage leaves
1 teaspoon salt
¼ cup shredded Parmesan
　cheese

About 1 hour before serving: In medium saucepan, combine 3 cups water and all remaining ingredients but cheese; cover; simmer 45 minutes. Serve sprinkled with grated Parmesan cheese. Makes 4 servings of about 1 cup each.

**Diabetic diet:** Prepare as directed but omit Parmesan. Exchanges per serving = 1 "A" vegetable.
**Low-fat, low-cholesterol diet:** Prepare as directed but omit Parmesan. Negligible fat per serving.

### SOUTH-OF-THE-BORDER CHOWDER (120 calories per serving)

1 10¼-ounce can frozen con-
　densed New England clam-
　chowder soup
⅔ cup skimmed milk or re-
　liquefied nonfat dry milk
1 beef-bouillon cube
1 cup water
few dashes Tabasco
1 4½-ounce can shrimp,
　drained

Several hours before serving: In medium saucepan, heat chowder, milk, bouillon, water and Tabasco to boiling. Rinse shrimp, refrigerate 8 for garnish. In electric-blender container (with lid ajar to allow hot air to escape), at low speed, blend soup with rest of shrimp until smooth. Refrigerate mixture.

　　To serve: Pour chowder into glass mugs; garnish each with reserved shrimp, coarsely chopped. Makes four ¾-cup servings.

**Bland diet:** Prepare as directed but omit bouillon cube and Tabasco.
**Diabetic diet:** Exchanges per serving = ½ bread and 1 meat.
**Low-fat diet:** 5 grams fat per serving. Omit recipe from low-cholesterol diet.
**Low-fat, bland (gall bladder) diet:** Prepare as directed for bland diet.
**Low-residue diet:** Prepare as directed for bland diet.

## CHICKEN BROTH WITH MEATBALLS AND SPINACH (115 calories per serving)

½ pound ground round steak
¾ teaspoon salt
⅛ teaspoon pepper
2 tablespoons shredded
　Parmesan cheese
1 tablespoon chopped parsley
1 tablespoon packaged dried-
　bread crumbs
3 tablespoons water
7 to 8 cups canned chicken
　broth (about 4 13¾-ounce
　cans)
1 10-ounce package frozen
　chopped spinach, thawed

About 1 hour before serving: In medium bowl, combine round steak with salt, pepper, Parmesan, parsley, bread crumbs and water. With a ½-teaspoon measuring spoon, form into small balls. Bring chicken broth to boiling. Drop meatballs into broth and cook, uncovered, about 10 minutes. Then add spinach and continue cooking about 5 minutes, or until meatballs and spinach are tender. Makes eight 1-cup servings.

**Diabetic diet:** Exchanges per serving = 1 meat and 1 "A" vegetable.
**Low-fat, low-cholesterol diet:** Prepare as directed but omit Parmesan. 5 grams fat per serving.
**High-iron diet:** 4 milligrams iron per serving.

## JELLIED TOMATO BOUILLON (40 calories per serving)

2 envelopes unflavored gelatin
1 tablespoon lemon juice
4 beef-bouillon cubes
1 19-ounce can tomato juice
½ teaspoon grated lemon peel
1 teaspoon Worcestershire
6 onion rings

At least 3 hours before serving: In medium saucepan, stir gelatin into ½ cup cold water; let stand 5 minutes to soften. Stir in lemon juice, bouillon cubes, tomato juice, 2 cups water and lemon peel. Stirring occasionally, bring mixture to boiling. Stir in Worcestershire. Refrigerate until set.

　To serve: Stir jellied soup, then ladle into cups. Serve immediately. Garnish with onion rings. Makes six ¾-cup servings.

**Diabetic diet:** Exchanges per serving = 1 "A" vegetable.
**Low-fat, low-cholesterol diet:** Negligible fat per serving.

## BEEFY-FLAVORED GREEN-BEAN SOUP (15 calories per serving)

1 15½-ounce can green beans
1 cup water
2 beef-bouillon cubes
salt and pepper to taste

About 15 minutes before serving: In electric-blender container, at high speed, blend green beans and their liquid until smooth. (Or press mixture through food mill.) In saucepan, heat blended green beans and remaining ingredients, stirring occasionally, for 10 minutes. Makes four ¾-cup servings.

**Diabetic diet:** Exchanges per serving = 1 "A" vegetable.
**Low-fat, low-cholesterol diet:** Negligible fat per serving.
**Low-residue diet:** Prepare as directed but omit pepper.

## BEEF BROTH WITH MEATBALLS (110 calories per serving)

½ pound ground round steak
¾ teaspoon salt
⅛ teaspoon pepper
¼ teaspoon thyme leaves
1 beaten egg
2 teaspoons flour
2 tablespoons water
2 10½-ounce cans condensed
　beef broth

About 25 minutes before serving: In medium bowl, combine all ingredients but beef broth. With wet hands, form heaping teaspoonful of this meat mixture into small ball; repeat with rest of meat. In large saucepan, dilute beef broth as label directs; heat. Drop meatballs into boiling broth; cover; simmer 15 minutes, or until meatballs are tender. Makes six 1-cup servings.

**Diabetic diet:** Exchanges per serving = 1 meat.
**Low-fat, low-cholesterol diet:** Prepare as directed but use only white of the egg. 5 grams fat per serving.
**High-iron diet:** 1.5 milligrams iron per serving.

## 1-2-3  GAZPACHO  (70 calories per serving)

1 medium cucumber
1 quart (4 cups) chilled canned
    tomato juice
⅓ cup wine vinegar
1½ tablespoons salad oil
½ teaspoon oregano leaves
dash Tabasco
12 ice cubes

About 10 minutes before serving: Pare cucumber. Cut 6 thin slices, then dice remaining cucumber. In electric blender container, at high speed, blend diced cucumber and remaining ingredients except ice cubes until smooth.

To serve: Pour soup over ice cubes in chilled bowls; garnish with cucumber slices. Makes six ¾-cup servings.

**Diabetic diet:** Exchanges per serving = 1 "A" vegetable and 1 fat.
**Egg-, gluten-, milk- and wheat-free diet:** Prepare as directed.
**Low-fat, low-cholesterol diet:** 4 grams fat per serving.
**Low-purine diet:** Prepare as directed.
**Low-sodium diet:** Prepare as directed but substitute low-sodium tomato juice for regular and omit Tabasco. 10 milligrams sodium per serving.

## STRAWBERRY-RHUBARB  SOUP  (115 calories per serving)

1 pint strawberries, sliced
1 pound rhubarb, chopped
1¼ cups orange juice
about ½ cup granulated sugar
¼ cup chopped orange seg-
    ments

About 3 hours before serving: In medium pan, combine strawberry slices (reserve 6 for garnish), rhubarb and orange juice; simmer 10 minutes. Stir in ½ cup sugar or sugar to taste; cool.

In covered electric-blender container, at low speed, blend strawberry mixture one-half at a time. (Or put berries through a food mill.) Then fold in chopped orange segments; refrigerate, covered.

To serve: Garnish soup with reserved strawberry slices. Makes 6 servings.

**Egg-, gluten-, milk- and wheat-free diet:** Prepare as directed.
**Low-fat, low-cholesterol diet:** Negligible fat per serving.
**Low-purine diet:** Prepare as directed.
**Low-sodium diet:** Negligible sodium per serving.

## HOLIDAY  TOMATO  SOUP  (115 calories per serving)

1 6-ounce can frozen orange-
    juice concentrate
3 juice-cans water
2 10¾-ounce cans condensed
    tomato soup

About 15 minutes before serving: In large saucepan, heat all ingredients to a gentle simmer. Serve hot or cold. Makes six 1-cup servings.

**Diabetic diet:** Exchanges per serving = 1 bread and 1 fruit.
**Low-fat, low-cholesterol diet:** 1 gram fat per serving.
**Low-purine diet:** Prepare as directed.

## TOMMY'S  TARRAGON  SOUP  (70 calories per serving)

1 tablespoon butter or
    margarine
2 tablespoons minced onion
2 tablespoons minced celery
2 cups canned tomato juice
½ teaspoon salt
½ teaspoon tarragon
⅛ teaspoon pepper
dash Tabasco

About 25 minutes before serving: In heavy saucepan over medium heat, in butter or margarine, sauté onion and celery until onion turns golden. Add remaining ingredients; bring to boiling; lower heat and simmer 5 minutes. Makes three ⅔-cup servings.

**Diabetic diet:** Exchanges per serving = 1 "A" vegetable and 1 fat.
**Low-fat, low-cholesterol diet:** Prepare as directed but sauté vegetables in only 1 teaspoon margarine. 2 grams fat per serving.
**Low-purine diet:** Prepare as directed.

## FRESH VEGETABLE SOUP (125 calories per serving)

1 quart water
1 tablespoon salt
1 cup sliced carrots
1 cup diced potatoes
1 cup diced fresh tomatoes
1 cup chopped green onions
½ 10-ounce package frozen
   baby lima beans
½ pound fresh green beans,
   cut into 1-inch pieces
½ cup corn, scraped from cob
2 teaspoons salt
1 cup hot fluffy rice (packaged
   precooked, regular or processed kind)

About 1 hour before serving: In large kettle or Dutch oven, simmer, covered, all ingredients but corn, 2 teaspoons salt and rice for 30 minutes. After soup has simmered 30 minutes, add corn and 2 teaspoons salt. Simmer, covered, 15 minutes longer.

To serve: Spoon some rice into each bowl; ladle soup over it. Makes about six 1-cup servings.

**Diabetic diet:** Exchanges per serving = 2 bread and 1 "A" vegetable.
**Low-fat, low-cholesterol diet:** Negligible fat per serving.
**Low-purine diet:** Prepare as directed.
**Low-sodium diet:** Prepare as directed but omit lima beans and salt; cook rice without adding salt. 15 milligrams sodium per serving.

## RED CABBAGE SOUP (70 calories per serving)

2 tablespoons butter or margarine
2 medium onions, sliced
8 cups (about 1½ pounds)
   shredded red cabbage
2 potatoes, sliced
1 apple, sliced
2 quarts water
1 10½-ounce can condensed
   beef broth
3½ teaspoons salt
¼ to ½ teaspoon pepper
⅛ teaspoon thyme leaves
⅛ teaspoon garlic powder
1 small bay leaf

About 3 hours before serving: In large kettle, in butter or margarine, sauté onions until golden. Add remaining ingredients. Stir; then simmer, covered, 2 hours. In electric-blender container (with lid ajar to allow hot air to escape), blend one-sixth of soup at low speed until creamy. Repeat until all of soup is blended. (Or press through food mill.) Makes twelve 1-cup servings.

**Diabetic diet:** Exchanges per serving = 1 "A" and 1 "B" vegetable.
**Low-fat, low-cholesterol diet:** Prepare as directed but use margarine instead of butter. 1 gram fat per serving.

## WESTERN CORN CHOWDER (130 calories per serving)

1 tablespoon butter or margarine
2 tablespoons minced onion
2 tablespoons minced green
   pepper
½ cup thinly sliced green
   celery
2 tablespoons flour
1 10½-ounce can condensed
   cream-of-chicken soup
2½ cups skimmed milk or reliquefied nonfat dry milk
⅛ teaspoon sage leaves
dash cayenne
1 8-ounce can whole-kernel
   corn, undrained
chopped parsley for garnish

About 25 minutes before serving: In medium saucepan, in butter or margarine, sauté onion, green pepper and celery until golden. Stir in flour, then soup, then milk. Heat, stirring, to boiling. Add sage, cayenne and corn; heat to boiling. Serve garnished with parsley. Makes six ¾-cup servings.

**Diabetic diet:** Exchanges per serving = 1 "B" vegetable and ½ milk.
**Low-fat diet:** Prepare as directed but use margarine instead of butter. 5 grams fat per serving. Omit recipe from low-cholesterol diet.

## SHERRIED VICHYSSOISE (115 calories per serving)

2 10¼-ounce cans frozen condensed cream-of-potato
soup, thawed
2 cups skimmed milk or reliquefied nonfat dry milk
¼ cup cooking sherry
chopped chives for garnish

About 20 minutes before serving: Prepare soup as label directs, but use skimmed milk and add cooking sherry. Garnish with chopped chives. Makes 6 servings of a scant cup each.

**Diabetic diet:** Exchanges per serving = ½ milk and ½ bread.
**Low-fat diet:** 5 grams fat per serving. Omit recipe from low-cholesterol diet.
**Low-purine diet:** Prepare as directed. Omit recipe if sherry is forbidden on diet.

## MANHATTAN SUPPER SOUP (150 calories per serving)

½ pound ground round steak
2 cups coarsely chopped cabbage (about ¼ of a small
cabbage)
1 large onion, thinly sliced
1 stalk green celery, sliced
3 carrots, cut into 1-inch slices
1 medium potato, cubed
1 tablespoon parsley flakes
3 ounces tomato paste (½ 6-
ounce can)
1 16-ounce can tomatoes
1 10½-ounce can condensed
beef broth
2 soup-cans water
1½ teaspoons salt
⅛ to ¼ teaspoon pepper
1½ teaspoons granulated sugar
1 10-ounce package frozen peas

At least 1½ hours before serving: In large kettle or Dutch oven, cook meat until it loses its red color. Add remaining ingredients except frozen peas; simmer, uncovered, 50 minutes. Add peas; cover; cook 10 minutes, or until peas are tender. Makes 8 servings of about 1 cup each.

**Diabetic diet:** Prepare as directed but omit sugar. Exchanges per serving = 1 meat, 1 bread and 1 "A" vegetable.
**Low-fat, low-cholesterol diet:** 5 grams fat per serving.

## TOMATO AND EGG SOUP (Sopa de Tomate e Ovos) (100 calories per serving)

butter or margarine
1 large onion, thinly sliced
2 pounds fresh tomatoes, sliced
salt
¼ cup chopped parsley
½ teaspoon granulated sugar
⅛ teaspoon pepper
2 hard-cooked eggs, sliced

About 1½ hours before serving: In large kettle, in 1 tablespoon butter or margarine, sauté onion until soft. Add tomatoes and 1 teaspoon salt; simmer 10 minutes. Now add 1 quart water and parsley; simmer, covered, 1 hour. Press soup through food mill, then add ½ teaspoon salt, sugar and pepper. Heat, then stir in 1 tablespoon butter or margarine. Arrange sliced eggs in bottom of soup tureen; pour in soup and serve. Makes six 1-cup servings.

**Diabetic diet:** Prepare as directed but omit sugar. Exchanges per serving = 1 "A" and 1 "B" vegetable and 1 fat.
**Gluten-, milk- and wheat-free diet:** Prepare as directed but use milk-free margarine on milk-free diet.
**High-iron diet:** 1.5 milligrams iron per serving.
**Low-purine diet:** Prepare as directed.
**Low-sodium diet:** Prepare as directed but use unsalted butter or margarine; omit salt. 30 milligrams sodium per serving. If eggs are also omitted, 5 milligrams sodium per serving.

## ROYAL CONSOMMÉ (70 calories per serving)

2 10½-ounce cans condensed
    beef broth
4 peppercorns
3 whole cloves
2 bay leaves
¼ teaspoon grated lemon peel
½ avocado, cut into 6 thin
    slices

About 10 minutes before serving: In medium saucepan, combine beef broth with 2 soup-cans water. Add peppercorns, cloves, bay leaves and lemon peel. Cover and heat to boiling; simmer 1 or 2 minutes. Strain, then float avocado slices on top. Makes six 1-cup servings.

**Diabetic diet:** Exchanges per serving = 1 "free" and 1 fat.
**Low-fat, low-cholesterol diet:** Omit avocado. Negligible fat per serving.

## HOT TOMATO SOUP VERDI (50 calories per serving)

1 46-ounce can vegetable-juice
    cocktail
½ cup dry sherry
1 tablespoon brown sugar
½ cup chopped green onions
    for garnish

About 15 minutes before serving: In large saucepan, heat vegetable juice, sherry and sugar to boiling. Serve in mugs, topped with green onions. Makes six 1-cup servings.

**Diabetic diet:** Prepare as directed but omit sugar; use saccharin equivalent to 1 tablespoon sugar. Exchanges per serving = 1 "A" vegetable.
**Low-fat, low-cholesterol diet:** Negligible fat per serving.
**Low-purine diet:** Prepare as directed.

## TOMATO SIP (40 calories per serving)

2 10½-ounce cans condensed
    beef bouillon
1 19-ounce can tomato juice
2 lemon slices
6 whole cloves
⅛ teaspoon basil
2 tablespoons dry sherry

About 15 minutes before serving: In saucepan, heat all ingredients to boiling; simmer 5 minutes; strain out spices. Serve in mugs or cups. Makes 6 servings of a scant cup each.

**Diabetic diet:** Exchanges per serving = 1 "A" vegetable.
**Low-fat, low-cholesterol diet:** Negligible fat per serving.

## POTATO-MUSHROOM SOUP (105 calories per serving)

1 cup mixed slivered carrots,
    celery and parsnips
3 cups cubed potatoes
salt
butter or margarine
½ pound fresh mushrooms,
    sliced
pepper
¼ cup flour
1 garlic clove, minced
1 teaspoon marjoram leaves

About 2 hours before serving: In large kettle, combine mixed vegetables with potatoes, 2½ teaspoons salt and 2 quarts boiling water; simmer, covered, about 30 minutes. In skillet, in 1 tablespoon butter or margarine, sauté mushrooms 5 minutes; sprinkle with ½ teaspoon salt and ⅛ teaspoon pepper. Add to soup and let simmer. Meanwhile, in same skillet, melt 2 tablespoons butter or margarine; stir in flour until smooth; continue stirring until mixture is light brown. Remove from heat and slowly stir in 1 cup cold water. Now pour this mixture through a strainer into soup; add garlic and marjoram. Simmer, stirring occasionally, until vegetables are tender and soup is thickened—about 45 minutes. Makes 8 servings of a scant 1½ cups each.

**Diabetic diet:** Exchanges per serving = 1 "A" vegetable, 1 bread and 1 fat.
**Egg-, gluten-, milk- and wheat-free diet:** Prepare as directed but use a milk-free margarine on milk-free diet; substitute 2 tablespoons cornstarch for flour on gluten- and wheat-free diets.
**Low-fat, low-cholesterol diet:** Prepare as directed but use margarine instead of butter. 5 grams fat per serving.
**Low-sodium diet:** Prepare as directed but use unsalted butter or margarine; omit salt. 15 milligrams sodium per serving.

## RANCH-STYLE VEGETABLE SOUP (170 calories per serving)

½ pound ground round steak
2 medium potatoes, cubed
1 small sweet potato, cubed
3 medium carrots, cut into ½-inch slices
2 teaspoons salt
½ teaspoon monosodium glutamate (optional)
1 tablespoon parsley flakes
2 tablespoons barley
6 cups water
½ 9-ounce package frozen cut green beans

About 1 hour and 15 minutes before serving: In large saucepan, cook beef, stirring constantly, until well browned. Add remaining ingredients except green beans. Cover; simmer 45 minutes. Add green beans. Simmer, uncovered, 15 minutes. Makes 6 servings of about 1½ cups each.

**Bland diet:** Prepare as directed. Omit parsley flakes if forbidden on diet.
**Diabetic diet:** Exchanges per serving = 1 meat, 1 "B" vegetable and 1 bread.
**Low-fat, low-cholesterol diet:** 5 grams fat per serving.
**Low-fat, bland (gall bladder) diet:** Prepare as directed.
**Low-residue diet:** Prepare as directed but omit parsley flakes.
**Low-sodium diet:** Prepare as directed but omit monosodium glutamate and salt. 55 milligrams sodium per serving.

## CHICKEN CORN SOUP (105 calories per serving)

1 10½-ounce can condensed chicken-with-rice soup
1 soup-can skimmed milk or re-liquefied nonfat dry milk
1 8-ounce can cream-style corn
2 tablespoons coarsely chopped parsley
¼ teaspoon salt
generous dash thyme leaves

About 15 minutes before serving: In medium saucepan, heat all ingredients to boiling; simmer 5 minutes. Makes four ¾-cup servings.

**Diabetic diet:** Exchanges per serving = 1 bread and ½ skim milk.
**Low-fat diet:** 1 gram fat per serving. Omit recipe from low-cholesterol diet.

## CURRIED APPLE SOUP (90 calories per serving)

1 tablespoon salad oil
1 medium onion, chopped
3 cups chicken broth
3 tablespoons cornstarch
1 to 2 teaspoons curry
⅔ cup evaporated skimmed milk, chilled
2 apples, peeled
salt

Early in day: In large skillet, in oil, sauté onion until transparent. Add chicken broth, cornstarch, dissolved in small amount of water, and curry. Heat to boiling, stirring constantly. Cover and simmer 8 minutes. Refrigerate.

Just before serving: In electric-blender container, at high speed, blend cold broth mixture, milk and one apple, quartered, until smooth. (Or puree mixture with food mill.) Dice remaining apple and add to soup. Salt to taste. Serve cold. Makes 6 servings.

**Diabetic diet:** Exchanges per serving = 1 "B" vegetable and ½ milk.
**Low-fat, low-cholesterol diet:** 2 grams fat per serving.

## WATERCRESS VICHYSSOISE (95 calories per serving)

1 10¼-ounce can frozen condensed cream-of-potato soup, thawed
1 soup-can water
½ cup firmly packed, coarsely chopped watercress

Up to 20 minutes before serving: In electric-blender container, at low-speed, blend all ingredients 1 minute, or until smooth. In medium saucepan, simmer mixture 5 minutes. Makes three ¾-cup servings.

**Diabetic diet:** Exchanges per serving = 1 "A" vegetable, 1 bread and 1 fat.
**Low-fat diet:** 5 grams fat per serving. Omit recipe from low-cholesterol diet.
**Low-purine diet:** Prepare as directed.

## QUICK SENEGLASE (120 calories per serving)

1 cup skimmed milk or reliquefied nonfat dry milk
2 teaspoons curry
1 10½-ounce can condensed cream-of-chicken soup
3 lemon slices for garnish

About 10 minutes before serving: In electric-blender container, at low speed, blend skimmed milk, curry and undiluted cream-of-chicken soup about 10 seconds, or until smooth. Garnish with lemon slices and serve cold. Makes 3 servings of a scant cup each.

**Diabetic diet:** Exchanges per serving = 1 milk.
**Low-fat diet:** 5 grams fat per serving. Omit recipe from low-cholesterol diet.

## JELLIED BOUILLON (20 calories per serving)

1 envelope unflavored gelatin
3 beef-bouillon cubes
1 thin slice boiled ham (about 1 ounce), trimmed of fat
6 thin cucumber slices
¼ carrot, cut into short thin strips
1 tablespoon lemon juice
½ teaspoon Worcestershire

Early in day: Sprinkle gelatin on ½ cup cold water to soften. In saucepan, simmer bouillon cubes in 2½ cups water until dissolved. Roll ham tightly into a pinwheel, then cut crosswise into thin slices. Meanwhile, in medium baking dish, place rolled ham, cucumber and carrot strips in a single layer. Stir gelatin, lemon juice and Worcestershire into bouillon. Pour mixture over ham and vegetables; refrigerate until consistency of soft jelly.

To serve: Spoon into chilled soup bowls. Makes 6 servings.

**Diabetic diet:** Prepare as directed but omit ham. Exchanges per serving = 1 "A" vegetable.
**Low-fat, low-cholesterol diet:** 1 gram fat per serving.

## CAN OPENER MINESTRONE (120 calories per serving)

1 10¾-ounce can condensed vegetarian-vegetable soup
1 10½-ounce can chicken-noodle soup
1 16-ounce can kidney beans
1 garlic clove, minced
⅓ cup chopped parsley

About 15 minutes before serving: In large saucepan, simmer all ingredients with 1 soup-can water for 10 minutes. Makes 6 servings of a scant cup each.

**Low-fat, low-cholesterol diet:** 2 grams fat per serving.
**High-iron diet:** 2 milligrams iron per serving.

## OXFORD CIRCLE CORN CHOWDER (130 calories per serving)

1 8¾-ounce can cream-style corn
1 cup skimmed milk or reliquefied nonfat dry milk
¼ cup shredded American cheese
chopped parsley for garnish

About 15 minutes before serving: In medium pan, combine corn, skimmed milk and cheese. Cook over low heat, stirring, until mixture just begins to bubble. Sprinkle with parsley. Makes 3 servings.

**Diabetic diet:** Exchanges per serving (⅔ cup) = 1 bread and ½ milk.
**High-iron diet:** 1 milligram iron per serving.
**Low-purine diet:** Prepare as directed.

## OYSTER STEW SPECIAL (205 calories per serving)

1 10¾-ounce can frozen condensed oyster stew
1 soup-can skimmed milk or reliquefied nonfat dry milk
2 ounces process cheese spread

About 15 minutes before serving: In medium saucepan, heat oyster stew and milk until soup melts and mixture simmers. Stir in process cheese spread and heat gently until it just melts. Makes 3 servings.

**Bland diet:** Prepare as directed.
**Diabetic diet:** Exchanges per serving = 1 meat, ½ bread and ½ milk.

## TAVIA'S LENTIL SOUP (100 calories per serving)

½ cup dry lentils
1 quart water
1 cup canned tomatoes
1 onion, thinly sliced
1 stalk celery, thinly sliced
1 teaspoon salt
¼ teaspoon garlic powder
⅛ teaspoon pepper
2 dashes aromatic bitters

Day before or early in day: In large covered saucepan, simmer all ingredients 1 hour, or until lentils are tender. In electric-blender container (with lid ajar to allow hot air to escape), blend soup one-quarter at a time until smooth. Or press through a food mill until smooth. Reheat and serve hot. Makes four 1-cup servings.

**Diabetic diet:** Exchanges per serving = 1 "A" vegetable and 1 bread.
**Low-fat, low-cholesterol diet:** Negligible fat per serving.
**High-iron diet:** 2 milligrams iron per serving.
**Low-sodium diet:** Prepare as directed but substitute low-sodium canned tomatoes for regular; omit salt. 20 milligrams sodium per serving.

## CHICKEN BORSCHT (145 calories per serving)

1 16-ounce can julienne beets, undrained
2 10½-ounce cans condensed beef bouillon
1 tablespoon flour
¼ teaspoon pepper
1 cup cut-up cooked or canned chicken
⅓ cup lemon juice

About 15 minutes before serving: In large saucepan, combine beets, bouillon and 1½ cups water. Stir a small amount of this mixture into flour and pepper to form a smooth paste; stir into remaining mixture. Simmer, covered, 10 minutes, then stir in chicken and lemon juice. Makes 4 servings.

**Low-fat, low-cholesterol diet:** 5 grams fat per serving.

## FRENCH ONION SOUP (90 calories per serving)

2 tablespoons butter or margarine
4 cups sliced onions
5 beef-bouillon cubes
¼ teaspoon salt
¼ teaspoon pepper
½ teaspoon Worcestershire
½ teaspoon bottled sauce for gravy
6 Melba-toast rounds
1 tablespoon shredded Parmesan cheese

About 45 minutes before serving: In large skillet, in butter or margarine, sauté onions until tender. Dissolve bouillon cubes in 4 cups boiling water; add to onion with salt, pepper, Worcestershire and bottled sauce for gravy. Simmer, covered, about 30 minutes. Before serving, top each serving with a Melba-toast round and sprinkle it with Parmesan cheese. Makes 6 servings.

**Low-fat diet:** 5 grams fat per serving. Omit recipe from low-cholesterol diet.

## VEGETABLE SHRIMP SOUP (65 calories per serving)

1 small onion, thinly sliced
1 carrot, thinly sliced
1 stalk celery, thinly sliced
1 tablespoon soy sauce
1 teaspoon salt
½ teaspoon granulated sugar
¼ teaspoon monosodium glutamate
1 tablespoon lemon juice
2 7-ounce packages frozen shelled and deveined shrimp
parsley for garnish

About 30 minutes before serving: In medium saucepan, combine onion, carrot, celery, soy sauce, salt, sugar and monosodium glutamate with 4 cups water. Simmer until vegetables are tender. Add lemon juice and shrimp; cook until shrimp curl and turn pink—about 5 minutes. Garnish with parsley. Makes 4 servings.

**Diabetic diet:** Prepare as directed but omit sugar. Exchanges per serving = 1 meat and 1 "A" vegetable.
**Low-fat diet:** 1 gram fat per serving. Omit recipe from low-cholesterol diet.

## FISH AND SEAFOOD

### BROILED MACKEREL PLATTER (345 calories per serving)

2 1-pound fresh mackerels,
  filleted*
1 teaspoon salt
¼ teaspoon pepper
2 10-ounce packages frozen
  broccoli spears
7 small mushrooms
salad oil
3 tablespoons low-calorie
  Italian dressing
1½ slices day-old bread,
  finely crumbled
6 to 8 thin tomato slices
1 ounce shredded Cheddar or
  American cheese

About 25 minutes before serving: Preheat broiler 10 minutes if manufacturer directs. Sprinkle fillets with salt and pepper. Broil, flesh side up, 4 to 5 inches from heat for 7 minutes. Meanwhile, cook broccoli as label directs. Prepare mushrooms for broiling: with sharp knife, remove 3 thin curved strips, equidistantly apart, from around top of each mushroom cap; then brush lightly with salad oil.

At end of 7 minutes, carefully turn fillets over. Brush skin of each with low-calorie Italian dressing; sprinkle with bread crumbs. Arrange mushrooms beside fillets. Broil 3 to 5 minutes, or until fish flakes easily with fork. Meanwhile, arrange broccoli in baking dish; top with tomato slices; sprinkle cheese down center; broil just until cheese melts.

To serve: Place fish in center of platter and arrange broccoli around edges. Makes 4 servings.

**Bland diet:** Prepare as directed but omit pepper; brush fish with salad oil instead of Italian dressing; omit broccoli, tomatoes and cheese.
**Diabetic diet:** Exchanges per serving = 4 meat and 1 "A" and 1 "B" vegetable.
**Low-fat, low-cholesterol diet:** Prepare as directed but use flounder, sole or haddock fillets; omit cheese. 2 grams fat per serving.
**Low-fat, bland (gall bladder) diet:** Prepare as directed for bland diet.
**Low-residue diet:** Prepare as directed for bland diet.
**Low-sodium diet:** Prepare as directed but use fresh flounder fillets (4 ounces each); omit salt; cook broccoli without added salt; brush fish with salad oil (not Italian dressing); use unsalted bread; omit cheese. 110 milligrams sodium per serving. (If prepared with regular bread, 155 milligrams sodium per serving.)

* Or use two 16-ounce packages frozen cod, haddock, sole or flounder fillets; thaw for several hours so fish separates easily, then prepare as directed above. 290 calories per serving.

### BAKED SWORDFISH AU GRATIN (260 calories per serving)

1 pound fresh swordfish steaks,
  ½- to ¾-inch thick (or frozen
  swordfish steaks, thawed)
½ cup salad oil
½ cup sauterne
1 teaspoon parsley flakes
¼ teaspoon thyme leaves
1 bay leaf, crumbled
6 peppercorns
1 small onion, thinly sliced
⅓ cup packaged dried-bread
  crumbs
⅓ cup shredded Parmesan
  cheese
¼ teaspoon oregano leaves
½ teaspoon salt

About 2½ hours before serving: Cut swordfish steaks into 4 portions. In medium baking pan, combine marinade of salad oil, sauterne, parsley, thyme, bay leaf, peppercorns and onion; lay fish on top; refrigerate at least 2 hours, occasionally spooning marinade over fish.

Preheat oven to 350°F. Combine bread crumbs, cheese, oregano and salt. Coat fish with this mixture; place in baking dish; cover; bake 20 minutes. Uncover and bake 15 minutes longer, or until fish flakes easily with fork. If browner surface is desired, place under broiler until light brown. Makes 4 servings.

**Diabetic diet:** Exchanges per serving = 3 meat and ½ bread.

## FLORENTINE FILLETS (230 calories per serving)

1 4-ounce can chopped mushrooms
salad oil
½ cup chopped onion
1 cup crushed saltines (about
 20)
¼ teaspoon pepper
⅛ teaspoon sage leaves
⅛ teaspoon mace
6 4-ounce fresh sole
 or flounder fillets
salt
1 10-ounce package frozen
 chopped spinach, thawed,
 thoroughly drained
4 teaspoons lemon juice
4 medium tomatoes
low-calorie Italian dressing

About 40 minutes before serving: Preheat oven to 325°F. Make stuffing: Drain mushrooms, reserving juice. In skillet over medium heat, in 1 tablespoon salad oil, sauté onion and mushrooms until onion is golden. Remove from heat; stir in crushed saltines, pepper, sage, mace and 2 tablespoons reserved mushroom juice.

Sprinkle sole fillets with salt. Spread with drained spinach; sprinkle with lemon juice; top with stuffing. Roll up each fillet; secure with toothpicks. Arrange, side by side, in medium baking dish; brush with 1 tablespoon salad oil. Cut tops from tomatoes; place in pan; sprinkle with salt; brush with low-calorie dressing. Bake fillets and tomatoes 15 minutes, or until fish flakes easily with fork. Remove picks. Makes 6 servings.

**Diabetic diet:** Exchanges per serving = 3 meat, 1 "A" vegetable and 1 bread.
**Low-fat, low-cholesterol diet:** 10 grams fat per serving.
**High-iron diet:** Prepare as directed and be sure to use enriched saltines. 3 milligrams iron per serving.

## GREEK BAKED HALIBUT (320 calories per serving)

½ tablespoon salad oil
2 medium onions, thinly sliced
1 garlic clove, crushed
½ cup chopped parsley
½ teaspoon salt
⅛ teaspoon pepper
1 16-ounce can tomatoes
1 tablespoon tomato paste
 (optional)
2 chicken-bouillon cubes
3 fresh halibut steaks, cut
 about ¾-inch thick (about
 1½ pounds)
3 thin tomato slices
3 thin lemon slices

About 1 hour before serving: In large skillet over medium heat, in oil, sauté onions and garlic until golden. Add parsley, salt, pepper, canned tomatoes, tomato paste and bouillon cubes; simmer, uncovered, 20 minutes.

Preheat oven to 350°F. Place fish steaks in medium (about 12″ by 8″ by 2″) baking dish; cover with tomato sauce; top with tomato and lemon slices. Bake 20 to 25 minutes, or until fish flakes with a fork. Makes 3 servings.

**Egg-, gluten-, milk- and wheat-free diet:** Prepare as directed but omit bouillon cubes.
**Low-fat, low-cholesterol diet:** 5 grams fat per serving.

## TOMATO-TOPPED FISH FILLETS (165 calories per serving)

1 16-ounce package frozen cod,
 perch or flounder fillets,
 thawed and drained
onion salt
½ teaspoon salt
¼ teaspoon pepper
2 tablespoons lemon juice
1 tablespoon melted butter or
 margarine
1 medium tomato, sliced

About 30 minutes before serving: Preheat oven to 400°F. In greased large shallow baking dish, arrange fillets. Sprinkle with ½ teaspoon onion salt, salt and pepper. Combine lemon juice and butter; pour over fish. Place tomato slices on top; sprinkle with ¼ teaspoon onion salt. Bake 20 to 25 minutes, or until fish flakes easily when tested with a fork. Makes 3 servings.

**Diabetic diet:** Exchanges per serving = 4 meat and 1 "A" vegetable.
**Egg-, gluten-, milk- and wheat-free diet:** Prepare as directed but use milk-free margarine for milk-free diet.
**Low-fat, low-cholesterol diet:** Prepare as directed but use salad oil or margarine in place of butter. 5 grams fat per serving.
**Low-sodium diet:** Prepare as directed but use only fresh (not frozen) fish; substitute onion powder for onion salt; omit salt; use unsalted butter or margarine. 120 milligrams sodium per serving.

## BOSTON FISH SALAD (235 calories per serving)

1 16-ounce package frozen cod, perch or flounder fillets, thawed and drained
1 cup low-calorie (imitation) mayonnaise
1 cup minced celery
½ cup grated carrot
1 tablespoon capers
2 teaspoons lemon juice
½ teaspoon salt
¼ teaspoon onion salt
1 small head Boston lettuce
2 hard-cooked eggs, sliced
1 cup sliced cooked beets

About 1 hour before serving: Bake fish as label directs. In large bowl, flake fish and combine with next 7 ingredients. Refrigerate.

To serve: Line salad platter with lettuce leaves; spoon fish mixture over top. Arrange egg slices on top of fish and beets around sides of platter. Makes 4 servings.

**Diabetic diet:** Carefully divide salad into 4 equal individual servings. Exchanges per serving = 3 meat and 1 "A" and 1 "B" vegetable. **Low-fat, low-cholesterol diet:** Prepare as directed but omit egg. 10 grams fat per serving.

## CAPE COD FLOUNDER (240 calories per serving)

1 10½-ounce can frozen clam chowder, thawed
½ cup skimmed milk or reliquefied nonfat dry milk
1 16-ounce package frozen flounder fillets, thawed
lemon wedges for garnish

About 20 minutes before serving: Preheat oven to 350°F. In heatproof medium shallow casserole dish over medium heat, heat clam chowder and milk, stirring until smooth; remove from heat. Separate pieces of flounder and roll up each one; place single layer in casserole. Spoon clam-chowder mixture over fish, coating completely. Bake 10 minutes, or until fish flakes easily with a fork. Serve fish with gravy. Garnish with lemon. Makes 3 servings.

**Bland diet:** Prepare as directed.
**Diabetic diet:** Exchanges per serving = 3 meat and 1 skim milk.
**Low-fat diet:** 10 grams fat per serving. Omit recipe from low-cholesterol diet.
**Low-fat, bland (gall bladder) diet:** Prepare as directed.
**Low-residue diet:** Prepare as directed.

## ALOHA FLOUNDER (220 calories per serving)

1 8½-ounce can pineapple tidbits
2 carrots, sliced diagonally
1 16-ounce package frozen flounder fillets, thawed (or 3 small fresh fillets)
1 teaspoon granulated sugar
1 teaspoon cornstarch
½ teaspoon soy sauce
½ green pepper, cut into thin strips
3 slices onion, separated into rings

About 30 minutes before serving: Preheat oven to 425°F. Drain syrup from pineapple into medium pan; reserve tidbits. Add carrot slices and cook, covered, until tender-crisp—about 15 minutes.

Meanwhile, place fillets in buttered medium baking pan; bake 20 minutes. In cup, mix sugar, cornstarch and soy sauce. When carrots are almost tender, add pineapple tidbits, green pepper, onion rings and cornstarch mixture. Cook, stirring constantly, until vegetables are tender-crisp and glazed—about 5 minutes. Serve vegetables over fish. Makes 3 servings.

**Diabetic diet:** Prepare as directed but for regular pineapple, substitute 1 cup pineapple and juice from 1 15¾-ounce can pineapple packed in pineapple juice; omit sugar; carefully divide into 3 equal servings. Exchanges per serving = 4 meat, 1 "A" and 1 "B" vegetable and 1 fruit.
**Egg-, gluten-, milk- and wheat-free diet:** Prepare as directed but omit soy sauce.
**Low-fat, low-cholesterol diet:** 1 gram fat per serving.
**Low-sodium diet:** Prepare as directed but use fresh instead of frozen fish; omit soy sauce. 105 milligrams sodium per serving.

## BAKED STRIPED BASS WITH CLAMS (155 calories per serving)

1 dozen hard-shelled clams
1 4-pound striped bass, dressed
   and boned, but with tail on
1 teaspoon salt
¼ teaspoon basil
⅛ teaspoon pepper
½ cup parsley sprigs
1 medium onion, thinly sliced
2 celery stalks with leaves,
   chopped
1 garlic clove, halved
2 bay leaves
½ cup dry white wine
2 tablespoons butter or margarine, melted

About 50 minutes before serving: Preheat oven to 350°F. Scrub clams under cold running water; set aside. Sprinkle inside of fish with salt, basil and pepper. Arrange parsley and half of onion slices inside fish; place fish in large shallow baking pan or ovenproof serving dish.

Around fish, place clams, remaining onion, celery, garlic and bay leaves. Pour wine and butter or margarine over fish. Cover pan with foil and bake 40 to 50 minutes, or until fish flakes easily when tested with a fork and shells of clams are open. Discard garlic and bay leaves. Makes 8 servings.

**Egg-, gluten-, milk- and wheat-free diet:** Prepare as directed but use milk-free margarine on milk-free diet.
**Low-fat diet:** 5 grams fat per serving. Omit recipe from low-cholesterol diet.

## BAKED FLOUNDER FILLETS SUPREME (300 calories per serving)

8 flounder fillets (about 2
   pounds)
seasoned salt
1 medium tomato,
   halved
4 slices natural Swiss cheese,
   halved
2 tablespoons butter or margarine
1 3- or 4-ounce can sliced
   mushrooms, drained (reserve
   liquid)
2 small onions, sliced
1½ tablespoons flour
chopped parsley
1 cup skimmed milk or reliquefied nonfat dry milk
6 tablespoons sherry
2 cups packaged precooked rice

About 45 minutes before serving: Sprinkle flounder fillets lightly on both sides with seasoned salt, then roll up each. Cut tomato into 8 slices. Arrange flounder rolls, seam side down, alternately with tomato and cheese slices, down center of large (about 13″ by 9″ by 2″) baking dish. Preheat oven to 400°F. In large skillet, in butter or margarine, sauté mushrooms and onions until golden. Now stir in flour, 1½ teaspoons seasoned salt and ¼ cup parsley, then skimmed milk, mushroom liquid combined with enough water to make ½ cup, and sherry. Bring to boiling, then pour over fish. Bake 20 minutes, or until fillets are golden and easily flaked with fork. Meanwhile, prepare rice as label directs; stir in ½ cup parsley. When fish is done, spoon rice around sides. Makes 8 servings.

**Diabetic diet:** Carefully divide into 8 equal servings. Exchanges per serving = 3 meat, 1 "A" vegetable and 2 bread.

## HALIBUT STEAK WITH EGGPLANT AND TOMATO SAUCE (280 calories per serving)

2 tablespoons salad oil
1 large green pepper, cut into
   ½-inch strips
1 large onion, thinly sliced
1 1-pound eggplant, peeled,
   cubed
2 8-ounce cans tomato sauce
½ cup dry white wine
1 garlic clove, minced
1 bay leaf
2 tablespoons butter or margarine
2 tablespoons lemon juice
salt and pepper
1 2-pound halibut steak

About 30 minutes before serving: In large skillet over medium-high heat, in oil, cook green pepper and onion until tender; add eggplant, tomato sauce, wine, garlic and bay leaf; simmer 15 minutes. Meanwhile, preheat broiler if manufacturer directs. In small saucepan over low heat, melt butter or margarine with lemon juice, ½ teaspoon salt and ¼ teaspoon pepper. Place fish in broiling pan and brush with butter mixture. Broil 5 minutes; turn and brush with butter mixture. Broil 5 minutes longer, or until fish flakes easily when tested with fork. Serve fish with sauce. Makes 6 servings.

**Diabetic diet:** Exchanges per serving = 1 "B" vegetable for ⅔ cup sauce, and 1 meat for each ounce of fish.
**Low-fat, low-cholesterol diet:** Prepare as directed but use margarine instead of butter. 10 grams fat per serving.

## FLOUNDER FOR A FEW (295 calories per serving)

4 carrots, cut into ½-inch slices
2 medium potatoes, cubed
2 medium onions, cut into thin
    rings
2 large celery stalks, cut into
    ½-inch slices
2 tablespoons finely chopped
    pimento
¼ medium green pepper,
    finely chopped
1 16-ounce package frozen
    flounder fillets
1 to 1½ teaspoons salt
¼ teaspoon poultry seasoning
3 tablespoons flour
1 8-ounce tube refrigerated
    biscuits (10 biscuits)

Day before: Place carrots, potatoes, onions, celery, pimento and green pepper in large saucepan. Cut frozen fillet into 1-inch cubes. Place cubes over vegetables in saucepan; add salt and 1 cup water; cover. Bring water to boiling, then simmer 15 to 20 minutes, or until vegetables are tender-crisp. Cool; refrigerate.

About 45 minutes before serving: Preheat oven to 425° F. Heat vegetables and fish to boiling. Thoroughly drain off broth; reserve; place drained stew in 2-quart casserole. Measure 1½ cups of broth, adding water if necessary. In medium saucepan, stirring constantly, slowly stir broth into poultry seasoning and flour. Cook, stirring constantly, until thickened and smooth. Pour sauce over stew. Top with biscuits. Bake 15 to 20 minutes, or until biscuits are a dark golden-brown. Makes 5 servings.

**Diabetic diet:** Prepare as directed but divide stew among 5 individual casserole dishes, and top with 2 biscuits each; bake as directed. Exchanges per serving = 2 meat, 1 "A" and 1 "B" vegetable and 2 bread.
**Low-fat diet:** 5 grams fat per serving. Omit recipe from low-cholesterol diet.

## CURRIED SWORDFISH AND RICE (265 calories per serving)

1 pound swordfish steak, cut
    into 4 pieces
1 teaspoon lemon juice
6 peppercorns
1 teaspoon salt
1 bay leaf
1 tablespoon salad oil
1 tablespoon minced onion
1 tablespoon cornstarch
1 teaspoon curry
2 cups cooked rice

About 30 minutes before serving: In medium skillet over high heat, heat 3 cups water to boiling; reduce heat to medium-low. Add swordfish, lemon juice, peppercorns, salt and bay leaf; simmer, covered, 10 to 15 minutes, or until fish flakes easily when tested with fork. With pancake turner, place fish on warm platter. Strain skillet liquid, reserving 1 cup. In same skillet over medium heat, in oil, cook onion until limp. In small bowl, stir reserved fish liquid into cornstarch; pour into skillet and cook until thickened, stirring frequently; blend in curry.

To serve: Pour sauce over fish and rice. Makes 4 servings.

**Diabetic diet:** Exchanges per serving = 3 meat and 1 bread.
**Egg-, gluten-, milk- and wheat-free diet:** Prepare as directed.
**Low-fat, low-cholesterol diet:** 10 grams fat per serving.

## PERCH À LA GRECQUE (250 calories per serving)

2 tablespoons salad oil
5 medium onions, sliced
5 large tomatoes
2 garlic cloves, minced
½ cup chopped parsley
2 16-ounce packages frozen
    ocean perch fillets, thawed
2 teaspoons salt
¼ teaspoon pepper
3 tablespoons lemon juice
2 lemons, sliced

About 1½ hours before serving: Preheat oven to 375° F. In large skillet over medium heat, in oil, sauté onions until tender; add 3 tomatoes (peeled and chopped), garlic and parsley; simmer 5 minutes. Sprinkle fillets with salt and pepper and lemon juice; arrange in medium baking dish; cover with onion mixture. Slice rest of tomatoes; arrange alternately with lemon slices on perch. Bake 45 minutes. Makes 6 servings.

**Diabetic diet:** Exchanges per serving = 4 meat, 1 "A" vegetable and 1 bread.
**Egg-, gluten-, milk- and wheat-free diet:** Prepare as directed.
**Low-fat, low-cholesterol diet:** 5 grams fat per serving.
**Low-sodium diet:** Prepare as directed but use only fresh (not frozen) perch; omit salt. 120 milligrams sodium per serving.

## FILLETS SUPREME (180 calories per serving)

1 tablespoon salad oil
1 large onion, sliced
½ cup white wine
½ teaspoon paprika
½ teaspoon salt
1 16-ounce package frozen
   flounder or sole fillets,
   thawed

About 30 minutes before serving: In medium skillet over medium heat, in oil, cook onion until limp. Add ½ cup water, wine, paprika and salt. Cover and simmer 20 minutes, stirring occasionally. Add fish; simmer 6 to 9 minutes, or until fish flakes with a fork. Serve sauce over fish. Makes 3 servings.

**Egg-, gluten-, milk- and wheat-free diet:** Prepare as directed.
**Low-fat, low-cholesterol diet:** 5 grams fat per serving.
**Low-sodium diet:** Prepare as directed but omit salt; use only fresh (not frozen) fish fillets. 120 milligrams sodium per serving.

## COD WITH SPANISH SAUCE (240 calories per serving)

1 tablespoon salad oil
1 large onion, sliced
1 16-ounce can tomatoes
⅛ teaspoon oregano leaves
salt
1 16-ounce package frozen cod
   fillets, thawed
pepper
1 tablespoon lemon juice
1 tablespoon butter or margarine

About 45 minutes before serving: In skillet, in oil, sauté onion until golden; stir in tomatoes, oregano and ½ teaspoon salt; simmer, uncovered, 30 minutes. Meanwhile, preheat oven to 350° F. Sprinkle cod with pepper, ½ teaspoon salt, and lemon juice; dot with butter or margarine. Bake 20 minutes, or until cod flakes easily when tested with a fork; top with sauce and bake 5 minutes more. Makes 3 servings.

**Diabetic diet:** Exchanges per serving = 3 meat and 1 "A" and 1 "B" vegetable.
**Egg-, gluten-, milk- and wheat-free diet:** Prepare as directed but use milk-free margarine on milk-free diet.
**Low-fat, low-cholesterol diet:** Prepare as directed but use margarine or salad oil instead of butter. 10 grams fat per serving.
**Low-sodium diet:** Prepare as directed but use low-sodium packed canned tomatoes; omit salt; use fresh (not frozen) fillets and unsalted butter or margarine. 100 milligrams sodium per serving.

## BAKED COD WITH GRAPEFRUIT (210 calories per serving)

2 16-ounce packages frozen cod
   fillets, thawed
1 large grapefruit
¾ teaspoon salt
⅛ teaspoon pepper
1 cup day-old bread crumbs
2 tablespoons butter or margarine, melted
¼ teaspoon thyme leaves

About 40 minutes before serving: Preheat oven to 350° F. Into small bowl, section grapefruit; let stand 5 minutes to collect juice. Brush cod fillets generously with juice from grapefruit; sprinkle with salt and pepper. Place in medium (about 12" by 8") baking pan.

In small bowl, combine bread crumbs, 1 tablespoon melted butter or margarine and thyme leaves; sprinkle over fish. Arrange grapefruit sections over bread crumbs; drizzle with remaining butter. Bake 25 to 30 minutes, or until fish flakes easily when tested with fork. Makes 6 servings.

**Diabetic diet:** Exchanges per serving = 4 meat and 1 bread.
**Low-fat, low-cholesterol diet:** Prepare as directed but use margarine instead of butter. 5 grams fat per serving.
**Low-sodium diet:** Prepare as directed but use fresh (not frozen) fillets; omit salt; use unsalted butter or margarine. 145 milligrams sodium per serving. If also prepared with unsalted bread, 105 milligrams sodium per serving.

## HALIBUT BAKED IN FOIL (285 calories per serving)

2 fresh halibut steaks, cut ¾-
    inch thick (about 1 pound)
salad oil
4 small potatoes, thinly sliced
2 medium onions, thinly sliced
2 carrots, thinly sliced
salt and pepper to taste
chopped parsley for garnish

About 50 minutes before serving: Preheat oven to 450° F. Remove skin from halibut steaks. Cut meat from bone and halve, lengthwise, to make 4 serving pieces.

For each serving: Pour 1 teaspoon salad oil in center of 18-inch square of heavy-duty foil. Top with one piece of fish, then one quarter of potatoes, onions and carrots, sprinkling each layer with salt and pepper to taste. Wrap, using double folds. Place on cookie sheet. Bake 25 minutes, or until fish flakes easily with fork. Sprinkle with parsley. Makes 4 servings.

**Bland diet:** Prepare as directed but omit onion, pepper and parsley.
**Diabetic diet:** Exchanges per serving = 3 meat, 1 "B" vegetable and 1 bread.
**Egg-, gluten-, milk- and wheat-free diet:** Prepare as directed.
**Low-fat, low-cholesterol diet:** 5 grams fat per serving.
**Low-fat, bland (gall bladder) diet:** Prepare as directed but omit onion, pepper and parsley.
**High-iron diet:** 3 milligrams iron per serving.
**Low-residue diet:** Prepare as directed but omit oinion, pepper and parsley.
**Low-sodium diet:** Prepare as directed but use only fresh (not frozen) halibut; omit salt. 80 milligrams sodium per serving.

## PERCH FILLETS WITH DIABLO SAUCE (175 calories per serving)

1 16-ounce package frozen
    perch fillets, thawed
1 teaspoon seasoned salt
¼ teaspoon seasoned pepper
1 slice white bread
butter or margarine
⅓ cup chili sauce
1½ teaspoons lemon juice
½ teaspoon Worcestershire

About 25 minutes before serving: Preheat oven to 350° F. Arrange fillets in greased ovenproof shallow dish; sprinkle with seasoned salt and pepper. Spread bread with butter, and cut into cubes; sprinkle over fish. Bake 15 minutes, or until fish flakes easily when tested with fork. Meanwhile, in cup, combine chili sauce, lemon juice and Worcestershire. Serve fillets with sauce. Makes 3 servings.

**Diabetic diet:** Exchanges per serving = 3 meat and 1 "B" vegetable.
**Low-fat, low-cholesterol diet:** Prepare as directed but use margarine instead of butter. 5 grams fat per serving.

## MAMBO FLOUNDER (215 calories per serving)

1 16-ounce package frozen
    flounder fillets, thawed (or
    3 small fresh fillets)
½ cup canned tomato sauce
2 tablespoons grated Parmesan
    cheese
1 16-ounce can small whole
    white potatoes, drained
¼ teaspoon oregano leaves
¼ teaspoon basil
chopped parsley

About 30 minutes before serving: Preheat oven to 425° F. In medium baking pan, arrange fillets in single layer. Pour tomato sauce over fish; sprinkle with cheese. Place potatoes around fish, and sprinkle seasonings and parsley over cheese and potatoes. Bake 20 minutes, or until fish flakes easily with fork. Makes 3 servings.

**Diabetic diet:** Exchanges per serving = 4 meat, 1 "A" and 1 "B" vegetable and 1 bread.
**Egg-, gluten- and wheat-free diet:** Prepare as directed.
**Low-fat, low-cholesterol diet:** Prepare as directed but omit cheese. 1 gram fat per serving.

## STUFFED FLOUNDER LORRAINE (170 calories per serving)

2 tablespoons salad oil
¼ cup chopped celery
2 tablespoons chopped parsley
2 tablespoons minced onion
1 cup (about ¼ pound) finely
   chopped fresh mushrooms
1 cup packaged stuffing mix
salt
6 small fresh flounder fillets
   (about 1½ pounds)
paprika and chopped parsley
   for garnish

About 40 minutes before serving: Preheat oven to 350° F. In medium skillet over medium heat, in oil, sauté celery, parsley, onion and mushrooms until golden. Turn off heat; add ⅓ cup water and stuffing mix; mix thoroughly. Lightly salt each fillet on both sides. Place one-sixth stuffing mixture toward thinner end of dark side of each fillet. Roll up; place each roll, not touching, open side down, in medium (about 9-inch square) baking dish. Pour ⅓ cup water over fish. Cover; bake 10 minutes; remove cover and bake 10 to 14 minutes more, or until fish flakes easily when tested with fork. Garnish with paprika and parsley. Makes 6 servings.

**Diabetic diet:** Exchanges per serving = 3 meat, 1 "A" vegetable and ½ bread.
**Low-fat, low-cholesterol diet:** 5 grams fat per serving.

## SOLE À LA PARISIENNE (260 calories per serving)

2 tablespoons finely minced
   onion
4 small fresh sole fillets
   (about 1½ pounds)
salt and pepper to taste
½ cup dry white wine
1 tablespoon butter or margarine
2 tablespoons flour
½ cup half-and-half
⅛ teaspoon nutmeg
½ teaspoon salt
dash pepper
½ cup grated Swiss cheese

About 30 minutes before serving: Preheat oven to 350° F. In range-top casserole, sprinkle onions, then top with fillets (in a single layer). Sprinkle with salt and pepper; add wine, and heat on top of range until liquid is just boiling. Then bake in oven for 10 minutes. Remove fish from oven; turn oven setting to "broil."

Drain all liquid from fish, reserving ½ cup. In medium saucepan, melt butter; stir in flour. Slowly stir in reserved cooking liquid, half-and-half, nutmeg, salt and pepper. Cook, stirring constantly, until thickened and smooth; stir in ⅓ cup grated cheese. Pour sauce over fish; top with remaining cheese. Run under broiler until brown. Makes 4 servings.

**Diabetic diet:** Prepare as directed, but after fish has been cooked, divide it among 4 individual broiler-proof casseroles; cover with sauce and broil as directed. Exchanges per serving = 4 meat and ½ milk.
**Egg-, gluten- and wheat-free diet:** Prepare as directed but substitute 1 tablespoon cornstarch for flour in gluten- and wheat-free diets.

## STUFFED BAKED SWORDFISH (270 calories per serving)

1 swordfish steak, cut 1-inch
   thick (about 1½ pounds)
1½ teaspoons salad oil
1 tiny onion, finely chopped
⅛ pound fresh mushrooms,
   finely chopped (about 4
   medium mushrooms)
½ large stalk green celery with
   leaves, chopped
½ teaspoon salt
⅛ teaspoon pepper
⅛ teaspoon poultry seasoning
1½ cups fresh bread cubes
salt and pepper to taste
paprika, chopped parsley and
   lemon slices for garnish

About 45 minutes before serving: Preheat oven to 375° F. Remove skin from swordfish steak. Cut pocket in swordfish just as you would for stuffed pork chops. In skillet over medium heat, in oil, sauté onion, mushrooms and celery until onion is golden. Stir in salt, pepper, poultry seasoning and bread cubes. Use mixture to stuff swordfish. Sprinkle on both sides with salt and pepper to taste.

Place fish in large (about 13" by 9" by 2") baking dish; cover with foil or lid. Bake 20 minutes, or until fish flakes easily with fork.

To serve: Cut steak into 4 equal servings; sprinkle with paprika and parsley; top with lemon slices. Makes 4 servings.

**Egg-, gluten-, milk- and wheat-free diet:** Prepare as directed but substitute 1 cup cooked rice for bread cubes for gluten- and wheat-free diet; use rice with milk-free margarine for milk-free diet.
**Low-fat, low-cholesterol diet:** 10 grams fat per serving.
**Low-sodium diet:** Prepare as directed but use only fresh instead of frozen swordfish; omit salt; substitute 1 cup unsalted cooked rice for bread cubes. 145 milligrams sodium per serving.

## SAUTÉED SOLE IN EGG SAUCE (Chi Tan Ch'ao Pan-Yu) (275 calories per serving)

1¼ pounds fresh sole fillets
3 eggs
1 teaspoon salt
2 tablespoons cornstarch
3 tablespoons salad oil
2 green onions (both tops and
    bulbs), thinly sliced crosswise
1 piece crystallized ginger,
    finely minced
1 tablespoon dry sherry

About 30 minutes before serving: Cut fillets, across the grain, into 2-inch-wide strips. In medium bowl, beat together eggs, salt and cornstarch. Add strips of sole and coat completely with egg mixture.

In large skillet, heat one tablespoon salad oil until sizzling. Drain excess egg mixture from sole. Taking care not to let pieces touch, add one-third of sole, one piece at a time, to skillet. Cook over high heat until fish just begins to turn white around sides and top—about 2 minutes; with spatula, turn each piece and cook one minute more. Remove pieces to warm platter.

Repeat until all fish is cooked. Stir sliced green onions, ginger, sherry and 2 tablespoons water into egg remaining in bowl. Remove skillet from heat; pour in egg-onion mixture; top with cooked sole. Cover; let stand about 2 minutes more, or until egg has set slightly. Serve immediately. Makes 4 servings.

**Diabetic diet:** Prepare as directed but substitute ¼ teaspoon ground ginger for crystallized ginger. Carefully divide into 4 equal servings. Exchanges per serving = 4 meat.
**Milk- and wheat-free diet:** Prepare as directed.
**Low-sodium diet:** Prepare as directed but use only fresh sole; omit salt. 165 milligrams sodium per serving.

## CURRIED STUFFED BASS (205 calories per serving)

1½ cups water
1 6-ounce package curried-rice
    mix
1 2-pound dressed striped bass
    or other dressed whole fish
juice of 1 lime or lemon
2 teaspoons salt
pepper to taste

About 50 minutes before serving: Preheat oven to 500°F. In medium saucepan, heat water to boiling; add rice mix; cover; simmer 10 minutes. Meanwhile, sprinkle fish inside and out with lime juice, salt and pepper. Place on cookie sheet, lined with large sheet of wide foil.

Use hot rice to fill cavity of fish. Wrap fish in foil, using double folds. Bake 10 minutes, then turn down heat to 425°F. and bake 25 minutes more, or until fish flakes easily with fork. Open foil carefully and pour off excess liquid. Makes 6 servings.

**Egg-, gluten-, milk- and wheat-free diet:** Prepare as directed but use rice mix not containing monosodium glutamate on gluten-free diet.
**Low-fat, low-cholesterol diet:** 5 grams fat per serving.

## FLOUNDER IN VELVET SAUCE (195 calories per serving)

2 16-ounce packages frozen
    flounder fillets, thawed
2 tablespoons butter or mar-
    garine
3 tablespoons flour
1½ cups skimmed milk or re-
    liquefied nonfat dry milk
¾ teaspoon salt
¼ teaspoon white pepper
2 tablespoons shredded Par-
    mesan cheese
paprika

About 45 minutes before serving: Preheat oven to 400°F. Place fillets in layers in medium (about 12" by 8" by 2") baking dish. In small saucepan, melt butter; blend in flour; gradually add milk, stirring constantly, until mixture thickens. Stir in salt, pepper and Parmesan; pour mixture evenly over fish. Sprinkle with paprika. Bake 30 minutes, or until fish flakes easily with fork. Makes 6 servings.

**Bland diet:** Prepare as directed but omit pepper.
**Diabetic diet:** Carefully divide into 6 equal servings. Exchanges per serving = 3 meat and ½ milk.
**Low-fat, bland (gall bladder) diet:** Prepare as directed, but omit pepper and cheese if forbidden on diet.
**Low-residue diet:** Prepare as directed but omit pepper.

## BAKED FISH WITH HORSERADISH SAUCE (180 calories per serving)

salt and pepper to taste
1 16-ounce package frozen fish
  fillets, partially thawed (cod,
  flounder, sole)
½ cup creamed cottage
  cheese*
½ tablespoon skimmed milk or
  reliquefied nonfat dry milk
2 tablespoons prepared horseradish
1 tablespoon lemon juice
1 tablespoon honey or granulated sugar
2 teaspoons chopped chives

About 30 minutes before serving: Preheat oven to 450°F. Salt and pepper each side of fish fillets; then place in lightly greased shallow baking dish. Tightly cover dish and bake for 15 to 20 minutes, or until fish flakes easily with fork.

Meanwhile, in electric-blender container, place cottage cheese, milk, horseradish, lemon juice and honey; at low speed, blend until smooth; stir in chives. (Or cottage cheese may be pressed through a fine sieve and mixed with other ingredients.) Serve sauce over hot fillets. Makes 3 servings.

**Diabetic diet:** Prepare as directed but omit honey or sugar; use saccharin equivalent to 1 tablespoon sugar. Top each serving fish with 3 tablespoons sauce. Exchanges per serving = 4 meat.
**Egg-, gluten- and wheat-free diet:** Prepare as directed.
**Low-fat, low-cholesterol diet:** 5 grams fat per serving.
* For smoothest sauce, use a brand of cottage cheese which has a soft curd.

## FLOUNDER TURBOTS (290 calories per serving)

1 tablespoon salad oil
¼ cup chopped onion
¼ cup chopped celery
2 cups packaged herb-seasoned
  bread-stuffing mix
1 16-ounce package frozen
  flounder fillets, thawed
salt and pepper to taste
chopped parsley for garnish
lemon wedges for garnish

About 40 minutes before serving: In skillet over medium heat, in oil, sauté onion and celery until onion is golden. Stir in ⅔ cup water, then stuffing mix until evenly moistened.

Meanwhile, preheat oven to 350°F. Lightly oil three 1-pint ovenproof casseroles. Lightly sprinkle fillets with salt and pepper; arrange along sides and part of bottom of casseroles. Divide stuffing mix among casseroles. Cover with foil; bake 20 minutes, or until fish flakes with fork.

To serve: Turn turbots out of casseroles onto serving plates; garnish with parsley and lemon wedges. Makes 3 servings.

**Diabetic diet:** Exchanges per serving = 4 meat, 1 "B" vegetable and 1 bread.
**Low-fat, low-cholesterol diet:** 5 grams fat per serving.

## FISH WITH FRESH MUSHROOMS (Ikan Masak Djamur) (160 calories per serving)

1 tablespoon salad oil
1 medium onion, thinly sliced
¾ pound fresh mushrooms,
  thinly sliced
1 pound fresh flounder fillets,
  cut crosswise into 1-inch
  slices
salt and pepper
1 tablespoon soy sauce
1 tablespoon dry sherry
1 large stalk green celery, cut
  into thin crosswise slices

About 25 minutes before serving: In large skillet over medium heat, in oil, sauté onion 1 minute. Add mushrooms and sauté, stirring constantly, 2 minutes, or until mushrooms are wilted. Spread a layer of fillet slices on mushrooms; sprinkle with salt and pepper. Top with remaining fillet slices; season them. Add soy sauce, sherry and celery; cover; simmer 10 minutes. Makes 4 servings.

**Diabetic diet:** Carefully divide into 4 equal servings. Exchanges per serving = 3 meat and 1 "A" and 1 "B" vegetable.
**Egg- and milk-free diet:** Prepare as directed.
**Low-fat, low-cholesterol diet:** 5 grams fat per serving.
**Low-sodium diet:** Prepare as directed but use only fresh flounder; omit salt and soy sauce. 115 milligrams sodium per serving.

## ZESTY SAUCED HADDOCK (200 calories per serving)

1 pound fresh haddock fillets
   (or 1 16-ounce package frozen haddock fillets, thawed,
   drained)
salt
½ cup sour cream
⅛ teaspoon dry mustard
⅛ teaspoon ginger
generous dash thyme leaves
paprika for garnish
chopped parsley for garnish

About 30 minutes before serving: Preheat oven to 400°F. Lightly grease medium (about 10″ by 6″ by 2″) baking dish. Divide haddock into 3 serving pieces; sprinkle on both sides with salt; place, in single layer, in baking dish.

In small bowl, mix sour cream, mustard, ginger and thyme; spread mixture on top of fillets. Bake 20 to 25 minutes, or until fish flakes easily with a fork. Serve sprinkled with paprika and parsley. Makes 3 servings.

**Bland diet:** Prepare as directed but omit mustard, ginger and parsley; use ground thyme.
**Diabetic diet:** Prepare as directed but divide into 4 equal servings. Exchanges per serving = 3 meat.
**Low-residue diet:** Prepare as directed for bland diet.
**Low-sodium diet:** Prepare as directed but use only fresh haddock; omit salt. 135 milligrams sodium per serving.

## CHERVIL BAKED SOLE (170 calories per serving)

2 16-ounce packages frozen
   fillets of sole, trimmed
1 teaspoon chervil
1 teaspoon salt
¼ teaspoon pepper
¼ teaspoon paprika
1 medium onion, sliced
½ cup skimmed milk or re-
   liquefied nonfat dry milk
¼ cup chicken broth
2 tablespoons butter or margarine

About 30 minutes before serving: Preheat oven to 400°F. In buttered large shallow baking dish, place fillets; sprinkle on both sides with combined chervil, salt, pepper and paprika. Separate onion into rings and place over fillets. Pour milk and broth over fish; dot with butter. Bake 20 to 25 minutes, or until fish flakes easily with fork. Makes 6 servings.

**Diabetic diet:** Carefully divide into 6 equal servings. Exchanges per serving = 3 meat.
**Egg-, gluten- and wheat-free diet:** Prepare as directed, but use homemade chicken broth for gluten- and wheat-free diets.
**Low-fat, low-cholesterol diet:** Prepare as directed but use salad oil or margarine instead of butter. 5 grams fat per serving.

## COD CASSEROLE (Cod à la Gomes de Sa) (225 calories per serving)

1½ cups water
salt
1 carrot, sliced
4 medium onions, thinly sliced
3 or 4 peppercorns
2 or 3 whole allspice
1 bay leaf
1 16-ounce package frozen cod
   fillets, thawed
2 tablespoons salad oil
1 garlic clove, sliced
4 medium potatoes, boiled,
   peeled, sliced ½-inch thick
½ teaspoon pepper
⅓ cup sliced ripe olives
½ cup dry white wine
3 hard-cooked eggs, shelled
½ cup chopped parsley

About 1 hour before serving: In large saucepan, combine water, 1 teaspoon salt, carrot, 1 sliced onion, peppercorns, allspice and bay leaf; bring to boiling. Add fish fillets and cook about 10 minutes. Drain; remove any bones; flake.

Preheat oven to 400°F. In large skillet over medium heat, in oil, sauté garlic until golden. Remove garlic; then, in same oil, sauté 3 sliced onions until tender. Add potatoes; sprinkle with 1 teaspoon salt, and pepper; add cod, olives and wine; heat about 5 minutes, stirring occasionally.

Arrange mixture in greased 2-quart casserole; bake 10 minutes. Chop 1 hard-cooked egg; cut rest into quarters. Before serving, garnish center of casserole with chopped egg, chopped parsley and egg quarters. Makes 6 servings.

**Diabetic diet:** Prepare as directed but divide mixture among 6 individual casseroles; bake and garnish as directed. Exchanges per serving = 2 meat, 1 "B" vegetable and 1 bread.
**Gluten-, milk-, and wheat-free diet:** Prepare as directed.

## HERB'S FAVORITE FLOUNDER (200 calories per serving)

1 tablespoon salad oil
1 onion, minced
1 16-ounce package frozen
    flounder fillets, thawed
1 teaspoon salt
¼ teaspoon basil
¼ teaspoon garlic powder
⅛ teaspoon pepper
2 medium fresh tomatoes,
    chopped

About 25 minutes before serving: In large skillet over medium heat, in oil, sauté onion until golden; lay fillets in skillet; cook, uncovered, 5 minutes. Add remaining ingredients; cover; cook, over low heat, 15 minutes, or until fish flakes easily with a fork. Makes 3 servings.

**Diabetic diet:** Exchanges per serving = 3 meat and 1 "A" and 1 "B" vegetable.
**Egg-, gluten-, milk- and wheat-free diet:** Prepare as directed.
**Low-fat, low-cholesterol diet:** 5 grams fat per serving.
**Low-sodium diet:** Prepare as directed but use fresh (not frozen) fillets; omit salt. 125 milligrams sodium per serving.

## BAKED FISH À LA GRAPEFRUIT (205 calories per serving)

1 4-pound cleaned striped bass
salt
butter or margarine
1 small onion, minced
4 slices bread, crumbled
¼ teaspoon pepper
½ teaspoon basil
2 tablespoons chopped parsley
1 grapefruit
parsley sprigs

About 1 hour before serving: Sprinkle bass, inside and out, with 1 teaspoon salt. Preheat oven to 400° F. In small skillet over medium heat, in 2 tablespoons butter or margarine, sauté onion until golden; stir in bread, ½ teaspoon salt, pepper, basil and chopped parsley. Use this bread mixture to loosely stuff fish, then fasten opening with toothpicks.

Line a large roasting pan with foil; place fish on pan. Pare and section grapefruit, squeezing any juice into a small bowl containing 2 tablespoons melted butter or margarine. Brushing fish often with this mixture, bake 45 minutes, or until fish flakes easily with a fork. Lay grapefruit sections over fish and bake 5 minutes more. Remove toothpicks; garnish with parsley sprigs.

To serve: Cut top side of fish into 4 servings, just down to backbone. Remove stuffing to serving plates, then discard backbone. Serve lower section of fish in same way. Makes 8 servings.

**Egg-, gluten-, milk- and wheat-free diet:** Prepare as directed but use milk-free margarine and bread on milk-free diet; use 1 cup cooked rice (in place of bread cubes) on gluten- and wheat-free diets.
**Low-fat, low-cholesterol diet:** Prepare as directed but use salad oil or margarine instead of butter. 10 grams fat per serving.

## SALMON FROID SMITHANE (240 calories per serving)

4 1-inch-thick fresh salmon
    steaks (about 1½ pounds)
½ cup diced celery
few parsley sprigs
1 medium onion, thinly sliced
6 peppercorns
2 bay leaves
½ teaspoon basil
salt
1 8-ounce container (1 cup)
    small-curd creamed cottage
    cheese
dash Tabasco
2 teaspoons white horseradish
watercress, lemon and lime
    wedges for garnish

Day before serving: In large skillet, place salmon steaks, celery, parsley, onion, peppercorns, bay leaves, basil and 1 teaspoon salt. Cover with boiling water; simmer, covered, 10 minutes, or until fish flakes easily when tested with fork. Remove from liquid; drain well. Arrange on platter; cover; refrigerate.

Just before serving: In electric-blender container, at low speed, blend cottage cheese, Tabasco, 1 teaspoon salt and horseradish until smooth. (Add a tablespoon or two of milk if needed to obtain a smooth consistency.) Spoon cottage-cheese mixture into opening between "legs" of salmon steaks. Garnish with watercress and lemon and lime wedges. Makes 4 servings.

**Diabetic diet:** Exchanges per serving = 4 meat and ½ skim milk.
**Low-fat, low-cholesterol diet:** 10 grams fat per serving.

## SPICY TUNA CHOWDER (260 calories per serving)

1 6½- or 7-ounce can tuna,
  drained and flaked
1 small onion, sliced
1 potato, cubed
1 carrot, diced
¼ cup diced celery
1 16-ounce can tomatoes
½ teaspoon salt
¼ teaspoon thyme leaves
⅛ teaspoon pepper
chopped parsley for garnish

About 1 hour before serving: In skillet, in 1 tablespoon oil drained from tuna, sauté onion until golden. Stir in potato, carrot, celery, tomatoes, ¾ cup water, salt, thyme and pepper; simmer, covered, 35 to 40 minutes, or until vegetables are tender. Add tuna and heat; sprinkle with parsley. Makes 2 servings.

**Diabetic diet:** Exchanges per serving = 3 meat, 1 "A" and 1 "B" vegetable and 1 bread.
**Egg-, gluten-, milk- and wheat-free diet:** Prepare as directed but use tuna not containing monosodium glutamate on gluten-free diet.
**Low-fat, low-cholesterol diet:** 5 grams fat per serving.
**Low-sodium diet:** Prepare as directed but use low-sodium packed canned tuna and tomatoes; omit salt. 70 milligrams sodium per serving.

## TUNA-CURRY SOUFFLÉ (260 calories per serving)

2 tablespoons butter or margarine
2 tablespoons minced onion
1 garlic clove, minced
1 teaspoon parsley flakes
¼ teaspoon ginger
¼ teaspoon salt
1 teaspoon curry
¼ cup flour
1 cup skimmed milk or reliquefied nonfat dry milk
1 6½- or 7-ounce can tuna, well drained, flaked
4 eggs, separated

About 1 hour and 20 minutes before serving: Preheat oven to 325°F. Grease 2-quart casserole. In medium skillet over medium heat, in butter, sauté onion, garlic and parsley flakes until onion is lightly browned; stir in ginger, salt and curry. Make a smooth paste with flour and a bit of milk; stir in remaining milk; add mixture to sautéed onions in skillet. Stirring constantly, cook until mixture thickens; remove from heat. Stir in tuna, then egg yolks, until sauce is smooth.

In large bowl, beat egg whites until stiff peaks form. Pour sauce mixture over egg whites; gently fold together until smooth; pour into casserole. Bake 50 to 60 minutes, or until surface is brown and rebounds when lightly touched. Serve immediately. Makes 4 servings.

**Bland diet:** Prepare as directed but omit onion, garlic, ginger and curry.
**Diabetic diet:** Exchanges per serving = 2 meat and ½ milk.
**Low-fat diet:** Prepare as directed but use water-packed tuna in place of regular. 10 grams fat per serving. Omit recipe from low-cholesterol diet.
**Low-residue diet:** Prepare as directed for bland diet.
**Low-sodium diet:** Prepare as directed but use unsalted butter or margarine; omit salt; use curry not containing salt; use low-sodium canned tuna. 130 milligrams sodium per serving.

## TUNA-VEGETABLE RAREBIT (300 calories per serving)

1 10-ounce package frozen mixed vegetables
1 10½-ounce can condensed cream-of-celery soup
¼ cup skimmed milk or reliquefied nonfat dry milk
2 6½- or 7-ounce cans tuna, drained
1 cup shredded Cheddar cheese
¼ teaspoon oregano leaves
¼ teaspoon dry mustard
dash Tabasco
dash pepper
3 English muffins, split and toasted

About 30 minutes before serving: Cook mixed vegetables as label directs; drain. In large skillet over low heat, stir together mixed vegetables and remaining ingredients except English muffins; heat. Serve over the toasted muffins. Makes 6 servings.

**Diabetic diet:** Exchanges per serving = 3 meat and 2 bread.
**Low-purine diet:** Prepare as directed but omit tuna. Makes 3 to 4 servings.

## TUNA SCRAMBLE SALAD (320 calories per serving)

1 tablespoon salad oil
1 medium onion, chopped
1⅓ cups packaged precooked
   rice
1 teaspoon seasoned salt
1 10-ounce package frozen
   chopped spinach
2 6½- or 7-ounce cans tuna,
   drained, flaked
⅛ teaspoon seasoned pepper
½ cup shredded process
   Cheddar cheese

About 25 minutes before serving: In skillet, in oil, sauté onion until golden. Stir in rice, 1½ cups water and seasoned salt. Bring rice to boiling. Cover; remove from heat; let stand 10 minutes. Meanwhile, cook spinach as label directs; drain. Add to rice with tuna and seasoned pepper; toss lightly. Top with cheese. Makes 5 servings of about 1 cup each.

**Diabetic diet:** Exchanges per serving = 3 meat, 1 "A" vegetable and 2 bread.
**Low-fat, low-cholesterol diet:** Prepare as directed but omit cheese. 10 grams fat per serving.

## TEMPTING TUNA TOSS (220 calories per serving)

2 hard-cooked eggs, shelled
2 6½- or 7-ounce cans tuna,
   drained and flaked
¼ teaspoon oregano leaves
scant ½ teaspoon onion salt
⅛ teaspoon garlic powder
½ cup low-calorie (imitation)
   mayonnaise
4 lettuce cups

About 20 minutes before serving: In medium bowl, finely chop eggs. Toss eggs with remaining ingredients except lettuce. Serve in lettuce cups. Makes 4 servings.

**Diabetic diet:** Exchanges per serving = 3 meat and 1 "A" vegetable.
**Low-fat, low-cholesterol diet:** 10 grams fat per serving.

## CREAMED TUNA ROCKEFELLER (280 calories per serving)

1 10-ounce package frozen
   chopped spinach, thawed
¼ cup cooked salad dressing
5 tablespoons flour
1 teaspoon salt
2 cups skimmed milk or reliquefied nonfat dry milk
¼ green pepper, minced
2 tablespoons minced onion
1 6½- or 7- ounce can tuna,
   thoroughly drained
½ cup grated Cheddar cheese

About 45 minutes before serving: Preheat oven to 350°F. Lightly grease 4 ovenproof 1-cup casserole dishes. Carefully press all liquid from thawed spinach, then divide it evenly among casseroles.

In medium saucepan, mix cooked salad dressing, flour and salt to form a smooth paste; slowly stir in milk until smooth; add green pepper and onion. Then, stirring constantly, heat until thickened and smooth. Divide sauce among casseroles. Break tuna into small pieces; divide among casseroles. Sprinkle cheese on tuna. Bake 20 minutes, or until cheese sauce bubbles. Makes 4 servings.

**Diabetic diet:** Exchanges per serving = 2 meat, 1 "A" vegetable and 1 skimmed milk.
**High-iron diet:** 3 milligrams iron per serving.

## TUNA-TOPPED APPLE SALAD (280 calories per serving)

1 6½- or 7-ounce can tuna,
   drained and flaked
⅓ cup low-calorie (imitation)
   mayonnaise
2 stalks celery, minced
1 large red apple
lemon juice
2 lettuce leaves
paprika for garnish

About 10 minutes before serving: In small bowl, combine tuna, low-calorie mayonnaise and celery. Core apple and slice crosswise into 4 slices. Sprinkle or brush with lemon juice. Place 2 apple slices on each lettuce leaf; top with mound of tuna salad; sprinkle with paprika. Makes 2 servings.

**Diabetic diet:** Exchanges per serving = 3 meat, 1 "A" vegetable and 1 fruit.
**Low-fat, low-cholesterol diet:** Prepare as directed but use water-packed tuna. 5 grams fat per serving.
**Low-sodium diet:** Prepare as directed but use low-sodium canned tuna, low-sodium mayonnaise (see recipe page 317); omit celery. 70 milligrams sodium per serving.

## GOLDEN GARDEN TUNA PIE (330 calories per serving)

4 medium carrots, cut into 1-
inch pieces
1 pound (about 3 medium)
potatoes, cut into large cubes
½ teaspoon salt
1 teaspoon celery salt
1 10-ounce package frozen
peas
3 tablespoons flour
⅓ cup nonfat dry-milk powder
1 cup skimmed milk or reliquefied nonfat dry milk
2 6½- or 7-ounce cans water-
or broth-packed tuna,
drained, flaked
1 8-ounce tube refrigerated
crescent rolls

About 30 minutes before serving: Preheat oven to 375°F. In medium saucepan, in 1 cup water, cook carrots, potatoes, salt and celery salt, covered, 5 minutes. Add frozen peas; cover; boil 10 minutes more.

Meanwhile, in 1½-quart casserole, mix flour and dry-milk powder. Slowly stir in skimmed milk to form a smooth paste. When vegetables are cooked, stir in flour-milk mixture; cook until thickened and smooth; stir in tuna. Return mixture to casserole. Cut crescent rolls (still rolled as they come from package) crosswise into ¼-inch slices; use to top tuna mixture. (Bake leftover slices on cookie sheet at the same time.) Bake 12 to 15 minutes, or until golden brown. Makes 6 servings of about 1 cup each.

**High-iron diet:** Prepare as directed but use crescent rolls made with enriched flour. 3 milligrams iron per serving.

## TUNA, SPANISH STYLE (265 calories per serving)

2 tablespoons salad oil
1 cup packaged precooked rice
1 medium onion, thinly sliced
⅓ cup chopped green pepper
1 teaspoon salt
dash cayenne
1 garlic clove, minced
1 20-ounce can tomatoes
½ cup tomato juice
2 4-ounce cans sliced mushrooms, undrained
1 6½- or 7-ounce can tuna,
drained

About 50 minutes before serving: In large skillet, in oil, brown rice, stirring constantly, until golden. Add 1 cup water, then all remaining ingredients but tuna. Cook, covered, over low heat, adding more water if necessary, 35 to 40 minutes. Break tuna into large pieces; place on top of rice mixture; heat, covered, 5 minutes. Makes 4 servings.

**Diabetic diet:** Exchanges per serving = 2 meat, 1 "A" vegetable and 1 bread.
**Low-fat, low-cholesterol diet:** 10 grams fat per serving.
**Low-sodium diet:** Prepare as directed but omit salt; use low-sodium canned tomatoes, tomato juice and tuna; substitute fresh mushrooms for canned. 35 milligrams sodium per serving.

## TUNA-POTATO PATTIES (260 calories per serving)

1 6½- or 7-ounce can tuna,
drained
1 tablespoon lemon juice
instant mashed potatoes for 4
servings
1 teaspoon parsley flakes
1 tablespoon instant minced
onion
1 egg, beaten
1 teaspoon salt
¼ teaspoon pepper
flour
2 tablespoons salad oil
1 8-ounce can tomato sauce
with cheese

About 20 minutes before serving: In medium bowl, flake tuna; sprinkle with lemon juice. Make up instant mashed potatoes as label directs but omit salt and butter and use skimmed milk; add to tuna with parsley flakes, minced onion, egg, salt and pepper; mix well. With floured hands, shape into 8 patties; coat each with flour. In medium skillet over medium heat, in oil, brown patties on both sides. Meanwhile, heat tomato sauce. Serve patties with tomato sauce. Makes 4 servings.

**Bland diet:** Prepare as directed but omit onion, pepper and tomato sauce with cheese.
**Diabetic diet:** Exchanges per serving = 2 meat, 1 "B" vegetable and 1 bread.
**Low-fat, low-cholesterol diet:** Prepare as directed but use only white of egg; use plain tomato sauce (not tomato sauce with cheese). 10 grams fat per serving.
**Low-fat, bland (gall bladder) diet:** Prepare as directed but use only white of egg; omit onion, pepper and tomato sauce with cheese.
**Low-residue diet:** Prepare as directed for bland diet.

## ZESTY TUNA BUNS (270 calories per serving)

⅔ cup evaporated skimmed
   milk
2 cups fresh bread cubes
2 6½- or 7-ounce cans tuna,
   drained, flaked
1 tablespoon catchup
1 tablespoon prepared mustard
1 tablespoon pickle relish
2 teaspoons lemon juice
½ teaspoon salt
½ teaspoon grated onion
⅛ teaspoon pepper
3 split hamburger buns
6 tender lettuce leaves
1 medium tomato, cut into 6
   slices

About 25 minutes before serving: Preheat broiler 10 minutes if manufacturer directs. In medium bowl, combine milk and bread cubes; with fork, beat until almost smooth. Then mix in tuna, catchup, mustard, pickle relish, lemon juice, salt, grated onion and pepper.

Separate split hamburger buns. Spread tuna mixture over bun halves; broil 5 inches from heat until light golden— about 8 minutes. Then transfer to warm platter and top each with a lettuce leaf and a tomato slice. Makes 6 servings.

**Diabetic diet:** Prepare as directed but omit pickle relish. Exchanges per serving = 1 meat, 1 bread and ½ skimmed milk.
**Low-fat, low-cholesterol diet:** 5 grams fat per serving.

## TOMATO-TUNA CHOWDER (250 calories per serving)

1 tablespoon salad oil
⅓ cup chopped onion
1 garlic clove, minced
1 stalk celery, chopped
2 tablespoons minced green
   pepper
2 medium potatoes, diced
1 teaspoon salt
2 6½- or 7-ounce cans tuna,
   drained, flaked
1 19-ounce can tomato juice
½ teaspoon poultry seasoning
dash cayenne

About 30 minutes before serving: In large saucepan, in oil, sauté onion, garlic, celery and green pepper until onion is golden. Add potatoes, 2 cups water and salt; cover; boil gently 20 minutes, or until potatoes are almost tender. Add remaining ingredients; cover; boil gently 10 minutes longer. Makes 4 servings of about 2 cups each.

**Diabetic diet:** Exchanges per serving = 3 meat, 1 "A" vegetable and 1 bread.
**Egg-, gluten-, milk- and wheat-free diet:** Prepare as directed but use tuna and tomato juice not containing monosodium glutamate on gluten-free diet.
**Low-fat, low-cholesterol diet:** Prepare as directed but use water-packed tuna. 10 grams fat per serving.
**Low-sodium diet:** Prepare as directed but omit salt; use low-sodium canned tuna and tomato juice. 75 milligrams sodium per serving.

## SWEET-AND-SOUR TUNA, ORIENTAL STYLE (295 calories per serving)

1 tablespoon salad oil
1 green pepper, cut into thin
   strips
1 large onion, thinly sliced
1 tablespoon cornstarch
1 13-ounce can pineapple
   chunks
2 tablespoons granulated sugar
2 tablespoons vinegar
2 6½- or 7-ounce cans tuna,
   drained, flaked
1 teaspoon salt
⅛ teaspoon pepper
3 cups cooked rice

About 30 minutes before serving: In large skillet over medium heat, in oil, sauté green pepper strips and onion until onion is just limp. Mix in cornstarch. Add syrup drained from pineapple, then cook, stirring constantly, until thickened and smooth. Add pineapple chunks, sugar, vinegar, tuna, salt and pepper. Cook 5 minutes, stirring regularly. Serve over rice. Makes 6 servings.

**Egg-, gluten-, milk- and wheat-free diet:** Prepare as directed but use tuna not containing monosodium glutamate on gluten-free diet.
**Low-fat, low-cholesterol diet:** 10 grams fat per serving.
**Low-sodium diet:** Prepare as directed but use low-sodium packed tuna; omit salt; serve over unsalted rice. 65 milligrams sodium per serving.

## BAKED TUNA-CHEESE CASSEROLE (300 calories per serving)

1 cup elbow macaroni
1 tablespoon butter or margarine
¼ cup finely chopped onions
¼ cup flour
½ teaspoon salt
⅛ teaspoon pepper
1 teaspoon dry mustard
2 cups skimmed milk or reliquefied nonfat dry milk
2 6½- or 7-ounce cans tuna, thoroughly drained
1 8-ounce can diced carrots, drained
½ cup grated sharp Cheddar cheese

About 45 minutes before serving: Cook macaroni as label directs, but use minimum recommended cooking time; drain. Preheat oven to 375°F. In medium saucepan over medium heat, in butter, sauté onion until golden. Stir in flour, salt, pepper and mustard. Stirring constantly, slowly stir in milk until mixture is smooth and has thickened slightly. Add drained macaroni, tuna and carrots; heat to simmering. Pour mixture into 1½-quart casserole; top with grated cheese. Bake 20 minutes, or until cheese browns slightly. Makes 6 servings of about 1 cup each.

**Diabetic diet:** Prepare as directed but divide mixture among 6 individual casseroles, top with cheese; bake 15 minues. Exchanges per serving = 2 meat, 1 bread and 1 skim milk.
**Low-fat, low-cholesterol diet:** Prepare as directed but use salad oil or margarine instead of butter; omit cheese. 10 grams fat per serving.

## TIP-TOP TUNA CASSEROLE (265 calories per serving)

1 tablespoon salad oil
½ cup chopped onion
1 cup chopped green pepper
2 tablespoons flour
1 29-ounce can tomatoes (about 3½ cups)
1 tablespoon Worcestershire
1 teaspoon dry mustard
½ teaspoon salt
½ teaspoon granulated sugar
¼ teaspoon pepper
2 6½- or 7-ounce cans chunk-style tuna, drained
1 8-ounce can refrigerated buttermilk biscuits

About 45 minutes before serving: Preheat oven to 375°F. In medium saucepan, in oil, sauté onion until limp; add green pepper and continue cooking until tender—about 5 minutes. Stir in flour. Add tomatoes, Worcestershire, mustard, salt, sugar and pepper; simmer, covered, 10 minutes. Add tuna and pour into 2½-quart casserole.

For topping: Cut each biscuit into sixths. Arrange pieces on casserole with points up. Bake 25 minutes. Cover lightly with foil if biscuits brown too soon. Makes 6 servings.

**Diabetic diet:** Prepare as directed but omit sugar; divide mixture among 6 individual casserole dishes, then top with biscuit pieces; bake as directed. Exchanges per serving = 2 meat and 1½ bread.
**Low-fat diet:** 10 grams fat per serving. Omit recipe from low-cholesterol diet.

## CLASSIC TUNA DINNER (335 calories per serving)

4 ounces spaghetti
1 6½- or 7-ounce can chunk-style tuna, drained
1 tablespoon parsley flakes
1 tablespoon lemon juice
2 tablespoons olive oil
salt and pepper to taste

About 15 minutes before serving: Cook spaghetti as label directs. Meanwhile, in small bowl, chop tuna finely; mix in parsley and lemon juice. In medium saucepan, heat oil and tuna mixture; simmer until bubbly and heated through. Toss spaghetti with tuna sauce. Season with salt and pepper if desired. Makes 3 servings.

**Bland diet:** Prepare as directed but omit pepper.
**Diabetic diet:** Carefully divide into 3 equal servings. Exchanges per serving = 2 meat, 2 bread and 1 fat.
**Egg-, gluten-, milk- and wheat-free diet:** Prepare as directed, but use bean threads or transparent noodles instead of spaghetti, and tuna not containing monosodium glutamate, for wheat- and gluten-free diets.
**Low-fat, low-cholesterol diet:** Prepare as directed but substitute salad oil for olive oil. 15 grams fat per serving.
**Low-residue diet:** Prepare as directed but omit pepper.

## PALOS VERDES STEW (270 calories per serving)

1 tablespoon salad oil
1 medium onion, minced
1 cup chopped celery
3 potatoes, quartered, then
    thinly sliced
1½ teaspoons oregano
    leaves
1½ teaspoons salt
1 19-ounce can tomato juice
1 6- or 7-ounce can water- or
    broth-packed tuna, drained,
    flaked

About 35 minutes before serving: In large skillet over medium heat, in oil, sauté onion and celery until onion is golden. Add potatoes, 1 cup water, oregano and salt; cover; simmer 10 minutes, or until potatoes are almost tender. Add tomato juice and tuna; simmer 10 minutes more, or until potatoes are done. Serve in soup bowls. Makes 4 servings.

Diabetic diet: Carefully divide into 4 equal servings. Exchanges per serving = 4 meat, 1 "B" vegetable and 1 bread.
Egg-, gluten-, milk- and wheat-free diet: Prepare as directed but use tomato juice and tuna not containing monosodium glutamate on gluten-free diets.
Low-fat, low-cholesterol diet: 5 grams fat per serving.
High-iron diet: 3.5 milligrams iron per serving.
Low-sodium diet: Prepare as directed but omit salt; use low-sodium canned tomato juice and tuna. 45 milligrams sodium per serving.

## TUNA BARBECUE (225 calories per serving)

1 teaspoon butter or margarine
1 garlic clove, minced
5 stuffed olives, chopped
1 teaspoon Worcestershire
⅓ cup catchup
½ teaspoon dry mustard
1 6½- or 7-ounce can tuna,
    drained and flaked
4 hamburger buns, split

About 30 minutes before serving: In medium saucepan, in butter, sauté garlic until soft; add ⅓ cup water, olives, Worcestershire, catchup, mustard and tuna. Simmer, uncovered, 15 minutes.

To serve: Use to fill buns. Makes 4 servings.

Low-fat, low-cholesterol diet: Prepare as directed but use margarine instead of butter; omit olives. 5 grams fat per serving.

## TUNA IN A SPINACH NEST (330 calories per serving)

2 10-ounce packages frozen leaf
    spinach
1 tablespoon butter or mar-
    garine
1 green pepper, slivered
1 10½-ounce can condensed
    mushroom soup
2 pimentos, cut into strips
2 6½- or 7-ounce cans tuna,
    drained and flaked
⅛ teaspoon pepper
1 cup soft day-old bread crumbs

About 20 minutes before serving: Cook spinach as label directs; drain. Meanwhile, in skillet, in butter, sauté green pepper until tender. Add mushroom soup, stirring until smooth; add pimentos, tuna and pepper; simmer 5 minutes. Add bread crumbs to spinach; toss well. Spoon onto serving dish in shape of ring; spoon tuna mixture into center. Makes 4 servings.

Diabetic diet: Prepare as directed but divide spinach and tuna mixture among 4 individual casserole dishes. Exchanges per serving = 3 meat, 1 "A" vegetable and 1 bread.
High-iron diet: 5 milligrams iron per serving.

## PIQUANT SALAD (250 calories per serving)

4 medium carrots, sliced
    diagonally
½ pound tiny white onions
1 cup white vinegar
¾ cup granulated sugar
1 tablespoon pickling spice
¾ teaspoon salt
2 medium tomatoes, sliced
2 6½- or 7-ounce cans tuna,
    drained and cut into chunks
1 8-ounce can ripe extra-large
    pitted olives, drained
6 hard-cooked eggs, halved

Day before serving: In medium saucepan, heat carrots and onions with water to cover; cover and boil 20 minutes or until tender-crisp. Meanwhile, in small saucepan, stir vinegar, 1 cup water, sugar, pickling spice and salt; heat to boiling; cool.

Arrange tomatoes, tuna, olives and eggs in large shallow dish. Add drained carrots and onions. Pour pickling liquid over all; cover dish and refrigerate. To serve: With slotted spoon, arrange salad on salad plate. Makes 6 servings.

Diabetic diet: Prepare as directed but omit sugar; add saccharin equivalent to ¼-cup sugar to pickling mixture. Carefully divide into 6 equal servings. Exchanges per serving = 3 meat and 1 "A" and 1 "B" vegetable.
Low-fat, low-cholesterol diet: Prepare as directed but omit olives and hard-cooked eggs. 5 grams fat per serving.
High-iron diet: 3 milligrams iron per serving.

## CRAB-ASPARAGUS CASSEROLE (260 calories per serving)

2 tablespoons butter or margarine
¼ cup flour
1¼ cups milk
seasoned salt
seasoned pepper
4 teaspoons grated Parmesan cheese
2 6-ounce packages frozen King crab, thawed, drained
2 15-ounce cans colossal white asparagus spears, drained
paprika

About 1 hour before serving: Preheat oven to 375°F. In small saucepan over low heat, melt butter; stir in flour until blended smooth. Slowly add milk, stirring constantly to avoid lumps. Then add 1 teaspoon seasoned salt, ½ teaspoon seasoned pepper, grated cheese. Cook sauce, stirring until smooth and thickened; set aside.

Line bottom of buttered 1½-quart casserole with crab; sprinkle lightly with seasoned salt and seasoned pepper, then add 6 tablespoons cheese sauce; mix lightly with fork. Arrange asparagus spears on top of crab mixture. Spoon remaining cheese sauce over asparagus, covering it entirely. Sprinkle with paprika. Bake 40 minutes, or until bubbly. Makes 4 servings.

**Bland diet:** Prepare as directed but omit pepper.
**Diabetic diet:** Prepare as directed but carefully divide into 4 equal servings. Exchanges per serving = 2 meat and 1 skim milk.
**Low-fat diet:** Prepare as directed but use skimmed milk in place of whole. 10 grams fat per serving. Omit recipe from low-cholesterol diet.
**High-iron diet:** 4.5 milligrams iron per serving.
**Low-residue diet:** Prepare as directed but omit pepper.

## TOMATO-CURRY LOBSTER TAILS (260 calories per serving)

6 large frozen rock-lobster tails (10 ounces each)
2 tablespoons butter or margarine
½ cup minced onion
1 garlic clove
½ cup chopped green pepper
1 16-ounce can tomatoes
2 teaspoons curry
1 teaspoon salt
1 bay leaf

About 1 hour before serving: Boil lobster tails as label directs. Cut away underside membrane and remove meat from shells; cut meat into bite-size pieces and reserve shells.

In large saucepan over medium heat, in butter, cook onion, garlic and green pepper until onion and green pepper are tender but not brown. Add tomatoes, curry, salt and bay leaf. Cover and cook over low heat 10 minutes, stirring occasionally.

Add lobster meat and cook until heated through, about 5 minutes.

To serve: Remove garlic and bay leaf. Fill reserved shells with lobster mixture. Makes 6 servings.

**Low-fat diet:** 10 grams fat per serving. Omit recipe from low-cholesterol diet.

## ALASKA CRAB NEWBURG SALAD (205 calories per serving)

1 6-ounce package frozen King crab, thawed and thoroughly drained
1 teaspoon lemon juice
¼ teaspoon salt
dash pepper
¼ pound fresh mushrooms, thinly sliced
¼ cup low-calorie (imitation) mayonnaise
1 tablespoon dry sherry
2 slices hot toast
paprika for garnish

About 1½ hours before serving: In medium bowl, toss crab with all remaining ingredients but toast and paprika; cover; refrigerate.

At serving time: Heap salad generously onto hot toast; sprinkle with paprika. Makes 2 servings.

**Diabetic diet:** Exchanges per serving = 3 meat and 1 bread.
**Low-fat diet:** 5 grams fat per serving. Omit recipe from low-cholesterol diet.

## SALMON PUFF (270 calories per serving)

1 16-ounce can salmon
2 tablespoons butter or margarine
3 tablespoons flour
1 teaspoon salt
½ teaspoon dry mustard
½ teaspoon Worcestershire
1 cup skimmed milk or reliquefied nonfat dry milk
4 eggs, separated

About 1 hour and 15 minutes before serving: Preheat oven to 375°F. Grease 1½-quart soufflé dish or casserole. In medium saucepan over medium heat, melt butter; stir in flour, salt, mustard and Worcestershire until blended. Slowly stir in milk and cook, stirring constantly, until thickened; cool about 10 minutes.

Beat in egg yolks, one at a time. In medium bowl, flake salmon and remove bone (do not drain); stir into egg mixture.

In large bowl, with electric mixer at high speed, beat egg whites until stiff peaks form; fold gently into mixture. Lightly pour into dish and bake 40 to 45 minutes, or until puffy and golden. Serve at once. Makes 6 servings.

**Diabetic diet:** Exchanges per serving = 2 meat and ½ milk.
**High-iron diet:** 3 milligrams iron per serving.

## NIPPY SHRIMP (155 calories per serving)

1 tablespoon salad oil
2 7-ounce packages frozen
   shelled deveined shrimp,
   thawed, drained
2 tablespoons soy sauce
2 tablespoons vinegar
2 tablespoons catchup
2 teaspoons granulated sugar
½ teaspoon ginger
½ teaspoon garlic salt
2 scallions, chopped

About 10 minutes before serving: In medium skillet over low heat, in oil, cook shrimp 4 minutes. Add remaining ingredients; simmer 5 minutes. Makes 4 servings.

**Low-fat diet:** 5 grams fat per serving. Omit recipe from low-cholesterol diet.

## SHRIMP BOUQUET PLATTER (285 calories per serving)

2 pounds large shrimp, shelled,
   deveined and cooked
salt
lemon juice
1 10-ounce package frozen
   peas, cooked
1½ pounds small shrimp,
   shelled, deveined and cooked,
   cut into chunks
10 hard-cooked eggs, cut into
   chunks
½ cup diced celery
3 medium potatoes, cooked,
   cut into chunks
¼ cup milk
1¼ cups low-calorie (imitation)
   mayonnaise
¼ teaspoon pepper
parsley sprigs for garnish
fluted, halved lemon slices
   for garnish

Day before serving: Toss large whole shrimp with 1 teaspoon salt and 1 tablespoon lemon juice; refrigerate. Separate ¼ cup of cooked peas; wrap; refrigerate. In large bowl, toss together cut-up shrimp, remaining peas, egg chunks, diced celery, potato chunks, milk, low-calorie mayonnaise, 2½ teaspoons salt, 1 tablespoon lemon juice, pepper.

Grease inside of 3-quart mixing bowl; line bottom with waxed paper; cover with single layer of whole shrimp. Line sides of bowl with one row of whole shrimp, then spoon in some potato-shrimp mixture and press level with shrimp. To sides of bowl add second row of shrimp, then spoon rest of salad into bowl and press firmly until level with shrimp circle. Refrigerate, covered. (Shrimp sizes vary, so some salad may be left over; refrigerate to serve next day.)

About 15 minutes before serving: Run spatula around inside of bowl to loosen salad; invert round platter on top of bowl; invert both; remove waxed paper. Garnish center of each shrimp with refrigerated pea; top salad with parsley sprigs; circle with fluted lemon slices. Makes 10 servings.

**High-iron diet:** 3.5 milligrams iron per serving.

## FRAGRANT SHRIMP RAREBIT (290 calories per serving)

1 tablespoon butter or margarine
½ teaspoon dried dill weed
½ teaspoon salt
dash cayenne
2 tablespoons flour
1½ cups skimmed milk or reliquefied nonfat dry milk
1 chicken-bouillon cube
1 pound fresh shrimp, shelled and deveined (or 2 7-ounce packages frozen shelled deveined shrimp, thawed and drained)
¾ cup grated mild Cheddar cheese
4 slices toast, cut into triangles

About 20 minutes before serving: In medium saucepan, melt butter; stir in dill weed, salt, cayenne and flour; cook, stirring constantly, 1 minute. Slowly stir in milk; cook until thickened and smooth. Add bouillon cube and shrimp; cook, stirring constantly, until shrimp curl and turn pink—about 5 minutes. Remove from heat; stir in cheese until melted. Divide cheese-shrimp mixture among 4 individual 1-cup casseroles; serve with toast triangles. Makes 4 servings.

**Bland diet:** Prepare as directed but omit dill, cayenne and bouillon cube.
**Diabetic diet:** Exchanges per serving = 3 meat, 1 bread and ½ skim milk.
**Low-residue diet:** Prepare as directed for bland diet.

## DIFFERENT SHRIMP CURRY (325 calories per serving)

½ cup flaked coconut
1½ cups uncooked long-grain rice
1 tablespoon salad oil
3 medium onions, thinly sliced
1 carrot, thinly sliced
1 garlic clove, minced
1 green pepper, coarsely chopped
1 red eating apple, thinly sliced
1 tablespoon curry
4 whole cloves
1 stick cinnamon
2 7-ounce packages frozen shelled deveined shrimp
2 tablespoons cornstarch

About 30 minutes before serving: In medium saucepan, heat coconut and 2 cups water; cover and simmer 10 minutes. Drain coconut, reserving liquid.

Cook rice as label directs but omit butter. In large skillet over medium heat, in oil, sauté onions, carrots and garlic until onion is limp. Add green pepper, apple slices, liquid drained from coconut, curry, 2 teaspoons salt, cloves and cinnamon stick; cover; simmer 3 minutes. Add frozen shrimp; cover; cook 5 to 10 minutes, or until shrimp have curled and are pink.

Meanwhile, stir enough water into cornstarch to form a smooth paste. Slowly stir into curry mixture; heat until smooth and thickened; remove cloves and cinnamon stick. Serve curry over rice. Top with flaked coconut. Makes 6 servings.

**Low-fat diet:** Prepare as directed but omit coconut. 5 grams fat per serving. Omit recipe from low-cholesterol diet.

## SHRIMP, SAILOR STYLE (245 calories per serving)

1 17-ounce can Italian tomatoes, undrained
2 tablespoons chopped parsley
2 cups sliced celery
¼ teaspoon basil
1½ teaspoons salt
⅛ teaspoon pepper
½ teaspoon oregano leaves
½ 6-ounce can tomato paste
1 cup uncooked long-grain rice
2 7-ounce packages frozen shelled deveined shrimp

About 45 to 50 minutes before serving: In large skillet or Dutch oven, simmer tomatoes, parsley, celery, basil, salt, pepper, oregano and tomato paste, uncovered, stirring occasionally, 30 minutes, or until celery is almost tender. Meanwhile, cook rice as label directs but omit butter. When tomato sauce is cooked, stir in frozen shrimp. Simmer 5 to 10 minutes, or until shrimp turn pink and curl. Serve over rice. Makes 5 servings.

**Egg-, gluten-, milk- and wheat-free diet:** Prepare as directed.
**Diabetic diet:** Prepare as directed but serve shrimp sauce over ½ cup rice. Exchanges per serving = 2 meat, 1 "B" vegetable and 1 bread.
**Low-fat diet:** 1 gram fat per serving. Omit recipe from low-cholesterol diet.

## CRAB THERMIDOR (275 calories per serving)

**4 slices white bread**
**1 tablespoon butter or margarine**
**1½ tablespoons flour**
**⅔ cup half-and-half**
**½ teaspoon salt**
**⅛ teaspoon nutmeg**
**dash paprika**
**generous dash pepper (preferably white pepper)**
**dash garlic salt**
**2 tablespoons dry sherry or water**
**2 6-ounce packages frozen King crab, thawed, thoroughly drained (or 2 6½- to 7½-ounce cans King crab, thoroughly drained)**
**⅓ cup grated mild process Cheddar cheese**

About 30 minutes before serving: Preheat oven to 350°F. Toast bread in oven until golden-brown on one side; turn; toast other side.

Meanwhile, in medium saucepan, melt butter; stir in flour. Stirring constantly, slowly add half-and-half. Cook, stirring, until thickened and smooth. Stir in salt, nutmeg, paprika, pepper, garlic salt and sherry. Add crab; heat, stirring, to simmering. Turn mixture into 1-quart ovenproof casserole; sprinkle with grated cheese. Run under broiler until cheese melts and is golden.

To serve: Cut each slice of toast into quarters. Use as a "nest" for the Crab Thermidor. Makes 4 servings.

**Bland diet:** Prepare as directed but omit nutmeg and pepper; use water (not sherry).
**Diabetic diet:** Exchanges per serving = 2 meat, 1 bread and ½ milk.
**Low-residue diet:** Prepare as directed for bland diet.

## TOMATO BAKED SHRIMP (175 calories per serving)

**1 10-ounce package frozen shelled deveined shrimp**
**½ cup canned condensed tomato soup**
**2 teaspoons parsley flakes**
**½ teaspoon oregano leaves**
**¼ teaspoon paprika**
**⅛ teaspoon garlic powder**
**1 4-ounce can mushrooms, drained**

About 25 minutes before serving: Cook shrimp as label directs; drain. Meanwhile, in medium saucepan, combine undiluted tomato soup and remaining ingredients. Heat to boiling, stirring occasionally. Add shrimp to sauce. Makes 2 servings.

**Diabetic diet:** Exchanges per serving = 4 meat and 1 "B" vegetable.
**Low-fat diet:** 2 grams fat per serving. Omit recipe from low-cholesterol diet.

## CRAB-CHEESE PILAF (295 calories per serving)

**2 tablespoons salad oil**
**1 cup chopped onion**
**1 cup sliced celery**
**¼ cup diced green pepper**
**¼ pound fresh mushrooms, sliced**
**½ cup thinly sliced carrots**
**1 teaspoon salt**
**1 bay leaf**
**1 tablespoon granulated sugar**
**2 16-ounce cans tomatoes**
**¾ cup packaged precooked rice**
**2 6½- to 7½-ounce cans King crab, thoroughly drained (or 2 6-ounce packages frozen King crab, thawed, thoroughly drained)**
**½ cup grated Cheddar cheese**

About 45 minutes before serving: Preheat oven to 350°F. In large ovenproof skillet over medium heat, in oil, sauté onion, celery, green pepper, mushrooms and carrots until onion is golden; add salt, bay leaf, sugar and tomatoes; simmer 5 minutes. Stir rice and crab into tomato mixture; sprinkle cheese on top. Bake 20 to 25 minutes. Serve in soup bowls, if desired. Makes 5 servings of about 1 cup each.

**Diabetic diet:** Prepare as directed but omit sugar. Exchanges per serving = 3 meat, 1 "A" and 1 "B" vegetable and 1 bread.
**Egg-, gluten-, milk- and wheat-free diet:** Prepare as directed but omit cheese on milk-free diet.

## SCALLOPS VINAIGRETTE (230 calories per serving)

1 pound potatoes, thinly sliced
1 pound fresh scallops (or frozen scallops, thawed)
1 cup thinly sliced green celery
2 tablespoons chopped pimento
2 tablespoons minced onion
2 tablespoons chopped parsley
¼ cup vinegar
2 tablespoons salad oil
1 teaspoon salt
⅛ teaspoon pepper
4 lettuce cups

At least 4 hours before serving: In medium saucepan, in salted boiling water to cover, simmer potatoes 10 minutes, or until almost tender.

Meanwhile, slice scallops, across the grain, into thin disks. Add scallops to potatoes; bring water back to boiling; cover; simmer 5 minutes, or until scallops are cooked. Carefully drain off liquid and reserve (it's an excellent base for soups); let potatoes and scallops cool slightly, then cover and refrigerate.

Meanwhile, in large bowl, toss together celery, pimento, onion, parsley, vinegar, oil, salt and pepper. Cover; refrigerate.

To serve: Toss scallops and potatoes with vinaigrette dressing. Arrange on lettuce cups. Makes 4 servings.

**Diabetic diet:** Carefully divide into 4 equal servings. Exchanges per serving = 2 meat, 1 "A" vegetable and 1 bread.
**Egg-, gluten-, milk- and wheat-free diet:** Prepare as directed.
**Low-fat diet:** 5 grams fat per serving. Omit recipe from low-cholesterol diet.

## PAELLA PRONTO (325 calories per serving)

2 6-ounce packages curried-rice mix
8 scrubbed cherrystone clams in shells
3 frozen rock-lobster tails, partially thawed, cut into 1-inch pieces (about 6 ounces)
1 green pepper, cut into eighths
1 15-ounce can asparagus or hearts of artichoke, drained
4 canned pimentos, quartered

About 30 minutes before serving: In very large skillet or Dutch oven, prepare rice mix as label directs, but reduce total amount of water by 1 cup; omit butter. To rice as it cooks, add clams, lobster tails and green pepper. When seafood is done, add asparagus and pimentos. Makes 4 servings.

**Egg-, gluten-, milk- and wheat-free diet:** Prepare as directed. For gluten-free diet, select rice mix which does not contain monosodium glutamate.
**Low-fat diet:** 2 grams fat per serving. Omit recipe from low-cholesterol diet.
**High-iron diet:** 5 milligrams iron per serving.

## BOUILLABAISSE, AMERICAN STYLE (210 calories per serving)

1 tablespoon salad oil
1 cup chopped onions
½ cup chopped celery
2 16-ounce cans tomatoes
1 garlic clove, minced
1 tablespoon chopped parsley
1½ teaspoons seasoned salt
¼ teaspoon thyme leaves
1 teaspoon monosodium glutamate
2½ pounds striped or sea bass fillets, cut into large pieces (or 2½ pounds halibut steak cut into chunks)
1½ dozen clams (little necks) in shell
1 tablespoon cornstarch
1 pound fresh or frozen shrimp, shelled and deveined

About 1 hour before serving: In Dutch oven, in oil, sauté onion with celery until tender—about 5 minutes. Stir in tomatoes, garlic, parsley, seasoned salt, thyme and monosodium glutamate. Simmer, covered, 10 minutes. Add bass and cook 10 minutes, or until fish flakes with fork.

Meanwhile, scrub clams under running water; place them in small kettle with ½ inch boiling water. Cover and steam until shells just open—about 5 minutes. Strain hot broth through cheesecloth; reserve 1 cup. Keep clams warm.

Blend cornstarch with clam juice; stir into tomato mixture; heat to boiling. Add shrimp and simmer about 5 minutes, or until shrimp have turned pink and are tender. Add reserved clams. Makes 10 servings.

**Egg-, gluten-, milk- and wheat-free diet:** Prepare as directed but substitute regular salt for seasoned salt; omit monosodium glutamate on gluten-free diet.
**Low-fat diet:** 5 grams fat per serving. Omit recipe from low-cholesterol diet.
**High-iron diet:** 3.5 milligrams iron per serving.

## SEAFOOD BOATS  (220 calories per serving)

2 teaspoons salt
8 peppercorns
2 whole allspice
1 bay leaf
4 chicken-bouillon cubes
2 summer squash
2 zucchini
¼ cup low-calorie (imitation) mayonnaise
2 teaspoons granulated sugar
½ teaspoon prepared mustard
¼ cup lemon juice
1 cup cooked, shelled, deveined shrimp
1 6-ounce package frozen King crab, thawed, drained
¼ cup drained cooked peas
½ cup canned hearts of palm, sliced
¼ pound fresh mushrooms, quartered
1 hard-cooked egg, chopped
curly endive
cherry tomatoes
1 lemon, cut into wedges for garnish

Early in day: In large kettle, heat 2 quarts water, salt, peppercorns, allspice, bay leaf and bouillon cubes to boiling; simmer 10 minutes.

Cut thin lengthwise slice from each squash and zucchini; scoop out some of pulp. Cook vegetables in seasoned water 10 to 15 minutes, or until tender-crisp; drain well; refrigerate.

Up to 1 hour before serving: In small bowl, combine low-calorie mayonnaise, sugar, mustard and lemon juice. Halve all but 4 shrimp. In medium bowl, toss halved shrimp, crab, peas, hearts of palm, mushrooms and egg with mayonnaise mixture. Fill each zucchini and squash with crab mixture; garnish with whole shrimp; arrange on platter with endive, tomatoes and lemon wedges for garnish. Makes 4 servings.

**Diabetic diet:** Prepare as directed but omit sugar. Exchanges per serving = 3 meat, 1 "A" vegetable and 1 bread.
**Low-fat diet:** 5 grams fat per serving. Omit recipe from low-cholesterol diet.
**High-iron diet:** 5 milligrams iron per serving.

## CRAB BISQUE  (195 calories per serving)

1 10¾-ounce can condensed tomato soup
1 11¼-ounce can condensed pea soup
2 cups skimmed milk or re-liquefied nonfat dry milk
1 teaspoon curry
1 teaspoon salt
¼ teaspoon pepper
2 6½- to 7½-ounce cans King crab, drained

About 15 minutes before serving: In large saucepan, mix together all ingredients but crab; simmer 5 minutes. Then add crab and simmer, over medium heat, about 10 minutes. Makes six 1-cup main-dish servings.

**Diabetic diet:** Exchanges per serving = 2 meat, ½ skim milk and 1 bread.
**Low-fat diet:** 3 grams fat per serving. Omit recipe from low-cholesterol diet.

## COUNTRY SCALLOPS  (290 calories per serving)

4 bacon slices, cut into small pieces
2 tablespoons diced onion
⅓ cup catchup
2 teaspoons Worcestershire
¼ teaspoon salt
⅛ teaspoon pepper
1 16-ounce package frozen scallops, thawed, drained

About 20 minutes before serving: In medium skillet over medium heat, fry bacon pieces until limp. Drain off fat; add onion; continue cooking 5 minutes longer, or until bacon is lightly browned. Stir in catchup, Worcestershire, salt and pepper. Add scallops and cook until tender—about 5 to 8 minutes—stirring occasionally. Makes 3 servings.

**High-iron diet:** 4 milligrams iron per serving.

## OYSTER STEW (200 calories per serving)

1 10-ounce can frozen condensed oyster stew
1 soup-can skimmed milk or reliquefied nonfat dry milk
2 thin lemon or fresh tomato slices for garnish
chopped parsley or dried parsley flakes for garnish

About 20 minutes before serving: Prepare stew as label directs, but substitute skimmed milk for water.

To serve: Divide stew between 2 soup bowls; top each with lemon or tomato slice and sprinkling of parsley. Makes two 1¼-cup servings.

**Bland diet:** Prepare as directed but omit garnish.
**Diabetic diet:** Exchanges per serving = 1 meat, 1 bread and ½ milk.
**Low-fat diet:** 10 grams fat per serving. Omit recipe from low-cholesterol diet.
**Low-fat, bland (gall bladder) diet:** Prepare as directed but omit garnish. If oysters cause "gas" omit recipe.
**Low-residue diet:** Prepare as directed but omit garnish.

## OYSTERS DIABLE (190 calories per serving)

16 large shucked raw oysters (or 2 7½-ounce cans oysters)
skimmed milk or reliquefied nonfat dry milk
2½ tablespoons flour
¾ teaspoon salt
⅛ teaspoon pepper
¼ teaspoon paprika
¼ teaspoon prepared or dry mustard
2 tablespoons horseradish
1 teaspoon Worcestershire
2 teaspoons lemon juice
2 cups toasted ½-inch bread squares
¾ cup chopped celery
celery leaves

About 45 minutes before serving: Preheat oven to 400°F. Drain oysters; add enough milk to liquid to make 2 cups. In saucepan, mix flour, salt, pepper, paprika and mustard. Gradually add liquid, stirring until smooth. Stir in horseradish, Worcestershire and lemon juice. Cook, stirring, over low heat, until thickened. In each of four 12-ounce casseroles, arrange layer of bread squares; cover with layers of celery, drained oysters and sauce. Top with remaining bread squares. Bake 20 to 25 minutes, or until bubbling. Garnish with celery leaves. Makes 4 servings.

**Diabetic diet:** Exchanges per serving = 1 meat, 1 "B" vegetable and 1 bread.
**Low-fat diet:** 3 grams fat per serving. Omit recipe from low-cholesterol diet.
**High-iron diet:** 7 milligrams iron per serving.

## SCALLOPS EN BROCHETTE (265 calories per serving)

12 small mushrooms
½ large green pepper
2 tablespoons melted butter or margarine
2 tablespoons lemon juice
¼ teaspoon salt
dash pepper
1 pound sea scallops (about 12)
4 slices bacon
2 slices process Cheddar cheese

About 1 hour and 15 minutes before serving: Remove stems from mushrooms. (Refrigerate stems for use in soup another day.) Cut green pepper into 8 pieces about 1-inch square. In pie plate, combine butter, lemon juice, salt and pepper. Add scallops, mushrooms and green pepper pieces; cover; refrigerate 30 minutes, tossing occasionally.

Preheat broiler if manufacturer directs. In medium skillet over medium-high heat, fry bacon until light-golden but still limp; drain on paper towels.

Run a skewer through one end of a bacon slice, then lace bacon through a fourth of the scallops, mushrooms and green-pepper pieces, alternating foods. Repeat with 3 more skewers. Place skewers on broiling pan and broil 10 minutes, turning frequently.

Cut cheese slices into fourths. When skewered food is done, place cheese strips on top of skewers. Broil just until cheese melts. Makes 4 servings.

**Diabetic diet:** Exchanges per serving = 3 meat and 1 "A" vegetable.
**Egg-, gluten- and wheat-free diet:** Prepare as directed.

## CAPRICIOUS CRAB CASSEROLE (240 calories per serving)

1 6-ounce package seasoned white-and-wild-rice mix
2 tablespoons salad oil
1 large onion, finely chopped
1 large stalk green celery with leaves, chopped
1 eating apple, chopped
1 to 2 teaspoons curry
½ teaspoon monosodium glutamate
3 6-ounce packages frozen King crab, thawed, thoroughly drained (or 3 6½- to 7½-ounce cans King crab, thoroughly drained)
2 tablespoons raisins

About 1 hour before serving: Cook rice mix as label directs but omit butter and decrease cooking time to 20 minutes. (Rice will be moist.) Preheat oven to 375°F. In large skillet over medium heat, in oil, sauté onion and celery until onion is golden. Stir in apple, curry, monosodium glutamate, drained crab, raisins and cooked rice. Turn into 2-quart casserole; cover; bake 20 minutes. Makes 6 one-cup servings.

**Diabetic diet:** Prepare as directed but divide mixture among 6 individual casseroles; bake only 15 minutes. Exchanges per serving = 2 meat, 1 bread and 1 fruit.
**Low-fat diet:** 5 grams fat per serving. Omit recipe from low-cholesterol diet.
**Egg-, gluten-, milk- and wheat-free diet:** Prepare as directed but omit monosodium glutamate and use rice mix not containing MSG on gluten-free diet.

## CRAB-MUSHROOM OMELET MINIATURES (200 calories per serving)

3 eggs
2 tablespoons flour
1 6-ounce package frozen King crab, thoroughly drained (or 1 6½- to 7½-ounce can King crab, drained)
1 cup cooked frozen peas (or 1 8-ounce can peas, thoroughly drained)
1 cup finely chopped fresh mushrooms
1 tablespoon minced onion
½ teaspoon salt
generous dash curry
2 tablespoons salad oil

About 20 minutes before serving: In medium bowl, beat eggs and flour until smooth. Mix in crab, peas, mushrooms, onion, salt and curry. In medium skillet over medium heat, in oil, drop egg mixture by heaping tablespoonfuls. Cook about 2 minutes, or until egg is lightly browned; turn, cook other side. Makes 4 servings.

**Bland diet:** Prepare as directed but omit onion and curry.
**Diabetic diet:** Exchanges per serving = 2 meat and 1 "B" vegetable.
**Low-residue diet:** Prepare as directed for bland diet.

## LOBSTER, ITALIAN STYLE (195 calories per serving)

salt
6 8-ounce frozen rock-lobster tails
2 tablespoons olive oil
2 tablespoons minced onion
½ garlic clove, minced
1 16-ounce can whole tomatoes
1 teaspoon lemon juice
¼ teaspoon oregano leaves
⅛ teaspoon pepper
parsley and lemon wedges for garnish

About 1 hour before serving: In 10-quart pot, heat 4 or 5 quarts water and 1 tablespoon salt to boiling. Add frozen lobster tails. When water reboils, lower heat and simmer 10 minutes. Drain lobster; then drench with cold water; drain again. With kitchen shears, cut away underside membrane. Grasp tail meat and gently pull it from shell in one piece, reserving whole shells. Dice meat.

In large skillet, in hot oil, sauté onion and garlic. Drain tomatoes and cut into pieces. Add tomatoes, ½ cup tomato liquid (use leftover tomato juice as beverage another day), lemon juice, 1 teaspoon salt, oregano and pepper; simmer 5 minutes. Add diced lobster, heating only until mixture is hot and bubbling. Fill reserved shells with mixture; garnish with parsley and lemon wedges. Makes 6 servings.

**Diabetic diet:** Exchanges per serving = 4 meat and 1 "A" vegetable.
**Egg-, gluten-, milk- and wheat-free diet:** Prepare as directed.
**High-iron diet:** 3 milligrams iron per serving.

## WHALER'S INN SHRIMP CHOWDER (250 calories per serving)

1 tablespoon butter or margarine
½ cup finely chopped onion
2 medium potatoes, cut into ½-inch cubes
salt
½ 10-ounce package frozen peas
2 7-ounce packages frozen shelled deveined shrimp, thawed
1 tablespoon flour
2 cups skimmed milk or reliquefied nonfat dry milk, scalded
pepper
thin tomato slices for garnish

About 45 minutes before serving: In large saucepan in butter, sauté onion until golden. Add potatoes, 2 tablespoons salt and 2 cups water; bring to boiling; cover; cook 15 to 20 minutes, or until potatoes are tender. Add peas and shrimp, stirring occasionally; boil gently 5 minutes, or until shrimp are pink and cooked. Meanwhile, stir just enough water into flour to make a smooth paste. Stir into potato mixture. Stir in scalded milk, then salt and pepper to taste. Makes 4 servings of about 1½ cups each.

**Bland diet:** Prepare as directed but omit onion, pepper and tomato slices.
**Diabetic diet:** Exchanges per serving = 2 meat, 1 bread and 1 milk.
**Low-fat diet:** 5 grams fat per serving. Omit recipe from low-cholesterol diet.
**Low-fat, bland (gall bladder) diet:** Prepare as directed but omit onion, pepper and tomato slices.
**Low-residue diet:** Prepare as directed for bland diet.

## CALIFORNIA SCALLOPS (165 calories per serving)

1 pound scallops
1 tablespoon salad oil
1 garlic clove, minced
2 medium tomatoes, halved
pepper
salt
1½ tablespoons lemon juice
1 tablespoon melted butter or margarine
lemon twists for garnish
chopped parsley for garnish

About 50 minutes before serving: Let scallops stand in oil and garlic about 30 minutes. Preheat broiler 10 minutes if manufacturer directs. Meanwhile, sprinkle tomato halves with pepper and ½ teaspoon salt. In shallow roasting pan, arrange with scallops. Over scallops pour butter, ½ teaspoon salt and ⅛ teaspoon pepper. Broil about 10 minutes, turning once. Serve garnished with lemon twists and parsley. Makes 4 servings.

**Diabetic diet:** Exchanges per serving = 3 meat and 1 "A" vegetable.
**Egg-, gluten-, milk- and wheat-free diet:** Prepare as directed but use milk-free margarine on milk-free diet.
**Low-fat diet:** Prepare as directed but use margarine instead of butter. 5 grams fat per serving. Omit recipe from low-cholesterol diet.

## SHRIMP-AND-FLOUNDER MAYONNAISE (Mayonnaise de Camarão e Linguado)
(225 calories per serving)

⅔ cup lemon juice
6 tablespoons chopped parsley
1 tablespoon granulated sugar
1 teaspoon salt
6 whole peppercorns
2 bay leaves
2 16-ounce packages frozen flounder fillets, thawed
¼ teaspoon seasoned salt
1 7-ounce package frozen shelled deveined shrimp, cooked
3 hard-cooked eggs
low-calorie (imitation) mayonnaise
rolled anchovy fillets
romaine leaves

At least 6 hours before serving: In large skillet, bring ⅓ cup lemon juice, ¼ cup parsley, sugar, salt, peppercorns and bay leaves to boiling. Lay fillets in mixture in skillet; cover; simmer 5 minutes. Refrigerate in skillet. Combine ⅓ cup lemon juice, 2 tablespoons parsley, seasoned salt and cooked shrimp. Refrigerate.

About 30 minutes before serving: Halve hard-cooked eggs lengthwise; top each with ¼ teaspoon low-calorie mayonnaise, then a rolled anchovy. Cut up half refrigerated shrimp and toss with 1 cup finely sliced romaine and ¼ cup low-calorie mayonnaise. Arrange fish in 6 romaine cups. Top with shrimp mixture and a dollop of low-calorie mayonnaise. Garnish with remaining shrimp and egg halves. Makes 6 servings.

## CURRIED SHRIMP WITH HONEYDEW (210 calories per serving)

2 teaspoons salt
2 peppercorns
1 16-ounce package frozen
  shelled deveined shrimp
½ cup low-calorie (imitation)
  mayonnaise
¼ cup sour cream
1 teaspoon curry
1 ripe medium honeydew melon
8 lettuce leaves

About 45 minutes before serving: In medium saucepan, bring 2 cups cold water to boiling; add salt, peppercorns and shrimp; cook until shrimp are pink and tender; drain; let cool slightly; then split each lengthwise. In medium bowl, combine low-calorie mayonnaise, sour cream and curry. Add shrimp; toss well; set aside.

Quarter honeydew melon lengthwise; remove seeds and pare each wedge; then cut across each wedge a few times, almost through melon. Arrange lettuce on serving plates; top each with melon wedge and fill with one-fourth of shrimp mixture. Makes 4 servings.

**Diabetic diet:** Exchanges per serving = 3 meat and 1 fruit.
**High-iron diet:** 3 milligrams iron per serving.

## LUNCHEON SCALLOP CHOWDER (195 calories per serving)

1 teaspoon lemon juice
1 teaspoon salt
generous dash pepper
¼ teaspoon celery salt
¼ teaspoon onion salt
1 pound fresh scallops (or frozen scallops, thawed)
2 tablespoons butter or margarine
3 tablespoons flour
2 cups milk
2 cups skimmed milk or reliquefied nonfat dry milk
salt and pepper to taste
chopped parsley

About 20 minutes before serving: In medium saucepan, heat 1 cup water, lemon juice, salt, pepper, celery salt and onion salt to boiling. Add scallops (halve large ones); cover; gently boil 3 to 5 minutes, or until scallops are just cooked. Remove from heat.

Meanwhile, in large saucepan, melt butter; stir in flour. Slowly add milk and cook, stirring constantly, until mixture thickens. Add cooked scallops and cooking broth; season to taste with salt and pepper. Serve sprinkled with parsley. Makes 6 luncheon main-course servings of 1 cup each.

**Bland diet:** Prepare as directed but omit pepper, celery salt, onion salt and parsley.
**Diabetic diet:** Exchanges per serving = 1 meat and 1 milk.
**Low-fat diet:** Prepare as directed but use all skimmed milk. 5 grams fat per serving. Omit recipe from low-cholesterol diet.
**Low-fat, bland (gall bladder) diet:** Prepare as directed for bland diet.
**Low-residue diet:** Prepare as directed for bland diet.

## SHRIMP AND TUNA GOURMET (230 calories per serving)

1 tablespoon butter or margarine
1 4-ounce can mushrooms,
  drained
⅓ cup chopped green onions
1 10½-ounce can condensed
  cream-of-chicken soup
1 teaspoon Worcestershire
¼ teaspoon salt
4 drops Tabasco
¼ cup diced canned pimentos
½ cup pitted ripe olives
1 cup cooked, deveined, shelled
  shrimp
1 6½- or 7-ounce can chunk-
  style tuna, drained
½ cup skimmed milk or reliquefied nonfat dry milk

About 30 minutes before serving: In medium skillet over medium heat, in butter, cook mushrooms and green onions, stirring occasionally, 5 minutes. Stir in undiluted soup, Worcestershire, salt and Tabasco and continue cooking, stirring occasionally, until mixture is hot and bubbly. Reduce heat to low and stir in remaining ingredients, stirring until mixture is hot. Makes 4 servings.

## MARLISE'S CREAMY RING WITH CRABMEAT (220 calories per serving)

1 3-ounce package lime gelatin
1 cup low-calorie (imitation) mayonnaise
1 8-ounce container small curd creamed cottage cheese
1 teaspoon white horseradish
¾ cup finely chopped peeled cucumber
¼ cup chopped red onion
2 7½-ounce cans King crab, well drained and flaked (or 2 6-ounce packages frozen King crab, thawed and well-drained)
½ cup low-calorie Italian dressing
½ head lettuce, shredded
parsley for garnish

Early in day: In medium bowl, dissolve lime gelatin in ¾ cup boiling water; refrigerate at least 30 minutes, stirring occasionally, or until gelatin is consistency of unbeaten egg whites. In large bowl, mix low-calorie mayonnaise, cottage cheese and horseradish until well blended. Stir in cucumber, onion and gelatin. Pour into 6-cup ring mold. Refrigerate until firm.

About 10 minutes before serving: Marinate crab in low-calorie Italian dressing about 10 minutes. Unmold gelatin onto shredded lettuce. Stir crab to mix in dressing; place in center of ring and garnish with parsley. Makes 6 servings.

**Diabetic diet:** Prepare as directed but substitute 1 4-serving envelope dietetic-pack lemon gelatin for regular. Exchanges per serving = 2 meat, 1 "A" vegetable and ½ skim milk.
**Low-fat, low-cholesterol diet:** Prepare as directed but substitute 2 6½- or 7-ounce cans tuna (well drained and in chunks) for crab. 10 grams fat per serving.

## SCALLOPS IN THE GARDEN (265 calories per serving)

2 9-ounce packages frozen cut green beans
1 cup uncooked long-grain rice
2 tablespoons butter or margarine
1½ pounds fresh sea scallops, split crosswise
1 teaspoon salt
⅛ teaspoon pepper
2 tomatoes, cut into wedges
1 tablespoon soy sauce
1 teaspoon cornstarch

About 30 minutes before serving: In separate saucepans, cook green beans and rice as labels direct but omit butter or margarine. In large skillet over medium heat, in butter, sauté scallops 8 minutes. Sprinkle with salt and pepper; toss with drained green beans and tomatoes; heat. Mix soy sauce, cornstarch and ¼ cup water until smooth; stir into scallop mixture. Serve on heated platter, with a border of hot fluffy rice. Pass soy sauce. Makes 6 servings.

**Bland diet:** Prepare as directed but omit pepper, tomatoes and soy sauce.
**Diabetic diet:** Carefully divide scallop mixture into 6 equal servings (about ¾ cup each). Exchanges per serving = 3 meat and 1 "A" and 1 "B" vegetable plus 1 bread for each ½-cup rice used.
**Egg-, gluten-, milk- and wheat-free diet:** Prepare as directed but use milk-free margarine for milk-free diet; omit soy sauce on gluten- and wheat-free diet.
**Low-fat diet:** 5 grams fat per serving. Omit recipe from low-cholesterol diet.
**Low-fat, bland (gall bladder) diet:** Prepare as directed but omit pepper, tomatoes and soy sauce.
**High-iron diet:** 3 milligrams iron per serving.
**Low-residue diet:** Prepare as directed for bland diet.

## SHRIMP AMANDINE (245 calories per serving)

butter or margarine
½ cup roasted slivered almonds
2½ pounds fresh medium shrimp, shelled, deveined
1 teaspoon salt
dash pepper
2 tablespoons chopped chives

About 15 minutes before serving: In medium skillet over medium heat, in 1 tablespoon butter, sauté almonds until golden; remove; drain on paper toweling. In same skillet, in 1 tablespoon butter, sauté half of shrimp, stirring constantly, a few minutes, or until they turn pink and are tender. Repeat with remaining shrimp. Sprinkle with salt and pepper.

To serve: Sprinkle shrimp with almonds and chives. Makes 6 servings.

**Diabetic diet:** Carefully divide into 6 equal servings. Exchanges per serving = 3 meat.

## PACIFIC SEAFOOD IN OLIVE-RICE RING (315 calories per serving)

1 16-ounce can tomatoes
¼ cup catchup
1 medium onion, sliced
⅛ teaspoon instant minced
    garlic
2 teaspoons granulated sugar
½ teaspoon Tabasco
2 tablespoons butter or mar-
    garine
¼ cup flour
1 tablespoon chili powder
½ cup bottled clam juice
1 6-ounce package frozen King
    crab, thawed and drained
1 7-ounce package frozen
    shrimp, thawed
2 7¾-ounce cans oysters,
    drained
½ teaspoon salt
3 cups hot fluffy rice
¼ cup sliced stuffed olives

About 45 minutes before serving: In saucepan, simmer tomatoes with catchup, onion, garlic, sugar and Tabasco 15 minutes; strain. In same saucepan, melt butter; stir in flour and chili powder until smooth; gradually stir in bottled clam juice and strained tomato sauce; boil 5 minutes. Add crab meat, shrimp and oysters; simmer 10 minutes or until shrimp turn pink and curl. Add salt. Toss hot rice with sliced stuffed olives; arrange in ring on heated platter. Pour seafood mixture in center. Makes 6 servings.

Diabetic diet: Prepare as directed but omit sugar.
   To serve: Top ½ cup (1 bread exchange) or 1 cup (2 bread exchanges) rice with a generous cup of seafood mixture (3 meat and 1 bread exchange).
Low-fat diet: Prepare as directed but omit olives. 5 grams fat per serving. Omit recipe from low-cholesterol diet.
High-iron diet: 6 milligrams iron per serving.

## SHRIMP-AND-COTTAGE-CHEESE SALAD (195 calories per serving)

½ pound cooked, shelled, de-
    veined shrimp, chilled
1 8-ounce container creamed
    cottage cheese
¼ cup chopped pecans
1 tablespoon minced onion
3 tablespoons low-calorie (imi-
    tation) mayonnaise
3 tablespoons low-calorie
    French dressing
4 large lettuce cups
8 tomato wedges for garnish
parsley sprigs for garnish

Up to 30 minutes before serving: Cut shrimp into bite-size pieces. In medium bowl, mix shrimp, cottage cheese, pecans, onion, low-calorie mayonnaise and French dressing. Cover; refrigerate until serving time.
   To serve: Heap shrimp mixture in lettuce cups; garnish with tomatoes and parsley. Makes 4 servings.

Diabetic diet: Exchanges per serving = 2 meat, 1 "A" vegetable and ½ skim milk.
Low-fat diet: 10 grams fat per serving. Omit recipe from low-cholesterol diet.
Low-purine diet: Prepare as directed but omit shrimp. Makes 3 servings.

## LOBSTER TAILS WITH SPICY RICE (235 calories per serving)

4 3-ounce frozen rock-lobster
    tails
melted butter or margarine
¼ teaspoon onion salt
pepper to taste
1 tablespoon chopped parsley
¾ cup uncooked long-grain
    rice
2 tablespoons minced
    onion
garlic salt to taste

About 30 minutes before serving: Boil frozen lobster tails as label directs. When lobster tails are cooked, cut away thin undershell; bend back tail until shell cracks. Brush with 1 tablespoon melted butter; sprinkle with onion salt and pepper.
   Meanwhile, cook rice as label directs but omit butter. Then stir in onion, 1 tablespoon butter or margarine and garlic salt to taste.
   To serve: Arrange lobster tails on serving dish; spoon rice around them. Makes 4 servings.

Diabetic diet: Exchanges per serving = 2 meat and 1 bread.
Egg-, gluten-, milk- and wheat-free diet: Prepare as directed but use milk-free margarine on milk-free diet.
Low-fat diet: 5 grams fat per serving. Omit recipe from low-cholesterol diet.

**POULTRY**

## OVEN-BAKED CHICKEN SUPREME (250 calories per serving)

2 tablespoons butter or margarine, melted
¼ cup flour
1 teaspoon seasoned salt
1 egg, beaten
1 tablespoon water
¼ cup packaged dried-bread crumbs
¼ cup grated Parmesan cheese
2 whole chicken breasts (about 1½ pounds), split, skinned and boned

About 1 hour before serving: Preheat oven to 350°F. In each of 4 cereal bowls, place butter or margarine, mixtures of flour and seasoned salt, beaten egg and water and bread crumbs and cheese. Beginning with butter, dip chicken breasts into each of 4 bowls, consecutively, ending with crumb-cheese mixture. On rack in shallow baking dish, arrange breasts close together. Bake 45 minutes, or until chicken is tender when pierced with fork. Remove from oven; turn heat to "broil"; slip chicken under broiler for a few minutes to lightly brown crust. Makes 4 servings.

**Bland diet:** Prepare as directed but substitute salt for seasoned salt.
**Diabetic diet:** Exchanges per serving = 4 meat and 1 "B" vegetable.
**Low-residue diet:** Prepare as directed for bland diet.

## CHICKEN-AND-PEA SALAD (260 calories per serving)

4 medium tomatoes
seasoned salt
seasoned pepper
bottled low-calorie Italian dressing
⅓ cup low-calorie (imitation) mayonnaise
1 teaspoon prepared mustard
½ cup cooked peas
2 cups cooked chicken chunks

At least 2 hours before serving: Cut ¼-inch slice from stem end of each tomato; scoop out pulp, reserving some. Sprinkle each tomato shell with seasoned salt and pepper and some low-calorie Italian dressing; refrigerate.

In medium bowl, combine low-calorie mayonnaise, mustard, ⅓ cup peas, and chicken; season to taste with seasoned salt and pepper; stir in ¼ cup reserved tomato pulp. Fill drained tomato shells with chicken salad; garnish with rest of peas and cut-up tomato. Makes 4 servings.

**Diabetic diet:** Exchanges per serving = 3 meat and 1 "A" and 1 "B" vegetable.
**Low-fat, low-cholesterol diet:** 10 grams fat per serving.

## CHICKEN-COD CHOWDER (170 calories per serving)

1 14½-ounce can chicken-noodle soup
1 10½-ounce can condensed chicken broth
1 16-ounce package frozen cod fillets, partially thawed

About 20 minutes before serving: In medium saucepan, heat soup and undiluted broth to boiling. Meanwhile, cut cod fillets into 1-inch cubes. Add to soup and cook 10 minutes, or until fish flakes easily with fork. Makes 3 servings.

**Diabetic diet:** Exchanges per serving (1 cup) = 4 meat and ½ bread.
**Low-fat, low-cholesterol diet:** 2 grams fat per serving.

## QUICK AVOCADO-CHICKEN SALAD (280 calories per serving)

2 cups cut-up cooked chicken
¼ cup low-calorie (imitation) mayonnaise
salt
⅛ teaspoon seasoned pepper
⅓ cup diced celery
3 small avocados
lemon juice
6 large pitted ripe olives, quartered
watercress for garnish

About 1 hour before serving: In medium bowl, toss together chicken, low-calorie mayonnaise, ½ teaspoon salt, seasoned pepper and celery; refrigerate, covered. Halve avocados; remove pits; brush with lemon juice; sprinkle with salt. Then fill each avocado half with chicken salad; garnish with 4 ripe olive quarters and cress. Refrigerate until served. Makes 6 servings.

**Diabetic diet:** Exchanges per serving = 2 meat and 1 fat.

## CHICKEN OCEANIA (250 calories per serving)

⅓ cup flour
½ teaspoon salt
¼ teaspoon celery salt
¼ teaspoon garlic salt
¼ teaspoon nutmeg
2 whole chicken breasts (about
   1½ pounds), split, skinned
   and boned
2 tablespoons salad oil
2 tablespoons soy sauce
1 8½-ounce can sliced pineapple

About 30 minutes before serving: Stir together flour, salt, celery salt, garlic salt and nutmeg; use to coat chicken, shaking off excess. In large skillet over medium heat, in oil, cook chicken until fork-tender—5 to 7 minutes on each side. Pour soy sauce, pineapple slices (and syrup) over chicken; stir gently to loosen any particles from bottom of skillet. Cover; simmer 10 minutes, or until gravy has thickened slightly. Top chicken with pineapple slices, then gravy. Makes 4 servings.

**Diabetic diet:** Prepare as directed but substitute, for sweetened pineapple, one 15¾-ounce can pineapple slices packed in pineapple juice. Serve ½ cup pineapple with chicken. Exchanges per serving = 3 meat and 1 fruit.
**Low-fat, low-cholesterol diet:** 10 grams fat per serving.

## PINEAPPLE CHICKEN (275 calories per serving)

1 6-ounce can frozen pineapple-
   juice concentrate
2 whole chicken breasts (about
   1½ pounds), split
salt and pepper
2 tablespoons butter or margarine

Early in day: Remove juice from freezer to thaw.

About 1 hour before serving: Season chicken with salt and pepper. In medium skillet over medium heat, in butter or margarine, brown on both sides. Drain on paper towels; wipe excess fat from pan.

Return chicken to pan; sprinkle with 1 teaspoon salt and ¼ teaspoon pepper; add juice concentrate. Cover; cook over low heat until tender—20 to 30 minutes. Remove chicken to platter; keep warm. Cook liquid in pan to consistency of medium sauce. Pour over chicken. Makes 4 servings.

**Egg-, gluten-, milk- and wheat-free diet:** Prepare as directed but use milk-free margarine on milk-free diet.
**Low-fat, low-cholesterol diet:** Prepare as directed but use salad oil or margarine instead of butter; dieter should not eat skin of chicken. 10 grams fat per serving.
**Low-sodium diet:** Prepare as directed but omit salt; use unsalted butter or margarine. 80 milligrams sodium per serving.

## GINGER SKILLET CHICKEN (275 calories per serving)

1½ tablespoons flour
2 teaspoons salt
1½ teaspoons granulated
   sugar
1 teaspoon ginger
1 3-pound broiler-fryer, cut up
2 tablespoons salad oil
1 16-ounce jar refrigerated
   fruit salad
about ½ cup orange juice

About 1 hour before serving: Combine flour, salt, sugar and ginger; use to coat chicken. (Reserve flour.) In large skillet over medium heat, in oil, brown chicken. Into measuring cup, drain liquid from fruit; add enough orange juice to make 1 cup. Add to chicken. (Reserve fruit.) Simmer, covered, 30 to 45 minutes, or until fork-tender.

In cup, mix leftover flour with 3 tablespoons water until smooth; stir into liquid in skillet; cook, stirring, until thickened. Add drained fruit and heat about 1 minute. Makes 6 servings.

**Diabetic diet:** Prepare as directed but omit sugar and use an unsweetened refrigerated fruit salad. Serve chicken with ½ cup fruit and juice. Exchanges per serving = 3 meat and 1 fruit.
**Egg-, gluten-, milk- and wheat-free diet:** Prepare as directed but coat chicken with cornstarch for gluten- and wheat-free diets.
**Low-fat, low-cholesterol diet:** Dieter should not eat skin of chicken. 10 grams fat per serving.
**High-iron diet:** 3 milligrams iron per serving.
**Low-sodium diet:** Prepare as directed but omit salt. 95 milligrams sodium per serving.

## MUSHROOM-STUFFED ROAST CHICKEN (325 calories per serving)

3 cups day-old bread crumbs
2 tablespoons finely chopped
  parsley
½ medium onion, minced
½ teaspoon salt
pepper
½ pound fresh mushrooms,
  chopped
½ teaspoon ground thyme
melted butter or margarine
1 3-pound broiler-fryer
2 tablespoons lemon juice
3 tablespoons flour
2 cups chicken broth
1 teaspoon marjoram leaves
½ teaspoon salt

About 2 hours before serving: Preheat oven to 375°F. Mix crumbs, parsley, onion, salt, ⅛ teaspoon pepper, mushrooms, thyme and 2 tablespoons melted butter or margarine. Use to stuff chicken, closing openings with toothpicks.

Place chicken in baking pan; brush with mixture of 2 tablespoons melted butter or margarine and 2 tablespoons lemon juice. Bake 1 hour and 15 minutes, or until golden brown and tender. When chicken is done, remove to heated platter; remove toothpicks. From pan pour off all but 2 tablespoons fat. Place pan over medium-high heat; stir in flour, then chicken broth, marjoram, salt and ⅛ teaspoon pepper. Cook, stirring, until slightly thickened; pass in gravy boat. Makes 6 servings.

**Diabetic diet:** Exchanges per serving = 1 bread and 1 fat for ⅓ cup stuffing; 1 meat for each ounce of chicken; up to ¼ cup gravy = 1 "free."
**Low-fat, low-cholesterol diet:** Prepare as directed but use salad oil or margarine instead of butter; dieter should not eat skin of chicken. 10 grams fat per serving.
**High-iron diet:** 4 milligrams iron per serving.

## BARBECUED CHICKEN IN A SACK (300 calories per serving)

2 clean medium brown-paper
  bags
salad oil
2 3-pound broiler-fryers
¼ cup chili sauce
¼ cup bottled barbecue sauce
12 ears corn in husks (optional)

About 2¼ hours before serving: Preheat oven to 375°F. Rub paper bags, inside and out, with salad oil. Place a chicken in each bag; set, side by side, in covered roaster or shallow roasting pan. Stir chili sauce and barbecue sauce together. Pour half over each chicken, right in bags; close bags. Run ears of corn (in their husks) under cold water; place around chicken for baking at same time. Place cover on roaster (or cover shallow roasting pan with foil). Bake chickens 1½ to 2 hours, or until fork-tender. Makes 12 servings.

**Low-fat, low cholesterol diet:** Prepare as directed, dieter should not eat skin of chicken. 10 grams fat per serving.
**High-iron diet:** 3.5 milligrams iron per serving.

## SKILLET PINEAPPLE CHICKEN (205 calories per serving)

3 large whole chicken breasts
  (about 2½ pounds), split,
  skinned and boned
1½ teaspoons salt
2 tablespoons butter or margarine
1 tablespoon instant minced
  onion
1 cup diagonally sliced celery
1 green pepper, cut into strips
1 8-ounce can pineapple tidbits
1½ teaspoons soy sauce
½ teaspoon cinnamon
2 teaspoons cornstarch

About 35 minutes before serving: Cut each chicken-breast half into 10 to 12 crosswise strips. Sprinkle with salt. In large skillet over high heat, in butter or margarine, brown chicken strips 3 minutes, stirring constantly. Add onion, celery and green pepper; continue cooking 2 minutes. Add pineapple, soy sauce, cinnamon and ¼ cup cold water; stir; cover; simmer 4 minutes. Blend cornstarch with 2 tablespoons cold water; stir into skillet. Cook, stirring, until thickened. Makes 6 servings.

**Low-fat, low-cholesterol diet:** Prepare as directed but use salad oil or margarine instead of butter. 5 grams fat per serving.

## OVEN-FRIED CHICKEN (255 calories per serving)

1½ cups packaged cornflake
   crumbs
2 teaspoons seasoned salt
½ teaspoon seasoned pepper
2 eggs
4 whole chicken breasts (about
   3 pounds), split
6 tablespoons butter or margarine

Up to 1½ hours before serving: Preheat oven to 350°F. On piece of waxed paper, combine crumbs, seasoned salt and pepper. In small bowl, beat eggs with 2 tablespoons water. Dip chicken, first into egg mixture, then into crumb mixture. Meanwhile, in each of 2 shallow baking pans in oven, melt 3 tablespoons butter; in it, arrange chicken. Bake about 1 hour, or until fork-tender. Makes 8 servings.

**Bland diet:** Prepare as directed but omit pepper and substitute salt for seasoned salt.
**Diabetic diet:** Exchanges per serving = 4 meat and ½ bread.
**Low-residue diet:** Prepare as directed for bland diet.

## CHICKEN-STUFFED ORANGES (180 calories per serving)

6 oranges
½ cup low-calorie (imitation)
   mayonnaise
grated orange peel
1½ teaspoons orange juice
⅛ teaspoon white pepper
3 cups cooked chicken chunks
½ cup cut-up orange sections
½ cup green grapes, halved
¼ to ½ teaspoon salt

About 2 hours before serving: Slice top from each orange, about one-third way down; with sharp knife, cut out orange sections from both the tops and bottoms; reserve ½ cup. Make shallow saw-toothed edge around top of each orange shell. In medium bowl, combine low-calorie mayonnaise, 1 teaspoon grated orange peel, orange juice and pepper. Mix in chicken, then ¼ cup reserved orange sections and some grapes; add salt to taste. Heap into orange shells; garnish with remaining orange sections and grapes; sprinkle with orange peel. Refrigerate. Makes 6 servings.

**Diabetic diet:** Exchanges per serving = 3 meat and ½ fruit.
**Low-fat, low-cholesterol diet:** 5 grams fat per serving.

## CHICKEN PORTUGAIS (280 calories per serving)

2 tablespoons bacon fat
4 whole chicken breasts (about
   3 pounds), split, boned and
   skinned
pinch instant minced garlic
¼ cup chopped onion
2 teaspoons flour
½ cup white wine
1 10½-ounce can condensed
   beef broth
2 tomatoes
4 cups hot fluffy rice

About 25 minutes before serving: In large skillet over medium heat, in bacon fat, brown chicken breasts 2 minutes on each side. Add garlic and onion; cook 3 minutes; stir in flour, then wine and undiluted broth. Let all simmer, uncovered, 10 minutes, or until chicken is fork-tender.

   Meanwhile, chop tomatoes coarsely. Add to chicken; continue boiling 5 minutes. Serve over hot fluffy rice. Makes 8 servings.

**Diabetic diet:** Serve chicken with ½ cup gravy over ½ cup rice. Exchanges per serving = 4 meat, 1 bread and 1 "B" vegetable.
**Low-fat, low-cholesterol diet:** Prepare as directed but use salad oil (not bacon fat). 5 grams fat per serving.

## CHICKEN-WATERCRESS SOUP (180 calories per serving)

1 10½-ounce can condensed
   chicken broth
½ teaspoon salt
2 tablespoons finely minced
   onion
¼ cup diced celery
1½ cups cooked diced chicken
   or turkey (about ½ pound)
1 cup firmly packed coarsely
   chopped watercress
1 tablespoon cornstarch

About 15 minutes before serving: In medium saucepan, simmer chicken broth, 1 cup water, salt, onion, celery and chicken 10 minutes. Add watercress and simmer again until just wilted. Meanwhile, mix cornstarch with enough water to form a smooth paste. Stir into soup; cook a few seconds until clear and smooth. Makes 3 servings of 1 cup each.

**Diabetic diet:** Exchanges per serving = 4 meat and 1 "B" vegetable.
**Egg-, gluten-, milk- and wheat-free diet:** Prepare as directed but use homemade chicken broth.
**Low-fat, low-cholesterol diet:** 5 grams fat per serving.
**High-iron diet:** 3 milligrams iron per serving.

## SAVORY CHICKEN (300 calories per serving)

3 tablespoons flour
1 teaspoon salt
1/4 teaspoon paprika
3 whole chicken breasts (about
  2 1/2 pounds), split, skinned
  and boned
2 tablespoons salad oil
1 envelope (.6 ounces) old-
  fashioned French-dressing
  mix
1 13 3/4-ounce can chicken broth
1 medium onion, quartered
6 medium new potatoes
6 carrots
chopped parsley for garnish

About 1 1/4 hours before serving: Combine flour, salt and paprika; use to coat chicken on all sides. In Dutch oven over medium heat, in oil, brown chicken on all sides; then sprinkle with French-dressing mix and add broth and onion.

Scrub new potatoes; cut carrots into thirds, lengthwise; add both to chicken. Simmer, covered, about 50 minutes, or until all are tender. Arrange on heated platter; then sprinkle with parsley. Spoon juices from Dutch oven over chicken and vegetables. Makes 6 servings.

**Diabetic diet:** Exchanges per serving = 4 meat for each half chicken breast; 1 bread for a potato; 1 "B" vegetable for 1 carrot; up to 3 tablespoons gravy = 1 "free" exchange.
**Low-fat, low-cholesterol diet:** 5 grams fat per serving.

## SIMMERED CHICKEN IN LEMON (255 calories per serving)

1 3-pound broiler-fryer, cut up
2 bay leaves
1 teaspoon monosodium glutamate
2 teaspoons salt
12 small white onions, peeled
1 9-ounce package frozen artichoke hearts
2 tablespoons flour
2 egg yolks
2 tablespoons lemon juice
paprika for garnish

About 1 hour and 10 minutes before serving: Place chicken in Dutch oven; add 2 cups water, bay leaves, monosodium glutamate and salt; cover; bring to boiling, then simmer 1 hour. At end of first 30 minutes, add onions; at end of next 20 minutes, add artichoke hearts; cook all until tender. Blend flour, 1/2 cup water, egg yolks, lemon juice; stir into liquid in Dutch oven, and cook, stirring, until thickened. Sprinkle with paprika. Makes 6 servings.

**Diabetic diet:** Serve 2 tablespoons gravy with each serving. Exchanges per serving = 1 "B" vegetable for 2 onions; 1 "A" vegetable for artichoke hearts; 1 meat for each ounce of cooked chicken; up to 2 tablespoons gravy = 1 "free" exchange.
**High-iron diet:** 4 milligrams iron per serving.

## CHICKEN, HUNTER STYLE (315 calories per serving)

2 2 1/2-pound broiler-fryers,
  quartered
1 teaspoon monosodium glutamate
1 teaspoon paprika
seasoned salt
1/4 teaspoon seasoned pepper
2 tablespoons salad oil
10 white onions, peeled
1/2 pound mushrooms, sliced
1 small eggplant, pared, cut
  into 1/2-inch strips
1 green pepper, cut into strips
1/8 teaspoon pepper
1/2 teaspoon thyme leaves
1 teaspoon basil
2 garlic cloves, minced
2 bay leaves
1/2 cup sherry
4 tomatoes, quartered

About 2 1/2 hours before serving: Sprinkle chicken with monosodium glutamate, paprika, 1 1/4 teaspoons seasoned salt and pepper. Preheat oven to 375°F. Meanwhile, in large skillet, in oil, brown chicken on all sides. Arrange in 3-quart casserole.

In fat left in skillet, sauté onions until golden. Now add mushrooms, eggplant, green pepper, 1 1/4 teaspoons seasoned salt, pepper, thyme, basil and garlic and sauté 2 or 3 minutes. Add to chicken in casserole with bay leaves and sherry. Bake, covered, 45 minutes. Add tomatoes and bake 20 minutes longer. Makes 8 servings.

**Egg-, gluten-, milk- and wheat-free diet:** Prepare as directed but for gluten-free diets use plain salt and pepper (not seasoned salt and pepper) and omit monosodium glutamate.
**Low-fat, low-cholesterol diet:** Prepare as directed; dieter should not eat skin of chicken. 15 grams fat per serving.
**High-iron diet:** 4.5 milligrams iron per serving.

## PRESSURE-COOKED PIMENTO CHICKEN (300 calories per serving)

1/4 cup flour
1 tablespoon seasoned salt
1/4 teaspoon seasoned pepper
1 tablespoon paprika
1 3½-pound chicken, cut up
2 tablespoons salad oil
2 4-ounce cans pimentos,
   drained
1 large onion, sliced
1/8 teaspoon instant minced
   garlic
1 bay leaf
1 stalk celery, chopped
1 teaspoon Worcestershire
1/2 cup water
2 teaspoons cornstarch

About 45 minutes before serving: Combine flour, seasoned salt, seasoned pepper and paprika; coat chicken with flour mixture. In pressure cooker, in oil, brown until golden.

Add pimentos, onion, garlic, bay leaf, celery, Worcestershire and water; close cover securely. Place pressure regulator on vent pipe as manufacturer directs; bring up to 15 pounds pressure. Cook chicken 15 minutes, then let pressure reduce of its own accord. With slotted spoon, remove chicken and vegetables to heated platter. Stir cornstarch into a little water until smooth, then stir mixture into gravy in cooker. Cook until thickened; pour some over chicken; pass rest in gravy boat. Makes 6 servings.

**Low-fat, low-cholesterol diet:** Prepare as directed; dieter should not eat skin of chicken. 15 grams fat per serving.
**High-iron diet:** 4 milligrams iron per serving.

## CHICKEN BREASTS AMANDINE (265 calories per serving)

2 tablespoons butter or margarine
2 large whole chicken breasts
   (about 1½ pounds), split,
   skinned and boned
1 small garlic clove, minced
1/4 cup canned roasted,
   blanched slivered almonds
1 fresh mushroom, sliced
1/2 teaspoon salt
1/4 teaspoon pepper
1 10½-ounce can condensed
   chicken broth
1 tablespoon cornstarch
parsley sprigs for garnish

About 40 minutes before serving: In skillet over medium heat, in butter or margarine, brown chicken breasts, garlic, almonds and mushroom slices, stirring occasionally, until all are golden. Now add salt, pepper and chicken broth; simmer, covered, 30 minutes, or until chicken is tender. Then mix cornstarch with a little water; stir into liquid in skillet; cook, stirring constantly, until thickened. Garnish chicken with parsley sprigs. Makes 4 servings.

**Diabetic diet:** Carefully divide into 4 equal servings. Exchanges per serving = 4 meat and 1 "B" vegetable.
**Low-fat, low-cholesterol diet:** Prepare as directed but use salad oil or margarine instead of butter. 10 grams fat per serving.
**Low-sodium diet:** Prepare as directed but use salad oil or unsalted butter or margarine; omit salt; use 1¼ cups unsalted chicken broth or water in place of canned broth. 70 milligrams sodium per serving.

## CHICKEN WITH BUTTERMILK GRAVY (250 calories per serving)

1 tablespoon butter or margarine
1 small garlic clove
1 medium onion, chopped
4 chicken legs with thighs
   (about 1½ pounds)
1/4 teaspoon ginger
1½ teaspoons curry
1 teaspoon salt
2 tablespoons chopped al-
   monds (optional)
2 cups buttermilk
2 tablespoons flour
paprika for garnish
dried parsley flakes for garnish

About 1 hour before serving: In large skillet, in butter or margarine, sauté garlic and onion until onion is lightly browned; remove garlic and discard. Brown chicken until golden, then remove. Add ginger, curry, salt and almonds to skillet; stir in 1 cup buttermilk; stirring constantly, bring mixture to boiling. Return chicken to skillet; cover; simmer, turning occasionally, 40 minutes, or until tender.

Remove chicken to warm platter. Stirring constantly, slowly mix remaining 1 cup of buttermilk into flour to form smooth paste; add paste to stock in skillet, still stirring constantly. Heat mixture almost to boiling—do not boil or mixture (which is never absolutely smooth) will separate.

To serve: Sprinkle chicken with paprika and garnish with parsley flakes. Pass remaining gravy. Makes 4 servings.

**Diabetic diet:** Prepare as directed; serve ½ cup gravy with each serving. Exchanges per serving = 3 meat, 1 "B" vegetable and ½ skim milk.
**Low-fat, low-cholesterol diet:** Prepare as directed but remove skin from chicken and use margarine or salad oil instead of butter. 10 grams fat per serving.

## CHICKEN ITALIANO (245 calories per serving)

1 3-pound broiler-fryer, skinned
  and cut up
1 teaspoon salt
⅛ teaspoon pepper
1 16-ounce can spaghetti sauce
  with mushrooms

About 1 hour and 15 minutes before serving: Preheat oven to 350°F. In large shallow baking dish, arrange chicken pieces so they do not overlap. Sprinkle with salt and pepper. Pour tomato sauce over chicken. Bake 1 hour, or until chicken is fork-tender, basting occasionally. Makes 4 servings.

**Diabetic diet:** Exchanges per serving = 1 meat for each ounce cooked chicken, plus 1 "B" vegetable for ⅓ cup sauce.
**Egg- and milk-free diet:** Prepare as directed but select a spaghetti sauce not containing cheese.
**Low-fat, low-cholesterol diet:** Prepare as directed but select spaghetti sauce not containing cheese. 10 grams fat per serving.

## FORK-AND-SPOON CHICKEN CANTALOUPE SALAD (275 calories per serving)

½ cup bottled low-calorie
  Italian dressing
¼ cup low-calorie (imitation)
  mayonnaise
⅛ teaspoon seasoned pepper
⅓ cup diced celery
2 tablespoons sliced scallions
3 cups cut-up cooked chicken
2 cantaloupes
watercress for garnish

Early in day, or at least 2 hours before serving: In medium bowl, stir together low-calorie dressings, seasoned pepper, celery and scallions. Add chicken; toss well; refrigerate, covered. Halve cantaloupes; remove seeds; refrigerate, covered.

To serve: Fill cantaloupe halves with chicken salad; garnish each half with 4 sprigs of cress. Makes 4 servings.

**Diabetic diet:** Prepare as directed but use mixture to fill 6 small cantaloupe halves. Exchanges per serving = 3 meat and 1 fruit.
**Low-fat, low-cholesterol diet:** 10 grams fat per serving.

## QUICK CUCUMBER BOATS (125 calories per serving)

3 cucumbers
2 9-ounce packages frozen cut
  green beans, cooked
chopped dill
1 to 2 tablespoons cocktail
  onions
2 cups julienne strips of cooked
  chicken breasts
low-calorie Italian dressing
salt

About 1 hour before serving: Cut cucumbers in half lengthwise; with pointed knife, remove and discard seeds. Scoop out cucumber shells; cut meat scooped from shells into strips. In medium bowl, toss green beans with 1 tablespoon chopped dill, cocktail onions, chicken, low-calorie dressing to taste and cucumber strips. Sprinkle cucumber shells lightly with salt; fill with salad mixture. Garnish with chopped dill. Refrigerate. Makes 6 servings.

**Diabetic diet:** Exchanges per serving = 2 meat and 1 "B" vegetable.
**Low-fat, low-cholesterol diet:** 5 grams fat per serving.
**High-iron diet:** 3 milligrams iron per serving.

## SPICY BAKED CHICKEN (205 calories per serving)

1 3-pound broiler-fryer, cut up
¾ cup chicken broth
1 teaspoon instant minced
  onion
½ teaspoon salt
¼ teaspoon thyme leaves
⅛ teaspoon seasoned pepper
⅛ teaspoon instant minced
  garlic
2 teaspoons cornstarch
½ cup seedless grapes

About 1½ hours beore serving: Preheat oven to 400°F. In shallow open roasting pan, arrange chicken pieces; pour broth over them. Combine instant minced onion, salt, thyme, seasoned pepper and instant minced garlic; sprinkle over chicken. Bake, uncovered, 1 hour, or until fork-tender, basting frequently. Transfer to warm platter. Stir cornstarch into a little water until smooth, then stir into gravy in pan. Cook until thickened; add grapes. Pass as gravy for chicken. Makes 6 servings.

**Diabetic diet:** Exchanges per serving = 4 meat plus 1 "free" for ¼ cup gravy.
**Low-fat, low-cholesterol diet:** Prepare as directed; dieter should not eat skin of chicken. 10 grams fat per serving.
**High-iron diet:** 3 milligrams iron per serving.

## MIRIAM'S CHICKEN (270 calories per serving)

**1 3-pound broiler-fryer, cut up**
**salt**
**¼ teaspoon pepper**
**2 tablespoons salad oil**
**2 cups diced onion**
**1 cup diced green pepper**
**1 garlic clove, minced**
**1 cup chopped fresh tomatoes**
**¼ cup chopped parsley**

About 1 hour before serving: Sprinkle chicken with 1 teaspoon salt and the pepper. In large skillet over medium heat, in oil, brown with diced onion until golden; add green pepper and garlic; sauté a few minutes longer. Stir in chopped tomatoes, parsley and 1 teaspoon salt; simmer, covered, 45 minutes or until tender, adding ¼ to ½ cup water if needed. Before serving, skim off any surface fat from gravy. Makes 6 servings.

**Diabetic diet:** Include ⅓ cup gravy with each serving. Exchanges per serving = 1 "B" vegetable and 1 meat for each ounce of cooked chicken.
**Low-fat, low-cholesterol diet:** Prepare as directed; dieter should not eat skin of chicken. 10 grams fat per serving.
**High-iron diet:** 3.5 milligrams iron per serving.
**Low-sodium diet:** Prepare as directed but omit salt. 100 milligrams sodium per serving.

## CHICKEN À L'ORANGE (270 calories per serving)

**2½ tablespoons flour**
**1 teaspoon chili powder**
**½ teaspoon salt**
**2 whole chicken breasts (about 1½ pounds), split**
**2 tablespoons salad oil**
**1 tablespoon grated orange peel**
**1 cup orange juice**
**1 teaspoon granulated sugar**
**1 orange, sectioned**

About 1 hour before serving: Combine flour with chili powder and salt; coat chicken with mixture. In large skillet over medium heat, in oil, brown on all sides. Stir in remaining flour mixture, orange peel, orange juice and sugar; simmer, covered, 45 minutes, or until chicken is tender. Remove cover; add orange sections and heat 5 minutes. Makes 4 servings.

**Diabetic diet:** Prepare as directed but omit sugar. Include ¼ cup gravy and orange slices with each serving. Exchanges per serving = 4 meat and 1 fruit.
**Egg-, gluten-, milk- and wheat-free diet:** Prepare as directed but flour chicken with cornstarch (not flour) for gluten- and wheat-free diets.
**Low-fat, low-cholesterol diet:** Prepare as directed but remove skin from chicken before preparing. 10 grams fat per serving.
**Low-sodium diet:** Prepare as directed but use chili powder not containing salt; omit salt. 60 milligrams sodium per serving.

## BAKED BROILERS WITH CRAB (320 calories per serving)

**2 2-pound broiler-fryers (backbones removed), quartered**
**butter or margarine**
**seasoned salt**
**pepper and paprika**
**¼ cup chili sauce**
**2 7½-ounce cans King crab, drained (or 2 6-ounce packages frozen King crab, thawed, thoroughly drained)**
**3 slices bread, cubed**
**1 teaspoon poultry seasoning**
**parsley for garnish**

About 1¼ hours before serving: Preheat oven to 375°F. Rub chicken with softened butter or margarine, then with 1 teaspoon seasoned salt, pepper and paprika. Lay, skin side up, in roasting pan; roast, uncovered, 35 minutes. In small saucepan, melt 2 tablespoons butter or margarine; stir in chili sauce; spread mixture over chicken and bake 10 minutes longer.

Meanwhile, in large bowl, flake crab; toss with bread cubes, poultry seasoning, 1 teaspoon seasoned salt and 2 tablespoons melted butter. Turn chicken skin side down; pile some crab mixture onto each piece; bake 20 minutes longer. Garnish with parsley. Makes 8 servings.

**Low-fat diet:** Prepare as directed; dieter should not eat skin of chicken. 15 grams fat per serving. Omit recipe from low-cholesterol diet.
**High-iron diet:** 3 milligrams iron per serving.

## EASY CHICKEN PARTS, COMPANY STYLE (250 calories per serving)

¾ teaspoon salt
⅛ teaspoon pepper
¼ teaspoon paprika
1 3-pound broiler-fryer, skinned, cut up
1 10½-ounce can condensed cream-of-chicken soup
½ cup skimmed milk or reliquefied nonfat dry milk
1 cup chopped green pepper

About 1 hour before serving: Preheat oven to 375°F. Combine salt, pepper and paprika; sprinkle over chicken. Arrange meat-side down in large (about 13" by 9" by 2") baking dish. Blend chicken soup with milk; pour over chicken. Top with chopped green pepper. Bake 45 minutes, or until fork-tender. Makes 6 servings.

**Diabetic diet:** Include ⅓ cup gravy with each serving. Exchanges per serving = ½ skim milk plus 1 meat for each ounce cooked chicken.
**Low-fat diet:** 5 grams fat per serving. Omit recipe from low-cholesterol diet.
**High-iron diet:** 3.5 milligrams iron per serving.

## CHICKEN WITH WALNUTS (Hop Po Gai Ding) (300 calories per serving)

1 teaspoon granulated sugar
1 teaspoon salt
1 tablespoon soy sauce
2 tablespoons dry sherry
3 whole chicken breasts (about 2½ pounds), split, skinned and boned
cornstarch
1 egg, beaten
3 tablespoons salad oil
½ cup walnut halves
½ teaspoon ginger
2 garlic cloves, minced
1 teaspoon monosodium glutamate
2 5-ounce cans sliced bamboo shoots, drained

About 45 minutes before serving: In medium bowl, combine sugar, salt, soy sauce and sherry. Cut chicken into 1- to 1½-inch slices, then let stand in sherry mixture about 15 minutes. Remove, reserving sherry mixture. Sprinkle chicken lightly with cornstarch, then toss with beaten egg.

In skillet over medium heat, in oil, lightly toast walnuts, stirring constantly; remove; drain. To oil remaining in skillet, add ginger, garlic and chicken. Cook, stirring constantly, until chicken is well browned on all sides. Now add ¾ cup water, monosodium glutamate and sherry mixture. Simmer, covered, until chicken is tender—about 20 minutes. Then stir in bamboo shoots and walnuts and simmer 5 minutes more. Makes 6 servings.

**Diabetic diet:** Prepare as directed but omit sugar; carefully divide into 6 equal servings. Exchanges per serving = 4 meat and 1 "B" vegetable.
**Low-fat, low-cholesterol diet:** Prepare as directed but omit egg. 15 grams fat per serving.

## CHICKEN WITH ORANGE SAUCE (250 calories per serving)

¼ cup cornstarch
salt and pepper
2 whole chicken breasts (about 1½ pounds), split and skinned
2 tablespoons salad oil
1 10½-ounce can condensed chicken broth
½ cup orange juice
½ unpeeled orange, thinly sliced
½ green pepper, chopped
¼ cup finely diced pimento
¼ pound medium mushrooms, quartered
¼ teaspoon ginger

About 1 hour before serving: Mix cornstarch, 1 teaspoon salt and generous dash pepper; use to coat chicken. In large skillet over medium heat, in oil, brown chicken until golden. Turn, skin side up, then add remaining ingredients. Cover; simmer, stirring occasionally, 30 minutes, or until chicken is tender. Season gravy with salt and pepper to taste. Makes 4 servings.

**Diabetic diet:** Prepare as directed; serve ½ cup gravy with each serving. Exchanges per serving = 4 meat and 1 fruit.
**Low-fat, low-cholesterol diet:** 10 grams fat per serving.

## BAKED CHICKEN CASSEROLE (250 calories per serving)

1 cup uncooked elbow macaroni
2 cups skimmed milk or reliquefied nonfat dry milk
¼ cup flour
2 chicken-bouillon cubes
2 cups diced cooked chicken
½ teaspoon marjoram leaves
dash pepper
¼ cup chopped parsley
¼ cup chopped onion
1 cup diced celery
5 mushrooms, thinly sliced
2 tablespoons chopped green
  pepper
2 teaspoons salt
1 tablespoon chopped pimento
  (optional)

About 1 hour before serving: Preheat oven to 350°F. Cook macaroni as label directs; drain. In 2-quart ovenproof sauce-pan, slowly add milk to flour, stirring constantly to form a smooth paste. Add bouillon cubes; cook on range top, still stirring constantly, until sauce is thickened and smooth. Stir in cooked macaroni, chicken and remaining ingredients. Bake, uncovered, 25 to 30 minutes, or until bubbly. Makes 5 servings of about 1 cup each.

**Diabetic diet:** Prepare as directed but divide mixture among 5 in-dividual casseroles; bake 20 minutes. Exchange per serving = 2 meat, 1 "B" vegetable, 1 bread and ½ skim milk.
**Low-fat, low-cholesterol diet:** 5 grams fat per serving.

## CHICKEN OLÉ (280 calories per serving)

1 3-pound broiler-fryer, cut up
¼ cup flour
2 tablespoons salad oil
½ medium onion, chopped
1 medium tomato, chopped
½ cup raisins
¼ cup sliced stuffed olives
¾ teaspoon salt
dash pepper

About 1½ hours before serving: Coat chicken with flour. In large skillet over medium heat, in oil, brown chicken on both sides. Remove from skillet. In same skillet, sauté onion until transparent. Add tomatoes, then browned chicken, raisins, olives, salt, pepper and 1 cup water. Bring to boiling; reduce heat and simmer, covered, 45 minutes, or until chicken is fork-tender. Arrange chicken on heated large platter; pour on sauce. Makes 6 servings.

**Egg-, gluten-, milk- and wheat-free diet:** Prepare as directed but sprinkle chicken with cornstarch instead of flour for gluten- and wheat-free diets.
**Low-fat, low-cholesterol diet:** Prepare as directed; dieter should not eat skin of chicken. Omit recipe if olives are forbidden on diet. 10 grams fat per serving.
**High-iron diet:** 3.5 milligrams iron per serving.
**Low-sodium diet:** Prepare as directed but omit olives and salt. 100 milligrams sodium per serving.

## CHICKEN À LA KING (230 calories per serving)

1 10½-ounce can condensed
  chicken broth
1 10-ounce package frozen peas
¼ chopped onion
7 tablespoons flour
⅛ teaspoon pepper
1 teaspoon salt
1 teaspoon granulated sugar
1 tablespoon butter or margarine
2 cups cup-up cooked chicken
2 canned pimentos, finely
  minced
1 egg yolk
6 slices toasted rye bread,
  quartered

About 20 minutes before serving: In medium saucepan, heat chicken broth to boiling; add peas and onion; cover; simmer 3 minutes. Meanwhile, in medium bowl, mix flour, pepper, salt and sugar. Slowly stir in 1½ cups water to form thin smooth paste. Stirring constantly, stir paste into chicken broth; cook until thickened. Add butter or margarine, chicken and pimentos; cook 5 minutes. Mix a bit of sauce with egg yolk, then stir into chicken mixture. Serve immediately in in-dividual 1-cup casseroles with toast quarters to one side. Makes 6 servings.

**Diabetic diet:** Prepare as directed but omit sugar. Exchanges per serving = 3 meat, 1 bread and 1 "B" vegetable.
**Low-fat, low-cholesterol diet:** Prepare as directed but use skimmed milk in place of water; use margarine instead of butter; omit egg yolk. 5 grams fat per serving.

## QUICK CAMP-STYLE CHICKEN LEGS (230 calories per serving)

1 envelope instant meat marinade
½ cup orange juice
2 tablespoons soy sauce
2 tablespoons honey
1 tablespoon lemon juice
½ teaspoon ginger
8 chicken legs with thighs (about 4 pounds)
½ cup bottled barbecue sauce

About 1 hour before serving: In shallow baking pan, combine meat marinade with orange juice, soy sauce, honey, lemon juice and ginger. Arrange chicken in marinade; prick with fork, then let stand 10 minutes, turning a few times.

Meanwhile, preheat broiler 10 minutes if manufacturer directs. Remove chicken from marinade and place, skin side down, on broiler rack (reserve marinade). Brush with barbecue sauce, then broil, about 7 inches from heat, brushing occasionally with marinade and sauce. When chicken is almost fork-tender, turn, skin side up, and brush with rest of marinade and barbecue sauce. Continue broiling until tender when pierced with fork. Makes 8 servings.

**Low-fat, low-cholesterol diet:** Dieter should not eat skin of chicken. 10 grams fat per serving.
**High-iron diet:** 3 milligrams iron per serving.

## CHICKEN IN A JIFFY (195 calories per serving)

2 large whole chicken breasts (about 1½ pounds) split, skinned and boned
2 tablespoons butter or margarine
½ teaspoon monosodium glutamate
½ teaspoon salt
1 teaspoon tarragon
⅔ cup dry vermouth
2 thin lemon slices
chopped parsley for garnish

About 30 minutes before serving: Cut each chicken-breast half into 10 to 12 strips. In skillet over high heat, in butter or margarine, cook chicken, monosodium glutamate, salt and tarragon 3 minutes, stirring occasionally. Add dry vermouth and lemon slices; cover and cook 5 minutes. Sprinkle with parsley. Makes 4 servings.

**Diabetic diet:** Carefully divide into 4 equal servings. Exchanges per serving = 3 meat.
**Egg-, gluten-, milk- and wheat-free diet:** Prepare as directed but use milk-free margarine on milk-free diet; omit monosodium glutamate on gluten-free diets.
**Low-fat, low-cholesterol diet:** Prepare as directed but use salad oil or margarine instead of butter. 10 grams fat per serving.
**Low-sodium diet:** Prepare as directed but use unsalted butter or margarine; omit monosodium glutamate and salt. 70 milligrams sodium per serving.

## INDIAN CHICKEN KABOBS (240 calories per serving)

4 large whole chicken breasts (about 3 pounds) split, skinned and boned
½ teaspoon ginger
⅛ teaspoon crushed red pepper
⅛ teaspoon prepared mustard
⅛ teaspoon ground cardamom
⅛ teaspoon turmeric
1 teaspoon curry
2 teaspoons lemon juice
1½ teaspoons salt
1 tablespoon salad oil
1 small onion, quartered
paprika
1 20-ounce can cling-peach halves, drained
1 lemon, cut into sixths
2 tablespoons chopped parsley for garnish

About 1¾ hours before serving: Flatten halved chicken breasts with hand, then cut each crosswise into thirds. In medium bowl, combine ginger, pepper, mustard, cardamom, turmeric, curry, lemon juice, salt, salad oil and 1 tablespoon water; add chicken; mix well. Refrigerate 1 hour.

Preheat broiler 10 minutes if manufacturer directs. On six 8-inch skewers, alternate 2 pieces of chicken with piece or two of onion from one of quarters. Repeat until each skewer is loosely filled, then sprinkle lightly with paprika. Place kabobs in jelly-roll pan; broil 15 minutes, turning once, or until chicken is cooked. Heat peaches under broiler for a minute or two. Serve garnished with lemon wedges and sprinkled with parsley. Makes 6 servings.

**Diabetic diet:** Prepare as directed but use water-packed peaches. Include 2 peach halves with each serving. Exchanges per serving = 4 meat and 1 fruit.
**Egg-, gluten-, milk- and wheat-free diet:** Prepare as directed.
**Low-fat, low-cholesterol diet:** 5 grams fat per serving.
**Low-sodium diet:** Prepare as directed but use dry mustard (not prepared); use curry which does not contain salt; omit salt. 95 milligrams sodium per serving.

## CHICKEN ALGERIAN (260 calories per serving)

1 3-pound broiler-fryer, cut up
paprika
salt
¼ teaspoon pepper
2 tablespoons butter or margarine
½ cup chicken broth
1 garlic clove
1 medium eggplant, pared, cubed
1 medium onion, chopped
2 tomatoes, peeled, diced
¼ teaspoon ground thyme
1 tablespoon chopped parsley

About 1 hour before serving: Sprinkle chicken with paprika, 1 teaspoon salt and pepper. In large skillet over medium heat, in butter or margarine, brown chicken. Stir in broth, scraping brown particles from bottom of skillet. Stick toothpick into garlic, then add to skillet with eggplant, 1 teaspoon salt and remaining ingredients. Simmer, covered, 30 minutes, or until chicken is tender. Remove garlic.

To serve: Turn into heated small soup tureen. Makes 6 servings.

**Egg-, gluten-, milk- and wheat-free diet:** Prepare as directed but use milk-free margarine on milk-free diet; water in place of broth on gluten- and wheat-free diets.
**Low-fat, low-cholesterol diet:** Use margarine or salad oil instead of butter; dieter should not eat skin of chicken. 10 grams of fat per serving.
**Low-sodium diet:** Prepare as directed but omit salt; use unsalted butter or margarine; substitute water for chicken broth. 100 milligrams sodium per serving.

## CURRIED CHICKEN KABOBS (270 calories per serving)

2 whole chicken breasts (about 1½ pounds) split, skinned and boned
1 8-ounce container plain yogurt
2 tablespoons minced onion
1½ teaspoons curry
½ to 1 teaspoon salt
2 tablespoons lemon juice
2 tablespoons granulated sugar
32 cherry tomatoes or 8 large tomatoes, quartered
¾ pound fresh medium mushrooms

About 45 minutes before serving: Cut chicken into 32 pieces. Cover large cookie sheet with foil, turning up foil edges to prevent spilling. In medium bowl, let chicken stand in mixture of yogurt, onion, curry, salt, lemon juice and sugar for about 10 minutes.

Preheat broiler 10 minutes if manufacturer directs. Thread eight 8-inch skewers with chicken, alternating with tomatoes and mushrooms. Place kabobs on cookie sheet; coat with half of remaining yogurt mixture. Broil 7 minutes; turn; coat with rest of yogurt mixture, then broil 7 minutes more until chicken is tender and lightly browned. Makes 4 servings.

**Diabetic diet:** Prepare as directed but omit sugar and add liquid nonnutritive sweetener equivalent to 2 tablespoons sugar. Exchanges per serving = 4 meat, 1 "A" vegetable and ½ skim milk.
**Egg-, gluten- and wheat-free diet:** Prepare as directed.
**Low-fat, low-cholesterol diet:** 5 grams fat per serving.
**Low-sodium diet:** Prepare as directed but use curry which does not contain salt; omit salt. 120 milligrams sodium per serving.

## CHILI CHICKEN (220 calories per serving)

2 whole chicken breasts (about 1½ pounds), split and skinned
2 tablespoons flour
1 tablespoon salad oil
1 8-ounce can tomato sauce with cheese
1 tablespoon granulated sugar
1 tablespoon parsley flakes
1 teaspoon salt
½ to 1 teaspoon chili powder

About 35 minutes before serving: Coat chicken lightly with flour; shake off excess. In medium skillet over medium heat, in oil, brown 5 minutes on each side. Add remaining ingredients. Cover and simmer 20 minutes, or until chicken is tender. Makes 4 servings.

**Diabetic diet:** Prepare as directed but omit sugar. Exchanges per serving = 3 meat and 1 "A" and 1 "B" vegetable.
**Egg-, gluten-, milk- and wheat-free diet:** Prepare as directed but substitute cornstarch for flour on gluten- and wheat-free diets; use plain tomato sauce in place of tomato sauce with cheese on milk-free diet.
**Low-fat, low-cholesterol diet:** Prepare as directed but use plain tomato sauce instead of tomato sauce with cheese. 5 grams fat per serving.

## EASY CHICKEN SAUTÉ (225 calories per serving)

2 whole chicken breasts (about 1½ pounds), split and skinned
2 tablespoons salad oil
½ pound fresh mushrooms, thinly sliced
1 onion, thinly sliced
1 teaspoon salt

About 30 minutes before serving: In medium skillet over medium heat, in oil, brown chicken well. Add remaining ingredients; cover; cook over low heat, turning chicken occasionally, until tender. Makes 4 servings.

**Bland diet:** Prepare as directed but omit onion.
**Diabetic diet:** Exchanges per serving = 4 meat and 1 "A" vegetable.
**Low-fat, low-cholesterol diet:** 10 grams fat per serving.
**Low-residue diet:** Prepare as directed but omit onion.
**Low-sodium diet:** Prepare as directed but omit salt. 80 milligrams sodium per serving.

## SEAFARING CHICKEN POTPIE (350 calories per serving)

3 tablespoons butter or margarine
1 large stalk green celery, thinly sliced
1 medium onion, thinly sliced
¼ cup flour
1 teaspoon salt
1 teaspoon poultry seasoning
1 8-ounce can sliced carrots, undrained
1 8-ounce can baby peas, undrained ·
2 7½-ounce cans minced clams, undrained
2 cups coarsely chopped cooked chicken or turkey (about 8 ounces)
2 hard-cooked eggs, thinly sliced
pepper to taste
1 8-ounce package refrigerated crescent rolls

About 30 minutes before serving: Preheat oven to 350°F. In medium skillet over medium heat, in butter or margarine, sauté celery and onion until onion is golden. Stir in flour, salt and poultry seasoning. Cook, stirring constantly, about 1 minute. Add undrained carrots, peas, clams and chicken. Cook, stirring constantly, until liquid thickens slightly and boils. Turn mixture into 2-quart casserole; top with egg slices. Sprinkle with pepper to taste.

Cut crescent rolls (still rolled as they come from the package) crosswise into 12 rounds. Place on top of potpie. Bake 15 to 20 minutes, or until rolls are a dark golden-brown. (Place piece of foil under casserole to catch any drippings.) Makes 6 servings of about 1 cup each.

**Diabetic diet:** Carefully divide stew among 6 individual casseroles; top with 2 biscuit slices; bake as directed. Exchanges per serving = 3 meat and 2 bread.
**High-iron diet:** 5.5 milligrams iron per serving.

## CURRIED CHICKEN SALAD (265 calories per serving)

¾ cup packaged precooked rice
¼ cup thinly-sliced carrots
¼ cup low-calorie creamy-style French dressing
2 tablespoons low-calorie (imitation) mayonnaise
¾ teaspoon curry
¾ teaspoon salt
dash pepper
2 tablespoons milk
2 cups cooked chicken or turkey, cut into cubes (about 10 ounces)
¼ cup thin green-pepper strips
romaine or lettuce
1 small red onion, thinly sliced

Early in day: Cook rice as label directs; toss rice with carrots and low-calorie French dressing; cover; refrigerate at least 2 hours.

Meanwhile, in medium bowl, combine low-calorie mayonnaise, curry, salt and pepper; slowly stir in milk; add chicken and green pepper; toss. Refrigerate, covered, at least 2 hours.

To serve: Combine rice and chicken mixtures. Arrange on romaine; garnish with onion. Makes 4 servings of a scant cup each.

**Diabetic diet:** Exchanges per serving = 3 meat, 1 "A" and 1 "B" vegetable and 1 bread.
**Low-fat, low-cholesterol diet:** Prepare as directed but use skimmed milk (not whole). 5 grams fat per serving.

## CHICKEN CURRY—IN A HURRY (270 calories per serving)

1 cup uncooked long-grain rice
1 tablespoon salad oil
2 whole chicken breasts (about
   1½ pounds), split, skinned,
   boned and cut into bite-size
   pieces
½ pound fresh mushrooms,
   thinly sliced
⅓ cup chopped onion
3 tablespoons flour
1 chicken-bouillon cube
1 teaspoon salt
1½ teaspoons curry
1 apple, quartered, thinly sliced
¼ cup chopped parsley
¾ cup skimmed milk or re-
   liquefied nonfat dry milk

About 30 minutes before serving: Cook rice as label directs but omit butter. In large skillet over medium heat, in oil, brown chicken, mushrooms and onion until chicken is golden and completely cooked—about 10 minutes. Stir in flour, bouillon cube, salt and curry to form a smooth paste. Add apple and parsley, then stir in milk and 1 cup water. Cook, stirring constantly, until thickened; still stirring, simmer 3 minutes, or until apple is tender-crisp. Makes 6 servings.

**Diabetic diet:** Serve ½ cup curry sauce over ½ cup rice. Exchanges per serving = 3 meat, 1 bread and 1 "B" vegetable.
**Egg-, gluten- and wheat-free diet:** Prepare as directed but use 1½ tablespoons cornstarch in place of flour; omit chicken-bouillon cube on gluten- and wheat-free diet.
**Low-fat, low-cholesterol diet:** 5 grams fat per serving.

## WAISTLINE BARBECUED CHICKEN (245 calories per serving)

2 tablespoons salad oil
4 whole chicken breasts (about
   3 pounds), split
3 cups tomato juice
½ cup vinegar
1 tablespoon granulated sugar
4 medium onions, sliced
3 tablespoons Worcestershire
½ cup catchup
4 teaspoons prepared mustard
1 teaspoon pepper
2 teaspoons salt

About 1 hour before serving: Preheat oven to 350°F. In skillet, in oil, brown chicken well on all sides. Remove to shallow baking pan. In saucepan, heat tomato juice and remaining ingredients; pour over chicken. Bake, uncovered, 40 minutes, or until tender, basting every 10 minutes with sauce. Makes 8 servings.

**Low-fat, low-cholesterol diet:** Prepare as directed; dieter should not eat skin of the chicken. 5 grams fat per serving.

## CHICKEN TROPICALE (285 calories per serving)

¼ cup flour
salt
¼ teaspoon pepper
4 small whole chicken breasts
   (about 3 pounds), split,
   skinned and boned
1½ tablespoons salad oil
1 cup orange juice
2 tablespoons brown sugar
2 tablespoons vinegar
¼ teaspoon nutmeg
1 teaspoon basil
8 new potatoes, pared
1 16-ounce can freestone peach
   halves, drained
chopped parsley for garnish

About 1 hour and 10 minutes before serving: Mix flour, 1 teaspoon salt and pepper; dip chicken breasts in mixture; shake off excess. In large skillet or Dutch oven over medium heat, in oil, brown chicken breasts a few at a time on both sides. Return to skillet; add orange juice, brown sugar, vinegar, 1 teaspoon salt, nutmeg, basil and potatoes; cover; simmer 40 minutes, or until potatoes are tender. Add drained peach halves; heat to boiling. Sprinkle with parsley. Makes 8 servings.

**Diabetic diet:** Prepare as directed but omit sugar; use dietetic-packed canned peaches. Exchanges per serving = 3 meat, 1 bread and 1 fruit.
**Egg-, gluten-, milk- and wheat-free diet:** Prepare as directed but sprinkle chicken with cornstarch instead of flour for gluten- and wheat-free diets.
**Low-fat, low-cholesterol diet:** 5 grams fat per serving.
**Low-sodium diet:** Prepare as directed but omit salt. 75 milligrams sodium per serving.

## SPEEDY CHICKEN CREOLE (305 calories per serving)

3 large whole chicken breasts
   (about 2½ pounds), split,
   skinned and boned
2 tablespoons butter or margarine
2 teaspoons salt
1 medium onion, minced
1 cup sliced celery
1 10-ounce package frozen
   whole okra, thawed, sliced
1 16-ounce can tomatoes
1 8-ounce can tomato sauce
1 teaspoon ground thyme
1 teaspoon parsley flakes
¼ teaspoon Tabasco
6 slices toast

About 45 minutes before serving: Cut each chicken breast half into 10 or 12 strips. In large skillet over medium heat, in butter, brown chicken and salt, stirring constantly, 3 minutes. Add onion, celery and okra; cook 2 minutes, stirring. Add tomatoes, tomato sauce, thyme, parsley and Tabasco; stir; bring to boiling; cover; cook 5 minutes. Serve over toast slices. Makes 6 servings.

**Diabetic diet:** Carefully divide into 6 equal servings. Exchanges per serving — 4 meat, 1 "B" vegetable, 1 bread.
**Egg-, gluten-, milk- and wheat-free diet:** Prepare as directed but use milk-free margarine on milk-free diets. Serve over cooked rice instead of toast for gluten- and wheat-free diets.
**Low-fat, low-cholesterol diet:** Prepare as directed but use salad oil or margarine instead of butter. 10 grams fat per serving.
**High-iron diet:** 3.5 milligrams iron per serving.

## CHICKEN SALAD IN PINEAPPLE (305 calories per serving)

2 medium pineapples
3 cups cut-up cooked chicken
1 cup diced celery
½ to ¾ cup low-calorie Italian
   dressing
¼ cup salted peanuts
2 tablespoons slivered crystallized ginger

Early in day: Halve each pineapple lengthwise through green crown. With long sharp knife, cut around each half pineapple, ½ inch in from edge, to free meat; do not cut through rind. Cut pineapple meat crosswise into slices about ¾-inch thick; then run knife under meat down full length of center; lift out chunks; cut off core.

Toss together chicken, celery, low-calorie Italian dressing, half the peanuts and half the slivered ginger. Spoon a little into each pineapple shell; then arrange pineapple chunks, broad-side up, around sides of each. Place rest of chunks in center. Top with rest of chicken salad, peanuts and ginger. refrigerate. Makes 4 servings.

**Low-fat, low-cholesterol diet:** 15 grams fat per serving.

## PLYMOUTH CHICKEN SPECIAL (270 calories per serving)

2 cups uncooked egg noodles
1 tablespoon salad oil
½ pound fresh mushrooms,
   thinly sliced
2 tablespoons flour
½ teaspoon salt
½ teaspoon monosodium glutamate (optional)
½ teaspoon celery salt
1½ cups skimmed milk or reliquefied nonfat dry milk
2 cups cubed cooked chicken
   or turkey (about 10 ounces)
2 slices day-old bread, cubed

About 40 minutes before serving: Preheat oven to 375°F. Cook noodles as label directs; drain. Meanwhile, in large saucepan over medium heat, in oil, sauté mushrooms until golden. Stir in flour, salt, monosodium glutamate and celery salt. Slowly add milk; cook, stirring constantly, until thickened and smooth. Stir in chicken; heat to boiling. In 2-quart casserole, mix noodles and mushroom-chicken mixture. Top with bread cubes. Bake 15 minutes, or until cubes are golden brown. Makes 6 servings of about 1 cup each.

**Bland diet:** Prepare as directed but omit celery salt if forbidden; ½ teaspoon ground thyme may be substituted.
**Diabetic diet:** Exchanges per serving = 3 meat and 2 bread.
**Low-fat, low-cholesterol diet:** 5 grams fat per serving.
**Low-fat, bland (gall bladder) diet:** Prepare as directed for bland diet.
**Low-residue diet:** Prepare as directed for bland diet.
**Low-sodium diet:** Prepare as directed but cook noodles and chicken without adding salt; omit salt and monosodium glutamate; substitute celery seed for celery salt. 110 milligrams sodium per serving. If prepared with low-sodium bread, 75 milligrams sodium per serving.

## DEVILED CHICKEN (295 calories per serving)

2 whole chicken breasts (about 1½ pounds), split and skinned
2 tablespoons salad oil
2 teaspoons Worcestershire
1 teaspoon dry mustard
1 tablespoon parsley flakes
1 teaspoon salt
¼ teaspoon pepper
2 cups fresh bread crumbs

About 1 hour before serving: Preheat oven to 350°F. In medium baking dish, place chicken, skin side down. In medium bowl, mix remaining ingredients. Spread evenly over surface of chicken. Cover; bake 30 minutes; uncover and bake 15 minutes more, or until chicken is tender and bread crumbs are crisp. Makes 4 servings.

**Diabetic diet:** Exchanges per serving = 4 meat and 1 bread.
**Low-fat, low-cholesterol diet:** 5 grams fat per serving.

## BAKED CHICKEN WITH PEACHES (260 calories per serving)

1 3-pound broiler-fryer, cut up
1 tablespoon flour
1 teaspoon salt
1 tablespoon butter or margarine
1 16-ounce can cling-peach halves
½ teaspoon cinnamon
½ teaspoon nutmeg
chopped parsley for garnish

About 1 hour before serving: Preheat oven to 400°F. Place chicken in shallow open roasting pan. Combine flour and salt; use to sprinkle chicken; dot chicken with butter. Bake, uncovered, 30 minutes. Place drained peach halves around chicken (reserve ½ cup peach syrup); sprinkle with combined cinnamon and nutmeg; spoon on reserved syrup. Bake 20 minutes longer, or until chicken is fork-tender. Arrange on platter; pour pan juices over all; sprinkle with parsley. Makes 6 servings.

**Bland diet:** Prepare as directed but omit nutmeg and parsley.
**Egg-, gluten-, milk- and wheat-free diet:** Prepare as directed but use cornstarch instead of flour on gluten- and wheat-free diets; use milk-free margarine on milk-free diet.
**Diabetic diet:** Prepare as directed but use water-packed peaches. Include 2 peach halves with each serving. Exchanges per serving = 1 fruit plus 1 meat for each ounce of cooked chicken.
**Low-fat, low-cholesterol diet:** Prepare as directed but use salad oil or margarine instead of butter; dieter should not eat skin of chicken. 10 grams fat per serving.
**Low-fat, bland (gall bladder) diet:** Prepare as directed but omit nutmeg and parsley.
**High-iron diet:** 3 milligrams iron per serving.
**Low-residue diet:** Prepare as directed but omit nutmeg and parsley.
**Low-sodium diet:** Prepare as directed but omit salt and use unsalted butter or margarine. 90 milligrams sodium per serving.

## CHICKEN-VEGETABLE MEDLEY (260 calories per serving)

2 tablespoons salad oil
½ cup thinly sliced onion
½ cup thinly sliced celery
1 4-ounce can sliced mushrooms, drained
1 5-ounce can water chestnuts, sliced
¼ teaspoon salt
1½ cups cooked or canned chicken, in chunks
½ cup chicken broth
1 teaspoon cornstarch
soy sauce
1 16-ounce can bean sprouts, drained
3 cups hot fluffy rice
¼ cup toasted almonds

About 30 minutes before serving: In large skillet over medium heat, in oil, sauté onion, celery, mushroom and water chestnut slices 5 minutes. Add salt, chicken and broth; simmer, covered, 10 minutes.

Meanwhile, combine cornstarch with 1 teaspoon soy sauce and 2 tablespoons cold water; stir into chicken. Bring to boiling; add drained bean sprouts; then stir until thickened and bean sprouts are hot. Serve on rice, sprinkled with almonds. Pass soy sauce. Makes 6 servings.

**Diabetic diet:** Carefully divide chicken mixture into 6 equal servings, and serve each over ½ cup rice. Exchanges per serving = 3 meat, 1 bread and 1 "A" and 1 "B" vegetable.
**Low-fat, low-cholesterol diet:** 10 grams fat per serving.
**High-iron diet:** 3.5 milligrams iron per serving.

## CHICKEN IN WINE (Coq au Vin) (310 calories per serving)

2 strips bacon, cut into ½-inch slices
2 small broiler-fryers (about 2 pounds each), quartered
1 tablespoon salad oil
1 pound mushrooms
1 pound small white onions
3 carrots, cut into 1-inch slices
2 garlic cloves, minced
2 medium onions, chopped
¼ cup chopped parsley
salt
1½ teaspoons marjoram leaves
1 teaspoon thyme leaves
1 bay leaf
pepper
2 beef-bouillon cubes
1½ cups dry red wine (preferably Burgundy)
⅓ cup flour

Day before serving: In large Dutch oven, fry bacon until almost crisp, remove bacon. In bacon fat, brown a few chicken pieces at a time until golden. In same Dutch oven over medium heat, in oil, sauté mushrooms, white onions and carrots until onions brown lightly; remove all. Sauté garlic and chopped onions in remaining fat until golden.

Return chicken pieces to Dutch oven and cover with vegetables. Add parsley, 2 tablespoons salt, marjoram, thyme, bay leaf, ⅛ teaspoon pepper, bouillon cubes, wine and 1½ cups water. Cover; boil gently 20 minutes. Cool slightly; refrigerate, covered.

About 1 hour and 10 minutes before serving: Heat chicken mixture to boiling; then simmer, covered, 40 minutes, or until chicken is tender. Mix enough water with flour to form a smooth paste. Remove chicken to warm platter. Add flour paste to stock, stirring constantly; simmer until thickened. Add salt and pepper to taste. Remove vegetables from gravy and arrange around chicken. Spoon on some gravy; pass remaining gravy. Makes 8 servings.

**Egg-, gluten-, milk- and wheat-free diet:** Prepare as directed but omit bouillon cubes; thicken gravy with 2 tablespoons cornstarch (not flour) for gluten- and wheat-free diets.
**Low-fat, low-cholesterol diet:** Prepare as directed but omit bacon; add an extra 2 tablespoons salad oil. Dieter should not eat skin of chicken. 10 grams fat per serving.
**High-iron diet:** 4 milligrams iron per serving.

## BEAN-AND-CHICKEN SALAD (210 calories per serving)

2 whole chicken breasts (about 1½ pounds), split, skinned and boned
2 16-ounce cans whole green beans, chilled and drained
½ teaspoon seasoned salt
¼ teaspoon seasoned pepper
½ cup bottled low-calorie Italian dressing
chopped dill
1 apple, cut into thin wedges for garnish
lemon juice for garnish

Early in day: Cook chicken in salted boiling water until tender —about 20 minutes; drain; refrigerate.

About 1½ hours before serving: Cut chicken into thin strips. In large salad bowl, toss with green beans, seasoned salt, seasoned pepper, low-calorie dressing and 1 teaspoon dill. Toss apple wedges with lemon juice and use to garnish salad. Sprinkle with another teaspoon dill. Refrigerate until serving time. Makes 4 servings.

**Diabetic diet:** Carefully divide into 4 equal servings. Exchanges per serving = 3 meat and 1 bread.
**Low-fat, low-cholesterol diet:** 5 grams fat per serving.
**High-iron diet:** 4 milligrams iron per serving.

## CHICKEN JAMBALAYA (310 calories per serving)

1 6-ounce package Spanish-rice mix
½-pound slice boiled ham, trimmed of fat, cubed
1 tablespoon salad oil
1 cup chopped celery
1 cup coarsely chopped green pepper
¼ cup chopped scallions
1 cup cubed cooked chicken
dash pepper
1 cup canned tomatoes, drained

About 1 hour before serving: In large skillet, cook Spanish-rice mix as label directs but omit butter. Stir in ham. In skillet over medium heat, in oil, sauté celery and green peppers until tender. Add scallions and sauté a few minutes longer. Add to rice mixture with chicken, pepper and tomatoes; heat to boiling. Makes 5 servings.

**Diabetic diet:** Carefully divide into 5 equal servings (about 1 cup each). Exchanges per serving = 3 meat, 1 "A" vegetable and 2 bread.
**Low-fat, low-cholesterol diet:** 10 grams fat per serving.
**High-iron diet:** 3.5 milligrams iron per serving.

## CHICKEN AND TOMATOES (255 calories per serving)

2 whole chicken breasts (about 1½ pounds), split, skinned and boned
1 tablespoon sherry (optional)
2 tablespoons soy sauce
2 tablespoons cornstarch
2 tablespoons salad oil
1 medium onion, diced
1 teaspoon salt
1 teaspoon granulated sugar
¾ cup chicken broth
1 16-ounce can stewed tomatoes

About 30 minutes before serving: Cut chicken into 1-inch cubes. In medium bowl, blend sherry and 1 tablespoon soy sauce with 1 tablespoon cornstarch. Toss with chicken; let stand 15 minutes.

In medium skillet over medium heat, in oil, brown chicken, stirring occasionally; add onion and cook 2 minutes more. In bowl, mix remaining soy sauce and cornstarch, salt, sugar and broth; pour over chicken and cook, stirring, until mixture thickens. Add tomatoes; simmer 2 minutes to heat through. Makes 4 servings.

**Diabetic diet:** Prepare as directed but omit sugar. Exchanges per serving = 3 meat and 1 "A" and 1 "B" vegetable.
**Low-fat, low-cholesterol diet:** 10 grams fat per serving.

## CHICKEN IN MUSTARD SAUCE (Pollo en Salsa de Mostaza)
(205 calories per serving)

¼ cup flour
½ teaspoon salt
¼ teaspoon garlic salt
¼ teaspoon onion salt
2 whole chicken breasts (about 1½ pounds), split, skinned and boned
2 tablespoons butter or margarine
1 chicken-bouillon cube
½ tablespoon lemon juice
¾ teaspoon dry mustard
1 teaspoon granulated sugar
1½ teaspoons cornstarch

About 45 minutes before serving: Mix flour, salt, garlic salt and onion salt. Use to coat chicken, shaking off excess. In large skillet over medium heat, in butter or margarine, brown chicken until golden—about 5 minutes to a side. Add bouillon cube and ¾ cup water; cover; simmer 20 minutes. Meanwhile, mix remaining ingredients with 1 tablespoon water to form a smooth paste. Remove chicken to warm platter; stir lemon-cornstarch mixture into chicken broth; stirring constantly, cook until thickened and smooth. Pour gravy over chicken. Makes 4 servings.

**Diabetic diet:** Prepare as directed but omit sugar; do not serve extra gravy with chicken. Exchanges per serving = 3 meat.
**Egg-, gluten-, milk- and wheat-free diet:** Prepare as directed but coat chicken with cornstarch instead of flour and omit bouillon cube on gluten- and wheat-free diets; use milk-free margarine on milk-free diet.
**Low-fat, low-cholesterol diet:** Prepare as directed but use margarine or salad oil instead of butter. 10 grams fat per serving.
**Low-sodium diet:** Prepare as directed but omit salt; use garlic powder and onion powder (not the salts); use unsalted butter or margarine; omit bouillon cube. 70 milligrams sodium per serving.

## CHICKEN WITH VEGETABLES (170 calories per serving)

4 large whole chicken breasts (about 3 pounds), split, skinned and boned
paprika
salt and pepper
2 tablespoons butter or margarine
3 medium yellow summer squash or zucchini, sliced diagonally ⅛-inch thick
5 scallions, tops and all, finely sliced
½ teaspoon basil

About 30 minutes before serving: Sprinkle chicken with paprika, ¾ teaspoon salt and ⅛ teaspoon pepper. In large skillet over medium heat, in butter, brown chicken until golden on both sides; add ½ cup water and simmer, covered, 15 minutes. Now another ½ cup water, squash, scallions, ¾ teaspoon salt, ⅛ teaspoon pepper, and basil. Cover; cook 10 minutes, or until vegetables are tender. Makes 8 servings.

**Diabetic diet:** Exchanges per serving = 3 meat and 1 "A" vegetable.
**Egg-, gluten-, milk- and wheat-free diet:** Prepare as directed but use milk-free margarine for milk-free diet.
**Low-fat, low-cholesterol diet:** Prepare as directed but use margarine or salad oil instead of butter. 5 grams fat per serving.
**Low-sodium diet:** Prepare as directed but omit salt and use unsalted butter or margarine. 70 milligrams sodium per serving.

## CHICKEN IN ASPIC (195 calories per serving)

3 whole chicken breasts (about
2½ pounds) cut in half
½ teaspoon seasoned salt
¼ teaspoon seasoned pepper
1½ teaspoons unflavored
gelatin
1½ tablespoons water
2 10½-ounce cans condensed
beef consommé
2 heads romaine
fresh dill sprigs
your favorite low-calorie salad
dressing

Day before or early in day: Preheat broiler 10 minutes if manufacturer directs. Place chicken in jelly-roll pan, skin side down. Sprinkle with seasoned salt and seasoned pepper. Broil until golden-brown—about 18 minutes; then turn and broil until second side is golden-brown. Cool, then place, skin side down, in medium baking dish. In cup, mix gelatin with water; set in hot water and stir until dissolved. Stir into undiluted consommé, then pour over chicken. Refrigerate until consommé is partially set. Turn chicken over; spoon consommé over it; refrigerate until consommé sets a bit more, then continue spooning consommé over chicken; allow it to set until chicken is coated.

To serve: Arrange chicken breasts on platter, spoke fashion. Remove outer leaves of romaine; cut head into sixths; arrange between chicken breasts; top with dill. Pass salad dressing to spoon over romaine. Makes 6 servings.

**Diabetic diet:** Exchanges per serving = 4 meat and 1 "A" vegetable.
**Low-fat, low-cholesterol diet:** Prepare as directed but remove skin from cooked chicken before glazing with aspic. 2 grams fat per serving.
**High-iron diet:** 3 milligrams iron per serving.

## HERBED CHICKEN IN WINE (245 calories per serving)

1 3-pound broiler-fryer, cut up
¼ cup flour
2 teaspoons salt
¼ teaspoon pepper
2 tablespoons salad oil
1 cup dry white wine
1 cup sliced mushrooms (about
¼ pound)
1 teaspoon tarragon
1 teaspoon thyme leaves
1 teaspoon chopped chives
(optional)

About 45 minutes before serving: Skin and trim fat from chicken. In plastic or paper bag, combine flour, salt and pepper; shake a few pieces of chicken at a time in flour mixture until coated. In large skillet over medium heat, in hot oil, brown chicken on all sides—about 15 minutes. Reduce heat to low; add wine, mushrooms, tarragon, thyme and chives; cover and simmer 20 minutes, or until chicken is fork-tender. Makes 6 servings.

**Egg-, gluten-, milk- and wheat-free diet:** Prepare as directed but use cornstarch instead of flour on gluten- and wheat-free diets.
**Low-fat, low-cholesterol diet:** Prepare as directed. 10 grams fat per serving.
**Low-sodium diet:** Prepare as directed but omit salt. 105 milligrams sodium per serving.

## CHICKEN LIVERS IN WINE (315 calories per serving on toast)

½ pound chicken livers (or
frozen livers, thawed)
1 tablespoon salad oil
¼ cup thinly sliced celery
½ teaspoon parsley flakes
½ teaspoon dried minced
chives
2 whole cloves
¾ cup dry sherry
1 red-skinned cooking apple,
chopped
1 teaspoon flour
salt
toast points prepared from 2
slices bread

About 20 minutes before serving: Remove connective tissue or fat from livers. In medium skillet over medium heat, in oil, sauté livers, celery, parsley and chives; remove from pan; add cloves, sherry and apples; simmer, covered, 5 minutes, or until apples are almost tender. Make paste of flour and a few drops of water; stir into apple mixture; simmer until thickened; return livers to pan; heat; add salt to taste. Serve on toast points. Makes 2 servings.

**Diabetic diet:** Exchanges per serving = 3 meat, 1 "B" vegetable and 1 bread.
**Egg-, gluten-, milk- and wheat-free diet:** Prepare as directed but use cornstarch in place of flour; serve livers over rice (not toast points) for gluten- and wheat-free diets.
**High-iron diet:** 9.5 milligrams iron per serving.
**Low-sodium diet:** Prepare as directed but omit salt. 195 milligrams sodium per serving. If served with low-sodium bread, 75 milligrams sodium per serving.

## CHICKEN KABOBS ITALIANO (240 calories per serving)

2 whole chicken breasts (about 1½ pounds), split, skinned and boned
1 cup low-calorie Italian dressing
2 green peppers, cut into 1-inch slices
8 fresh medium mushrooms
8 small white onions, sliced
4 fresh medium tomatoes, quartered

About 4 hours before serving: Cut chicken into 1-inch pieces. Marinate in low-calorie Italian dressing, in refrigerator, at least 3½ hours.

About 30 minutes before serving: Preheat broiler 10 minutes if manufacturer directs. In water to cover, boil green peppers, mushrooms and onions 5 minutes. Line large baking or jelly-roll pan with foil; turn up edges to prevent spilling.

On eight 8-inch skewers, alternate chicken with tomatoes, green peppers, onions and mushrooms. Brush with remaining low-calorie Italian dressing. Place skewers, not touching, on lined baking pan. Place under broiler with skewers 3 to 5 inches from heat; broil 7 minutes; turn; brush again with dressing. Broil 7 minutes on other side, or until chicken is done but still tender. Makes 4 servings.

**Diabetic diet:** Exchanges per serving = 4 meat and 1 "A" and 1 "B" vegetable.
**Low-fat, low-cholesterol diet:** 5 grams fat per serving.
**High-iron diet:** 3 milligrams iron per serving.
**Low-sodium diet:** Prepare as directed but marinate chicken in homemade low-sodium dressing (such as ⅓ cup vinegar, ⅔ cup salad oil, ⅛ teaspoon paprika, ¼ teaspoon dry mustard, ⅛ teaspoon black pepper and 1 teaspoon minced onion). 90 milligrams sodium per serving.

## CHICKEN LIVER SAUTÉ WITH ONION-CURRY SAUCE (235 calories per serving)

2 tablespoons butter or margarine
1 pound fresh chicken livers or frozen livers, thawed
1 medium onion, thinly sliced
⅓ cup nonfat dry-milk powder
1 tablespoon flour
¼ teaspoon curry
½ teaspoon salt
dash pepper

About 25 minutes before serving: In skillet over low heat, in butter or margarine, cook livers about 5 minutes, turning often. Remove. In same skillet, cook onion slices with ½ cup boiling water, uncovered, 10 minutes, or until onions are tender. Stir together dry-milk powder, ½ cup water, and remaining ingredients. Gradually stir into onion mixture; cook, stirring constantly, until thickened. Serve over chicken livers. Makes 4 servings.

**Diabetic diet:** Exchanges per serving = 3 meat and 1 "B" vegetable.
**Low-fat diet:** 10 grams fat per serving. Omit recipe from low-cholesterol diet.
**High-iron diet:** 9 milligrams iron per serving.
**Low-sodium diet:** Prepare as directed but use unsalted butter or margarine; use curry not containing salt; omit salt. 115 milligrams sodium per serving.

## JULES' CHICKEN LIVERS (210 calories per serving)

1 pound fresh chicken livers (or 1 pound frozen chicken livers, thawed)
2 tablespoons salad oil
1 teaspoon flour
2 tablespoons to ⅓ cup wine vinegar
garlic and onion salt to taste

About 20 minutes before serving: Wash chicken livers and cut away any fat or filament; dry livers on paper toweling. In medium skillet over medium heat, in oil, brown about 2 minutes on each side, or until almost to desired degree of doneness. Stir in flour; add vinegar. Stirring constantly, simmer 2 minutes; then add garlic and onion salt to taste. Makes 4 servings.

**Diabetic diet:** Exchanges per serving = 3 meat.
**Egg-, gluten-, milk- and wheat-free diet:** Prepare as directed but use cornstarch in place of flour on gluten- and wheat-free diets.
**High-iron diet:** 9 milligrams iron per serving.
**Low-sodium diet:** Prepare as directed but use garlic and onion powder in place of the salts. 80 milligrams sodium per serving.

## BAKED CHICKEN DINNER (220 calories per serving)

8 celery stalks
8 large carrots
¾ pound small white onions
   (about 12)
4 chicken breasts, halved
   (about 3 pounds)
¼ cup chopped parsley
2 10½-ounce cans condensed
   cream of mushroom soup
paprika

About 1 hour and 45 minutes before serving: Preheat oven to 350°F. Cut celery and carrots into chunks. In covered medium saucepan over medium heat, in 1 cup boiling salted water, cook celery, carrots and onions 15 minutes; drain.

Remove skin from chicken breasts; place chicken in large baking dish; sprinkle with parsley. Arrange vegetables around chicken.

In small bowl, stir undiluted soup until smooth; pour evenly over chicken and vegetables. Sprinkle generously with paprika. Cover, and bake 1 hour or until chicken and vegetables are fork-tender. Makes 8 servings.

To do ahead: Early in day, prepare recipe as above but, instead of baking it, cover and refrigerate. About 1 hour and 15 minutes before serving, bake in preheated 350°F. oven until fork-tender.

**Bland diet:** Prepare as directed but omit celery and onions.
**Low-fat diet:** 10 grams fat per serving. Omit recipe from low-cholesterol diet.
**Low-residue diet:** Prepare as directed but omit celery and onions.

## ORANGE BAKED CHICKEN (255 calories per serving)

5 whole chicken breasts (about
   4 pounds), skinned and split
¼ cup minced onion
½ teaspoon paprika
1 teaspoon salt
¼ teaspoon rosemary
⅛ teaspoon pepper
2 tablespoons flour
2 cups orange juice
1 8-ounce package noodles

About 1 hour and 15 minutes before serving: Preheat oven to 350°F. Spread chicken breasts in large shallow baking pan, not overlapping. Sprinkle with onion and seasonings. In medium bowl, blend flour with about ½ cup orange juice to form a smooth paste; stir in remaining juice; pour over chicken. Bake, uncovered, 1 hour or until tender, basting occasionally with juice in pan. Meanwhile, cook noodles as label directs; drain. Serve chicken and gravy over noodles. Makes 10 servings.

**Bland diet:** Prepare as directed but omit onion, rosemary and pepper.
**Low-fat, low-cholesterol diet:** 5 grams fat per serving.
**Low-fat, bland (gall bladder) diet:** Prepare as directed for bland diet.
**Low-residue diet:** Prepare as directed for bland diet.

## TURKEY ORIENTALE (255 calories per serving)

1 tablespoon butter or margarine
1 medium onion, sliced
1 green pepper, sliced
2 stalks celery, sliced
1 3-ounce can sliced mushrooms
1 16-ounce can bean sprouts
1 5¼-ounce can bamboo
   shoots, drained
1½ cups leftover roast turkey,
   cut into strips
5 teaspoons soy sauce
2 tablespoons cornstarch

About 25 minutes before serving: In large skillet, in butter or margarine, sauté onion, green pepper and celery until tender. Add mushrooms and bean sprouts with their liquids, bamboo shoots and turkey. Cook, covered, over low heat, 15 minutes. Gradually stir ⅓ cup water and soy sauce into cornstarch. Stir into turkey-vegetable mixture; cook, stirring, until thickened. Makes 3 servings.

**Low-fat, low-cholesterol diet:** Prepare as directed but use margarine or salad oil instead of butter. 10 grams fat per serving.

## HAM-AND-CHICKEN CROWN (220 calories per serving)

1 envelope unflavored gelatin
1 10½-ounce can condensed
  cream-of-celery soup
1 tablespoon lemon juice
dash pepper
1 cup diced cooked or canned
  chicken or turkey
2 tablespoons chopped onion
3 slices (3 ounces) boiled ham
8 stuffed olives, sliced
lettuce

Early in day: In double boiler, sprinkle gelatin onto ½ cup cold water; let stand 5 minutes; cook over hot water until gelatin is dissolved. Combine soup, ¼ cup water, lemon juice and pepper; add to gelatin; stir in chicken and onion. Trim fat from ham; use to line sides of three 12-ounce custard cups; cover bottoms with sliced olives. Fill with chicken mixture. Refrigerate until firm.

To serve: Unmold on crisp lettuce. Makes 3 servings.

**Diabetic diet:** Exchanges per serving = 3 meat and 1 "A" and 1 "B" vegetable.
**Low-fat diet:** 10 grams fat per serving. Omit recipe from low-cholesterol diet.

## SAVORY CHICKEN BAKE (255 calories per serving)

1 10-ounce package frozen
  broccoli spears
¼ cup skimmed milk or re-
  liquefied nonfat dry milk
2 cups cubed cooked or canned
  chicken
1 10¾-ounce can condensed
  cream-of-chicken soup
⅛ teaspoon savory
¼ cup grated Cheddar cheese

About 45 minutes before serving: Preheat oven to 350°F. Cook broccoli as label directs; drain. Combine milk, chicken, soup and savory. In each of four 2-cup casseroles, place layer of broccoli; cover with chicken mixture; top with remaining broccoli; sprinkle with cheese. Bake, covered, 20 minutes, or until bubbling. Makes 4 servings.

**Diabetic diet:** Exchanges per serving = 4 meat, 1 "A" vegetable and ½ skim milk.
**Low-fat diet:** 10 grams fat per serving. Omit recipe from low-cholesterol diet.

## CHOPPED CHICKEN LIVERS (130 calories per serving)

½ pound fresh chicken livers
  (or frozen chicken livers,
  thawed)
1 medium onion, finely
  chopped
1 tablespoon rendered chicken
  or bacon fat
1 hard-cooked egg
¼ cup chopped parsley
½ teaspoon salt
½ teaspoon lemon juice

At least 3 hours before serving: Wash and remove any fat from livers. In medium skillet, in rendered chicken or bacon fat, sauté onion until well browned. (Take care not to burn fat.) Add chicken livers and brown 3 to 5 minutes.

In electric-blender container, at low speed, blend livers with fat, cooked onion and remaining ingredients until smooth. (Add small amount of water if needed.) Transfer to small container; cover; refrigerate until serving time. Makes filling for four sandwiches or serve on lettuce as appetizer.

**Diabetic diet:** Exchanges per serving = 2 meat.
**Gluten-, milk- and wheat-free diet:** Prepare as directed; serve as appetizer.
**High-iron diet:** 5 milligrams iron per serving.
**Low-sodium diet:** Prepare as directed but cook livers in chicken fat and omit salt. 60 milligrams sodium per serving.

## FRUITED TURKEY SALAD (245 calories per serving)

2 cups cubed cooked turkey or
  chicken
½ cup chopped celery
½ cup drained canned mandarin-orange sections
½ cup halved seedless grapes
½ teaspoon salt
¼ cup low-calorie (imitation)
  mayonnaise
3 lettuce cups

At least 2 hours before serving: Toss together all ingredients but lettuce. Refrigerate to allow flavors to blend. Serve in lettuce cups. Makes 3 servings.

**Low-fat, low-cholesterol diet:** 5 grams fat per serving.

## ROAST TURKEY-ROLL PLATTER (70 calories for each thin slice turkey; 170 calories per Stuffing Ball; 20 calories per ¼ cup gravy)

1 4-pound frozen turkey roll
1 teaspoon seasoned salt
6 strips bacon
½ cup chopped onion
1 cup chopped celery
1 cup chopped fresh
  mushrooms
1 8-ounce package herb-
  seasoned stuffing mix
1 cup canned chicken broth,
  heated
2 tablespoons flour
parsley for garnish

2 days before serving: Thaw turkey roll by storing in refrigerator for 1½ to 2 days.

About 3 hours before serving: Remove wrapping from thawed turkey roll. Preheat oven to 375°F. Place turkey roll on rack in shallow roasting pan; sprinkle with seasoned salt; cover with foil; then insert roast-meat thermometer into center. Roast 1½ hours. Open foil and pour off drippings, reserving 6 tablespoons. Arrange bacon strips on roll; cover again with foil; roast 30 minutes longer. Uncover; roast until meat thermometer reads 175°F.—about 35 minutes per pound.

Meanwhile, prepare Stuffing Balls. In medium skillet over medium heat, in ¼ cup turkey drippings, sauté onion, celery and mushrooms till tender. In medium bowl, mix stuffing mix with chicken broth and onion mixture until moist. Form into 8 balls; arrange on greased cookie sheet.

About 15 minutes before turkey is done, spoon 1 teaspoon drippings over each stuffing ball. Bake balls, with turkey, for 15 minutes; then remove turkey to hot platter and bake balls 10 minutes longer.

Meanwhile, prepare gravy as follows: In roasting pan, mix 1 tablespoon drippings and flour, scraping up brown bits from bottom of pan. Slowly stir in 2 cups water and cook, stirring constantly, until thickened.

To serve: Carve turkey into thin slices; surround with stuffing balls; garnish with parsley. Pass gravy in gravy boat. Makes 8 servings.

**Diabetic diet:** Exchanges per stuffing ball = 1 "B" vegetable, 1 bread and 1 fat. Count turkey as 1 meat exchange for each ounce. Up to ¼ cup gravy = 1 "free" exchange.

## BRAISED CHICKEN LIVERS (265 calories per serving)

1 pound fresh chicken livers
  (or frozen livers, thawed)
¼ cup flour
½ teaspoon salt
1 tablespoon salad oil
⅔ to 1 cup canned tomato
  juice
4 slices toast, quartered

About 30 minutes before serving: Remove any fat from livers. Toss livers with flour, mixed with salt, just to coat; shake off excess. In medium skillet over medium heat, in oil, brown livers well on both sides. Add tomato juice; cover; boil gently 10 minutes, or until livers are done and tomato sauce has thickened slightly.

To serve: Top toast points with livers and sauce. Makes 4 servings.

**Bland diet:** Prepare as directed.
**Diabetic diet:** Exchanges per serving = 3 meat and 1 bread.
**Egg-, gluten-, milk- and wheat-free diet:** Prepare as directed but dust livers with cornstarch (not flour); serve over rice (not toast) for gluten- and wheat-free diets.
**Low-fat, bland (gall bladder) diet:** Prepare as directed.
**High-iron diet:** 10 milligrams iron per serving.
**Low-residue diet:** Prepare as directed.
**Low-sodium diet:** Prepare as directed but omit salt and use water instead of tomato juice. 195 milligrams sodium per serving. If served on low-sodium bread, 80 milligrams sodium per serving.

## EASYGOING DINNER PLATTER (325 calories per serving)

**1 10-ounce package frozen peas**
**1 tablespoon granulated sugar**
**butter or margarine**
**6 carrots, sliced**
**1 teaspoon seasoned salt**
**seasoned pepper**
**1 9-ounce package frozen whole green beans**
**dash nutmeg**
**2 summer squash, thinly sliced**
**3 small tomatoes**
**½ cup low-calorie (imitation) mayonnaise**
**1 teaspoon prepared mustard**
**18 slices cold roast turkey or sliced turkey roll (about 1¼ pounds)**
**parsley sprigs for garnish**

About 35 minutes before dinner: Cook peas as label directs, adding sugar; drain, then add 1 teaspoon butter or margarine; keep warm. Cook sliced carrots in 1 inch boiling water, covered, until fork-tender; drain; add seasoned salt, a dash of seasoned pepper and 1 teaspoon butter or margarine; keep warm.

Cook whole green beans as label directs; drain; add nutmeg with 1 teaspoon butter or margarine; keep warm. Cook sliced summer squash in 1 inch boiling salted water, covered, until fork-tender; drain, then add dash of seasoned pepper and 1 teaspoon butter or margarine; keep warm.

Cut slice from top of each tomato; hollow out; fill with low-calorie mayonnaise mixed with mustard (to spoon onto sliced turkey later). Arrange tomatoes in center of round platter. Then arrange turkey slices in 4 overlapping rows with hot vegetables in between the slices. Tuck parsley sprigs around tomatoes. Makes 6 servings.

**Low-fat, low-cholesterol diet:** Prepare as directed but use margarine instead of butter. 10 grams fat per serving.
**High-iron diet:** 3.5 milligrams iron per serving.

## QUICK CHICKEN LIVERS (265 calories per serving)

**1 tablespoon butter or margarine**
**2 large onions, thinly sliced**
**2 large stalks green celery, thinly sliced**
**1 pound fresh chicken livers (or frozen livers, thawed)**
**salt, pepper and garlic salt to taste**

About 15 minutes before serving: In large skillet over medium heat, in butter or margarine, sauté onion and celery slices until onion is just wilted. Push onions to one side; turn up heat to high. Add chicken livers; top with onions; cook, turning livers once or twice, until done as you like them—3 to 5 minutes. Season to taste with salt, pepper and garlic salt. Makes 3 servings.

**Diabetic diet:** Exchanges per serving = 4 meat and 1 "B" vegetable.
**Egg-, gluten-, milk- and wheat-free diet:** Prepare as directed but use milk-free margarine for milk-free diet.
**Low-fat diet:** 10 grams fat per serving. Omit recipe from low-cholesterol diet.
**High-iron diet:** 12.5 milligrams iron per serving.
**Low-sodium diet:** Prepare as directed but use unsalted butter or margarine; omit salt; use garlic powder (not garlic salt). 135 milligrams sodium per serving.

## BURGER POT-AU-FEU (305 calories per serving)

6 carrots, halved lengthwise
2 quarts (8 cups) hot water
6 chicken-bouillon cubes
2 medium leeks, halved lengthwise
1 pound ground round steak
½ cup seasoned dried bread
crumbs
1 teaspoon cornstarch
½ cup skimmed milk or reliquefied nonfat dry milk
1 egg
1 tablespoon salad oil
1 15½-ounce can small white
onions, drained
1 16-ounce can potatoes,
drained
2 small tomatoes, cut into
thirds crosswise
chopped parsley for garnish

About 45 minutes before serving: In covered Dutch oven, cook carrots in water with bouillon cubes for 10 minutes. Then add leeks; cover; cook 10 minutes, or until carrots are almost tender.

Meanwhile blend together meat, bread crumbs, cornstarch, milk and egg. Form mixture into 18 meatballs. In large skillet over medium heat, in oil, brown on all sides. Turn off heat; cover; keep warm. To carrots in broth add onions, potatoes and tomatoes; heat. Add meatballs; sprinkle with parsley. Makes 6 servings.

**Diabetic diet:** One serving = 2 carrot halves, 2 potatoes, 2 onions and 3 meatballs plus broth. Exchanges per serving = 2 meat, 1 "A" and 1 "B" vegetable and 1 bread.
**Low-fat, low-cholesterol diet:** Prepare as directed but use only white of egg. 10 grams fat per serving.
**High-iron diet:** 4 milligrams iron per serving.

## LEMON-BARBECUED MEAT LOAVES (325 calories per serving)

1½ pounds ground round steak
3 slices day-old bread, diced
¼ cup lemon juice
¼ cup minced onion
1 egg, slightly beaten
2 teaspoons seasoned salt
½ cup catchup
¼ cup brown sugar
1 teaspoon dry mustard
¼ teaspoon allspice
¼ teaspoon ground cloves
6 thin lemon slices

About 50 minutes before serving: Preheat oven to 350°F. In large bowl, combine meat, bread, lemon juice, onion, egg and salt. Mix well and shape into 6 individual loaves; place in greased medium (about 13" by 9") baking pan. Bake 15 minutes.

In small bowl, combine remaining ingredients except lemon slices. Use to cover loaves; top each with lemon slice; bake 30 minutes longer, basting occasionally with sauce from pan. Serve sauce over loaves. Makes 6 servings.

**Low-fat, low-cholesterol diet:** Prepare as directed but use only white of egg. 15 grams fat per serving.
**High-iron diet:** 4 milligrams iron per serving.

## FAMILY HAMBURGER (245 calories per serving)

1½ pounds ground round steak
1½ teaspoons salt
½ teaspoon pepper
¼ teaspoon garlic powder
1 teaspoon Worcestershire
2 teaspoons butter or margarine
1 onion, cut into rings

About 30 minutes before serving: Preheat broiler if manufacturer directs. In bowl, mix meat, salt, pepper, garlic powder and Worcestershire. Shape into one large patty, about 1½-inches thick. Broil about 7 minutes on each side for medium-rare, or until done as desired.

Meanwhile, in small skillet over medium heat, in butter, sauté onion rings until golden; arrange over patty on heated platter. Cut into 12 slices. Makes 6 servings.

**Diabetic diet:** Carefully divide into 6 equal servings. Exchanges per serving = 3 meat.
**Egg-, gluten-, milk- and wheat-free diet:** Prepare as directed but use milk-free margarine for milk-free diet.
**Low-fat, low-cholesterol diet:** Prepare as directed but use margarine instead of butter. 15 grams fat per serving.
**High-iron diet:** 3.5 milligrams iron per serving.
**Low-sodium diet:** Prepare as directed but omit salt and Worcestershire; use unsalted butter or margarine. 75 milligrams sodium per serving.

## SWEET-AND-SOUR MEAT LOAF (230 calories per serving)

1 pound ground round steak
1 medium onion, minced
12 individual saltine crackers,
    crushed
dash pepper
½ teaspoon salt
1 8-ounce can tomato sauce
2 egg whites
2 tablespoons vinegar
¼ teaspoon dry mustard
2 tablespoons brown sugar

About 1 hour and 10 minutes before serving: Preheat oven to 350°F. In 9-inch pie plate or baking dish, mix meat, onion, crackers, pepper, salt, ½ cup tomato sauce, and egg whites; form round loaf. Mix remaining tomato sauce, vinegar, mustard and brown sugar; pour over meat loaf; pour ⅔ cup water around edge of loaf. Bake 1 hour, or to desired doneness.

To serve: Let cool 5 minutes, then cut into serving pieces. Makes 6 servings.

**Diabetic diet:** Prepare as directed but omit sugar, and use saccharin equivalent to 1 tablespoon sugar. Exchanges per serving = 2 meat and 1 bread.
**Low-fat, low-cholesterol diet:** 10 grams fat per serving.
**High-iron diet:** Prepare as directed but use enriched saltines. 3 milligrams iron per serving.

## SURPRISE HAMBURGERS (225 calories per serving)

1¼ pounds ground round steak
1 teaspoon salt
1 teaspoon Worcestershire
½ teaspoon dry mustard
¼ teaspoon nutmeg
3 hard-cooked eggs

About 30 minutes before serving: Preheat broiler 10 minutes if manufacturer directs. Combine meat, salt, Worcestershire, mustard and nutmeg; shape into 12 patties.

Cut eggs in half lengthwise. Place one half, cut side down, on a patty; top with another patty; press firmly together. Repeat with remaining patties. Place on broiler rack. Broil 4 minutes; turn and broil 4 minutes longer, or to desired doneness. Makes 6 servings.

**Diabetic diet:** Exchanges per serving = 3 meat.
**Gluten-, milk- and wheat-free diet:** Prepare as directed.
**High-iron diet:** 4 milligrams iron per serving.

## HAMBURGER CHOP SUEY (300 calories per serving)

1 pound ground round steak
1 onion, sliced
1 cup chopped celery
1 16-ounce can bean sprouts,
    drained
1 10½-ounce can condensed
    beef broth
1 3- or 4-ounce can mushrooms
2 tablespoons cornstarch
¼ cup soy sauce
3 cups hot cooked rice

About 25 minutes before serving: In skillet, stirring constantly, cook meat with onion and celery until meat loses its red color. Add bean sprouts, beef broth and mushrooms (including liquid); cover; simmer 10 minutes. Mix cornstarch with soy sauce and stir into meat mixture; simmer 5 minutes. Serve over rice. Makes 6 servings of ¾ cup meat sauce and ½ cup rice each.

**Diabetic diet:** Exchanges per serving = 2 meat, 1 "A" vegetable and 2 bread.
**Low-fat, low-cholesterol diet:** 10 grams fat per serving.
**High-iron diet:** 3.5 milligrams iron per serving.

## HAMBURGER, SPANISH STYLE (310 calories per serving)

1 pound ground round steak
1 small onion, chopped
1 8-ounce can tomato sauce
dash Tabasco
½ teaspoon prepared mustard
dash pepper
1 8-ounce can French-style
    green beans, drained
4 slices toast

About 25 minutes before serving: In skillet over medium heat, cook meat and onion until meat loses red color. Stir in ¼ cup water, tomato sauce, Tabasco, mustard and pepper; cook, covered, 10 minutes. Add green beans and simmer 5 minutes. Serve on toast. Makes 4 servings.

**Diabetic diet:** Exchanges per serving = 3 meat, 1 "A" vegetable and 1 bread.
**Low-fat, low-cholesterol diet:** 15 grams fat per serving.
**High-iron diet:** 4.5 milligrams iron per serving.

## GREEK PARSLEY MEATBALLS (235 calories per serving)

⅓ cup packaged dried bread
   crumbs
¼ cup skimmed milk or reliquefied nonfat dry milk
1 medium onion, chopped
1 pound ground round steak
chopped parsley
1 egg
1 garlic clove, minced
¼ teaspoon oregano leaves
1 teaspoon salt
⅛ teaspoon pepper
2 tablespoons salad oil
2 tablespoons lemon juice or
   red wine vinegar

About 1 hour before serving: Let bread crumbs soak in milk until soft. In small saucepan, combine onion and ¼ cup water; cook, covered, until water has almost boiled away and onions are transparent. In medium bowl, mix meat, ½ cup parsley, egg, garlic, oregano, salt, pepper, soaked bread crumbs and cooked onion. Form into 12 meatballs.

About 30 minutes before serving: In large skillet, in oil, brown meatballs on all sides. Transfer to heated serving dish or platter. Pour lemon juice into hot skillet; scrape up and blend drippings with juice; pour over meatballs. Sprinkle with a little parsley. Makes 6 servings.

**Diabetic diet:** Exchanges per serving = 2 meat and 1 "B" vegetable.
**Low-fat, low-cholesterol diet:** Prepare as directed but use only white of egg. 15 grams fat per serving.

## POLENTA MEAT PIE (330 calories per serving)

1 tablespoon salad oil
¼ cup finely chopped onion
1 garlic clove, finely minced
1 pound ground round steak
1 cup fresh bread crumbs
1 egg
buttermilk
¼ cup catchup
salt
⅛ teaspoon pepper
½ cup yellow cornmeal
1 teaspoon granulated sugar
½ teaspoon baking soda
2 eggs, separated
¼ cup grated sharp Cheddar
   cheese

About 1 hour before serving: Preheat oven to 350°F. In medium skillet over medium heat, in oil, sauté onion and garlic until golden; remove from heat. Stir in meat, bread crumbs, egg, ¼ cup buttermilk, catchup, 1½ teaspoons salt, and pepper; mix thoroughly. Use to line bottom and sides of 10-inch pie plate. Bake 15 minutes; pour off liquid.

Meanwhile, in medium saucepan, mix 2 cups buttermilk, cornmeal, sugar, 1 teaspoon salt, and baking soda. Cook, stirring constantly, until thickened. Remove from heat; stir in egg yolks. In small bowl, beat egg whites until stiff peaks form; fold into cornmeal mixture. Use to fill meat-pie shell; top with grated cheese. Bake 30 minutes, or until cheese is lightly browned. Let cool 5 minutes before cutting. Makes 6 servings.

**Diabetic diet:** Prepare as directed but omit sugar. Exchanges per serving = 3 meat, 1 bread and ½ skim milk.
**High-iron diet:** 3.5 milligrams iron per serving.

## HAMBURGER SHELL PIE (230 calories per serving)

1 pound ground round steak
⅓ cup packaged dried bread
   crumbs
¼ teaspoon garlic salt
¼ teaspoon celery salt
dash pepper
1 small onion, chopped
⅓ cup canned tomato juice
dash of Tabasco
2 17-ounce cans Italian
   tomatoes, well drained
seasoned salt
oregano leaves
¼ cup grated Parmesan cheese

About 50 minutes before serving: Preheat oven to 375°F. In 9-inch (preferably glass) pie plate, thoroughly mix meat, bread crumbs, garlic and celery salts, pepper, onion, tomato juice and Tabasco. Press mixture into plate, building up sides to about ½-inch thickness. Bake 15 minutes, placing piece of foil on oven rack to catch drippings. At end of 15 minutes, remove meat shell from oven; drain off drippings.

Now arrange drained tomatoes in shell, making overlapping rows and sprinkling each tomato with seasoned salt. Sprinkle with oregano to taste; top with ring of grated cheese. Return to 375°F. oven for 15 to 20 minutes. Cool one minute; drain well again. Cut into 6 wedges. Makes 6 servings.

**Diabetic diet:** Exchanges per serving = 2 meat, 1 "A" vegetable and ½ bread.
**Low-fat, low-cholesterol diet:** Prepare as directed but omit Parmesan. 10 grams fat per serving.
**High-iron diet:** 3 milligrams iron per serving.

## CHILEAN BEEF AND CORN (Pastel de Choclo) (330 calories per serving)

1 tablespoon salad oil
1 large onion, chopped
1 12-ounce can whole-kernel corn
1 cup canned tomatoes
salt
¾ pound ground round steak
1 teaspoon granulated sugar
¼ cup raisins
4 green olives, sliced

About 25 minutes before serving: In large skillet, in oil, sauté onion until golden; add corn, canned tomatoes and 1 teaspoon salt; cook, over low heat, about 8 to 10 minutes. Meanwhile, in medium skillet, cook meat with sugar and ½ teaspoon salt, stirring occasionally, until meat loses its red color; add raisins and olives; cook 2 minutes longer. In 8-inch round or square dish, alternate wide rows of meat and corn mixtures, 4 in all. Makes 4 servings.

**Egg-, gluten-, milk- and wheat-free diet:** Prepare as directed.
**Low-fat, low-cholesterol diet:** Prepare as directed but omit olives. 15 grams fat per serving.
**High-iron diet:** 4 milligrams iron per serving.

## TAMALE CASSEROLE (330 calories per serving)

¾ cup uncooked instant whole-wheat cereal
2 teaspoons salt
2 teaspoons chili powder
1 tablespoon butter or margarine
1 medium onion, sliced
¾ pound ground round steak
1½ cups well-drained canned tomatoes

About 1 hour before serving: Preheat oven to 350°F. Into 2 cups boiling water in saucepan, stir cereal, 1 teaspoon salt and 1 teaspoon chili powder; boil 1 to 2 minutes. Remove from heat; cool.

Meanwhile, in skillet, in butter, sauté onion until soft; add meat and continue cooking until meat loses its red color; drain well. Add tomatoes and remaining 1 teaspoon salt and 1 teaspoon chili powder; blend well. Line bottom of 1½-quart casserole with half of cereal; cover with meat mixture; top with remaining cereal. Bake, uncovered, 45 minutes. Makes 4 servings.

**Diabetic diet:** Exchanges per serving = 2 meat, 1 "A" vegetable, 2 bread and 1 fat.
**Low-fat, low-cholesterol diet:** Prepare as directed but use margarine instead of butter. 15 grams fat per serving.
**High-iron diet:** 3.5 milligrams iron per serving.

## STROGANOFF SKILLET DINNER (320 calories per serving)

1 pound ground round steak
1 small onion, chopped
1½ cups uncooked noodles
1½ cups tomato juice
1 teaspoon Worcestershire
1 teaspoon celery salt
½ teaspoon salt
dash pepper
⅓ cup sour cream
chopped parsley for garnish

About 45 minutes before serving: In skillet, cook meat with onion until meat loses its red color. Add noodles and remaining ingredients except sour cream and parsley; cover; simmer 25 minutes, stirring occasionally, or until noodles are tender. Stir in sour cream and sprinkle with parsley (do not boil again). Makes 5 servings.

**Diabetic diet:** Exchanges per serving = 3 meat, 1 "A" and 1 "B" vegetable and 1 bread.
**High-iron diet:** 3.5 milligrams iron per serving.

## MARVELOUS MUENSTER BURGER (280 calories per serving)

1 pound ground round steak
2 teaspoons prepared mustard
½ teaspoon salt
½ teaspoon Worcestershire
⅛ teaspoon pepper
2 ounces (or slices) Muenster cheese, chopped

About 20 minutes before serving: Combine meat with mustard, salt, Worcestershire and pepper; mix well and shape into 8 thin patties. Divide cheese among 4 patties; top each with another patty. Seal edges carefully. Panbroil 5 minutes on each side, or until done as desired. Makes 4 servings.

**Bland diet:** Prepare as directed but omit mustard, Worcestershire and pepper.
**Diabetic diet:** Exchanges per serving = 4 meat.
**High-iron diet:** 3.5 milligrams iron per serving.
**Low-residue diet:** Prepare as directed for bland diet.

## CUCUMBER COOL BURGERS (290 calories per serving)

1 pound ground round steak
1 teaspoon salt
¼ teaspoon pepper
2 tablespoons chopped parsley
⅓ cup chopped, pared cucumber
4 slices rye toast, quartered

About 25 minutes before serving: Combine all ingredients but bread. Shape into 4 patties, then broil or panfry to desired doneness. Serve on rye toast quarters. Makes 4 servings.

**Diabetic diet:** Exchanges per serving = 3 meat, 1 "A" vegetable and 1 bread.
**Egg-, gluten-, milk- and wheat-free diet:** Prepare as directed but omit toast.
**Low-fat, low-cholesterol diet:** 15 grams fat per serving.
**High-iron diet:** 4 milligrams iron per serving.
**Low-sodium diet:** Prepare as directed but omit salt. 190 milligrams sodium per serving. If served on low-sodium bread, 75 milligrams sodium per serving.

## MEAT-AND-POTATO PIE (300 calories per serving)

1 14½-ounce can tomato slices in tomato juice
1 pound ground round steak
1 egg
⅓ cup packaged dried bread crumbs
1 teaspoon oregano leaves
1 teaspoon salt
¼ teaspoon pepper
instant mashed potatoes for 6 servings
skimmed milk or reliquefied nonfat dry milk
2 tablespoons butter or margarine
¼ teaspoon celery seed

About 50 minutes before serving: Preheat oven to 350°F. Thoroughly drain sliced tomatoes, reserving ⅓ cup juice. In 9-inch pie plate, mix meat, egg, bread crumbs, ⅓ cup tomato juice, oregano, salt and pepper. Line bottom and sides of pie plate with mixture, mounding up sides about 1 inch above edge of plate. Bake 15 minutes; pour off liquid.

Meanwhile, prepare instant potatoes as label directs but use skimmed milk and only 2 tablespoons butter or margarine; stir in celery seed. Heap mixture into baked meat shell. Overlap tomato slices around edge of potatoes. Bake 15 minutes more. Let stand 5 minutes, then slice. Makes 6 servings.

**Bland diet:** Prepare as directed but omit tomato slices, oregano, pepper and celery seed. Add ⅓ cup milk to meat mixture. Drain one 16-ounce can green beans; toss with 1 tablespoon butter or margarine; use, in place of tomatoes, to ring potatoes.
**Diabetic diet:** Exchanges per serving = 2 meat, 1 "A" vegetable, 1 bread and 1 fat.
**Low-fat, low-cholesterol diet:** Prepare as directed but use 2 egg whites in place of whole egg; use margarine instead of butter. 15 grams fat per serving.
**High-iron diet:** 3.5 milligrams iron per serving.

## CHILI-MEATBALL-AND-VEGETABLE SOUP (220 calories per serving)

1 pound ground round steak
¼ cup packaged dried bread crumbs
¼ cup tomato juice
2 tablespoons minced onion
4 to 5 teaspoons chili powder
salt and pepper
1 tablespoon salad oil
2 10½-ounce cans condensed beef broth
1 16-ounce can tomatoes
1 10-ounce package frozen mixed vegetables
1 medium onion, sliced
½ cup packaged precooked rice

About 45 minutes before serving: In medium bowl, combine meat, crumbs, tomato juice, onion, chili powder, 1½ teaspoons salt and ¼ teaspoon pepper. Shape into 1-inch balls. In large skillet, in oil, brown meatballs. Drain; set aside.

In large kettle, combine beef broth with 2 soup-cans water, 1 teaspoon salt and remaining ingredients. Cover and heat to boiling; reduce heat; add meatballs; let simmer 10 minutes. Makes 8 main-dish servings of about 1¼ cups each.

**Diabetic diet:** Exchanges per serving = 2 meat and 1 bread.
**Low-fat, low-cholesterol diet:** 10 grams fat per serving.
**High-iron diet:** 3 milligrams iron per serving.

## MEXICAN CHILI (290 calories per serving)

¾ pound ground round steak
½ cup thinly sliced onions
1 to 1½ tablespoons chili powder
1 cup canned tomatoes
½ teaspoon salt
1 teaspoon granulated sugar
1 garlic clove, minced
1 16-ounce can kidney beans

About 1 hour and 45 minutes before serving: In large skillet, cook meat with onion until meat loses its red color. Add 1 cup water and remaining ingredients except kidney beans; cover; simmer 1 hour. Uncover; add kidney beans; simmer 30 minutes more. Makes 4 servings of about 1 cup each.

**Diabetic diet:** Prepare as directed but omit sugar. Exchanges per serving = 3 meat, 1 "A" and 1 "B" vegetable and 1 bread.
**Egg-, gluten-, milk- and wheat-free diet:** Prepare as directed.
**Low-fat, low-cholesterol diet:** 10 grams fat per serving.
**High-iron diet:** 5 milligrams iron per serving.

## CHILI CON CARNE (280 calories per serving)

1 tablespoon salad oil
1 garlic clove, thinly sliced
1 cup chopped onion
2 cups sliced celery
½ cup chopped green pepper
1 pound ground round steak
1 16-ounce can kidney beans, thoroughly drained
2 16-ounce cans tomatoes
½ teaspoon salt
chili powder

About 1 hour and 15 minutes before serving: In large kettle over medium heat, in oil, sauté garlic, onion, celery and green pepper until onion is golden; add meat; cook until it is well browned. Stir in kidney beans, tomatoes, salt and 1½ teaspoons chili powder; simmer, uncovered, at least 45 minutes to blend flavors. Just before serving, stir in enough chili powder to give desired "hotness." Makes 6 servings of about 1½ cups each.

**Diabetic diet:** Exchanges per serving = 2 meat, 1 "A" and 1 "B" vegetable and 1 bread.
**Egg-, gluten-, milk- and wheat-free diet:** Prepare as directed.
**Low-fat, low-cholesterol diet:** 10 grams fat per serving.
**High-iron diet:** 4.5 milligrams iron per serving.
**Low-sodium diet:** Cook 1 cup dried kidney beans in 1 quart water for 1½ hours, or until almost tender; drain, reserving ½ cup liquid. Use liquid and beans in place of canned beans. Use low-sodium canned tomatoes; omit salt and celery; use chili powder not containing salt. 60 milligrams sodium per serving.

## SAUCY CRANBERRY BURGERS (330 calories per serving)

1 pound ground round steak
1 tablespoon parsley flakes
½ teaspoon celery salt
½ to 1 teaspoon salt
1½ teaspoons salad oil
1 8-ounce can jellied cranberry sauce
¼ cup orange juice

About 20 minutes before serving: In medium bowl, mix meat, parsley flakes, celery salt and salt; form into 4 patties. In skillet over medium heat, in oil, brown 5 minutes on each side. Meanwhile, in small bowl, beat cranberry sauce and orange juice until smooth. Add to skillet; cover; simmer 5 minutes. Makes 4 servings.

**Bland diet:** Prepare as directed but omit celery salt if forbidden on diet.
**Egg-, gluten-, milk- and wheat-free diet:** Prepare as directed.
**Low-fat, low-cholesterol diet:** 20 grams fat per serving.
**Low-fat, bland (gall bladder) diet:** Prepare as directed for bland diet.
**High-iron diet:** 3.5 milligrams iron per serving.
**Low-sodium diet:** Prepare as directed but omit celery salt and salt. 75 milligrams sodium per serving.

## 20-MINUTE HASH (280 calories per serving)

1 pound ground round steak
2 cups cubed cooked potatoes
½ cup minced onion
1 teaspoon salt
1 tablespoon Worcestershire

About 20 minutes before serving: In skillet, stirring constantly, cook meat with potatoes and onion until meat loses its red color. Add salt and Worcestershire; cook, over low heat, 15 minutes, stirring often. Makes 4 servings of about 1 cup each.

**Diabetic diet:** Exchanges per serving = 3 meat and 1 bread.
**Low-fat, low-cholesterol diet:** 15 grams fat per serving.
**High-iron diet:** 4 milligrams iron per serving.

## CHILIBURGERS (270 calories per serving)

1 pound ground round steak
½ cup chili sauce

About 20 minutes before serving: Mix meat with chili sauce. Form into 4 patties. In medium skillet, over medium heat, pan-broil on each side to desired doneness. Makes 4 servings.

**Egg-, gluten-, milk- and wheat-free diet:** Prepare as directed.
**Low-fat, low-cholesterol diet:** 15 grams fat per serving.
**High-iron diet:** 3.5 milligrams iron per serving.

## HAMBURGER-VEGETABLE SOUP (210 calories per serving)

6 beef bouillon cubes
1 16-ounce can tomatoes
1 large onion, diced
¾ cup diced celery
1 medium carrot, diced
1 garlic clove, crushed
1 bay leaf
½ teaspoon salt
⅛ teaspoon pepper
1 pound ground round steak
1 10-ounce package frozen peas
3 tablespoons chopped parsley
    for garnish

About 1 hour before serving: In large saucepan over high heat, heat 5 cups water to boiling; add bouillon cubes, and stir until dissolved. Add next 8 ingredients; cover and simmer over low heat 20 minutes.

Meanwhile, in small skillet over medium-high heat, cook meat, stirring constantly, until it loses its bright red color. Add meat and peas to soup and cook 10 minutes, or until peas are fork-tender; discard bay leaf. Stir in parsley just before serving. Makes 6 servings.

**Low-fat, low-cholesterol diet:** 10 grams fat per serving.

## TOMATO-BAKED MEAT LOAF (265 calories per serving)

3 cups soft bread crumbs
1 cup canned tomatoes
¼ green pepper, chopped
1 medium onion, finely
    chopped
dash pepper
½ teaspoon prepared horse-
    radish
1½ teaspoons salt
2 eggs
1 pound ground round steak
¼ cup catchup

About 1 hour and 20 minutes before serving: Preheat oven to 375°F. In medium baking pan, mix all ingredients but catchup; form mixture into 9″ by 5″ loaf. Bake 50 to 60 minutes, or to desired doneness.

To serve: Let cool 10 minutes, then cut into 12 equal slices. Serve with catchup. Makes 6 servings of 2 slices each.

**Diabetic diet:** Prepare as directed but omit catchup. Exchanges per serving = 2 meat and 1 bread.
**Low-fat, low-cholesterol diet:** Prepare as directed but use only white of egg. 10 grams fat per serving.
**High-iron diet:** 3.5 milligrams iron per serving.

## ITALIANA MEAT LOAF (290 calories per serving)

1 pound ground round steak
1 cup fresh bread crumbs
¼ cup grated Parmesan cheese
¼ cup chopped parsley
2 tablespoons instant minced
    onion
basil
salt and pepper
3 eggs
1½ cups well-drained creamed
    cottage cheese
1 teaspoon granulated sugar

About 1 hour and 15 minutes before serving: Preheat oven to 350°F. In large bowl, mix meat with crumbs, cheese, parsley, onion, 1 teaspoon basil, 1 teaspoon salt, ¼ teaspoon pepper and 2 eggs.

In medium bowl, beat remaining egg with cottage cheese, ½ teaspoon salt, ¼ teaspoon basil and sugar until well blended. In lightly greased 9″ by 5″ loaf pan, spread cheese mixture evenly over bottom. On waxed paper, shape meat mixture into oblong to fit into pan. Using 2 pancake turners, lift meat onto cheese mixture. Bake 1 hour. Drain off liquid. Makes 6 servings.

**Diabetic diet:** Prepare as directed but omit sugar. Exchanges per serving = 4 meat and ½ bread.
**High-iron diet:** 3 milligrams iron per serving.

## BACON-STUFFED BURGERS (255 calories per serving)

2 strips bacon
1 pound ground round steak
1 teaspoon salad oil
salt to taste

About 20 minutes before serving: Cook bacon until almost crisp; crumble. Form beef into 8 thin patties. Top each of 4 of the patties with one quarter of crumbled bacon. Cover with rest of patties; carefully seal edges together. In medium skillet over medium heat, in oil, cook burgers until well done. Sprinkle with salt to taste. Makes 4 servings.

**Bland diet:** Prepare as directed.
**Diabetic diet:** Exchanges per serving = 3 meat.
**Egg-, gluten-, milk- and wheat-free diet:** Prepare as directed.
**High-iron diet:** 4 milligrams iron per serving.
**Low-residue diet:** Prepare as directed.

## QUICK CHILI LOAF (300 calories per serving)

1 pound ground round steak
½ cup chili sauce
2 slices bread, finely cubed
1 egg
¼ teaspoon garlic salt

About 45 minutes before serving: Preheat oven to 350°F. In medium baking pan, mix all ingredients. Shape into 4 loaves. Bake 30 minutes, or until meat is done as you like it. Makes 4 servings.

**Low-fat, low-cholesterol diet:** Prepare as directed but use 2 egg whites in place of whole egg. 15 grams fat per serving.
**High-iron diet:** 4 milligrams iron per serving.

## PEPPERCORN STEAK (200 calories per serving)

1 2½-pound boneless round steak
instant meat tenderizer
⅓ cup Burgundy wine
¼ cup minced onion
1 tablespoon salad oil
2 teaspoons peppercorns

About 50 minutes before serving: Trim excess fat from meat. Prepare steak with meat tenderizer as label directs. Place steak in large baking dish. In small measuring cup, combine wine, onion and salad oil. Pour over steak; refrigerate, loosely covered, 30 minutes turning occasionally.

Preheat broiler if manufacturer directs. Coarsely crush peppercorns in pepper mill or wrap peppercorns in cloth, then crush coarsely with rolling pin; press pepper well into both sides of steak. Place steak on broiling pan; pour remaining marinade over steak. Broil about 15 minutes or until of desired doneness, turning once. Serve steak cut in very thin slices. Makes 8 servings.

**Diabetic diet:** Exchanges = 1 meat for each ounce of meat.
**Low-fat, low-cholesterol diet:** 10 grams fat per serving.
**High-iron diet:** 4.5 milligrams iron per serving.
**Low-sodium diet:** Prepare as directed but omit meat tenderizer. 95 milligrams sodium per serving.

## PINEAPPLE BEEF LOAF (290 calories per serving)

½ cup fresh bread crumbs
¼ cup skimmed milk or re-liquefied nonfat dry milk
1 pound ground round steak
2 teaspoons Worcestershire
1 egg, slightly beaten
1½ teaspoons salt
¼ teaspoon pepper
1 4-ounce can mushroom slices, drained
1 8¼-ounce can pineapple slices, drained and halved

About 1 hour before serving: Preheat oven to 375°F. In bowl, let bread crumbs and milk stand 5 minutes. With fork, mix in meat and all remaining ingredients but pineapple. Pack meat into 1½-quart loaf pan. Bake 50 minutes; remove from oven and let stand 5 minutes.

To serve: Pour off meat-loaf juices, then turn loaf onto heated platter. Lay overlapping pineapple slices on loaf. Makes 4 servings.

**Low-fat, low-cholesterol diet:** Prepare as directed but use only white of egg. 15 grams fat per serving.
**High-iron diet:** 4 milligrams iron per serving.

## DELUXE PINEAPPLE MEAT LOAF (240 calories per serving)

1 pound ground round steak
1 8-ounce can crushed pine-
    apple (do not drain off syrup)
bread cubes made from 2 slices
    day-old bread
2 eggs
¼ cup minced onion
⅛ teaspoon prepared horse-
    radish
1 teaspoon salt
catchup
¼ cup orange or pineapple
    juice

About 1 hour and 15 minutes before serving: Preheat oven to 350°F. In 9-inch baking pan, mix meat, pineapple, bread cubes, eggs, onion, horseradish, salt and 2 tablespoons catchup. Form into long narrow loaf. Bake 60 minutes. Meanwhile, prepare sauce by stirring together 2 tablespoons catchup with orange juice. Cut meat loaf into 12 slices; top with sauce. Makes 6 servings.

**Diabetic diet:** Prepare as directed but use crushed pineapple packed in pineapple juice. Exchanges per serving = 2 meat and 1 bread.
**Low-fat, low-cholesterol diet:** Prepare as directed but use only whites of eggs. 10 grams fat per serving.
**High-iron diet:** 3 milligrams iron per serving.

## CHINESE BEEF AND PEPPERS (290 calories per serving)

1½ pounds ground round steak
2 tablespoons salad oil
½ teaspoon minced garlic
2 beef-bouillon cubes
1 teaspoon salt
¼ teaspoon pepper
½ teaspoon ginger
6 to 8 whole green onions, cut
    into ¼-inch pieces
4 celery stalks, cut diagonally
    into ¼-inch pieces
3 medium green peppers, cut
    into ½-inch strips
2 tablespoons cornstarch
1 tablespoon soy sauce

About 40 minutes before serving: Shape meat into 18 small patties. In large skillet over medium meat, in hot oil, brown patties and garlic; pour off fat. Add beef bouillon, salt, pepper, ginger and 1¾ cups hot water. Simmer, uncovered, 15 minutes. Add vegetables; simmer 5 minutes, stirring occasionally. In cup, combine cornstarch, soy sauce and ¼ cup water; stir into mixture in skillet. Cook, covered, 7 to 10 minutes until celery is tender-crisp. Makes 6 servings.

**Diabetic diet:** Exchanges per serving = 3 meat and 1 "A" vegetable.
**Egg-, gluten-, milk- and wheat-free diet:** Prepare as directed but omit bouillon cubes and soy sauce for gluten- and wheat-free diets.
**Low-fat, low-cholesterol diet:** 10 grams fat per serving.
**High-iron diet:** 4 milligrams iron per serving.

## FLANK STEAK ROLLED AND FILLED (Chilean Malaya) (250 calories per serving)

1 2-pound flank steak
½ teaspoon salt
½ teaspoon thyme leaves
⅛ teaspoon pepper
1 medium onion
3 tablespoons chopped parsley
3 tablespoons red wine vinegar
½ cup fresh bread crumbs
½ cup chopped cooked
    spinach
½ cup cooked or canned peas
¼ cup finely grated carrot
1 tablespoon grated Cheddar
    cheese
1 hard-cooked egg, chopped
2 cooked bacon slices,
    crumbled
2 tablespoons salad oil
1 10½-ounce can condensed
    beef broth

Day before serving: With sharp knife score one side of flank steak in diamond pattern. Then sprinkle both sides with salt, thyme and pepper. In large bowl, place flank steak with onion, parsley and vinegar; cover; refrigerate.

About 2 hours before serving: In large bowl, lightly combine bread crumbs, spinach, peas, carrot, cheese, chopped egg and bacon; spoon onto scored side of steak; pat until it extends nearly to edges. Then roll up, jelly-roll fashion, and tie securely with string at 1-inch intervals.

In Dutch oven, in oil, brown on all sides. Add onion-vinegar mixture in which meat was marinated, also broth. Simmer, covered, 1½ hours, or until meat is fork-tender. Arrange on heated platter; remove strings; slice. Skim surface fat from gravy and pass. Makes 8 servings.

**Low-fat, low-cholesterol diet:** Prepare as directed but omit egg and bacon. 10 grams fat per serving.
**High-iron diet:** 4.5 milligrams iron per serving.

## ROLLED FLANK STEAK (270 calories per serving)

1 10-ounce package frozen
mixed vegetables
½ cup chopped onion
½ cup chopped celery
1 teaspoon salt
2 slices white bread
2 tablespoons chopped parsley
1 teaspoon seasoned salt
¼ teaspoon seasoned pepper
¼ teaspoon nutmeg
1 2½-pound flank steak
1 tablespoon bottled sauce for
gravy
2 tablespoons butter or margarine

About 1 hour and 40 minutes before dinner: Cook frozen mixed vegetables with onion, celery and salt as label directs; drain. Meanwhile, into large bowl, crumble bread slices; add parsley, seasoned salt and pepper and nutmeg; add drained vegetables; toss well.

Score flank steak crosswise in diamond pattern, on both sides. Spread with vegetable mixture, patting until mixture spreads nearly to edges of meat. Roll up, jelly-roll fashion; secure with string. Brush outside with bottled sauce for gravy. In Dutch oven over medium heat, in butter, brown steak on all sides. Add ¾ cup water and simmer, covered, 1 hour, or until fork-tender. Place on heated platter. Remove string, then cut steak into 8 slices; pass any gravy left in Dutch oven. Makes 8 servings.

**Low-fat, low-cholesterol diet:** Prepare as directed but use salad oil or margarine instead of butter. 10 grams fat per serving.
**High-iron diet:** 5 milligrams iron per serving.

## BERGENFIELD POTTED BEEF (310 calories per serving)

1 2-pound rump beef
¼ cup flour
1 tablespoon salad oil
1 envelope dried onion-soup
mix
8 carrots, cut into 1-inch pieces
8 small white potatoes, pared
16 small white onions
1 16-ounce can tomatoes
1 teaspoon oregano leaves
2 tablespoons cornstarch

About 4½ hours before serving: Trim fat from meat. Sprinkle meat with flour; shake off excess. In Dutch oven over medium heat, in oil, brown meat on all sides. Add onion-soup mix and 2 cups water; cover; boil gently 2 to 3 hours, or until meat is fork-tender.

About one hour before meat is done, add carrots, potatoes, onions, tomatoes and oregano. Continue cooking until vegetables are tender. Mix enough water with corn-starch to form a smooth paste. Remove meat from Dutch oven; slice and arrange on serving platter; surround with vegetables. Stirring constantly, mix cornstarch with gravy in Dutch oven; cook until thickened and smooth.

To serve: Top meat and vegetables with a little hot gravy; pass rest of gravy. Makes 8 servings.

**Diabetic diet:** Carefully divide into 8 equal servings. Exchanges per serving = 3 meat, 1 "B" vegetable and 2 bread.
**Low-fat, low-cholesterol diet:** 10 grams fat per serving.
**High-iron diet:** 5 milligrams iron per serving.

## SKILLET BURGER LOAF (270 calories per serving)

¾ pound ground round steak
1 egg
¾ teaspoon salt
2 tablespoons instant minced
onion
3 packages process Cheddar-
cheese slices
¼ teaspoon pepper
chopped parsley for garnish

About 20 minutes before serving: Combine meat, egg, salt and instant minced onion. Grease 8-inch skillet; lightly pat one-half of meat over bottom; arrange cheese slices on top. Cover with rest of meat, patting smooth. Sprinkle with pepper; cut into 4 pie-shaped wedges. Cook, on top of range, over fairly high heat, until browned on bottom. Turn; brown other side; cook until done as desired. Garnish with parsley. Makes 4 servings.

**Bland diet:** Prepare as directed but omit onion, pepper and parsley.
**Diabetic diet:** Exchanges per serving = 3 meat.
**High-iron diet:** 3 milligrams iron per serving.
**Low-residue diet:** Prepare as directed for bland diet.

## HERB-STUFFED FLANK STEAK (335 calories per serving)

butter or margarine
1 medium onion, chopped
1 4-ounce can mushroom stems
  and pieces, drained
¼ cup chopped parsley
1½ cups fresh bread crumbs
1 teaspoon poultry seasoning
½ teaspoon salt
dash pepper
1 egg, slightly beaten
1 2-pound flank steak
1 10½-ounce can condensed
  beef broth

About 2 hours before serving: In skillet over medium heat, in 1 tablespoon butter, sauté onion and mushrooms until golden. In bowl, combine parsley, crumbs, poultry seasoning, salt, pepper and egg; then mix in onion and mushrooms. Remove fat from steak; score surface, in diamond pattern, on both sides. Place mushroom mixture lengthwise down center, then bring both ends together on top; fasten with string, tied at 1-inch intervals.

In skillet over medium heat, in 2 tablespoons butter, brown steak well on all sides; add broth; simmer, covered, 1½ hours, or until meat is fork-tender.

To serve: Remove meat to heated platter; remove strings; cut into 1-inch pieces. Thicken pan juices, if desired, and pass with meat. Makes 6 servings.

**Low-fat, low-cholesterol diet:** Prepare as directed but use only white of egg; use margarine instead of butter. 15 grams fat per serving.
**High-iron diet:** 5.5 milligrams iron per serving.

## BOILED BEEF WITH DILL (Kikt Biff Med Dillsäs) (240 calories per serving)

2 pounds boneless sirloin beef
1 tablespoon salad oil
1 10½-ounce can condensed
  beef broth
1 teaspoon salt
¼ teaspoon pepper
1 bay leaf
1 teaspoon dried dill weed
1 tablespoon cornstarch
1 tablespoon vinegar
2 tablespoons granulated sugar
chopped parsley for garnish

About 2 hours before serving: Trim fat from meat; cut meat into 6 serving pieces. In large skillet over medium heat, in oil, brown on both sides. Add beef broth, 1 cup water, salt, pepper, bay leaf and dill; cover; simmer gently 1½ hours, or until meat is tender. Drain off broth; measure 1 cup into a small saucepan. Mix cornstarch, vinegar and sugar to form smooth paste. Stir into broth; cook, stirring constantly, until thickened and smooth. Serve meat topped with gravy; sprinkle with parsley. Makes 6 servings.

**Diabetic diet:** Prepare as directed but omit sugar. Exchanges per serving = 4 meat.
**Low-fat, low-cholesterol diet:** 10 grams fat per serving.
**High-iron diet:** 4.5 milligrams iron per serving.

## STUFFED CUCUMBERS (325 calories per serving)

4 large cucumbers
1 pound ground round steak
¼ cup chopped celery
¼ cup chopped onions
1 teaspoon salt
½ teaspoon ginger
3 tablespoons cornstarch
4 tablespoons soy sauce
1½ cups beef broth
3 cups cooked rice

About 1 hour before serving: Peel cucumbers and cut each in half crosswise, then lengthwise. With spoon, scoop out seeds. In medium bowl, mix meat, celery, onions, salt, ginger, 1 tablespoon cornstarch and 1 tablespoon soy sauce. Stuff cucumbers with mixture.

In large skillet over medium heat, in broth, arrange cucumbers, stuffed side up; simmer, covered, 35 minutes. Place on warm platter on bed of rice. Pour off pan liquid, reserving 1 cup; return it to skillet.

In cup, dissolve 2 tablespoons cornstarch in 3 tablespoons soy sauce. Gradually add to skillet and cook over medium heat, stirring constantly until thickened. Pour over cucumbers and rice. Makes 6 servings.

**Low-fat, low-cholesterol diet:** 10 grams fat per serving.

## PEACHY MEAT LOAF (335 calories per serving)

2 pounds ground round steak
1 cup packaged dried bread crumbs
1 2¾-ounce package onion soup mix
1 cup skimmed milk or reliquefied nonfat dry milk
1 16-ounce can cling-peach halves, drained
chili sauce

About 1 hour before serving: Preheat oven to 425°F. Combine meat, crumbs, soup mix and milk; place in cake pan and shape into mound. With back of large spoon, make 3 indentations in meat; set peach, hollow side up, in each indentation; bake 50 minutes. Heat remaining peaches in oven with meat for last 10 minutes.

To serve: Remove loaf to heated platter; top peaches with chili sauce. Cut into 8 wedges. Makes 8 servings.

**Low-fat, low-cholesterol diet:** 15 grams fat per serving.
**High-iron diet:** 4 milligrams iron per serving.

## FLANK STEAK WITH BLUE-CHEESE BUTTER (280 calories per serving)

1 2-pound flank steak
⅔ cup bottled low-calorie Italian dressing
¼ cup crumbled blue cheese
2 tablespoons butter or margarine
2 teaspoons chopped chives

About 4 hours before serving: Trim fat from steak, then score each side in diamond pattern, about ⅛-inch deep. Place in baking dish; pour on dressing; refrigerate, covered, turning once.

About ½ hour before serving: Preheat broiler if manufacturer directs. Meanwhile, mash blue cheese smooth with butter and chives; set aside. Lay flank steak on rack in broiler pan; broil about 5 minutes on each side for medium rare. Spread immediately with blue-cheese butter.

To serve: Cut on angle into thin slices. Makes 6 servings.

**Diabetic diet:** Each ounce meat = 1 meat exchange. One tablespoon blue-cheese topping = 2 fat exchanges.
**High-iron diet:** 5 milligrams iron per serving.

## MEATBALLS PIEMONTE (315 calories per serving)

1 pound ground round steak
¼ teaspoon garlic salt
1 medium onion, finely chopped
salt
¼ cup packaged dried bread crumbs
1 teaspoon dry mustard
1 egg
1 tablespoon salad oil
1 tablespoon instant coffee powder
½ teaspoon granulated sugar
1 tablespoon cornstarch

About 50 minutes before serving: In medium bowl, mix meat, garlic salt, chopped onion, ½ teaspoon salt, bread crumbs, mustard and egg. Form into 12 medium meatballs. In medium skillet over medium heat, in oil, brown on all sides. Add coffee powder, 1 cup water, ½ teaspoon salt, and sugar; cover; simmer 30 minutes. Meanwhile, stir ¾ cup water into cornstarch until smooth. Add to meatballs; cook, stirring, until thickened. Makes 4 servings.

**Diabetic diet:** Prepare as directed but omit sugar. Exchanges per serving = 3 meat, 1 "B" vegetable and 1 fat.
**Low-fat, low-cholesterol diet:** Prepare as directed but use only white of egg. 20 grams fat per serving.
**High-iron diet:** 4 milligrams iron per serving.

## JOHNNY APPLESEED MEAT LOAF (320 calories per serving)

1 pound ground round steak
½ cup packaged dried bread crumbs
¾ cup applesauce
¼ cup catchup
¾ teaspoon salt
¼ teaspoon cinnamon
⅛ teaspoon nutmeg

About 1 hour before serving: Preheat oven to 350°F. In 1-quart casserole, mix all ingredients and smooth top. Bake 50 minutes. Makes 4 servings.

**Diabetic diet:** Prepare as directed but use unsweetened applesauce. Carefully divide into 4 equal servings. Exchanges per serving = 3 meat and 1 fruit.
**Low-fat, low-cholesterol diet:** 15 grams fat per serving.
**High-iron diet:** 3.5 milligrams iron per serving.
**Low-sodium diet:** Prepare as directed but omit salt; use low-sodium catchup. 105 milligrams sodium per serving. Or make with bread crumbs from unsalted Melba toast. 75 milligrams sodium per serving.

## STEAK-AND-POTATO CASSEROLE (325 calories per serving)

2 pounds round steak, ½-inch thick
¼ cup flour
4 teaspoons salt
½ teaspoon pepper
2 tablespoons salad oil
8 medium carrots, thickly sliced
8 medium potatoes, thickly sliced
1 1⅜-ounce envelope onion-soup mix
chopped parsley for garnish

About 2½ hours before serving: Preheat oven to 350°F. Cut meat into 8 serving pieces, trimming fat and bone. On board or waxed paper, using meat mallet or edge of saucer, pound mixture of flour, salt and pepper into meat.

In large heavy skillet over medium heat, in oil, brown meat well on both sides. Arrange in 3-quart casserole; place carrots and potato slices on top. Sprinkle with onion-soup mix and cover with 3½ cups water.

Bake, covered, 2 hours, or until meat is fork-tender. Skim off any fat. If desired, thicken gravy with 2 tablespoons flour mixed with ¼ cup cold water; return casserole to oven for a few minutes. Sprinkle parsley on top. Makes 8 servings.

**Low-fat, low-cholesterol diet:** 10 grams fat per serving.
**High-iron diet:** 4.5 milligrams iron per serving.

## MANDARIN SKILLET BEEF (350 calories per serving)

2 pounds boneless sirloin, cut 1- to 1½-inches thick
1 tablespoon salad oil
¼ teaspoon ginger
1 teaspoon chili powder
¼ teaspoon garlic powder
1 small onion, finely minced
3 beef-bouillon cubes
1 tablespoon plum jam
1 tablespoon vinegar
1 cup uncooked rice
1 tablespoon cornstarch

About 1 hour and 20 minutes before serving: Trim all fat from meat. Cut meat against grain, into very thin strips about ⅛-inch thick. Cut long strips in half. In large skillet over medium heat, in oil, brown meat, a few strips at a time. Add ginger, chili and garlic powders, onion, bouillon cubes, 2 cups water, plum jam and vinegar; cover; simmer 40 minutes, or until meat is tender.

Meanwhile, cook rice as label directs but omit butter. Stir 1 tablespoon water into cornstarch; stir into meat mixture until slightly thickened.

To serve: Top rice with beef mixture. Makes 6 servings.

**Diabetic diet:** Prepare as directed but omit jam. One serving = one-sixth meat mixture served on ½ cup rice. Exchanges per serving = 4 meat and 1 bread.
**Low-fat, low-cholesterol diet:** 10 grams fat per serving.
**High-iron diet:** 4.5 milligrams iron per serving.
**Low-sodium diet:** Prepare as directed but omit bouillon cubes or use low-sodium bouillon cubes; omit salt when cooking rice; use chili powder not containing salt. 85 milligrams sodium per serving.

## CHINESE PEPPER STEAK (290 calories per serving)

2 pounds boneless round steak, cut ½-inch thick
¼ cup soy sauce
1 beef-bouillon cube
½ teaspoon ginger
½ teaspoon garlic powder
2 tablespoons salad oil
3 large green peppers, cut into thin strips
3 tablespoons cornstarch
4 cups cooked rice

Day before or early in day: Trim any fat from meat; cut meat into strips about ¼-inch wide. In medium bowl, combine soy sauce, bouillon cube, ginger, garlic powder and 1 cup boiling water. Add meat strips; cover and refrigerate.

About 1 hour and 15 minutes before serving: Drain meat, reserving ½ cup marinade. In large skillet over high heat, in oil, cook meat until it loses its red color. Add reserved marinade and 1 cup water; reduce heat; simmer, covered, 1 hour. Add green pepper; cook 15 minutes, or until meat is tender.

To make gravy: In measuring cup, combine ¼ cup cold water and cornstarch. Gradually stir into skillet liquid; cook, stirring, until mixture thickens slightly. Serve over rice. Makes 8 servings.

**Diabetic diet:** Carefully divide meat into 8 equal servings; serve over ½ cup rice. Exchanges per serving = 3 meat and 1 bread.
**Low-fat, low-cholesterol diet:** 10 grams fat per serving.
**High-iron diet:** 4 milligrams iron per serving.

## SPICY BEEF (250 calories per serving)

**2 pounds round steak**
**¼ cup flour**
**1 tablespoon salt**
**¼ teaspoon pepper**
**2 tablespoons salad oil**
**2 medium onions, sliced**
**1 tablespoon Worcestershire**
**1 teaspoon curry**
**1 teaspoon molasses**
**dash ginger**

About 3 hours before serving: Preheat oven to 350°F. Trim all fat from meat; cut into 1½-inch cubes. Mix flour, salt and pepper; coat meat with mixture. In Dutch oven over medium heat, in oil, brown meat well on all sides. Add remaining ingredients and 1 cup water.

Cover; bake 2½ hours, or until meat is fork-tender. Pass gravy. Makes 6 servings.

**Diabetic diet:** Prepare as directed but omit molasses; use saccharin equivalent to 1 teaspoon sugar. Exchanges for 1 slice (1 ounce) beef = 1 meat, and for up to ¼ cup gravy = 1 "free" exchange.
**Egg-, gluten-, milk- and wheat-free diet:** Prepare as directed but use cornstarch in place of flour on gluten- and wheat-free diets.
**Low-fat, low-cholesterol diet:** 10 grams fat per serving.
**High-iron diet:** 4.5 milligrams iron per serving.
**Low-sodium diet:** Prepare as directed but omit salt and Worcestershire; use curry not containing salt. 90 milligrams sodium per serving.

## SPICY CHUCK ROAST (325 calories per serving)

**½ cup bottled thick meat sauce**
**1 tablespoon salad oil**
**1 cup canned tomato puree**
**1 tablespoon prepared mustard**
**¼ cup maple-flavored syrup**
**2 tablespoons vinegar**
**1 tablespoon Worcestershire**
**⅛ teaspoon garlic salt**
**1 3-pound boneless round roast**

Day before serving: In large bowl, combine all ingredients but meat. Trim all fat from meat. Place meat in this marinade; refrigerate. Turn occasionally, until needed next day.

About 1¼ hours before serving: Preheat oven to 325°F. Place meat in foil-lined shallow open roasting pan; insert roast-meat thermometer in center of meatiest part. Spoon some marinade over meat, then roast 1 hour, or to 140°F. on meat thermometer, occasionally basting with marinade. When meat is done, remove to heated platter.

To serve: Slice thinly; pass hot marinade as gravy. Makes 8 servings.

**Low-fat, low-cholesterol diet:** 15 grams fat per serving.
**High-iron diet:** 5 milligrams iron per serving.

## CUBED-STEAK SANDWICHES (265 calories per serving)

**6 slices French bread, cut on**
**diagonal, ¾-inch thick**
**2 teaspoons prepared mustard**
**6 4-ounce cubed round steaks**
**instant meat tenderizer**
**seasoned pepper**
**2 tablespoons butter or mar-**
**garine**
**6 lettuce leaves**
**6 tomato slices**
**salt**

About 15 minutes before serving: Preheat broiler 10 minutes if manufacturer directs. Broil bread slices until golden on one side; spread other side with mustard and broil until golden; keep warm. Sprinkle cubed steaks with meat tenderizer as label directs, then some seasoned pepper. In large skillet, in butter, brown steaks about 2 minutes on each side. Now, on mustard side of each bread slice, arrange lettuce leaf, cubed steak and tomato slice. Sprinkle with salt and seasoned pepper. Makes 6 servings.

**Diabetic diet:** Exchanges per serving = 3 meat, 1 "A" vegetable and 1 bread.
**Low-fat, low-cholesterol diet:** Prepare as directed but use salad oil or margarine instead of butter. 10 grams fat per serving.
**High-iron diet:** 4 milligrams iron per serving.

## BRAISED BEEF WITH GINGER (255 calories per serving)

1 pound round steak
1 tablespoon salad oil
1 medium onion, thinly sliced
2 garlic cloves, minced
¼ teaspoon ginger
1 tablespoon soy sauce
½ cup uncooked white rice
2 stalks celery, cut into thin
   crosswise slices
salt to taste

About 50 minutes before serving: Trim as much fat from meat as possible. Cut meat, against grain, into julienne strips. In large skillet over medium heat, in oil, sauté meat, onion and garlic until meat browns. Add ginger, soy sauce and ⅔ cup water; cover; simmer 25 minutes, or until meat is tender. Meanwhile, cook rice as label directs but omit butter. Add celery to meat mixture; cover; simmer 5 minutes more; salt to taste. Serve on hot fluffy rice. Makes 4 servings.

**Diabetic diet:** One serving = ¼ meat mixture and ½ cup cooked rice. Exchanges per serving = 3 meat, 1 "A" vegetable and 1 bread.
**Low-fat, low-cholesterol diet:** 10 grams fat per serving.
**High-iron diet:** Prepare as directed but be certain to use enriched rice. 3 milligrams iron per serving.
**Low-sodium diet:** Prepare as directed but omit soy sauce and salt. 105 milligrams sodium per serving.

## BEEF BOURGUIGNON (310 calories per serving)

1 pound round steak
flour
butter or margarine
3 tablespoons cognac
1 garlic clove, minced
2 carrots, thinly sliced
2 cups thinly sliced celery
1 cup chopped onions
1 tablespoon parsley flakes
1 bay leaf, crumbled
½ teaspoon thyme leaves
2 teaspoons salt
½ teaspoon hickory-smoked
   salt
1 pound small white onions
1 pound fresh mushrooms
1 teaspoon lemon juice

At least 3 hours before serving: Preheat oven to 350°F. Trim fat from meat; cut meat into 1-inch cubes. Toss in flour to coat. In Dutch oven in 1 tablespoon butter, brown on all sides. Add cognac; ignite. When flames have subsided, add garlic, carrots, celery, onions, parsley flakes, bay leaf, thyme, 2 cups water, salt and hickory salt. Stir; simmer 2 to 3 minutes; cover tightly; bake 2 hours, or until meat is tender.

One-half hour before meat is done, cook onions, in salted water to cover, until tender—about 20 minutes. Wash and stem mushrooms (halve larger ones). Sauté caps and stems in 1 tablespoon butter and lemon juice until golden—about 15 minutes. Make a smooth paste with 2 tablespoons flour and ¼ cup water. Add with drained onions, mushrooms and ¾ cup water to meat mixture. Stirring constantly, simmer until gravy thickens. Makes 4 servings.

**Diabetic diet:** Carefully divide into 4 equal servings. Exchanges per serving = 3 meat, 1 "B" vegetable and 1 bread.
**Low-fat, low-cholesterol diet:** Prepare as directed but use margarine instead of butter. 10 grams fat per serving.
**High-iron diet:** 5.5 milligrams iron per serving.

## HAMBURGER ROLLS (245 calories per serving)

1 pound ground round steak
1 cup fresh bread crumbs
½ cup skimmed milk or re-
   liquefied nonfat dry milk
1 tablespoon lemon juice
½ cup shredded Cheddar
   cheese
¼ cup chopped stuffed olives
1 teaspoon salt
3 bacon slices, halved

About 45 minutes before serving: Preheat oven to 400°F. Combine all ingredients but bacon. Divide mixture into sixths; form each portion into rolls about 4" by 1½". Wrap each with bacon strip. Place in medium baking dish; bake 30 minutes. Broil an additional 2 to 3 minutes to crisp bacon. Makes 6 servings.

**Diabetic diet:** Exchanges per serving = 3 meat and ½ bread.

## LEMON-BARBECUED POT ROAST  (220 calories per serving)

1 3-pound sirloin tip
seasoned instant meat tenderizer
1 tablespoon salad oil
½ cup lemon juice
2 garlic cloves, minced
¼ cup minced onion
salt
½ teaspoon celery salt
½ teaspoon pepper
¼ teaspoon ground thyme
1½ teaspoons cornstarch
½ teaspoon bottled meat sauce
for gravy
1 lemon, thinly sliced

Day before: Trim fat from meat. Sprinkle with meat ten-derizer as label directs. In small Dutch oven over medium heat, in oil, brown meat on all sides. Add 2 cups water; cover; simmer 1 hour. Cool; then cover and refrigerate over-night.

In jar, combine lemon juice, garlic, onion, ½ teaspoon salt, celery salt, pepper and thyme; refrigerate, covered.

About 3 hours before serving: Strain lemon-garlic sauce and add to stock in Dutch oven. Simmer, covered, 2½ hours, or until meat is tender. (Replenish water if neces-sary.) Remove meat from Dutch oven; carve, against the grain, into 16 slices. Arrange on heated platter; keep hot.

Add enough water to liquid in Dutch oven to make 1 cup. Slowly mix in cornstarch, then return to Dutch oven. Stir in bottled meat sauce for gravy. Cook, stirring, until thickened. Pass with meat. Makes 8 servings.

**Diabetic diet:** Count each ounce of meat as 1 meat exchange; use up to ¼ cup gravy as 1 "free" exchange.
**Low-fat, low-cholesterol diet:** 10 grams fat per serving.
**High-iron diet:** 4.5 milligrams iron per serving.
**Low-sodium diet:** Prepare as directed but use low-sodium meat ten-derizer; omit salt and bottled sauce for gravy; use celery seed in place of celery salt. 90 milligrams sodium per serving.

## TRANSPARENT NOODLES WITH BEEF (Sun-Hie's Chopchae)
(280 calories per serving)

1 pound round of beef, thinly
sliced
3 scallions, chopped
¼ cup imported soy sauce
1 teaspoon granulated sugar
¼ teaspoon monosodium
glutamate
¼ teaspoon pepper
¼ teaspoon garlic powder
6 medium carrots, scraped
8 fresh medium mushrooms
1 6-ounce container dried mushrooms
1 10-ounce package frozen
chopped spinach
sesame-seed oil*
salt
4 ounces bean threads (transparent noodles)*
4 cups water

Day before or at least 3 hours before serving: Trim fat from meat, then slice meat into thin strips (about ¼-inch wide); place in medium bowl.

In small bowl, combine scallions, soy sauce, sugar, mono-sodium glutamate, pepper and garlic powder. Pour over meat; cover; refrigerate. Cut carrots into very thin strips, 2 inches long. Wash, then thinly slice fresh mushrooms; soak dried mushrooms as label directs; then cut into thin slices. Wrap and refrigerate carrots and mushrooms.

About 20 minutes before serving: Cook spinach as label directs. In large skillet over medium heat, in 4 teaspoons sesame-seed oil, sauté carrot strips until tender-crisp. Place in mixing bowl; sprinkle lightly with salt. In 1 tablespoon sesame-seed oil, in same skillet, sauté fresh and dried mushrooms until lightly browned. Add to carrots; sprinkle with salt. Again in same skillet, in another 4 teaspoons sesame-seed oil, quickly brown meat on both sides. Add to carrots; sprinkle with salt.

Meanwhile, in medium saucepan, soak bean threads in water for 15 minutes. Bring water to boiling and cook bean threads until transparent; drain. Combine all ingredients and toss well. Makes 6 servings.

**Low-fat, low-cholesterol diet:** 10 grams fat per serving.
* Available in gourmet sections of many large department stores, or Chinese or Japanese groceries.

## PIQUANT-SAUCED STEAK (310 calories per serving)

3 tablespoons packaged onion-
soup mix
2 tablespoons granulated sugar
½ teaspoon salt
⅛ teaspoon pepper
1 tablespoon prepared mustard
½ cup catchup
¼ cup cider vinegar
1 tablespoon lemon juice
1 2½-pound boned chuck steak,
about 1½ inches thick
instant meat tenderizer

About 30 minutes before serving: Preheat broiler if manufacturer directs. In small saucepan, combine onion-soup
mix, sugar, salt, pepper, mustard, catchup, vinegar, lemon
juice and ¾ cup cold water. Simmer, covered, 10 minutes.
    Meanwhile, trim fat from meat. Apply meat tenderizer as
label directs. Then broil meat, 4 inches from heat, about
10 minutes on each side, or to desired doneness. Arrange
on board; cut diagonally across grain into thin slices. Pass
sauce. Makes 6 servings.

**Diabetic diet:** Prepare as directed but omit sugar. Each ounce meat =
1 meat exchange. One-quarter cup gravy = ½ bread or 1 "B"
vegetable.
**Low-fat, low-cholesterol diet:** 10 grams fat per serving.
**High-iron diet:** 5 milligrams iron per serving.

## MEAT-AND-FRUIT STEW (Carbonada Criolla) (300 calories per serving)

1½ pounds boneless sirloin
beef
1 tablespoon salad oil
1 cup chopped onion
1 tablespoon canned tomato
paste
1 bay leaf
½ teaspoon salt
¼ teaspoon pepper
¼ teaspoon thyme leaves
1 10½-ounce can condensed
beef broth
2 medium potatoes, cut into
large cubes
½ medium acorn squash, cut
into large cubes
1 medium sweet potato, cut into
large cubes
1 pear, pared, cubed
1 medium apple, pared, cubed
2 tablespoons raisins
1 tablespoon chopped parsley

About 2 hours before serving: Trim fat from meat; cut meat
into 1-inch cubes. In large skillet over medium heat, in oil,
brown on all sides. Add onion, tomato paste, bay leaf, salt,
pepper, thyme, beef broth and 2½ cups water; cover; simmer 1 hour and 15 minutes, or until meat is almost tender.
Add potatoes, squash and sweet potato; cover; cook 20
minutes longer. Add pear, apple and raisins; cover; cook
10 minutes more. Serve in soup bowls; sprinkle with parsley.
Makes 6 servings of about 1½ cups each.

**Diabetic diet:** Exchanges per serving = 3 meat, 1 bread, 1 "B"
vegetable and 1 fruit.
**Low-fat, low-cholesterol diet:** 10 grams fat per serving.
**High-iron diet:** 4.5 milligrams iron per serving.

## STUFFED BURGERS (250 calories per serving)

2 pounds ground round steak
¼ cup prepared mustard
8 large stuffed green olives,
minced
salt and pepper to taste

About 20 minutes before serving: Preheat broiler if manufacturer directs. Shape meat into 16 thin patties. In small
bowl, combine mustard and olives; place heaping spoonful
in center of each of 8 patties. Top with rest of patties and
pinch edges together to seal. Sprinkle with salt and pepper
to taste. Broil patties about 5 minutes on each side, or
until of desired doneness. Makes 8 servings.

**Diabetic diet:** Exchanges per serving = 3 meat.
**High-iron diet:** 3.5 milligrams iron per serving.

## ROAST-BEEF DINNER WITH FRESH VEGETABLES (365 calories per serving)

1 4-pound eye round roast
12 small (about 2 pounds) new
   potatoes
butter or margarine
salt
1½ pounds fresh green beans
2 pounds carrots
1 teaspoon granulated sugar
½ teaspoon nutmeg
2 pounds zucchini
½ teaspoon basil
 6 ears corn
seasoned salt

About 3 to 5 hours before serving: Trim fat from meat. Preheat oven to 325°F. Insert roast-meat thermometer into center of meat; place on rack in shallow open pan. Roast, uncovered, as follows:

|  | time at 325°F. | internal temperature |
|---|---|---|
| rare | 2¾ to 3½ hours | 140°F. |
| medium | 3¼ to 4¼ hours | 160°F. |
| well done | 3½ to 4¾ hours | 170°F. |

Let stand 15 minutes before carving.

About 1½ hours before meat is done: Place potatoes in ovenproof dish; add ¼ cup water, 1 teaspoon butter and 2 teaspoons salt. Cover; bake 1½ hours, or until fork-tender; drain.

Place green beans in ovenproof dish. Add ¼ cup water, 1 teaspoon butter and 2 teaspoons salt. Cover and bake 1½ hours; drain.

Slice carrots into 3-inch chunks; place in ovenproof dish. Add ¼ cup water, 1 teaspoon butter, sugar, 1 teaspoon salt and nutmeg. Cover and bake 1½ hours; drain.

Cut zucchini into 1-inch chunks; place in ovenproof dish. Add 1 teaspoon butter, 2 tablespoons water, 1 teaspoon salt and basil. Cover and bake 1 to 1½ hours, or until tender; drain.

Cut corn ears in half. Spread each lightly with butter; sprinkle with seasoned salt. Wrap in foil, 2 chunks at a time, twisting foil ends. Bake 1 hour. Makes 12 servings.

**Bland diet:** Prepare as directed but cook meat well done and serve only potatoes, green beans and carrots.
**Diabetic diet:** Prepare as directed but omit sugar from carrots; increase butter in each vegetable to 1 tablespoon. Count one ounce meat as 1 meat exchange, and vegetables according to exchanges as follows: 1 potato and 1 piece corn = 1 bread and 1 fat; green beans and zucchini = 1 "A" vegetable and 1 fat; ½ cup carrots = 1 "B" vegetable and 1 fat.
**Egg-, gluten-, milk- and wheat-free diet:** Prepare as directed but use milk-free margarine on milk-free diet; substitute regular salt for seasoned salt on gluten-free diet.
**Low-fat, low-cholesterol diet:** Prepare as directed but use margarine or salad oil instead of butter. 10 grams fat per serving.
**Low-fat, bland (gall bladder) diet:** Prepare as directed for bland diet.
**High-iron diet:** 1.5 milligrams iron per serving of vegetables; 4 milligrams iron per serving of meat.
**Low-residue diet:** Prepare as directed for bland diet.
**Low-sodium diet:** Prepare as directed but omit salts, and use unsalted butter or margarine. 35 milligrams sodium per serving vegetables, or 5 milligrams per serving if carrots are omitted. Meat provides 75 milligrams sodium per 4-ounce serving.

## ROAST BEEF PIQUANT (275 calories per serving)

2 pounds small potatoes,
    cooked, peeled and sliced
salt
seasoned pepper
1 tablespoon chopped fresh dill
1 cup low-calorie French dress-
    ing
1 9-ounce package frozen whole
    green beans
1 9-ounce package frozen cut
    wax beans
1 16-ounce can small whole
    carrots, drained
2 pounds cold sliced roast beef
    (about 20 slices)
3 small tomatoes, sliced
¼ cup chopped parsley for
    garnish
1 small red onion, sliced for
    garnish

At least 6 hours before serving: In medium bowl, toss potatoes with ½ teaspoon salt, ¼ teaspoon seasoned pepper, chopped dill and some low-calorie French dressing; refrigerate, covered.

Boil green and wax beans as labels direct; drain; cool; toss together with some dressing. Cut carrots into julienne strips; toss with some dressing. Refrigerate beans, carrots and leftover dressing.

About 1 hour before serving: Fold each roast-beef slice in quarters. Lay slices in one row down center of large rectangular tray. Then arrange bean, potato and carrot salads, as well as tomato slices, on opposite sides of roast beef. Garnish tray with parsley and onion rings. Refrigerate, covered, until served. Pass leftover dressing. Makes 10 servings.

**Diabetic diet:** Two slices meat = 2 meat exchanges. Select vegetables and count according to exchange system—carrots = "B" vegetable, potatoes = bread exchange, green beans and tomatoes = "A" vegetables.
**Low-fat, low-cholesterol diet:** 5 grams fat per serving.
**High-iron diet:** 4.5 milligrams iron per serving.

## BEEF-AND-CABBAGE CASSEROLE (310 calories per serving)

2 pounds round of beef, cut
    into 1-inch cubes
2 tablespoons salad oil
1 tablespoon bottled sauce for
    gravy
4 medium onions, sliced
1 teaspoon salt
¼ teaspoon pepper
1 bay leaf
1½ teaspoons caraway seed
10 gingersnaps, finely crushed
½ cup cider vinegar
2 tablespoons granulated sugar
½ head green cabbage
seasoned salt and pepper

About 2 hours before serving: Trim all fat from meat. In large ovenproof skillet over medium-high heat, in oil, brown meat cubes. Add bottled sauce for gravy, 3 cups water, 2 sliced onions, salt, pepper, bay leaf and caraway seed. Simmer, covered, 1 hour, or until meat is fork-tender.

Stir in gingersnap crumbs, then cook, stirring, until dissolved; remove bay leaf. Preheat oven to 400°F. Stir in vinegar and sugar; cut cabbage into 6 thin wedges, then lay in row on top of meat; sprinkle with seasoned salt and seasoned pepper. Slice 2 onions into rings and scatter over top. Cover and bake 30 minutes, or until cabbage is tender-crisp.

To serve: Pour some of gravy over cabbage wedges. Makes 6 servings.

**Low-fat, low-cholesterol diet:** 10 grams fat per serving.
**High-iron diet:** 5 milligrams iron per serving.

## POTTED BEEF (265 calories per serving)

1 tablespoon salad oil
2 pounds boneless chuck beef,
    trimmed of all fat, cut into
    2-inch cubes
1 medium onion, sliced
1 tablespoon salt
¼ teaspoon pepper
6 large carrots, cut into chunks
6 stalks celery, cut into chunks
1 teaspoon dill weed
1 bay leaf

About 30 minutes before serving: In 4-quart pressure cooker, in hot oil, brown meat and onion. Add remaining ingredients and ¾ cup water. (Use 1 cup if recommended in pressure-cooker manual.) Bring to 15 pounds pressure as manufacturer directs; cook 15 minutes. Remove from heat; reduce pressure quickly as manufacturer directs before uncovering. Makes 6 servings.

**Egg-, gluten-, milk- and wheat-free diet:** Prepare as directed.
**Low-fat, low-cholesterol diet:** 10 grams fat per serving.
**High-iron diet:** 5 milligrams iron per serving.

## FLEMISH OVEN POT ROAST (245 calories per serving)

1 cup cider vinegar
salt
seasoned pepper
1 tablespoon whole allspice
¼ teaspoon nutmeg
1 3-pound round steak
3 bread slices
1 egg
1 tablespoon instant minced
   onion
1½ teaspoons mixed dried
   herbs
1 6-ounce can tomato paste
1 tablespoon flour

About 3½ hours before serving: Heat vinegar with 2 teaspoons salt, ¾ teaspoon seasoned pepper, allspice and nutmeg 5 minutes. Trim fat from meat. Pour seasoning mixture over meat and let stand.

To prepare stuffing: With fork, pull bread into crumbs; mix with egg, onion, ½ teaspoon salt, ⅛ teaspoon seasoned pepper, mixed herbs and tomato paste. Preheat oven to 350°F. Remove meat from vinegar mixture; discard vinegar; gash meat deeply with sharp knife, then fill slit with stuffing; repeat on all sides until all stuffing is used. In Dutch oven, brown meat on all sides—about 10 to 15 minutes; pour off fat; add ¼ cup hot water; cover and bake 3 hours, or until tender.

When meat is tender, pour juices from Dutch oven into measuring cup; skim off fat. Return all but ¼ cup juices to Dutch oven. Stir reserved juices into flour and ½ teaspoon salt; stir this mixture into Dutch-oven juices. Cook, stirring, until thickened.

To serve: Cut meat into thin slices; pass gravy. Makes 8 servings.

**Low-fat, low-cholesterol diet:** Prepare as directed but use only white of egg. 10 grams fat per serving.
**High-iron diet:** 5.5 milligrams iron per serving.
**Low-sodium diet:** Prepare as directed but omit salt; use tomato paste not containing added salt. 145 milligrams sodium per serving. If also prepared with low-sodium bread, 100 milligrams sodium per serving.

## HEARTY BEEF-AND-VEGETABLE CASSEROLE (305 calories per serving)

1½ pounds boneless round of
   beef
unseasoned meat tenderizer
salad oil
1 pound onions, thinly sliced
5 fresh medium tomatoes
salt
pepper
½ pound green beans, cut up
2 carrots, sliced
1½ cups diced green peppers
1½ cups pared cubed eggplant
½ cup uncooked long-grain
   rice

Day before: Trim all fat from meat; sprinkle with meat tenderizer as label directs; cut into 1-inch cubes. In medium skillet over medium heat, in 2 tablespoons oil, sauté onions until tender; remove. In same skillet, brown meat; add ¼ cup water, then simmer, covered, ½ hour. Refrigerate, covered.

About 2½ hours before serving: Preheat oven to 375°F. Lightly oil medium baking dish; line bottom with half of onions and 3 tomatoes in ½-inch slices. Sprinkle with ½ teaspoon salt, ⅛ teaspoon pepper. Cover with half of each of following: beans, carrots, green peppers and eggplant. Top with rice, 1 teaspoon salt, dash pepper, meat and juices. Top meat with rest of vegetables, then ½ teaspoon salt. Pour ⅔ cup water over all. Arrange remaining sliced tomatoes down middle; sprinkle with ¼ teaspoon salt. Cover with foil and bake 2 hours, or until tender. Makes 6 servings.

**Egg-, gluten-, milk- and wheat-free diet:** Prepare as directed.
**Low-fat, low-cholesterol diet:** 10 grams fat per serving.
**High-iron diet:** 4 milligrams iron per serving.
**Low-sodium diet:** Prepare as directed but use low-sodium meat tenderizer; omit salt. 105 milligrams sodium per serving.

Halibut with Buttery Lemon Sauce, page 173
Chicken with Honolulu Sauce, page 175
Rib Steak with Mexicali Marinade, page 174
Hamburger Patties with Chili-Pineapple Sauce, page 172

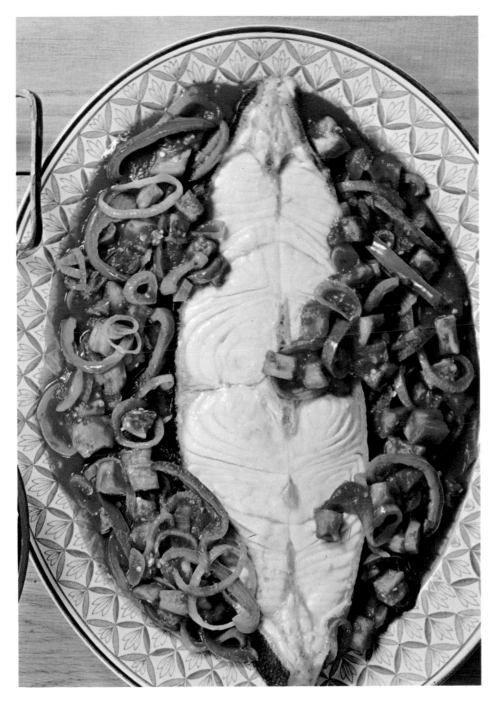

Above: Halibut Steak with Eggplant
and Tomato Sauce, page 84

Opposite: Peas and Celery, page 178,
Country Scallops, page 104, and
Potato Soup Laced with Lime, page 72

Turkey Roll with Cranberry Sauce,
page 172
Side Sauces, page 172–175

Barbecued Chicken in a Sack, page 113

Above: Liver Jardinière, page 164

Right: Minute Meat Loaves,
page 155

Opposite: Roast Beef Dinner
with Fresh Vegetables,
page 152

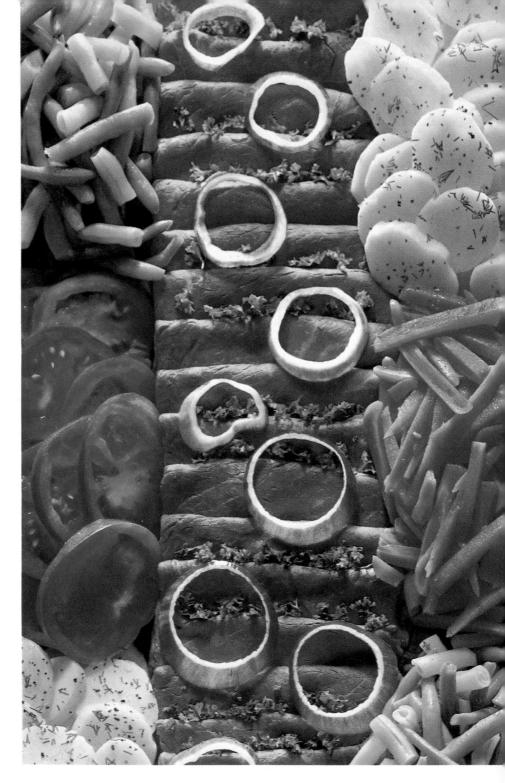

Roast Beef Piquant, page 153

Steak-and-Potato Casserole, page 147

Indian Egg-Meat
Balls, page 157

Snack Suggestions: Cherry tomatoes, zucchini sticks, celery and
endive hearts, cauliflowerets, cucumber coins, green-pepper rings,
radishes. Fresh fruits like pears, oranges, apples, strawberries,
blackberries and grapes. Also yogurt, herring in mustard sauce,
eggs, ham, Melba rounds—all shown above.

Below: Hamburger-Vegetable Soup,
page 141

Opposite, top: Harvest Vegetables,
page 182

Opposite, bottom: Watermelon Cooler,
page 69

Garlicky Cherry
Tomatoes, page 177

Apple-Juice Acorn
Squash, page 186

Autumn Vegetable
Salad, page 202

Rainbow Angel Cake, page 237

Left, above: Brie with Buttery Baked Pears, page 212

Left, below: Angel-Berry Shortcake, page 236

Above: Cherry-Banana Festive Parfait, page 224

Sherbet Blueberry Festive Parfait, page 229,

Melon Festive Parfait, page 210

## NETHERLANDS BEEF BIRDS WITH ONIONS (230 calories per serving)

1½ pounds round steak, cut
   ½-inch thick
salt and pepper
¼ teaspoon marjoram leaves
6 small white onions, halved
flour
2 tablespoons salad oil
1 8-ounce can stewed tomatoes
   (1 cup)
2 tablespoons horseradish

About 1 hour and 45 minutes before serving: Trim fat from meat; cut into 6 serving pieces. With mallet, edge of plate or dull edge of French knife, pound meat until thin. Salt and pepper on both sides; sprinkle top with marjoram. Place 2 onion halves on each piece and roll up; secure with string or toothpicks. Roll in flour. In large skillet over medium heat, in hot oil, brown meat rolls; pour off any fat. Add tomatoes and horseradish; simmer covered, 1½ hours, or until meat is tender. Makes 6 servings.

**Diabetic diet:** Exchanges per serving = 3 meat and 1 "A" and 1 "B" vegetable.
**Egg-, gluten-, milk- and wheat-free diet:** Prepare as directed but dredge meat in cornstarch instead of flour for gluten- and wheat-free diets.
**Low-fat, low-cholesterol diet:** 10 grams fat per serving.
**High-iron diet:** 4 milligrams iron per serving.

## MINUTE MEAT LOAVES (295 calories per serving)

1½ pounds ground round steak
2 cups fresh bread crumbs
1 10½-ounce can condensed
   onion soup, undiluted
6 stuffed olives, halved

About 30 minutes before serving: Preheat oven to 400°F. Meanwhile, combine all ingredients but olive halves. Spoon meat mixture into 12 ungreased, 3-inch cupcake cups; lightly press to shape. Top each with olive half. Bake 15 minutes, or until well done. Makes 12 individual loaves or 6 servings.

**Diabetic diet:** Exchanges per serving = 3 meat and ½ bread.
**Low-fat, low-cholesterol diet:** Prepare as directed but omit olives. 15 grams fat per serving.
**High-iron diet:** 4 milligrams iron per serving.

## SAUCY SWISS STEAK (230 calories per serving)

1 pound boneless round steak,
   1 inch thick
1½ tablespoons flour
salt and pepper
1 tablespoon salad oil
1 16-ounce can tomatoes
1 medium onion, sliced
1½ teaspoons basil
½ small green pepper, sliced

About 2 hours and 15 minutes before serving: Trim fat from meat; cut meat into serving pieces. Combine flour with 1 teaspoon salt and ⅛ teaspoon pepper. Place meat on chopping board; sprinkle with half flour mixture and pound with meat mallet, edge of plate or dull edge of French knife. Turn meat and repeat on other side. In medium skillet over medium heat, in oil, brown meat well on both sides. Add tomatoes, onion and basil. Simmer, covered, about 2 hours, or until meat is fork-tender, adding green pepper during last 30 minutes. Makes 4 servings.

**Diabetic diet:** Carefully divide into four equal portions. Exchanges per serving = 3 meat and 1 "A" and 1 "B" vegetable.
**Egg-, gluten-, milk- and wheat-free diet:** Prepare as directed but use cornstarch in place of flour on gluten- and wheat-free diet.
**Low-fat, low-cholesterol diet:** 10 grams fat per serving.
**High-iron diet:** 4.5 milligrams iron per serving.
**Low-sodium diet:** Prepare as directed but omit salt; use low-sodium canned tomatoes in place of regular. 80 milligrams sodium per serving.

## HUNTER'S HARVEST STEW (275 calories per serving)

1½ pounds boneless chuck
  beef
3 tablespoons flour
1 teaspoon salt
⅛ teaspoon pepper
2 tablespoons butter or margarine
1 16-ounce can tomatoes
2 teaspoons Worcestershire
6 medium carrots, scraped and
  cut into 1-inch slices
12 small white onions
½ pound fresh medium mushrooms

About 2 hours and 45 minutes before serving: Trim fat from meat; cube meat into 1-inch pieces. Coat with mixture of flour, salt and pepper.

In large skillet over medium heat, in butter, brown meat cubes. Add 1 cup water, tomatoes and Worcestershire; cover; simmer one hour. Add carrots and white onions; simmer 45 minutes more. Add quartered mushrooms; continue cooking 15 minutes. If stew is too thin, stir enough water into flour, left over from coating meat, to form a thin paste; use to thicken stew to desired consistency. Makes 5 servings.

**Diabetic diet:** Exchanges per serving = 3 meat, 1 "A" and 1 "B" vegetable and 1 bread.
**Egg-, gluten-, milk- and wheat-free diet:** Prepare as directed but substitute cornstarch for flour on gluten- and wheat-free diets; use milk-free margarine on milk-free diet.
**Low-fat, low-cholesterol diet:** Prepare as directed but use margarine or salad oil instead of butter. 15 grams fat per serving.
**High-iron diet:** 5 milligrams iron per serving.
**Low-sodium diet:** Prepare as directed but omit salt and Worcestershire; use unsalted butter or margarine and low-sodium tomatoes. 95 milligrams sodium per serving.

## "PORCUPINE" LAMB BURGERS (225 calories per serving)

1 pound ground lean lamb
½ cup uncooked white rice
⅔ cup minced onion
1 teaspoon salt
½ teaspoon pepper
1 teaspoon garlic salt
salad oil
1 10½-ounce can condensed
  beef or chicken broth
½ cup catchup
½ teaspoon basil or thyme
  leaves or savory or marjoram
  leaves

About 1¼ hours before serving: Thoroughly combine meat, rice, onion, salt, pepper and garlic salt; form into eighteen 1-inch balls. Lightly rub bottom of skillet with oil; add balls and sauté until browned, shaking skillet to turn balls. Add remaining ingredients; cover; simmer 1 hour. Makes 6 servings.

**Diabetic diet:** Exchanges per serving (3 meatballs) = 2 meat and 1 bread.
**Low-fat, low-cholesterol diet:** 10 grams fat per serving.

## GLORIFIED ROAST LAMB (220 calories per 4-ounce serving)

½ cup Dijon-style prepared
  mustard
2 tablespoons imported soy
  sauce
1 teaspoon garlic powder
1 teaspoon rosemary
¼ teaspoon ginger
2 teaspoons salad oil
6 pound leg of lamb, trimmed
  of excess fat

Early in day: With electric-blender at low speed, blend mustard, soy sauce, garlic powder, rosemary and ginger, just until combined. On medium speed, blend in oil by droplets until smoothly mixed. Place meat in shallow pan and brush with sauce. Cover and refrigerate several hours.

About 3 hours before serving: Preheat oven to 325°F. Place meat on rack in shallow open pan and roast 2½ to 3 hours or until done as desired—175°F. internal temperature on roast-meat thermometer for medium-done, 180°F. for well-done. Makes 12 servings.

**Diabetic diet:** Exchanges = 1 meat for each ounce of meat in serving.
**Egg- and milk-free diet:** Prepare as directed.
**Low-fat, low-cholesterol diet:** 15 grams fat per serving.
**Low-sodium diet:** Prepare as directed but omit prepared mustard and soy sauce. For marinade, mix 1 cup dry mustard with ½ cup water and other seasonings. 140 milligrams sodium per serving.

## INDIAN EGG-MEATBALLS (Nargis Kofta) (300 calories per serving)

4 eggs, hard-cooked
1 pound lean ground lamb
2 teaspoons dried mint flakes,
    crumbled
2 teaspoons salt
1/4 teaspoon pepper
1 tablespoon salad oil
1 large onion, sliced thin
1/2 fresh red pepper, cut into
    1/2-inch strips (optional)
1/4 to 1/2 teaspoon chili powder
1 teaspoon turmeric
1 teaspoon ginger
1/4 teaspoon garlic salt
1/2 cup chicken broth

About 30 minutes before serving: Cut hard-cooked eggs in half crosswise. Mix meat with mint, 1 1/2 teaspoons salt and pepper. Divide into 8 parts; mold each into thin patty, then wrap patty around egg-half, covering it completely.

In large skillet, in oil, cook meatballs (kofta), onion and red pepper. Add chili powder, turmeric, ginger, garlic salt, 1/2 teaspoon salt and chicken broth; simmer 5 minutes. Makes 4 servings.

**Diabetic diet:** Exchanges per serving = 4 meat.
**High-iron diet:** 3 milligrams iron per serving.

## LAMB-AND-PINEAPPLE BURGERS (280 calories per serving)

1 15 1/4-ounce can sliced pine-
    apple packed in pineapple
    juice
3 slices white bread
1 1/2 pounds lean lamb, ground
1 egg, beaten
1/2 cup chopped onion
1 1/2 teaspoons salt
1/2 teaspoon pepper
1/2 teaspoon rosemary
6 stuffed olives for garnish

About 30 minutes before serving: Drain can of sliced pine-apple, reserving 2/3 cup juice. Preheat broiler if manufac-turer directs. Soak bread slices in reserved pineapple juice; mix in remaining ingredients except olives. Shape mixture into 6 patties. Broil, 3 to 4 inches from heat, 6 to 8 minutes. Turn; top each patty with pineapple slice and broil 6 min-utes. If desired, top center of each pineapple slice with stuffed olive. Makes 6 servings.

**Diabetic diet:** Prepare as directed. Exchanges per serving = 3 meat, 1 bread and 1/2 fruit.
**Low-fat, low-cholesterol diet:** Prepare as directed but use only white of egg. 10 grams fat per serving. Omit olive if forbidden on diet.
**Low-sodium diet:** Prepare as directed but omit salt and olives. 155 milligrams sodium per serving. If also prepared with low-sodium bread, 100 milligrams sodium per serving.

## LAMB-AND-CARROT MEATBALLS (305 calories per serving)

1 pound lean lamb, ground
1 cup finely grated carrots
1 medium onion, finely chopped
1/4 cup packaged dried bread
    crumbs
1 egg
2 teaspoons salt
1/4 teaspoon pepper
1/2 teaspoon basil
1/4 teaspoon thyme leaves
2 tablespoons butter or mar-
    garine
2 tablespoons flour

About 1 hour before serving: In large bowl, mix lamb, car-rots, onion, bread crumbs, egg, salt, pepper, basil and thyme; form into 8 balls. In large skillet or Dutch oven over medium heat, in butter, cook lamb balls until well browned.

Meanwhile, in small bowl, slowly add 1 1/2 cups water to flour, stirring well. Stir mixture into skillet until smooth; cover, simmer 40 minutes. Arrange meatballs on small platter. Skim fat from gravy, then pour a little gravy over each meatball; pass rest. Makes 4 servings.

**Diabetic diet:** Exchanges per serving = 3 meat and 1 bread.
**Low-fat, low-cholesterol diet:** Prepare as directed but use only white of egg; use margarine instead of butter. 15 grams fat per serving.
**Low-sodium diet:** Prepare as directed but use ground unsalted Melba rounds instead of bread crumbs; omit salt; use unsalted butter or margarine. 115 milligrams sodium per serving.

## MARINATED LAMB PATTIES (290 calories per serving)

½ cup soy sauce
1 garlic clove crushed
1 teaspoon curry
¼ teaspoon ginger
1 pound ground lean lamb

At least 1½ hours before serving: In small bowl, combine soy sauce, garlic, curry and ginger. Shape meat into 4 patties and place in baking dish. Pour marinade over patties; refrigerate at least 1 hour, turning once, basting occasionally.

About 25 minutes before serving: Preheat broiler 10 minutes if manufacturer directs. Place patties on broiler pan; spoon half of marinade over them. Broil 5 minutes; turn; spoon on remaining marinade and broil 5 minutes more, or until done as desired. Makes 4 servings.

**Diabetic diet:** Exchanges per serving = 3 meat.

## VEAL POLONAISE (295 calories per serving)

4 small loin veal chops (about
  5 ounces each)
1 tablespoon salad oil
1 medium onion, minced
seasoned salt
flour
1 8-ounce can tomato sauce
1 beef-bouillon cube
½ cup buttermilk
2 tablespoons dry white wine
chopped parsley for garnish

About 45 minutes before serving: Trim fat from chops. In large skillet over medium heat, in oil, sauté onion. Meanwhile, sprinkle chops with seasoned salt; lightly dust with flour; brown on both sides in skillet with onion. Stir in tomato sauce, bouillon cube and ½ cup water. Bring to boiling; then simmer, covered, about 30 minutes, or until chops are fork-tender. Place chops on serving platter. Stir buttermilk and wine into liquid in skillet; do not boil; pour gravy over chops. Sprinkle with parsley. Makes 4 servings.

**Diabetic diet:** Exchanges per serving = 3 meat and 1 "B" vegetable.
**Low-fat, low-cholesterol diet:** 15 grams fat per serving.
**High-iron diet:** 4.5 milligrams iron per serving.

## DEVILED VEAL CUTLET (265 calories per serving)

1½ pounds veal cutlets, thinly
  sliced
2 tablespoons flour
1 teaspoon salt
1 teaspoon paprika
2 tablespoons butter or margarine
1 cup minced onions
1 beef-bouillon cube
1 teaspoon prepared mustard
2 teaspoons prepared horseradish
⅓ cup sour cream

About 45 minutes before serving: Cut meat into serving-size pieces; roll in flour mixed with salt and paprika. In skillet, in butter, sauté onions; remove; set aside. In same skillet, brown meat well. Dissolve bouillon cube in 1½ cups boiling water; pour over meat. Add sautéed onions, mustard, horseradish; simmer, covered, 25 minutes, or until meat is tender. Remove to serving dish. Gradually stir sour cream into gravy; spoon over meat. Makes 6 servings.

**Diabetic diet:** Carefully divide into 6 equal servings. Exchanges per serving = 3 meat and 1 "B" vegetable.

## VEAL TARRAGON (250 calories per serving)

1 pound veal cutlets, thinly
sliced
1 tablespoon flour
1 tablespoon butter or margarine
juice of ½ lemon
2 teaspoons tarragon
½ teaspoon salt
⅛ teaspoon pepper

About 20 minutes before serving: On board, pound cutlets with meat mallet or edge of saucer; cut into serving pieces. Dust with flour. In large skillet, in butter, brown quickly on both sides. Add 2 tablespoons water and remaining ingredients; cover; cook until tender—7 to 10 minutes. Makes 4 servings.

**Diabetic diet:** Exchanges per serving = 3 meat.
**Egg-, gluten-, milk- and wheat-free diet:** Prepare as directed but substitute cornstarch for flour on gluten- and wheat-free diets; use milk-free margarine on milk-free diet.
**Low-fat, low-cholesterol diet:** Prepare as directed but use margarine or salad oil instead of butter. 15 grams fat per serving.
**Low-sodium diet:** Prepare as directed but use unsalted butter or margarine; omit salt. 100 milligrams sodium per serving.

## VEAL SCALOPPINI (260 calories per serving)

1½ pounds veal steak, cut
¼-inch thick
2 tablespoons flour
2 teaspoons seasoned salt
¼ teaspoon pepper
2 tablespoons salad oil
1 garlic clove
1 1½-ounce package spaghetti-
sauce mix
1 20-ounce can tomatoes
2 tablespoons sherry

About 30 minutes before serving: Cut meat into 1½-inch pieces; roll in flour combined with seasoned salt and pepper. In large skillet, in oil, heat garlic clove until light brown; remove. Then brown meat in oil; remove from skillet; set aside. Add spaghetti-sauce mix and tomatoes to skillet; stir thoroughly; simmer, covered, 15 minutes. Return meat to sauce; simmer, covered, 45 minutes longer. Add wine just before serving. Makes 6 servings.

**Diabetic diet:** Carefully divide into 6 equal servings. Exchanges per serving = 3 meat and 1 "A" and 1 "B" vegetable.
**Low-fat, low-cholesterol diet:** 15 grams fat per serving.

## VEAL WITH MARSALA WINE (230 calories per serving)

1 pound veal round, cut about
¼-inch thick for scaloppini
¼ cup flour
1 teaspoon salt
generous dash pepper
1½ tablespoons butter or margarine
¼ cup dry Marsala wine
¼ cup water

About 45 minutes before serving: If necessary, cut meat into pieces about 3-inches square. Cut away any white skin, connective tissue and fat. With mallet or bottom of bottle, pound meat into very thin slices—about ⅛-inch thick.

About 20 minutes before serving: Dip meat into mixture of flour, salt and pepper. In large skillet over medium heat, in butter, cook on both sides until lightly browned—about one minute on each side; remove pieces from pan as they are done. Return all meat to skillet; add Marsala and water; cook, gently scraping bottom of skillet to loosen browned particles until gravy thickens slightly—about 5 minutes. Makes 4 servings.

**Egg-, gluten-, milk- and wheat-free diet:** Prepare as directed but use cornstarch instead of flour for gluten- and wheat-free diets; use milk-free margarine on milk-free diet.
**Low-fat, low-cholesterol diet:** Prepare as directed but use margarine instead of butter. 15 grams fat per serving.
**High-iron diet:** 3.5 milligrams iron per serving.
**Low-sodium diet:** Prepare as directed but use unsalted butter or margarine; omit salt. 105 milligrams sodium per serving.

## CURRIED VEAL CHOPS WITH APPLES (350 calories per serving)

4 veal chops, ¾-inch thick
  (1½ pounds)
2 tablespoons flour
2 tablespoons salad oil
¾ cup chopped onions
2 to 3 teaspoons curry
1½ teaspoons salt
¼ teaspoon pepper
1 medium red apple
lemon juice

About 1 hour before serving: Trim all fat from chops; coat chops with flour. In large skillet over medium heat, in oil, brown on both sides. Spoon onions around chops, then sauté, stirring occasionally, until onions are browned. Sprinkle with curry, salt and pepper; add ¼ cup water. Cover and cook, over medium heat, 45 minutes, or until chops are tender.

Meanwhile, core apple (do not remove skin); cut into 8 wedges; brush with lemon juice; place around chops. Cover and cook 10 minutes, or until apples are tender-crisp.

To serve: Remove chops and apples to heated platter; spoon pan juices over them. Makes 4 servings.

**Diabetic diet:** Exchanges per serving = 4 meat and 1 fruit.
**Egg-, gluten-, milk- and wheat-free diet:** Prepare as directed but use cornstarch in place of flour for gluten- and wheat-free diets.
**Low-fat, low-cholesterol diet:** 15 grams fat per serving.
**High-iron diet:** 4 milligrams iron per serving.

## POTTED VEAL CHOPS (355 calories per serving)

4 ¾-inch loin veal chops
  (about 1½ pounds)
¼ cup flour
1 teaspoon seasoned salt
¼ teaspoon seasoned pepper
1 tablespoon salad oil
1 16-ounce can stewed
  tomatoes
3 tablespoons canned tomato
  paste
¼ teaspoon basil
oregano leaves
4 ounces spaghetti

About 2 hours before serving: Trim fat from chops. Combine flour, seasoned salt and pepper; rub into chops. Set electric skillet at 300°F. In oil, brown chops on both sides— about 20 minutes. Stir in tomatoes, tomato paste, basil and ½ teaspoon oregano. Turn control to 215°F.; simmer, covered, 1 hour, or until chops are fork-tender.

About 15 minutes before chops are done, cook spaghetti as label directs; drain; keep hot.

To serve: Arrange hot spaghetti on heated platter; sprinkle with oregano. Top with chops and tomato sauce. Makes 4 servings.

**Diabetic diet:** Serve chops on ½ cup (1 bread) or 1 cup (2 bread) spaghetti. Exchanges per serving = 3 meat and 1 "A" vegetable plus bread exchanges from spaghetti.
**Low-fat, low-cholesterol diet:** 15 grams fat per serving.
**High-iron diet:** 5 milligrams iron per serving.

## VEAL STEAK WITH HAM AND MUSHROOMS (280 calories per serving)

1 veal steak, ¾-inch thick (1½
  pounds)
½ teaspoon salt
¼ teaspoon seasoned pepper
1 tablespoon salad oil
1½ tablespoons bottled garlic
  spread
15 ½-inch cubes lean ham
  (about ½ pound)
2 fresh mushrooms, sliced
1 tablespoon lemon juice
1 teaspoon coarsely grated
  lemon peel

About 1 hour before serving: Trim all fat from veal; sprinkle veal with salt and seasoned pepper. In skillet over medium heat, in oil, brown on both sides and smooth garlic spread over top. Add 2 tablespoons water to skillet; cover tightly, then simmer 45 minutes, or until veal is fork-tender.

Uncover, pour off, then measure drippings; add water to make ⅔ cup, return to skillet and add ham cubes and mushroom slices; then cook 5 minutes, stirring occasionally. Remove veal to heated platter; add lemon juice to skillet and spoon sauce over veal. Sprinkle with lemon peel. Makes 6 servings.

**Low-fat, low-cholesterol diet:** 15 grams fat per serving.
**High-iron diet:** 4 milligrams iron per serving.

## FRUITED RABBIT (245 calories per serving)

1 package frozen tender young
    rabbit (about 2½ pounds),
    thawed
salt
¼ teaspoon pepper
1 cup orange juice
2 tablespoons brown sugar
2 tablespoons wine vinegar
1 teaspoon nutmeg
1 teaspoon basil
⅛ teaspoon garlic salt
¼ cup flour
2 tablespoons salad oil
1 cup fresh orange sections
1 cup fresh grapefruit sections
2 tablespoons chopped parsley
    for garnish

About 1¾ hours before serving: Sprinkle rabbit with 1½ teaspoons salt and pepper; refrigerate 30 minutes. Meanwhile, in small bowl, combine orange juice, brown sugar, vinegar, nutmeg, basil, garlic salt and ¾ teaspoon salt. Combine flour and ½ teaspoon salt; use to coat rabbit evenly.

In large skillet over medium heat, in oil, brown rabbit on all sides until golden. Add orange-juice mixture; simmer, covered, 1 hour or until rabbit is fork-tender, stirring occasionally and turning once. Now lay orange and grapefruit sections over surface of rabbit; cook, covered, without stirring, until just heated through. Garnish with parsley. Makes 6 servings.

**Egg-, gluten-, milk- and wheat-free diet:** Prepare as directed but use cornstarch in place of flour on gluten- and wheat-free diets.
**Low-fat, low-cholesterol diet:** 10 grams fat per serving.
**Low-sodium diet:** Prepare as directed but omit salt and use garlic powder in place of garlic salt. 40 milligrams sodium per serving.

## ITALIAN FRANKFURTERS (295 calories per serving)

1 tablespoon butter or mar-
    garine
1 pound frankfurters, sliced
    into 1-inch lengths
1 10½-ounce can condensed
    beef broth
1 soup-can water
½ to 1 teaspoon oregano
    leaves
1 16-ounce can tomatoes
2 cups uncooked egg noodles
2 medium zucchini, sliced
    crosswise into ½-inch pieces
1 10-ounce package frozen
    Italian beans
2 tablespoons flour

About 30 minutes before serving: In large skillet over medium heat, in butter, brown franks. Add broth, water, oregano and tomatoes; bring to boiling, then stir in noodles. Bring to a simmer again, then top with zucchini; cover; simmer 5 minutes. Now add Italian beans (still frozen); cover; simmer 10 minutes more, or until zucchini is tender.

Meanwhile, stir a few tablespoons water into flour to form a smooth paste; stir into stew. Makes 8 servings of about 1 cup each.

**Diabetic diet:** Exchanges per serving = 2 meat, 1 "A" vegetable, 2 bread and 1 fat.

## SAY MORE FRANKS (155 calories per frank)

1 tablespoon butter or mar-
    garine
¾ medium onion, chopped
¾ cup water
3 tablespoons catchup
2 tablespoons vinegar
1 tablespoon brown sugar
1 tablespoon prepared mustard
2 teaspoons Worcestershire
¾ teaspoon salt
¾ teaspoon prepared horse-
    radish
dash pepper
12 frankfurters

About 45 minutes before serving: In small saucepan in butter, sauté onion until tender. Stir in all remaining ingredients except frankfurters; simmer mixture 20 minutes, stirring occasionally. Preheat oven to 400°F. Place frankfurters in lightly oiled casserole; pour on sauce. Bake 20 minutes, basting occasionally.

To serve: Spoon sauce over frankfurters. Makes 6 servings.

**Diabetic diet:** Prepare as directed but omit brown sugar. Exchanges per serving (2 franks) = 2 meat and 1 "B" vegetable.

## FOIL-BLANKETED FRANKS (235 calories per serving)

frankfurter buns
prepared mustard
chili sauce
frankfurters
scallions

About 30 minutes before serving: Preheat oven to 400°F. On each frankfurter bun spread some mustard and chili sauce; insert frankfurter and scallion. Wrap in foil; lay on cookie sheet; bake 15 to 20 minutes. Unwrap to serve.

## QUICK FRANK DINNER (350 calories per serving)

4 medium carrots, quartered
   lengthwise
1 cup chicken broth
1 small onion
1 bay leaf
1 small head cabbage (about 2
   pounds), quartered
salt
8 frankfurters

About 40 minutes before serving: In large skillet, place carrots, broth, onion and bay leaf; cover and cook over medium heat 5 minutes. Arrange cabbage wedges next to carrots; cover and continue cooking 5 minutes. Turn cabbage wedges. Sprinkle vegetables with salt. Add frankfurters and simmer 5 to 10 minutes longer, or until vegetables are tender. Makes 4 servings.

**Diabetic diet:** Exchanges per serving = 2 meat and 1 "A" and 1 "B" vegetable.

## FRANKFURTER-AND-BEAN CASSEROLE (270 calories per serving)

1 9-ounce package frozen cut
   green beans
1 tablespoon butter or margarine
1 tablespoon flour
1 cup skimmed milk or reliquefied nonfat dry milk
½ teaspoon salt
dash pepper
dash paprika
4 frankfurters, cut into ½-inch
   slices
1 slice toast, cubed
½ cup shredded Cheddar
   cheese

About 50 minutes before serving: Preheat oven to 350°F. Cook green beans as label directs, but only for 3 minutes; drain. In same saucepan, over medium heat, blend butter and flour; slowly stir in milk, salt, pepper and paprika; cook until thickened. Add frankfurters and green beans; pour into 1 quart casserole; top with bread cubes and cheese. Bake 30 minutes. Makes 4 servings.

**Diabetic diet:** Exchanges per serving = 2 meat, 1 "A" vegetable, 1 bread and 1 fat.

## FRANKFURTER STEW (310 calories per serving)

1 19-ounce can tomatoes
2 beef-bouillon cubes
2 cups cubed pared potatoes
2 medium onions, cut into
   eighths
3 medium carrots, thinly
   sliced
3 stalks green celery, cut into
   1-inch pieces
1 tablespoon parsley flakes
½ pound frankfurters, cut into
   1-inch pieces
3 tablespoons flour
¼ teaspoon thyme leaves
salt and pepper to taste

About 40 minutes before serving: In large saucepan or Dutch oven, mix tomatoes, 3 cups water, bouillon cubes, potatoes, onions, carrots, celery and parsley; simmer 20 minutes, or until vegetables are almost tender. Add frankfurters, then simmer 10 minutes more, or until vegetables are tender.

Mix water with flour and thyme to make a smooth paste. Stir into stew, and heat until thickened. Add salt and pepper to taste. Serve in soup bowls. Makes 5 servings of a scant 2 cups each.

**Diabetic diet:** Exchanges per serving = 2 meat, 1 "A" vegetable and 2 bread.

## LIVER AND ONIONS AU FROMAGE (250 calories per serving)

1 pound beef liver, sliced ½-inch thick
flour
salt
garlic salt
pepper
2 tablespoons butter or margarine
¼ cup shredded Cheddar cheese
1 scallion, cut into thin rounds

About 20 minutes before serving: Remove skin and veins from liver; cut into serving pieces. Sprinkle lightly with flour (shake off excess); sprinkle to taste with salt, garlic salt and pepper. In medium skillet over medium heat, in butter, brown liver 2 to 3 minutes; turn and continue cooking until almost done as you like. Turn off heat, pour off most of butter and return skillet to burner. Sprinkle liver pieces with shredded cheese, then scallion. Cover; let stand 2 to 3 minutes, or until cheese is just melted. Makes 4 servings.

**Bland diet:** Prepare as directed but omit garlic salt, pepper and scallions; top with mild Cheddar cheese.
**Diabetic diet:** Prepare as directed but omit dredging liver in flour. Exchanges per serving = 3 meat.
**Egg-, gluten- and wheat-free diet:** Prepare as directed but omit dredging liver in flour for gluten- and wheat-free diets.
**High-iron diet:** 8 milligrams iron per serving.
**Low-residue diet:** Prepare as directed for bland diet.

## ENGLISH LIVER BAKE (245 calories per serving)

1 pound beef liver
flour
1 teaspoon salt
¼ teaspoon pepper
1 4-ounce package Canadian bacon (about 10 to 12 slices)
1 large onion, sliced

About 1 hour and 45 minutes before serving: Preheat oven to 350°F. Cut liver into 4 serving pieces. Dredge in 2 tablespoons flour mixed with salt and pepper. Trim fat from Canadian bacon.

In 2-quart casserole, place layers of liver, Canadian bacon and onion slices; add 1½ cups water. Bake, uncovered, 1½ hours. For a thicker gravy, make a smooth paste with 2 tablespoons flour and 2 tablespoons water; stir in about 10 minutes before end of cooking time. Makes 4 servings.

**Bland diet:** Prepare as directed but omit pepper and onion.
**Diabetic diet:** Exchanges per serving = 4 meat and 1 "B" vegetable.
**Egg-, gluten-, milk- and wheat-free diet:** Prepare as directed but dredge liver in cornstarch instead of flour for gluten- and wheat-free diets.
**Low-fat, bland (gall bladder) diet:** Prepare as directed for bland diet.
**High-iron diet:** 8.5 milligrams iron per serving.
**Low-residue diet:** Prepare as directed for bland diet.

## LEMONY LIVER (220 calories per serving)

1½ tablespoons flour
½ teaspoon salt
¼ teaspoon pepper
1 pound calves' liver, thinly sliced
2 tablespoons butter or margarine
1 tablespoon lemon juice
1 tablespoon chopped parsley for garnish

About 10 minutes before serving: Combine flour, salt and pepper; use to coat liver. In medium skillet over high heat, in butter, cook liver until tender—about 2 minutes on each side. Sprinkle with lemon juice and parsley. Makes 4 servings.

**Diabetic diet:** Exchanges per serving = 3 meat.
**Egg-, gluten-, milk- and wheat-free diet:** Prepare as directed but use cornstarch in place of flour on gluten- and wheat-free diets; use milk-free margarine on milk-free diet.
**High-iron diet:** 10 milligrams iron per serving.
**Low-sodium diet:** Prepare as directed but omit salt; use unsalted butter or margarine. 85 milligrams sodium per serving.

## LIVER CREOLE (230 calories per serving)

1 pound calves' liver, thinly
  sliced
1 tablespoon flour
1 tablespoon butter or margarine
1 16-ounce can tomatoes
1 medium onion, sliced
1 green pepper, cut into thin
  strips
½ cup diced celery
½ teaspoon salt
dash pepper
2 teaspoons cornstarch

About 30 minutes before serving: Cut liver into 1-inch strips; sprinkle lightly with flour. In medium skillet, in butter, quickly brown liver; add remaining ingredients except cornstarch. Simmer, covered, 15 minutes. Mix cornstarch with a little water to form a smooth paste. Stir into liver mixture; simmer, stirring, until sauce thickens. Makes 4 servings.

**Diabetic diet:** Exchanges per serving = 3 meat, 1 "A" and 1 "B" vegetable.
**Egg-, gluten-, milk- and wheat-free diet:** Prepare as directed but use cornstarch in place of flour to dredge liver for gluten- and wheat-free diets; use milk-free margarine on milk-free diet.
**Low-fat diet:** 10 grams fat per serving. Omit recipe from low-cholesterol diet.
**High-iron diet:** 11 milligrams iron per serving.
**Low-sodium diet:** Prepare as directed but use unsalted butter or margarine; use low-sodium-packed canned tomatoes; omit salt. 95 milligrams sodium per serving.

## LIVER JARDINIÈRE (275 calories per serving)

2 pounds beef liver, sliced
3 tablespoons flour
8 strips bacon
3 medium onions, thinly sliced
3 large green peppers, thinly
  sliced
2 teaspoons salt
¼ teaspoon pepper
1 16-ounce can whole tomatoes

About 1 hour and 15 minutes before serving: Lightly coat liver slices with flour. In large skillet over medium heat, fry bacon until crisp; drain on paper towels. Pour off bacon drippings and reserve. Over medium heat, in 2 tablespoons bacon drippings, fry liver, a few pieces at a time, until lightly browned on both sides. Remove from pan.

Meanwhile, to skillet, add 1 tablespoon more bacon drippings, onions, green peppers, salt and pepper; brown lightly. Add juice from tomatoes (reserve tomatoes); place liver on top; cover and cook over low heat 25 minutes, or until liver is tender. During last minutes of cooking, add tomatoes and bacon slices to heat through. Makes 8 servings.

**Diabetic diet:** Count one meat exchange for each ounce of cooked liver, and 1 bread exchange for about ½ cup tomatoes and sauce.
**Egg-, gluten-, milk- and wheat-free diet:** Prepare as directed but use cornstarch in place of flour to coat liver for gluten- and wheat-free diets.
**High-iron diet:** 8 milligrams iron per serving.

## YANKEE HAM (160 calories per serving)

1 1½-pound center-cut ham
  steak, cut about ½-inch
  thick
Worcestershire
chopped parsley for garnish

About 20 minutes before serving: Preheat broiler 10 minutes if manufacturer directs. Trim fat from ham. Place ham on broiler rack; brush with Worcestershire. Broil, 3 inches from heat, 4 minutes; turn; brush again; broil 4 minutes more. Sprinkle with chopped parsley. Makes 6 servings.

**Diabetic diet:** Exchanges per serving = 1 meat for each ounce cooked ham.
**Low-fat, low-cholesterol diet:** 10 grams fat per serving.

## HAM STEAK WITH CURRANT GLAZE (225 calories per serving)

**1 2-pound ham steak**
**¼ cup currant jelly**

About 40 minutes before serving: Preheat oven to 325°F. Trim fat from ham; place ham in shallow baking pan. Spoon jelly over it and bake 30 minutes, basting several times with jelly. Makes 6 servings.

**Egg-, gluten-, milk- and wheat-free diet:** Prepare as directed.
**Low-fat, low-cholesterol diet:** 10 grams fat per serving.
**High-iron diet:** 3 milligrams iron per serving.

## BARBECUED HAM (300 calories per serving)

**2 tablespoons salad oil**
**2 teaspoons salt**
**2 tablespoons prepared mustard**
**2 tablespoons white vinegar**
**2 tablespoons paprika**
**1 cup white corn syrup**
**¼ cup catchup**
**1 48-ounce (3-pound) canned ham**
**heavy cord**

About 1¼ hours before serving: In medium saucepan, combine oil, salt, mustard, vinegar, paprika, corn syrup and catchup. Heat slowly until time to use as glaze. Preheat oven to 350°F.

Open ham; scrape off "jelly," and trim extra fat; cut, crosswise, into ¼-inch-thick slices. Reshape slices; tie together, lengthwise, with heavy cord; place on rack in foil-lined shallow roasting pan. Brush liberally with glaze. Roast about 1 hour; spoon on glaze 2 or three times. Transfer to platter; remove cord. Makes 10 servings.

**Low-fat, low-cholesterol diet:** 15 grams fat per serving.
**High-iron diet:** 4 milligrams iron per serving.

## EGG-ON-HAM TOAST (210 calories per serving)

**1 10-ounce package frozen chopped spinach**
**3 slices bread**
**1 teaspoon horseradish**
**½ teaspoon prepared mustard**
**3 eggs**
**3 slices boiled ham (about 3 ounces)**
**paprika**

About 20 minutes before serving: Cook spinach as label directs; drain. Under broiler, toast bread on 1 side, then spread with blend of horseradish and mustard. Meanwhile, poach eggs until whites are firm.

Trim fat from ham; place ham on untoasted sides of bread; run under broiler until hot. Top each slice with poached egg; then sprinkle with paprika. Serve surrounded with spinach. Makes 3 servings.

**Diabetic diet:** Exchanges per serving = 2 meat, 1 "A" vegetable and 1 bread.
**Low-fat diet:** 10 grams fat per serving. Omit recipe from low-cholesterol diet.
**High-iron diet:** 4.5 milligrams iron per serving.

## OPEN-FACED HAM-AND-SWISS SANDWICHES (275 calories per serving)

**4 large slices rye bread**
**low-calorie (imitation) mayonnaise**
**4 ¼-inch-thick slices canned or boiled ham (about ½ pound)**
**4 rectangular slices (about 4 ounces) Swiss cheese, halved crosswise**
**¾ cup shredded cabbage**
**salt and pepper to taste**

Just before serving: Spread each slice rye bread with 1 tablespoon low-calorie mayonnaise; top with slice canned or boiled ham. Roll cheese slices and place on top of ham—three slices for each sandwich. Toss cabbage with 2 tablespoons low-calorie mayonnaise and salt and pepper to taste. Arrange over cheese slices. Serve with knife and fork. Makes 4 servings.

**Diabetic diet:** Exchanges per serving = 3 meat and 1 bread.

## HAM AND BANANAS (330 calories per serving)

1 2-pound center-cut ham steak
6 whole cloves
½ cup grapefruit juice
brown sugar
½ teaspoon dry mustard
4 medium bananas

About 1 hour and 15 minutes before serving: Preheat oven to 325°F. Trim fat from ham; place ham in shallow baking dish; stud with cloves. In cup, combine grapefruit juice, 2 tablespoons brown sugar and mustard; pour over ham. Bake 50 minutes, basting frequently with sugar mixture. Cut bananas lengthwise; arrange, cut sides down, on top of ham; brush with sugar mixture, then sprinkle with an additional ¼ cup brown sugar. Bake 10 to 15 minutes more, or heat under broiler 5 to 10 minutes until brown sugar melts and forms glaze over bananas. Makes 8 servings.

**Egg-, gluten-, milk- and wheat-free diet:** Prepare as directed.
**Low-fat, low-cholesterol diet:** 10 grams fat per serving.

## APRICOT-TOPPED HAM (210 calories per serving)

¾ pound fully cooked boned
   ham slices (4 slices, each
   about ⅓-inch thick)
1 tablespoon salad oil
3 tablespoons apricot preserves

About 5 minutes before serving: Trim fat from ham. In large skillet, heat oil and preserves until bubbly. Add ham slices; cook, turning once, until heated through. Roll up ham; serve with sauce from pan. Makes 4 servings.

**Egg-, gluten-, milk- and wheat-free diet:** Prepare as directed.
**Low-fat, low-cholesterol diet:** 10 grams fat per serving.

## SWEET-AND-TART TROPICAL HAM (290 calories per serving)

1 16-ounce canned ham
1 16-ounce can tropical fruit
   salad
1 tablespoon vinegar

About 20 minutes before serving: Drain ham, reserving gelatin; trim fat and slice ham into 4 serving pieces. Drain fruit, reserving ¼ cup syrup. In medium skillet over high heat, bring reserved gelatin and syrup to boiling; cook 5 minutes, or until reduced to half of original volume. Add vinegar and ham; simmer 5 minutes more, turning ham once or twice. Add fruit to skillet; heat. Serve sauce over ham. Makes 4 servings.

**Egg-, gluten-, milk- and wheat-free diet:** Prepare as directed.
**Low-fat, low-cholesterol diet:** 10 grams fat per serving.

## HAM-AND-POTATO CASSEROLE (310 calories per serving)

1 tablespoon butter or margarine
1 12-ounce can spiced luncheon
   meat, cut into ½-inch cubes
1 small onion, minced
2 tablespoons chopped green
   pepper
1 cup sliced celery
¼ cup flour
2 cups skimmed milk or reliquefied nonfat dry milk
5 cups diced potatoes
1 teaspoon parsley flakes

About 1 hour and 10 minutes before serving: Preheat oven to 375°F. In large ovenproof skillet, in butter, cook meat cubes, onion, green pepper and celery until onion is lightly browned. Mix flour with bit of milk to form a smooth paste; add remaining milk. Stir flour-milk mixture into skillet; cook until thickened. Stir in potatoes and parsley flakes. Reheat to a simmer. Bake, uncovered, 40 to 50 minutes, or until potatoes are tender and lightly browned on surface. Makes 6 servings.

**Diabetic diet:** Carefully divide into 6 equal servings (about 1 cup each). Exchanges per serving = 1 meat, 1 bread and ½ milk.

## PORK CHOPS IN MUSHROOM GRAVY (245 calories per serving)

2 tablespoons salad oil
8 thin center-cut pork chops
(about two pounds), trimmed
of all fat
1 medium onion, sliced
1 10½-ounce can mushroom
gravy
1 tablespoon brown sugar
¼ teaspoon salt
1 teaspoon lemon juice
½ teaspoon Worcestershire
dash Tabasco
2 8¼-ounce cans pineapple
slices, drained

About 1 hour before serving: In large skillet over medium heat, in oil, brown chops on both sides. Pour off fat; add remaining ingredients except pineapple. Simmer, covered, 40 minutes. Uncover; simmer until gravy thickens, stirring often. Add pineapple and heat through; transfer to heated platter. Makes 8 servings.

**Diabetic diet:** Prepare as directed but omit sugar and pineapple. One serving equals 1 chop and ¼ cup gravy. Exchanges per serving = 2 meat, 1 fat, and 1 "B" vegetable.
**High-iron diet:** 3 milligrams iron per serving.

## SMOKED PORK FLORENTINE (310 calories per serving)

1 2-pound smoked pork butt
2 10-ounce packages frozen
chopped spinach
1 10½-ounce can condensed
cream-of-mushroom soup
¼ cup grated Parmesan cheese
1 cup skimmed milk or reliquefied nonfat dry milk

About 2 hours before serving: In large kettle, place pork butt (remove any casing or stockinette covering first and trim away fat) and cover with hot water; cover and cook, over low heat, 2 hours, or until fork-tender; drain. Near end of cooking time, in medium saucepan, cook spinach as label directs but use no salt; drain.

In small saucepan over medium heat, combine undiluted soup and cheese; slowly stir in milk; heat through. Slice meat and place on platter; arrange spinach on top and pour on soup. Makes 8 servings.

**Diabetic diet:** Prepare as directed. Serve with ½ cup spinach and ⅓ cup soup-cheese mixture = 1 "A" vegetable and ½ milk exchange. Count each ounce cooked pork as 1 meat exchange.
**High-iron diet:** 5 milligrams iron per serving.

## PORK CHOPS JARDINIÈRE (275 calories per serving)

4 pork chops, ¾-inch thick
(about 1¼ pounds)
1 tablespoon salad oil
1 13¾-ounce can chicken
broth
¼ teaspoon salt
⅛ teaspoon pepper
⅛ teaspoon granulated sugar
2 medium stalks celery
1 carrot
1 tablespoon flour

About 1 hour and 20 minutes before serving: Trim fat from chops. In medium skillet over medium heat, in oil, brown chops on both sides. Pour off fat. Add chicken broth, salt, pepper and sugar. Simmer, covered, 1 hour, or until chops are almost fork-tender.

Cut celery and carrot into thin strips. Push chops to one side of skillet; add celery and carrot. Simmer, covered, 5 minutes, or until vegetables are tender. Place chops on warm platter. Using slotted spoon, place vegetables on chops.

In measuring cup, blend flour and 2 tablespoons water until smooth; gradually stir in broth. Cook over medium heat, stirring often, until liquid is thickened; pour over vegetables. Makes 4 servings.

**Diabetic diet:** Prepare as directed but omit sugar and cook 4 carrots. One serving = 1 chop plus ½ cup carrots. Exchanges per serving = 3 meat and 1 "B" vegetable.
**Low-fat, low-cholesterol diet:** 15 grams fat per serving.
**High-iron diet:** 4.5 milligrams iron per serving.
**Low-sodium diet:** Prepare as directed but use unsalted chicken broth and omit salt. 110 milligrams sodium per serving.

## EGGS AND CHEESE MAIN DISHES

### DEVILED-EGG RAREBIT (315 calories per serving)

⅔ cup nonfat dry-milk powder
¼ cup flour
½ teaspoon salt
2 hard-cooked eggs, sliced
1 4½-ounce can deviled ham
2 tablespoons grated process
    Cheddar cheese
2 English muffins, split

About 20 minutes before serving: In double-boiler top, beat 2 cups water, dry-milk powder, flour and salt until smooth. Cook over hot, not boiling, water, stirring until thickened. Then stir in eggs, ham and cheese; continue cooking until cheese is melted. Serve ½ cup sauce on split toasted English muffin. Makes 4 servings.

**Diabetic diet:** Exchanges per serving = 1 meat, ½ bread, ½ milk and 1 fat.

### SURPRISE EGGS (160 calories per serving)

2 10-ounce packages frozen
    broccoli spears
shredded Parmesan cheese
1 tablespoon butter or mar-
    garine
6 eggs
½ teaspoon salt

About 45 minutes before serving: Cook broccoli as label directs; drain. Cut into 1-inch pieces and arrange evenly over bottom of 10-inch pie plate. Preheat oven to 350°F. Sprinkle with 4 tablespoons Parmesan cheese and dot with butter. Separate eggs, leaving each yolk in one half of shell. Beat egg whites with salt until stiff. Spread half over broccoli; sprinkle with 4 tablespoons Parmesan; then top with rest of whites; shape 6 "nests" in whites with back of spoon. Bake 10 minutes. Carefully slide one egg yolk into each "nest." Cover all with foil; bake about 15 minutes, or until eggs reach desired doneness. Makes 6 servings.

**Diabetic diet:** Exchanges per serving = 2 meat and 1 "A" vegetable.
**High-iron diet:** 3 milligrams iron per serving.
**Low-purine diet:** Prepare as directed.

### TOMATO-MACARONI CHEESE (250 calories per serving)

2 cups uncooked macaroni
2 bacon slices
1 11-ounce can condensed
    Cheddar-cheese soup
¼ teaspoon paprika
¼ cup skimmed milk or re-
    liquefied nonfat dry milk
3 tomatoes, thinly sliced
2 tablespoons shredded Par-
    mesan cheese

About 1 hour before serving: Cook macaroni as label directs; drain. Fry bacon slices until crisp; crumble. Preheat oven to 350°F. Combine drained macaroni, cheese soup, paprika and milk. In 2-quart casserole, layer macaroni with crumbled bacon and tomato slices. Top with Parmesan cheese. Bake 30 minutes. Makes 5 servings of about 1 cup each.

**Diabetic diet:** Exchanges per serving = 1 meat, 1 "A" vegetable, 2 bread and 1 fat.
**Low-purine diet:** Prepare as directed but omit bacon.

### EGGS IN RICE NESTS (280 calories per serving)

1 10-ounce package frozen
    mixed vegetables
2 cups cooked rice
½ cup shredded process
    Cheddar cheese
¼ teaspoon salt
⅛ teaspoon pepper
4 eggs

About 30 minutes before serving: Preheat oven to 400°F. Meanwhile, cook mixed vegetables as label directs; drain. In 1-quart casserole, combine cooked vegetables with remaining ingredients except eggs. With spoon, make 4 "nests" in rice mixture; break eggs into them. Bake, covered, 15 minutes, or until eggs are done as you like them. Makes 4 servings.

**Diabetic diet:** Exchanges per serving = 2 meat and 2 bread.
**Low-fat diet:** 10 grams fat per serving. Omit recipe from low-cholesterol diet.

## MUSHROOM CHEESE SOUFFLÉ (260 calories per serving)

2 eggs, separated
2 tablespoons milk
3 tablespoons flour
½ teaspoon salt
dash pepper
1 8-ounce container (1 cup)
  creamed cottage cheese
2 tablespoons minced onion
1 3- or 4-ounce can sliced
  mushrooms, drained

About 1 hour and 10 minutes before serving: Preheat oven to 300°F. In medium bowl, beat egg yolks until light and foamy.

Stir milk gradually into flour, then add to egg yolks and beat well. Beat in salt, pepper and cottage cheese; stir in onion and mushrooms.

Beat egg whites until stiff peaks form; fold into yolk mixture. Turn into greased 1-quart casserole. Bake 50 minutes, or until golden brown. Makes 2 servings.

**Bland diet:** Prepare as directed but omit pepper and onions.
**Diabetic diet:** Exchanges per serving = 1 meat, ½ bread and 1 milk.
**Low-purine diet:** Prepare as directed but omit mushrooms.
**Low-residue diet:** Prepare as directed but omit pepper and onion.

## CURRIED EGGS AND MUSHROOMS (320 calories per serving)

1 tablespoon butter or margarine
½ pound fresh mushrooms, thinly sliced
1 10½-ounce can condensed cream-of-celery soup
½ cup skimmed milk or reliquefied nonfat dry milk
1 teaspoon curry
2 tablespoons slivered toasted almonds
4 hard-cooked eggs, sliced
2 English muffins, split and toasted
2 tablespoons chopped parsley for garnish

About 10 minutes before serving: In skillet over medium heat, in butter, sauté mushrooms until limp. Stir in soup, milk and curry; stir in almonds and egg slices and heat to boiling. Serve over English muffin halves. Garnish with parsley. Makes 4 servings.

**Diabetic diet:** Exchanges per serving (a scant cup sauce over muffin half) = 1 meat, 1 "A" vegetable, 1 bread and 1 fat.
**High-iron diet:** 3.5 milligrams iron per serving.
**Low-purine diet:** Prepare as directed but omit mushrooms.

## ZUCCHINI OMELET (140 calories per serving)

2 tablespoons butter or margarine
1 medium onion, sliced thinly
1 garlic clove, minced
2 pounds zucchini, coarsely grated
1½ teaspoons salt
¼ teaspoon pepper
2 eggs
½ cup skimmed milk or reliquefied nonfat dry milk
½ cup shredded Parmesan cheese
paprika

About 35 minutes before serving: Preheat oven to 350°F. In large skillet, in butter or margarine, sauté onion slices and garlic until golden. Remove garlic; add grated zucchini, salt and pepper; cook, covered, 5 to 7 minutes or until zucchini is fork-tender. Meanwhile, beat together eggs, milk and cheese. In 1½-quart shallow casserole or ovenproof skillet, combine zucchini and egg mixture. Sprinkle with paprika. Bake about 20 minutes, or until firm. Serve at once. Makes 6 servings.

**Diabetic diet:** Exchanges per serving = 1 meat and 1 "A" and 1 "B" vegetable.
**Low-purine diet:** Prepare as directed.

## PETAL CHEESE SALAD (145 calories per serving)

1 8-ounce container creamed
   cottage cheese
1 8-ounce container large-curd
   cottage cheese
½ cup coarsely grated carrot
2 tablespoons minced celery
½ teaspoon celery salt
2 teaspoons chopped watercress
½ teaspoon salt
¼ teaspoon onion powder
dash pepper
1½ carrots, thinly sliced
   crosswise
watercress sprigs
4 cherry tomatoes or 1 medium
   tomato, thinly sliced

About 30 minutes before serving: Mix cottage cheese with carrot, celery, celery salt, watercress, salt, onion powder and pepper. Divide among 4 salad bowls, or arrange on medium round plate; lay carrot slices around outside edge, just touching cottage cheese and overlapping slightly. Radiate watercress sprigs from center of cottage cheese; place tomato slices in center. Makes 4 servings.

**Diabetic diet:** Exchanges per serving = 2 meat and 1 "A" and 1 "B" vegetable.
**Egg-, gluten- and wheat-free diet:** Prepare as directed.
**Low-fat, low-cholesterol diet:** 5 grams fat per serving.
**Low-purine diet:** Prepare as directed.

## GARDEN CHEESE SALAD (200 calories per serving)

1 16-ounce container creamed
   cottage cheese
½ to ¾ teaspoon salt
⅛ teaspoon white pepper
chopped chives
1 cucumber
3 medium tomatoes

About 1 hour before serving: In medium bowl, combine cottage cheese with salt, pepper and ¼ cup chives. Run tines of fork lengthwise along unpared cucumber, all around; cut into thin slices. Slice tomatoes thin, then cut slices in half. Arrange cottage cheese on 3 salad plates, reserving a bit for garnish. Around edge of each plate, alternate tomato and cucumber slices; in center of each cheese mound, arrange 4 cucumber and 2 tomato slices. Dot center tomato slices with reserved cheese mixture; sprinkle with more chives. Makes 3 servings.

**Diabetic diet:** Exchanges per serving = 2 meat, 1 "A" vegetable and ½ skim milk.
**Egg-, gluten- and wheat-free diet:** Prepare as directed.
**Low-fat, low-cholesterol diet:** 5 grams fat per serving.
**Low-purine diet:** Prepare as directed.

## COTTAGE-CHEESE PANCAKES (300 calories per serving)

1 cup sifted all-purpose flour
½ teaspoon salt
1½ teaspoons double-acting
   baking powder
1 egg, slightly beaten
1½ cups skimmed milk or reliquefied nonfat dry milk
1 tablespoon melted butter or
   margarine
2 8-ounce containers creamed
   cottage cheese

About 30 minutes before serving: Preheat griddle until drop of water "dances" on it. Sift together flour, salt and baking powder. In bowl, combine egg and milk; gradually beat milk mixture into dry ingredients. Stir in butter (batter will be quite thin). Bake pancakes, using a scant ¼ cup batter for each, until bubbles break in top; turn; bake other side. Spread each pancake with cottage cheese; roll up. Makes 4 servings of 3 pancakes each.

**Bland diet:** Prepare as directed.
**Diabetic diet:** Exchanges per serving = 2 meat, 1 bread and 1 skim milk.
**Low-fat, low-cholesterol diet:** Prepare as directed but use only white of egg, use salad oil or margarine instead of butter. 10 grams fat per serving.
**Low-fat, bland (gall bladder) diet:** Prepare as directed.
**Low-purine diet:** Prepare as directed.
**Low-residue diet:** Prepare as directed.

## DIETER'S LINGUINE ALFREDO (300 calories per serving)

**4 ounces linguine**
**1 cup creamed cottage cheese**
**½ cup shredded Parmesan cheese**
**dash salt**
**2 tablespoons butter or margarine**

About 15 minutes before serving: Cook linguine as label directs; drain. In small bowl, cream cottage cheese with Parmesan and salt. In small saucepan, melt butter; toss cooked linguine with melted butter, then with cheese mixture. Makes 3 servings.

**Bland diet:** Prepare as directed.
**Diabetic diet:** Carefully divide into 3 equal servings. Exchanges per serving = 3 meat and 2 bread.
**Egg-, gluten- and wheat-free diet:** Prepare as directed but for gluten- and wheat-free diets use bean threads or transparent noodles in place of linguine.
**Low-purine diet:** Prepare as directed.
**Low-residue diet:** Prepare as directed.

# GRAVIES AND SAUCES

## GREEN SAUCE (5 calories per tablespoon)

1 13¾-ounce can chicken
  broth
3 tablespoons flour
½ teaspoon salt
dash white pepper
2½ cups coarsely chopped
  watercress

About 15 minutes before serving: In medium saucepan, heat chicken broth to boiling. Combine flour with ¼ cup water to form a smooth paste. Slowly stir into broth; cook, stirring, until thickened and smooth. Add remaining ingredients; simmer 2 minutes. Makes about 2 cups.

**Diabetic diet:** Up to 3 tablespoons sauce = 1 "free" exchange.
**Low-fat, low-cholesterol diet:** Negligible fat per serving.

## CRANBERRY SAUCE (20 calories per tablespoon)

2 tablespoons cornstarch
1 teaspoon lemon juice
1 teaspoon finely grated lemon
  peel
½ teaspoon ground cloves
⅛ teaspoon salt
1 16-ounce can whole cranberry sauce

About 10 minutes before serving: In medium saucepan, combine all ingredients and heat to boiling. Makes about 2½ cups.

**Egg-, gluten-, milk- and wheat-free diet:** Prepare as directed.
**Low-fat, low-cholesterol diet:** Negligible fat per serving.
**Low-purine diet:** Prepare as directed.
**Low-sodium diet:** Prepare as directed but omit salt. Negligible sodium per serving.

## CREAMY-HAM SAUCE (15 calories per tablespoon)

2 tablespoons butter or margarine
¼ cup flour
1 cup chicken broth
1 cup skimmed milk or reliquefied nonfat dry milk
1 cup finely chopped boiled
  ham
¼ cup sliced pitted ripe olives
⅛ teaspoon pepper
salt to taste

About 10 minutes before serving: In medium saucepan over medium heat; melt butter; stir in flour. Stirring constantly, slowly blend in milk and cook until thickened and smooth. Add ham, olives and pepper. Cook, stirring, about 5 minutes; add salt to taste. Makes about 2½ cups.

**Low-fat, low-cholesterol diet:** Prepare as directed but use margarine or salad oil instead of butter; omit olives. 1 gram fat per tablespoon sauce.

## CURRY SAUCE (15 calories per tablespoon)

2 tablespoons butter or margarine
¼ cup flour
1 teaspoon curry
¾ teaspoon salt
2 cups skimmed milk or reliquefied nonfat dry milk

About 5 minutes before serving: In medium saucepan, melt butter or margarine; stir in flour, curry and salt. Slowly stir in milk and cook, stirring, until thickened and smooth. Makes about 2 cups.

**Egg-, gluten- and wheat-free diet:** Prepare as directed but use 2 tablespoons cornstarch in place of flour for gluten- and wheat-free diets.
**Low-fat, low-cholesterol diet:** Prepare as directed but use margarine or salad oil instead of butter. 1 gram fat per tablespoon.

## CHILI-PINEAPPLE SAUCE (15 calories per tablespoon)

1 14-ounce bottle catchup
1 cup pineapple juice
¾ cup chopped scallions
½ teaspoon chili powder

About 10 minutes before grilling meat: In medium bowl, combine all ingredients. Use to baste meat, fish or poultry during grilling. Serve additional sauce with meat. Makes about 2½ cups.

**Low-fat, low-cholesterol diet:** Negligible fat per serving.

## FRUIT SAUCE (10 calories per tablespoon)

1½ tablespoons cornstarch
¼ teaspoon cinnamon
1 tablespoon finely grated
    orange peel
¾ teaspoon salt
1½ cups orange juice
1 16-ounce can fruit cocktail,
    drained

About 10 minutes before serving: In medium saucepan, combine cornstarch, cinnamon, orange peel, salt and orange juice; cook, stirring constantly, until thickened and smooth. Stir in drained fruit cocktail and heat to boiling. Makes about 2½ cups.

**Diabetic diet:** Prepare as directed but use dietetic-packed fruit cocktail. Exchanges per serving = 1 fruit for ½ cup sauce.
**Egg-, gluten-, milk- and wheat-free diet:** Prepare as directed.
**Low-fat, low-cholesterol diet:** Negligible fat per serving.
**Low-purine diet:** Prepare as directed.
**Low-sodium diet:** Prepare as directed but omit salt. Negligible sodium per serving.

## SOY-SESAME MARINADE (35 calories per tablespoon)

¼ cup chopped onion
¼ cup soy sauce
1 tablespoon light brown
    sugar
1 tablespoon sesame seed
1 tablespoon salad oil
1 teaspoon salt
1 teaspoon lemon juice
¼ teaspoon pepper
¼ teaspoon ginger

Just before marinating meat: Combine all ingredients in small bowl. Brush on beef or lamb before marinating in refrigerator or immediately before grilling. Makes ½ cup.

**Diabetic diet:** Prepare as directed but omit sugar; use saccharin equivalent to 2 teaspoons sugar. 2 tablespoons sauce = 1 fat exchange.
**Low-fat, low-cholesterol diet:** 5 grams fat per 2 tablespoons marinade.

## BUTTERY LEMON SAUCE (35 calories per tablespoon)

½ cup melted butter or mar-
    garine
1 cup lemon juice
¼ cup chopped parsley
1 tablespoon grated lemon
    peel
1 tablespoon salt
1 teaspoon granulated sugar
¼ teaspoon pepper

About 10 minutes before grilling: In medium bowl, combine all ingredients. Use to baste fish during grilling. Makes 1½ cups.

**Diabetic diet:** Prepare as directed but omit sugar. Exchanges per tablespoon = 1 fat.
**Egg-, gluten-, milk- and wheat-free diet:** Prepare as directed but use milk-free margarine on milk-free diet.
**Low-fat, low-cholesterol diet:** Prepare as directed but use margarine or salad oil instead of butter. 5 grams fat per tablespoon.
**Low-sodium diet:** Prepare as directed but use unsalted butter or margarine; omit salt. Negligible sodium per serving.

## HORSERADISH SAUCE (10 calories per tablespoon)

⅓ cup low-calorie (imitation)
    mayonnaise
¼ cup minced dill pickle
2 tablespoons horseradish
1 tablespoon milk
dash pepper

At least 2 hours before serving: In small container, combine all ingredients. Cover; refrigerate. Makes ¾ cup sauce.

**Low-fat, low-cholesterol diet:** Prepare as directed but use skimmed milk. 1 gram fat per serving.

## PIQUANT SAUCE (35 calories per tablespoon)

1½ cups catchup
3 tablespoons vinegar
2 tablespoons dark corn syrup
2 teaspoons salt
1 teaspoon paprika
¾ teaspoon chili powder
¼ teaspoon pepper

Just before grilling meat: In medium bowl, combine all ingredients. Use to baste lean beef or lamb patties during grilling. Makes 1¾ cups.

**Egg-, gluten-, milk- and wheat-free diet:** Prepare as directed but be certain catchup does not contain forbidden ingredients.
**Low-fat, low-cholesterol diet:** Negligible fat per serving.

## HOMEMADE TARTAR SAUCE (15 calories per tablespoon)

½ cup low-calorie (imitation) mayonnaise
2 tablespoons minced parsley
2 tablespoons minced sweet gherkins
1½ tablespoons lemon juice
1 tablespoon minced onion

At least 2 hours before serving: In small container, stir together all ingredients. Cover; refrigerate. Makes about ¾ cup sauce.

**Low-fat, low-cholesterol diet:** 1 gram fat per tablespoon.

## GIBLET GRAVY (10 calories per tablespoon)

giblets and neck from turkey
2 small onions, thinly sliced
2 large stalks celery, thinly sliced
1 to 1½ teaspoons salt
¼ teaspoon pepper
¼ cup fat from roast turkey
½ cup flour
drained pan drippings
salt and pepper to taste

Early in day: Trim extra fat from gizzard and heart. In medium saucepan, simmer giblets (except liver) and neck, 3 cups water, onions, celery, salt and pepper, covered, 1 to 2 hours, or until tender. In the last 15 minutes, add liver; simmer until just done. Cool enough to handle, then trim gristle from gizzard; cut meat from giblets and neck into small pieces. Refrigerate, covered, in cooking liquid.

When ready to make gravy: Drain as much fat as possible from drippings in pan used to roast turkey; measure ¼ cup. Pour into saucepan; add flour and cook 1 minute. Measure pan drippings, giblets, cooking liquid and vegetables; add enough water to make 6 to 7 cups. Slowly stir into flour mixture. Cook, stirring constantly, until thickened and smooth. Season to taste with salt and pepper. Makes about 1½ quarts.

**Diabetic diet:** Use up to ¼ cup as "free" exchange. Count ½ cup gravy as ½ meat and ½ bread exchanges.
**Egg-, gluten-, milk- and wheat-free diet:** Prepare as directed but substitute 2 tablespoons cornstarch for flour on gluten- and wheat-free diets.
**Low-fat, low-cholesterol diet:** Prepare as directed but cook only neck with vegetables; omit giblets. Substitute margarine for turkey fat. Carefully drain all fat from pan drippings and discard. If desired, add a drop or two of brown sauce for gravy. 3 grams fat per ¼-cup serving.
**Low-sodium diet:** Prepare as directed but omit salt in cooking turkey, giblets and in making gravy. 15 milligrams sodium per ¼-cup serving.

## MEXICALI MARINADE (25 calories per tablespoon)

2 tablespoons olive oil
2 garlic cloves, crushed
¼ cup vinegar
¼ cup apple juice
1 teaspoon chili powder
1 teaspoon granulated sugar
1 teaspoon salt
¼ teaspoon pepper

At least 24 hours before grilling meat: In medium saucepan over medium heat, in oil, cook garlic until golden. Stir in remaining ingredients and heat to boiling. Use to marinate lean beef, pork, lamb or veal and to baste also during cooking. Makes ¾ cup.

**Diabetic diet:** Prepare as directed but omit sugar. Exchanges per tablespoon = 1 fat.
**Egg-, gluten-, milk- and wheat-free diet:** Prepare as directed.
**Low-fat, low-cholesterol diet:** Prepare as directed but use salad oil instead of olive oil. 5 grams fat per tablespoon.
**Low-sodium diet:** Prepare as directed but use chili powder not containing salt; omit salt. Negligible sodium per tablespoon.

## GRAVY JARDINIÈRE (20 calories per ¼-cup serving)

**1 medium onion, thinly sliced**
**2 stalks celery, diced**
**1 10½-ounce can beef con-
  sommé**
**2 tablespoons cornstarch**
**¼ teaspoon bottled sauce for
  gravy**

About 20 minutes before serving: In medium saucepan, combine onion, celery, consommé and 1 soup-can water; cover; boil gently, over low heat, until onion is transparent. Strain consommé, reserving vegetables; return consommé to saucepan. Mix cornstarch with a little water and bottled sauce for gravy to form a smooth paste; slowly stir into consommé; heat to boiling. Serve over beef or other meat, garnishing with cooked onions and celery. Makes 2 cups.

**Diabetic diet:** Exchanges per ¼ cup serving = 1 "free."
**Low-fat, low-cholesterol diet:** Negligible fat per serving.

## HONOLULU SAUCE (10 calories per tablespoon)

**2 tablespoons butter or mar-
  garine**
**½ cup catchup**
**½ cup orange juice**
**⅓ cup honey**
**¼ cup lemon juice**
**2 tablespoons soy sauce**
**½ teaspoon ginger**

About 10 minutes before grilling poultry: In medium saucepan, heat all ingredients until blended. Use to baste poultry, pork or ham during grilling. Makes about 2 cups.

**Low-fat, low-cholesterol diet:** Prepare as directed but use margarine or salad oil instead of butter. 1 gram fat per tablespoon.

## VEGETABLES

### STEWED TOMATOES (70 calories per serving)

1 tablespoon butter or margarine
1 stalk green celery, cut into ½-inch slices
1 small onion, sliced into rings
¼ pound mushrooms, thinly sliced
1 20-ounce can tomatoes, undrained
1 tablespoon flour
1 tablespoon granulated sugar
1 slice slightly stale bread, cubed
½ to 1 teaspoon prepared horseradish
1 teaspoon salt
dash pepper

About 25 minutes before serving: In medium saucepan, in butter, sauté celery, onion and mushrooms until onion is golden. Add tomatoes; simmer mixture about 5 minutes. Meanwhile, mix flour with sugar; stirring constantly, add enough water to form a smooth paste; stir paste into tomato mixture. Return to boiling; add bread cubes, horseradish, salt and pepper; boil 5 minutes more. Makes 6 servings.

**Diabetic diet:** Prepare as directed but increase butter to 2 tablespoons; omit sugar; add saccharin equivalent to 1 tablespoon sugar. Exchanges per serving = 1 "A" and 1 "B" vegetable and 1 fat.
**Low-fat, low-cholesterol diet:** Prepare as directed but use salad oil or margarine instead of butter. 2 grams fat per serving.

### SCALLOPED TOMATOES (115 calories per serving)

2 tablespoons butter or margarine
2 stalks green celery, thinly sliced
1 medium onion, thinly sliced
1 29-ounce can tomatoes
1 tablespoon brown sugar
1 beef-bouillon cube
3 slices toast, cubed

About 20 minutes before serving: In medium saucepan, in butter, sauté celery and onion until onion is golden. Add tomatoes, sugar and bouillon cube; simmer 5 minutes. Add toast cubes; simmer 5 minutes more. Makes six ¾-cup servings.

**Diabetic diet:** Prepare as directed but omit sugar; use saccharin equivalent to 2 teaspoons sugar. Exchanges per serving = 1 "A" vegetable, 1 bread and 1 fat.
**Low-fat, low-cholesterol diet:** Prepare as directed but use only 1 tablespoon margarine or salad oil instead of butter. 3 grams fat per serving.
**High-iron diet:** 1 milligram iron per serving.
**Low-purine diet:** Prepare as directed but omit bouillon cube.

### OVEN-BAKED SCALLOPED TOMATOES (100 calories per serving)

1 28-ounce can tomatoes
1 medium cucumber, pared and thinly sliced
1 medium onion, thinly sliced
1½ cups cubed bread, toasted
salt
pepper
½ cup grated Cheddar cheese

About 1 hour before serving: Preheat oven to 375°F. Drain off 1½ cups of juice from tomatoes (use later for stew or drinking). In 2-quart casserole, place half of tomatoes; add a layer of half of the cucumber slices, onion and bread cubes. Sprinkle generously with salt and lightly with pepper. Repeat layering with remaining tomatoes, cucumber, onion and bread cubes. Sprinkle with salt and pepper, then with cheese. Bake 40 to 45 minutes, or until mixture is bubbly and cheese begins to brown. Makes 6 servings.

**Diabetic diet:** Prepare as directed but omit cheese. Exchanges per serving = 1 bread and 1 "A" vegetable.
**Low-fat, low-cholesterol diet:** Prepare as directed but omit cheese. Negligible fat per serving.
**High-iron diet:** 1.5 milligrams iron per serving.
**Low-purine diet:** Prepare as directed.

## GARLICKY CHERRY TOMATOES (50 calories per serving)

1 tablespoon butter or margarine
1 small garlic clove, minced
1 pint cherry tomatoes, stemmed

About 10 minutes before serving: In large skillet over low heat, in butter, sauté garlic 2 to 3 minutes. Add tomatoes and cook 6 or 7 minutes, shaking skillet frequently. Makes 4 servings.

**Diabetic diet:** Divide into 3 servings. Exchanges per serving = 1 "A" vegetable and 1 fat.
**Egg-, gluten-, milk- and wheat-free diet:** Prepare as directed but use milk-free margarine on milk-free diet.
**Low-fat, low-cholesterol diet:** Prepare as directed but use margarine or salad oil instead of butter. 3 grams fat per serving.
**Low-sodium diet:** Prepare as directed but use unsalted butter or margarine. 5 grams sodium per serving.

## ITALIAN-STYLE TOMATOES (40 calories per serving)

2 16-ounce cans Italian plum tomatoes
1 small onion, minced
2 tablespoons granulated sugar
1 tablespoon basil
1 teaspoon salt
⅛ teaspoon pepper
1 teaspoon Worcestershire

About 20 minutes before serving: In saucepan, combine all ingredients; simmer 5 minutes. Makes 8 servings of ½-cup each.

**Diabetic diet:** Omit sugar; add saccharin equivalent to 2 tablespoons sugar; prepare as directed. Exchanges per serving = 1 "A" vegetable.
**Egg-, gluten-, milk- and wheat-free diet:** Prepare as directed.
**Low-fat, low-cholesterol diet:** Negligible fat per serving.

## SEASONED ASPARAGUS SPEARS (20 calories per serving)

2 pounds fresh asparagus
nutmeg

About 20 minutes before serving: In large covered skillet over high heat, in 1-inch boiling salted water, cook asparagus 12 to 15 minutes, or until tender; drain. Sprinkle lightly with nutmeg. Makes 6 servings.

**Diabetic diet:** Exchanges per serving = 1 "A" vegetable.
**Low-fat, low-cholesterol diet:** Negligible fat per serving.
**Low-sodium diet:** Prepare as directed but cook in unsalted water. Negligible sodium per serving.

## CHINESE-STYLE ASPARAGUS (50 calories per serving)

1½ pounds fresh asparagus
1 tablespoon butter or margarine
½ teaspoon salt
dash pepper

Up to 45 minutes before serving: Cut off tough white part of asparagus stalks and discard; wash spears and remove scales. Lay 2 or 3 spears together on board; with sharp knife, cutting diagonally, make bias slices about ¼-inch thick and 1½ inches long.

About 10 minutes before serving: In large skillet; place butter and ¼ cup water; cover; heat to boiling. Add asparagus, salt and pepper. Cook, covered, over high heat for 5 minutes, shaking skillet occasionally and checking water once. Cook until just tender-crisp. Makes 4 servings.

**Bland diet:** Prepare as directed but omit pepper.
**Diabetic diet:** Exchanges per serving = 1 "A" vegetable and 1 fat.
**Egg-, gluten-, milk- and wheat-free diet:** Prepare as directed but use milk-free margarine on milk-free diet.
**Low-fat, low-cholesterol diet:** Prepare as directed but use margarine or salad oil instead of butter. 3 grams fat per serving.
**Low-sodium diet:** Prepare as directed but omit salt; use unsalted butter or margarine. 2 milligrams sodium per serving.

## ASPARAGUS AUX HERBES (40 calories per serving)

1 10-ounce package frozen
asparagus spears
1½ teaspoons butter or margarine
¼ cup water
½ teaspoon salt
2 tablespoons chopped chives

About 20 minutes before serving: Run water over asparagus just enough to separate spears. Meanwhile, in medium skillet, bring butter, water, salt and chives to boiling. Immediately add asparagus; cover; simmer 15 minutes, or until tender-crisp. Makes 3 servings.

**Bland diet:** Prepare as directed but omit chives.
**Diabetic diet:** Prepare as directed but increase butter to 1 tablespoon. Exchanges per serving = 1 "A" vegetable and 1 fat.
**Egg-, gluten-, milk- and wheat-free diet:** Prepare as directed but use milk-free margarine on milk-free diet.
**Low-fat, low-cholesterol diet:** Prepare as directed but use margarine instead of butter. 2 grams fat per serving. (Or omit margarine for negligible fat per serving.)
**Low-fat, bland (gall bladder) diet:** Prepare as directed; omit chives.
**High-iron diet:** 1 milligram iron per serving.
**Low-residue diet:** Prepare as directed but omit chives.
**Low-sodium diet:** Prepare as directed but use unsalted butter or margarine; omit salt. 2 milligrams sodium per serving.

## CELERY WITH CARAWAY SEED (25 calories per serving)

3 cups diagonally sliced celery
1 teaspoon salt
1 tablespoon butter or margarine
½ teaspoon caraway seed
dash pepper

About 30 minutes before serving: In medium saucepan, combine celery, salt and enough water to cover. Simmer, covered, 15 to 20 minutes; drain. Add remaining ingredients; toss until well mixed. Makes 6 servings.

**Diabetic diet:** Prepare as directed but increase butter to 2 tablespoons. Exchanges per serving = 1 "A" vegetable and 1 fat.
**Egg-, gluten-, milk- and wheat-free diet:** Prepare as directed but use milk-free margarine on milk-free diet.
**Low-fat, low-cholesterol diet:** Prepare as directed but use margarine or salad oil instead of butter. 2 grams fat per serving.
**Low-purine diet:** Prepare as directed.

## PEAS AND CELERY (105 calories per serving)

⅓ cup coarsely chopped
celery
1 10-ounce package frozen
peas
½ teaspoon thyme leaves
¼ teaspoon salt
1 tablespoon butter or margarine

About 20 minutes before serving: In medium saucepan over medium heat, cook celery, covered, in ½ cup water, 5 minutes, or until tender-crisp. Add peas; cover and cook 8 to 10 minutes; drain. Sprinkle with thyme and salt; toss with butter. Makes 3 servings of about ½ cup each.

**Diabetic diet:** Exchanges per serving = 1 "A" and 1 "B" vegetable and 1 fat.
**Low-fat, low-cholesterol diet:** Prepare as directed but omit butter or margarine. Negligible fat per serving.
**High-iron diet:** 2 milligrams iron per serving.

## CREAMED CELERY (45 calories per serving)

1 tablespoon butter or margarine
2 cups chopped green celery
2 tablespoons finely minced
onion
½ teaspoon salt
1 teaspoon cornstarch
¼ cup skimmed milk or re-
liquefied nonfat dry milk
generous dash pepper

About 25 minutes before serving: In skillet over low heat, in butter, sauté celery and onion until onion is golden. Add ¼ cup water and salt; cover; simmer gently 10 minutes, or until celery is tender but still quite crisp.

Meanwhile, stir together cornstarch, milk and pepper. Stirring constantly, add to cooked celery; heat until thickened and smooth. Makes four ½-cup servings.

**Diabetic diet:** Exchanges per serving = 1 "A" vegetable and 1 fat.
**Egg-, gluten- and wheat-free diet:** Prepare as directed.
**Low-fat, low-cholesterol diet:** Prepare as directed but use margarine instead of butter. 3 grams fat per serving.
**Low-purine diet:** Prepare as directed.

## BRAISED CELERY AMANDINE (60 calories per serving)

4 small bunches green celery
1 10½-ounce can condensed chicken broth
2 tablespoons melted butter or margarine
paprika
1 tablespoon blanched slivered almonds

About 30 minutes before serving: From each celery bunch pull off outer stalks; then cut off tops, leaving about 5 inches on each; split each lower section in half, lengthwise. (Refrigerate outer celery stalks and tops for use another day.)

Place split celery stalks in skillet; pour on undiluted chicken broth; simmer, covered, 25 minutes, or until tender. Arrange in serving dish; pour melted butter over them, then sprinkle lightly with paprika and slivered almonds. Makes 8 servings.

**Diabetic diet:** Exchanges per serving = 1 "A" vegetable and 1 fat.
**Low-fat, low-cholesterol diet:** Prepare as directed but use margarine instead of butter. 3 grams fat per serving.

## SPINACH GOURMET STYLE (70 calories per serving)

1 tablespoon butter or margarine
½ pound fresh mushrooms, thinly sliced
1 garlic clove, minced
1 small onion, chopped
1 10-ounce package frozen chopped spinach
⅛ teaspoon pepper
⅓ cup sour cream
salt to taste

About 25 minutes before serving: In medium skillet over medium heat, in butter, sauté mushrooms, garlic and onion until golden. Place frozen spinach and pepper on top of mushroom mixture; cover. Stirring occasionally, cook 7 minutes, or until spinach is just heated through. Stir in sour cream; add salt to taste; serve immediately. Makes 6 servings.

**Diabetic diet:** Exchange per serving = 1 "A" vegetable and 1 fat.
**Egg-, gluten-, and wheat-free diet:** Prepare as directed.
**Low-fat, low-cholesterol diet:** Prepare as directed but use salad oil instead of butter; omit sour cream. 2 grams fat per serving.
**High-iron diet:** 1 milligram iron per serving.

## SOUTHERN SPINACH (40 calories per serving)

1 10-ounce package frozen chopped spinach
1 8-ounce can grapefruit sections
½ teaspoon salt
1 teaspoon lemon juice
cinnamon
pepper

About 20 minutes before serving: Cook spinach according to package directions, but substitute juice drained from grapefruit for water. During last minutes of cooking time, add grapefruit sections to heat through. Drain and toss with lemon juice. Serve in warm bowl; sprinkle lightly with cinnamon and pepper. Makes 6 servings.

**Egg-, gluten-, milk- and wheat-free diet:** Prepare as directed.
**Low-fat, low-cholesterol diet:** Negligible fat per serving.
**High-iron diet:** 1 milligram iron per serving.

## CURRIED SPINACH (55 calories per serving)

2 10-ounce packages frozen chopped spinach
2 tablespoons butter or margarine
⅛ teaspoon pepper
⅛ teaspoon nutmeg
¼ teaspoon curry

About 15 minutes before serving: Cook spinach as label directs. Meanwhile, in small saucepan, melt butter; remove from heat; stir in pepper, nutmeg and curry. Drain spinach well through fine strainer. Return to original pan and toss with butter mixture. Makes 6 servings.

**Diabetic diet:** Exchanges per serving = 1 "A" vegetable and 1 fat.
**Egg-, gluten-, milk- and wheat-free diet:** Prepare as directed but use milk-free margarine on milk-free diet.
**Low-fat, low-cholesterol diet:** Prepare as directed but use margarine or salad oil instead of butter. 5 grams fat per serving.
**High-iron diet:** 2 milligrams iron per serving.

## CRUNCHY PEAS (55 calories per serving)

1 10-ounce package frozen
 peas
1 cup chopped lettuce

About 10 minutes before serving: Cook peas as label directs. Add lettuce; simmer until wilted and transparent. Makes 4 servings.

**Diabetic diet:** Exchanges per serving (about ½ cup) = 1 "B" vegetable. (If desired, stir in 4 teaspoons butter or margarine and add 1 fat exchange.)
**Egg-, gluten-, milk- and wheat-free diet:** Prepare as directed.
**High-iron diet:** Make only 3 servings. 2 milligrams iron per serving.

## ZUCCHINI PARMIGIANA (90 calories per serving)

2 medium zucchini, cut into
 ½-inch slices
½ teaspoon oregano leaves
2 medium tomatoes, cut into
 eighths
salt
½ cup grated Parmesan
 cheese

About 20 minutes before serving: In salted water to cover, simmer zucchini slices and oregano 10 minutes, or until tender. Preheat broiler 10 minutes if manufacturer directs. In shallow baking pan, arrange drained zucchini and tomatoes; sprinkle with salt, then cheese. Broil 3 to 5 minutes, or until cheese browns lightly. Makes 4 servings.

**Diabetic diet:** Exchanges per serving = 1 "A" vegetable and ½ milk.
**Egg-, gluten-, and wheat-free diet:** Prepare as directed.
**Low-purine diet:** Prepare as directed.

## ITALIAN MEDLEY (75 calories per serving)

1 12-ounce can whole-kernel
 corn, undrained
1 16-ounce can tomatoes
2 medium zucchini, thinly
 sliced
1½ teaspoons salt
½ teaspoon whole cumin seed
⅛ teaspoon pepper

About 20 minutes before serving: In medium saucepan, mix all ingredients. Bring to boiling; cover; simmer 10 minutes; drain. Makes six ¾-cup servings.

**Diabetic diet:** Exchanges per serving = 1 "A" vegetable and 1 bread.
**Egg-, gluten-, milk- and wheat-free diet:** Prepare as directed.
**Low-fat, low-cholesterol diet:** Negligible fat per serving.
**High-iron diet:** 1 milligram iron per serving.
**Low-purine diet:** Prepare as directed.

## SPICY EGGPLANT (40 calories per serving)

½ medium eggplant (about ¾
 pound)
1 medium onion, thinly sliced
1 8-ounce can meatless spaghetti sauce
¼ teaspoon garlic salt

About 30 minutes before serving: Slice, peel, then cut eggplant into 1-inch cubes. In medium skillet over medium heat, cover and cook eggplant and onion slices in ½ cup water until onion is tender—about 10 minutes. Stir in spaghetti sauce and garlic salt; cook, stirring constantly, 5 minutes. Makes 6 servings.

**Diabetic diet:** Exchanges per serving = 1 "A" and 1 "B" vegetable.
**Low-fat, low-cholesterol diet:** 1 gram fat per serving.
**Low-purine diet:** Prepare as directed.

## EGGPLANT AND POTATO ALEXANDRIA (85 calories per serving)

2 teaspoons salad oil
¼ cup finely chopped onion
2 cups peeled diced eggplant
1 medium potato, finely diced
 (about 1 cup)
1 teaspoon salt
¼ teaspoon dry mustard
¼ teaspoon turmeric
dash ginger
dash cayenne

About 25 minutes before serving: In saucepan, in oil, sauté onion until golden. Stir in ½ cup water and remaining ingredients; cover; simmer 15 to 20 minutes, or until potatoes are tender. Makes three ¾-cup servings.

**Diabetic diet:** Prepare as directed but use 1 tablespoon salad oil. Exchanges per serving = 1 "A" and 1 "B" vegetable and 1 fat.
**Egg-, gluten-, milk- and wheat-free diet:** Prepare as directed.
**Low-fat, low-cholesterol diet:** 3 grams fat per serving.
**Low-sodium diet:** Prepare as directed but omit salt. 5 milligrams sodium per serving.

## SPICY ITALIAN CASSEROLE (120 calories per serving)

1 medium eggplant, peeled if desired (¾ pound)
1 small zucchini, thinly sliced
3 small onions, thinly sliced
1 cup spaghettini, broken into 3-inch pieces
3 cups canned vegetable-juice cocktail
1 tablespoon Worcestershire
1 teaspoon salt
1 teaspoon garlic salt
¼ teaspoon oregano leaves

About 1½ hours before serving: Preheat oven to 325°F. Slice eggplant ¼-inch thick. In 1½-quart casserole, place succeeding layers of eggplant, zucchini, onions and spaghettini. Repeat layering until casserole is full.

Combine vegetable-juice cocktail, Worcestershire, salt, garlic salt and oregano. Pour over eggplant and zucchini; cover. Bake 1¼ hours, or until vegetables are tender, placing foil, edges turned up, on lower rack to catch juices.

To serve: Spoon some of juice in casserole over top of zucchini and eggplant. Makes 6 servings.

**Dabetic diet:** Exchanges per serving (about 1 cup) = 1 bread and 1 "A" and 1 "B" vegetable.
**Low-fat, low-cholesterol diet:** Negligible fat per serving.
**High-iron diet:** 1.5 milligrams iron per serving. (Be sure to use enriched spaghettini.)
**Low-purine diet:** Prepare as directed.

## CARAWAY RED CABBAGE (55 calories per serving)

2 tablespoons butter or margarine
1 cup chopped onion
4 teaspoons granulated sugar
2½ teaspoons salt
1½ teaspoons caraway seed
4 teaspoons white vinegar
1 large red cabbage (about 3 pounds), shredded

About 1 hour before serving: In large saucepan, in hot butter, sauté onions until golden; stir in sugar. Add 1 cup water and remaining ingredients. Simmer, covered, stirring occasionally, about 35 minutes, or until cabbage is tender. Makes 12 servings.

**Diabetic diet:** Prepare as directed but omit sugar; at end of cooking time, add saccharin equivalent to 4 teaspoons sugar; increase butter to 3 tablespoons. Exchanges per serving = 1 "B" vegetable and 1 fat.
**Egg-, gluten-, milk- and wheat-free diet:** Prepare as directed but use milk-free margarine on milk-free diet.
**Low-fat, low-cholesterol diet:** Prepare as directed but use margarine or salad oil instead of butter. 2 grams fat per serving.

## SKILLET CHINESE CABBAGE (35 calories per serving)

1 small head Chinese cabbage
1 tablespoon salad oil
½ teaspoon salt

About 15 minutes before serving: Wash and cut Chinese cabbage into 1-inch crosswise slices. In large skillet, heat oil, ½ cup water and salt to boiling; add cabbage; cover; simmer 10 minutes, or until tender-crisp. Makes 6 servings.

**Diabetic diet:** Prepare as directed but increase oil to 2 tablespoons. Exchanges per serving = 1 "A" vegetable and 1 fat. (Or omit oil and count as 1 "A" vegetable.)
**Egg-, gluten-, milk- and wheat-free diet:** Prepare as directed.
**Low-fat, low-cholesterol diet:** Prepare as directed but omit oil. Negligible fat per serving.
**Low-purine diet:** Prepare as directed.
**Low-sodium diet:** Prepare as directed but omit salt. 15 milligrams sodium per serving.

## BROCCOLI WITH MUSTARD SAUCE (60 calories per serving)

2 10-ounce packages frozen broccoli spears
1 tablespoon butter or margarine
1 tablespoon flour
1 tablespoon prepared mustard
1 cup skimmed milk or re-liquefied nonfat dry milk
1½ teaspoons lemon juice

About 15 minutes before serving: Cook broccoli as label directs; drain. Meanwhile, in small saucepan over medium heat, melt butter; stir in flour and mustard. Slowly add milk; cook, stirring, until smooth and thickened. Remove from heat; stir in lemon juice. Serve on broccoli. Makes 6 servings.

**Low-fat, low-cholesterol diet:** Prepare as directed but use margarine instead of butter. 2 grams fat per serving.
**High-iron diet:** 1.5 milligrams iron per serving.

## HARVEST VEGETABLES (95 calories per serving)

3 medium zucchini
salt
butter or margarine
2 cups peeled small white
  onions
1 16-ounce can small whole
  carrots
2 tablespoons orange juice
seasoned pepper

About 30 minutes before serving: Diagonally slice unpared zucchini about 1/4-inch thick. Place in skillet with about 1 cup hot water; sprinkle with 1 teaspoon salt. Cover; cook 15 minutes, or until tender. Drain; add 1 tablespoon butter, then toss. Meanwhile, cook peeled small white onions in 1/2 inch hot water, with 1/2 teaspoon salt, covered, about 15 minutes, or until tender. Drain; add 1 tablespoon butter or margarine and toss lightly. Drain carrots; in uncovered saucepan, heat with 1 teaspoon butter or margarine and orange juice. Arrange hot vegetables in large round serving dish, with onions in center, carrots around them, and zucchini in ring around outside. Sprinkle all generously with seasoned pepper. Makes 6 servings.

**Diabetic diet:** Count vegetables according to exchanges: zucchini = "A" vegetable and 1 fat; 1/2 cup onions or carrots = 1 "B" vegetable and 1 fat.
**Egg-, gluten-, milk- and wheat-free diet:** Prepare as directed but use milk-free margarine on milk-free diet.
**Low-fat, low-cholesterol diet:** Prepare as directed but use margarine instead of butter. 5 grams fat per serving.
**High-iron diet:** 1 milligram iron per serving.
**Low-purine diet:** Prepare as directed.

## CAULIFLOWER PARMESAN (65 calories per serving)

1 medium fresh cauliflower
1/2 teaspoon salt
4 teaspoons olive oil
1 garlic clove, minced
1 tablespoon chopped parsley
1/4 cup grated Parmesan
  cheese

About 30 minutes before serving: Wash cauliflower; divide into flowerets; boil, in salted water to cover, 15 to 20 minutes, or until almost tender; drain. In medium skillet, in oil, sauté garlic and parsley 2 minutes; add cauliflower and sauté 2 minutes more. Remove from heat; sprinkle with cheese. Makes 6 servings of about 1/2 cup each.

## ONIONS WITH A ZEST (60 calories per serving)

16 small white onions, peeled
  or 1 15 1/2-ounce can white
  onions, drained
1 tablespoon brown sugar
1/2 teaspoon Worcestershire
2 teaspoons butter or margarine
1 chicken-bouillon cube
1/2 teaspoon salt

About 20 minutes before serving: In saucepan, mix all ingredients with 1 cup water. Cook, covered, stirring occasionally, 20 minutes, or until onions are tender. Makes 4 servings.

**Diabetic diet:** Prepare as directed but omit sugar; add saccharin equivalent to 1 tablespoon sugar; use 1 tablespoon butter or margarine. Exchanges per serving = 1 "B" vegetable and 1 fat.
**Low-fat, low-cholesterol diet:** Prepare as directed but omit butter. Negligible fat per serving.

## GINGER-GLAZED CARROTS (70 calories per serving)

8 medium carrots, pared
1/2 teaspoon salt
1 stick cinnamon
1 tablespoon butter or margarine, melted
1/4 teaspoon ginger
2 teaspoons granulated sugar
1 teaspoon chopped parsley

About 30 minutes before serving: In medium saucepan over low heat, cook carrots with salt, cinnamon, and enough water to cover, 20 minutes, or until tender-crisp. In small bowl, combine butter, ginger, sugar and parsley; toss lightly with drained carrots. Makes 4 servings.

**Low-fat, low-cholesterol diet:** Prepare as directed but omit butter or margarine. Negligible fat per serving.

## CARROTS MEDLEY (80 calories per serving)

1 pound carrots, pared, cut into ¼-inch slices
1 medium onion, thinly sliced
3 large stalks celery, cut into 1-inch slices
1 tablespoon butter or margarine

About 25 minutes before serving: In medium saucepan, in salted water, cook carrots, onion and celery until tender—about 15 minutes; drain; stir in butter. Makes 4 servings.

**Diabetic diet:** Exchanges per serving (about ¾ cup) = 1 bread and 1 fat.
**Egg-, gluten-, milk- and wheat-free diet:** Prepare as directed but use milk-free margarine on milk-free diet.
**Low-fat, low-cholesterol diet:** Prepare as directed but omit butter or margarine. Negligible fat per serving.
**High-iron diet:** 1 milligram iron per serving.
**Low-purine diet:** Prepare as directed.

## BRUSSELS SPROUTS WITH BABY CARROTS (75 calories per serving)

1 10-ounce package frozen Brussels sprouts
½ cup chicken broth
1 tablespoon butter or margarine
1 8-ounce can tiny whole carrots, drained
dash ginger
⅛ teaspoon seasoned salt

About 15 minutes before serving: Cook Brussels sprouts as label directs but use chicken broth as cooking "water." Meanwhile, in large skillet, in butter, sauté carrots with ginger about 5 minutes; add cooked Brussels sprouts and sauté a few minutes longer. Sprinkle with seasoned salt. Makes 4 servings.

**Diabetic diet:** Exchanges per serving = 1 "B" vegetable and 1 fat.
**Low-fat, low-cholesterol diet:** Prepare as directed but use margarine or salad oil instead of butter. 3 grams fat per serving.
**High-iron diet:** 1 milligram iron per serving.

## CURRIED CARROTS AND PINEAPPLE (70 calories per serving)

1 15½-ounce can pineapple chunks packed in pineapple juice
8 medium carrots, cut into strips
½ teaspoon curry
½ teaspoon salt
dash pepper

About 20 minutes before serving: Into measuring cup, drain pineapple juice, reserving pineapple chunks. Add enough water to make 1 cup liquid; pour into medium skillet. Add carrot strips, curry, salt and pepper. Cook, covered, over medium heat about 20 minutes, or until fork-tender. Stir in reserved pineapple chunks and cook, covered, a few minutes longer to heat through. Makes 6 servings.

**Low-fat, low-cholesterol diet:** Negligible fat per serving.
**Low-purine diet:** Prepare as directed.

## CARROTS À L'ORANGE (125 calories per serving)

salt
6 medium carrots, thinly sliced diagonally
2 tablespoons granulated sugar
1 teaspoon butter or margarine
4 small oranges, sectioned

About 20 minutes before serving: In covered medium saucepan, in salted water to just cover, boil carrots until tender—about 15 minutes; drain. Add 1 teaspoon salt, sugar, butter, orange sections; heat gently. Makes four ¾-cup servings.

**Bland diet:** Prepare as directed.
**Diabetic diet:** Prepare as directed but omit sugar; add saccharin equivalent to 1 tablespoon sugar; use 1 tablespoon butter or margarine. Exchanges per serving = 1 "B" vegetable, 1 fruit and 1 fat.
**Egg-, gluten-, milk- and wheat-free diet:** Prepare as directed but use milk-free margarine on milk-free diet.
**Low-fat, low-cholesterol diet:** Prepare as directed but omit butter or margarine. Negligible fat per serving.
**Low-fat, bland (gall bladder) diet:** Prepare as directed.
**High-iron diet:** 1 milligram iron per serving.
**Low-purine diet:** Prepare as directed.
**Low-residue diet:** Prepare as directed but substitute ½-cup strained orange juice for orange sections.

## CARROTS AND CELERY PLUS A SURPRISE (45 calories per serving)

1 pound carrots, cut diagonally
into ½-inch slices
6 stalks celery, cut into ½-inch
slices
1 to 2 teaspoons prepared
horseradish
½ teaspoon salt
½ tablespoon butter or
margarine

About 30 minutes before serving: In water to just cover, simmer carrots, celery, horseradish and salt 15 to 20 minutes, or until carrots are just tender-crisp. Drain; toss with butter. Makes 6 servings.

**Diabetic diet:** Prepare as directed but increase butter or margarine to 2 tablespoons. Exchanges per serving (about ¾ cup) = 1 "A" and 1 "B" vegetable and 1 fat.
**Egg-, gluten-, milk- and wheat-free diet:** Prepare as directed but use milk-free margarine on milk-free diet.
**Low-fat, low-cholesterol diet:** Prepare as directed but omit butter or margarine. Negligible fat per serving.
**Low-purine diet:** Prepare as directed.

## CHEESE-TOPPED CARROTS (80 calories per serving)

1 16-ounce jar or can sliced
carrots
¼ cup grated sharp Cheddar
cheese
salt and pepper
chopped parsley for garnish

About 10 minutes before serving: In saucepan, simmer carrots 5 minutes; turn off heat; thoroughly drain, then return carrots to saucepan. Sprinkle with cheese; cover; let stand until cheese is melted.

To serve: Sprinkle with salt and pepper to taste; stir to mix cheese; top with parsley. Makes three ½-cup servings.

**Bland diet:** Prepare as directed but use mild cheese; omit pepper and parsley.
**Diabetic diet:** Exchanges per serving = 1 "B" vegetable and 1 fat.
**Egg-, gluten- and wheat-free diet:** Prepare as directed.
**High-iron diet:** 1 milligram iron per serving.
**Low-purine diet:** Prepare as directed.
**Low-residue diet:** Prepare as directed for bland diet.

## JULIAN'S CARROTS (60 calories per serving)

10 medium carrots, thickly
sliced
1 15¼-ounce can pineapple
chunks packed in pineapple
juice
1 cup orange juice
1 tablespoon cornstarch
1 teaspoon salt
½ teaspoon cinnamon

About 20 minutes before serving: In medium saucepan, cook carrots in 1 inch of boiling water until tender—about 15 minutes; drain.

Into small saucepan, drain juice from pineapple and add orange juice. In small bowl, mix cornstarch, salt and cinnamon; stir in a few tablespoons juice; mix to smooth paste.

Heat juices, then stir in cornstarch mixture. Simmer, stirring constantly, until thickened. Add pineapple chunks and carrots; cook over low heat, stirring constantly, until hot and bubbly. Makes 10 servings.

**Diabetic diet:** Exchanges per serving (¾ cup carrots plus sauce) = 1 "B" vegetable and 1 fruit.
**Egg-, gluten-, milk- and wheat-free diet:** Prepare as directed.
**Low-fat, low-cholesterol diet:** Negligible fat per serving.
**Low-purine diet:** Prepare as directed.

## CARROTS CAROLINA (90 calories per serving)

2 16-ounce cans whole baby
carrots
⅓ cup brown sugar
2 tablespoons orange juice
dash salt

About 30 minutes before serving: Preheat oven to 375°F. Thoroughly drain carrots. In ovenproof saucepan, mix brown sugar, orange juice and salt. Cook, stirring constantly, until sugar is dissolved. Add carrots; stir to coat with sugar mixture. Bake, stirring occasionally, 20 minutes. Serve with syrup. Makes six ½-cup servings.

**Egg-, gluten-, milk- and wheat-free diet:** Prepare as directed.
**Low-fat, low-cholesterol diet:** Negligible fat per serving.
**High-iron diet:** 1.5 milligrams iron per serving.
**Low-purine diet:** Prepare as directed.

## VEGETABLES "CUNARD" (95 calories per serving)

1 pound carrots
1 pound white turnips
2 tablespoons granulated sugar
salt
½ teaspoon basil
⅛ teaspoon pepper
2 tablespoons bacon fat

About 45 minutes before serving: Wash, pare, finely dice carrots; prepare turnips in same way. Place vegetables in saucepan with 2 cups boiling water, sugar, 2 teaspoons salt, basil and pepper. Cover; cook until fork-tender—about 15 minutes.

When vegetables are fork-tender, drain well. Return to saucepan; toss with ½ teaspoon salt and bacon fat. Makes 6 servings.

**Diabetic diet:** Prepare as directed but omit sugar. Exchanges per serving = 1 "B" vegetable and 1 fat.
**Egg-, gluten-, milk- and wheat-free diet:** Prepare as directed.
**Low-fat, low-cholesterol diet:** Prepare as directed but substitute margarine for bacon fat. 5 grams fat per serving.

## FLORENTINE MUSHROOMS (Funghi Trifolati) (80 calories per serving)

1½ tablespoons butter or margarine
1 pound fresh mushrooms, thinly sliced
1 garlic clove, minced
4 anchovy fillets, finely chopped
2 tablespoons chopped parsley
½ tablespoon lemon juice
pepper

About 20 minutes before serving: In large skillet over medium heat, in butter, sauté mushrooms and garlic until lightly browned and liquid from mushrooms has evaporated.

Reduce heat to very low; cover; cook 5 minutes more, shaking skillet occasionally. Stir in chopped anchovies, parsley and lemon juice; add pepper to taste. Makes 4 servings.

**Diabetic diet:** Exchanges per serving = 1 "A" vegetable and 1 fat.
**Egg-, gluten-, milk- and wheat-free diet:** Prepare as directed but use milk-free margarine on milk-free diet.
**Low-sodium diet:** Prepare as directed but use unsalted butter or margarine; omit anchovies. 15 milligrams sodium per serving.

## FUN TWISTS (110 calories per serving)

¼ pound uncooked spaghetti twists
1 tablespoon salad oil
½ pound fresh mushrooms, thinly sliced
1 medium onion, thinly sliced
½ teaspoon salt
dash pepper

About 20 minutes before serving: Cook spaghetti as label directs; drain. Meanwhile, in medium skillet, in oil, sauté mushrooms and onion until golden; season with salt and pepper. In warm serving bowl, mix spaghetti and mushrooms. Makes six ½-cup servings.

**Diabetic diet:** Prepare as directed but sauté onion in 2 tablespoons oil. Exchanges per serving = 1 bread and 1 fat.
**Low-fat, low-cholesterol diet:** 3 grams fat per serving.
**High-iron diet:** Use enriched spaghetti. 1 milligram iron per serving.
**Low-sodium diet:** Prepare as directed but cook spaghetti without added salt; omit salt. 10 milligrams sodium per serving.

## HARVARD-STYLE BEETS (65 calories per serving)

1 16-ounce can sliced beets
2 tablespoons granulated sugar
½ teaspoon salt
½ teaspoon paprika
1½ teaspoons cornstarch
2 tablespoons lemon juice

About 10 minutes before serving: Drain beets, reserving ⅓ cup liquid. In medium saucepan, mix remaining ingredients with reserved beet juice. Heat, stirring constantly, until thickened and smooth. Add beets and bring to boiling. Makes 4 servings.

**Bland diet:** Prepare as directed.
**Egg-, gluten-, milk- and wheat-free diet:** Prepare as directed.
**Low-fat, low-cholesterol diet:** Negligible fat per serving.
**Low-fat, bland (gall bladder) diet:** Prepare as directed.
**Low-purine diet:** Prepare as directed.
**Low-residue diet:** Prepare as directed.

## APPLE-JUICE ACORN SQUASH (60 calories per serving)

2 cups apple juice
1¼ teaspoons salt
⅛ teaspoon cinnamon
⅛ teaspoon mace
⅛ teaspoon pepper
3 small acorn squash

About 1 hour and 15 minutes before serving: Preheat oven to 350°F. In large (about 15" by 10") roasting pan, combine all ingredients but squash. Cut squash in half; remove seeds.

Place, cut side down, in apple juice; bake 45 minutes. Turn, cut side up, and spoon a few tablespoons apple juice into cavity of each squash. Bake 10 minutes more, or until tender. Makes 6 servings.

**Diabetic diet:** Exchanges per serving = 1 bread.
**Egg-, gluten-, milk- and wheat-free diet:** Prepare as directed.
**Low-fat, low-cholesterol diet:** Negligible fat per serving.
**High-iron diet:** 1 milligram iron per serving.
**Low-sodium diet:** Prepare as directed but omit salt. 5 milligrams sodium per serving.

## DILLED BARLEY (145 calories per serving)

1 10½-ounce can condensed chicken broth
1 cup dry barley
1 tablespoon chopped fresh dill or 2 teaspoons dried dill weed
1 tablespoon butter or margarine
¼ teaspoon salt

About 1 hour before serving: In large saucepan, heat chicken broth and 1½ soup-cans water to boiling; add barley and dill; simmer until barley is tender and broth absorbed—45 minutes to 1 hour. Stir in butter, and salt if needed. Makes six ½-cup servings.

**Diabetic diet:** Prepare as directed but stir 2 tablespoons butter or margarine into cooked barley. Exchanges per serving = 1 "B" vegetable, 1 bread and 1 fat.
**Low-fat, low-cholesterol diet:** Prepare as directed but use margarine or salad oil instead of butter. 2 grams fat per serving. If desired, omit fat for negligible fat per serving.
**High-iron diet:** 1 milligram iron per serving.
**Low-sodium diet:** Prepare as directed but cook barley in unsalted homemade chicken broth; use unsalted butter or margarine; omit salt. Negligible sodium per serving.

## DUCHESS POTATO CROWNS (120 calories per serving)

3 small tomatoes
salt
instant mashed potatoes to make 4 servings
½ cup skimmed milk or reliquefied nonfat dry milk
½ teaspoon celery salt
½ cup grated mild Cheddar cheese

About 45 minutes before serving: Preheat oven to 400°F. Halve tomatoes; scoop out seeds; salt inside and out. Place, cut side up, in shallow baking pan.

Prepare instant potatoes as label directs but use skimmed milk and celery salt; omit butter; stir in cheese. Top tomatoes with potatoes.

Fill bottom of pan with ¼ inch water; bake 25 to 30 minutes, or until tops of potatoes have brown peaks. Makes 6 servings.

**Diabetic diet:** Exchanges per serving = 1 "A" vegetable, 1 bread and 1 fat.
**Low-fat, low-cholesterol diet:** Prepare as directed but omit cheese; stir 2 tablespoons margarine into potato mixture. 5 grams fat per serving.
**High-iron diet:** 1 milligram iron per serving.
**Low-purine diet:** Prepare as directed.

## LEMON-PARSLEY POTATOES (125 calories per serving)

12 medium potatoes (about 4 pounds), pared
1/4 cup butter or margarine
2 tablespoons chopped parsley
1 tablespoon lemon juice
lemon slices for garnish

About 50 minutes before serving: In large pan, in about 1 inch boiling salted water, cook potatoes until fork-tender; drain. In small saucepan, melt butter with parsley and lemon juice; pour over potatoes. Garnish with lemon slices, if desired. Makes 12 servings.

**Bland diet:** Prepare as directed but omit parsley.
**Diabetic diet:** Prepare as directed but use small potato for dieter. Exchanges per serving = 1 bread and 1 fat.
**Egg-, gluten-, milk- and wheat-free diet:** Prepare as directed but use milk-free margarine on milk-free diet.
**Low-fat, low-cholesterol diet:** Prepare as directed but use margarine instead of butter. 4 grams fat per serving.
**Low-fat, bland (gall bladder) diet:** Prepare as directed but omit parsley.
**Low-purine diet:** Prepare as directed.
**Low-residue diet:** Prepare as directed but omit parsley.
**Low-sodium diet:** Prepare as directed but cook potatoes in unsalted water; use unsalted butter or margarine. 5 milligrams sodium per serving.

## PAPRIKA POTATO BALLS (100 calories per serving)

2 16-ounce cans tiny whole potatoes, drained
2 tablespoons butter or margarine
1 teaspoon paprika
1 1/4 teaspoons salt

About 25 minutes before serving: Preheat oven to 425°F. Meanwhile, dry potatoes on paper towels. Place butter in large baking dish; set in oven to melt. Arrange potatoes in melted butter; sprinkle with paprika and salt; toss until evenly coated. Bake 10 minutes. Makes 6 servings.

**Bland diet:** Prepare as directed.
**Diabetic diet:** Exchanges per serving = 1 bread and 1 fat.
**Egg-, gluten-, milk- and wheat-free diet:** Prepare as directed but use milk-free margarine on milk-free diet.
**Low-fat, low-cholesterol diet:** Prepare as directed but use margarine instead of butter. 5 grams fat per serving.
**Low-fat, bland (gall bladder) diet:** Prepare as directed.
**Low-purine diet:** Prepare as directed.
**Low-sodium diet:** Prepare as directed but use canned potatoes not containing added salt; use unsalted butter or margarine; omit salt. 2 milligrams sodium per serving.

## BOHEMIAN MASHED POTATOES (120 calories per serving)

1/2 teaspoon salt
1 tablespoon butter or margarine
1/2 cup creamed cottage cheese
1/4 cup skimmed milk or reliquefied nonfat dry milk
mashed potatoes to make 4 servings
1/2 teaspoon poppy seed

About 15 minutes before serving: In medium saucepan, bring 1 1/2 cups water, salt and butter to boiling. Meanwhile, in electric-blender container, at low speed, blend cottage cheese and milk until smooth. Add to boiling water; gradually stir in instant mashed potatoes. Beat until smooth; mix in poppy seed. Makes 5 servings.

**Bland diet:** Prepare as directed but omit poppy seed.
**Diabetic diet:** Prepare as directed but make only 4 servings. Exchanges per serving = 1 bread and 1/2 milk.
**Low-fat, low-cholesterol diet:** Prepare as directed but use margarine instead of butter. 3 grams fat per serving.
**Low-fat, bland (gall bladder) diet:** Prepare as directed but omit poppy seed.
**Low-purine diet:** Prepare as directed.
**Low-residue diet:** Prepare as directed for bland diet.

## SALTED BAKED POTATOES (105 calories per serving)

4 small baking potatoes
salad oil
butter or margarine
salt

About 30 minutes before serving: Preheat oven to 425°F. Wash and dry potatoes, then brush with salad oil. Place in oven and bake 25 minutes, or until soft. Let cool slightly, then rub with a little butter and sprinkle generously with salt. Makes 4 servings.

**Bland diet:** Prepare as directed. Dieter should not eat skin of potato.
**Diabetic diet:** Exchanges per serving = 1 bread and 1 fat.
**Egg-, gluten-, milk- and wheat-free diet:** Prepare as directed but use milk-free margarine on milk-free diet.
**Low-fat, low-cholesterol diet:** Prepare as directed but use margarine instead of butter. 5 grams fat per serving.
**Low-fat, bland (gall bladder) diet:** Prepare as directed. Dieter should not eat skin of potato.
**Low-purine diet:** Prepare as directed.
**Low-residue diet:** Prepare as directed for bland diet.

## REBAKED POTATOES (150 calories per serving)

1 garlic clove, minced
½ teaspoon salt
2 tablespoons butter or margarine
2 tablespoons shredded Parmesan cheese
4 unpeeled cold baked small potatoes

About 30 minutes before serving: Preheat oven to 350°F. Blend together all ingredients but potatoes. Cut potatoes into ½-inch slices, almost all the way through. Spread garlic mixture between slices. Bake 20 minutes, or until hot. Makes 4 servings.

**Bland diet:** Prepare as directed but omit garlic.
**Diabetic diet:** Exchanges per serving = 1 bread and 2 fat.
**Egg-, gluten- and wheat-free diet:** Prepare as directed.
**Low-fat, low-cholesterol diet:** Prepare as directed but use margarine instead of butter; substitute dried bread crumbs for Parmesan cheese. 5 grams fat per serving.
**Low-fat, bland (gall bladder) diet:** Prepare as directed but omit garlic; substitute dried bread crumbs for cheese.
**High-iron diet:** Prepare as directed but use a large baking potato. 1 milligram iron per serving.
**Low-purine diet:** Prepare as directed.
**Low-residue diet:** Prepare as directed but omit garlic.

## TACY'S CREAMED POTATOES (125 calories per serving)

2½ pounds potatoes (8 medium), pared and cubed
1 medium onion, thinly sliced
1 cup thinly sliced celery
2 teaspoons salt
⅛ teaspoon pepper
2½ cups skimmed milk or reliquefied nonfat dry milk
1 tablespoon cornstarch

About 40 minutes before serving: In large saucepan, heat all ingredients but cornstarch to boiling; cover; simmer 20 minutes, or until potatoes are tender. Mix enough water with cornstarch to form a thin paste. Stir into potato-milk mixture; cook until thickened and smooth. Makes eight ¾-cup servings.

**Diabetic diet:** Exchanges per serving = 1 "A" vegetable, 1 bread and ½ skimmed milk.
**Egg-, gluten- and wheat-free diet:** Prepare as directed.
**Low-fat, low-cholesterol diet:** Negligible fat per serving.
**Low-purine diet:** Prepare as directed.

## HELPFUL BAKED BEANS (115 calories per serving)

½ cup chopped onion
½ cup chopped green pepper
½ cup catchup
1 16-ounce can vegetarian baked beans

About 20 minutes before serving: In medium saucepan, gently boil onion, pepper and ¾ cup water, covered, for 15 minutes. Add catchup and baked beans; bring to boiling. Makes 6 servings.

**Low-fat, low-cholesterol diet:** Negligible fat per serving.
**High-iron diet:** Make only 4 servings. 2 milligrams iron per serving.

## LEMON MINT BEANS (25 calories per serving)

1 9-ounce package frozen cut
  green beans
1 9-ounce package frozen cut
  wax beans
2 tablespoons lemon juice
1 teaspoon dried mint leaves
½ teaspoon grated lemon peel
½ teaspoon salt

About 15 minutes before serving: In medium saucepan, cook green beans and wax beans together as labels direct, but use 1 cup water; drain. Add remaining ingredients and toss well. Makes 6 servings.

**Diabetic diet:** Exchanges per serving = 1 "A" vegetable.
**Low-fat, low-cholesterol diet:** Negligible fat per serving.
**Low-purine diet:** Prepare as directed.

## GREEN BEANS WITH MARJORAM (30 calories per serving)

1 9-ounce package frozen
  green beans
2 chicken-bouillon cubes
½ teaspoon marjoram leaves

About 15 minutes before serving: Cook green beans as label directs but omit salt, add bouillon cubes and marjoram to cooking water. Drain before serving. Makes 3 servings.

**Diabetic diet:** Exchanges per serving = 1 "A" vegetable.
**Low-fat, low-cholesterol diet:** Negligible fat per serving.

## GREEN BEANS AND CELERY (25 calories per serving)

1 pound fresh green beans,
  trimmed
1 teaspoon salt
3 stalks celery, thinly sliced
pepper
2 tablespoons chopped parsley
  for garnish

About 20 minutes before serving: In saucepan, in 1 inch boiling water, simmer beans and salt, covered, 10 minutes. Add celery; sprinkle lightly with pepper. Simmer, covered, another 10 minutes; drain; sprinkle with parsley and serve. Makes 6 servings.

**Diabetic diet:** Exchanges per serving = 1 "A" vegetable.
**Egg-, gluten-, milk- and wheat-free diet:** Prepare as directed.
**Low-fat, low-cholesterol diet:** Negligible fat per serving.
**Low-purine diet:** Prepare as directed.
**Low-sodium diet:** Prepare as directed but omit salt. 30 milligrams sodium per serving.

## GREEN BEANS WITH MINT (45 calories per serving)

2 16-ounce cans Blue Lake
  green beans
¼ cup dried mint flakes
1 tablespoon butter or margarine
salt and pepper

About 15 minutes before serving: In medium saucepan, heat green beans and mint flakes to boiling. Drain; toss with butter, then salt and pepper to taste. Makes 6 servings.

**Diabetic diet:** Prepare as directed but use 2 tablespoons butter or margarine. Exchanges per serving = 1 "A" vegetable and 1 fat.
**Egg-, gluten-, milk- and wheat-free diet:** Prepare as directed but use milk-free margarine on milk-free diet.
**Low-fat, low-cholesterol diet:** Prepare as directed but use margarine or salad oil instead of butter. 2 grams fat per serving.
**Low-purine diet:** Prepare as directed.
**Low-sodium diet:** Prepare as directed but select brand of canned beans not containing added salt; use unsalted butter or margarine; omit salt. 3 milligrams sodium per serving.

## PLANTATION GREEN BEANS (60 calories per serving)

2 9-ounce packages frozen
  French-style green beans,
  thawed
2 slices bacon, diced
½ cup green onions, chopped
¼ teaspoon pepper

About 20 minutes before serving: Prepare beans as label directs, but cook only 5 minutes. In medium skillet over medium-high heat, fry bacon until crisp; remove and drain well on paper towels. Cook green onions in 1 tablespoon of bacon drippings until just tender. Add pepper and green beans; cook over medium heat, stirring occasionally, until tender. Stir in bacon. Makes 6 servings.

**Diabetic diet:** Exchanges per serving = 1 "A" vegetable and 1 fat.
**Egg-, gluten-, milk- and wheat-free diet:** Prepare as directed.

## WAX BEANS LYONNAISE (60 calories per serving)

1 tablespoon butter or margarine
2 medium onions, thinly sliced
2 15½-ounce cans whole wax beans, drained
⅛ teaspoon pepper

About 15 minutes before serving: In saucepan over medium heat, in butter, sauté onions until golden. Add drained wax beans and pepper; cover; heat, shaking saucepan, until hot. Makes 6 servings.

**Diabetic diet:** Prepare as directed but use 2 tablespoons butter or margarine. Exchanges per serving = 1 "A" and 1 "B" vegetable and 1 fat.
**Egg-, gluten-, milk- and wheat-free diet:** Prepare as directed but use milk-free margarine on milk-free diet.
**Low-fat, low-cholesterol diet:** Prepare as directed but use margarine instead of butter. 2 grams fat per serving.
**High-iron diet:** 2 milligrams iron per serving.

## ITALIAN GREEN BEANS WITH GRAPES (45 calories per serving)

1 9-ounce package frozen Italian green beans
1 cup seedless grapes
salt and pepper to taste

About 15 minutes before serving: Cook Italian green beans as label directs, but omit butter or margarine; add grapes during last 3 minutes of cooking. Drain; add salt and pepper to taste. Makes 4 servings.

**Bland diet:** Prepare as directed but omit pepper.
**Diabetic diet:** Exchanges per serving = 1 "B" vegetable.
**Egg-, gluten-, milk- and wheat-free diet:** Prepare as directed.
**Low-fat, low-cholesterol diet:** Negligible fat per serving.
**Low-fat, bland (gall bladder) diet:** Prepare as directed but omit pepper.
**Low-purine diet:** Prepare as directed.
**Low-residue diet:** Prepare as directed but omit pepper.
**Low-sodium diet:** Prepare as directed but omit salt. 5 milligrams sodium per serving.

## SAUTÉED GREEN BEANS (50 calories per serving)

1 9-ounce package frozen French-style green beans
2 teaspoons salad oil
1 teaspoon salt
2 teaspoons wine vinegar
⅛ teaspoon pepper

About 25 minutes before serving: Cook green beans as label directs until just tender-crisp; drain. In medium skillet over medium heat, in oil, sauté beans until they begin to brown. Season with salt, vinegar and pepper. Makes 3 servings.

**Bland diet:** Prepare as directed but omit vinegar and pepper.
**Diabetic diet:** Exchanges per serving = 1 "A" vegetable and 1 fat.
**Egg-, gluten-, milk- and wheat-free diet:** Prepare as directed.
**Low-fat, low-cholesterol diet:** 5 grams fat per serving.
**Low-purine diet:** Prepare as directed.
**Low-sodium diet:** Prepare as directed but cook green beans without adding salt; omit salt. Negligible sodium per serving.

## ONIONY GREEN BEANS (40 calories per serving)

1 tablespoon butter or margarine
1½ teaspoons instant minced onion
2 9-ounce packages frozen cut green beans
1 teaspoon salt

About 20 minutes before serving: In medium saucepan over medium heat, in butter, cook instant onion until browned. Add green beans, salt and ½ cup water; cook, covered, until tender—about 15 minutes. Makes 6 servings.

**Diabetic diet:** Prepare as directed but increase butter to 2 tablespoons. Exchanges per serving = 1 "A" vegetable and 1 fat.
**Egg-, gluten-, milk- and wheat-free diet:** Prepare as directed but use milk-free margarine on milk-free diet.
**Low-fat, low-cholesterol diet:** Prepare as directed but use margarine instead of butter. 2 grams fat per serving.
**Low-purine diet:** Prepare as directed.

## GREEN BEANS ITALIAN (70 calories per serving)

1 9-ounce package frozen
  Italian green beans
1 16-ounce can white onions,
  drained
½ teaspoon oregano leaves
1 tablespoon butter or margarine
salt and pepper to taste

About 15 minutes before serving: Cook Italian beans as label directs, but add drained white onions and oregano. Drain; toss with butter; add salt, pepper. Makes 4 servings.

**Diabetic diet:** Exchanges per serving (about ¾ cup) = 1 "A" and "B" vegetable and 1 fat.
**Egg-, gluten-, milk- and wheat-free diet:** Prepare as directed but use milk-free margarine on milk-free diet.
**Low-fat, low-cholesterol diet:** Prepare as directed but omit butter or margarine. Negligible fat per serving.
**High-iron diet:** 1.5 milligrams iron per serving.
**Low-purine diet:** Prepare as directed.
**Low-sodium diet:** Prepare as directed but select canned onions not containing added salt; use unsalted butter or margarine; omit salt. 15 milligrams sodium per serving.

## GREEN BEANS IN HERB SAUCE (65 calories per serving)

1 tablespoon butter or margarine
1 large onion, thinly sliced
1 large stalk green celery,
  thinly sliced
1 tablespoon parsley flakes
¼ teaspoon garlic salt
  (optional)
¾ teaspoon salt
dash pepper
1 tablespoon cornstarch
1 9-ounce package frozen cut
  green beans

About 25 minutes before serving: In saucepan over medium heat, in butter, sauté onion, celery and parsley flakes until onion is golden. Meanwhile, mix garlic salt, salt, pepper and cornstarch; slowly stir in 1 cup water to form a smooth paste. Add this mixture and green beans to onion; cover; boil gently 10 minutes, or until beans are tender-crisp and sauce has thickened slightly. Makes four ¾-cup servings.

**Diabetic diet:** Exchanges per serving = 1 "A" and 1 "B" vegetable and 1 fat.
**Egg-, gluten-, milk- and wheat-free diet:** Prepare as directed but use milk-free margarine on milk-free diet.
**Low-fat, low-cholesterol diet:** Prepare as directed but use margarine instead of butter. 3 grams fat per serving.
**Low-purine diet:** Prepare as directed.
**Low-sodium diet:** Prepare as directed but use unsalted butter or margarine; substitute garlic powder for garlic salt; omit salt. 15 milligrams sodium per serving.

## NOODLES WITH SESAME SEED (135 calories per serving)

½ 8-ounce package egg
  noodles
½ tablespoon butter or margarine
1½ tablespoons sesame seed

About 15 minutes before serving: Cook noodles as label directs; drain. Meanwhile, in small skillet, in butter, brown sesame seed; toss with noodles. Makes 4 servings.

**Diabetic diet:** Exchanges per serving (½ cup noodles) = 1 bread and 1 fat.
**Low-fat, low-cholesterol diet:** Prepare as directed but use margarine or salad oil instead of butter. 5 grams fat per serving.
**Low-sodium diet:** Prepare as directed but cook noodles without added salt; use unsalted butter or margarine. 2 milligrams sodium per serving.

## VIENNESE RICE (135 calories per serving)

1 cup uncooked long-grain rice
¼ teaspoon lemon juice
1 10-ounce package frozen
  peas
1 tablespoon salad oil
1 medium onion, diced
chopped parsley for garnish

About 30 minutes before serving: Cook rice as package directs, omitting butter but adding lemon juice. Meanwhile, cook peas as label directs. In medium skillet, in oil, sauté onion until golden. Toss rice with peas and onion; garnish with parsley. Makes 8 servings.

**Diabetic diet:** Prepare as directed but use 2 tablespoons salad oil. Exchanges per serving (⅔ cup) = 1 "B" vegetable, 1 bread, 1 fat.
**Egg-, gluten-, milk- and wheat-free diet:** Prepare as directed.
**High-iron diet:** Use enriched rice. 1 milligram iron per serving.

## BACON-TOMATO RICE (140 calories per serving)

2 bacon slices
1 cup chopped onions
2 8-ounce cans tomato sauce
1 teaspoon seasoned salt
⅛ teaspoon seasoned pepper
1 teaspoon granulated sugar
1 cup uncooked regular white
   rice

About 1 hour before serving: In medium skillet, sauté bacon slices until crisp; pour off and reserve bacon fat; drain, then crumble bacon. Preheat oven to 375°F.

In skillet, in 1 tablespoon bacon fat, sauté onions until tender; stir in tomato sauce, seasoned salt, seasoned pepper, sugar and 1½ cups water; simmer 10 minutes, then stir in rice. Pour rice mixture into 1½-quart casserole; bake, covered, 30 minutes; fluff up rice with fork; stir in bacon bits; then bake, uncovered, 5 minutes longer. Makes 6 servings.

**Diabetic diet:** Prepare as directed but omit sugar. Exchanges per serving (about ¾ cup) = 1 "B" vegetable, 1 bread and 1 fat.
**Egg-, gluten-, milk- and wheat-free diet:** Prepare as directed but use regular (not seasoned) salt and pepper on gluten-free diet.
**Low-fat, low-cholesterol diet:** Prepare as directed but omit bacon; sauté onion in 1 tablespoon salad oil. 2 grams fat per serving.
**High-iron diet:** Use enriched rice. 1.5 milligrams iron per serving.

## RICE WITH MUSHROOMS (120 calories per serving)

1 beef-bouillon cube
1 tablespoon butter or margarine
½ cup uncooked long-grain
   rice
½ cup coarsely chopped
   onion
¼ pound fresh mushrooms,
   sliced
½ teaspoon salt
¼ teaspoon pepper
⅛ teaspoon thyme leaves
½ cup coarsely chopped celery

About 1 hour before serving: Preheat oven to 350°F. In 1- or 1½-quart casserole, dissolve bouillon cube in 1¼ cups boiling water. In medium skillet over medium heat, in butter, sauté rice 5 minutes or until golden-brown, stirring constantly.

To broth in casserole, add rice, onion, mushrooms, salt, pepper and thyme. Bake, covered, stirring occasionally, 40 minutes; then stir in celery and bake, uncovered, 5 minutes longer. Makes four ½-cup servings.

**Diabetic diet:** Exchanges per serving = 1 bread and 1 fat.
**Egg-, gluten-, milk- and wheat-free diet:** Prepare as directed but omit bouillon cube from gluten- and wheat-free diet; use milk-free margarine on milk-free diet.
**Low-fat, low-cholesterol diet:** Prepare as directed but use margarine or salad oil instead of butter. 3 grams fat per serving.
**Low-sodium diet:** Prepare as directed but omit bouillon cube and salt; use unsalted butter or margarine. 15 milligrams sodium per serving.

## SAVORY LEMON RICE (130 calories per serving)

1 tablespoon butter or margarine
1½ cups packaged precooked
   rice
1½ cups chicken broth
½ teaspoon salt
2 tablespoons chopped parsley
1 tablespoon lemon juice
1 tablespoon grated lemon peel

About 15 minutes before serving: In saucepan, heat butter, rice, broth and salt to boiling; remove from heat; cover; let stand five minutes. Toss in parsley, lemon juice and peel. Makes six ½-cup servings.

**Diabetic diet:** Prepare as directed but cook rice with 2 tablespoons butter. Exchanges per serving = 1 bread and 1 fat.
**Egg-, gluten-, milk- and wheat-free diet:** Prepare as directed but use milk-free margarine on milk-free diet, use home-made chicken broth on gluten- and wheat-free diets.
**Low-fat, low-cholesterol diet:** Prepare as directed but omit butter or margarine. Negligible fat per serving.

## PINTO RICE (105 calories per serving)

4 cups hot fluffy cooked rice
3 tablespoons chopped green
  pepper
3 tablespoons chopped green
  onions
2 tablespoons chopped
  pimento
¼ teaspoon celery salt
⅛ teaspoon pepper
dash cayenne

About 10 minutes before serving: Toss hot rice with remaining ingredients. Makes eight ½-cup servings.

**Diabetic diet:** Exchanges per serving = 1 bread.
**Egg-, gluten-, milk- and wheat-free diet:** Cook rice without adding butter. Prepare as directed.
**Low-fat, low-cholesterol diet:** Negligible fat per serving.

# SALADS AND SALAD DRESSINGS

## NOVELTY SALAD (45 calories per serving)

1 medium green pepper, diced
1 medium tomato, cut into
   wedges (or 1 16-ounce can
   tomato slices, drained)
1 medium apple, thinly sliced
2 stalks celery, thinly sliced
2 tablespoons chopped parsley
   (optional)
2 tablespoons low-calorie (imitation) mayonnaise
½ tablespoon lemon juice

About 10 minutes before serving: In medium bowl, toss all ingredients until coated with mayonnaise. Makes four 1-cup servings.

**Diabetic diet:** Exchanges per serving = 1 "A" and 1 "B" vegetable.
**Low-fat, low-cholesterol diet:** 1 gram fat per serving.
**Low-purine diet:** Prepare as directed.

## SAVORY CARROT-AND-RAISIN SALAD (65 calories per serving)

2 cups grated carrots (4 to 6
   carrots)
⅓ cup raisins
1 8¾-ounce can crushed pineapple, thoroughly drained
⅛ teaspoon salt
⅓ cup low-calorie creamy
   French dressing
pepper to taste
6 small lettuce cups

At least 1 hour before serving: In medium bowl, toss together all ingredients but lettuce; refrigerate at least 1 hour to "marry" flavors.

   To serve: Divide salad among lettuce cups. Makes 6 servings.

**Diabetic diet:** Prepare as directed but substitute pineapple packed in pineapple juice for regular. Exchanges per serving = 1 "A" vegetable and 1 bread.
**Low-fat, low-cholesterol diet:** 1 gram fat per serving.
**Low-purine diet:** Prepare as directed.

## ASPARAGUS VINAIGRETTE SALAD (25 calories per serving)

3 10-ounce packages frozen
   jumbo asparagus spears
1 8-ounce bottle low-calorie
   Italian dressing

At least 4 hours before serving: Cook asparagus as label directs; drain. Place in shallow dish and pour on low-calorie dressing. Cover; refrigerate, turning spears occasionally.

   To serve: Arrange asparagus on serving platter, discarding dressing. Makes 12 servings.

**Diabetic diet:** Exchanges per serving = 1 "A" vegetable.
**Low-fat, low-cholesterol diet:** Negligible fat per serving.

## MEXICAN POTATO SALAD (135 calories per serving)

4 pounds potatoes
1 medium onion, chopped
½ medium green pepper,
   chopped
4 medium carrots, thinly sliced
⅓ cup chopped canned
   pimentos
1 medium head lettuce,
   shredded
1 cup low-calorie (imitation)
   mayonnaise
1 teaspoon salt
1 tablespoon lemon juice
chili powder

Early in day: Boil potatoes, in jackets, until fork-tender; cool; peel; cut into bite-size pieces. In large serving bowl, toss with onion, pepper, carrots, pimentos and lettuce. In small bowl, blend low-calorie mayonnaise with salt, lemon juice and 1 teaspoon chili powder; gently stir into potato mixture; refrigerate until serving time.

   To serve: Sprinkle salad lightly with more chili powder. Makes about 12 servings.

**Diabetic diet:** Carefully divide into 12 servings (about ¾ cup each). Exchanges per serving = 1 bread and 1 "B" vegetable.
**Low-fat, low-cholesterol diet:** 2 grams fat per serving.
**High-iron diet:** 1 milligram iron per serving.
**Low-purine diet:** Prepare as directed.

## DILLED MACARONI SALAD (150 calories per serving)

1 8-ounce package macaroni
1 cup low-calorie (imitation)
  mayonnaise
2 tablespoons vinegar
1¼ teaspoons salt
½ teaspoon dried dill weed
⅛ teaspoon pepper
1 cup coarsely chopped celery
½ cup coarsely chopped green
  pepper
2 tablespoons chopped onion
2 tablespoons chopped
  pimento
lettuce leaves

Several hours before serving: Cook macaroni as label directs; drain. In large bowl, combine mayonnaise, vinegar, salt, dill and pepper. Add macaroni, celery, green pepper, onion and pimento; toss well. Cover and refrigerate.

To serve: Arrange salad on lettuce leaves. Makes eight ½-cup servings.

**Diabetic diet:** Exchanges per serving = 1 "A" and 1 "B" vegetable, 1 bread and 1 fat.
**Low-fat, low-cholesterol diet:** 5 grams fat per serving.
**High-iron diet:** 1 milligram iron per serving.
**Low-purine diet:** Prepare as directed.

## APPLE SLAW (65 calories per serving)

4 cups finely shredded green
  cabbage
¼ cup low-calorie Italian
  dressing
¼ cup juice drained from
  sweet pickles
1 apple, cubed
¼ teaspoon salt

About 10 minutes before serving: In large bowl, toss together all ingredients. Makes 4 servings.

**Low-fat, low-cholesterol diet:** Negligible fat per serving.
**Low-purine diet:** Prepare as directed.

## HERBED TOMATO SALAD (40 calories per serving)

6 ripe medium tomatoes,
  peeled
4 tablespoons wine vinegar
1½ teaspoons oregano leaves
1½ teaspoons salt
6 small lettuce cups

About 30 minutes before serving: Finely chop 1½ tomatoes. In small bowl, combine chopped tomatoes, vinegar, oregano and salt. Thinly slice remaining tomatoes; divide among lettuce cups. Top with tomato-vinegar mixture. Refrigerate until serving time. Makes 6 servings.

**Diabetic diet:** Exchanges per serving = 1 "A" vegetable.
**Egg-, gluten-, milk- and wheat-free diet:** Prepare as directed.
**Low-fat, low-cholesterol diet:** Negligible fat per serving.
**High-iron diet:** 1 milligram iron per serving.
**Low-purine diet:** Prepare as directed.
**Low-sodium diet:** Prepare as directed but omit salt. 5 milligrams sodium per serving.

## SAVORY TOMATO ASPIC (30 calories per serving)

2 envelopes unflavored gelatin
1 quart (4 cups) tomato juice
2 tablespoons lemon juice
¼ teaspoon granulated sugar
¼ teaspoon Tabasco
6 to 8 sprigs parsley
¼ medium green pepper
½ cup celery leaves and stalks,
  finely chopped

Day before or early in day: Stir gelatin into ½ cup tomato juice to soften. In medium saucepan over medium heat, cook remaining tomato juice, lemon juice, sugar, Tabasco, parsley and green pepper 6 to 8 minutes, or until parsley loses its bright green color. Discard parsley and green pepper. Stir in gelatin until dissolved. Pour into 1½-quart mold and refrigerate until mixture reaches consistency of egg whites; stir in celery. Refrigerate 4 hours, or until firm. Makes 8 servings.

**Diabetic diet:** Prepare as directed but omit sugar. Exchanges per serving = 1 "A" vegetable.
**Low-fat, low-cholesterol diet:** Negligible fat per serving.
**Low-purine diet:** Prepare as directed.

## PEPPY CHIVE DRESSING (10 calories per tablespoon)

**1 8-ounce container plain
  yogurt
2 teaspoons lemon juice
1 teaspoon seasoned salt
2 tablespoons chopped chives**

At least 2 hours before serving: In small bowl, combine all ingredients. Refrigerate to blend flavors. Makes about 1 cup.

**Low-fat, low-cholesterol diet:** Negligible fat per serving.
**Low-purine diet:** Prepare as directed.

## RELISH SALAD (100 calories per serving)

**3 cups diced tomatoes
3 cups peeled, diced cucumbers
1 cup sliced radishes
⅓ cup sliced pitted ripe olives
1 carrot, grated
¼ cup chopped parsley
2 to 2½ teaspoons salt
¼ teaspoon pepper
3 tablespoons olive oil
2 hard-cooked eggs**

About 2 hours before serving: In large bowl, combine tomatoes, cucumbers, radishes, olives, carrot and parsley. Sprinkle with salt and pepper; toss with olive oil. Cover; refrigerate until serving time.

To serve: Toss salad again, then arrange in salad bowl; sprinkle center with one chopped egg. Cut other egg into wedges; use as garnish. Makes 8 servings.

**Diabetic diet:** Prepare as directed but omit eggs. Exchanges per serving = 1 "B" vegetable and 1 fat.
**Egg-, gluten-, milk- and wheat-free diet:** Prepare as directed but omit eggs.
**Low-fat, low-cholesterol diet:** Prepare as directed but omit eggs. 5 grams fat per serving. If olive oil is forbidden on diet, omit recipe.
**High-iron diet:** 2 milligrams iron per serving.
**Low-purine diet:** Prepare as directed.

## MARINATED SLICED TOMATOES (60 calories per serving)

**4 tomatoes
1 green onion
½ teaspoon salt
¼ teaspoon basil
½ cup low-calorie French
  dressing**

About 1 hour before serving: Thinly slice tomatoes and place in shallow dish. Thinly slice green onion (including top) and sprinkle on tomatoes with salt and basil. Top with French dressing; refrigerate.

To serve: Drain excess dressing from tomatoes and serve. Makes 4 servings.

**Diabetic diet:** Exchanges per serving = 1 "A" vegetable.
**Low-fat, low-cholesterol diet:** 1 gram fat per serving.
**High-iron diet:** 1 milligram iron per serving.
**Low-purine diet:** Prepare as directed.
**Low-sodium diet:** Prepare as directed but omit salt and use low-sodium French dressing. 5 milligrams sodium per serving.

## WATERMELON COMPOTE SALAD (65 calories per serving)

**½ small watermelon
escarole leaves
1 cucumber, cut into fingers
½ pear, thinly sliced, tossed
  with lemon juice
bottled low-calorie dressing
  (optional)**

Up to 1 hour before serving: With melon-baller, scoop meat from watermelon, seeding as you go, if desired. (For a prettier compote, separate more perfect balls, for use where they show.)

In compote or on platter, arrange bed of escarole leaves with cucumber fingers, spoke-fashion, around edge. Next, heap mound of watermelon balls in center, on top of cucumbers, with pear slices here and there. Pass dressing. Makes 6 servings.

**Diabetic diet:** Exchanges per serving = 1 "A" vegetable and 1 fruit.
**Egg-, gluten-, milk- and wheat-free diet:** Prepare as directed but omit salad dressing.
**Low-fat, low-cholesterol diet:** 1 gram fat per serving.
**High-iron diet:** 1.5 milligrams iron per serving.
**Low-purine diet:** Prepare as directed.
**Low-sodium diet:** Prepare as directed but omit salad dressing. 5 milligrams sodium per serving.

## ICY SPICY PEACH SALAD (90 calories per serving)

1 30-ounce can cling-peach
   halves
2 sticks cinnamon
1 teaspoon whole cloves
1 tablespoon vinegar
4 lettuce cups

At least 3 hours before serving: In medium saucepan, mix peach halves, cinnamon, cloves and vinegar. Over low heat, simmer 5 minutes; refrigerate.

To serve: Drain thoroughly; stud peach halves with whole cloves. Serve in lettuce cups. Makes 4 servings of 2 peach halves each.

**Diabetic diet:** Prepare as directed but substitute water-pack canned peaches for regular. Exchanges per serving = 1 fruit.
**Egg-, gluten-, milk- and wheat-free diet:** Prepare as directed.
**Low-fat, low-cholesterol diet:** Negligible fat per serving.
**Low-purine diet:** Prepare as directed.
**Low-sodium diet:** 3 milligrams sodium per serving.

## DILLED COTTAGE-CHEESE DRESSING (15 calories per tablespoon)

1 cup creamed cottage cheese
½ teaspoon salt
scant ⅛ teaspoon cayenne
¼ cup sour cream
¼ cup fresh dill, finely
   chopped

At least 2 hours before serving: In electric-blender container, at low speed, blend cottage cheese, salt, cayenne, sour cream and 2 tablespoons water until smooth. Transfer to glass jar; stir in dill; cover; refrigerate at least 2 hours to "marry" the flavors. Use as a dressing for lettuce. Makes about 1½ cups.

**Diabetic diet:** Exchanges per ¼-cup dressing = 1 meat.
**Egg-, gluten- and wheat-free diet:** Prepare as directed.
**Low-purine diet:** Prepare as directed.

## SUNSHINE SALAD (65 calories per serving)

2 envelopes unflavored gelatin
¼ cup lemon juice
2 15¼-ounce cans pineapple
   chunks packed in pineapple
   juice
2 tablespoons vinegar
½ teaspoon salt
2 cups grated carrots
lettuce, green pepper, parsley
   and maraschino cherry for
   garnish

At least 4 hours before serving: In large bowl, mix gelatin, lemon juice and a bit of juice from canned pineapple; let stand 5 minutes to soften. Remove 3 pineapple chunks from can; wrap; refrigerate. Stir in 1 cup boiling water, then vinegar, salt, carrots, pineapple chunks and rest of pineapple juice. Pour into rinsed 9" by 5" by 3" loaf pan. Refrigerate until firm—at least 3 hours.

About 15 minutes before serving. Arrange nest of lettuce on oval platter. Unmold salad onto lettuce. Decorate with flower made from thin strips of green pepper for stem, parsley for leaf and reserved pineapple chunks, cut in half, for bud. Use maraschino cherry for center of flower.

To serve: Cut into slices with very sharp knife. Makes 10 servings.

**Diabetic diet:** Exchanges per serving = 1 fruit.
**Egg-, gluten-, milk- and wheat-free diet:** Prepare as directed.
**Low-fat, low-cholesterol diet:** Negligible fat per serving.
**Low-sodium diet:** Prepare as directed but omit salt. 5 milligrams sodium per serving.

## CALORIE WATCHERS' DRESSING (10 calories per tablespoon)

1 10¾-ounce can condensed
   tomato soup, undiluted
¼ teaspoon garlic powder
¼ teaspoon onion salt
⅛ teaspoon pepper
1 tablespoon India relish
2 to 3 tablespoons wine vinegar

At least 8 hours before serving: In wide-mouth pint jar, stir all ingredients. Cover; refrigerate. Use as a dressing for salad greens. Makes 1½ cups dressing.

**Diabetic diet:** Exchanges per tablespoon = 1 "free."
**Low-fat, low-cholesterol diet:** Negligible fat per serving.

## SUMMER FRUIT SLAW (55 calories per serving)

1 large head cabbage
¾ cup low-calorie (imitation) mayonnaise
2 tablespoons vinegar
1½ teaspoons salt
1 teaspoon granulated sugar
1 13¼-ounce can pineapple tidbits, drained
1 peach, cut into thin wedges for garnish
2 purple plums, cut into thin wedges for garnish

About 20 minutes before serving: Spread apart several outer leaves of cabbage. Carefully cut out center of cabbage, leaving outer leaves as "bowl"; also leave core intact for about an inch. Finely shred cut-out cabbage.

Combine low-calorie mayonnaise, vinegar, salt and sugar; toss with pineapple tidbits and shredded cabbage. Pile into prepared "bowl." For pretty garnish, arrange peach and plum wedges around slaw. Makes 12 servings.

**Low-fat, low-cholesterol diet:** 2 grams fat per serving.

## PEACH SALAD (125 calories per serving)

2 teaspoons unflavored gelatin
⅛ teaspoon salt
2 tablespoons lemon juice
1 16-ounce can freestone-peach halves, drained (reserve syrup)
1 8-ounce container creamed cottage cheese
lettuce cups

At least 4 hours before serving: In small saucepan, sprinkle gelatin on ⅓ cup water to soften; add salt and lemon juice, then heat to dissolve gelatin. Refrigerate until consistency of unbeaten egg whites. Meanwhile, place 5 whole peach halves, smooth side down, in bottom of five ¾-cup custard cups.

When gelatin mixture has thickened, stir in cottage cheese and ⅔ cup peach syrup. Divide mixture among custard cups. Refrigerate until firm.

To serve: Turn out into lettuce cups. Makes 5 servings.

**Bland diet:** Prepare as directed but dieter should not eat lettuce unless allowed on diet.
**Diabetic diet:** Prepare as directed but substitute water-pack canned peach halves for regular. Exchanges per serving = 1 meat and 1 fruit.
**Egg-, gluten-, and wheat-free diet:** Prepare as directed.
**Low-fat, low-cholesterol diet:** 2 grams fat per serving.
**Low-fat, bland (gall bladder) diet:** Prepare as directed for bland diet.
**Low-purine diet:** Prepare as directed.
**Low-residue diet:** Prepare as directed for bland diet.

## MARINATED VEGETABLE SALAD (40 calories per serving)

1 9-ounce package frozen whole green beans
1 9-ounce package frozen cut wax beans
1 9-ounce package frozen artichoke hearts
1 pound zucchini, thickly sliced
1 small head cauliflower, cut into bite-size pieces
salt
1 8-ounce bottle low-calorie Italian salad dressing
½ pint cherry tomatoes

Day before: Cook green and wax beans and artichoke hearts as labels direct; drain well. In medium saucepan, cook zucchini and cauliflower in 1-inch boiling salted water until tender-crisp; drain.

Place cooked vegetables in individual containers. Pour Italian dressing over each vegetable. Cover and marinate in refrigerator overnight; stir once or twice.

To serve: Drain and discard marinade, then place vegetables in large serving jar and top with cherry tomatoes. Makes 12 servings.

**Diabetic diet:** Exchanges per serving = 1 "A" vegetable.
**Low-fat, low-cholesterol diet:** 1 gram fat per serving.
**High-iron diet:** 1 milligram iron per serving.
**Low-purine diet:** Prepare as directed but omit cauliflower. Makes 9 servings.

## ORANGES OREGANO (95 calories per serving)

1 tablespoon olive oil
1 teaspoon oregano leaves
½ teaspoon salt
4 black pitted olives, sliced
2 large oranges, sliced
lettuce leaves

About 10 minutes before serving: In small bowl, combine olive oil, 1 tablespoon hot water, oregano and salt; mix well. Add olives and orange slices and toss until well coated. Serve on lettuce leaves. Makes 4 servings.

**Diabetic diet:** Exchanges per serving = 1 "A" vegetable, 1 fruit and 1 fat.
**Egg-, gluten-, milk- and wheat-free diet:** Prepare as directed.
**Low-fat, low-cholesterol diet:** Prepare as directed but use salad oil instead of olive oil; omit olives. 4 grams fat per serving.
**Low-purine diet:** Prepare as directed.
**Low-sodium diet:** Prepare as directed but omit salt and olives. Negligible sodium per serving.

## FRESH MINTED PEAR SALAD (100 calories per serving)

1 tablespoon chopped fresh
  mint
1 tablespoon chopped parsley
½ teaspoon granulated sugar
2 tablespoons salad oil
1 tablespoon wine vinegar
3 large pears, sliced
lettuce leaves

About 10 minutes before serving: In small bowl, stir mint, parsley and sugar; crush lightly with back of spoon. Stir in oil, vinegar and 1 teaspoon water. Toss pears in dressing, a few slices at a time, until well coated. Serve on lettuce leaves. Makes 6 servings.

**Diabetic diet:** Prepare as directed but omit sugar. Exchanges per serving = 1 "A" vegetable, 1 fruit and 1 fat.
**Egg-, gluten-, milk- and wheat-free diet:** Prepare as directed.
**Low-fat, low-cholesterol diet:** 5 grams fat per serving.
**Low-purine diet:** Prepare as directed.
**Low-sodium diet:** Negligible sodium per serving.

## A & B SALAD (85 calories per serving)

2 tablespoons lemon juice
2 tablespoons honey
1 egg white
dash salt
about 2 cups shredded lettuce
1 large apple, thinly sliced
1 cup diced canned beets,
  drained

About 15 minutes before serving: In small bowl, combine lemon juice and honey; add egg white and salt; beat until blended. Cover bottom of serving platter with lettuce; arrange apple slices in pinwheel fashion and spoon beets in center. Then spoon honey dressing over salad. Makes 4 servings.

**Diabetic diet:** Prepare as directed but omit honey; add 2 tablespoons water and saccharin equivalent to 2 tablespoons sugar. Carefully divide into 4 equal individual servings. Exchanges per serving = 1 fruit.
**Low-fat, low-cholesterol diet:** Negligible fat per serving.
**Gluten-, milk- and wheat-free diet:** Prepare as directed.
**Low-purine diet:** Prepare as directed.
**Low-sodium diet:** Prepare as directed but omit salt and beets. 10 milligrams sodium per serving.

## BLUSHING GREEN SALAD (150 calories per serving)

½ cup Yogurt Dressing (page
  206)
2 cups seedless grapes
4 stalks celery, coarsely
  chopped
1 tablespoon lemon juice
2 fresh pears, diced
4 small lettuce cups

Up to 1 hour before serving: Make dressing. Toss grapes, celery and lemon juice with pears. Fill lettuce cups with salad mixture; refrigerate.

   To serve: Top each salad with dollop of dressing; pass the rest. Makes 4 servings.

**Diabetic diet:** Exchanges per serving = 1 "B" vegetable, 1 fruit and 1 fat.
**Egg-, gluten- and wheat-free diet:** Prepare as directed.
**Low-fat, low-cholesterol diet:** 5 grams fat per serving.
**High-iron diet:** 1 milligram iron per serving.
**Low-purine diet:** Prepare as directed.

## NEW YORK COLESLAW (85 calories per serving)

½ cup raisins
2 tablespoons flour
½ teaspoon salt
¼ teaspoon dry mustard
3 tablespoons vinegar
1 egg
3 cups shredded cabbage
2 carrots, grated
1 small onion, minced
3 stalks celery, thinly sliced

Day before or early in day: In small saucepan, heat raisins and 1 cup water to boiling; simmer 2 to 3 minutes; drain raisins thoroughly, reserving syrup. Cool, then refrigerate.

In medium saucepan, stir together flour, salt and mustard. Slowly stir in ¾ cup raisin syrup (if necessary, add enough water to syrup to make ¾ cup) and vinegar to form a smooth paste. Add egg; then beat until smooth. Cook over low heat, stirring constantly, until thickened.

Up to 1 hour before serving: In large bowl, toss cabbage with carrots, onion, celery and raisins; toss with chilled dressing. Makes 6 servings.

**Diabetic diet:** Exchanges per serving = 1 "A" and 1 "B" vegetable and 1 fruit.
**Gluten-, milk- and wheat-free diet:** Prepare as directed but substitute 1 tablespoon cornstarch for flour.
**High-iron diet:** 1 milligram iron per serving.
**Low-purine diet:** Prepare as directed.

## SIMPLE CAESAR SALAD (20 calories per serving)

1 tablespoon grated Parmesan
  cheese
2 tablespoons wine vinegar
1 tablespoon lemon juice
dash pepper
dash salt
dash Worcestershire
1 large head romaine, chopped

About 10 minutes before serving: In salad bowl, mix all ingredients but romaine. Toss romaine with this dressing. Makes 6 servings.

**Diabetic diet:** Exchanges per serving = 1 "A" vegetable.
**Low-fat diet:** 1 gram fat per serving. Omit recipe from low-cholesterol diet.

## FARMLAND PEPPER HASH (15 calories per serving)

1 quart (4 cups) very finely
  chopped fresh cabbage
½ cup finely chopped green
  pepper (for more color, use
  green peppers that are turning red)
½ cup cider vinegar
½ cup granulated sugar
½ cup water
2 teaspoons salt

At least 1 hour before serving: In large bowl, mix all ingredients. Let stand at least 1 hour to "marry" flavors. This salad may be kept, covered and refrigerated, for several weeks. Drain well before serving. Makes 16 servings.

**Diabetic diet:** Prepare as directed but omit sugar; substitute saccharin equivalent to ¼ cup sugar. Exchanges per serving = 1 "A" vegetable.
**Egg-, gluten-, milk- and wheat-free diet:** Prepare as directed.
**Low-fat, low-cholesterol diet:** Negligible fat per serving.
**Low-purine diet:** Prepare as directed.

## COLORFUL VEGETABLE SLAW (80 calories per serving)

3 tablespoons vinegar
1 tablespoon salad oil
1 tablespoon chopped parsley
½ teaspoon dry mustard
¼ teaspoon salt
dash pepper
¼ medium cabbage, shredded
1 8-ounce can diced carrots,
  drained
1 8-ounce can cut green beans,
  drained
1 medium green pepper, diced
¼ cup minced onion

About 20 minutes before serving: In medium bowl, stir vinegar, oil, parsley, mustard, salt and pepper. Add vegetables and toss lightly. Makes 4 generous 1-cup servings.

**Diabetic diet:** Exchanges per serving = 1 "B" vegetable and 1 fat.
**Egg-, gluten-, milk- and wheat-free diet:** Prepare as directed.
**Low-fat, low-cholesterol diet:** 5 grams fat per serving.
**High-iron diet:** 1.5 milligrams iron per serving.
**Low-purine diet:** Prepare as directed. Omit pepper if forbidden on diet.

## NIPPY COLESLAW (50 calories per serving)

1 medium cabbage
3 tablespoons white vinegar
1 tablespoon granulated sugar
1 teaspoon salt
1 egg, slightly beaten

About 1 hour before serving: Shred cabbage. In small saucepan, combine ¼ cup water, vinegar, sugar and salt; add egg; cook over very low heat, stirring constantly, until slightly thickened. Pour over cabbage and toss lightly. Chill. Makes 6 servings.

**Diabetic diet:** Prepare as directed but omit sugar; substitute saccharin equivalent to 1 tablespoon sugar. Exchanges per serving = 1 "A" vegetable.
**Low-fat diet:** 1 gram fat per serving. Omit recipe from low-cholesterol diet.
**Gluten-, milk- and wheat-free diet:** Prepare as directed.
**Low-purine diet:** Prepare as directed.

## CUCUMBER-CHIVE SALAD (55 calories per serving)

2 cucumbers
1 teaspoon salt
¼ cup white vinegar
2 tablespoons salad oil
2 teaspoons chopped chives
1 teaspoon granulated sugar

About 1 hour before serving: Peel, then cut cucumbers into thin slices; sprinkle with salt. Refrigerate, covered, one hour. Combine vinegar with ¼ cup water, oil, chives and sugar for dressing. Drain off any liquid from cucumbers, then toss with dressing. Makes 6 servings.

**Diabetic diet:** Prepare as directed but omit sugar; use saccharin equivalent to 1 teaspoon sugar. Exchanges per serving = 1 "A" vegetable and 1 fat.
**Egg-, gluten-, milk- and wheat-free diet:** Prepare as directed.
**Low-fat, low-cholesterol diet:** 5 grams fat per serving.
**High-iron diet:** 1 milligram iron per serving.
**Low-purine diet:** Prepare as directed.
**Low-sodium diet:** Prepare as directed but omit salt. 5 milligrams sodium per serving.

## PINEAPPLE-CARROT SLAW (60 calories per serving)

1 15¼-ounce can pineapple chunks packed in pineapple juice
¼ cup low-calorie Italian dressing
4 cups finely shredded green cabbage
1 small carrot, thinly sliced
¼ teaspoon tarragon
½ teaspoon salt

A few minutes before serving: Drain pineapple, reserving ¼ cup juice. Mix juice with low-calorie dressing; toss with pineapple chunks and remaining ingredients. Makes 6 servings.

**Low-fat, low-cholesterol diet:** Negligible fat per serving.
**Low-purine diet:** Prepare as directed.

## PIMENTO COLESLAW (60 calories per serving)

1 medium onion, minced
⅓ cup low-calorie (imitation) mayonnaise
2 tablespoons prepared mustard
1 teaspoon salt
¼ teaspoon pepper
⅓ cup juice from sweet pickles
4 cups finely shredded cabbage
1 4-ounce can pimentos, chopped

About 10 minutes before serving: Combine onion, low-calorie mayonnaise, mustard, salt, pepper and pickle juice. Toss with shredded cabbage, then sprinkle with chopped pimentos. Makes 6 servings.

**Low-fat, low-cholesterol diet:** 2 grams fat per serving.
**Low-purine diet:** Prepare as directed.

## SWEDISH CABBAGE SALAD (70 calories per serving)

3 cups finely chopped cabbage
1 cup canned whole cranberry
   sauce
¼ cup thawed frozen or fresh
   whole cranberries (optional)

About 1 hour before serving: In medium bowl, toss all but ¼ cup chopped cabbage with cranberry sauce. Then heap in salad bowl; sprinkle with rest of cabbage and whole cranberries, if desired. Refrigerate until serving time. Makes 6 servings.

**Egg-, gluten-, milk- and wheat-free diet:** Prepare as directed.
**Low-fat, low-cholesterol diet:** Negligible fat per serving.
**Low-purine diet:** Prepare as directed.

## AUTUMN VEGETABLE SALAD (55 calories per serving)

1 medium rutabaga, diced
1 cup bottled low-calorie Italian
   or French dressing
1 10-ounce package frozen
   Brussels sprouts
1 16-ounce can julienne beets

Day before serving: In medium saucepan, cook rutabaga in 1 inch boiling salted water until tender-crisp; drain. Place in small bowl and pour on ⅓ cup of dressing. Meanwhile, cook Brussels sprouts as label directs; drain and cut sprouts into halves. Place in small bowl and pour on ⅓ cup dressing. Drain beets well; place in small bowl; pour on ⅓ cup dressing. Refrigerate all vegetables, covered; toss them occasionally.

To serve: Drain vegetables and arrange in rows on platter. Makes 6 servings.

**Diabetic diet:** Exchanges per serving = 1 "A" and 1 "B" vegetable.
**Low-fat, low-cholesterol diet:** 2 grams fat per serving.
**High-iron diet:** 1 milligram iron per serving.

## PALISADES PICKLED BEETS (115 calories per serving)

2 16-ounce cans sliced beets
3 tablespoons granulated sugar
1 teaspoon salt
¼ teaspoon pepper
1 tablespoon pickling spice
½ cup vinegar
3 hard-cooked eggs, shelled

Day before serving: Drain beets, reserving ½ cup beet juice. In medium saucepan, mix juice, sugar, salt, pepper and pickling spice; simmer 5 minutes; strain. Stir in vinegar.

Place whole hard-cooked eggs and beet slices in flat baking dish; pour beet-juice marinade over them. Refrigerate overnight, turning eggs and beets occasionally.

To serve: Slice eggs with egg slicer. Top each serving of beet slices with bit of marinade, then egg slices. Makes 6 servings.

**Diabetic diet:** Prepare as directed but omit sugar; substitute saccharin equivalent to 2 tablespoons sugar; increase eggs to six. Exchanges per serving = 1 meat and 1 "B" vegetable.
**Gluten-, milk- and wheat-free diet:** Prepare as directed.
**High-iron diet:** 1.5 milligrams iron per serving.
**Low-purine diet:** Prepare as directed.

## ZUCCHINI SALAD (30 calories per serving)

½ cup pickle relish
2 tablespoons white vinegar
1 teaspoon granulated sugar
½ teaspoon salt
1 pound zucchini, sliced
   (about 3)
romaine or lettuce
1 tomato, cut in thin wedges

About 45 minutes before serving: In medium bowl, combine pickle relish, vinegar, sugar and salt. Add zucchini; toss gently. Refrigerate about 30 minutes.

To serve: Line salad bowl with romaine; add tomato wedges and toss with zucchini. Makes 6 servings.

**Egg-, gluten-, milk- and wheat-free diet:** Prepare as directed.
**Low-fat, low-cholesterol diet:** Negligible fat per serving.

## HOT GERMAN COLESLAW (40 calories per serving)

**4 slices bacon**
**¼ cup vinegar**
**¾ teaspoon salt**
**¼ teaspoon pepper**
**1 small cinnamon stick**
**1 small cabbage, shredded**

About 30 minutes before serving: In large saucepan over high heat, heat 1½ quarts water, bacon, vinegar, salt, pepper and cinnamon to boiling. Add cabbage, and cook until cabbage is tender-crisp; drain. Remove bacon and cinnamon stick. Makes 6 servings.

## RED-CABBAGE-GRAPE SLAW (45 calories per serving)

**4 cups shredded red cabbage**
**few ice cubes**
**½ cup apple juice**
**6 tablespoons cider vinegar**
**½ teaspoon seasoned salt**
**¼ teaspoon seasoned pepper**
**½ teaspoon basil**
**2 cups seedless grapes**

About 3 hours before serving: In large bowl, place shredded cabbage; top with a few ice cubes; refrigerate. Make dressing by combining apple juice, vinegar, seasoned salt and pepper and basil; refrigerate.

To serve: Drain cabbage well; toss with grapes and dressing. Makes 8 servings.

**Low-fat, low-cholesterol diet:** Negligible fat per serving.
**Low-purine diet:** Prepare as directed.

## SUSAN'S CALICO COLESLAW (85 calories per serving)

**5 cups shredded cabbage**
**2 tablespoons granulated sugar**
**1 teaspoon salt**
**½ teaspoon dry mustard**
**¼ teaspoon pepper**
**¼ cup minced green pepper**
**¼ cup shredded raw carrots**
**¼ cup coarsely diced pimentos**
**½ teaspoon grated onion**
**2 tablespoons salad oil**
**⅓ cup vinegar**

Just before serving: Toss cabbage with sugar, salt, mustard, pepper, green pepper, carrots, pimentos and onion. In small bowl, combine salad oil and vinegar; pour over cabbage mixture; toss well. Makes 6 servings.

**Diabetic diet:** Prepare as directed but omit sugar; add liquid saccharin equivalent to 2 tablespoons sugar with oil and vinegar. Exchanges per serving = 1 "A" vegetable and 1 fat.
**Egg-, gluten-, milk- and wheat-free diet:** Prepare as directed.
**Low-fat, low-cholesterol diet:** 5 grams fat per serving.
**Low-purine diet:** Prepare as directed.

## CAJIK (tsayik) (65 calories per serving)

**2 cucumbers**
**salt**
**¼ teaspoon garlic salt**
**1 tablespoon vinegar**
**1 tablespoon chopped fresh dill**
**2 8-ounce containers (2 cups) plain yogurt**
**1 tablespoon olive oil**
**fresh mint leaves for garnish**

About 30 minutes before serving: Pare cucumbers; quarter lengthwise, then slice crosswise into ¼-inch slices. Place in bowl; sprinkle with salt; refrigerate.

In another bowl, stir ¾ teaspoon salt, garlic salt, vinegar, dill and yogurt together until consistency of thick soup. Pour yogurt mixture over cucumbers; toss; sprinkle with olive oil; toss, then garnish with mint.

To serve: Spoon into bowl and serve as a refreshing cold soup or serve on lettuce leaves as an unusual salad. Makes 6 servings.

**Diabetic diet:** Make into 4 generous servings. Exchanges per serving = 1 "A" vegetable and ½ milk.
**Egg-, gluten- and wheat-free diet:** Prepare as directed.
**Low-fat, low-cholesterol diet:** Prepare as directed but use salad oil (not olive oil). 4 grams fat per serving.
**High-iron diet:** 1 milligram iron per serving.
**Low-purine diet:** Prepare as directed.

## MARINATED WHOLE MUSHROOMS (25 calories per serving)

⅔ cup tarragon vinegar
1 tablespoon salad oil
1 small garlic clove, crushed
1 bay leaf
¼ teaspoon thyme leaves
3 6-ounce cans whole mushrooms, drained

At least 1 hour and 15 minutes before serving: In large bowl, toss together all ingredients plus ⅓ cup water. Cover and refrigerate at least 1 hour. Drain marinade and discard bay leaf. Serve as salad. Makes 5 servings.

For fresh mushrooms: Prepare as directed above but substitute ¾ pound fresh mushrooms, thinly sliced, for canned mushrooms; season with salt, if desired.

**Diabetic diet:** Exchanges per serving = 1 "A" vegetable.
**Egg-, gluten-, milk- and wheat-free diet:** Prepare as directed.
**Low-fat, low-cholesterol diet:** Negligible fat per serving.
**Low-sodium diet:** Prepare as directed for fresh mushrooms; omit salt. 5 milligrams sodium per serving.

## DILLY CUKES (30 calories per serving)

3 cups peeled and chopped
  cucumber (2 small)
¼ teaspoon salt
1 8-ounce container plain
  yogurt
2 tablespoons chopped fresh
  dill
dash pepper

About 30 minutes before serving: In medium bowl, mix cucumbers and salt; set aside.

To serve: Drain cucumber and discard liquid; toss with yogurt, dill and pepper. Makes 6 servings.

**Egg-, gluten- and wheat-free diet:** Prepare as directed.
**Low-fat, low-cholesterol diet:** 1 gram fat per serving.
**Low-purine diet:** Prepare as directed. Omit pepper if forbidden on diet.

## CHILLED BEAN SPROUTS AND CUCUMBERS (100 calories per serving)

3 medium cucumbers, pared
1 16-ounce can bean sprouts
¼ cup soy sauce
2 tablespoons vinegar
1 tablespoon salad oil
2 tablespoons sesame oil*
1 teaspoon granulated sugar
2 tablespoons chopped green
  onions
1 tablespoon pimento strips for
  garnish

About 30 minutes before serving: Cut both tip ends from each cucumber. Then cut each cucumber into quarters lengthwise; scoop out all seeds; cut into julienne strips. Rinse sprouts under cold water; drain.

In small bowl, combine soy sauce, vinegar, oil, sesame oil and sugar; stir to mix well.

In serving bowl, combine cucumber strips, bean sprouts, soy-sauce mixture and chopped green onions; toss well. Garnish with pimento strips. Makes 6 servings.

**Diabetic diet:** Exchanges per serving = 1 "A" and 1 "B" vegetable and 1 fat.
**Low-fat, low-cholesterol diet:** 5 grams fat per serving.
**High-iron diet:** 1.5 milligrams iron per serving.
**Low-purine diet:** Prepare as directed.

* Available in specialty foodshops and Japanese and Chinese groceries.

## POTATO SALAD WITH CREAMY SAUERKRAUT DRESSING
(110 calories per serving)

5 cups sliced cold cooked
  potatoes
1½ tablespoons chopped
  onion
¼ cup chopped pimento
⅓ cup chopped parsley
⅓ cup canned sauerkraut juice
1 teaspoon salt
⅓ cup skimmed milk or re-
  liquefied nonfat dry milk
⅓ cup low-calorie (imitation)
  mayonnaise

About 15 minutes before serving: Combine potatoes, onion, pimento and parsley. In small bowl, blend sauerkraut juice, salt, milk and low-calorie mayonnaise. Toss with potato mixture. Makes 6 servings.

**Low-fat, low-cholesterol diet:** 2 grams fat per serving.
**Low-purine diet:** Prepare as directed.

## PIQUANT SALAD DRESSING (10 calories per tablespoon)

1 cup tomato juice
1 tablespoon cornstarch
2 tablespoons salad oil
¼ cup vinegar
1 teaspoon salt
¼ teaspoon prepared horseradish
¼ teaspoon paprika
¼ teaspoon onion salt
½ teaspoon Worcestershire
¼ teaspoon celery salt
scant ⅛ teaspoon dry mustard
2 dashes garlic salt

At least 2 hours before serving: In small saucepan, heat ½ cup water, tomato juice and cornstarch, stirring constantly, until thickened. Cool to lukewarm; add remaining ingredients and beat until blended. Refrigerate. Shake well before serving. Makes 1¾ cups.

**Diabetic diet:** Exchanges per tablespoon = 1 "free."
**Egg-, gluten-, milk- and wheat-free diet:** Prepare as directed.
**Low-fat, low-cholesterol diet:** 1 gram fat per tablespoon.

## TANGY CHEESE DRESSING (15 calories per tablespoon)

1 8-ounce container creamed
  cottage cheese*
⅓ cup evaporated skimmed
  milk
2 tablespoons water
1 teaspoon vinegar
½ teaspoon garlic salt
½ teaspoon onion salt
¼ teaspoon salt
dash Tabasco

About 1 hour before serving: In electric-blender container, at low speed, blend all ingredients until smooth—2 to 3 minutes. Chill until serving time. Delicious over salad greens. Makes 1¼ cups.

**Egg-, gluten- and wheat-free diet:** Prepare as directed.
**Low-fat, low-cholesterol diet:** 1 gram fat for 2 tablespoons dressing.
**Low-purine diet:** Prepare as directed.

* For smoothest dressing, use a soft-curd cottage cheese.

## HORSERADISH-HERB DRESSING (10 calories per tablespoon)

1 8-ounce container plain
  yogurt
½ to 1 tablespoon white prepared horseradish
1 tablespoon tarragon or garlic
  vinegar
1 tablespoon chopped chives
1 tablespoon fresh chopped
  dill
1 tablespoon granulated sugar
¾ teaspoon salt
¼ teaspoon paprika

At least 4 hours before serving: In medium bowl, stir together all ingredients. Cover; refrigerate until serving time. Dressing may be kept about 3 days. Makes about 1 cup.

**Egg-, gluten- and wheat-free diet:** Prepare as directed.
**Low-fat, low-cholesterol diet:** Negligible fat per serving.
**Low-purine diet:** Prepare as directed.

## WATERCRESS-ROQUEFORT DRESSING (15 calories per tablespoon)

2 tablespoons soft Roquefort
  cheese
⅓ cup low-calorie (imitation)
  mayonnaise
¼ cup skimmed milk or re-
  liquefied nonfat dry milk
2 tablespoons chopped watercress

At least 2 hours before serving: In small bowl, mash Roquefort, and blend with remaining ingredients until creamy. Refrigerate. Makes ⅔ cup. Nice served with tossed salad.

**Low-fat diet:** 1 gram fat per tablespoon. Omit recipe from low cholesterol diet.

## OLD-FASHIONED FRENCH DRESSING (10 calories per tablespoon)

⅔ cup creamed cottage cheese
½ cup canned tomato juice
1 envelope (.6 ounces) French
   salad-dressing mix

At least 1 hour before serving: In electric-blender container, blend all ingredients; refrigerate until serving time. Makes 1 cup.

**Low-fat, low-cholesterol diet:** Less than 1 gram fat per tablespoon.
**Low-purine diet:** Prepare as directed.

## YOGURT DRESSING (20 calories per tablespoon)

1 8-ounce container plain
   yogurt
2 tablespoons salad oil
1 tablespoon lemon juice
1 teaspoon paprika
1 teaspoon salt
¼ teaspoon garlic powder
dash Tabasco

At least 1 hour before serving: In jar, combine all ingredients; stir well; refrigerate. Makes 1 cup.

**Egg-, gluten- and wheat-free diet:** Prepare as directed.
**Low-fat, low-cholesterol diet:** 1 gram fat per tablespoon.
**Low-purine diet:** Prepare as directed.

## TORINO DRESSING (3 calories per tablespoon)

⅓ cup canned tomato juice
¼ cup vinegar
2 tablespoons water
1 envelope (.6 ounces) Italian
   salad-dressing mix

At least 1 hour before serving: Combine all ingredients in small bowl; refrigerate until serving time. Makes ⅔ cup.

**Diabetic diet:** Exchanges per tablespoon = 1 "free."
**Low-fat, low-cholesterol diet:** Negligible fat per serving.
**Low-purine diet:** Prepare as directed.

## DELICATE SALAD DRESSING (5 calories per tablespoon)

1 tablespoon granulated sugar
1½ teaspoons cornstarch
½ teaspoon salt
½ teaspoon dry mustard
⅓ cup vinegar
⅓ cup water
⅓ cup canned tomato juice
1 tablespoon minced onion

At least 1 hour before serving: In medium saucepan, mix sugar, cornstarch, salt and mustard; stir in rest of ingredients. Heat mixture just to boiling. Pour into jar; cover; refrigerate. Seasonings may be adjusted to taste, if desired. Makes 1 cup.

**Diabetic diet:** Prepare as directed but omit sugar; substitute saccharin equivalent to 1 tablespoon sugar. Exchanges per tablespoon = 1 "free."
**Egg-, gluten-, milk- and wheat-free diet:** Prepare as directed.
**Low-fat, low-cholesterol diet:** Negligible fat per serving.
**Low-purine diet:** Prepare as directed.
**Low-sodium diet:** Prepare as directed but omit salt; use low-sodium tomato juice. Negligible sodium per serving.

## ISLAND FRUIT DRESSING (20 calories per tablespoon)

1 cup drained canned crushed
   pineapple
1 tablespoon butter or margarine
1½ teaspoons curry
dash salt
1 teaspoon cornstarch

At least 3 hours before serving: In small saucepan, heat pineapple, butter or margarine, curry and salt to boiling. Blend cornstarch with ⅓ cup water; stir into pineapple mixture and cook, stirring, until thickened. Refrigerate; serve as dressing for crab or tuna salad. Makes 1 cup.

**Low-fat, low-cholesterol diet:** Prepare as directed but use margarine instead of butter. 1 gram fat per tablespoon.
**Low-sodium diet:** Prepare as directed but use unsalted butter or margarine; use curry mixture not containing salt; omit salt. Negligible sodium per tablespoon.

## HOT BREADS

### BUTTERMILK CARAWAY BISCUITS (85 calories per biscuit)

**2 cups sifted all-purpose flour**
**2 teaspoons double-acting**
**baking powder**
**¼ teaspoon baking soda**
**1 teaspoon salt**
**2 teaspoons caraway seed**
**⅔ cup buttermilk**
**⅓ cup salad oil**

About 30 minutes before serving: Preheat oven to 475°F. Sift dry ingredients into a bowl. To oil, add caraway seed and buttermilk (don't stir together). Pour, all at once, over flour mixture; mix with fork to make soft dough that rounds up into a ball.

Wipe work surface with damp cloth, then spread with sheet of waxed paper; turn dough onto paper. Knead lightly, without additional flour, 10 times, or until smooth. Flatten slightly, then top with second sheet of waxed paper; pat or roll dough ¼-inch thick. Remove top paper. Cut out with unfloured 3-inch biscuit cutter. Bake on ungreased cookie sheet 9 to 12 minutes, or until golden brown. Makes about 18.

**Diabetic diet:** Exchanges per serving = 1 bread and 1 fat.
**Low-fat, low-cholesterol diet:** 5 grams fat per biscuit.
**Low-purine diet:** Prepare as directed.

### . CRISP CRUSTS (45 calories each)

**1 12-ounce loaf French bread**
**2 tablespoons butter or mar-**
**garine**
**poppy or caraway or celery seed**

About 30 minutes before serving: Preheat oven to 375°F. With sharp knife, cut off oval-shaped pieces of crust, about 2-inches long and 1-inch wide, from entire surface of loaf of bread. Use center of bread for bread crumbs. Lightly spread each piece first with butter, then with poppy, caraway or celery seed. Place on cookie sheet, cut side up, and bake 5 to 10 minutes, or until butter is bubbly. Makes about 14.

**Bland diet:** Prepare as directed but substitute Parmesan cheese for poppy, caraway or celery seed.
**Diabetic diet:** Exchanges per serving (2 pieces) = 1 bread and 1 fat.
**Low-fat, low-cholesterol diet:** Prepare as directed but use margarine instead of butter. 2 grams fat per piece.
**Low-purine diet:** Prepare as directed.

### BUTTERMILK-PANCAKE COINS (150 calories per serving)

**½ cup packaged buttermilk-**
**pancake mix**
**⅓ cup skimmed milk or re-**
**liquefied nonfat dry milk**
**¼ cup cold water**
**¼ cup canned applesauce**
**cinnamon**

About 30 minutes before serving: Preheat griddle until drop of water "dances" on it; grease lightly. In small bowl, stir together pancake mix, milk and water until almost smooth but still slightly lumpy.

Pour batter, by level measuring tablespoons, onto hot griddle. Cook until pancakes are covered with bubbles and edges are cooked; turn; cook other side until golden-brown.

To serve: Top each serving of 4 pancakes with 2 tablespoons applesauce. If desired, sprinkle lightly with cinnamon. Makes 2 servings.

**Bland diet:** Prepare as directed.
**Diabetic diet:** Prepare as directed but substitue dietetic-pack applesauce for regular. Exchanges per serving = 2 bread.
**Low-fat, low-cholesterol diet:** 1 gram fat per serving.
**Low-fat, bland (gall bladder) diet:** Prepare as directed.
**High-iron diet:** 1 milligram iron per serving.
**Low-purine diet:** Prepare as directed.
**Low-residue diet:** Prepare as directed.

## WAFFLES (110 calories per waffle)

1½ cups sifted all-purpose
  flour
3 teaspoons double-acting
  baking powder
2 tablespoons granulated sugar
½ teaspoon salt
1 cup skimmed milk or reliquefied nonfat dry milk
2 eggs
3 tablespoons salad oil

About 30 minutes before serving: Preheat waffle iron as manufacturer directs. In medium bowl, sift together flour, baking powder, sugar and salt. In small bowl beat milk, eggs and salad oil together. Add to flour mixture; beat until all flour is wet and batter is almost smooth. Bake waffles until dark golden brown. Makes about twelve 4-inch waffles.

**Bland diet:** Prepare as directed.
**Diabetic diet:** Prepare as directed but omit sugar; substitute saccharin equivalent to 2 tablespoons sugar; increase salad oil to ¼ cup. Exchanges per serving = 1 bread and 1 fat.
**Low-fat, low-cholesterol diet:** Prepare as directed but substitute 3 egg whites for 2 whole eggs. 4 grams fat per serving.
**Low-purine diet:** Prepare as directed.
**Low-sodium diet:** Prepare as directed but substitute low-sodium baking powder for regular; omit salt; increase salad oil to ¼ cup. 25 milligrams sodium per serving.

## JAM ROLLS (65 calories per serving)

1 8-ounce can refrigerated
  crescent rolls
4 tablespoons apricot jam or
  preserves

About 25 minutes before serving: Preheat oven to 375°F. Unroll rolls; separate into 4 rectangles. Gently press seam together, across each rectangle. Spread each with 1 tablespoon jam; reroll to original shape; cut, crosswise, into 4 sections. Place on ungreased cookie sheet; bake 12 to 15 minutes, or until rich golden-brown. Makes 16.

**Bland diet:** Prepare as directed but substitute jelly for jam.
**Diabetic diet:** Prepare as directed but substitute sugar-free jam for regular. Exchanges per serving (2 rolls) = 1 bread and 1 fat.
**Low-purine diet:** Prepare as directed.
**Low-residue diet:** Prepare as directed for bland diet.

## FLOWER BUNS (80 calories per bun)

1 8-ounce can refrigerated
  buttermilk biscuits
milk
poppy seed

About 20 minutes before serving. Preheat oven to 450°F. Grease large cookie sheet. Separate biscuits, then press each until twice its original size. With kitchen scissors, make 5 to 6 snips, from outer edge almost to center. Place on cookie sheet and shape "petals" to form "flower." Repeat with remaining dough. Brush each "flower" with milk; sprinkle with poppy seed. Bake 6 to 8 minutes, or until golden-brown. Makes 8.

**Bland diet:** Prepare as directed but substitute Parmesan cheese for poppy seed.
**Diabetic diet:** Exchanges per bun = 1 bread.
**Low-purine diet:** Prepare as directed.
**Low-residue diet:** Prepare as directed for bland diet.

## "BREADBOARD" BISCUITS (80 calories per biscuit)

1 9.5-ounce package refrigerated artificial-butter-flavored
  biscuits
sesame seed or garlic salt or
  shredded Parmesan cheese

About 15 minutes before serving: Preheat oven to 450°F. On greased cookie sheet, roll each biscuit into oval about 4" by 6". Sprinkle with one of seasonings. Bake 8 minutes, or until golden brown. Makes 10.

**Diabetic diet:** Exchanges per biscuit = 1 bread.
**Low-purine diet:** Prepare as directed.

## PASTRY FINGERS (35 calories per finger)

**1 8-ounce package refrigerated crescent rolls**

About 15 minutes before serving: Preheat oven to 375°F. Unroll the 2 strips of perforated dough, but do **not** separate into triangles. Instead, cut crosswise, into strips 1-inch wide. Place on ungreased cookie sheet. Bake 5 to 7 minutes, or until golden-brown. Serve hot. Makes 24 fingers.

**Bland diet:** Prepare as directed.
**Diabetic diet:** Exchanges per serving (4 fingers) = 1 bread and 1 fat.
**Low-purine diet:** Prepare as directed.

## SEEDED BREADSTICKS (95 calories each)

**4 slices day-old bread**
**4 teaspoons butter or margarine**
**One of following: poppy seed, sesame seed, celery seed or grated Parmesan cheese**

About 25 minutes before serving: Preheat oven to 375°F. Trim crust from bread. Spread each slice with 1 teaspoon butter, then sprinkle with poppy, sesame or celery seed, or with Parmesan cheese. Roll, diagonally, to form "stick" and fix with toothpick. Place on cookie sheet, and bake until crisp and lightly toasted—10 to 15 minutes. Makes 4 sticks.

**Bland diet:** Prepare as directed but sprinkle only with Parmesan cheese.
**Diabetic diet:** Exchanges per serving = 1 bread and 1 fat.
**Low-fat, low-cholesterol diet:** Prepare as directed but use margarine instead of butter; omit Parmesan-cheese topping. 5 grams fat per serving.

## MUSHROOM PIZZETTES (75 calories per serving)

**1 15⅜-ounce package cheese-pizza mix**
**1 4-ounce can sliced mushrooms, thoroughly drained**

About 30 minutes before serving: Preheat oven to 425°F. Prepare flour mixture as label directs, but separate dough into 12 balls. Thoroughly grease cookie sheets and hands. On cookie sheets, with hands, spread each ball into paper-thin circle about 5 inches in diameter. (Circles may be close together, but not touching.) Spread each circle with heaping tablespoon tomato sauce from can. Divide mushroom slices among pizzettes; sprinkle each with a little Parmesan cheese. Bake 15 minutes, or until edges are brown. Makes 12 servings.

**Diabetic diet:** Exchanges per serving = 1 bread.
**Low-fat diet:** 1 gram fat per serving. Omit recipe from low-cholesterol diet.
**Low-purine diet:** Prepare as directed but omit mushrooms.

## BRUNCH DELIGHT (245 calories per serving)

**1 8-ounce container cottage cheese**
**2 tablespoons skimmed milk or reliquefied nonfat dry milk**
**4 teaspoons granulated sugar**
**¼ teaspoon vanilla extract**
**1 5-ounce package frozen waffles**
**1 cup frozen unsweetened strawberries, thawed**

About 15 minutes before serving: In electric-blender container, at low speed, blend cottage cheese, milk, sugar and vanilla. Toast waffles as label directs. Spoon cheese mixture over waffles, then top with strawberries. Makes 3 servings.

**Diabetic diet:** Prepare as directed but omit sugar; substitute saccharin equivalent to 1 tablespoon sugar. Exchanges per serving = 1 bread, 1 milk and 1 fruit.
**Low-fat, low-cholesterol diet:** 5 grams fat per serving.
**High-iron diet:** 1.5 milligrams iron per serving.
**Low-purine diet:** Prepare as directed.

## DESSERTS

### MELON FESTIVE PARFAIT (50 calories per serving)

cantaloupe
watermelon
honeydew
1½ cups pineapple juice
mint sprigs for garnish

About 30 minutes before serving: From each melon, make 1½ cups balls. In 6 parfait glasses, alternate layers of three types. Pour pineapple juice over them; garnish with mint sprigs. Makes 6 servings.

**Diabetic diet:** Exchanges per serving = 1 fruit.
**Egg-, gluten-, milk- and wheat-free diet:** Prepare as directed.
**Low-fat, low-cholesterol diet:** Negligible fat per serving.
**Low-sodium diet:** 5 milligrams sodium per serving.

### COMPOTE WAIKIKI (125 calories per serving)

¼ cup granulated sugar
1 tablespoon lemon juice
1 stick cinnamon
20 whole cloves
¾ teaspoon vanilla extract
1 15¼-ounce can pineapple chunks packed in pineapple juice, drained
1 30-ounce can freestone peach halves, drained

Early in day: In medium saucepan, stir together sugar, ½ cup water, lemon juice, cinnamon and cloves. Simmer 5 minutes; remove spices; stir in vanilla extract. Add pineapple chunks and peach halves; chill thoroughly before serving. Makes 6 servings.

**Egg-, gluten-, milk- and wheat-free diet:** Prepare as directed.
**Low-fat, low-cholesterol diet:** Negligible fat per serving.
**Low-sodium diet:** 2 milligrams sodium per serving.

### OUR FAVORITE FRUIT COMPOTE (80 calories per serving)

1 pint lime or orange sherbet
1 pint fresh strawberries, chilled
1 medium cantaloupe, chilled

Day before serving or early in day: Line cookie sheet with waxed paper; store in freezer at least 10 minutes. Dipping melon baller into warm water between each ball, scoop sherbet into balls. Place on chilled cookie sheet. Cover with second sheet of waxed paper; freeze.

About 15 minutes before serving: Wash and stem strawberries; scoop balls from cantaloupe. Divide cantaloupe balls, strawberries and sherbet balls among 8 dessert dishes. Makes 8 servings.

**Egg-, gluten- and wheat-free diet:** Prepare as directed but use gluten-free sherbet on gluten-free diet.
**Low-fat, low-cholesterol diet:** Negligible fat per serving.
**Low-purine diet:** Prepare as directed.
**Low-sodium diet:** 10 milligrams sodium per serving.

### MAPLE BAKED PEARS (120 calories per serving)

2 fresh ripe Bartlett pears
4 walnut halves
maple syrup

About 40 minutes before serving: Pare, then halve and core pears. (Scoop out seeds neatly with a half-teaspoon measuring spoon.) Preheat oven to 350°F.

In medium baking dish, place pears, cut side up; top each with walnut half. Pour 1 tablespoon maple syrup over each. Cover; bake 20 to 25 minutes, or until pears are just tender. Serve warm, spooning syrup over pears. Makes 4 servings.

**Egg-, gluten-, milk- and wheat-free diet:** Prepare as directed.
**Low-fat, low-cholesterol diet:** 1 gram fat per serving.
**Low-purine diet:** Prepare as directed.
**Low-sodium diet:** 2 milligrams sodium per serving.

## SPANISH CREAM WITH RASPBERRY SAUCE (150 calories per serving)

1½ teaspoons unflavored
  gelatin
granulated sugar
⅛ teaspoon salt
2 eggs, separated
1½ cups skimmed milk or reliquefied nonfat dry milk
½ teaspoon vanilla extract
1 10-ounce package frozen
  raspberries, thawed
1 tablespoon cornstarch

Early in day: In top of double boiler, mix gelatin, 2 table-spoons sugar, salt and egg yolks. In small saucepan, scald milk. Stirring constantly, slowly stir scalded milk into gela-tin-sugar mixture. Place over boiling water; stirring con-stantly, cook until custard just begins to coat spoon—do not overcook or custard will separate. Remove from heat; stir in vanilla; refrigerate until consistency of soft gelatin dessert.

Meanwhile, drain raspberries, reserving syrup. In small saucepan, slowly stir raspberry syrup into cornstarch. Heat, stirring constantly, until slightly thickened; stir in rasp-berries; refrigerate, covered, until serving time.

In medium bowl, beat egg whites until soft peaks form; then, beating constantly, slowly add ¼ cup sugar; beat un-til meringue forms stiff peaks. Beat custard until smooth, if necessary. Slowly pour custard over meringue; fold together until smooth. Divide among six ¾-cup custard cups. Re-frigerate until set—at least 2 hours.

To serve: Warm cups slightly over hot water; turn custard out into dessert dishes; spoon on raspberry sauce. Makes 6 servings.

**Low-fat diet:** 2 grams fat per serving. Omit recipe from low-choles-terol diet.
**Gluten- and wheat-free diet:** Prepare as directed.
**Low-purine diet:** Prepare as directed.
**Low-sodium diet:** Prepare as directed but omit salt. 45 milligrams sodium per serving.

## FRESH APPLE SNOW (130 calories per serving)

4 large apples, peeled
1 teaspoon ascorbic-acid mixture for fruit
granulated sugar
3 tablespoons lemon juice
¼ teaspoon nutmeg
dash salt
2 egg whites
6 thin unpeeled apple slices
  for garnish

Early in day: In electric-blender container or on grater, coarsely grate apples. In medium bowl, mix ascorbic-acid mixture with 1½ tablespoons water; add grated apples, 2 tablespoons sugar, lemon juice, nutmeg and salt; refriger-ate; stir occasionally.

Just before serving: With electric mixer at high speed, beat egg whites with ¼ cup sugar until soft peaks form. Drain apple mixture well; fold into egg whites; spoon into serving dishes; garnish with apple slices. Makes 6 servings.

**Low-fat, low-cholesterol diet:** Negligible fat per serving.
**Gluten-, milk- and wheat-free diet:** Prepare as directed.
**Low-purine diet:** Prepare as directed.

## PEACHES AMANDINE GLACÉ (145 calories per serving)

⅓ cup skimmed milk or re-
  liquefied nonfat dry milk
½ teaspoon almond extract
2 tablespoons granulated sugar
1 8-ounce container creamed
  cottage cheese
1 29-ounce can sliced peaches
2 tablespoons flaked coconut

About 2 to 3 hours before serving: In electric-blender con-tainer, at low speed, blend milk, almond extract, sugar and cottage cheese into a smooth sauce.

Drain peaches; cover with sauce; refrigerate.

To serve: Divide among 5 dessert dishes; top with coco-nut. Makes 5 servings.

**Bland diet:** Prepare as directed but omit coconut.
**Low-fat, low-cholesterol diet:** Prepare as directed but omit coconut. 2 grams fat per serving.
**Low-fat, bland (gall bladder) diet:** Prepare as directed for bland diet.
**Low-purine diet:** Prepare as directed.
**Low-residue diet:** Prepare as directed for bland diet.

## McINTOSH MERINGUE (90 calories per serving)

1 egg white
granulated sugar
dash ginger
2 8-ounce or 1 16-ounce can
    unsweetened applesauce

Early in day or up to 1 hour before serving: Preheat oven to 425°F. In a small bowl, beat egg white until soft peaks form; beating constantly, gradually add 4 teaspoons sugar and ginger; beat until stiff glossy peaks form.

Stir 2 tablespoons sugar into applesauce; divide among four ¾-cup custard cups; top each with dollop of meringue. Bake 4 to 6 minutes, or until nicely browned. Serve warm or cold. Makes 4 servings.

**Bland diet:** Prepare as directed but omit ginger.
**Low-fat, low-cholesterol diet:** Negligible fat per serving.
**Low-fat, bland (gall bladder) diet:** Prepare as directed for bland diet.
**Gluten-, milk- and wheat-free diet:** Prepare as directed.
**Low-purine diet:** Prepare as directed.
**Low-residue diet:** Prepare as directed for bland diet.
**Low-sodium diet:** 15 milligrams sodium per serving.

## BRIE WITH BUTTERY BAKED PEARS (125 calories per pear and about 100 for each cracker spread with cheese)

½ cup granulated sugar
2 tablespoons lemon juice
2 tablespoons butter or mar-
    garine
6 ripe pears, pared
1 round Brie cheese
sesame-seed crackers

Day before or early in day: Preheat oven to 350°F. Meanwhile, simmer sugar with lemon juice, butter, 1 cup boiling water for 5 minutes. Arrange pears in 3-quart casserole; add syrup. Bake, covered, 55 to 60 minutes, or until tender; refrigerate.

About 3 hours before serving: Arrange cheese and crackers on wooden board; set aside at room temperature.

To serve: Arrange pears in dishes; pass tray of cheese and crackers. Makes 6 servings.

**Diabetic diet:** Instead of pears baked as directed, substitute 12 water-packed pear halves that have been brushed with butter or margarine and lemon juice; refrigerate. Serve as above. One pear, a 1-inch cube of cheese and 3 crackers = 1 fruit, 1 meat and 1 bread exchange.
**Low-purine diet:** Prepare as directed.

## SPANISH PEACHES (about 60 calories per serving)

1 30-ounce can cling-peach
    halves
3 tablespoons dark brown
    sugar
2 tablespoons lime juice
¼ cup sherry (optional)
1 tablespoon grated lime peel

At least 2 hours before serving: Drain peaches, reserving ½ cup syrup. In small saucepan, combine peach syrup, brown sugar, lime juice and sherry; simmer 5 minutes.

Meanwhile, place peach halves, flat side down, side by side, in serving dish; pour syrup mixture over them. Sprinkle with grated lime peel. Refrigerate until serving time. Serve 1 peach half per serving. Makes 8 to 9 servings.

**Bland diet:** Prepare as directed but omit sherry and lime peel.
**Egg-, gluten-, milk- and wheat-free diet:** Prepare as directed.
**Low-fat, low-cholesterol diet:** Negligible fat per serving.
**Low-fat, bland (gall bladder) diet:** Prepare as directed for bland diet.
**Low-purine diet:** Prepare as directed but omit sherry.
**Low-residue diet:** Prepare as directed for bland diet.
**Low-sodium diet:** 2 milligrams sodium per serving.

## PINEAPPLE CUSTARD (Quesilla de Piña) (160 calories per serving)

1 cup canned pineapple juice
½ cup granulated sugar
6 eggs
generous dash salt
½ teaspoon vanilla extract

Early in day: In small saucepan, simmer pineapple juice with sugar for 15 minutes. Cool; refrigerate.

About 2 hours before serving: Preheat oven to 350°F. In large bowl, with electric mixer at high speed, beat eggs and salt until light and fluffy—at least 5 minutes. With mixer at medium speed, slowly beat in cold pineapple-sugar mixture, then vanilla. Turn into 2-quart casserole. Place casserole in shallow pan of hot water.

Bake 45 minutes, or until custard sinks in center, turns a dark golden-brown around edges, and is set. Serve warm. Makes 6 servings.

**Bland diet:** Prepare as directed. Omit recipe if pineapple juice is forbidden on diet.
**Gluten-, milk- and wheat-free diet:** Prepare as directed.
**Low-purine diet:** Prepare as directed.
**Low-residue diet:** Prepare as directed. Omit recipe if pineapple juice is forbidden on diet.

## PEACHES MERINGUE (135 calories per serving)

3 egg whites (at room temperature)
⅛ teaspoon salt
⅛ teaspoon cream of tartar
½ cup granulated sugar
1 29-ounce can peach halves
6 teaspoons red raspberry preserves

About 1 hour before serving: Preheat oven to 275°F. In small bowl, with electric mixer at high speed, beat egg whites with salt and cream of tartar until frothy; add sugar, a little at a time, beating well after each addition. Beat until stiff peaks form. Drain 6 peach halves on paper towels; place, cut side up, in shallow baking dish. Spoon teaspoon of preserves into each. Cover with meringue; bake 40 minutes. Serve warm. Makes 6 servings.

**Bland diet:** Prepare as directed but use strawberry jelly instead of raspberry preserves.
**Low-fat, low-cholesterol diet:** Negligible fat per serving.
**Low-fat, bland (gall bladder) diet:** Prepare as directed for bland diet.
**Gluten-, milk- and wheat-free diet:** Prepare as directed.
**Low-purine diet:** Prepare as directed.
**Low-residue diet:** Prepare as directed for bland diet.
**Low-sodium diet:** Prepare as directed but omit salt. 25 milligrams sodium per serving.

## GOLD-AND-WHITE COMPOTE (90 calories per serving)

2 13¼-ounce cans pineapple chunks, drained
1 cup orange juice
1 cup miniature marshmallows

At least 45 minutes before serving: Toss together all ingredients; refrigerate 45 minutes, or until marshmallows are softened. Makes 6 servings.

**Bland diet:** Prepare as directed, but substitute two 16-ounce cans peeled apricots for pineapple.
**Low-fat, low-cholesterol diet:** Negligible fat per serving.
**Low-fat, bland (gall bladder) diet:** Prepare as directed for bland diet.
**Low-purine diet:** Prepare as directed.
**Low-residue diet:** Prepare as directed for bland diet.
**Low-sodium diet:** Prepare as directed but use brand of marshmallows not containing salt or sodium-containing compounds. 5 milligrams sodium per serving.

## APPLES AMERICANA (125 calories per serving)

12 small McIntosh apples
1 cup granulated sugar
1 stick cinnamon
confectioners' sugar

Up to 4 hours before serving: In medium heavy-gauge saucepan, bring sugar, 2 cups water and cinnamon stick to boiling. Add apples, a few at a time, and cook until they are fork-tender but still shapely—about 3 to 5 minutes. Remove from syrup, one at a time. In heated compote filled with a cushion of crumpled foil, or on heated platter, arrange apples in pyramid—7 apples in bottom tier, 4 in second tier, and 1 on top.

Boil syrup to 234°F. on candy thermometer; pour over apples in very thin coating; lightly sift confectioners' sugar over all. Serve with fruit knife and fork. Makes 12 servings.

**Egg-, gluten-, milk- and wheat-free diet:** Prepare as directed.
**Low-fat, low-cholesterol diet:** Negiigible fat per serving.
**Low-purine diet:** Prepare as directed.
**Low-sodium diet:** 1 milligram sodium per serving.

## MARSHMALLOW APPLE BETTY (120 calories per serving)

4 medium cooking apples,
  peeled, coarsely chopped
¼ cup raisins
¼ cup granulated sugar
1 teaspoon lemon juice
½ teaspoon cinnamon
dash nutmeg
dash salt
1½ cups miniature marsh-
  mallows

About 45 minutes before serving: Preheat oven to 350°F. In medium baking dish, mix all ingredients but marshmallows. Cover and bake 30 minutes, or until apples are tender. Remove cover and stir ingredients well. Turn oven to broil. Sprinkle marshmallows on top of apples. Broil just until marshmallows are well browned—about 1 or 2 minutes. Serve either hot or cold. Makes 6 servings.

**Bland diet:** Prepare as directed but omit nutmeg and raisins.
**Low-fat, low-cholesterol diet:** Negligible fat per serving.
**Low-fat, bland (gall bladder) diet:** Prepare as directed for bland diet.
**Low-purine diet:** Prepare as directed.
**Low-residue diet:** Prepare as directed for bland diet.
**Low-sodium diet:** Prepare as directed but omit salt; use marshmallows not containing salt or sodium compounds (check label). 5 milligrams sodium per serving.

## MEXICAN FRUIT BOWL (50 to 100 calories per serving, depending on fruit)

1 fresh pineapple
1 melon (honeydew,
  cantaloupe or cranshaw)
2 seedless oranges
seedless grapes

Early in day or at least 1 hour before serving: Prepare pineapple as follows: Grasp by crown; then, holding firmly, cut off rind all around, from top down, following curve of fruit; remove eyes if desired. Cut into ¼-inch crosswise slices, then reassemble into pineapple shape. Pare skin from melon, just as if it were an apple; cut off top, 1 inch down; scrape out seeds. Cut melon into ¼-inch crosswise slices; reassemble, using picks if necessary. With sharp knife cut peel from oranges in a continuous spiral, to one-third of way down from top. Refrigerate all.

To serve: In fruit bowl assemble fruits, with pineapple and melon, side by side, and grapes and oranges tucked here and there. Makes 8 servings.

**Low-fat, low-cholesterol diet:** Negligible fat per serving.
**Low-purine diet:** Prepare as directed.
**Low-sodium diet:** 5 milligrams sodium per serving.

## AMBROSIA TROPICALE (145 calories per serving)

2 large seedless oranges
3 large bananas
3 tablespoons flaked coconut
½ pint orange sherbet

About 20 minutes before serving: Carefully peel and section oranges; press juice from remaining orange pieces; add to sections. Peel and slice bananas; add to orange; toss; divide among 6 dessert dishes. Sprinkle each serving with ½ tablespoon coconut; top with sherbet. Makes 6 servings.

**Egg-, gluten- and wheat-free diet:** Prepare as directed but use sherbet not containing gluten on gluten-free diet.
**Low-purine diet:** Prepare as directed.
**Low-sodium diet:** Use coconut not containing salt or sodium compounds. 5 milligrams sodium per serving.

## IRANIAN PINEAPPLE COMPOTE (120 calories per serving)

1 15¼-ounce can pineapple chunks packed in pineapple juice
⅓ cup plain yogurt
1 tablespoon granulated sugar
1½ tablespoons chopped walnuts

About 2 hours before serving: Drain pineapple chunks; toss with yogurt and sugar. Divide among 3 dessert dishes; top each with one-third of walnuts. Refrigerate until serving time to blend flavors. Makes 3 servings.

**Bland diet:** Toss yogurt with peach halves and sugar; omit walnuts.
**Diabetic diet:** Prepare as directed but omit sugar; use liquid saccharin equivalent to 2 teaspoons sugar. Exchanges per serving = 1 fruit. Makes 4 servings.
**Egg-, gluten- and wheat-free diet:** Prepare as directed.
**Low-fat, low-cholesterol diet:** 1 gram fat per serving.
**Low-fat, bland (gall bladder) diet:** Prepare as directed for bland diet.
**Low-purine diet:** Prepare as directed.
**Low-residue diet:** Prepare as directed for bland diet.
**Low-sodium diet:** 15 milligrams sodium per serving.

## BAKED APPLE SURPRISE (155 calories per serving)

2 medium bananas
1 tablespoon lemon juice
¼ cup granulated sugar
dash salt
¼ teaspoon nutmeg
6 medium baking apples
1 cup orange juice

At least 3 hours before serving: Preheat oven to 375°F. In medium bowl, mash bananas with fork and mix with lemon juice, sugar, salt and nutmeg. Wash and core apples; place in large baking dish. Fill with banana mixture; pour orange juice over them. Bake one hour, or until tender, basting occasionally with orange juice. Makes 6 servings.

**Bland diet:** Prepare as directed but substitute cinnamon for nutmeg.
**Egg-, gluten-, milk- and wheat-free diet:** Prepare as directed.
**Low-fat, low-cholesterol diet:** Negligible fat per serving.
**Low-fat, bland (gall bladder) diet:** Prepare as directed for bland diet.
**Low-purine diet:** Prepare as directed.
**Low-residue diet:** Prepare as directed for bland diet.
**Low-sodium diet:** Prepare as directed but omit salt. 5 milligrams sodium per serving.

## BAKED BANANA AMBROSIA (90 calories per serving)

3 bananas, peeled
1½ tablespoons melted butter or margarine
2 tablespoons lemon or lime juice
⅓ cup flaked coconut

About 30 minutes beore serving: Preheat oven to 375°F. Grease medium baking dish. Halve bananas crosswise, then lengthwise; place in dish. Brush with butter, then with juice; sprinkle with coconut. Bake 15 to 20 minutes, or until easily pierced with fork. Serve warm. Makes 6 servings.

**Egg-, gluten-, milk- and wheat-free diet:** Prepare as directed but use milk-free margarine on milk-free diet.
**Low-purine diet:** Prepare as directed.
**Low-sodium diet:** Prepare as directed but use unsalted butter or margarine; use coconut not containing added salt or sodium-containing compounds. 2 milligrams sodium per serving.

## GRAPEFRUIT BRÛLÉE (90 calories per serving)

2 medium grapefruit
4 teaspoons granulated sugar
⅛ teaspoon cinnamon
4 maraschino cherries

About 20 minutes before serving: Preheat broiler 10 minutes if manufacturer directs. Meanwhile, halve grapefruit; with knife, cut around each section. Mix sugar and cinnamon; sprinkle evenly over grapefruit halves. Broil 5 minutes, or until warm and bubbly; top each with maraschino cherry. Makes 4 servings.

**Diabetic diet:** Prepare as directed but omit sugar; sprinkle grapefruit halves lightly with granulated saccharin to taste. Exchanges per serving = 1 fruit.
**Egg-, gluten-, milk- and wheat-free diet:** Prepare as directed.
**Low-fat, low-cholesterol diet:** Negligible fat per serving.
**Low-purine diet:** Prepare as directed.
**Low-sodium diet:** Prepare as directed but omit cherries. Negligible sodium per serving.

## HOT-COLD SPICED FRUIT (70 calories per serving)

1 16-ounce can cling-peach
    slices, chilled
1 15¼-ounce can pineapple
    chunks, packed in pineapple
    juice, chilled
¼ teaspoon cinnamon

About 10 minutes before serving: Drain syrup from peaches and pineapple; reserve pineapple syrup. In medium saucepan, heat pineapple syrup and cinnamon to boiling.
    To serve: Place fruit in serving bowl; cover with hot pineapple syrup. Makes 6 servings.

**Bland diet:** Prepare as directed but substitute one 16-ounce can pear halves for pineapple chunks.
**Egg-, gluten-, milk- and wheat-free diet:** Prepare as directed.
**Low-fat, low-cholesterol diet:** Negligible fat per serving.
**Low-fat, bland (gall bladder) diet:** Prepare as directed for bland diet.
**Low-purine diet:** Prepare as directed.
**Low-residue diet:** Prepare as directed for bland diet.
**Low-sodium diet:** 1 milligram sodium per serving.

## APRICOT SNOWBALLS (35 calories per snowball)

24 large dried apricots
1 cup flaked coconut
2 teaspoons orange juice
confectioners' sugar

At least 1 hour before serving: Put apricots and coconut through food chopper. Blend in orange juice, confectioners' sugar. Shape into ¾-inch balls. Makes 2 dozen.

**Egg-, gluten-, milk- and wheat-free diet:** Prepare as directed.
**Low-purine diet:** Prepare as directed.
**Low-sodium diet:** Prepare as directed but use coconut not containing added salt or sodium-containing compounds. 2 milligrams sodium per serving.

## SNOW-PEAK RASPBERRY SAUCE (130 calories per serving)

1 egg white
2 tablespoons granulated sugar
dash salt
1 16-ounce can or jar
    raspberry applesauce, chilled

Up to 20 minutes before serving: Preheat oven to 375°F. In small bowl, beat egg white until soft peaks form. Slowly add sugar and salt, beating constantly, until stiff peaks form. Divide raspberry applesauce among four 6-ounce custard cups. Top with dabs of meringue. Bake 5 to 7 minutes, or until golden-brown on top. Serve warm or cold. Makes 4 servings.

**Bland diet:** Prepare as directed.
**Low-fat, low-cholesterol diet:** Negligible fat per serving.
**Low-fat, bland (gall bladder) diet:** Prepare as directed.
**Gluten-, milk- and wheat-free diet:** Prepare as directed.
**Low-purine diet:** Prepare as directed.
**Low-residue diet:** Prepare as directed.
**Low-sodium diet:** Omit salt. 15 milligrams sodium per serving.

## APRICOT DELIGHT (70 calories per serving)

2 egg whites
⅛ teaspoon salt
1 tablespoon granulated sugar
1 16-ounce can peeled apricots, pitted and drained

About 15 minutes before serving: In medium bowl, with electric mixer at high speed, beat egg whites and salt until frothy. Gradually add sugar, beating constantly for 2 minutes, or until sugar is dissolved. Then gradually beat in apricots until shredded. Makes 4 servings.

**Bland diet:** Prepare as directed.
**Low-fat, low-cholesterol diet:** Negligible fat per serving.
**Low-fat, bland (gall bladder) diet:** Prepare as directed.
**Gluten-, milk- and wheat-free diet:** Prepare as directed.
**Low-purine diet:** Prepare as directed.
**Low-residue diet:** Prepare as directed.

## FROSTED WATERMELON (90 calories per serving)

½ watermelon
1 pint raspberry sherbet
1 pint fresh raspberries, washed and hulled

Several hours ahead: With serving spoon, scoop meat from watermelon half in spoonfuls, reserving shell. If desired, with tip of paring knife, remove surface seeds from each spoonful of watermelon; then return watermelon to shell, with rounded side up; refrigerate.

To serve: Top watermelon with spoonfuls of raspberry sherbet; scatter raspberries over sherbet. Makes 16 servings.

**Low-fat, low-cholesterol diet:** Negligible fat per serving.
**Low-purine diet:** Prepare as directed.
**Low-sodium diet:** 5 milligrams sodium per serving.

## STRAWBERRIES IN ALMOND YOGURT (155 calories per serving)

2 pints fresh strawberries
1 8-ounce container plain yogurt
2 teaspoons vanilla extract
1½ or 2 teaspoons almond extract
5 tablespoons granulated sugar

Early in day: Wash and hull strawberries; drain on paper toweling. Mix together yogurt, extracts and sugar; taste, adding more almond extract, if desired. Fold in strawberries. Spoon strawberries into 4 champagne or sherbet glasses; cover with yogurt sauce. Refrigerate. Makes 4 servings.

**Diabetic diet:** Prepare as directed but omit sugar. Stir granulated or liquid saccharin equivalent to 3 tablespoons sugar into yogurt. Exchanges per serving = ¼ skimmed milk and 1 fruit.
**Egg-, gluten- and wheat-free diet:** Prepare as directed.
**Low-fat, low-cholesterol diet:** Prepare as directed. 1 gram fat per serving.
**Low-purine diet:** Prepare as directed.

## BAKED CHERRY TAPIOCA (125 calories per serving)

1 16-ounce can pitted red sour cherries, undrained
1 tablespoon lemon juice
⅓ cup granulated sugar
1 teaspoon salt
dash nutmeg
⅓ cup quick-cooking tapioca
½ cup whipped topping

At least 1½ hours before serving: Preheat oven to 350°F. In 1½-quart casserole, stir together ¾ cup hot water, cherries and all remaining ingredients but whipped topping. Stirring occasionally, bake 35 to 45 minutes, or until tapioca granules are clear and pudding has thickened. Serve warm, dabbed with whipped topping. Makes 6 servings.

**Egg-, gluten-, milk- and wheat-free diet:** Prepare as directed but omit whipped topping on milk-free diet.
**Low-fat, low-cholesterol diet:** Prepare as directed but omit whipped topping. Negligible fat per serving.
**Low-purine diet:** Omit whipped topping. Prepare as directed.
**Low-sodium diet:** Prepare as directed but omit salt and whipped topping. 5 milligrams sodium per serving.

## PEACH DUMPLINGS (150 calories per serving)

4 peach halves from 1 16-
   ounce can freestone peach
   halves
1 cup orange juice
3 tablespoons skimmed milk or
   reliquefied nonfat dry milk
1/4 teaspoon grated lemon peel
scant 1/8 teaspoon almond
   extract
1/2 cup packaged biscuit mix
1 teaspoon granulated sugar
pinch cinnamon

At least 1 hour before serving: Drain peach halves; reserve 1/2 cup syrup. In heavy skillet, heat 1/2 cup syrup and orange juice to boiling. Meanwhile, in medium bowl, slowly stir milk, lemon peel and almond extract into biscuit mix. Drop batter, in 4 tablespoonfuls, onto syrup. Simmer, covered, 10 minutes; then sprinkle with sugar, mixed with cinnamon; cover again; simmer 5 minutes more.

To serve: Top peach halves with dumplings and syrup from skillet. Makes 4 servings.

**Bland diet:** Prepare as directed. Omit recipe if orange juice is forbidden on diet.
**Low-fat, low-cholesterol diet:** 3 grams fat per serving.
**Low-fat, bland (gall bladder) diet:** Prepare as directed.
**Low-purine diet:** Prepare as directed.
**Low-residue diet:** Prepare as directed. Omit recipe if orange juice is forbidden on diet.

## CUSTARD RICE PUDDING (150 calories per serving)

1 cup hot cooked rice†
2 eggs
1/3 cup granulated sugar
dash salt
1/2 teaspoon vanilla extract
1/4 cup raisins‡
1/4 teaspoon cinnamon
2 cups skimmed milk or reliquefied nonfat dry milk,
   scalded

At least 1 1/2 hours before serving: Preheat oven to 350°F. In 1-quart casserole, mix all ingredients but milk. Slowly stir in hot milk.

Place casserole in shallow baking dish; fill baking dish 1-inch deep with water. Bake 30 minutes; stir well to prevent rice from settling to bottom. Bake, stirring occasionally, 20 to 30 minutes more, or until consistency of soft custard sauce. Serve warm or cold. Makes six 1/2-cup servings.

**Bland diet:** Prepare as directed but omit raisins.
**Diabetic diet:** Prepare as directed but omit sugar; substitute saccharin equivalent to 1/3 cup sugar. Exchanges per serving = 1/2 skim milk and 1 fruit.
**Gluten- and wheat-free diet:** Prepare as directed.
**Low-purine diet:** Prepare as directed.
**Low-residue diet:** Prepare as directed for bland diet.

† Use regular long-grain, packaged precooked or converted rice. Consistency of pudding varies, from relatively thin and saucy to quite firm, with cooking time and type of rice used. Thin puddings are best served cold; thick ones warm.
‡ If raisins are omitted, count 130 calories per serving.

## PINEAPPLE-TAPIOCA FLUFF (125 calories per serving)

1 egg, separated
2 cups skimmed milk or reliquefied nonfat dry milk
granulated sugar
1/8 teaspoon salt
2 tablespoons quick-cooking
   tapioca
1/4 teaspoon vanilla extract
1 8-ounce can pineapple tidbits, drained

At least 2 hours before serving: In saucepan, beat egg yolk with 1/2 cup milk. Add 1 1/2 cups milk, 1 tablespoon sugar, salt and tapioca. Cook mixture over medium heat, stirring constantly, until boiling—about 5 to 8 minutes. (Do not overcook; mixture thickens as it cools.) Remove from heat.

In medium bowl, beat egg white until foamy. Gradually add 2 teaspoons sugar, continuing to beat until mixture forms soft peaks. Add hot tapioca mixture, stirring constantly. Add vanilla; cool, stirring once after 15 to 20 minutes. Then stir in 1/3 cup pineapple tidbits. Refrigerate.

To serve: Top each serving with remaining pineapple. Makes 4 servings.

**Bland diet:** Prepare as directed but omit pineapple. Substitute 1/2 cup chopped, drained peach slices.
**Low-purine diet:** Prepare as directed.
**Low-residue diet:** Prepare as directed for bland diet.

## GEORGIA DELIGHT (135 calories per serving)

1 cup boiling water
1 20-ounce can sliced freestone peaches
1/4 teaspoon salt
1/8 teaspoon cinnamon
2 tablespoons lemon juice
1/4 cup quick-cooking tapioca
1/3 cup heavy or whipping
  cream, whipped and
  sweetened

At least 1½ hours before serving: Prepare as directed for Baked Cherry Tapioca (page 217). Makes 6 servings.

**Bland diet:** Prepare as directed.
**Egg-, gluten-, milk- and wheat-free diet:** Prepare as directed but omit whipped cream on milk-free diet.
**Low-fat, low-cholesterol diet:** Prepare as directed but omit whipped cream. Negligible fat per serving.
**Low-fat, bland (gall bladder) diet:** Prepare as directed but omit whipped cream.
**Low-purine diet:** Prepare as directed.
**Low-sodium diet:** Prepare as directed but omit salt. 5 milligrams sodium per serving.

## POLKA DOT PUDDING (155 calories per serving)

1 4-serving package regular
  vanilla-pudding mix
2 cups skimmed milk
1 tablespoon chocolate
  sprinkles

About 2 hours before serving: Prepare pudding as label directs but use skimmed milk. Cool slightly; stir in chocolate sprinkles; spoon into sherbet glasses; refrigerate. Makes 4 servings.

**Bland diet:** Prepare as directed. Omit recipe if chocolate is forbidden on diet.
**Low-fat, bland (gall bladder) diet:** Prepare as directed. 2 grams fat per serving.
**Low-residue diet:** Prepare as directed.

## DAISY PUDDING (125 calories per serving)

1 4-serving package regular or
  instant vanilla-pudding mix
2 cups skimmed milk
pineapple tidbits
5 maraschino-cherry halves
sprigs of mint

At least 1 hour before serving: Prepare pudding mix as directed but use skimmed milk. Divide among 5 dessert dishes. Top each with flower made of pineapple tidbits and maraschino-cherry half. Add sprigs of mint for leaf. Serve warm or cold. Makes 5 servings.

**Diabetic diet:** Prepare as directed but use one 4-serving envelope artificially sweetened vanilla-pudding mix, unsweetened canned pineapple in place of regular; divide into 4 servings. Exchanges per serving = ½ skim milk.
**Low-fat, low-cholesterol diet:** Negligible fat per serving.
**Low-purine diet:** Prepare as directed.

## TIP-TOP ORANGE PUDDING (155 calories per serving)

4 medium oranges
granulated sugar
2 cups skimmed milk or reliquefied nonfat dry milk
1 4-serving package regular
  vanilla-pudding mix
3 egg whites
generous dash salt
1/2 teaspoon vanilla extract

At least 1 hour before serving: Prepare ½ tablespoon finely grated orange peel. Peel oranges; section into 1½-quart casserole. Press remaining juice from pulp into casserole. Sprinkle orange sections with 2 tablespoons sugar.

Preheat oven to 325°F. In medium saucepan, slowly stir milk and grated orange peel into pudding mix. Cook, stirring constantly, as label directs; pour over orange sections.

In medium bowl, beat egg whites until soft peaks form. Beating constantly, slowly add 6 tablespoons sugar, salt and vanilla until stiff peaks form. Spread over top of pudding, sealing all around edges of casserole. Bake 15 minutes, or until peaks are golden-brown. Cool about 30 minutes and serve warm. Makes 8 servings.

**Low-fat, low-cholesterol diet:** Negligible fat per serving.
**Low-purine diet:** Prepare as directed.

## DANISH FRUIT PUDDING (Rogrod) (120 calories per serving)

2 10-ounce packages frozen
   raspberries, thawed
dash cinnamon
finely grated peel of ½ lemon
juice of ½ lemon
2 tablespoons cornstarch
½ teaspoon vanilla extract
generous dash salt
2 tablespoons slivered almonds

Early in day: Into medium saucepan, drain syrup from raspberries. Mix cinnamon, grated peel, lemon juice, cornstarch, vanilla and salt to form a smooth paste; stir into raspberry syrup. Cook, stirring constantly, until thickened. Stir in raspberries. Refrigerate.

To serve: Top with sprinkling of slivered almonds. Makes 6 servings.

**Egg-, gluten-, milk- and wheat-free diet:** Prepare as directed.
**Low-fat, low-cholesterol diet:** 2 grams fat per serving.
**Low-purine diet:** Prepare as directed.
**Low-sodium diet:** Prepare as directed but omit salt. 1 milligram sodium per serving.

## APRICOT-AND-PUDDING PLEASER (150 calories per serving)

1 16-ounce can peeled whole
   apricots
1 4-serving package regular or
   instant vanilla-pudding mix
2 cups skimmed milk

Early in day: Remove pits and thoroughly drain apricots. Meanwhile, prepare pudding as label directs, but use skimmed milk. Immediately stir in drained apricots. Divide among 5 dessert dishes. Refrigerate until serving time. Makes 5 servings.

**Bland diet:** Prepare as directed.
**Low-fat, low-cholesterol diet:** Negligible fat per serving.
**Low-fat, bland (gall bladder) diet:** Prepare as directed.
**Low-purine diet:** Prepare as directed.
**Low-residue diet:** Prepare as directed.

## BLUEBERRY COTTAGE PUDDING (190 calories per serving)

1¾ cups sifted all-purpose
   flour
2½ teaspoons double-acting
   baking powder
salt
¼ cup butter or margarine,
   softened
granulated sugar
1 egg
⅔ cup skimmed milk or re-
   liquefied nonfat dry milk
½ teaspoon lemon extract
1½ tablespoons cornstarch
1 tablespoon lemon juice
¾ cup orange juice
1½ 10-ounce boxes frozen
   blueberries, thawed and
   drained

Early in day: Preheat oven to 375°F. Grease, then lightly flour 9-inch square cake pan. Sift together flour, baking powder and ½ teaspoon salt. In medium bowl, with electric mixer at medium speed, cream butter with ½ cup sugar until almost cream-colored. Add egg, beating until smooth. Beat in one-third of flour mixture until smooth, then one-half milk and lemon extract until just smooth. Beat in remaining milk, then remaining one-third flour mixture. Beat for 30 seconds. Turn into prepared cake pan. Bake 30 to 35 minutes, or until a cake tester, inserted in center, comes out clean. Cool on rack 15 minutes; then turn cake out of pan onto rack.

About 1 hour before serving: In medium saucepan, mix cornstarch, ⅓ cup sugar and dash of salt; slowly stir in lemon juice, orange juice and blueberries. Cook, stirring, until sauce is thickened.

To serve: Cut cake into 12 servings. Place on dessert dishes; dribble scant ¼ cup of warm sauce over each. Makes 12 servings.

**Low-purine diet:** Prepare as directed.
**Low-sodium diet:** Prepare as directed but omit salt, use unsalted butter or margarine and substitute 2½ teaspoons low-sodium baking powder for double-acting. 10 milligrams sodium per serving.

## BLUEBERRY RICE PUDDING (150 calories per serving)

1 quart skimmed milk or reliquefied nonfat dry milk
5 tablespoons uncooked rice
1/4 cup nonfat dry-milk
powder
1/4 teaspoon cinnamon
1/4 teaspoon nutmeg
1/4 teaspoon salt
1/4 cup granulated sugar
1 cup fresh blueberries (or
frozen unsweetened blue-
berries, thawed, drained)

Early in day: Preheat oven to 325°F. Lightly grease 1½-quart casserole. In casserole, mix all ingredients but blueberries. Bake, uncovered, 1½ to 2 hours, or until rice is tender. Stir in surface skin whenever it forms. Refrigerate. Immediately before serving, stir in blueberries. Makes 6 servings.

**Diabetic diet:** Prepare as directed but omit sugar. Substitute saccharin equivalent to 1/4 cup sugar. Exchanges per serving = 1 skim milk and 1 fruit.
**Egg-, gluten- and wheat-free diet:** Prepare as directed.
**Low-fat, low-cholesterol diet:** Negligible fat per serving.
**Low-purine diet:** Prepare as directed.

## LIGHT-AND-LEMON PUDDING (175 calories per serving)

granulated sugar
3 tablespoons cornstarch
1/4 cup cake flour
1/4 teaspoon salt
1 tablespoon grated lemon
peel
1/2 cup lemon juice
3 eggs, separated

At least 1 hour before serving: In medium saucepan, stir together 1 cup sugar, cornstarch, cake flour and salt, until smooth. Stirring constantly, slowly add 3 cups boiling water; mix until smooth; add grated lemon peel. Stirring regularly, boil gently over medium heat for 10 minutes.

Preheat oven to 425°F. Beat lemon juice and egg yolks until smooth; stirring constantly, add to pudding. Still stirring, cook 2 minutes longer. Divide among eight 3/4-cup custard cups; place on cookie sheet.

In medium bowl, beat egg whites until soft peaks form; still beating, slowly add 6 tablespoons sugar; beat until glossy peaks form. Drop generous dollop of this meringue onto each pudding; bake 4 to 6 minutes, or until golden-brown. Serve warm or cold. Makes 8 servings.

**Low-purine diet:** Prepare as directed.
**Low-sodium diet:** Prepare as directed but omit salt. 25 milligrams sodium per serving.

## BAKED LEMON PUDDING (140 calories per serving)

2 eggs, separated
1/4 teaspoon salt
granulated sugar
1 tablespoon grated lemon peel
1½ tablespoons lemon juice
1 tablespoon melted butter or
margarine
2 tablespoons flour
1 cup skimmed milk or re-
liquefied nonfat dry milk

At least 2 hours before serving: Preheat oven to 350°F. Grease 1-quart casserole. Beat egg whites with salt until moist peaks form. Gradually add 1/4 cup sugar, beating until stiff. With same beater, beat yolks with lemon peel, lemon juice and melted butter until blended. Stir in 2 tablespoons sugar mixed with flour, then milk. Fold into beaten egg whites.

Pour batter into greased casserole. Set in pan containing 1/2 inch hot water. Bake, uncovered, 55 to 65 minutes, or until top of pudding is firm and brown (pudding will separate into cake and sauce layers). Serve warm or chilled. Makes 5 servings.

**Bland diet:** Prepare as directed but omit lemon peel.
**Low-purine diet:** Prepare as directed.
**Low-residue diet:** Prepare as directed but omit lemon peel.

## RHUBARB PUDDING (170 calories per serving)

1½ pounds fresh rhubarb
1 cup granulated sugar
4 teaspoons cornstarch
½ teaspoon vanilla extract
½ cup whipped topping

Early in day: Clean, then cut rhubarb into ½-inch slices. Combine rhubarb with 1 cup water and 1 cup granulated sugar; simmer 5 minutes, or until tender. Blend cornstarch, ¼ cup water; stir into rhubarb; cook, stirring, until thick and clear; stir in vanilla. Pour into serving dish; refrigerate, covered.

To serve: Top pudding with whipped topping. Makes 6 servings.

**Egg-, gluten- and wheat-free diet:** Prepare as directed.
**Low-fat, low-cholesterol diet:** Prepare as directed but omit whipped topping. Negligible fat per serving.
**Low-purine diet:** Prepare as directed but omit whipped topping if fat is restricted on diet.
**Low-sodium diet:** Prepare as directed but use whipped cream instead of whipped topping. 5 milligrams sodium per serving.

## BAKED CUSTARD (120 calories per serving)

4 eggs
¼ cup granulated sugar
¼ teaspoon salt
2½ cups skimmed milk or reliquefied nonfat dry milk
1 teaspoon vanilla extract

At least 2 hours before serving: Preheat oven to 300°F. In large bowl, beat eggs, sugar and salt until lemon-colored. Beat in milk and vanilla. Pour into greased custard cups. Set cups in shallow pan; place in oven and pour hot water to within ¾ inch of top of pan. Bake 1 hour, or until set; refrigerate. Makes 6 servings.

**Bland diet:** Prepare as directed.
**Low-fat diet:** 5 grams fat per serving. Omit recipe from low-cholesterol diet.
**Low-purine diet:** Prepare as directed.
**Low-residue diet:** Prepare as directed.

## RHUBARB WHIP (130 calories per serving)

1 pound rhubarb, cut into
½-inch cubes
½ cup granulated sugar
1 cup evaporated skimmed
milk
2 drops red food color

At least 2 hours before serving: In top of double boiler, mix rhubarb and sugar; cook, stirring occasionally, over rapidly boiling water until rhubarb is just tender—about 20 minutes. Refrigerate.

About 30 minutes before serving: In medium freezer-proof bowl, stir evaporated skimmed milk and food color; freeze until ice crystals form around edge of bowl.

To serve: With electric mixer at high speed, beat chilled milk until consistency of whipped cream. Fold in rhubarb (and its syrup). Serve immediately. Makes 4 servings.

**Egg-, gluten- and wheat-free diet:** Prepare as directed.
**Low-fat, low-cholesterol diet:** Negligible fat per serving.
**Low-purine diet:** Prepare as directed.

## LIME-GRAPE FRUIT SHIMMER (100 calories per serving)

1 3-ounce package lime-flavor gelatin dessert
1 tablespoon lime juice
⅔ cup whole or halved
seedless grapes

Early in day: Prepare lime gelatin as label directs, then stir in lime juice. Layer gelatin and grapes as directed in paragraph 2 of Lemon-Orange Fruit Shimmer (see recipe opposite). Makes 4 servings.

**Diabetic diet:** Prepare as directed but substitute one 4-serving envelope dietetic-packed lemon gelatin for regular lime gelatin. Exchanges per serving = ½ fruit.
**Egg-, gluten-, milk- and wheat-free diet:** Prepare as directed.
**Low-fat, low-cholesterol diet:** Negligible fat per serving.
**Low-purine diet:** Prepare as directed.

## LEMON-ORANGE FRUIT SHIMMER (120 calories per serving)

1 11-ounce can mandarin-
orange sections
1 3-ounce package lemon-flavored gelatin dessert

Early in day: Drain juice from mandarin-orange sections; add enough boiling water to make 2 cups liquid. Stir into lemon gelatin until dissolved.

Fill 4 parfait glasses or large goblets with one-third of gelatin dessert; add one-third fruit; refrigerate parfait glasses until gelatin mixture is just set, but not quite firm. (Refrigerate remaining gelatin and fruit as well.) Add half of remaining gelatin and fruit. Chill until just set, but not firm. Add remaining gelatin, then fruit; refrigerate. Makes 4 servings.

**Bland diet:** Prepare as directed.
**Egg-, gluten-, milk- and wheat-free diet:** Prepare as directed.
**Low-fat, low-cholesterol diet:** Negligible fat per serving.
**Low-fat, bland (gall bladder) diet:** Prepare as directed.
**Low-purine diet:** Prepare as directed.
**Low-residue diet:** Prepare as directed.

## MARASCHINO-CHERRY FRUIT SHIMMER (100 calories per serving)

1 3-ounce package cherry- or
watermelon-flavored gelatin
dessert
1 teaspoon lemon juice
⅓ cup maraschino cherries

Early in day: Prepare cherry or watermelon gelatin as label directs, then stir in lemon juice. Layer gelatin and cherries as directed in paragraph 2 of Lemon-Orange Fruit Shimmer (see recipe above). Makes 4 servings.

**Bland diet:** Prepare as directed.
**Egg-, gluten-, milk- and wheat-free diet:** Prepare as directed.
**Low-fat, low-cholesterol diet:** Negligible fat per serving.
**Low-fat, bland (gall bladder) diet:** Prepare as directed.
**Low-purine diet:** Prepare as directed.
**Low-residue diet:** Prepare as directed.

## CHERRY-PINEAPPLE FRUIT SHIMMER (145 calories per serving)

1 15¼-ounce can pineapple
chunks packed in pine-
apple juice
1 3-ounce package cherry-
flavored gelatin dessert

Early in day: Drain juice from pineapple and add enough boiling water to make 2 cups liquid. Stir into gelatin until dissolved. Layer gelatin and pineapple as directed in paragraph 2 of Lemon-Orange Fruit Shimmer (see recipe above). Makes 4 servings.

**Diabetic diet:** Prepare as directed but substitute one 4-serving envelope dietetic-packed cherry gelatin for regular. Exchanges per serving = 1 fruit.
**Egg-, gluten-, milk- and wheat-free diet:** Prepare as directed.
**Low-fat, low-cholesterol diet:** Negligible fat per serving.
**Low-purine diet:** Prepare as directed.

## CRANBERRY FROTH (85 calories per serving)

1 3-ounce package lemon-
flavored gelatin
1 cup cranberry-juice cocktail
2 egg whites

Several hours before serving: Dissolve gelatin in 1 cup boiling water; stir in cranberry juice. Refrigerate until slightly thickened, stirring occasionally. Beat egg whites stiff, but not dry; gradually pour in thickened gelatin mixture, beating until frothy. Spoon into 8 parfait glasses (mixture will separate into 2 layers). Refrigerate several hours before serving. Makes 8 servings.

**Bland diet:** Prepare as directed.
**Gluten-, milk- and wheat-free diet:** Prepare as directed.
**Low-fat, low-cholesterol diet:** Negligible fat per serving.
**Low-fat, bland (gall bladder) diet:** Prepare as directed.
**Low-purine diet:** Prepare as directed.
**Low-residue diet:** Prepare as directed.

## CHERRY-BANANA FESTIVE PARFAIT (110 calories per serving)

1 3-ounce package cherry-
flavor gelatin dessert
1 8-ounce can Bing cherries,
drained
4 medium bananas, halved,
then quartered
lemon juice
½ cup vanilla ice milk

At least 4 hours before serving: Prepare cherry gelatin as label directs, but stir in drained cherries; refrigerate until firm.

To serve: Dip banana quarters into lemon juice to prevent discoloration. Place 2 banana quarters along sides of each of 8 parfait glasses, then spoon in gelatin to top of glass. Top with small dollop of ice milk. Makes 8 servings.

**Bland diet:** Prepare as directed.
**Diabetic diet:** Prepare as directed, but substitute one 4-serving envelope strawberry-flavored dietetic-packed gelatin dessert for regular; omit cherries and ice milk. Exchanges per serving = 1 fruit.
**Egg-, gluten- and wheat-free diet:** Prepare as directed but use gluten-free ice milk on gluten-free diet.
**Low-fat, low-cholesterol diet:** Negligible fat per serving.
**Low-fat, bland (gall bladder) diet:** Prepare as directed.
**Low-purine diet:** Prepare as directed.
**Low-residue diet:** Prepare as directed.

## GOLDEN-GLOW PARFAIT (150 calories per serving)

2 3-ounce packages lemon-
flavored gelatin dessert
2 10-ounce containers frozen
raspberries, thawed
⅓ cup heavy cream, whipped
and sweetened to taste

Early in day: Prepare both packages gelatin, as label directs, but use only 1½ cups boiling water and 2½ cups cold water.

Drain 1 cup syrup from thawed raspberries. (Use this syrup later as a sauce for puddings or fruit.) Evenly divide one-half of raspberries and remaining syrup among 8 parfait glasses. Spoon 3 tablespoons gelatin into each glass; refrigerate until firm (tilt glass by catching base between bars of rack and leaning side against refrigerator wall, to make gelatin set at slant). Cover remaining gelatin and raspberries, and reserve at room temperature.

Add ¼ cup gelatin to firm gelatin in each parfait glass. Again refrigerate, with glass tipped at angle, until firm. Divide remaining gelatin, raspberries and syrup among glasses; refrigerate, not tipped this time, until firm.

To serve: Top each serving with a dab of whipped cream. Makes 8 servings.

**Egg-, gluten-, milk- and wheat-free diet:** Prepare as directed but omit whipped cream for milk-free diet.
**Low-fat, low-cholesterol diet:** Prepare as directed but omit whipped cream. Negligible fat per serving.
**Low-purine diet:** Prepare as directed.

## PARFAIT ROYALE (125 calories per serving)

1 16-ounce can raspberry
applesauce
1 package vanilla-rennet-
custard-dessert mix
2 cups skimmed milk

At least 4 hours before serving: Divide half of applesauce among six ¾-cup parfait glasses or custard cups. Prepare rennet mix as label directs but use skimmed milk. Immediately divide among parfaits; let stand in warm spot until firm—about 10 minutes. Spoon remaining applesauce on top of each serving; refrigerate. Makes 6 servings.

**Bland diet:** Prepare as directed.
**Egg-, gluten- and wheat-free diet:** Prepare as directed.
**Low-fat, low-cholesterol diet:** Negligible fat per serving.
**Low-fat, bland (gall bladder) diet:** Prepare as directed.
**Low-purine diet:** Prepare as directed.
**Low-residue diet:** Prepare as directed.
**Low-sodium diet:** 45 milligrams sodium per serving.

## RASPBERRY PARFAIT (150 calories per serving)

2 10-ounce packages frozen raspberries, thawed
1 package vanilla-rennet-custard-dessert mix
2 cups skimmed milk

At least 4 hours before serving: Prepare as directed for Parfait Royale (see recipe opposite), sustituting thawed raspberries for raspberry applesauce.

**Egg-, gluten- and wheat-free diet:** Prepare as directed.
**Low-fat, low-cholesterol diet:** Negligible fat per serving.
**Low-purine diet:** Prepare as directed.
**Low-sodium diet:** 45 milligrams sodium per serving.

## FESTIVE PINEAPPLE SNOW PARFAIT (75 calories per serving)

1 3-ounce package lime-flavor gelatin dessert
green food color (optional)
2 egg whites
1 15¼-ounce can pineapple slices packed in pineapple juice

At least 4 hours before serving: Prepare lime gelatin as label directs; stir in a few drops green food color, if desired. Refrigerate until consistency of thin pudding. Beat egg whites until stiff peaks form. Still beating, slowly add gelatin and continue to beat until light and frothy. Refrigerate until firm.

Drain pineapple; cut 4 slices in half and the rest into tidbits. Divide half of tidbits among 8 parfait glasses; top with layer of gelatin mixture. Repeat layers with remaining tidbits and gelatin to top of glass. Decorate with half-pineapple slice. Makes 8 servings.

**Bland diet:** Prepare as directed but substitute canned peaches for pineapple.
**Diabetic diet:** Prepare as directed but substitute one 4-serving envelope artificially sweetened lemon gelatin-dessert for regular. Exchanges per serving = ½ fruit.
**Low-fat, low-cholesterol diet:** Negligible fat per serving.
**Low-fat, bland (gall bladder) diet:** Prepare as directed but substitute peaches for pineapple.
**Gluten-, milk- and wheat-free diet:** Prepare as directed.
**Low-purine diet:** Prepare as directed.
**Low-residue diet:** Prepare as directed for bland diet.

## HEART OF CREAM (Coeur à la Crème) (160 calories per serving)

2 8-ounce containers creamed cottage cheese
2 3-ounce packages Neufchâtel cheese, softened slightly
½ teaspoon salt
¼ cup granulated sugar
3 cups fresh strawberries or Bing cherries, halved and pitted

Day before serving: In small bowl, thoroughly blend cottage cheese, Neufchâtel cheese, salt and sugar; refrigerate.

About 15 minutes before serving: On serving platter, form cheese mixture into heart shape; surround with berries. Makes 8 servings.

**Bland diet:** Prepare as directed but substitute two 16-ounce cans peeled apricots, peaches or pears for strawberries.
**Low-purine diet:** Prepare as directed.
**Low-residue diet:** Prepare as directed for bland diet.

## COTTAGE-CHEESE DESSERT-SALAD (about 100 calories per serving)

1 30-ounce can freestone peach halves
⅛ teaspoon cinnamon
1 8-ounce container creamed cottage cheese

About 10 minutes before serving: Drain peaches, reserving syrup. Mix ¼ cup reserved syrup with cinnamon and cottage cheese. Use as topping for peaches. Makes 6 servings.

**Bland diet:** Prepare as directed.
**Diabetic diet:** Prepare as directed but substitute water-packed peach halves for regular. Exchanges per serving (2 peach halves and ¼ cup cottage-cheese sauce) = 1 fruit and 1 meat.
**Egg-, gluten- and wheat-free diet:** Prepare as directed.
**Low-fat, low-cholesterol diet:** 2 grams fat per serving.
**Low-fat, bland (gall bladder) diet:** Prepare as directed.
**Low-purine diet:** Prepare as directed.
**Low-residue diet:** Prepare as directed.

## APRICOT CLOUD (140 calories per serving)

**24 dried apricot halves**
**¾ cup granulated sugar**
**2 envelopes unflavored gelatin**
**2 tablespoons lemon juice**
**6 egg whites**

At least 4 hours before serving: In medium saucepan, mix apricot halves, 1½ cups water and sugar; cover; simmer 45 minutes, or until apricots are tender; cool; refrigerate.

Reserve 8 apricot halves and ¼ cup syrup for garnish. In electric-blender container, at low speed, blend remaining apricots and syrup smooth. (Or press through food mill.)

In medium saucepan, mix gelatin into 1 cup water and let stand 5 minutes; heat just to boiling to dissolve; stir in lemon juice and apricot puree. Refrigerate, stirring occasionally, until mixture mounds when dropped from spoon.

In large bowl, beat egg whites until stiff peaks form. Add apricot puree, then continue beating until completely mixed. Divide among 8 dessert dishes; top each with reserved apricot half and bit of syrup. Refrigerate 3 hours, or until serving time. Makes 8 servings.

**Bland diet:** Prepare as directed.
**Diabetic diet:** Prepare as directed but omit sugar. Stir saccharin equivalent to ½ cup sugar into apricot puree before it is refrigerated. Exchanges per serving = 1 fruit.
**Low-fat, low-cholesterol diet:** Negligible fat per serving.
**Low-fat, bland (gall bladder) diet:** Prepare as directed.
**Gluten-, milk- and wheat-free diet:** Prepare as directed.
**High-iron diet:** 1 milligram iron per serving.
**Low-purine diet:** Prepare as directed.
**Low-residue diet:** Prepare as directed.
**Low-sodium diet:** 40 milligrams sodium per serving.

## FLUFFY GELATIN TREAT (55 calories per serving)

**1 3-ounce package cherry-**
**flavor gelatin dessert**
**2 egg whites**

About 3 to 4 hours before serving: In medium bowl, dissolve gelatin in 1 cup boiling water; stir in 1 cup cold water; refrigerate. When gelatin is consistency of unbeaten egg white, beat with egg beater or electric mixer until light and frothy. Then, in medium bowl, beat egg whites until soft peaks form. Fold beaten gelatin mixture into whites until smooth. Divide among 6 sherbet glasses; refrigerate until firm—2 to 3 hours. Makes 6 servings.

**Bland diet:** Prepare as directed.
**Diabetic diet:** Prepare as directed but use one 4-serving envelope artificially-sweetened strawberry gelatin for regular. Exchanges per serving = 1 "free."
**Low-fat, low-cholesterol diet:** Negligible fat per serving.
**Low-fat, bland (gall bladder) diet:** Prepare as directed.
**Gluten-, milk- and wheat-free diet:** Prepare as directed.
**Low-purine diet:** Prepare as directed.

## STRAWBERRY SPLIT (110 calories per serving)

**5 ladyfingers, split**
**1 package strawberry-rennet-**
**custard-dessert mix**
**2 cups skimmed milk**

About 2 hours before serving: Use ladyfingers to line sides of 5 parfait glasses. Prepare rennet pudding as label directs but use skimmed milk. Pour into prepared glasses; let stand 10 minutes; refrigerate. Makes 5 servings.

**Bland diet:** Prepare as directed.
**Low-fat, low-cholesterol diet:** 1 gram fat per serving.
**Low-fat, bland (gall bladder) diet:** Prepare as directed.
**Low-purine diet:** Prepare as directed.
**Low-residue diet:** Prepare as directed.

## MELON RINGS WITH STRAWBERRIES (35 calories per serving)

1 medium Spanish or honeydew
  melon
1 pint strawberries

About 30 minutes before serving: Cut melon crosswise into rings 1 inch thick; remove seeds.

Place slices on individual plates; with knife, carefully loosen meat by cutting around slice ¼ inch from rind; do not remove rind. Slice meat to make bite-size pieces, leaving rind intact.

Rinse strawberries under cold running water; do not hull. Arrange 5 or 6 berries in center of each melon slice. Makes 5 servings.

**Diabetic diet:** Exchanges per serving = 1 fruit.
**Egg-, gluten-, milk- and wheat-free diet:** Prepare as directed.
**Low-fat, low-cholesterol diet:** Negligible fat per serving.
**Low-purine diet:** Prepare as directed.
**Low-sodium diet:** 5 milligrams sodium per serving.

## BUTTERSCOTCH TREAT (140 calories per serving)

¾ cup graham-cracker crumbs
1 tablespoon butter or margarine, softened
1 4-serving package regular
  butterscotch pudding mix
2 cups skimmed milk or reliquefied nonfat dry milk
¾ cup frozen whipped topping,
  thawed

Early in day: Preheat oven to 350°F. In medium bowl, combine crumbs, 1 tablespoon water and butter or margarine. Line 9" by 5" by 3" loaf pan with foil; press crumb mixture in thin layer in bottom of pan. Bake 7 minutes; chill. Meanwhile, prepare pudding as label directs but use skimmed milk. Pour into crust; refrigerate.

To serve: Slice and place on chilled plates. Top each with dab of whipped topping. Makes 8 servings.

**Bland diet:** Prepare as directed.
**Low-fat, low-cholesterol diet:** Prepare as directed but use margarine instead of butter; substitute marshmallow cream for whipped topping. 1 gram fat per serving.
**Low-fat, bland (gall bladder) diet:** Prepare as directed for low-fat, low-cholesterol diet.
**Low-purine diet:** Prepare as directed but omit whipped topping.
**Low-residue diet:** Prepare as directed.

## PERSIAN RICE DESSERT (145 calories per serving)

2¼ cups skimmed milk or reliquefied nonfat dry milk
¼ cup uncooked long-
  grain rice
¼ teaspoon salt
¼ cup granulated sugar
2 tablespoons raisins
¼ teaspoon cinnamon
generous dash nutmeg
1½ teaspoons vanilla extract
½ cup creamed cottage
  cheese, sieved until smooth
½ teaspoon finely grated
  lemon peel

Early in day: In top of double boiler, mix milk, rice, salt and sugar; cover; cook over boiling water, stirring occasionally, 30 minutes.

Add raisins, cinnamon and nutmeg; cook, uncovered, 45 minutes longer, stirring every 10 minutes. Stir in vanilla. Refrigerate.

To serve: Mix sieved cottage cheese with lemon peel; fold into rice mixture until almost smooth. Makes five ½-cup servings.

**Bland diet:** Prepare as directed but omit raisins, nutmeg and lemon peel.
**Diabetic diet:** Prepare as directed but omit sugar; use saccharin equivalent to ¼ cup sugar. Exchanges per serving = ½ bread and ½ skim milk.
**Egg-, gluten- and wheat-free diet:** Prepare as directed.
**Low-fat, low-cholesterol diet:** Negligible fat per serving.
**Low-fat, bland (gall bladder) diet:** Prepare as directed for bland diet.
**Low-purine diet:** Prepare as directed.
**Low-residue diet:** Prepare as directed for bland diet.

## COCONUT-CREAM BANANA DESSERT (110 calories per serving)

3 under-ripe bananas
lemon juice
1 2-ounce envelope whipped-
    topping mix
1 tablespoon flaked coconut

About 25 minutes before serving: Preheat oven to 325°F. Slice bananas diagonally into 1-inch pieces; sprinkle with lemon juice. Arrange in lightly greased, shallow baking dish; bake 12 minutes to heat through.

Prepare whipped topping as label directs but use skimmed milk. (Refrigerate 1 cup topping in airtight container for later use with fruit or gelatin.) Fold coconut into remaining 1 cup topping; serve over bananas. Makes 6 servings.

**Bland diet:** Prepare as directed but omit coconut.
**Low-residue diet:** Prepare as directed but omit coconut.

## FROZEN DESSERTS CHURNED IN AN ICE-CREAM MAKER

General Instructions: The two recipes that follow were developed for the traditional crank-type ice-cream maker. Both hand-turned and electric makers come in 4- and 6-quart capacities. They are available in most large department stores and through mail-order houses. After freezing ice cream, place in freezer section in chilled bowl for a few hours, to allow ice cream to ripen. These recipes produce 1½ to 2 quarts of ice cream—fine for a 4-quart maker.

## APRICOT ICE (120 calories per serving)

2 30-ounce cans peeled whole
    apricots
2¼ cups orange juice
⅓ cup lemon juice
1 cup granulated sugar

About 2 to 3 hours before churning ice cream: Drain apricots; remove seeds. In electric-blender container, at low speed, puree apricots. Stir together with remaining ingredients. Refrigerate at least 1 hour.

Churn and freeze in ice-cream maker as manufacturer directs. Makes 1½ quarts or twelve ½-cup servings.

**Bland diet:** Prepare as directed.
**Egg-, gluten-, milk- and wheat-free diet:** Prepare as directed.
**Low-fat, low-cholesterol diet:** Negligible fat per serving.
**Low-fat, bland (gall bladder) diet:** Prepare as directed.
**Low-purine diet:** Prepare as directed.
**Low-residue diet:** Prepare as directed.
**Low-sodium diet:** 1 milligram sodium per serving.

## PINK MINT ICE CREAM* (90 calories per serving)

6 ounces peppermint-stick
    candy
2 cups skimmed milk or re-
    liquefied nonfat dry milk
2 cups evaporated skimmed
    milk

About 3 hours before churning ice cream: Crush candy to a fine powder by placing between sheets of waxed paper or in plastic bag and pounding with rolling pin. In medium bowl, mix candy with milk; refrigerate and let soak 2 hours, stirring occasionally. Stir together candy mixture and evaporated skimmed milk. Chill thoroughly—about 1 hour.

Churn and freeze in ice-cream maker as manufacturer directs. Makes 1½ quarts or twelve ½-cup servings.

**Egg-, gluten- and wheat-free diet:** Prepare as directed.
**Low-fat, low-cholesterol diet:** Negligible fat per serving.
**Low-purine diet:** Prepare as directed.
* This ice cream has a refreshing but sharp mint flavor. For a milder flavor, reduce candy to 4 ounces and add 1/3 cup granulated sugar; prepare as directed.

## SHERBET BLUEBERRY FESTIVE PARFAIT (150 calories per serving)

1 10-ounce package unsweetened frozen blueberries,
thawed
1 pint raspberry sherbet

To serve: In 4 parfait glasses, alternate layers of blueberries and sherbet. Makes 4 servings.

**Egg-, gluten- and wheat-free diet:** Prepare as directed but use gluten-free sherbet on gluten-free diet.
**Low-fat, low-cholesterol diet:** Negligible fat per serving.
**Low-purine diet:** Prepare as directed.
**Low-sodium diet:** 5 milligrams sodium per serving.

## RUBY ICE (130 calories per serving)

2 10-ounce packages frozen
raspberries, thawed
2 egg whites
¼ cup granulated sugar

At least 5 hours before serving: Press raspberries through sieve and discard seeds. In bowl to be used for freezing, beat egg whites until soft peaks form. Beating constantly, slowly beat in sugar until stiff peaks form. Fold in raspberry puree. Freeze, stirring occasionally, until consistency of soft sherbet. Makes 6 servings.

**Low-fat, low-cholesterol diet:** Negligible fat per serving.
**Gluten-, milk- and wheat-free diet:** Prepare as directed.
**Low-purine diet:** Prepare as directed.
**Low-sodium diet:** 15 milligrams sodium per serving.

## ORANGE FLOATS (85 calories per serving)

6 very large eating oranges
1½ cups orange sherbet
2 cups (from 2 12-ounce
bottles) orange carbonated
beverage

About 40 minutes before serving: Slice tops from oranges about one-fifth of the way down. Hollow out orange sections (use fruit for salads later), leaving shells intact. Cut very thin slice from bottom of each orange so it stands upright. Place 1 small scoop sherbet in each orange shell; fill with orange soda. Serve with straws. Makes 6 servings.

**Egg-, gluten- and wheat-free diet:** Prepare as directed but use gluten-free sherbet on gluten-free diet.
**Low-fat, low-cholesterol diet:** Negligible fat per serving.
**Low-sodium diet:** 5 milligrams sodium per serving.

## SHERBET LEMON CUPS (80 calories per serving)

6 large lemons
1 pint lemon sherbet, slightly
softened

About 45 minutes before serving: With sharp knife, slice tops from lemons, one-third of the way down. Slice a bit of peel from bottom of each so it stands upright. Then cut out all inside sections. Fill each shell with sherbet and mound up over rim. Freeze. Makes 6 servings.

**Bland diet:** Prepare as directed.
**Egg-, gluten- and wheat-free diet:** Prepare as directed but use gluten-free sherbet on gluten-free diet.
**Low-fat, low-cholesterol diet:** Negligible fat per serving.
**Low-fat, bland (gall bladder) diet:** Prepare as directed.
**Low-residue diet:** Prepare as directed.
**Low-sodium diet:** 5 milligrams sodium per serving.

## MIX-AND-FREEZE FROZEN DESSERTS

General Instructions: The 5 recipes that follow are for ice creams frozen in bowls. For the best results, have freezer as cold as possible and freeze mixture quickly. Freeze, uncovered, but cover before storing to prevent drying out. If you prefer to freeze this type of ice cream in ice-cube trays, keep special trays for this purpose. (Cubes will stick in trays which have been used previously for ice cream.)

## MILLICENT'S LEMON CRÈME (90 calories per serving)

1 lemon
1 cup granulated sugar
1 envelope unflavored gelatin
1½ cups skimmed milk or reliquefied nonfat dry milk
2 teaspoons vanilla extract
dash salt
1 cup evaporated skimmed
  milk

About 4 to 6 hours before serving: Finely grate all peel from lemon. Slice lemon, remove seeds, then finely snip lemon slices with scissors, reserving all juice. In small saucepan, mix grated lemon peel and juice of lemon with ½ cup sugar; heat gently until sugar is dissolved.

In large bowl, soften gelatin in ¾ cup skimmed milk for 5 minutes. Meanwhile, scald ¾ cup skimmed milk with ½ cup sugar. Stir hot milk into gelatin mixture until gelatin is dissolved. Slowly stir in sugar-lemon mixture, then vanilla and salt.

Freeze, in same bowl, until firm about 2 inches in around edge. Meanwhile, in medium bowl, freeze evaporated skimmed milk until ice crystals form 1 inch in from edge of bowl. Whip until consistency of whipped cream. Then beat lemon mixture until smooth. Carefully fold whipped evaporated milk into lemon mixture. Freeze until firm. Makes 1 quart or eight ½-cup servings.

**Egg-, gluten- and wheat-free diet:** Prepare as directed.
**Low-fat, low-cholesterol diet:** Negligible fat per serving.
**Low-purine diet:** Prepare as directed.

## GRAPE ICE CREAM (120 calories per serving)

¼ cup cornstarch
1 cup granulated sugar
dash cinnamon
dash nutmeg
1½ cups bottled grape juice
1 teaspoon vanilla extract
2 or 3 tablespoons lemon juice
1 14½-ounce can evaporated
  skimmed milk

Day before or early in day: In medium saucepan, mix cornstarch, sugar, cinnamon and nutmeg. Stir in a little grape juice to form a smooth paste; then add remaining grape juice, vanilla, ½ cup water and lemon juice. Cook, stirring constantly, until mixture boils and thickens. Refrigerate, stirring occasionally.

While grape mixture is chilling, freeze evaporated skimmed milk in large mixing bowl until ice crystals form ½-inch to 1-inch from edge of bowl.

When grape and milk mixtures are ready, beat milk with electric mixer at highest speed, until consistency of whipped cream. Beating continuously, slowly add grape-juice mixture. Mix completely. Freeze until firm—at least 4 hours. Makes 2 quarts or twelve ¾-cup servings.

For 6 servings: Use ¾ cup of skimmed evaporated milk; halve all other ingredients.

**Diabetic diet:** Prepare as directed but omit sugar. Substitute saccharin equivalent to ¾ cup sugar. Exchanges per serving = 1 fruit.
**Egg-, gluten- and wheat-free diet:** Prepare as directed.
**Low-fat, low-cholesterol diet:** Negligible fat per serving.
**Low-purine diet:** Prepare as directed.
**Low-sodium diet:** 40 milligrams sodium per serving.

## WINTER SHERBET (120 calories per serving)

2 8½-ounce cans crushed
  pineapple
1 16-ounce can peaches
2 tablespoons lemon juice
¼ teaspoon vanilla extract
dash salt

About 6 hours before serving: In electric-blender container, at low speed, blend crushed pineapple (and syrup) until smooth; pour into medium mixing bowl. Blend peaches (and syrup) until smooth; add to pineapple. Stir in remaining ingredients. Freeze, stirring occasionally, until mushy—about 2 hours. Again blend mixture, one-third at a time, until smooth. Freeze until consistency of sherbet. If softer texture is preferred, thaw at room temperature a few minutes before serving. Makes six ½-cup servings.

**Egg-, gluten-, milk- and wheat-free diet:** Prepare as directed.
**Low-fat, low-cholesterol diet:** Negligible fat per serving.
**Low-purine diet:** Prepare as directed.
**Low-sodium diet:** Prepare as directed but omit salt. 2 milligrams sodium per serving.

## STRAWBERRY ICE (90 calories per serving)

1 pint strawberries
½ cup granulated sugar
2 tablespoons orange juice
2 egg whites
¼ teaspoon salt

Early in day: With food mill or fork, puree strawberries. In medium pan, combine strawberries and sugar. Cover and simmer, over low heat, 5 minutes. Add ½ cup water and orange juice; cool slightly. Pour into freezer-proof medium bowl, and freeze until a thick mush throughout.

At least 3 hours before serving: In medium bowl, with electric mixer at high speed, beat egg whites and salt until stiff peaks form. Then beat strawberry mixture until light and frothy. Fold in egg whites; return to freezer until firm. Makes 6 servings.

**Low-fat, low-cholesterol diet:** Negligible fat per serving.
**Gluten-, milk- and wheat-free diet:** Prepare as directed.
**Low-purine diet:** Prepare as directed.
**Low-sodium diet:** Prepare as directed but omit salt. 15 milligrams sodium per serving.

## HOMEMADE PINEAPPLE SHERBET (105 calories per serving)

1 envelope unflavored gelatin
1 cup syrup drained from 20-
  ounce can crushed pineapple
¼ cup granulated sugar
1 teaspoon grated lemon peel
½ teaspoon vanilla extract
2 tablespoons lemon juice
dash salt
2 cups cold skimmed milk or
  reliquefied nonfat dry milk
drained pineapple from can of
  crushed pineapple

About 5 to 6 hours before serving: In small saucepan, sprinkle gelatin on pineapple syrup; let stand 5 minutes. Heat, stirring constantly, until gelatin is dissolved—do not boil. Stir in sugar, lemon peel, vanilla extract, lemon juice and salt. Place milk in medium bowl; slowly stir in gelatin mixture. (Mixture may appear curdled.) Freeze, stirring occasionally, until ice crystals form throughout most of mixture. Beat until smooth; fold in drained pineapple. Freeze until firm enough to spoon out. (If sherbet freezes too hard, let stand at room temperature to soften slightly.) Makes eight ½-cup servings.

**Egg-, gluten- and wheat-free diet:** Prepare as directed.
**Low-fat, low-cholesterol diet:** Negligible fat per serving.
**Low-purine diet:** Prepare as directed.
**Low-sodium diet:** Prepare as directed but omit salt. 35 milligrams sodium per serving.

## SHERBET ARRAY (120 calories per serving)

favorite sherbets
crushed ice
liquid food color
sprig of mint for garnish

Day before serving: Using ice-cream scoop, make large balls of orange, lime and raspberry sherbet. Place in freezer.

About 20 minutes before serving: Prepare about ½ cup crushed ice for each serving. Tint with liquid food color that matches sherbet, then place in bottom of seafood (or dessert) server. Now place ball of sherbet in cup of each seafood server; add sprig of mint and set cups in servers. Serve at once.

**Bland diet:** Prepare as directed.
**Egg-, gluten- and wheat-free diet:** Prepare as directed but use a gluten-free sherbet on gluten-free diet.
**Low-fat, low-cholesterol diet:** Negligible fat per serving.
**Low-fat, bland (gall bladder) diet:** Prepare as directed.
**Low-purine diet:** Prepare as directed.
**Low-residue diet:** Prepare as directed.
**Low-sodium diet:** 10 milligrams sodium per serving.

## SPECIAL STRAWBERRY FROST (65 calories per serving)

½ cup nonfat dry-milk powder
2 tablespoons lemon juice
¼ cup granulated sugar
1 pint fresh strawberries, stemmed

About 4 to 6 hours before serving: In large bowl, stir together milk powder, ½ cup cold water, lemon juice and sugar. Beat, with electric mixer at high speed (about 15 to 20 minutes), until consistency of whipped cream. Meanwhile, in electric-blender container, at low speed, blend strawberries; fold into milk mixture. (Or puree strawberries through food mill.)

Freeze, in same bowl, until mixture is solid about 3 inches in from sides of bowl. Then beat with electric mixer until smooth. Refreeze until firm. Makes 1 quart or eight ½-cup servings.

**Diabetic diet:** Prepare as directed but omit sugar; use saccharin equivalent to ¼ cup sugar. Exchanges per serving = 1 fruit.
**Egg-, gluten- and wheat-free diet:** Prepare as directed.
**Low-fat, low-cholesterol diet:** Negligible fat per serving.
**Low-purine diet:** Prepare as directed.
**Low-sodium diet:** Prepare as directed. 40 milligrams sodium per serving. If prepared with low-sodium nonfat dry-milk powder, 3 milligrams sodium per serving.

## BLUEBERRY SHERBET (120 calories per serving)

2 teaspoons unflavored gelatin
¼ cup granulated sugar
1 10-ounce package frozen unsweetened whole blueberries, thawed
3 tablespoons light corn syrup
3 tablespoon lemon juice

At least 6 hours before serving: Sprinkle gelatin on ⅓ cup water to soften. In saucepan, add sugar to ⅓ cup water; boil 5 minutes; add softened gelatin. In electric-blender container at low speed, blend sugar-gelatin mixture and blueberries until smooth. Strain to remove pulp; stir in corn syrup and lemon juice. Pour into ice-cube tray and fit with divider; freeze 5 to 6 hours.

To serve: Place sherbet cubes and ⅓ cup water in blender; blend until smooth. Serve immediately in sherbet glasses. Makes 4 servings.

**Egg-, gluten-, milk- and wheat-free diet:** Prepare as directed.
**Low-fat, low-cholesterol diet:** Negligible fat per serving.
**High-iron diet:** 1 milligram iron per serving.
**Low-purine diet:** Prepare as directed.
**Low-sodium diet:** 10 milligrams sodium per serving.

## FROZEN FRUIT MOUSSE (130 calories per serving)

⅓ cup cinnamon drops
1 envelope unflavored gelatin
2 16-ounce cans applesauce
1 teaspoon cinnamon
⅛ teaspoon mace
1 tablespoon lemon juice
1 2-ounce envelope whipped-
   topping mix

Up to 4 hours before serving: In small saucepan, simmer and stir cinnamon drops with ¼ cup water until drops dissolve completely. In measuring cup, stir gelatin into ¼ cup cold water; set cup in boiling water, and stir until gelatin is dissolved.

In large bowl, combine applesauce, cinnamon, mace, lemon juice, cinnamon-drop mixture and gelatin. Make up whipped-topping mix as label directs but use skimmed milk; fold into applesauce mixture. Turn into ice-cube trays; freeze until solid 1 inch in from edge. Turn into chilled bowl and beat with hand beater, or electric mixer at low speed, until smooth but not melted. Return mixture to trays; freeze until just firm enough to spoon out. Makes 12 servings.

**Low-purine diet:** Prepare as directed.
**Low-sodium diet:** Prepare as directed but use 2 cups whipped cream instead of whipped topping. 10 milligrams sodium per serving.

## RAINBOW WHIP (145 calories per serving)

1 3-ounce package lemon-
   flavor gelatin dessert
1 3-ounce package lime-
   flavor gelatin dessert
1 3-ounce package strawberry-
   punch-flavor gelatin dessert
1 cup whipped topping

Early in day: In 3 separate bowls, make up each of the gelatin flavors as label directs. Refrigerate until each mounds when dropped from spoon.

Then, with electric mixer at high speed, beat lemon-flavored gelatin until fluffy; spoon into 8 sherbet glasses. Refrigerate until gelatin sets a little. Top each with layer of lime gelatin; again refrigerate until gelatin sets a little. Use strawberry-punch gelatin for top layer; refrigerate until firm. Top each serving with dab of whipped topping. Makes 8 servings.

**Bland diet:** Prepare as directed.
**Egg-, gluten- and wheat-free diet:** Prepare as directed.
**Low-fat, low-cholesterol diet:** Prepare as directed but omit whipped topping. Negligible fat per serving.
**Low-fat, bland (gall bladder) diet:** Prepare as directed but omit whipped topping.
**Low-purine diet:** Prepare as directed but omit whipped topping if fat is restricted on diet.
**Low-residue diet:** Prepare as directed.

## BANANA POPS (90 calories per pop)

2 cups crushed bananas (approximately 3 bananas)
1 cup orange juice
2 tablespoons granulated sugar
1 teaspoon lemon juice

About 4 to 6 hours before serving: In medium bowl, combine ¼ cup water, bananas and remaining ingredients, mixing well. Divide among six 4-ounce paper cups. Freeze until firm. (If desired, add popsicle sticks or wooden spoons when semi-firm.)

To serve: Let stand at room temperature for 5 minutes; to eat, peel paper cup down from pop. Makes 6 servings.

**Bland diet:** Prepare as directed.
**Egg-, gluten-, milk- and wheat-free diet:** Prepare as directed.
**Low-fat, low-cholesterol diet:** Negligible fat per serving.
**Low-fat, bland (gall bladder) diet:** Prepare as directed.
**Low-sodium diet:** 1 milligram sodium per serving.

## LADYFINGERS PROFITEROLE (60 calories each)

1 3¾-ounce package chocolate
    whipped-dessert mix
skimmed milk or reliquefied
    nonfat dry milk
2 tablespoons instant-coffee
    powder
3 3-ounce packages ladyfingers
1 cup granulated sugar
¼ teaspoon cream of tartar

Day before serving or early in day: Prepare dessert mix as label directs, but use skimmed milk for regular milk and add coffee powder with water; refrigerate. Meanwhile, separate ladyfingers. Spread whipped dessert on bottom halves of ladyfingers; cover with tops.

In small skillet, mix sugar, ¾ cup water and cream of tartar; bring to boiling; lower heat to medium, then simmer until very light amber, stirring occasionally. Drizzle a bit of this caramel syrup over each ladyfinger; refrigerate.

To serve: Arrange ladyfingers on cake stand in pyramid. Makes 36.

**Bland diet:** Prepare as directed. (Substitute vanilla whipped-dessert mix for chocolate if chocolate is forbidden on diet.)
**Low-purine diet:** Prepare as directed but substitute vanilla whipped-dessert mix for chocolate if chocolate is forbidden on diet.
**Low-residue diet:** Prepare as directed. (See note for bland diet.)

## CHOCOLATE-VANILLA-PEACH GEM (155 calories per serving)

1 29-ounce can cling peaches,
    chilled
2 3¾-ounce packages vanilla
    whipped-dessert mix
1 cup skimmed milk or relique-
    fied nonfat dry milk
2 teaspoons almond extract
1 9-inch round chocolate-cake
    layer

Early in day: Drain peaches, reserving syrup. Dry peaches on paper towels; cube; set aside. Prepare 1 package whipped dessert mix as label directs, but use ½ cup peach syrup and ½ cup skimmed milk as liquid; stir in 1 teaspoon almond extract. Refrigerate 10 minutes, then fold in half of cubed peaches.

Cut chocolate-cake layer into 6 even wedges. Arrange 3 of these, spoke-fashion, on cake plate. Fold 30-inch piece of foil in half lengthwise; grease lightly, then coil around outside of cake wedges, forming collar; tape in place. Now spoon whipped dessert evenly into empty spaces; refrigerate.

Meanwhile, prepare other package of whipped-dessert mix, using ½ cup peach syrup, ½ cup skimmed milk and 1 teaspoon almond extract, as above. Now make second layer on top of first one by laying remaining 3 cake wedges on top of whipped-dessert wedges in first layer; spoon newly prepared whipped dessert into empty spaces. Refrigerate 2 hours. Just before serving, peel foil collar off cake. Cut into 16 wedges.

## MAX'S LOW-CALORIE CHEESECAKE (185 calories per serving)

Graham-Cracker Crust (see
    recipe page 239)
12 ounces creamed cottage
    cheese (1½ 8-ounce con-
    tainers)
2 eggs
½ cup granulated sugar
½ teaspoon vanilla extract

Early in day: Prepare Graham-Cracker Crust as directed but make 8-inch pie shell, and do not bake. In electric-blender container, at low speed, blend cottage cheese, eggs, sugar and vanilla. (Or sieve cottage cheese, then mix with other ingredients.) Pour into prepared pie shell. Bake 35 minutes in preheated 350°F. oven, or until filling puffs slightly and seems dry on top. Refrigerate at least 2 hours to chill thoroughly. Makes 8 servings.

**Bland diet:** Prepare as directed.
**Low-purine diet:** Prepare as directed.
**Low-residue diet:** Prepare as directed.

## LEAN MAN'S CAKE (130 calories per serving)

2 cups sifted cake flour
2½ teaspoons double-acting
  baking powder
¾ teaspoon salt
⅓ cup shortening
¾ cup granulated sugar
1 egg, unbeaten
1 cup less 2 tablespoons
  skimmed milk or reliquefied
  nonfat dry milk
1 teaspoon vanilla extract (or
  1 tablespoon grated orange
  or lemon peel)

At least 3 hours before serving: Preheat oven to 350°F. Grease bottom of 8-inch square cake pan, then line with waxed paper. Sift flour with baking powder and salt 3 times. In large bowl, with electric mixer at medium speed, cream shortening with sugar, then with egg, until **very light and fluffy**—about 4 minutes altogether. Then, at low speed, beat in alternately, **just until smooth**, flour mixture in fourths and combined milk and vanilla in thirds. Turn into pan. Bake 45 minutes, or until cake tester, inserted in center, comes out clean. Cool on rack about 10 minutes. Remove from pan; peel off paper; cool on rack. Makes 16 servings.

**Bland diet:** Prepare as directed.
**Low-purine diet:** Prepare as directed.
**Low-residue diet:** Prepare as directed.

## NUT-TOPPED LEAN MAN'S CAKE (160 calories per serving)

Lean Man's Cake batter (see
  recipe above)
¼ cup packed brown sugar
2 teaspoons cinnamon
2 tablespoons flour
1½ tablespoons melted butter
  or margarine
3 tablespoons chopped walnuts

At least 3 hours before serving: Make Lean Man's Cake as directed. Meanwhile, with fork, thoroughly mix remaining ingredients.

When cake is done, before cooling, sprinkle with topping. Bake at 350°F. 5 minutes more; cool as directed. Makes 16 servings.

## CHOCO-NUT CAKE (165 calories per serving)

1 cup flaked coconut
3 tablespoons water
¼ cup melted chocolate
  morsels
Lean Man's Cake batter (recipe
  above)

At least 2 hours before serving: Preheat oven to 375°F. Grease bottom of 8-inch square cake pan, then line with waxed paper. Combine coconut, water and chocolate. Prepare cake batter. Pour half into pan; sprinkle with half of coconut-chocolate mixture; repeat. Bake 35 minutes. Cool in pan, on rack, about 10 minutes. Remove from pan; peel off paper; cool on rack. Makes 16 servings.

## UPSIDE-DOWN SPICE CAKE (155 calories per serving)

2 16-ounce cans freestone
  peach halves, drained
6 maraschino cherries, halved
¼ cup packed brown sugar
1 19-ounce package spice-cake
  mix
water and 1 egg for cake mix

About 1½ hours before serving: Preheat oven to 350°F. In 12" by 8" by 2" baking dish, arrange 12 peach halves, cut side down. Tuck cherry half under each peach. Sprinkle with brown sugar.

Prepare half of cake mix according to package directions for one layer. Pour batter evenly over peach halves. Bake 30 to 35 minutes, or until cake is a rich golden-brown and just beginning to come away from edges of pan. Cool on rack 10 minutes; loosen sides with spatula. Place large serving plate over baking dish; invert both; let stand 2 minutes; remove baking dish. Serve cake warm. Makes 12 servings.

**Egg-free diet:** Prepare as directed but for cake batter use milk in place of water and omit egg.
**Low-purine diet:** Prepare as directed.

## SHERBET CAKE ROLL (150 calories per serving)

1 package angel-food cake mix
1½ pints sherbet, slightly
softened

Day before or early in day: Preheat oven to 375°F. Line bottom and sides of 15″ by 10″ by 1″ jelly-roll pan with waxed paper. Prepare angel-food cake as label directs; smoothly spread half of batter into jelly-roll pan; spoon remaining half into unlined 9″ by 5″ by 3″ loaf pan. Bake both until golden-brown—about 20 minutes for jelly roll; 25 minutes for loaf cake.

Immediately after removing jelly roll from oven, turn out of pan onto lightly sugared pastry cloth; peel waxed paper off bottom; let cool. To cool loaf cake: Suspend pan upside down. Loaf cake may be served topped with tangy fruit.

To prepare cake roll, gently spread sherbet over jelly-roll cake, leaving ½-inch border on three sides and 2-inch border on one short side. Starting with 2-inch border, roll up cake. Place on plate, seam side down; wrap; freeze until just before serving time.

To serve: Slice with very sharp knife into 1-inch pieces. Makes 10 servings.

**Bland diet:** Prepare as directed.
**Low-fat, low-cholesterol diet:** Negligible fat per serving.
**Low-fat, bland (gall bladder) diet:** Prepare as directed.
**Low-purine diet:** Prepare as directed.
**Low-residue diet:** Prepare as directed.

## ANGEL-BERRY SHORTCAKE (170 calories per serving)

1 package angel-food cake mix
confectioners' sugar
1 2-ounce envelope whipped-
topping mix
3 pints large strawberries,
halved
¼ cup fresh blueberries

Early in day: Preheat oven to 375°F. Line bottom of 15″ by 10″ by 1″ greased jelly-roll pan with waxed paper; grease well. Prepare angel-food cake mix as label directs. Spread batter evenly in jelly-roll pan; bake 20 minutes, or until done. Cover large rack with sheet of waxed paper, then lightly dust with confectioners' sugar. When cake is done, loosen from sides of pan; invert onto waxed paper. Lift off pan, and peel off paper. Let cake stand at room temperature until just cool; then return to clean jelly-roll pan; wrap; refrigerate.

About 30 minutes before serving: Prepare whipped-topping mix as label directs but use skimmed milk. Spread evenly on top of cake. Top with rows of strawberries; garnish with blueberries. Cut into 15 rectangles.

## SPECTATOR'S SPONGE CAKE (130 calories per serving)

1 6.5-ounce package fluffy
vanilla-frosting mix
1 10-ounce 6-inch square packaged sponge cake
9 large perfect fresh strawberries, washed and
stemmed

At least 20 minutes before serving: Into small bowl, measure ¼ cup plus 1 tablespoon frosting mix; stir in 2 tablespoons boiling water, then beat with electric mixer at highest speed until stiff peaks form—about 5 minutes. (Carefully seal remaining frosting mix for later use. To prepare it, use 6 tablespoons boiling water and follow label instructions. Makes enough frosting for two 8-inch layers.)

Use frosting to frost top of sponge cake; then, with knife, mark frosting into 2″ by 2″ squares to indicate serving sizes. Place strawberry, cut side down, in center of each square. Refrigerate until serving time. Makes 9 servings.

**Low-purine diet:** Prepare as directed but omit whipped topping.

## ANGEL DELIGHT (185 calories per serving)

2 tablespoons softened butter
   or margarine
2 tablespoons light-brown
   sugar
4 1-inch slices angel-food cake

About 20 minutes before serving: Preheat broiler if manufacturer directs. Mix butter and sugar; lightly spread over cake slices. Place on cookie sheet; broil 2 minutes, or until bubbly. Makes 4 servings.

**Bland diet:** Prepare as directed.
**Low-fat, low-cholesterol diet:** Prepare as directed but use margarine instead of butter. 5 grams fat per serving.
**Low-purine diet:** Prepare as directed.
**Low-residue diet:** Prepare as directed.

## DOUBLE APPLE UPSIDE-DOWN CAKE (170 calories per serving)

1 15-ounce jar raspberry applesauce
1 18½-ounce package apple-
   sauce-cake mix
2 eggs for cake mix

About 1½ hours before serving: In greased 13″ by 9″ by 2″ baking pan, spread applesauce. Prepare cake mix as label directs. Pour batter over applesauce, spreading it to edges. Bake 35 minutes, or until cake tester, inserted in center, comes out clean. Cool 10 minutes on rack. With spatula, loosen cake from sides of pan; place cake plate on top of pan; invert. Cool. Makes 16 servings.

**Bland diet:** Prepare as directed.
**Egg-free diet:** Prepare as directed but omit eggs; substitute milk for water in cake mix.
**Low-fat diet:** Prepare as directed but use only whites of eggs. 3 grams fat per serving. Omit recipe from fat-controlled diet.
**Low-fat, bland (gall bladder) diet:** Prepare as directed for low-fat diet.
**Low-purine diet:** Prepare as directed.
**Low-residue diet:** Prepare as directed.

## RAINBOW ANGEL CAKE (160 calories per serving)

1 package angel-food cake mix
2 tablespoons chocolate sauce
   (from a jar)
2 tablespoons skimmed milk
2 tablespoons caramel sauce
   (from a jar)
2 tablespoons cranberry-juice
   cocktail
red food color

Early in day: Make and bake angel-food cake in 10-inch tube pan as label directs. Cool; place, top side down, on wire rack. Into measuring cup, pour chocolate sauce and 1 tablespoon milk; set in a little boiling water in saucepan; heat to pouring consistency.

Mark top of cake into thirds. About ½ inch out from center of edge of cake, with wooden meat skewer, make deep hole; into it pour some chocolate sauce. Now, in same third of cake, make a number of holes, of varying depths. Fill each hole with chocolate sauce.

Make and fill holes in second third of cake, using caramel sauce.

In cup, tint cranberry-juice cocktail with few drops red food color. Make and fill holes in last third of cake, using tinted juice.

To serve: Cut into wedges. Makes 16 servings.

**Low-fat, low-cholesterol diet:** Prepare as directed. About 1 gram fat per serving.
**Low-purine diet:** Prepare as directed.

## RAINBOW CUPCAKES (100 calories per serving)

½ cup sifted cake flour
½ teaspoon double-acting
    baking powder
⅛ teaspoon salt
1 egg
3 tablespoons granulated sugar
¾ teaspoon lemon juice
2 tablespoons plus 1½ tea-
    spoons hot skimmed milk or
    reliquefied nonfat dry milk

At least 2 hours before serving: Preheat oven to 350°F. Lightly grease 8 medium muffin cups. Sift flour with baking powder and salt 3 times. With electric mixer at high speed, beat egg **until very thick and light**—about 5 minutes. Gradually add sugar, beating constantly. Beat in lemon juice. Fold in flour mixture, a small amount at a time. Add hot milk; stir quickly until blended. Immediately turn batter into prepared muffin cups. Bake 15 minutes, or until done. Cool in pans 10 minutes. Makes 8 cupcakes.

**Bland diet:** Prepare as directed.
**Low-purine diet:** Prepare as directed.
**Low-residue diet:** Prepare as directed.

## MINIATURE CUPCAKES (170 calories per serving)

1 package white-cake mix
1 cup confectioners' sugar,
    sifted
yellow, red and green food
    color

About 4 hours before serving: Make up cake mix as label directs. Divide batter in half. Bake half in 9-inch layer-cake pan as label directs (use later). Spoon other half into tiny greased gem cupcake pans, each measuring 1¾″ by ⅞″. Bake at 350°F. for 15 to 20 minutes, or until done. Loosen from pans; cool on racks. Repeat until all are baked.

Frost cooled cupcakes as follows: Into sifted confectioners' sugar, stir 4 teaspoons water until smooth. Divide frosting among 4 custard cups; leave one white; with food color, tint others yellow, pink and green. Frost cupcakes, alternating colors. Serve 4 apiece. Makes about 36.

**Egg-free diet:** Prepare cake mix as directed but omit eggs and substitute milk for water.
**Low-purine diet:** Prepare as directed.

## STRAWBERRY SHORTCAKES (190 calories per serving)

1 teaspoon cornstarch
¼ cup orange juice
1 14- or 16-ounce package
    frozen unsweetened whole
    strawberries, partially
    thawed
⅓ cup granulated sugar
2 baker's 6-inch sponge-cake
    layers
1 cup whipped topping

Early in day: Mix cornstarch with orange juice until smooth. In saucepan over medium heat, heat strawberries and sugar to boiling, then stir in orange-juice mixture. Cook, stirring, until slightly thickened; refrigerate.

About 30 minutes before serving: Place one cake layer on cake plate; spread with some of strawberry mixture; top with other cake layer, then with prepared whipped topping.

To serve: Cut shortcake into 8 wedges; serve each topped with some of remaining strawberry mixture. Makes 8 servings. (If whipped topping is omitted, 150 calories per serving.)

## GRAHAM-CRACKER CRUST (575 calories per pie crust)

¾ cup graham-cracker crumbs
1 tablespoon granulated sugar
2 tablespoons butter or
  margarine
1 tablespoon water
dash salt

About 1 hour before serving: Preheat oven to 350°F. In 9-inch pie plate, mix all ingredients. Press on bottom and sides of plate. Bake 6 to 8 minutes, or until brown around edges. Cool before filling.

**Bland diet:** Prepare as directed.
**Diabetic diet:** Prepare as directed but use cornflake crumbs; omit sugar; substitute granulated saccharin equivalent to 1 tablespoon sugar.
**Low-fat, low-cholesterol diet:** Prepare as directed but use margarine instead of butter. 3 grams fat per 1/10 crust.
**Low-fat, bland (gall bladder) diet:** Prepare as directed.
**Low-purine diet:** Prepare as directed.
**Low-residue diet:** Prepare as directed.

## LEMON PARFAIT PIE (160 calories per serving)

Graham Cracker Crust (see
  recipe above)
1 3-ounce package lemon-
  flavor gelatin dessert
1 teaspoon grated lemon peel
3 tablespoons lemon juice
1 pint vanilla ice milk

At least 2 hours before serving: Make, bake and cool Graham-Cracker Crust as directed. In 2-quart saucepan, dissolve lemon-flavor gelatin in 1¼ cups boiling water; add lemon peel and juice. Add vanilla ice milk by spoonfuls, stirring until melted. Refrigerate until mixture is thickened but not set—25 to 30 minutes. Turn into graham crust. Refrigerate until firm—at least 1 hour. Makes 8 servings.

**Bland diet:** Prepare as directed.
**Low-fat, bland (gall bladder) diet:** Prepare as directed.
**Low-purine diet:** Prepare as directed.
**Low-residue diet:** Prepare as directed.

## LEMON CHIFFON PIE (155 calories per serving)

1 envelope unflavored gelatin
granulated sugar
2 egg yolks
1 tablespoon finely grated
  lemon peel
¼ cup lemon juice
1 3½-ounce can flaked coconut
1 tablespoon butter or margarine, softened
4 egg whites
¼ teaspoon salt

Early in day: In small saucepan, mix gelatin, ¼ cup granulated sugar, egg yolks, lemon peel, lemon juice and ⅓ cup water. Cook over low heat, stirring constantly, until mixture just begins to boil around edges. Refrigerate, stirring occasionally, until mixture mounds slightly when dropped from spoon; beat smooth.

Meanwhile, preheat oven to 350°F. In 9-inch pie plate, mix coconut and butter. Then spread evenly over bottom and up the sides of pie plate. Bake 7 minutes, or until coconut is dark golden-brown around edges; cool.

When lemon mixture mounds slightly: In medium bowl, beat egg whites and salt until soft peaks form; slowly beat in ¼ cup sugar until stiff peaks form. Fold in lemon mixture; heap into pie shell. Refrigerate until serving time—at least 3 hours. Makes 8 servings.

**Low-purine diet:** Prepare as directed.

## MELON CHIFFON PIE (175 calories per serving)

Graham-Cracker Crust (see
recipe page 239)
2 tablespoons cornstarch
grated peel of ½ lemon
2 tablespoons lemon juice
½ cup granulated sugar
2 eggs
1½ teaspoons unflavored
gelatin
3 cups finely diced cantaloupe

Early in day: Prepare, bake and cool Graham-Cracker Crust as directed.

To make filling: In top of double boiler, mix cornstarch with 2 tablespoons water; stir in lemon peel and juice, sugar, egg yolks and gelatin. Beating with spoon, stir in 1 cup boiling water. Cook over boiling water, beating constantly with egg beater or electric mixer, until thickened. Refrigerate until consistency of soft pudding.

About 4 hours before serving: Beat egg whites until stiff peaks form. Into lemon mixture, fold in cantaloupe then egg whites. Turn into pie shell. Refrigerate until set. Makes 8 servings.

## FRUIT PINWHEELS (75 calories per serving)

1 package refrigerated
cherry, blueberry or apple
turnovers

Early in day, or several hours before serving: Preheat oven to 400°F. Remove turnover dough from tube; refrigerate half. Separate other half into 4 squares. With lightly-floured rolling pin, roll out one of squares until it measures 5" by 5"; cut into quarters. Transfer to cookie sheet. Make slits from each corner to ½ inch from center. Dot center with about ½ teaspoon of turnover filling. Now bring alternate corners to center, making pinwheel. Repeat with other 3 squares, then with reserved refrigerated dough. Bake 5 minutes, or until golden. Remove to racks to cool. Frost, if desired. Makes 16 servings of 2 pinwheels each.

**Low-purine diet:** Prepare as directed.

## APPLE DESSERT PANCAKES (155 calories per serving)

2 eggs
⅔ cup milk
1 tablespoon melted
shortening
¼ teaspoon salt
granulated sugar
⅔ cup sifted all-purpose flour
2 apples
butter or margarine

Early in day or at least 1½ hours before serving: In electric-blender container or electric mixer, beat eggs thoroughly. Add milk, shortening, salt and 1 teaspoon sugar, then beat once more. Add flour and beat until a smooth batter. Pare and core apples; slice very thin into 16 slices.

Heat 1 teaspoon butter in 7-inch skillet; add 2 apple slices; sauté until tender-crisp. Then, using ¼-cup measuring cup as scoop, pour scant ¼ cup batter over apple slices; tilt skillet to spread batter over bottom. Cook pancake until brown on bottom. With narrow spatula, loosen sides and under part of apple slices; now invert pancake into another hot buttered skillet; sauté until underside is golden-brown, then slip onto square of waxed paper, on rack. In same way, continue making pancakes (8 in all), placing each on waxed-paper square and piling one on top of another.

Now remove each pancake from waxed paper; carefully fold in half, then lay, in overlapping row, down center of cookie sheet or stainless-steel platter. Set aside.

Just before serving: Sprinkle pancakes with 2 tablespoons sugar; broil till hot and bubbly. If pancakes were broiled on cookie sheet, transfer to heated platter for serving. Makes 8 servings.

**Bland diet:** Prepare as directed.
**Low-fat diet:** 5 grams fat per serving. Omit recipe from low-cholesterol diet.
**Low-purine diet:** Prepare as directed.
**Low-residue diet:** Prepare as directed.
**Low-sodium diet:** Prepare as directed but omit salt and use unsalted butter or margarine. 35 milligrams sodium per serving.

## GERMAN DESSERT PANCAKE (140 calories per serving)

⅓ cup sifted all-purpose
  flour
¼ teaspoon double-acting
  baking powder
⅓ cup milk
2 eggs, slightly beaten
2 tablespoons butter or margarine
1 tablespoon confectioners'
  sugar
4 lemon wedges for garnish

About 25 minutes before serving: Preheat oven to 425°F. In small bowl, combine flour and baking powder. Beat in milk and eggs, leaving batter a bit lumpy. In 10-inch skillet with heat-proof handle, melt butter. When butter is very hot, pour in batter all at once. Bake in oven 15 to 18 minutes, or until pancake is golden. Sprinkle with sugar. Serve hot, with lemon wedges for squeezing over pancake. Makes 4 servings.

**Bland diet:** Prepare as directed.
**Low-fat diet:** 10 grams fat per serving. Omit recipe from low-cholesterol diet.
**Low-purine diet:** Prepare as directed.
**Low-residue diet:** Prepare as directed.

# Special Diets

Physicians prescribe special diets to treat many disorders. If you are following one of these prescriptions, you'll find here the reasons "why," suggestions to simplify planning and delicious recipes. See the index for recipes in the main section that can be adapted, as indicated at the end of each, for use in particular special diets.

The seven therapeutic diets discussed in this chapter are used to treat some common ailments and disorders. They are: Allergy Diets (pages 242–252) for those who are allergic to egg, gluten, milk or wheat; Bland Diets (pages 253–265) for ulcer, gall bladder and colitis sufferers; Diabetic Diet (pages 266–277), with an explanation of the "exchange" system; High-Iron Diet (pages 278–285) for sufferers from anemia; Low-Fat, Low-Cholesterol Diet (pages 286–296) for those who are concerned about heart attacks; Low-Purine Diet (pages 297–305) for people with chronic gout; Low-Sodium Diets (pages 306–318) for those who have kidney trouble.

Remember, these diets should be used only with your doctor's approval.

## ALLERGY DIETS

In terms of meal planning, the most difficult allergies to cope with are those involving egg, gluten, milk and wheat. Each is a basic food ingredient (gluten is found in wheat and several other grains); eliminating these ingredients in recipes requires careful planning. See page 244 for some guidelines to aid in adapting recipes for allergy diets. The recipes in this section are for baked goods—the problem area in cooking for egg-, gluten-, milk- and wheat-free diets. How to make egg-free cakes from cake mixes is discussed on page 245.

The questions and answers that follow cover the more general problems allergy-sufferers must face, along with some specific suggestions for treatment.

Q. *What is an allergy?*
A. An allergy is an unusual physical reaction to some substance in the environment that is normally harmless. The allergic reaction or sensitivity may be to food or to such substances as pollen, dust, feathers or fur. When the offending substance comes in contact with the skin or the mucous membrane lining the eyes, nose, lungs or digestive system of an allergic person, antibodies are formed; the interaction of the foreign substance with these antibodies results in a reaction. The reaction can show up as skin rashes, asthma, red nose, headaches, digestive upsets, and many other things.

Q. *Are allergies inherited?*
A. Allergies aren't inherited in the way that blue eyes and red hair are, but a predisposition or tendency to allergies does run in families. If both parents have allergies, there is a greater chance that their children will also have them. Pediatricians consider this tendency when prescribing formulas and introducing new foods.

Q. *Are people born with allergies?*
A. In most cases, allergies develop after birth—a person first must become sensitive to a food or other substance before an allergic reaction can develop. Though children are the most likely ones to develop allergies as they change from formula to regular food, allergies can develop at any time.

Q. *How can I recognize a food allergy?*
A. While it's not fair to blame all adverse reactions to food on allergies, it's essential to take a child to the doctor if he repeatedly suffers from any of the symptoms mentioned above. If the doctor suspects a food allergy, he will review the child's eating habits with you, and try to correlate the onset of reactions with the eating of certain foods. This is not always as simple as it may sound. In some cases, the allergic reaction begins as soon as the food is eaten. But in most cases, the food must be digested first; symptoms won't occur until hours later. In trying to pinpoint the cause of the reaction, the physicians will often suggest eliminating foods such as chocolate, nuts, milk or eggs from the diet for a week or two. If symptoms clear up, it's then relatively easy to pick out the offending food. The child is given the suspected food again; if symptoms return, the allergy is considered confirmed. For adults, too, recurring symptoms should be brought to a doctor's attention. He can help identify the allergens (the offending substances) if they are what is causing the reaction. But beware of jumping to conclusions about allergic reactions to foods. Food poisoning and overeating, among other things, cause similar symptoms.

Q. *Do children outgrow allergies?*
A. A true allergy is not outgrown. Often the reaction will be milder or "outgrown" if the offending food is omitted from the diet for several years. However, allergies can reappear later, indicating that they were dormant, not outgrown.

Q. *Are allergic reactions always equally severe?*
A. No. In the case of a mild allergy, it's possible to eat a small portion of a certain food with little reaction. Also, if the eating is paced (for instance, eggs twice a week, not every day), no reaction may occur.

Your emotional state can play a part in the degree of reaction, too. When you're tense or tired, reactions will often be more violent than usual.

Cooking some foods may change them enough to prevent a reaction to them. For instance, cooked vegetables and fruits are easier to tolerate than raw ones; some children who are allergic to fresh milk can tolerate evaporated milk.

Q. *Is there a common factor in food that causes allergic reactions?*
A. Although the most common offender is the protein portion of food, there is no one universal factor that causes allergies. In fact, it is often only one part of a particular food that causes a reaction. For example, in the case of a reaction to orange juice, it

may be oil from the orange peel that causes a reaction–not the orange juice itself.

Q. *If you are allergic to a certain food, what others should you suspect?*
A. Foods can be divided into common botanical and animal families, and allergic reactions often run in families. If you are allergic to peanuts, a legume, you'll also tend to be allergic to peas, beans and lentils. If onions are a problem, also suspect leeks, garlic and asparagus. Your doctor can give you a list of commonly associated food allergies.

Q. *How can you know what packaged foods contain?*
A. Read the list of ingredients on the label to be found on virtually all packaged foods.

In some cases, however, the listing is not specific enough. For example, "starch" may be wheat starch, cornstarch, potato starch, or other types. For more information write to the manufacturer. All large companies have consumer services departments. Several have also prepared lists of their products which may be used on various allergy diets.

Some products do not list their ingredients on the label. These products have federal "standards of identity" that limit the type and proportion of ingredients that may be used. Two examples are mayonnaise and ice cream. For these it is then necessary to write the manufacturer for information.

Q. *If you are allergic to gluten or wheat, what other grain products may be used?*
A. Gluten-free diets are primarily for treatment of children's celiac disease and adults' nontropical sprue. Wheat must be eliminated mainly because of allergic reactions.

On wheat-free diets, cornmeal and cornstarch, oatmeal, tapioca, rice and rice cereals are readily available. In addition, rye, barley, potato starch, rice and soybean flours may be used. They are available in some supermarkets and health-food stores.

Gluten is found in unrefined wheat, barley, rye and oats as well as in many of their common processed forms (bread, flour, cereal). If gluten must be avoided, you may still use arrowroot, cornstarch and wheat starch (the gluten has been removed, but in severe cases, wheat starch may not be tolerated). Corn flour and cornmeal, rice flour and rice in other forms, potato starch, tapioca, soybean flour may also be used. If you must avoid either gluten or wheat, you usually need special recipes, especially for baking.

## ADAPTING RECIPES FOR ALLERGY DIETS

Many favorite recipes can be adapted with only slight modifications for allergy diets. Here are some general guide lines.

- Look for recipes that either lack the allergenic food, or include it only in small quantities, so that a substitution can be easily made.
- When experimenting with cookies, bake just a few at first until you see that the recipe is right. You may find you should add more flour, liquid, etc. Also, bake the first few cookies in a pan with a rim—a cake pan or pie plate—rather than on a cookie sheet. This will save an oven-cleaning job if the cookies spread too much.

- Since cakes are particularly delicate, when making layer cakes, first grease pans, then line with waxed paper and grease again; then flour.

### FOR EGG-FREE DIETS:

- Recipes that call for no more than two eggs, plus relatively large amounts of baking powder (1½ to 2 teaspoons) or baking soda (1 to 1½ teaspoons), can often be made without eggs. The extra baking powder or soda helps to increase the volume and compensates for the lack of eggs.
- Egg-free cakes have a moist, chewy texture and a more "bready" flavor.

Compensate for this by adding more flavoring—spices, raisins, etc.

- Increase beating time by one-half minute after each step; beat batter an additional two minutes before adding any fruit or nuts. This will get more air into the batter and make the product higher and lighter. Then spoon batter or dough into baking pan or onto cookie sheet; handle as little as possible; bake immediately.

## FOR MILK-FREE DIETS:

- Look for recipes which require only small amounts of milk; substitute water or fruit juices for milk.
- Use only milk-free margarine for butter or margarine. There are several milk-free brands—check lists of ingredients.
- If evaporated milk can be tolerated on the diet (check with your doctor), use one part evaporated milk to one part water as a substitute for milk in recipes.
- Special non-milk formulas, generally used for infants allergic to milk, usually may be substituted for milk in recipes. Most coffee lighteners and other milk substitutes contain caseinates—often the allergenic factor in milk—and should be used only with your doctor's approval.

## FOR WHEAT-FREE DIETS:

- Try recipes using grain products that are readily available—cornstarch, cornmeal, oatmeal, etc.
- Look for recipes, such as corn bread, that use a small amount of wheat flour combined with another flour. This makes it easier to substitute another flour for the wheat flour.
- Use half the amount of wheat flour called for when substituting cornstarch, rice flour, potato flour or arrowroot starch in puddings, sauces and gravies.
- Use table below as a rough estimate of the amount of other flours to substitute for 1 cup all-purpose flour:

  1 cup barley flour
  1 cup corn flour
  ¾ cup cornmeal
  ⅞ cup rice flour
  1¼ cups rye flour
  1⅓ cups oat flour
  ⅜ cup potato-starch flour
  1 cup soybean flour, plus ¼ cup potato-starch flour

---

## MAKING EGG-FREE CAKES FROM MIXES

- *To choose a mix:* Read the list of ingredients; select one that doesn't contain eggs or egg products. Success can't be guaranteed with every brand and flavor of cake mix on the market, but most flavors of the four major brands in 16- to 19-ounce packages should give acceptable results.
- *To mix:* Prepare cake as label directs but omit eggs; substitute milk for water.
- *To select cake pans:* Do not use 8-inch layer-cake pans or cake will sink in center. Bake cakes in two 9-inch layer-cake pans, a 9-inch square pan or in 13" by 9" by 2" oblongs. Thoroughly grease and flour pans. Or use medium muffin cups and baking-cup liners; fill cups with only a heaping tablespoon of batter.
- *To bake:* Bake as label directs. Do not underbake. When cakes are done, they will come away from the edge of the pan.
- *To cool:* Cool and remove from pan as directed; cool on rack. Cakes made without eggs are very fragile, so handle with care.
- *To frost and store:* Cool completely before frosting. Spread frosting with a gentle touch. Keep cakes tightly covered. Freeze for long-term storage.
- *To freeze:* For unfrosted layers, cool completely, then wrap snugly with heavy-duty foil or saran, or put in plastic bags. For frosted layers, freeze cake, uncovered, one to two hours. Then wrap and replace in freezer. Freeze individual cake slices and cupcakes in the same way.

## ALLERGY DIETS: 25 Recipes for Baked Goods

### POTATO-FLOUR SPONGE CAKE (gluten-, milk- and wheat-free diet)

4 eggs, separated
granulated sugar
½ cup potato-starch flour
¾ teaspoon double-acting
   baking powder
⅛ teaspoon salt
½ teaspoon finely grated
   lemon peel
½ teaspoon lemon juice

About 4 hours before serving: Preheat oven to 325°F. In medium bowl, with electric mixer at high speed, beat egg yolks until thick and fluffy—at least 5 minutes. Gradually beat in ½ cup sugar. Then **fold** potato starch into yolk mixture.

In large bowl, with electric mixer at high speed, beat egg whites until almost stiff. Gradually beat in ¼ cup sugar mixed with baking powder and salt. Beat until stiff—but not dry—peaks form.

Fold yolk mixture, lemon peel and lemon juice into whites. Turn into ungreased 9-inch square cake pan. Bake 60 minutes, or until golden. Invert pan to cool. Cool thoroughly before removing from pan.

### CHERRY UPSIDE-DOWN CAKE (gluten-, milk- and wheat-free diet)

1 16-ounce can pitted tart
   red cherries
3 tablespoons milk-free margarine
¾ cup granulated sugar
¼ teaspoon cinnamon
2 eggs, separated
⅔ cup uncooked cream-of-
   rice cereal
½ teaspoon salt

About 1 hour before serving: Preheat oven to 350°F. Drain cherries, reserving ¼ cup liquid. In 9-inch round cake pan, in oven, melt milk-free margarine. In small bowl, combine cherries, ½ cup sugar and cinnamon; spread in cake pan. In small bowl, with electric mixer at high speed, beat egg whites until stiff peaks form; gradually add ¼ cup sugar. In another small bowl, with electric mixer at high speed, beat egg yolks until thick and lemon-colored. Blend reserved juice, cereal and salt into egg yolks; fold into whites until well blended. Pour batter over cherries, spreading evenly; bake 40 minutes, or until cake pulls away from sides of pan. Immediately loosen from pan with knife; invert on platter. Serve warm. Makes 8 servings.

### ORANGE-BLOSSOM CAKE (egg- and milk-free diet)

½ cup milk-free margarine
¾ cup granulated sugar
1¾ teaspoons vanilla extract
1 tablespoon grated orange
   peel
3 cups sifted cake flour
1¼ teaspoons salt
4 teaspoons double-acting
   baking powder
1¼ teaspoons baking soda
½ cup orange juice
yellow food color (optional)
Creamy Apricot Frosting (page
   248)

About 4 hours before serving: Preheat oven to 350°F. Grease two 8-inch layer-cake pans; line with waxed paper; grease and flour the paper.

In medium bowl, with electric mixer at medium speed, cream margarine with sugar until cream-colored, light and fluffy. Beat in vanilla and orange peel. Sift together flour, salt, baking powder and baking soda.

With electric mixer at medium speed, beat one-third flour mixture into margarine mixture until smooth; beat orange juice into batter until smooth. Repeat with second third of flour; beat in ½ cup plus 2 tablespoons water; beat in remaining flour mixture. Add yellow food color; beat one minute. Batter will be consistency of soft cookie dough.

Divide between pans; push batter slightly up around edges. Bake 30 to 35 minutes, or until cake shrinks from sides of pan. Let cool on rack about 30 minutes before turning out of pans. Fill and frost with Creamy Apricot Frosting.

## ORANGE CHIFFON CAKE  (gluten-, milk- and wheat-free diet)

¾ cup potato-starch flour
¾ cup granulated sugar
2 teaspoons double-acting baking powder
½ teaspoon salt
¼ cup salad oil
4 eggs, separated
1 tablespoon finely grated
   orange peel
⅓ cup orange juice
¼ teaspoon cream of tartar

About 5 hours before serving: Preheat oven to 350°F. Into small bowl, sift potato-starch flour with sugar, baking powder and salt. Make well in center; pour in (in order) salad oil, egg yolks, orange peel and orange juice. Beat, with electric mixer at medium speed, 1 minute.

In large bowl, beat egg whites with cream of tartar until whites are very stiff and almost dry. Carefully fold in yolk mixture. Divide batter evenly between 2 ungreased 8-inch layer-cake pans.* Bake 30 to 35 minutes, or until a cake tester, inserted in center, comes out clean. To cool, invert pans and suspend by rim. Cool completely, then carefully remove cake from pans—it will be delicate.

* This cake may also be baked in an 8-inch square cake pan. Baking time will be 5 to 10 minutes longer.

## GINGER CAKE  (egg- and milk-free diet)

2½ cups sifted all-purpose
   flour
1½ teaspoons double-acting
   baking powder
1 teaspoon baking soda
1 teaspoon salt
2 teaspoons cinnamon
1½ teaspoons ginger
½ teaspoon nutmeg
½ teaspoon ground cloves
½ cup raisins
½ cup chopped walnuts
   (optional)
1 cup packed brown sugar
⅔ cup molasses
⅔ cup shortening
confectioners' sugar

About 1 hour and 10 minutes before serving: Preheat oven to 350°F. Grease and flour 13" by 9" baking pan. On waxed paper, sift together flour, baking powder, baking soda, salt and spices. In small bowl, toss raisins and nuts with ¼ cup flour mixture until well coated. In large mixing bowl, with electric mixer at medium speed, blend brown sugar and molasses. Add shortening, then dry ingredients, beating well after each addition. Gradually beat in 1 cup boiling water until smooth. Beat 2 minutes more. Stir in raisin mixture. Pour into pan; bake 45 to 50 minutes, or until cake shrinks from sides of pan. Sprinkle with confectioners' sugar; serve warm. Makes 8 to 10 servings.

## APPLESAUCE SPICE CAKE  (egg-, milk- and wheat-free diet)

½ cup shortening
½ cup granulated sugar
½ cup sifted rye flour
1½ cups sifted barley flour
3 teaspoons double-acting
   baking powder
1 teaspoon baking soda
1 teaspoon salt
½ teaspoon cinnamon
¼ teaspoon nutmeg
1 cup minus 2 tablespoons
   canned applesauce
sifted confectioners' sugar

About 4 hours before serving: Preheat oven to 350°F. Grease bottom of 9-inch square cake pan; line with waxed paper; grease and flour (with barley flour) the paper.

In medium bowl, with electric mixer at medium speed, cream shortening with sugar until light and fluffy. Sift together: rye and barley flour, baking powder, baking soda, salt, cinnamon and nutmeg.

With electric mixer at medium speed, beat one-third of flour mixture into sugar mixture until smooth; beat in half of applesauce until smooth. Repeat with flour and remaining applesauce. Then beat in remaining flour. Beat one minute.

Turn batter into cake pan; smooth surface. Bake 30 to 35 minutes, or until cake shrinks from sides of pan. (Center of this cake will not be as firm as that of regular cake.) Let cool on rack 30 minutes; turn out of pan. Serve sprinkled with confectioners' sugar.

## FRUIT-AND-SPICE CAKE (egg- and milk-free diet)

2 cups raisins
1 cup packed dark brown sugar
½ cup shortening
½ teaspoon cinnamon
½ teaspoon allspice
½ teaspoon salt
⅛ teaspoon nutmeg
2 cups sifted cake flour
1 teaspoon double-acting
   baking powder
1 teaspoon baking soda
1 cup chopped pecans
   (optional)
confectioners' sugar

About 4 hours before serving: In medium saucepan, heat 1 cup water, raisins, brown sugar, shortening, cinnamon, allspice, salt and nutmeg to boiling; simmer, uncovered, 3 minutes. Cool to room temperature.

Grease 9-inch square cake pan. Preheat oven to 375°F. Sift together flour, baking powder and baking soda. In medium bowl, stir together raisin-sugar mixture, flour mixture and pecans. Beat, with electric mixer at medium speed, until smooth—about 1 minute.

Pour into cake pan; bake 35 to 40 minutes, or until cake just comes away from edge of pan. Cool about 15 minutes; turn out of pan. Cool completely, then sprinkle with confectioners' sugar. Cut into 16 squares.

**For gluten- and wheat-free diet:** Prepare as directed but substitute 1½ cups potato-starch or rice flour for cake flour.

## CREAMY COFFEE FROSTING (egg-, gluten-, milk- and wheat-free diet)

⅔ cup milk-free margarine
about 6 cups sifted confectioners' sugar (approximately
   1½ 16-ounce boxes)
6 tablespoons boiling water
1 tablespoon instant-coffee
   powder
2 teaspoons vanilla extract
¼ teaspoon salt

About 20 minutes before frosting cake: In medium bowl, with electric mixer at low speed, blend milk-free margarine and 4 cups sugar. Beat in remaining ingredients until smooth. With electric mixer at low speed, beat in enough confectioners' sugar to make frosting with a good spreading consistency. At high speed, beat 1 minute. Use to frost 36 cupcakes or one 13" by 9" by 2" oblong cake, or to fill and frost an 8- or 9-inch layer cake.

CREAMY APRICOT FROSTING: Prepare as directed, but heat one 4¾-ounce jar strained apricots with tapioca to boiling; use hot apricots and 2 teaspoons lemon juice in place of water and instant coffee.

CREAMY CHOCOLATE FROSTING: Prepare as directed, but mix 6 tablespoons cocoa with margarine and sugar; omit instant coffee.

## MOLASSES DROP COOKIES (egg- and wheat-free diet)

2 cups sifted rye flour
2 teaspoons double-acting
   baking powder
½ teaspoon salt
¼ teaspoon ginger
½ teaspoon nutmeg
½ cup shortening
½ cup granulated sugar
½ cup light molasses
½ cup evaporated milk
½ cup raisins or chopped nuts
   (optional)

At least 2 hours before serving: Preheat oven to 400°F. Lightly grease cookie sheets. Onto sheet of waxed paper, sift together rye flour, baking powder, salt, ginger and nutmeg. In medium bowl, with electric mixer at medium speed, cream together shortening and sugar until light and fluffy; beat in molasses until smooth.

Add one-third of rye-flour mixture to shortening; beat, at low speed, until smooth. Add one-half evaporated milk; beat until smooth. Repeat, then beat in remaining flour mixture until smooth. Beat in raisins or nuts, if desired.

Drop, by level tablespoonfuls, 2 inches apart, onto cookie sheets. Bake 7 minutes, or until browned around the edges and cookies feel "set." Makes 3½ to 4 dozen.

**For milk-free diet:** Prepare as directed but substitute ½ cup canned applesauce for evaporated milk.

## PEANUT-BUTTER COOKIES (gluten-, milk- and wheat-free diet)

½ cup creamy- or chunky-style peanut butter
½ cup shortening
½ cup granulated sugar
½ cup packed dark brown sugar
½ teaspoon double-acting baking powder
1 egg

About 4 hours before serving: Preheat oven to 350°F. In medium bowl, with electric mixer at medium speed, cream peanut butter, shortening and sugars until fluffy. Add baking powder and egg; beat until smooth.

Drop batter, by level tablespoonfuls, 2 inches apart, onto ungreased cookie sheets. Bake 15 minutes, or until edges of cookies brown. Allow to cool on sheets 2 to 3 minutes before removing. Makes 2½ dozen.

## BUTTERBALLS (egg- and milk-free diet)

1½ cups sifted all-purpose flour
½ cup granulated sugar
¼ teaspoon salt
2 teaspoons instant-coffee powder
1 cup milk-free margarine, softened to room temperature*
¾ cup chopped walnuts (optional)
granulated sugar

About 1 hour before serving: Preheat oven to 300°F. In medium bowl, sift together flour, sugar, salt and instant coffee. With pastry blender, cut in margarine until the size of peas. Press together dough to form large ball. Break off pieces size of small walnuts; roll in chopped walnuts. (Or omit nuts and bake plain, as directed.)

Place cookies, about 2 inches apart, on ungreased cookie sheet. Dip flat-bottomed glass in water, then sugar; use to flatten cookies. Bake 20 to 25 minutes, or until cookies feel "set." (They will brown only slightly.) Cool a minute; remove from cookie sheets. Makes 2 to 3 dozen.

\* Do **not** use shortening.

## FORGOTTEN COOKIES (gluten-, milk- and wheat-free diet)

2 egg whites
¾ cup granulated sugar
1 6-ounce package semisweet-chocolate pieces

At least 6 hours before serving: Preheat oven to 375°F. Grease 2 cookie sheets. In deep medium bowl, with mixer at high speed, beat egg whites until soft peaks form; continuing to beat, slowly add sugar. Beat until stiff meringue forms. Fold in chocolate pieces.

Drop, by level tablespoonfuls, onto greased cookie sheets. Place in oven, then turn off heat. Let remain in oven until it cools to room temperature. Remove from cookie sheet. Store in an air-tight container. Makes 2½ dozen.

If you wish, substitute 1 cup raisins or chopped nuts for the chocolate pieces; prepare as directed.

## APRICOT CANDY COOKIES (egg-, gluten-, milk- and wheat-free diet)

24 large dried apricots
1 3½-ounce can flaked coconut
2 teaspoons orange juice
confectioners' sugar

About 1 day before serving: With food grinder, grind together apricots, coconut and orange juice at least 2 times to mix thoroughly. Form mixture into about 24 small balls. Roll in confectioners' sugar to coat completely. Keep in airtight container until ready to serve. Makes about 24.

## OVERNIGHT SURPRISES (milk- and wheat-free diet)

2 cups uncooked rolled oats
1 cup packed light brown sugar
½ cup salad oil
1 egg
½ teaspoon salt
½ teaspoon almond extract

Night before: In medium bowl, with electric mixer at low speed, mix rolled oats, sugar and salad oil about 3 minutes. Cover; refrigerate overnight.

When ready to bake cookies: Preheat oven to 350°F. Generously grease 2 cookie sheets. To oatmeal mixture, add egg, salt and almond extract. Beat, with mixer at lowest speed, until mixture just begins to form a ball and stick together. Drop batter by level tablespoonfuls, 2 inches apart, onto cookie sheets. Bake 10 minutes or until golden-brown around the edges; let cool 2 to 3 minutes before removing from sheets. Makes about 2 dozen.

## APPLE-OATMEAL DESSERT (egg-, milk- and wheat-free diet)

2½ cups uncooked rolled oats
⅔ cup packed light brown sugar
¼ teaspoon salt
1 teaspoon cinnamon
½ cup milk-free margarine, melted
1 cup applesauce
cinnamon and nutmeg for garnish

At least 2 hours before serving: Preheat oven to 375°F. In electric-blender container, coarsely chop half the oats. (Or chop oatmeal in nut chopper.) In medium bowl, mix all oats together with brown sugar, salt and cinnamon. Add melted margarine; blend well. Pack firmly into bottom of well-greased 9-inch pie plate. Bake 12 to 15 minutes. Cool. Then slice; top each serving with applesauce; sprinkle with cinnamon and nutmeg, if desired. Makes 6 servings.

## APPLE, SPICE AND EVERYTHING NICE (egg- and milk-free diet)

2 cups sifted all-purpose flour
1 teaspoon baking soda
½ teaspoon salt
1 teaspoon cinnamon
1 teaspoon ground cloves
½ teaspoon nutmeg
½ cup shortening
1⅓ cups packed light brown sugar
⅓ cup apple juice or water
1 cup chopped walnuts (optional)
1 cup finely chopped cooking apples
1 cup raisins

About 1 hour before serving: Preheat oven to 400°F. Grease two large cookie sheets. On sheet of waxed paper, sift flour with baking soda, salt, cinnamon, cloves and nutmeg. In medium bowl, with electric mixer at medium speed, cream shortening with sugar until light, fluffy and cream-colored; beat in apple juice until smooth. Stir in flour mixture until dampened, then mix, at medium speed, until smooth. (Mixture will be extremely thick.) Stir in walnuts, apples and raisins.

Drop dough, by level tablespoonfuls, about 2 inches apart, onto greased cookie sheets. Bake 8 to 10 minutes, or until golden-brown around edges and cookies feel "set." Cool slightly; remove from cookie sheet; cool completely, then store in an airtight container. Makes about 3 dozen.

## AMAZING PANCAKES (gluten-, milk- and wheat-free diet)

2 eggs
2 medium bananas
2 teaspoons granulated sugar
maple-flavored syrup for topping

Just before serving: Preheat griddle until a drop of water "dances" on it; grease lightly. In electric-blender container, at low speed, blend eggs, bananas and sugar until smooth. (Or mash bananas; add eggs and sugar; mix until smooth.) Pour batter by ¼-cup portions onto hot griddle. Cook until edges of pancakes are browned; turn; cook other side until golden-brown. Serve with maple-flavored syrup. Makes six 4-inch pancakes.

## APPLESAUCE PANCAKES (gluten- and wheat-free diet)

1½ cups unsifted rice flour
2 tablespoons unsifted potato-
   starch flour
3 tablespoons cornstarch
1½ teaspoons double-acting
   baking powder
½ teaspoon salt
1 teaspoon lemon juice
1 cup canned applesauce
3 tablespoons butter or margarine, melted
1 cup milk
2 eggs, separated
bananas (optional)
maple-flavored syrup (optional)

About 45 minutes before serving: Preheat lightly greased griddle until a drop of water "dances" on it. In medium bowl, stir together dry ingredients. Add lemon juice, applesauce, melted butter or margarine, milk and egg yolks; mix only until dry ingredients are dampened.

In small bowl, beat egg whites until stiff peaks form; fold beaten egg whites into pancake batter. Drop batter, by ¼-cupfuls, onto heated griddle; spread each pancake with back of spoon into circle about 4 inches in diameter. Cook until rim of each cake is full of broken bubbles and underside is brown. Turn and brown other side. Makes about 16. Serve with freshly sliced bananas and syrup, if desired.

## CORNMEAL WAFFLES (gluten- and wheat-free diet)

½ cup yellow cornmeal
½ cup potato-starch flour
2 tablespoons cornstarch
1½ teaspoons double-acting
   baking powder
¼ teaspoon salt
1 tablespoon granulated sugar
1 egg
½ cup milk*
3 tablespoons melted butter or
   margarine*

About 30 minutes before serving: Preheat waffle iron if manufacturer directs. In medium bowl, stir together dry ingredients. Beat egg until light, then stir in milk and butter. Gradually beat into dry ingredients until smooth. Bake waffles as usual. Makes 2 to 3 waffles.

* For milk-free diet, substitute water for milk and milk-free margarine for regular.

## CARAWAY SPONGE BREAD (gluten-, milk- and wheat-free diet)

6 eggs, separated
¾ cup potato-starch flour
½ cup rice flour
2 teaspoons double-acting baking powder
1¼ teaspoons salt
⅛ teaspoon pepper
6 tablespoons granulated
   sugar
caraway seed*

About 6 hours before serving: Separate eggs and let warm to room temperature. When ready to make bread, preheat oven to 350°F. Line bottom of 8" by 4" by 3" loaf pan with waxed paper. Sift together, twice, potato-starch flour, rice flour, baking powder, salt and pepper. In large bowl, beat egg whites until soft mounds form; beat in sugar, a tablespoon at a time, then continue to beat until stiff peaks form. In medium bowl, beat egg yolks until light, creamy and fluffy—at least 5 minutes at high speed.

Sprinkle about one-third flour mixture over whites; fold together; repeat two times; fold in 1 tablespoon caraway seed. Carefully fold beaten yolks into flour mixture.

Pour batter into pan. (Pan will be very full.) Lightly sprinkle top of bread with caraway seed. Bake 45 to 50 minutes, or until top is golden-brown and crisp. Cool 1 hour before removing from pan. Center of bread may shrink slightly during cooling. Let bread stand about 3 hours before slicing.

* Poppy or sesame seed may be substituted for caraway seed.

## 100% RYE BREAD (egg-, milk- and wheat-free diet)

1 envelope active dry yeast
2 teaspoons salt
1 tablespoon dark brown sugar
unsifted rye flour*
salad oil

At least 6 hours before serving: Dissolve yeast in ¼ cup lukewarm water. Combine salt, sugar and 1 cup water; stir in 4 cups rye flour; beat smooth. Turn out onto rye-floured board, then knead (at least 10 minutes), using additional flour as necessary to make a firm elastic dough. Place in greased bowl; brush top with oil; cover; let rise in warm (about 85° to 95°F.) place until double in bulk.

Knead as before. Place in bowl and let rise again 1 hour. Preheat oven to 450°F. Shape dough into loaf; place in greased 9" by 5" by 3" loaf pan. Cover with clean towel; let rise until double in bulk. Bake 15 minutes; reduce heat to 350°F. and bake 55 minutes longer. Cool slightly, then turn out of pan to complete cooling. Makes 1 loaf.

* Finely milled rye flour gives best results.

## RYE BAKING-POWDER BISCUITS (egg-, milk- and wheat-free diet)

1 cup unsifted rye flour
1½ teaspoons double-acting
   baking powder
¼ teaspoon salt
3 tablespoons shortening

About 30 minutes before serving: Preheat oven to 450°F. Grease baking sheet. Sift together rye flour, baking powder and salt. Cut in shortening until mixture is like coarse cornmeal. Stir in 3 to 4 tablespoons water to form a thick pliable dough. Turn onto lightly rye-floured board; roll about ½-inch thick. Cut with 2-inch cutter; place on sheet; bake 12 to 16 minutes. Makes 6.

## CORN MUFFINS (gluten-, and wheat-free diet)

1 cup cornmeal
¾ cup unsifted rice flour
4 teaspoons double-acting
   baking powder
½ teaspoon salt
¼ cup granulated sugar
1 egg, separated
¼ cup butter or margarine,
   melted
1 cup milk

About 45 minutes before serving: Preheat oven to 425°F. Grease 12 medium muffin-pan cups. In medium bowl, stir together cornmeal, rice flour, baking powder, salt and sugar. Beat egg white until stiff peaks form. Stir egg yolk, butter and milk into dry ingredients until smooth. Fold in beaten egg white.

Divide batter among muffin cups (a scant ¼ cup of batter per cup). Bake 25 minutes, or until sides of muffins brown lightly and pull away from edges. Makes 12.

## ONION-POTATO MUFFINS (gluten-, milk- and wheat-free diet)

½ cup potato-starch flour
2 tablespoons granulated sugar
1 teaspoon double-acting
   baking powder
½ teaspoon salt
2 teaspoons instant minced
   onion (optional)
4 eggs separated

About 40 minutes before serving: Preheat oven to 375°F. Sift together dry ingredients; add onion. In small bowl, beat egg whites until stiff. In cup, beat egg yolks lightly, then fold into whites. Fold in flour mixture slowly, not more than 2 tablespoons at a time, until blended. Sprinkle on 2 tablespoons ice water, then gently fold in. Spoon into greased 2-inch muffin cups—about ⅔ full; bake 20 minutes, or until golden brown. Turn out immediately. Makes about 10.

## RYE-AND-RICE MUFFINS (egg-, milk- and wheat-free diet)

⅔ cup unsifted rye flour
⅓ cup rice flour
2 teaspoons double-acting baking powder
¼ teaspoon salt
4 teaspoons granulated sugar
3 tablespoons melted shortening

About 50 minutes before serving: Preheat oven to 400°F. Grease 6 cups of medium muffin pans. In medium bowl, stir together dry ingredients. Stir ½ cup water and shortening into flour mixture until mixed but still lumpy. Divide batter among muffin cups. Bake 30 to 35 minutes, or until muffins pull away from edge of pan. Makes 6.

# BLAND, LOW-RESIDUE AND GALL-BLADDER DIETS

A trio of chronic conditions—hiatal hernias, ulcers or simply "touchy" stomachs; gall bladder upsets; and colitis are treated with bland diets. Although the outline for all three is essentially the same, they vary in their application. For example, the ulcer patient must eat six to eight meals a day; the patient with colitis can eat the broths and gravies denied to the ulcer patient but may need his vegetables pureed; the gall bladder sufferer must severely limit fat intake. In each case, the restrictions will vary with the severity of the condition. At the acute stages the emphasis is on limiting foods to the mildest and least irritating. But as the patient improves, the diet can be liberalized.

Precise diet restrictions vary from hospital to hospital and doctor to doctor, but they are all similar in rationale. The three outlines that follow are composites of the "maintenance" or "discharge" diets given in the diet manuals of several large teaching hospitals. Ask your doctor to check the outline for your problem; if he eliminates some foods, avoid the recipes that contain them. (See 24 main dish recipes beginning on page 259.) The "Outline of Allowed Foods" and the "Week of Menus" on the following pages are designed for all three diets; necessary adaptations for specific problems are indicated.

## BUYING AND COOKING CUES

*Main Dishes for Bland Diets:*

- Season meat, fish or poultry main dishes with ground thyme, sage, parsley and paprika. For the more liberal bland diet, add celery salt, oregano and basil.
- Serve sandwiches on a variety of breads, filled with sliced hard-cooked eggs, roast beef, chicken or turkey, or tuna. Use butter on the bread. Add lettuce if allowed on diet.
- Pan-broil meats by placing meat in skillet before heating; heat quickly to cooking temperatures and cook, draining away fat as it accumulates.
- Use seafood regularly. Clams, oysters, lobster, shrimp and crab all have distinct flavors, yet are perfect for a bland diet. *To serve:* Make chowders, broil or pan-broil, or dip seafood in butter or margarine, then bake.

- Liver is another meat with a distinctive flavor that should be used often. Broil or pan-broil with bacon or mushrooms rather than onion.
- Use canned chicken in casseroles; keep frozen quick steaks on hand for quick meals; try unbreaded frozen shrimp and crab; use canned tuna or salmon (pick out the bones and skin).
- Make homemade-creamed soups in a blender with canned peas or asparagus and half-and-half or light cream.

*Vegetables:*

- Top potatoes, vegetables or fruit with sour cream. To save calories (or for gall bladder diets), substitute cottage cheese pureed smooth in a blender, or yogurt.
- To puree vegetables at home, place cooked (or canned) drained vegetables

in electric-blender container with 2 table-spoons cooking liquid for each cup of vegetables. Blend until smooth.
- Mashed squash is now available frozen.
- Canned boiled potatoes need only be heated for an "instant" vegetable.
- Use packaged precooked rice and instant mashed potatoes for quick-to-fix vegetables.

*Milk:*

- Buttermilk has more tang than plain milk.
- To save calories, drink skimmed milk. The modified skimmed milks have more "body" than the regular kind. Or make your own modified-skimmed milk by adding 1 or 2 tablespoons extra dry-milk powder for each glass reliquefied nonfat dry milk.

*Breads:*

- Use the full range of allowed breads—white or rye (without seeds), hard rolls, refrigerated biscuits and rolls, hamburger and frankfurter rolls, Melba toast or breadsticks (not salted).
- Toasting bread adds textural appeal. Make homemade Melba toast by thinly slicing French bread and toasting in 250°F. oven 15 minutes, or until crisp.

*Desserts:*

- Use cinnamon, allspice and mace to season desserts.
- Make fruit toppings from pureed canned peaches, pears, apricots, etc. for ice cream and ice milk. For gall bladder diet, use as topping for sherbets.
- To puree fruits, place drained cooked or canned fruit in blender container, and blend until smooth. There's no need to add extra liquid.
- Try the new canned and frozen puddings for a quick dessert.
- Use the sponge-cake and chiffon-cake mixes as well as angel-food mix.

*Miscellaneous:*

- Try freeze-dried decaffeinated instant coffee.
- Try a wide variety of flavors in jellies. They make an excellent substitute for butter on a gall bladder diet.
- Use yogurt plain, or try vanilla or coffee as a tangy snack. Make your own flavored yogurts with jellies. Use yogurts made with partially skimmed milk on gall bladder diets.

## OUTLINE OF ALLOWED FOODS

**BLAND DIET (for peptic ulcers, hiatal hernias and gastric indigestion):**
Foods are smooth and bland in consistency and texture; their flavor is bland and chemically non-irritating. Choose meals from the following. Follow your doctor's advice concerning the number and timing of meals.

### SOUPS
Creamed soups using allowed vegetables
**Avoid:** All meat-stock-based soups

### FISH, MEAT AND POULTRY
Fish: All boned fish fillets or steaks
Seafood prepared with allowed ingredients
Meat: Very tender cuts of beef, lamb, mild fresh pork and veal—all cooked "well done"

Variety meats including heart, liver and sweetbreads
Poultry: All forms of poultry prepared with allowed ingredients
**Avoid:** Tough, stringy meat
Highly seasoned, salted or smoked meats
Excessively fatty meats

### CHEESE AND EGGS
Cheese: Cottage cheese, cream cheese, mild-flavored hard cheese used in cooking
Eggs: Any style but fried. Do not over-cook the eggs
**Avoid:** Strong cheeses and those containing spices. Fried eggs.

## VEGETABLES

Tender, well-cooked asparagus, beets, carrots, green beans, green peas, mushrooms, potatoes (sweet and white), spinach (chopped), squash (acorn or yellow) and tomato juice

Lettuce or tomatoes with skin and seeds removed if approved by doctor

Pureed or baby-food versions of other vegetables not specifically forbidden

**Avoid:** Strong-flavored vegetables: Brussels sprouts, cabbage, cauliflower, cucumber, onion, peppers, radishes, turnips

All raw vegetables (note exceptions above) and those containing seeds, skins or tough fibers

## BREADS AND CEREALS

Breads: plain rolls, rye (without seeds), enriched white, biscuits, muffins

Cereals: Cornflakes, puffed rice, rice flakes, farina, grits, strained oatmeal

Pastas: Macaroni, noodles, spaghetti, etc.

Specialty breads: Melba toast, rusk, saltines (unsalted), soda crackers, zwieback

Rice: White only

**Avoid:** Coarse-grained breads and cereals, pretzels, salty crackers, sweet rolls

## FATS

Butter, cream, margarine, vegetable fats, oils

**Avoid:** Excessive fats, mineral oil, salad dressings

## FRUITS

Canned or cooked: Apricots, apples, peaches, pears, plums and Royal Anne cherries

Juices: Apple, apricot, grapefruit, lemon (in moderation), orange, pineapple and prune (in moderation)

Strained: All others

Raw: Avocado and banana

Pared and seeded apple, if doctor approves

**Avoid:** All other raw fruit

Fruit containing seeds, skin or fibers

## DESSERTS

Cakes and cookies: All plain and not excessively sweet or rich

Gelatin: Plain or with allowed fruits

Ice cream, ice milk or sherbet: Plain without seeds or nuts (in moderation)

Puddings: Blanc mange, custards, junkets, etc. All plain without seeds or nuts

**Avoid:** All excessively sweet desserts. All containing nuts, seeds, etc.

## BEVERAGES

Coffee or tea, only if doctor approves

Decaffeinated coffee

Milk and milk drinks: Buttermilk, evaporated, skimmed, whole, yogurt, etc.

**Avoid:** Alcoholic beverages, carbonated beverages

## MISCELLANEOUS

Candy: Gum drops, hard candy, marshmallows, etc. (all in moderation)

Jellies: No jams or preserves

Seasonings: Allspice, cinnamon, lemon, mace, monosodium glutamate, paprika, parsley, sage, salt, thyme (all in moderation)

Sugar: Corn syrup, granulated sugar, honey, molasses, etc. (all in moderation)

**Avoid:** Condiments and highly seasoned foods

Gravies and all meat stocks

Nuts, salty foods—pickles, smoked fish, etc.

Seasonings: Particularly garlic, onion and pepper

LOW-RESIDUE DIET (for colitis and similar conditions):

Foods are extremely smooth and bland in consistency and form a minimum of residue in the large intestine. To choose meals, follow bland diet (page 254), but make the following adjustments:

## SOUPS

Meat-stock-based soups are allowed

## FISH, MEAT AND POULTRY

No changes

## CHEESE AND EGGS

No changes unless milk products are limited on diet. Check with physician

**Vegetables**

Omit all raw vegetables, spinach and squash

## BREADS AND CEREALS

No changes

## FATS

No changes

## FRUITS

Omit all raw fruits. Strain fruit juices

## DESSERTS

No changes unless milk products are limited on diet

## BEVERAGES

No changes unless milk products are limited on diet

(Check specifically with your doctor; milk and milk products are occasionally restricted on a low-residue diet. Include them unless specifically forbidden.)

## MISCELLANEOUS

Herbs and spices are allowed in moderation, with the following exceptions:
Any seeds or coarse leaves, garlic, mustard, onion and pepper

LOW-FAT, BLAND DIET (for gall bladder conditions):
Foods are bland in nature, and the total fat content of the diet is restricted. Choose meals from the following:

## SOUPS

Mildly seasoned meat-stock-based soups
Creamed soups prepared with skimmed milk and allowed vegetables
**Avoid:** Soups containing fat and forbidden foods

## FISH, MEAT AND POULTRY

Fish: Boned fish fillets or steaks from low-fat fish. Seafood prepared with allowed ingredients
Meat: Tender or well-cooked cuts of lean beef, lamb and veal
Variety meats low in fat, including heart, liver and sweetbreads
Poultry: Chicken, turkey and game birds prepared with allowed ingredients
**Avoid:** Fatty fish such as herring, mackerel, salmon, trout, etc.
Tough, stringy meat; fatty meats; highly seasoned, salted or smoked meats
Duck and goose

## CHEESE AND EGGS

Cheese: Cottage cheese (uncreamed cottage cheese allowed at all times; fat in creamed cottage cheese must be calculated into diet)
Eggs: Prepared with no added fat. Avoid egg yolks if they cause distress
**Avoid:** Cream cheese, hard cheeses
Fried eggs and egg yolks if necessary

## VEGETABLES

Tender, well-cooked asparagus, beets, carrots, green beans, green peas, mushrooms, potatoes (sweet and white), spinach (chopped), squash (acorn and yellow) and tomato juice
Lettuce or tomatoes with skin and seeds removed if doctor approves
**Avoid:** Strong-flavored vegetables: Brussels sprouts, cabbage, cauliflower, cucumber, onion, peppers, radishes, turnips
All raw vegetables (note exceptions above) and those containing seeds, skins or fibers

## BREADS AND CEREALS

Bread: Plain rolls, rye (without seeds), enriched white bread
Cereals: Cornflakes, puffed rice, rice flakes, farina, grits, strained oatmeal
Pastas: Macaroni, noodles, spaghetti, etc.
Specialty breads: Melba toast, rusk, saltines, soda crackers, zwieback
**Avoid:** Coarse-grained breads and cereals, hot breads, pretzels, salty crackers, sweet rolls

## FATS

Butter, cream, margarine, vegetable fats and oils—a maximum of 3 teaspoons a day
**Avoid:** Excessive fats, mineral oil, salad dressings

## FRUITS

Canned or cooked: Apricot, apple, peach and pear
Juices: Apple, apricot, grapefruit, lemon (in moderation), orange, pineapple and prune (in moderation)
Raw: Bananas
**Avoid:** All other raw fruits, avocado, fruits containing seeds, skins or fiber

## DESSERTS

Cakes: Angel-food cake only
Gelatin: Plain or with allowed fruits
Puddings: Plain puddings prepared with skimmed milk
Sherbet
**Avoid:** All desserts containing fats
All desserts containing nuts, seeds, etc.
All excessively sweet desserts

## BEVERAGES

Coffee or tea as doctor approves; no cream
Decaffeinated coffee; no cream

Milk and milk drinks: Buttermilk, skimmed milk, skimmed-milk yogurt

**Avoid:** Alcoholic and carbonated beverages
All beverages containing fat

## MISCELLANEOUS

Candy: Gum drops, hard candy, marshmallows, etc. (in moderation)

Jellies: No jams or preserves

Seasonings: Cinnamon, lemon, monosodium glutamate, nutmeg, oregano, paprika, poultry seasoning, sage, salt and thyme (all in moderation)

Sugar: Corn syrup, granulated sugar, honey, molasses, etc. (in moderation)

**Avoid:** Condiments and highly seasoned foods

Gravies and sauces rich in fat

Nuts, salty foods, pickles, smoked fish

Seasonings: Particularly garlic, onion and pepper

## A WEEK OF MENUS

### BREAKFAST

orange juice
baked eggs on toast
milk
coffee or tea*

orange-pineapple juice
oatmeal with brown sugar
toast with butter or jelly
milk

applesauce
cornflakes with bananas and sugar
milk

apricot nectar
scrambled eggs on toast with bacon
milk

canned whole apricots
soft-cooked eggs
English muffins with butter and jelly
milk

orange juice
cream of rice with light cream
toasted hard roll with butter
milk

sliced bananas in orange juice
shirred eggs
toasted French bread with butter
milk

### LUNCH OR SUPPER

pan-broiled minute steaks on open-faced sandwich
buttered green beans
tapioca pudding (topped with peach slices)
milk

* Use coffee or tea as recommended by physician.

cream-of-pea soup (made from pureed canned peas)
chicken sandwich on roll (with lettuce if allowed on diet)
purple plums
milk

scrambled egg-and-bacon sandwich on toast
canned apricots
milk

roast-beef sandwich on rye bread (with lettuce if allowed)
applesauce sprinkled with cinnamon
buttermilk

stew of hamburger, potatoes and peas
French bread and butter
raspberry applesauce
milk

cheese soufflé
chopped spinach
buttered refrigerated biscuits
Royal Anne cherries
milk

broiled hamburger on hard roll
buttered carrots
vanilla-rennet custard pudding
butterscotch cookies

### DINNER

oven-fried chicken parts
buttered peas
cranberry sauce
rice pudding

broiled minute veal steaks (sprinkled with mild Cheddar cheese)
buttered green beans and mushrooms
buttered rice
angel-food cake

meat loaf
baked potatoes with butter or sour cream
buttered Italian green beans
breadsticks
vanilla ice cream and raspberry sherbet
(mixed)

baked swordfish steaks
buttered carrots
buttered green beans
buttered clover-leaf roll
baked apple

broiled chicken livers (on toast points)
pan-sautéed mushroom slices
buttered peas
peach-and-cottage-cheese salad-dessert

broiled hamburgers (stuffed with cottage
cheese)
buttered whipped squash
buttered asparagus or green beans
buttered toast fingers
hot canned apricots (with vanilla wafers)

leg of lamb (with pear halves filled with
jelly)
buttered beets
buttered parslied potatoes
fruited gelatin

## LOW-RESIDUE DIET

Follow menus as given but:
strain fruit juices
use pureed vegetables if necessary
add seasonings as allowed on diet

## LOW-FAT, BLAND (GALL BLADDER) DIET

Follow menus as given but:
use skimmed milk in place of whole
omit eggs and bacon (substitute hot and
cold cereals or cottage cheese)
omit buttering of foods, or limit as diet
prescribes
prepare puddings with skimmed milk
substitute bread or plain rolls for quick
breads
omit cheese (except cottage cheese) and
sour cream
substitute sherbet for ice cream

## BLAND, LOW-RESIDUE AND GALL-BLADDER DIETS: 24 Recipes for Main Dishes

### STEAK ROLL-UPS (bland and low-residue diets)

4 slices white bread, cut into
    small cubes
1 egg
¼ teaspoon ground sage
¼ teaspoon ground thyme
salt
2 pounds round steak, cut into
    6 pieces, ¼-inch thick
2 tablespoons butter or mar-
    garine
1 10½-ounce can condensed
    cream-of-mushroom soup
1 4-ounce can mushrooms,
    drained (optional)
½ cup plain yogurt (optional)

About 1 hour and 30 minutes before serving: In medium bowl, combine bread cubes, egg, sage, thyme and ½ teaspoon salt. Place ⅓ cup bread mixture down center of each steak; roll; secure with toothpicks or skewers.

In medium skillet over medium heat, in heated butter, brown roll-ups; remove to plate. Pour soup and ½ cup water into skillet; heat to boiling, stirring occasionally. Return roll-ups to skillet; cook, covered, over low heat 1 hour, or until meat is tender.

Occasionally spoon sauce over meat. Place meat on warm platter; remove toothpicks. To sauce in skillet, add mushrooms and yogurt; heat. Spoon sauce over roll-ups. Makes 6 servings.

### POLISH VEAL SCALLOPS (bland, low-residue and gall bladder* diets)

1 20-ounce can sliced apples
2 tablespoons butter or mar-
    garine
1 pound veal cutlets
¼ cup packed brown sugar
1 tablespoon flour
½ teaspoon cinnamon
½ teaspoon allspice

About 30 minutes before serving: Drain apples, reserving syrup. In large skillet over medium heat, in butter, brown veal on both sides; place on warm platter. Add reserved syrup to skillet. Stir in sugar, flour, cinnamon and allspice; cook until slightly thickened. Return veal to skillet; add apple slices and simmer, covered, 5 minutes. Makes 4 servings.

* 15 grams fat per serving.

### RICE-A-ROUND LAMB STEW (bland, low-residue and gall bladder* diets)

2 pounds lean lamb stew meat
1 tablespoon salad oil
½ pound mushrooms, sliced
3 tablespoons parsley flakes
1 teaspoon ground sage
2 teaspoons salt
5 carrots, diced
4 cups hot cooked rice
1 10-ounce package frozen
    peas, cooked and drained (or
    1 16-ounce can peas,
    drained)
flour or cornstarch to thicken
    gravy

About 1 hour and 45 minutes before serving: In large saucepan over medium heat, in oil, brown meat. Add 2 cups water, one-half mushrooms, parsley, sage and salt. Simmer, covered, 1 hour. Add carrots and remaining mushrooms; cook 15 minutes, or until meat and vegetables are fork-tender.

Grease 1½-quart ring mold. Combine rice and peas; pack into mold; then unmold onto warm large platter. With slotted spoon, spoon stew into center and around rice ring. If desired, thicken liquid with flour or cornstarch. Serve as gravy. Makes 6 to 8 servings.

* 15 grams fat per serving.

## SAUCY SWEDISH MEATBALLS (bland and low-residue diets)

2 pounds ground round steak
½ cup unseasoned dried
  bread crumbs
tomato juice
1 teaspoon salt
2 eggs
2 tablespoons salad oil
1 tablespoon cornstarch
¼ to ½ cup sour cream
hot cooked noodles or rice

About 45 minutes before serving: In medium bowl, mix meat, bread crumbs, ½ cup tomato juice, salt and eggs. Form into 24 meatballs. In large skillet, in oil, brown well on all sides; remove from skillet; pour off remaining oil. Return meatballs to skillet; add 2 cups tomato juice; cover; boil gently 30 minutes, or until meat is done and tender.

Meanwhile, mix cornstarch with ¼ cup water to form a smooth paste. Remove meatballs to warm platter. Stir cornstarch mixture into tomato juice until sauce is thickened and smooth.

Remove skillet from heat. Stir in sour cream until just smooth. Do not boil. Use as gravy for meatballs, served with noodles or rice. Makes 6 servings.

## PEEKABOO BURGER (bland and low-residue diets)

1½ pounds ground round
  steak
5 eggs
salt
¼ teaspoon ground sage
¼ teaspoon ground thyme
½ cup unseasoned packaged
  dried bread crumbs
¼ cup tomato juice
1½ cups sifted all-purpose
  flour
1½ teaspoons double-acting
  baking powder
1½ cups milk
3 tablespoons melted butter or
  margarine

About 1 hour and 30 minutes before serving: Preheat oven to 350°F. Grease 13" by 9" baking pan. In medium bowl, combine ground round, 1 egg, 1 teaspoon salt, sage, thyme, bread crumbs and tomato juice. Shape mixture into 24 small meatballs; place in 4 rows in baking pan. On waxed paper, sift together flour, baking powder and 1 teaspoon salt. In medium bowl, beat 4 eggs until foamy; beat in milk and butter. Beat in flour mixture until smooth. Pour over meatballs. Bake 50 to 60 minutes, or until lightly browned on top. Remove from oven and allow to stand 5 minutes before serving. Makes 8 servings.

## HAMBURG DUMPLING STEW (bland and low-residue diets)

1 pound ground round steak
salt
flour
½ teaspoon ground sage
1 tablespoon granulated sugar
1 20-ounce can tomato juice
2 teaspoons double-acting
  baking powder
2 tablespoons butter or margarine
½ cup milk

About 40 minutes before serving: In large skillet, brown round with 1 teaspoon salt; stir in 1 tablespoon flour. Add sage, sugar and tomato juice; cover; simmer gently 10 minutes.

Meanwhile, in medium bowl, sift together 1 cup sifted flour, baking powder and ¼ teaspoon salt. Cut in butter or margarine until like coarse corn meal; stir in milk to make a soft dough. Make 4 dumplings by dropping dollops of dough into hot hamburg mixture; cover; simmer 14 minutes. Serve in soup bowls with dumplings on top. Makes 4 servings.

## OVEN-BAKED CRANBERRY POT ROAST (bland, low-residue and gall bladder* diets)

1 pound top-round beef, cut
  ½- to ¾-inch thick
2 tablespoons salad oil
1 tablespoon flour
1 7-ounce can jellied cranberry
  sauce
½ teaspoon salt
1 tablespoon granulated sugar
3 medium potatoes, quartered

About 2 hours before serving: Preheat oven to 350°F. Trim fat from beef; cut into 3 serving portions. In ovenproof skillet, in oil, brown meat on both sides; mix 1 tablespoon flour with oil in pan. Mash cranberry sauce into small pieces; then add, with ½ cup water, salt and sugar, to meat. Bake, covered, 30 minutes; then add potatoes and turn meat. Bake 1 hour longer, or until potatoes and meat are tender. Makes 3 servings.

* 15 grams fat per serving.

## BRAISED CHICKEN LIVERS (bland, low-residue and gall bladder* diets)

1 pound fresh chicken livers (or frozen livers, thawed)
¼ cup flour
½ teaspoon salt
1 tablespoon salad oil
⅔ to 1 cup canned tomato juice
4 slices toast, quartered

About 30 minutes before serving: Remove any fat from livers. Toss livers with flour, mixed with salt, to just coat; shake off excess. In medium skillet, in oil, brown livers well on both sides. Pour off any oil remaining in skillet. Add tomato juice; cover; boil gently 10 minutes, or until livers are done and tomato sauce has thickened slightly.

To serve: Cover toast points with livers and sauce. Makes 4 servings.

* 10 grams fat per serving.

## BROILED CHICKEN BREASTS (bland, low-residue and gall bladder* diets)

3 whole chicken breasts, halved (about 3 pounds)
salad oil
salt
paprika or monosodium gluta-mate

About 60 minutes before serving: Preheat broiler 10 minutes if manufacturer directs. Remove rack from broiler pan, then line pan with foil. Arrange halved chicken breasts, skin side down, in pan. Brush with salad oil; sprinkle with salt and paprika or monosodium glutamate. Place pan in broiler so surface of chicken is 7 to 9 inches from heat. If it is impossible to place broiler pan this low in your range, lower heat. (If broiler-oven is thermostatically controlled, turn temperature to about 350°F.) Broil chicken 30 minutes on one side; turn; brush with salad oil; sprinkle with salt and paprika; then broil 15 to 20 minutes, or until fork-tender, nicely browned and crisp. Makes 6 servings.

* 5 grams fat per serving. Don't eat chicken skin.

## CHICKEN AND SHRIMP ON RICE (bland, low-residue and gall bladder* diets)

½ cup flour
1 teaspoon ground thyme
1 teaspoon salt
4 whole chicken breasts (about 3 pounds), split, skinned and boned
3 tablespoons salad oil
2 cups uncooked long-grain rice
1 19-ounce can tomato juice
¼ cup parsley flakes
2 7-ounce packages frozen shelled, deveined shrimp, thawed and drained

About 30 minutes before serving: On waxed paper, mix flour, thyme and salt. Dip chicken in mixture to coat. In large skillet, in oil, brown chicken on all sides. Pour off any excess oil.

Meanwhile, cook rice as label directs. Add tomato juice and parsley flakes to chicken in skillet; cover; simmer 10 minutes. Add shrimp; simmer 5 minutes more, or until shrimp curl and turn pink. Add salt to taste. Serve on rice. Makes 6 to 8 servings.

* 10 grams fat per serving.

## SPANISH CHICKEN AND EGGPLANT (bland and gall bladder* diets)

1 teaspoon salt
½ teaspoon ground thyme
1 small or ½ medium eggplant, peeled and thinly sliced
1 8-ounce can tomato sauce
1 9-ounce package frozen whole green beans, separated
2 chicken breasts, split and skinned

About 1 hour and 15 minutes before serving: Preheat oven to 350°F. Mix salt and thyme. In greased casserole, layer eggplant, half of tomato sauce, half of seasoning mixture, green beans and chicken; top with remaining tomato sauce and seasonings. Bake, covered, 1 hour. Makes 4 servings.

* 10 grams fat per serving.

## CHICKEN-AND-SWEET-POTATO SHORTCAKE (bland and low-residue diets)

2 cups sifted all-purpose flour
1 tablespoon granulated sugar
2½ teaspoons double-acting
   baking powder
1½ teaspoons salt
¼ cup shortening
½ cup mashed sweet potatoes
1 cup milk
1 10½-ounce can condensed
   cream-of-chicken soup
1 cup cubed cooked chicken
paprika for garnish

About 40 minutes before serving: Preheat oven to 450° F. In medium bowl, sift together 1½ cups flour, sugar, baking powder and salt; with pastry blender or 2 knives used scissor fashion, cut in shortening until mixture resembles coarse crumbs.

In small bowl, combine sweet potatoes and ½ cup milk; stir into flour mixture just until dry ingredients are moistened. Place remaining flour on work surface and knead dough about 10 times. Roll dough ¼-inch thick; fold in half. Cut 6 biscuits with 3-inch round cutter. Place, almost touching, on ungreased cookie sheet; bake 15 to 20 minutes, or until golden brown.

In medium saucepan over medium heat, stir ½ cup milk, undiluted soup and chicken until boiling. Split biscuits; top with chicken mixture. Sprinkle with paprika. Makes 6 servings.

## BAKED CHICKEN CASSEROLE (bland and low-residue diets)

½ 8-ounce package elbow
   macaroni (about 1 cup)
2 tablespoons butter or margarine
2 tablespoons flour
1½ cups milk
½ teaspoon salt
½ teaspoon ground thyme
¼ teaspoon paprika
1 cup grated mild Cheddar
   cheese
1 8-ounce can sliced carrots,
   drained
1 8-ounce can peas, drained
2 cups cubed cooked chicken

About 45 minutes before serving: Preheat oven to 350°F. Cook macaroni as label directs; drain. Meanwhile, in small saucepan, melt butter or margarine. Stir in flour, then slowly add milk, salt, thyme and paprika. Cook, stirring constantly, until thickened. Stir in ½ cup cheese until just melted.

In 2-quart casserole, toss together drained macaroni, cheese sauce, carrots, peas and chicken. Top with remaining cheese. Cover; bake 20 minutes. Makes 4 servings.

## CHICKEN-MUSHROOM SOUFFLÉ (bland and low-residue diets)

3 tablespoons butter or margarine
¼ cup flour
1 cup milk
½ cup chopped fresh mush-
   rooms
1 cup finely diced cooked
   chicken
½ teaspoon celery salt
½ teaspoon salt
4 eggs, separated

About 1 hour before serving: Preheat oven to 350°F. Grease 1½-quart casserole. In medium saucepan, melt butter; stir in flour. Stirring constantly, add milk and cook until thickened and smooth. Stir in mushrooms, chicken, celery salt and salt until smooth; stir in egg yolks.

In large bowl, beat egg whites until stiff peaks form. Fold chicken mixture into egg whites. Turn into casserole; bake 45 to 55 minutes, or until soufflé is golden-brown. Serve immediately. Makes 4 servings.

## LIVER-AND-RICE SKILLET DINNER (bland and low-residue diets)

1/4 pound sliced bacon
1 pound fresh chicken livers
  (or frozen livers, thawed)
1 cup uncooked long-grain rice
3 tablespoons chopped parsley
2 or 3 carrots, thinly sliced
1/4 teaspoon salt
1 teaspoon ground thyme

About 40 minutes before serving: In medium skillet, fry bacon until crisp; remove; drain and crumble. In bacon fat in same skillet, sauté livers until brown but still slightly pink in center; remove. Add rice, parsley, carrots, salt, thyme, crumbled bacon and 2½ cups water to skillet; bring water to boiling; add livers; cover; cook 14 minutes, or until rice is tender and most of the water absorbed. Makes 4 to 6 servings.

## DEVONSHIRE DEVILED CRAB (low-residue diet)

1 cup milk
2 tablespoons flour
1 chicken-bouillon cube
2 hard-cooked eggs, chopped
3 slices day-old bread, finely
  cubed
1 cup grated raw carrots
2 6½- to 7½-ounce cans King
  crab, drained (or 2 6-ounce
  packages frozen King crab,
  thawed, drained)
1 tablespoon butter or margarine

About 50 minutes before serving: Preheat oven to 350°F. In medium saucepan, slowly stir milk into flour to form a smooth paste; add chicken bouillon. Cook, stirring constantly, until thickened. Stir in eggs, 2 slices cubed bread, carrots and crab. Turn mixture into 1-quart casserole; sprinkle with remaining cubed bread; dot with butter or margarine. Bake 30 to 35 minutes, or until bread crumbs are dark golden-brown. Makes 4 servings of about 1 cup each.

## CRAB AND DUMPLINGS (bland and low-residue diets)

2 tablespoons butter or margarine
2 tablespoons flour
½ teaspoon salt
1½ cups milk
1¼ cups shredded American
  cheese
1 6½- to 7½-ounce can King
  crab, drained and flaked (or
  1 6-ounce package frozen
  King crab, thawed and
  drained)
1 cup sifted all-purpose flour
2 teaspoons double-acting baking powder
½ teaspoon salt
2 tablespoons shortening

About 1 hour before serving: Preheat oven to 450°F. In double boiler over boiling water, melt butter or margarine. Stir in 2 tablespoons flour and salt until blended; add 1 cup milk and cook, stirring, until thickened. Stir in 1 cup cheese until melted; add crabmeat. Pour mixture into 1½-quart casserole. Sift together 1 cup flour, baking powder and salt; with pastry blender, or 2 knives used scissor-fashion, cut in shortening until mixture resembles coarse crumbs. Stir in remaining ¼ cup cheese. Add ½ cup milk and mix, just until moistened. Drop mixture by teaspoonfuls on top of crab mixture. Bake 25 minutes, or until dumplings are dark golden-brown. Makes 6 to 8 servings.

## SALMON BALLS (bland and low-residue diets)

1 cup instant potato flakes
1 7¾-ounce can salmon,
  drained, boned and flaked
2 eggs
1 teaspoon salt
½ teaspoon ground thyme
¼ cup unseasoned packaged
  dried-bread crumbs

About 45 minutes before serving: Preheat oven to 375°F. Lightly grease medium baking pan. In medium bowl, combine potato flakes with ¾ cup boiling water. Stir in salmon, then beat in eggs, salt and thyme until fluffy. Shape mixture in 4 to 6 balls (mixture may be sticky). Roll in bread crumbs until well coated. Place in pan; bake 30 minutes, or until light brown. Makes 4 servings.

## NEPTUNE KABOBS (bland and low-residue diets)

**1 pint shucked oysters (about one dozen)**
**1 pound fresh large shrimp, shelled and deveined**
**½ pound bacon**
**½ pound small mushrooms**
**salad oil**
**2 cups hot buttered rice**

About 45 minutes before serving: Wash oysters, removing sand and pieces of shell; rinse shrimp. Cook bacon until almost crisp; cut in half crosswise. Wrap some shrimp and oysters with bacon; hold in place with toothpicks.

Preheat broiler 10 minutes if manufacturer directs. Thread six 8-inch skewers alternately with wrapped shrimp, mushrooms and oysters. (For non-dieters in family, also include cherry tomatoes and small canned onions on kabobs, if desired.) Brush generously with salad oil.

Broil, 3 to 4 inches from heat, 4 to 5 minutes; turn; brush again with oil and broil other side for 4 minutes more, or until oysters are tender but still moist, shrimp have turned pink and bacon is crisp; remove toothpicks. Serve on rice. Makes 3 to 4 servings.

## BAKED FLOUNDER, SOUTHERN STYLE (bland and low-residue diets)

**8 strips bacon**
**4 small fresh flounder fillets (about 1½ pounds)\***
**salt**
**lemon juice**

About 40 minutes before serving: Preheat oven to 375°F. Cook bacon until almost crisp; drain. Place two strips bacon along length of each flounder fillet. Roll up; place, seam side down, in medium baking dish. Cover; bake 20 to 25 minutes, or until fish flakes easily with fork. Sprinkle with salt and lemon juice to taste. Makes 4 servings.

\* Or use 1 16-ounce package frozen flounder fillets. Thaw as label directs; roll each fillet with bacon and bake as directed above.

## BAKED FISH WITH SOUR CREAM (bland, low-residue and gall bladder\* diets)

**1 16-ounce package frozen fish fillets, thawed**
**½ teaspoon salt**
**½ cup sour cream**
**1 teaspoon parsley flakes**
**¼ teaspoon paprika**

About 40 minutes before serving: Preheat oven to 350°F. Grease medium baking pan. Sprinkle fish fillets with salt; place in single layer in baking pan. Spread with sour cream; sprinkle with parsley and paprika. Bake, covered, 30 minutes, or till fish flakes easily with fork. Makes 3 to 4 servings.

\* Prepare as directed but use vanilla yogurt instead of sour cream. 2 grams fat per serving.

## BREADED CHEESE SOUFFLÉ (bland and low-residue diets)

1 cup milk
1 tablespoon butter or margarine
1/4 teaspoon salt
1 1/2 cups fresh bread crumbs
1 1/2 cups (about 6 ounces) shredded process Cheddar cheese
3 eggs, separated

About 1 hour and 5 minutes before serving: Preheat oven to 375°F. Place large pan, filled 1/2-inch deep with hot water, in oven.

In medium saucepan, scald milk; add butter and salt; stir to melt butter. Remove from heat; stir in bread crumbs and cheese until melted; stir in egg yolks.

In medium bowl, beat egg whites until stiff peaks form. Fold milk-bread mixture into whites. Pour into 2-quart casserole. Bake, in pan of hot water, 45 minutes, or until nicely browned. Serve immediately. Makes 4 servings.

## EGGS MORNAY (bland and low-residue diets)

2 tablespoons butter or margarine
2 tablespoons flour
1/2 teaspoon salt
1/2 teaspoon paprika
1 1/2 cups milk
1 cup shredded American cheese (4 ounces)
8 eggs

About 1 hour before serving: Preheat oven to 350°F. Grease four 10-ounce custard cups. In double boiler, over boiling water, melt butter; stir in flour, salt and paprika until blended; stir in milk. Stirring constantly, cook until thickened. Add cheese; stir until melted and well blended. In each custard cup, pour thin layer of sauce; top with 2 eggs. Add remaining sauce, leaving yolks partially uncovered. Bake 20 to 25 minutes, or until eggs are of desired doneness. Makes 4 servings.

## LINGUINI ALFREDO (Alfred's linguine) (bland and low-residue diets)

1 8-ounce package linguine (very thin, flat spaghetti)
1/4 pound butter or margarine, softened
3 tablespoons heavy or whipping cream
1/2 cup grated Parmesan cheese
salt to taste

About 30 minutes before serving: Cook linguine as label directs; drain; keep warm. Meanwhile, cream butter with heavy cream and Parmesan cheese until light, fluffy and smooth.

To serve: Toss linguine with butter mixture. Sprinkle with salt to taste. Makes 6 appetizer servings or 3 main-dish servings.

# DIABETIC DIET

The meal plan used by diabetics is a typical diet grounded on the Basic Four building blocks (see page 37), with the following exceptions: pure sugar is reduced to a minimum; other forms of carbohydrate are divided among the three meals and one or two snacks; the diet is slightly restricted in fat content to 30 to 35 percent of the calories from fat.

A number of years ago the American Dietetic Association, American Diabetes Association and the Public Health Service developed the exchange system, a simplified form of diet calculation which virtually eliminated the need to weigh foods. This system is based on the fact that similar foods (the fruits as a group, for example), in varying amounts, are virtually identical in calories and the other nutrients calculated in the diabetic's diet—protein, fat and carbohydrate—and can therefore be exchanged for one another. The system is built on the seven food categories listed below. One serving in each category contains approximately the same number of calories and the same amount of protein, fat or carbohydrate.

Meat: 7 grams protein, 5 grams fat

Vegetables:
"A" vegetables: virtually no calories or protein, fat or carbohydrate
"B" vegetables: 2 grams protein, 7 grams carbohydrate
Bread and cereals: 2 grams protein, 15 grams carbohydrate
Fruit: 10 grams carbohydrate
Fat: 5 grams fat
Milk: 8 grams protein, 10 grams fat, 12 grams carbohydrate
"Free": Like "A" vegetables, these contain too few nutrients to need to be counted.

The diabetic's diet prescription is determined by taking the estimated number of calories he needs each day, based on sex, age, activity and current weight, and dividing them among the three nutrient groups, allowing 15 to 20 percent for protein, 30 to 35 percent for fat, and 45 to 55 percent for carbohydrate. This gives a diet prescription which might look like this: Calories 1500, protein 70 grams, fat 65 grams, carbohydrate 150 grams. The dietitian takes this prescription, and after discussing the individual's food preferences, devises a meal plan which allows the patient to enjoy his regular foods as much as possible, yet keep a good nutritional balance. A typical meal plan might look like this:

Breakfast:

1 fruit, 1 meat, 1 bread, 1 fat and 1 milk exchange.

Lunch:

2 meat, 1 "A" vegetable, 2 bread, 1 fat, 1 fruit and ½ milk exchange

Dinner:

3 meat, 1 or 2 "A" vegetables, 1 "B" vegetable, 2 bread, 1 fat and 1 fruit exchange.

Snack:

½ milk and 1 bread exchange

The next step is to go to the lists of foods in each "exchange" group and choose the meals for the day. A typical simple menu might include:

Breakfast:

½ cup orange juice (1 fruit), 1 poached egg (1 meat) on 1 slice toast (1 bread), 2 strips bacon (1 fat) and 1 cup milk (1 milk). (Coffee or tea sweetened with saccharin can be "freely" added to the menu.)

Lunch:

Sandwich: 1 slice ham (1 meat) and 1 slice cheese (1 meat) on 2 slices rye bread (2 bread) spread with 1 teaspoon butter (1 fat), lettuce (1 "A" vegetable), 1 apple (1 fruit) and ½ cup milk (½ milk).

Dinner:

3 ounces broiled halibut (3 meat) topped with lemon and tomato slices (1 "free" and 1 "A" vegetable), 1 large baked potato (2 bread) with 1 tablespoon sour cream (1 fat), carrot sticks (1 "B" vegetable) and dietetic gelatin dessert with ½ banana (1 fruit).

Snack:

10 oyster crackers (1 bread) and ½ cup milk (½ milk).

Unfortunately, far too many diabetics limit their meal planning to very basic meals of this type. With a good collection of recipes like those that follow, and no more effort, the variety of meals can be infinite. Each of the "diabetic" exchanges per serving is marked. Use them to fit the recipes into your diet outline.

To add full variety to the recipes allowed on the diet, the exchanges for the recipes have been calculated to allow full accuracy in the exchange system with a minimum of restriction in foods used in recipes. The protein, fat and carbohydrate values for all the ingredient foods are totaled, and divided by the number of servings (fractional amounts are ignored). Then the exchanges are assigned, keeping in mind the classifications of the ingredient foods. For example:

| POTATO SOUP WITH OREGANO | protein (grams) | fat (grams) | carbohydrate (grams) |
|---|---|---|---|
| 1 10¼-ounce can frozen cream-of-potato soup | 8 | 13 | 30 |
| 1¼ cups skim milk | 11 | — | 15 |
| total | 19 | 13 | 45 |
| divided by 3 servings | 6 | 4 | 15 |
| Exchanges:  ½ milk | 4 | 5 | 6 |
|       ½ bread | 1 | – | 7 |
| | 5 | 5 | 13 |

There are 2 grams of carbohydrate left over, but this small amount is not significant. The individual food items that go into the bread exchanges vary from about 12 grams carbohydrate (1 slice bread) to 22 (½ cup rice) per serving. The system assumes that the highs and lows balance one another out by the end of the day.

## How to Use Saccharin

To determine the amount of saccharin to use in a recipe, check the label for the amount equivalent to 1 cup of sugar. Then calculate, by proportions, the amount to use. For example, if a recipe calls for saccharin equivalent to 1½ cups sugar and 1 tablespoon of saccharin is equivalent to ½ cup sugar, three times as much (3 tablespoons) would be needed for sweetness equal to 1½ cups sugar.

To help to make the calculations, use the table below:

    3 teaspoons   = 1 tablespoon
    4 tablespoons = ¼ cup
    16 tablespoons = 1 cup
    48 teaspoons   = 1 cup

Cyclamate-based sweeteners are no longer available but saccharin is available in three forms—tablets, granulated and liquid.* The granulated and liquid forms are easier to measure and mix in the quantities needed for cooking. Saccharin may be substituted for sugar for use in beverages, on cereals, and in most puddings. Brands vary in sweetening power or concentration so the levels used in the "diabetic" recipes are given in terms of sugar equivalents. Special recipes are needed for cakes, cookies and most baked goods and for sugar-free jellies, candies, etc. (see pages 270–277).

* Some sweeteners are a mixture of nutritive (sugar or a near relative) and saccharin. They should not be used by a diabetic, unless doctor approves.

## CUES FOR COOKING AND PLANNING MEALS

*Planning Meals:*

- Plan meals several days at a time to assure variety, and to make shopping easier. One way to do this is to prepare homemade TV dinners containing the meat, vegetables and bread exchanges called for on the menu outline, then freeze them. Also, have treats ready to serve in a few minutes by freezing extra servings of sugar-free cake or cookies.
- Follow your physician's or dietitian's advice in using convenience foods. Don't assume a "dietetic" food is fine for a diabetic.
- In addition to the recipes in this book, make use of the recipe booklets published by the manufacturers of saccharin and of sugar-free products. These include exchanges per serving.
- Exchanges are based on accurate servings. Divide recipes carefully into the exact number of servings specified. To simplify the problem, try preparing casserole dishes in individual serving casseroles.
- As a rule, meat, fish and poultry shrink about 25 percent during cooking, so 4 ounces of uncooked meat gives 3 ounces of cooked.

*Vegetables:*

- If it is difficult to include a "B" vegetable each day, substitute ½ bread exchange. For example: ½ slice bread equals 1 "B" vegetable. Limit the "A" vegetables at a meal to 1 cup cooked vegetables or 2 cups raw.
- For a richer flavor, with no added fat, add a bouillon cube to cooking water for vegetables and pastas.
- Try vegetable- as well as beef- and chicken-flavored bouillon cubes or powder. Count as a "free" exchange.

*Milk:*

- If diet plan calls for whole milk, substitute skimmed milk, and then add 2 fat exchanges to meal.
- Use evaporated skimmed milk in place of regular evaporated milk in cooking. Count ½ cup (undiluted) as 1 skimmed-milk exchange.

*Desserts:*

- Try unsweetened canned pineapple packed in juice rather than water—the flavor is fuller and delightfully tart.
- Make homemade rennet custard pudding by using plain rennet tablets (not pudding mix); prepare as directed, but instead of sugar, try saccharin equivalent to ¼ cup sugar for each 2 cups milk.
- Look for unsweetened frozen strawberries, cherries, raspberries and blackberries. They thaw to form their own syrup.

*Miscellaneous:*

- Flavor plain yogurt with dietetic jams or jellies. Or make coffee or vanilla yogurt by adding coffee powder or vanilla extract and saccharin to taste. One cup (8 ounces) equals 1 skimmed milk exchange.
- Low-calorie mayonnaises contain some fat. Count 1½ tablespoons as 1 fat exchange.
- Diet margarine has half the fat of regular margarine—2 teaspoons equal 1 fat exchange.
- Use the low-calorie pourable dressings (up to 2 tablespoons) as a "free" exchange.
- Try the aromatic teas. They don't need sweetening to have a full, mellow flavor.

DIABETIC DIET: 23 Recipes for Sugar-Free Desserts, Jams and Jellies

### BIG ORANGE-CHIFFON CAKE (exchanges per serving = 1 bread and 1 fat)

8 egg whites
5 egg yolks
2¼ cups sifted cake flour
3 teaspoons double-acting
  baking powder
1 teaspoon salt
3 tablespoons orange peel
orange juice
saccharin equivalent to 1½
  cups sugar
½ teaspoon cream of tartar
½ cup salad oil

At least 3 hours before serving: Place egg whites in large bowl, yolks in small bowl; let warm to room temperature. Meanwhile, in medium bowl, sift together flour, baking powder and salt. Finely grate 3 tablespoons orange peel. Squeeze enough orange juice to mix with saccharin to make ¾ cup of liquid.

When ready to bake cake: Preheat oven to 325°F. Rinse 9-inch square cake pan; shake out excess water. Add cream of tartar to egg whites in large bowl and beat, with electric mixer at highest speed, until very stiff peaks form. (They should be stiffer than for angel-food cake or meringue.) Then make well in center of sifted dry ingredients; add salad oil, egg yolks, juice-saccharin mixture and orange peel. Stir to blend; beat, with mixer at medium speed, 1 minute. Slowly add yolk-orange mixture to whites; fold together until smooth. Pour into cake pan. Bake 35 minutes, or until cake tester, inserted in center, comes out clean. Invert pan to cool cake.

After 20 minutes, remove cake from pan by cutting around edge with knife. With fingertips, gently pull cake away from edge of pan, lifting slightly to loosen bottom. Turn onto rack to cool completely. Makes 16 servings.

### BANANA CREAM CAKE (exchanges per serving = 1 bread and 3 fat)

Big Orange-Chiffon Cake batter
  (see recipe above)
1 cup heavy cream
liquid saccharin equivalent to 2
  tablespoons sugar
2 medium bananas
juice of half a lemon

At least 4 hours before serving: Prepare cake batter as directed, but bake for 30 minutes at 325°F. in 2 rinsed 8-inch round layer-cake pans. Cool and remove from pans as directed.

About 30 minutes before serving: In chilled bowl, whip cream and saccharin. Into medium bowl, peel and thinly slice bananas; add lemon juice and enough water to cover completely. Thoroughly drain banana slices on paper toweling. Place cake layer on cake plate; **lightly** frost with whipped cream; cover with single layer of sliced bananas. Add second cake layer; frost sides, then top, with remaining whipped cream. Circle top of cake with rest of banana slices; refrigerate until serving time. Makes 16 servings.

### CHOCOLATE-SPICE COOKIES (exchanges for 3 cookies = ½ bread and 1 fat)

⅓ cup butter or margarine
1 cup sifted cake flour
¼ teaspoon double-acting
  baking powder
2 tablespoons cocoa
¼ teaspoon salt
1 tablespoon water
granulated saccharin equivalent
  to ⅓ cup sugar
½ teaspoon cinnamon
1 teaspoon vanilla extract

At least 2 hours before serving: Preheat oven to 375°F. In medium bowl, with electric mixer, cream butter until light and fluffy. Stir together cake flour, baking powder, cocoa and salt; blend into butter until smooth. Mix water, saccharin, cinnamon and vanilla; beat into flour-butter mixture until smooth. (Dough will be very stiff.) Shape into balls a scant ¾ inch in diameter. Place on cookie sheet and flatten with fork that has been dipped into cold water. Bake 15 minutes, or until cookies seem "set." Remove from sheet; cool. Makes about 2 dozen.

## BROWNIES (exchanges per brownie = ½ bread and 2 fat)

½ cup butter or margarine
saccharin equivalent to ¾ cup
    sugar
2 squares unsweetened choco-
    late, melted
2 eggs
½ teaspoon vanilla extract
¾ cup sifted all-purpose flour
1 teaspoon double-acting
    baking powder
½ cup chopped walnuts

About 1 hour before serving: Preheat oven to 350°F. In large bowl, cream butter and saccharin until light and fluffy; add chocolate; beat until smooth. Beat in eggs and vanilla; beat in flour, baking powder and walnuts. Spread batter in greased 8-inch square pan. Bake 30 minutes, or until surface is shiny. Cool in pan; cut into 16 pieces.

## ORANGE NUT COOKIES (exchanges for 2 cookies = ½ bread and 1 fat)

¼ cup butter or margarine
granulated saccharin equivalent
    to ¼ cup sugar
½ teaspoon orange extract
½ teaspoon vanilla extract
1 cup sifted cake flour
½ teaspoon double-acting
    baking powder
¼ teaspoon salt
¼ cup finely chopped pecans
1 tablespoon finely grated
    orange peel

About 6 hours before serving: In medium bowl, cream butter with saccharin, 2 tablespoons hot water, orange and vanilla extracts until fluffy. Combine flour, baking powder and salt, then add pecans and orange peel; blend with butter mixture until smooth. Shape dough into long roll about 5″ by 1½″; wrap in waxed paper and refrigerate until well chilled.

About 1 hour before serving: Preheat oven to 400°F. Lightly grease cookie sheet. Cut roll into 24 cookies, each about ⅛-inch thick. Bake, on cookie sheet, 12 to 15 minutes, or until brown around edges. Makes about 2 dozen.

## STRAWBERRY-GLAZED CHEESECAKE (exchanges per serving = 2 meat and 1 fruit)

Cornflake Crust (see recipe
    below)
3 envelopes unflavored gelatin
saccharin
1 cup orange juice
1 teaspoon grated lemon peel
2 tablespoons lemon juice
2 8-ounce containers creamed
    cottage cheese
¾ cup heavy cream
3 egg whites
¼ teaspoon salt
2 cups hulled fresh straw-
    berries, partially crushed (or
    2 cups frozen unsweetened
    whole strawberries, thawed,
    then crushed slightly)

At least 6 hours before serving: Prepare Cornflake Crust as directed but press in bottom of 8-inch square cake pan; bake and cool as directed. In medium saucepan, mix 2 envelopes gelatin, granulated or liquid saccharin equivalent to ½ cup sugar, orange juice, lemon peel and juice; let stand 5 minutes to soften gelatin. Meanwhile, sieve cottage cheese. Heat mixture until gelatin is dissolved; beat in cottage cheese and heavy cream. Refrigerate until the consistency of soft pudding.

In medium bowl, beat egg whites with salt until stiff peaks form. Fold in gelatin mixture. Turn into cooled crumb mixture; smooth surface. Refrigerate until set.

While cheesecake is setting, prepare strawberry glaze. In medium saucepan, mix 1½ teaspoons gelatin with ¼ cup water and saccharin equivalent to 2 tablespoons sugar. Let stand 5 minutes, then bring just to simmer. Stir in crushed strawberries. Pour glaze over cake and gently spread with spatula to edges. Refrigerate until completely set—about 3 hours. Makes 9 servings.

## CORNFLAKE CRUST (exchanges per ⅛ crust = ½ bread and 1 fat)

3 tablespoons butter or mar-
    garine
liquid saccharin equivalent to 1
    tablespoon sugar
¾ cup packaged cornflake
    crumbs

At least 1 hour before filling: Preheat oven to 375°F. In 9-inch pie plate, mix all ingredients, then press on sides and up edges of pie plate. Bake 8 minutes; cool, then fill as desired.

## CHOCOLATE CHIFFON PIE (exchanges per serving = 1 meat, 1 bread and 2 fat)

Cornflake Crust (see recipe
    page 271)
1 4-serving envelope dietetic-
    pack chocolate-pudding mix
⅓ cup cocoa
2 envelopes unflavored gelatin
1¾ cups skimmed milk or re-
    liquefied nonfat dry milk
saccharin equivalent to ½
    cup sugar
3 egg whites
1 cup heavy cream

About 4 hours before serving: Mix, bake and cool Cornflake Crust as recipe directs. In medium saucepan, mix pudding mix, cocoa and gelatin. Stirring constantly, slowly stir in enough milk to form a smooth paste. Add remaining milk and saccharin. Stir until smooth; let stand 5 minutes to soften gelatin. Heat, stirring constantly, until mixture boils. Cool slightly, then cover pudding with waxed paper. Refrigerate until cold. Beat until consistency of soft whipped cream.

In medium bowl, beat egg whites until stiff peaks form. Whip cream; fold 1 cup into chocolate mixture. Then fold in beaten egg whites. Pour into crumb shell. Refrigerate until firm—about 2 hours. Spread remaining whipped cream attractively on top of pie. Refrigerate until serving time. Makes 8 servings.

## PUMPKIN PIE (exchanges per serving = 1 fruit, 1 fat and 1 milk)

9-inch single crust Flaky Pie-
    crust (see recipe page 292)
saccharin equivalent to 1 cup
    sugar
½ teaspoon salt
1½ teaspoons cinnamon
½ teaspoon ginger
½ teaspoon nutmeg
½ teaspoon allspice
½ teaspoon ground cloves
1½ cups canned pumpkin
1⅔ cups evaporated milk
2 eggs, well beaten

At least 4 hours before serving: Prepare Flaky Piecrust as directed. Preheat oven to 425°F. In medium bowl, combine saccharin, salt, cinnamon, ginger, nutmeg, allspice and cloves; beat in pumpkin, milk and eggs until smooth. Pour mixture into pie shell. Bake at 425°F. for 15 minutes; then reduce heat to 350°F. and bake 35 minutes, or until silver knife, inserted in center, comes out clean. Cool; refrigerate. Makes 8 servings.

## APPLE PIE (exchanges per serving = 1½ bread, 3 fat and 1 fruit)

8-inch double-crust Flaky Pie-
    crust (see recipe page 292)
1 quart (about 2 pounds)
    thinly sliced tart cooking
    apples
liquid saccharin equivalent to
    ¾ cup sugar
2 tablespoons cornstarch
¼ teaspoon finely grated
    lemon peel
1 to 2 teaspoons lemon juice
¼ teaspoon nutmeg
½ teaspoon cinnamon

At least 4 hours before serving: Prepare double-crust Flaky Piecrust; use half to line 8-inch pie plate. Preheat oven to 425°F. In large bowl, toss together remaining ingredients. Fill crust with apple mixture; top with second crust. Flute edges; cut air vents. To prevent excessive browning of crust, lightly cover fluted edges with foil. Bake 40 to 50 minutes, or until apples are tender. Remove foil after 30 minutes baking time. Cool. Makes 8 servings.

BLUEBERRY PIE (exchanges per serving = 1½ bread, 3 fat and 1 fruit)
Substitute 1 quart fresh blueberries for apples; prepare and bake pie as directed for Apple Pie, above. Makes 8 servings.

FRUIT-COCKTAIL PIE (exchanges per serving = 1½ bread, 3 fat and 1 fruit)
Substitute 1 quart mixed sliced fresh fruit (choose from pears, peaches, seedless grapes, apples and pineapple) for apples; prepare and bake pie as directed for Apple Pie, above. Makes 8 servings.

## FRUITFUL COBBLER (exchanges per serving = 1 bread, 1 fat and 1 fruit)

½ teaspoon salt
½ tablespoon cornstarch
saccharin
1 quart sliced fresh peaches
1 cup packaged biscuit mix
½ cup light cream
½ teaspoon vanilla extract
1 teaspoon grated lemon peel

At least 1½ hours before serving: Preheat oven to 425°F. In 1½ quart casserole, combine salt, cornstarch, saccharin equivalent to ½ cup sugar and ½ cup water; add peach slices. In medium bowl, mix biscuit mix, light cream, vanilla, saccharin equivalent to 2 tablespoons sugar and lemon peel. Spread mixture over peaches. Bake, uncovered, 40 minutes, or until topping is golden-brown and peaches are bubbly and tender. Serve warm or cold. Makes 8 servings.

## BLUEBERRY MUFFINS (exchanges per serving = 1 bread and 1 fat)

⅓ cup butter or margarine, melted
saccharin equivalent to ⅓ cup sugar, plus water to make ¼ cup
2 eggs
1¼ cups cornmeal
¾ cup sifted all-purpose flour
2½ teaspoons double-acting baking powder
¾ teaspoon salt
¾ cup skimmed milk or re-liquefied nonfat dry milk
½ cup fresh blueberries (or ½ cup unsweetened frozen blue-berries, thawed and drained)

About 35 minutes before serving: Preheat oven to 400°F. Grease 15 cups of muffin pans. In medium bowl, beat butter, saccharin dissolved in water, and eggs; stir in corn-meal. Sift flour, baking powder and salt; stir a third of this mixture into cornmeal mixture; stir in half of milk; repeat, then stir in remaining third of flour mixture. Gently fold in blueberries. Place scant ¼ cup of batter in each muffin cup. Bake 20 to 25 minutes, or until muffins are golden-brown. Makes 15.

## CREAMY RICE PUDDING (exchanges per serving = 1 bread, 1 fat and ½ milk)

⅔ cup packaged precooked rice
⅓ cup raisins
2 cups milk
saccharin equivalent to ⅓ cup sugar
1 teaspoon vanilla extract
½ teaspoon salt
⅛ teaspoon nutmeg
⅛ teaspoon cinnamon
½ cup heavy cream, whipped

About 3 hours before serving: In medium saucepan, combine rice, raisins and milk; bring to boiling; simmer, loosely covered, 15 minutes, fluffing rice occasionally with fork. Stir in saccharin, vanilla, salt, nutmeg and cinnamon. Refrigerate, covered, until cold. Fold in whipped cream. Makes 6 servings.

## BAKED CUSTARD (exchanges per serving = ½ milk)

4 eggs
saccharin equivalent to ¼ cup sugar
¼ teaspoon salt
2 cups milk
1 teaspoon vanilla extract
nutmeg

At least 4 hours before serving: Preheat oven to 300°F. Butter six ¾-cup custard cups. In medium bowl, beat eggs, saccharin, ¼ cup water and salt until smooth. Scald milk, then slowly stir hot milk and vanilla into egg mixture. Divide among custard cups; sprinkle with nutmeg. Set custard cups in baking pan; place in oven and fill pan with hot water to ¾ inch from top of cups. Bake about 1½ hours, or until custard leaves thick coating on knife inserted in center. Cool; refrigerate. Makes 6 servings.

## BUTTERMILK-OAT CRISPS (exchanges for 4 crisps = 1 bread and 1 fat)

1 cup sifted all-purpose flour
½ teaspoon salt
¼ teaspoon baking soda
½ cup uncooked rolled oats
saccharin equivalent to 3
    tablespoons sugar
¼ cup buttermilk
¼ cup butter or margarine,
    melted

At least 1 hour before serving: Preheat oven to 400°F. In medium bowl, stir flour, salt, baking soda and oatmeal. Stir saccharin, buttermilk and butter into flour-oat mixture until dry ingredients are just moistened. On well-floured pastry board or cloth, knead dough lightly for a few seconds. Then roll out into rectangle 10" by 12". Cut into 2" by 2" squares. Bake on ungreased cookie sheets 10 to 12 minutes, or until crisps are golden-brown. Serve hot or cold. Makes 30.

## CHOCOLATE-CHIP-MINT ICE CREAM (exchanges per serving = ½ milk)

1 square unsweetened choco-
    late
1 tablespoon cornstarch
1½ teaspoons spearmint or
    peppermint extract
1 tablespoon lemon juice
saccharin equivalent to ½ cup
    sugar
½ teaspoon vanilla extract
dash salt
green food color
¾ cup evaporated skimmed
    milk

At least 6 hours before serving: Refrigerate square of chocolate. In small saucepan, stir ½ cup water into cornstarch to form a smooth paste. Add spearmint or peppermint extract, lemon juice, saccharin, vanilla and salt. Stir in enough food color to turn mixture kelly-green. Cook, stirring constantly, until mixture boils and thickens. (Mixture will then be forest-green.) Refrigerate, stirring occasionally.

Place milk (in medium bowl) and electric mixer beaters in freezer until ice crystals form ½ to 1 inch from edge of bowl. Shave or grate chilled chocolate. With electric mixer at highest speed, beat milk until consistency of whipped cream. Gradually beat cornstarch mixture into whipped milk; mix in chocolate. Turn into baking dish; smooth surface; cover with waxed paper. Freeze hard—3 to 4 hours. About 15 to 20 minutes before serving, remove ice cream from freezer; let warm to good spooning temperature. Makes 6 servings.

## PEACH AND ORANGE SHERBET (exchanges per serving = 1 fruit)

2 16-ounce cans dietetic-pack
    peach slices
saccharin equivalent to ½ cup
    sugar
¼ teaspoon grapefruit juice
½ cup orange juice
1 tablespoon lemon juice
2 egg whites

About 6 hours before serving: Drain juice from peaches. In electric-blender container at low speed, blend enough peaches to make 1¾ cups puree. In medium bowl, mix this puree, saccharin, ¼ cup water, grapefruit juice, orange juice and lemon juice. (Or press peaches through sieve and mix with other ingredients.) Freeze until firm about 1 inch from edge of bowl—about 30 minutes. Then, with electric mixer, beat egg whites until stiff peaks form. Beat fruit mixture until smooth. Fold egg whites into fruit. Freeze until just firm. If sherbet gets too hard to serve, let soften slightly, then beat with electric mixer until smooth. Makes 1 quart or six ⅔-cup servings.

## FROSTY POP (exchanges per serving = 1 "free")

2 4-serving envelopes dietetic-
    packed cherry-, orange-, or
    lemon-flavor gelatin
1 cup boiling water
1 cup cold water

About 4 to 6 hours before serving: In medium bowl, stir together gelatin and boiling water until all gelatin is dissolved. Stir in cold water. Divide mixture among six 3-ounce paper cups. Freeze until firm. (If desired, wooden sticks may be added when mixture is semifirm.)

To serve: Let stand at room temperature for 5 minutes; peel paper cup down from pop to eat. Makes 6 servings.

## ORANGE BAGATELLE (exchanges per serving = 1 fruit and 1 fat)

1 4-serving envelope orange-
    flavored dietetic-pack gelatin
2 8-ounce cans dietetic-pack
    applesauce
nutmeg
dash salt
coarsely grated orange peel
heavy cream, whipped and
    seasoned to taste with liquid
    saccharin and vanilla

About 4 hours before serving: In medium bowl, dissolve gelatin in ½ cup boiling water. Stir in applesauce, ⅛ teaspoon nutmeg, salt and 2 tablespoons grated orange peel. Pour into 9″ by 5″ by 3″ pan; refrigerate.

A few minutes before serving: Cut jelly into 1-inch squares; heap into 4 sherbet glasses; sprinkle with more grated orange peel and nutmeg, if desired. Top each serving with 2-tablespoon dab whipped cream. Makes 4 servings.

## SUGAR-FREE JAMS AND JELLIES (General Instructions)

- Sterilize jelly jars as follows:
  1. Boil, completely covered with water, for 15 minutes.
  2. Remove from water with tongs that have been held in boiling water at least one minute.
  3. Let drain, upside down, on clean paper toweling until immediately before using, then turn right-side up.
- Sweeten jam or jelly with liquid or granulated saccharin, or if tablets are used, pulverize to a fine powder.
- Carefully calculate the amount of saccharin to use.* Stir into hot fruit until completely mixed and dissolved. Do not boil again.
- Melt paraffin in top of double boiler or in saucepan, over **very low heat**—paraffin burns easily.
- Pour jam or jelly into jars without smearing sides. Wipe away any dribbles.
- Pour on melted paraffin, covering jam or jelly with layer about ⅛- to ¼-inch thick. Set to one side to cool, then refrigerate.
- After jam or jelly has been opened the first time, store, covered with lid or foil.
- Keep refrigerated. Use within 3 to 4 weeks, then prepare fresh batch.

* The first time, use the sweetening levels suggested. Later you may want to adjust them to your personal taste.

## BLUEBERRY JELLY-JAM (exchanges per tablespoon = 1 "free")

1 tablespoon lemon juice
1½ teaspoons cornstarch
1½ teaspoons unflavored
    gelatin
dash salt (optional)
1 10-ounce package frozen
    unsweetened blueberries,
    partially thawed
saccharin equivalent to ¾ cup
    sugar

Prepare two 1-cup jelly jars as directed in General Instructions (above). In medium saucepan, mix lemon juice, cornstarch, gelatin and salt; add blueberries. Stirring constantly, heat to boiling; boil gently 3 minutes, or until blueberry syrup thickens slightly and turns a rich shade of royal blue.

In electric-blender container at low speed (keep lid ajar to allow steam to escape), blend blueberry mixture until smooth. (Or mixture may be strained through food mill.) Return to saucepan; stirring constantly, bring to boiling; boil 2 minutes. Stir in saccharin. Fill jelly jars; seal and store as directed in General Instructions. Makes slightly more than 1 cup of jelly-jam.

## PINEAPPLE-APRICOT PRESERVES (exchanges per tablespoon = ½ fruit)

½ 8-ounce package dried
  apricots
1 cup pineapple (from 15¼-
  ounce can pineapple tidbits
  packed in pineapple juice)
1 tablespoon lemon juice
dash salt (optional)
saccharin equivalent to ½ cup
  sugar

In medium saucepan, simmer apricots with 1 cup water 20 minutes, or until tender. Meanwhile, prepare two 1-cup jelly jars as directed in General Instructions (page 275). Drain pineapple tidbits and cut each, crosswise, into 3 pieces.

In electric-blender container, at low speed (cover ajar to allow steam to escape), blend apricots and cooking water with lemon juice and salt. (Mixture may also be strained through food mill.) Return to saucepan; stir in pineapple pieces. Simmer, stirring occasionally, 5 minutes. Remove from heat; stir in saccharin. Fill jelly jars; seal and store as directed in General Instructions. Makes generous cup of preserves.

PINEAPPLE-APRICOT CONSERVES (exchanges per tablespoon = ½ fruit

Prepare Pineapple-Apricot Preserves as directed above, but stir in ¼ cup finely chopped, blanched almonds with pineapple pieces.

## APPLE JELLY (exchanges per tablespoon = 1 "free")

1 tablespoon lemon juice
1 teaspoon unflavored gelatin
1 teaspoon cornstarch
dash salt (optional)
1 cup canned apple juice
saccharin equivalent to ¾ cup
  sugar

Prepare one 1-cup jelly jar as directed in General Instructions (see page 275). In small saucepan, mix lemon juice, gelatin, cornstarch and salt; stir in apple juice. Stirring constantly, heat to boiling; boil 2 minutes. Remove from heat; stir in saccharin. Fill jelly jar; seal and store as directed in General Instructions. Makes full cup of jelly.

# SUGAR-FREE CANNING

Canning fruits can be done successfully in water or unsweetened fruit juice, rather than the traditional sugar syrup, if you use proper techniques and adequate processing times. To assure good results, get one of the complete booklets on canning published by canning-equipment manufacturers or the U.S. Department of Agriculture,* and follow directions explicitly. These booklets give instructions for both water-bath and pressure-cooker methods of canning. When serving, count fruit exchanges as you would for fresh or commercially prepared sugar-free fruit.

If only one family member is eating sugar-free fruits, cut waste by using pint, or even half-pint, jars for canning. To keep fruit from darkening as you prepare it (apples, pears, peaches), soak it in an ascorbic-acid or lemon-juice solution.†

* For Home Canning of Fruits and Vegetables, send 15 cents (in coin) to: Superintendent of Documents, U.S. Government Printing Office, Washington, D.C. 20402. Include your ZIP code.
† Ascorbic-acid solution: 1 teaspoon crystalline ascorbic acid for each quart of water or fruit juice. Lemon juice solution: 2 tablespoons lemon juice for each quart of water or fruit juice.

You'll need much less sweetener than would be equivalent to the amount of sugar used in a traditional sugar syrup. We recommend saccharin equivalent to 2 to 4 cups of sugar for every 2 to 3 quarts of liquid. Try this proportion first, then make any adjustments necessary to suit your taste. You can add saccharin during canning, but the sweetness seems more natural when added at serving time. (Saccharin can be in liquid or dry form.)

In canned fruit or vegetable relishes, unlike canned fruits, sugar does contribute to the texture and preservation of the ingredients. Experiment with recipes, but don't be too discouraged if some prove disappointing. (Fruits or vegetables can turn mushy, or have an unsuitable flavor.) Relishes aren't as suited to sugar-free canning as plain fruits are. To preserve sugar-free relishes, use the water-bath method of canning—you can't depend on open-kettle heating.

*Pears or Peaches:* Vary the pieces (halves, quarters or slices) so you'll have some variety. Small pieces pack best in small jars; halves in quart jars.

Use unsweetened orange or pineapple juice as the canning liquid to gain unusual flavor. *Note:* These juices will settle to the bottom of the jar. Before you serve, shake the jar to mix. For delicious variation, blend a 50-50 mixture of peaches and pears.

*Raspberries and Strawberries:* Mash berries; strain off and save juice. Use mixture of juice and water as canning liquid. The fruit will retain a richer color.

*Fruit Cocktail:* Mix peaches, pears, pineapple, apples, seedless oranges and grapes. Beware of adding banana slices—they get too soft, and their flavor changes. Since juices of strawberries, raspberries, blueberries, plums and cherries "weep," avoid using them in fruit cocktails.

*Plums:* Most plums can well, but take the advice of your canning booklet when selecting varieties. Halve large plums, or only 2 or 3 will fit into a pint jar. A mixture of strained plum juice and water, used as the canning liquid, cuts down on loss of color.

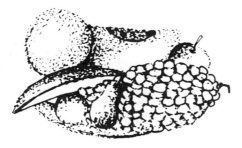

# HIGH-IRON DIET

A high-iron diet is used to treat iron-deficiency anemia. Anemia is a general term used to describe the condition of the body when there are too few functioning blood cells. There are at least six different types of anemia, but the most common is caused by too little iron in the diet.

Everyone needs iron for blood-cell formation and function. The need is greatest in women of child-bearing age, for some of the body's supply of iron is depleted during menstruation and pregnancy. The blood stream is the main storage house for iron, but iron is also stored in body tissue—liver, bone marrow and spleen. When iron levels in the blood are lowered, iron is pulled from the body's tissue stores.

Men must absorb 1 milligram of iron per day and women 1.8 milligrams to replace the iron lost through perspiration, urine, and in women, menstruation. However, relatively little—about 10 percent—of the iron in food eaten daily is absorbed, so the Recommended Daily Allowance for iron is 10 milligrams a day for men, 18 for women of child-bearing age. Note that while a woman's iron needs are higher than a man's, her caloric needs are lower, making it necessary for her to get more iron for her calorie "dollar."

If your physician has warned you that you are anemic, carefully follow all his instructions about iron supplements, medication and meal planning. Avoid eating a meal with huge "doses" of iron, and then one with little or no iron. Keep your iron intake at a steady pace and you will absorb more of it.

The foods that follow are all good sources of iron. Unfortunately, the very richest sources are relatively unpopular (liver), expensive (oysters), or difficult to obtain (dandelion greens). So don't underestimate the importance of vegetables, fruits and enriched or whole-grain breads in adding iron to the diet. These old faithfuls do the job unobtrusively. See pages 342 to 351 for the specific iron content of various foods.

Apricots (dried)
Beans, baked
Beef (trimmed meat)
Beet greens
Blackberries
Blueberries
Bran cereal
Breads (enriched or whole grain)
Broccoli
Brussels sprouts
Chard
Chinese cabbage
Clams
Collards
Cowpeas (black-eyed peas)
Dandelion greens
Egg yolks
Kale
Kidney
Liver
Mushrooms
Mustard greens
Oysters
Pastas (enriched)
Peaches (dried)
Plums
Pork (trimmed meat)
Rice (enriched)
Spinach
Squash (winter)
Strawberries
Sweet potatoes
Tongue
Turnip greens
Veal

If you are taking special care to meet the Recommended Daily Allowance for iron, some of the suggestions that follow will be helpful.

• Products with the words enriched, whole-grain and fortified on their labels are all good sources of iron. For example, enriched refrigerator biscuits, rolls and sweet bread; enriched saltines; enriched or whole-grain bread; ready-to-eat cereals fortified with iron as well as vitamins; whole-grain crackers; enriched white rice (don't rinse the rice before or after cooking—the enrichment mixture is on the surface); biscuits and quick breads made from enriched biscuit mix; juice drinks and synthetic drinks fortified with iron.

- Use dried fruits. Add prunes, dates and dried apricots to fruit cocktails and salads; use as condiments for curries; make raisin sauces for ham; add raisins to cookies.
- If you like fresh fruit, the berries—blackberries, blueberries, strawberries, etc.—are among the fruits highest in iron content (1 milligram iron per cup).
- Try "Southern" vegetables—kale, chard, collards, dandelion greens, okra. They are available frozen as well as fresh. (Don't overcook!) Other vegetable suggestions: Steam mushrooms in broth with a few onion slices; Mixed-Bean Salad (see recipe on page 283).
- If you hate liver (one of the highest sources of iron), try chicken livers—the flavor is mild. Cook them smothered in onions. Chopped chicken livers come frozen so no preparation is needed. Use as a salad or in sandwiches. And don't forget *pork* liver; it's higher in iron content than beef or calves' liver and *much cheaper.*
- If you love chocolate, you will be glad to know that cocoa and chocolate (particularly unsweetened) are rich in iron, too. A cup of prepared cocoa will provide 1 milligram of iron. Make it with skimmed milk and the calories are about the same as plain whole milk.
- Snack on delicious instant breakfast made with skimmed milk (225 calories and 2½ milligrams of iron per serving). Try it as a milkshake: Mix instant breakfast, 1 cup skimmed milk and 3 or 4 ice cubes; buzz in blender until smooth.
- When making turkey gravy, use the giblets. Cook the gizzard and heart until tender; add the liver for the last 15 minutes. Trim away the tough parts of the gizzard and heart, and chop with the liver. Make gravy as usual; add giblets.
- Try baked eggs on toast: Beat 2 egg whites until stiff; spread on a slice of enriched or whole-wheat bread; nest yolks into the whites. Bake at 350°F. until done as you like—about 10 minutes. (3 milligrams iron and 220 calories per serving.)

## HIGH-IRON DIET: 24 Recipes

### KASHMIR SPLIT-PEA SOUP (2 milligrams iron per serving)

1 medium onion, sliced
1 medium carrot, sliced
1 cup dried green split peas
3 chicken-bouillon cubes
1 teaspoon salt
generous dash cayenne
1 teaspoon curry (optional)
green food color (optional)
¾ cup packaged croutons

About 1 hour before serving: In medium saucepan, heat 5 cups water, onion, carrot, peas, bouillon cubes, salt and cayenne to boiling; cover; simmer 50 minutes, or until peas are soft. Stir in curry if desired.

Press mixture through sieve or food mill. Return puree to saucepan; stir in few drops green food color to brighten color. Serve topped with croutons. Makes 4 servings.

### OYSTER-CORN CHOWDER (9 milligrams iron per serving)

1 medium onion, thinly sliced
½ cup chopped celery
½ teaspoon salt
generous dash garlic salt
generous dash pepper
generous dash nutmeg
1 16-ounce can cream-style corn
1 10½-ounce can condensed chicken broth
1 soup-can liquid from oysters
2 hard-cooked eggs, thinly sliced
2 dozen shucked oysters

About 30 minutes before serving: In large saucepan, simmer, uncovered, all ingredients but hard-cooked eggs and oysters, for 20 minutes. Add egg slices and oysters; simmer 3 minutes, or until oysters curl and are just cooked. Makes 4 main-dish servings.

### LINGUINE WITH CLAM SAUCE (9 milligrams iron per serving)

½ 16-ounce package enriched linguine
2 7½-ounce cans minced clams
about 1 cup bottled clam juice
¼ cup butter or margarine
1 garlic clove, minced
2 tablespoons flour
about ¼ cup chopped parsley
1½ teaspoons thyme leaves
salt and pepper to taste

About 30 minutes before serving: Cook linguine as label directs. Meanwhile, drain clams, reserving liquid. Add enough bottled clam juice to liquid to make 2 cups. In large skillet over medium heat, in butter, sauté garlic until golden. Blend flour into butter. Slowly stir in liquid and seasonings until smooth. Cover and simmer 10 minutes, stirring occasionally. Add clams to sauce and heat; season with salt and pepper. Pour over drained linguine; toss. Makes 4 servings.

### CLAM FRITTERS (4.5 milligrams iron per serving)

oil or fat for deep frying
1½ cups sifted enriched all-purpose flour
2 teaspoons double-acting baking powder
¾ teaspoon salt
2 eggs, separated
1 cup milk
1 teaspoon lemon juice
2 7½-ounce cans minced clams, thoroughly drained
catchup (optional)

About 1 hour before serving: Preheat oil or fat in deep fat fryer to 375°F. Stir together flour, baking powder and salt. In small bowl, beat egg whites until stiff peaks form. In medium bowl, beat together flour mixture, egg yolks, milk and lemon juice. Fold in egg whites, then drained clams.

Drop batter, ¼ cup per fritter, into hot oil and cook until golden brown and bubbles stop forming in top of batter; turn and brown other side. Drain on paper toweling. Serve hot; pass catchup if desired. Makes 6 servings of 2 fritters each.

## CLAM-AND-CHEESE SANDWICHES (3 milligrams iron per serving)

1 3-ounce package Neufchâtel
   cheese
1 7- or 7½-ounce can minced
   clams, drained
1 teaspoon soy sauce
1 teaspoon prepared mustard
¼ teaspoon salt
2 teaspoons instant minced
   onion
8 square slices pumpernickel
   bread

About 1 hour before serving: In small bowl, mix all ingredients but bread. Use to fill bread slices making 4 sandwiches.

## OYSTER-MUSHROOM KABOBS (8 milligrams iron per serving)

12 slices bacon (about ¾
   pound)
2 8-ounce cans large oysters
½ pound medium mushrooms

About 40 minutes before serving: Preheat broiler if manufacturer directs. In medium skillet, cook bacon until slices are slightly browned but not yet crisp.

Drain oysters; wrap slice of bacon around each. Alternating oysters with mushrooms, place on four skewers. Broil, turning once, until bacon is crisp. Makes 4 servings.

## HAZEL'S OYSTERS ROCKEFELLER (8 milligrams iron per serving)

1 10-ounce package frozen,
   chopped spinach, thawed
½ cup chopped parsley leaves
½ cup chopped celery leaves
¼ cup minced onion
1 bay leaf
salt
1 tablespoon Worcestershire
dash cayenne
butter or margarine
4 slices whole-wheat toast
1 cup shucked oysters (about
   2 dozen oysters), carefully
   washed, with any pieces of
   shell removed
1 cup large bread cubes
   made with enriched bread

About 1 hour before serving: In electric-blender container, at low speed, combine spinach, parsley, celery leaves, onion, bay leaf, ½ teaspoon salt, Worcestershire and cayenne. In medium saucepan, heat puree, with 1 tablespoon butter, just to boiling. Preheat oven to 350°F. Into 8-inch pie plate, press toast slices to form 4 wedges. Spread puree on toast; then arrange oysters over puree; sprinkle with salt, if desired. Top oysters with bread cubes, then dot with 2 tablespoons butter or margarine. Bake 25 minutes, or until bread cubes are a dark golden-brown and oysters are easily pierced with a fork. Makes 4 servings.

## LIVER EMPANADAS (6 milligrams iron per serving)

1 9.5-ounce can enriched refrigerated flaky buttermilk
   biscuits
1 6-ounce container frozen,
   seasoned chopped chicken
   liver, thawed
1 8- or 10¼-ounce can
   spaghetti sauce with mushrooms

About 25 minutes before serving: Preheat oven to 450°F. Separate biscuits; roll or press each into oval about 3" by 3½". In center of each biscuit, place 1 tablespoon chopped liver. Moisten edges slightly with water, then fold long end over and press edges together with tines of fork. Shape ends toward each other, forming crescent. Bake on greased cookie sheet 10 minutes, or until golden. Meanwhile, heat spaghetti sauce. Serve empanadas with sauce. Makes 3 main-course servings.

## LIVERBURGERS  (6 milligrams iron per serving)

½ pound beef liver
½ pound ground chuck
¾ cup enriched dried bread
  crumbs
2 eggs
1 teaspoon salt
½ teaspoon Tabasco
½ teaspoon celery salt
¼ cup minced onion
bacon fat

About 1 hour and 45 minutes before serving: Remove skin and large veins from liver. Using a fine blade, grind liver. Thoroughly mix liver, chuck, bread crumbs, eggs, salt, Tabasco, celery salt and onion. Form mixture into 8 patties; refrigerate about one hour, or until ready to fry. In large skillet, in bacon fat, fry patties until done. Makes 4 servings of 2 patties each.

## EGGS À LA RUSSE  (3 milligrams iron per serving)

½ cup mayonnaise
2 tablespoons chili sauce
1 teaspoon chopped chives
few drops lemon juice
dash Tabasco
10 hard-cooked eggs
5 small lettuce cups

At serving time: In medium bowl, stir together mayonnaise, chili sauce, chives, lemon juice and Tabasco. Cut eggs with egg slicer and "fan" attractively; place on lettuce cups and spoon on dressing. Makes 5 servings.

## MUSHROOM DEVILED EGGS  (1.5 milligrams iron per egg)

2 tablespoons butter or margarine
¼ pound mushrooms, minced
2 tablespoons minced onion
8 hard-cooked eggs
2 tablespoons mayonnaise
2 tablespoons prepared
  mustard
1 tablespoon lemon juice
½ teaspoon celery salt
⅛ teaspoon pepper
paprika for garnish

About 30 minutes before serving: In skillet, in butter, sauté mushrooms and onion until onion is transparent. Meanwhile, halve eggs lengthwise; remove yolks, keeping whites intact. Mash yolks with fork; combine with mushroom mixture and remaining ingredients except paprika. Use mixture to refill hollows in whites, rounding each. Sprinkle with paprika. Makes 16 halves.

## MODERN-DAY KNISHES  (.5 milligram iron per knish)

1 8-ounce can enriched refrigerated crescent rolls
1 6-ounce container frozen
  seasoned chopped chicken
  liver, thawed
1 egg, lightly beaten

About 35 minutes before serving: Preheat oven to 375°F. Unroll rolls; separate into 4 rectangles; pinch diagonal seams together. Cut each rectangle in half lengthwise, then thirds crosswise. Fill each tiny rectangle with about 1 tea-spoon chopped chicken liver; roll up and place, seam side down, on ungreased cookie sheet. Brush each knish with beaten egg, then bake 12 to 15 minutes, or until a rich golden-brown. Serve immediately. Makes 24.

## BAKED-BEAN SURPRISE  (2.5 milligrams iron per serving)

1 16-ounce can vegetarian
  baked beans
1 15¼-ounce can pineapple
  chunks packed in pineapple
  juice, drained
⅓ cup chili sauce

About 10 minutes before serving: In medium saucepan, mix ingredients; simmer 5 minutes. Makes 4 servings.

## QUICK BAKED BEANS (4 milligrams iron per serving)

¼ pound sliced bacon, cut into
   1-inch pieces
1 large onion, thinly sliced
1 garlic clove, minced
1 tablespoon cornstarch
2 16-ounce cans kidney beans,
   drained
1 16-ounce can tomatoes
½ teaspoon salt
½ teaspoon dry mustard
½ teaspoon chili powder
generous dash pepper
1½ teaspoons Worcestershire
½ cup dark molasses

About 1 hour before serving: Preheat oven to 375°F. In medium skillet, cook bacon until almost crisp; remove. In bacon fat, sauté onion and garlic until golden—do not brown. Pour most of fat from skillet, then stir in cornstarch; mix in 1 can drained kidney beans. In 2-quart casserole, stir together bacon, onion mixture, remaining kidney beans, tomatoes, salt, mustard, chili powder, pepper, Worcestershire and molasses. Bake 45 minutes, or until bubbly and lightly browned on top. Makes eight 1-cup servings.

## MIXED BEAN SALAD (4 milligrams iron per serving)

1 cup drained canned red
   kidney beans
1 cup drained canned white
   kidney beans
1 cup drained canned chick
   peas
1 small green pepper, chopped
¾ cup chopped onions
3 tablespoons wine vinegar
½ cup olive oil
1 teaspoon salt
½ teaspoon garlic powder
dash pepper
4 lettuce leaves

About 1 hour before serving: In medium bowl, toss together all ingredients but lettuce; refrigerate.

   To serve: Drain mixture, then spoon into lettuce leaves. Makes 4 servings.

## SALAD—TIVOLI GARDEN (4 milligrams iron per serving)

¾ pound fresh spinach, cut
   into bite-size pieces
1 small head red cabbage, cut
   into thin strips
3 scallions, chopped
2 6½- or 7-ounce cans tuna,
   drained and separated into
   chunks
¼ cup salad oil
½ teaspoon salt
¼ teaspoon dry mustard
¼ cup vinegar
2 tablespoons grated
   Parmesan cheese
2 hard-cooked eggs, sliced for
   garnish

About 30 minutes before serving: In large bowl, toss spinach, cabbage and scallions with tuna. Stir together oil, salt, mustard and vinegar until smooth; then toss with greens and tuna. Sprinkle with Parmesan and garnish with egg slices. Makes 6 servings.

## SPINACH SPECIAL (2.5 milligrams iron per serving)

1 16-ounce bag spinach, washed
1½ teaspoons salt
1 large carrot, coarsely grated
1 apple, grated
½ teaspoon lemon juice

About 15 minutes before serving: In large kettle, cook spinach and salt, in water that still clings to leaves, 6 minutes, or until just tender-crisp. Drain; return to kettle; stir in grated carrot, apple and lemon juice. Simmer, covered, a few minutes, or until heated through. Makes 6 servings.

## BROCCOLI WITH HOLLANDAISE (1 milligram iron per serving)

2 10-ounce packages frozen cut broccoli
½ cup butter or margarine
3 egg yolks
2 tablespoons lemon juice
¼ teaspoon salt
¼ teaspoon onion salt
dash cayenne

About 15 minutes before serving: Cook broccoli as label directs; drain. Meanwhile, in small pan, heat butter or margarine until just bubbling, but not brown. In electric-blender container, at low speed, blend remaining ingredients until mixed. Still at low speed, remove center of cover and slowly pour in all hot butter in low, steady stream; turn off immediately. Serve over broccoli. Makes 6 servings.

## HOT CUCUMBERS WITH DILL (1 milligram iron per serving)

5 medium cucumbers, pared
salt
1 cup plain yogurt
½ cup mayonnaise
⅛ teaspoon white pepper
2 egg yolks, lightly beaten
1 tablespoon chopped fresh dill

About 30 minutes before serving: Cut cucumbers into 1-inch crosswise chunks; cook, uncovered, in boiling salted water, 7 minutes, or until just fork-tender; drain. In double boiler, over simmering water, combine yogurt with mayonnaise, ¼ teaspoon salt, pepper and beaten egg yolks. Stir constantly for about 10 minutes, or until slightly thickened; do not boil. Turn drained cucumbers into serving dish; top with sauce; sprinkle with the dill. Makes 6 servings.

## SOFT MOLASSES COOKIES (.5 milligram iron per cookie)

2¼ cups sifted enriched all-purpose flour
1 teaspoon ginger
1 teaspoon cinnamon
¼ teaspoon salt
2 teaspoons baking soda
½ cup shortening
½ cup packed dark-brown sugar
½ cup dark molasses
1 egg
1½ cups raisins

About 2 hours before serving: Preheat oven to 400°F. Lightly grease cookie sheets. Stir together flour, ginger, cinnamon and salt. Dissolve soda in 2 tablespoons hot water.

In medium bowl, with electric mixer at medium speed, cream shortening, brown sugar, molasses and egg until fluffy and golden-brown. Beat in flour mixture alternately with 6 tablespoons cold water. Beat in soda mixture and raisins.

Drop, by rounded tablespoonfuls, 2 inches apart, onto greased cookie sheets. Bake 10 to 12 minutes, or until done. Makes about 3½ dozen.

## APRICOT BROWN BETTY (3 milligrams iron per serving)

1 cup dried apricot halves
½ cup packed dark brown sugar
2 cups fresh bread cubes (made from enriched bread)
2 tablespoons butter or margarine
cinnamon
ginger
light cream or whipped cream

About 1½ hours before serving: In medium saucepan, simmer apricot halves, brown sugar and 1½ cups water, covered, 20 minutes. Preheat oven to 350°F. In 1-quart casserole, place half of bread cubes; dot with half of butter; top with several dashes of cinnamon and ginger to taste. Top with hot apricot halves, lightly drained. Add remaining bread cubes; top with butter, cinnamon and ginger as before. Pour syrup used to cook apricots over bread cubes. Bake 30 minutes, or until brown. Cool until serving time.

To serve: Pass light cream, or top each serving with dab of whipped cream. Makes 4 servings.

## PRUNE-FILLED BRAID (2.5 milligrams iron per serving)

½ 12-ounce package pitted
  prunes
¼ cup orange marmalade
⅓ cup chopped walnuts
2 8-ounce cans enriched crescent dinner rolls
¼ cup raisins
½ cup confectioners' sugar
1 tablespoon milk

About 1½ hours before serving: In medium saucepan, heat prunes and 2 cups water to boiling. Cover and simmer 20 to 25 minutes; drain. In medium bowl, mash prunes with fork. Stir in orange marmalade and walnuts.

Preheat oven to 375°F. On ungreased large cookie sheet, unroll both cans crescent rolls; form into one large rectangle, about 14" by 12", overlapping edges slightly; press together seams and perforated edges.

Spread prune filling in 2-inch wide strip, lengthwise, down center of dough to about ½ inch from each end; sprinkle with raisins. Make cuts 2 inches apart diagonally along both sides of filling. Alternating sides, fold strips across filling. Fold ends under to seal. Bake 25 minutes, or until dark golden-brown. Combine sugar and milk. Drizzle over braid. Makes 8 servings.

## SHOOFLY PIE (2.5 milligrams iron per serving)

1 cup sifted enriched all-
  purpose flour
½ cup packed dark brown
  sugar
½ teaspoon salt
½ teaspoon cinnamon
⅛ teaspoon nutmeg
⅛ teaspoon ground cloves
2 tablespoons butter or margarine
½ teaspoon baking soda
½ cup dark molasses
1 egg
unbaked 9-inch pie shell
vanilla ice cream or whipped
  cream (optional)

About 4 hours before serving: Preheat oven to 375°F. In small bowl, mix flour, brown sugar, salt, cinnamon, nutmeg, cloves and butter to make crumb mixture.

In small bowl, stir together baking soda and ¾ cup hot water. Then beat in molasses and egg until smooth. Sprinkle one-quarter of crumb mixture in pie shell; carefully pour in one-third of molasses mixture. Repeat two more times, then top with remaining crumb mixture. Bake 35 minutes, or until pie is firm in center. Cool and serve warm, topped with dollops of ice cream. Or chill and serve cold, topped with whipped cream. Makes 8 servings.

## APRICOT CHIFFON PIE (4 milligrams iron per serving)

½ pound dried apricots
2 teaspoons unflavored gelatin
granulated sugar
3 eggs, separated
2 tablespoons lemon juice
⅛ teaspoon salt
4 drops almond extract
½ cup heavy cream, whipped
1 9-inch pie shell

About 4 hours before serving: In medium saucepan, soak apricots in 1 cup water 1 hour; then cook, in same water, covered, 10 minutes, or until tender. In electric-blender container, at low speed, blend apricots and cooking liquid. Measure one cup of this puree. (Or press apricots through food mill.)

In top of double boiler, mix gelatin, ¼ cup sugar, egg yolks, lemon juice, salt, almond extract and apricot puree; let stand 5 minutes to soften gelatin. Cook mixture over boiling water, stirring constantly for 5 minutes. Let cool to lukewarm.

About 2 hours before serving: In medium bowl, with electric mixer at high speed, beat egg whites until soft peaks form; then beat in, a tablespoon at a time, ½ cup sugar; continue to beat until stiff peaks form. Fold cooled apricot mixture into beaten whites; then fold whipped cream into apricot-egg mixture. Pour into prepared pie shell. Refrigerate until firm. Makes 6 servings.

PRUNE CHIFFON PIE: Prepare as directed above, but substitute ½ pound pitted prunes for apricots.

# LOW-FAT, LOW-CHOLESTEROL DIET

Low-fat, low-cholesterol diet is the general term for a family of diets all designed to help prevent arteriosclerosis, embolisms or coronary thrombosis—in two words, "heart attacks."

It became apparent 30 years ago that Americans had an abnormally high rate of heart attacks and circulatory diseases. Studies also showed that Americans are more apt to be overweight, to eat more fat, to get less exercise and to live under more stressful conditions than virtually any other people. Then studies in experimental animals demonstrated that high blood-cholesterol levels (an indicator of abnormalities in the circulatory system) could be reduced by a diet rich in polyunsaturated fats.

Diets now being prescribed are based on this work plus later studies which showed that, for best results, total fat should not exceed 30 to 35 percent of the calories in the diet,* and that cholesterol from foods should also be limited. These diets:

1. Restrict the total amount of fat—particularly that from saturated fats
2. Increase the use of polyunsaturated fats
3. Restrict cholesterol-rich foods

Some also restrict the use of pure carbohydrates (i.e., sugar), but relatively few doctors add this restriction to a patient's diet. (See the Low-Fat, Low-Cholesterol Diet Outline that follows.)

The most restricted diet is used to treat those who have already had a heart attack. The emphasis is placed on reducing weight to normal by the severe restriction of total fat intake as well as over-all calories. Cholesterol-rich foods are also severely limited, and the polyunsaturated fats are used wherever possible. The doctor often recommends increased regular exercise such as walking, bowling or cycling. The same diet is also prescribed for the special-risk groups—those with a family history of heart disease, diabetes or high-blood pressure, or those who are overweight or are moderate to heavy smokers.

The American Heart Association has taken the diet one step further by recommending that everyone follow the AHA plan called "the fat-controlled diet." This diet places less restriction on the total amount of fat in the diet but severely limits saturated fats and substitutes polyunsaturated fats. Cholesterol-rich foods and pure sugars are also limited.

Not all recognized authorities agree on the scientific relationship of diet to heart disease. They do agree that a calorie surplus leads to overweight, which is a major factor in heart disease. Since the easiest way to cut calories is to eliminate fat from the diet, any well-balanced diet will limit fat intake to a certain extent. In short, it makes sense for everyone to avoid overrich foods.

* A "normal" diet obtains 40 to 45 percent of its calories from fat.

## DIET OUTLINE

This diet is designed to limit fat to 45 to 50 grams a day, cholesterol to less than 300 milligrams. Polyunsaturated fats are substituted for saturated wherever possible.

**FOODS ALLOWED**

**MILK**

Skimmed milk; modified skimmed milk; buttermilk made from skimmed milk; evaporated skimmed milk

**CHEESE**

Cottage cheese

**FATS**

(Up to 3 teaspoons—about 15 grams fat a day)
"Special" margarine (those with liquid oil listed first in ingredients)
Corn, safflower, cottonseed or soybean oils

**EGGS**

Egg whites allowed freely; egg yolks up to 2 to 4 a week

**MEAT AND POULTRY**

(Up to 15 grams fat per serving)
Lean cooked meat only—one serving equals 3 ounces cooked meat. Use lean trimmed beef, pork, lamb and veal
Chicken and turkey—do not eat skin

**FISH**

Any of the following:
Cod, flounder, haddock, hake, halibut, ocean perch, pickerel, pollock, red snapper, sand dabs, sea bass, sole, tuna
Moderate amounts of: bluefish, brook trout, lake herring, smelt and swordfish

**SHELLFISH**

Other than those forbidden (see right) in moderation

**VEGETABLES**

All

**FRUIT**

All except avocado, olives and coconut

**BREAD**

Cracked wheat, French or Italian, rye, white and whole-wheat breads
Homemade quick breads made with allowed oil or "special" margarine and no egg yolks
Angel-food cake

**FOODS FORBIDDEN**

**MILK**

Whole milk; evaporated milk; buttermilk or yogurt made from whole milk

**CHEESE**

Cream cheese; hard cheeses

**FATS**

Butter; regular margarine; cooking fat; lard; olive oil; coconut oil

**EGGS**

More than 2 to 4 yolks a week

**MEAT AND POULTRY**

Fatty cuts of meat such as short ribs, fatty hamburger, bacon, shoulder lamb chops
Frankfurters, luncheon meats
Duck and goose
Skin of poultry

**FISH**

Herring, lake trout, mackerel, rainbow trout, salmon, shad

**SHELLFISH**

Oysters, lobster, shrimp

**VEGETABLES**

No restrictions

**FRUIT**

Avocado, olives and coconut

**BREAD**

Commercial quick breads, pastries, cakes and pies, most crackers and doughnuts

## FOODS ALLOWED

### CEREALS AND PASTAS
All

### DESSERTS
Fruit; sherbet and Italian ices; puddings made with skimmed milk; gelatin; angel-food cake

### BEVERAGES
Coffee; tea; carbonated beverages; beer and liquor as physician permits

### MISCELLANEOUS
Herbs and spices
Condiments such as catchup, mustard, pickles
Sugar, honey, syrups, hard candy

## FOODS FORBIDDEN

### CEREALS AND PASTAS
No restrictions

### DESSERTS
Ice cream and ice milk; others not specifically mentioned

### BEVERAGES
Any containing forbidden foods

### MISCELLANEOUS
Chocolate; olives; nuts

### FAT-CONTROLLED DIET OUTLINE
Follow the low-fat, low-cholesterol diet as given above but:
1. Limit servings of meat to 3 times a week
2. Use fish, poultry or cottage cheese for remaining 11 lunch and dinner main dishes
3. Increase allowed fats to 2 to 4 tablespoons a day as allowed by doctor
4. Restrict starchy vegetables, breads and cereals as needed to adjust calories

## QUESTIONS MOST OFTEN ASKED

Q. *What is the difference between saturated fats and polyunsaturated fats?*
A. The terms saturated and polyunsaturated describe the chemical structure of the fats. The names also give a clue to the form and origin of the fats. Saturated fats, usually solid at room temperature, are mainly fats of animal origin, such as those found in meat, cheese (except cottage cheese), egg yolk and butter, though coconut oil and hydrogenated vegetable oils are also relatively saturated. Polyunsaturated fats are generally of vegetable origin and are liquid at room temperature. These include corn, cottonseed, soybean and safflower oils.

Q. *What is cholesterol? Where is it found?*
A. Cholesterol is a natural fat-like substance in cell tissue that plays a fundamental role in the body functions of both animals and man. It is manufactured in body tissue and can also be obtained from food we eat. It's not possible (except with medication) to control the amount the body manufactures, but the amount from food can be limited. Cholesterol is found only in animal food products. The foods highest in cholesterol include egg yolks, oysters, liver and other variety meats. Cholesterol is not found in plant foods such as vegetables, fruits, grain and cereal products and nuts.

Q. *What is meant by the term "special margarine?"*
A. See page 287 for the difference between regular and "special" margarine.

Q. *May coffee lighteners and sour-cream substitutes be used on the low-fat, low-cholesterol diet?*
A. No, they may not. Virtually all the coffee lighteners and sour-cream substitutes on the market today are made with saturated fat and so are forbidden. The fat content of these products is high enough to eliminate them for this reason also. Since they are made with vegetable fat, they do not contain any cholesterol.

Q. *May filled milk or imitation milk be used on the diet?*
A. Filled milks are made by substituting another fat (usually partially hydrogenated soybean or coconut oil) for butterfat. Since filled milks contain saturated fats, they are not allowed on the diet. Imitation milk does not have a skimmed-milk base but it does contain a relatively high fat content; saturated fats are ordinarily used. It is forbidden also.

Q. *Which frozen desserts are suitable for low-fat, low-cholesterol diets?*
A. On a strict low-fat, low-cholesterol diet, sherbets and fruit ices only. On a low-cholesterol diet with no restrictions in the total amount of fat, mellorine (ice cream made with other fats besides butterfat) is allowable. On a diet only slightly restricted in fat and cholesterol, moderate amounts of ice milk may be eaten if your doctor allows.

Q. *What's the difference in fat and cholesterol content of an 8-ounce container of these cheeses: ricotta, unsalted, uncreamed and creamed cottage cheese?*
A. The fat content depends on the kind of milk from which the cheese is made. All of the above except ricotta are made with the curd of skimmed milk. Creamed cottage cheese does have some cream added; this makes it richer and the texture smoother. Creamed cottage cheese has 10 grams fat per 8-ounce container; uncreamed cottage cheese has negligible fat per 8-ounce container. Unsalted cottage cheese is usually uncreamed, but there may be some creamed,

unsalted types on the market—check the label. Ricotta cheese is produced from either partially skimmed or whole milk. Partially skimmed ricotta has 20 grams fat and whole-milk ricotta 30 grams fat per 8 ounces.

Uncreamed cottage cheese is allowed on all low-fat, low-cholesterol diets. Creamed cottage cheese is allowed on all but the most restricted; it provides 35 milligrams cholesterol per 8 ounces. Ricotta cheese is too high in cholesterol and fat to be recommended on the diet.

Q. *Will mushrooms harm someone who is on an exceptionally low-cholesterol diet?*
A. Actually, mushrooms are ideal for such a diet because they, like all fruits and vegetables, contain no cholesterol at all. Also, their fat and calorie content is very low.

Q. *May cocoa and chocolate be used on a low-cholesterol diet?*
A. Cocoa and chocolate do not contain cholesterol, but both are high in fat content. There are 6 grams of fat in ¼ cup cocoa, 15 grams in 1 ounce of chocolate. All but the most restricted diets allow small amounts of cocoa and chocolate-pudding mixes; chocolate is usually forbidden.

Q. *Are there any substitutes for sour-cream dips and gravies, bananas with sour cream, etc. for those on a low-fat, low-cholesterol diet?*
A. Since the fat content of the diet is limited, sour cream (at 48 grams of fat per cup) is definitely out. However, the situation isn't hopeless. Try these ideas: In gravies calling for a small amount of sour cream, substitute buttermilk. Add it at the last minute to the gravy—never boil buttermilk or it will curdle. Serve sliced bananas in pineapple or orange juice. The flavor is a long way from that of sour cream, but it's delicious in its own way. Or enjoy fruits with cottage cheese instead of sour cream. A creamed cottage cheese (or uncreamed, if fat in a diet is extremely limited) can be whirled in a blender to become a base for

dips or salad dressings ordinarily containing sour cream.

Q. *Is it true that food preservatives are high in cholesterol?*
A. Preservatives used in foods do not contain cholesterol. There is no reason to avoid foods with preservatives, if they are otherwise appropriate for the diet.

Q. *My doctor has told me to avoid fatty fish, but I am allowed to have the leanest ones. Which fish are right for the diet?*
A. The various fish fall into three main categories by fat content. Those containing up to 7 grams of fat per pound of flesh include cod, flounder, haddock, hake, halibut, ocean perch, pickerel, pollock, red snapper, sand dabs, sea bass, sole and water-packed tuna. At 10 to 20 grams per pound are bluefish, brook trout, lake herring, smelt, swordfish and fresh tuna. Fish with fat content of 45 grams per pound and up are herring, lake trout, mackerel, rainbow trout, Chinook (king) salmon and shad. Use the first two groups on your diet.

Q. *Is it the white or the yolk of an egg that contains cholesterol? If egg yolks are not eaten, would any nutrients be missing from the diet?*
A. The yolk has all the cholesterol. It also happens to have more iron, calcium and Vitamin A than the white. But don't worry if the doctor forbids yolks—you can get adequate amounts of the nutrients they contain from other foods.

Q. *My husband is on a low-fat diet following a heart attack. He is much improved and has returned to work. Don't you think I could begin using salad oils in food preparation, baking, etc.?*
A. Your doctor must decide. Consult him before making *any* change in your husband's diet. Although many doctors allow, even encourage, the use of oils in the diet of heart patients, the doctor in charge must be the one to make the decision for his patient.

Q. *When polyunsaturated salad oil is used to fry foods, does it become saturated fat? If not, why are fried foods forbidden on fat-restricted diets?*
A. No. Frying does not turn such oils into saturated fat. Fat-restricted diets limit the total intake of all fats, so naturally, fried foods are forbidden.

Q. *If a doctor recommends a diet high in polyunsaturated oils, may olive oil be used in cooking rather than vegetable oils?*
A. Use only the oils the doctor recommends. Experiments have shown that monounsaturated oils, of which olive oil is the best-known example, have no significant effect on lowering blood-cholesterol levels.

Q. *Vegetable fats are stressed in my diet. May I always bake with oils?*
A. If a small amount of melted shortening is called for in a recipe, you may use salad oil. But, in practically all baked goods, you will need special recipes calling for salad oil. Write salad-oil manufacturers for help along this line, and try the following recipes.

Q. *Is it true that the easiest way to lose weight is to go on a low-cholesterol diet?*
A. The cholesterol content of foods has nothing to do with gaining or losing weight. However, most individuals on low-cholesterol diets must also restrict the total fat and calories in their diet. But don't confuse the separate factors and assume that reducing cholesterol will also reduce the calories and fat content of the diet.

## LOW-FAT, LOW-CHOLESTEROL DIET: 25 Recipes

### CHERRY-GLAZED PINEAPPLE-CHEESE PIE (5 grams fat per serving)

**Graham-Cracker Crust (see recipe below)**
**1 8-ounce container creamed cottage cheese**
**1 envelope unflavored gelatin**
**granulated sugar**
**1 cup canned pineapple juice**
**1 teaspoon grated lemon peel**
**lemon Juice**
**3 egg whites**
**1/4 teaspoon salt**
**1 tablespoon cornstarch**
**1 16-ounce can pitted red sour cherries, drained (reserve liquid)**
**1/4 teaspoon almond extract**
**few drops red food color**

About 5 hours before serving: Prepare and cool Graham-Cracker Crust. Press cottage cheese through fine sieve. In medium saucepan, stir together gelatin, 1/4 cup sugar, pineapple juice, lemon peel and 2 tablespoons lemon juice; let stand 5 minutes. Stirring constantly, heat mixture until gelatin just dissolves; stir in cottage cheese. Refrigerate until slightly thicker than consistency of unbeaten egg whites.

Beat egg whites and salt until whites form soft peaks; beating constantly, gradually add 1/4 cup sugar until stiff peaks form. Fold gelatin mixture into whites. Turn into Graham-Cracker Crust; refrigerate until set—1 to 2 hours.

While pie is setting, prepare cherry glaze. In small saucepan, mix cornstarch with 2 tablespoons sugar; slowly stir in 1/2 cup liquid drained from canned cherries. Simmer mixture, stirring constantly, until clear and thickened. Stir in thoroughly drained cherries, 1 tablespoon lemon juice, almond extract and food color; cool to room temperature.

When pie has set, pour on glaze; spread to edges of pie; refrigerate at least 2 hours. Makes 10 servings.

### SPRINGTIME STRAWBERRY PIE (3 grams fat per serving)

**Graham-Cracker Crust (see recipe below)**
**2 10-ounce packages frozen sweetened strawberries, thawed**
**1 envelope unflavored gelatin**
**1/3 cup fresh lemon juice**
**2 egg whites**

About 6 hours before serving: Prepare, bake and cool Graham-Cracker Crust. In small saucepan, drain syrup from thawed strawberries. Stir in gelatin; let stand 5 minutes. Heat, stirring constantly, until gelatin just dissolves; stir in lemon juice. Refrigerate, stirring occasionally, until thickened to consistency of unbeaten egg white; then stir in egg whites. With electric mixer at high speed, beat mixture until light and fluffy. Fold in drained strawberries. Heap in pie shell; refrigerate until serving time—at least 3 hours. Makes 8 servings.

### GRAHAM-CRACKER CRUST (3 grams fat per 1/8 crust)

**3/4 cup graham-cracker crumbs**
**1 tablespoon granulated sugar**
**2 tablespoons special margarine**
**1 tablespoon water**
**dash salt**

About 1 hour before filling: Preheat oven to 350°F. In 9-inch pie plate, mix all ingredients. Press on bottom and up sides of plate. Bake 6 to 8 minutes. Cool before filling.

### BAKED ALASKA (negligible fat per serving)

**3 egg whites**
**6 tablespoons granulated sugar**
**1/4 teaspoon vanilla extract**
**dash salt**
**1 pint raspberry or lime sherbet**
**4 1-inch thick slices angel-food cake**

About 15 minutes before serving: Preheat oven to 450°F. Line cookie sheet with double thickness of brown paper. In medium bowl, beat egg whites until soft peaks form. Gradually beat in sugar, then vanilla and salt until stiff peaks form. Cut sherbet into 4 pieces. Place cake slices on brown paper; top each with 1/4 sherbet. Cover with meringue, taking care to seal meringue all around edges of cake. Bake 4 to 5 minutes, or until golden-brown. Serve immediately. Makes 4 servings.

## PUMPKIN CHIFFON PIE (5 grams fat per serving)

Graham-Cracker Crust (see recipe page 291)
dark brown sugar
1 envelope unflavored gelatin
½ teaspoon salt
½ teaspoon nutmeg
½ teaspoon cinnamon
¼ teaspoon ginger
1 tablespoon cornstarch
1 cup evaporated skimmed milk
2 egg whites
1¼ cups canned mashed pumpkin

Early in day: Prepare, bake and cool Graham Cracker Crust. In top of double boiler, combine ½ cup brown sugar, gelatin, salt, nutmeg, cinnamon, ginger, cornstarch, evaporated skimmed milk and ½ cup water; beat smooth with an egg beater. Over boiling water, cook, stirring regularly, 10 minutes. Cool until consistency of thin pudding.

In medium bowl, with electric mixer at high speed, beat egg whites until soft peaks form. Beating constantly, gradually beat in ¼ cup brown sugar until stiff peaks form. Beat pumpkin into gelatin mixture. Fold this mixture into meringue. Pour into pie shell; refrigerate until firm—at least 2 hours. Makes 8 servings.

## FLAKY PIECRUST (10 grams fat for ⅛ crust)

1⅓ cups sifted all-purpose flour
½ teaspoon salt
⅓ cup salad oil
2 tablespoons cold water

About 1 hour before filling: Preheat oven to 450°F. In medium bowl, sift together flour and salt. Dribble salad oil over flour, then mix, with fork, until flour and oil are completely mixed. Dribble water over this mixture and stir to form smooth dough that can easily be formed into a ball. Dampen work surface, then press on sheet of waxed paper about 15-inches long. Place ball of dough in center of paper; cover with second sheet at right angles to first. Gently roll dough into 12-inch circle. Peel off top sheet of paper. Turn dough into 8- or 9-inch pie plate; peel off paper. Gently shape crust into plate; flute or finish edge. Prick bottom and sides of crust at least every ½ inch. Bake 12 to 15 minutes, or until light golden-brown. Cool before filling.

FLAKY PIECRUST FOR 2-CRUST PIE: Use 2 cups sifted all-purpose flour, 1 teaspoon salt, ½ cup salad oil and 3 tablespoons cold water. Prepare as above; divide in half and roll as directed. Bake according to instructions for filling.

## LEMON-CHIFFON PIE (10 grams fat per serving)

single crust 9-inch Flaky Piecrust (see recipe above)
1½ teaspoons unflavored gelatin
granulated sugar
1 tablespoon grated lemon peel
⅓ cup lemon juice
¼ cup water
7 egg whites
¼ teaspoon salt

About 6 hours before serving: Prepare, bake and cool Flaky Piecrust. In top of double boiler, combine gelatin, ⅓ cup sugar, lemon peel, lemon juice, water and 3 egg whites. Beat thoroughly; let stand 5 minutes to soften gelatin. Cook, over boiling water, 5 minutes, or until thickened. Remove from heat; cool slightly; refrigerate, stirring occasionally, until consistency of soft gelatin dessert.

In medium bowl, beat 4 egg whites until soft peaks form. Gradually beat in ½ cup granulated sugar and salt, then beat until soft peaks form. Beat gelatin mixture until smooth; fold into egg whites until smooth. Turn into pie shell; swirl topping. Refrigerate until firm—2 to 3 hours. Makes 8 servings.

## CRANBERRY ANGEL CAKE (negligible fat per serving)

1 8-ounce can whole cranberry sauce
⅓ cup raisins
¼ teaspoon vanilla extract
6 1-inch slices angel-food cake

Day before serving: In small saucepan, heat and stir whole-cranberry sauce with raisins until sauce has melted; stir in vanilla. Cover; refrigerate.

To serve: Top each slice of angel-food with dab of sauce. If desired, sauce may be heated and served warm. Makes 6 servings.

## BUTTERMILK-PINEAPPLE ICE MILK (negligible fat per serving)

2 envelopes unflavored gelatin
2 8½-ounce cans crushed
    pineapple
1 cup granulated sugar
1 quart buttermilk
¼ cup lemon juice
2 teaspoons vanilla extract

About 2 hours before churning ice cream: In medium saucepan, soften gelatin in syrup drained from pineapple. Stir in sugar; heat until sugar and gelatin are just dissolved. Refrigerate in mixing bowl until lukewarm. Slowly stir in buttermilk, then lemon juice, vanilla and crushed pineapple. Refrigerate at least 1 hour. Churn and freeze in ice-cream maker as manufacturer directs. Makes 2 quarts or sixteen ½-cup servings.

## CREAMY PEACH ICE CREAM (negligible fat per serving)

1 14½-ounce can evaporated
    skimmed milk
1 envelope unflavored gelatin
2 tablespoons lemon juice
2 cups sliced fresh peaches
1 cup granulated sugar
1 teaspoon vanilla extract

About 1 hour before churning ice cream: Pour evaporated skimmed milk into large bowl. Place bowl and electric-mixer beater blades in freezer until ice crystals have formed about 1 inch in from edge of bowl.

Meanwhile, in small saucepan, mix gelatin and lemon juice; let stand 5 minutes to soften. Stirring constantly, heat gently over low heat until gelatin has just dissolved. In electric-blender container at high speed, blend gelatin mixture and peaches to form smooth puree. Add sugar and vanilla; blend until sugar is dissolved. (Or peaches may be pureed with sieve or food mill, then mixed with gelatin mixture, sugar and vanilla.) With electric mixer at high speed, beat chilled milk until the consistency of whipped cream. Gently fold in peach mixture; refrigerate 1 hour.

Churn and freeze in ice-cream maker as manufacturer directs. Makes 1½ quarts or twelve ½-cup servings.

CREAMY STRAWBERRY ICE CREAM (negligible fat per serving) Substitute 1 pint fresh strawberries for peaches; prepare as directed for Creamy Peach Ice Cream, above.

## RAINBOW ROLLS (1 gram fat per serving)

2 pints raspberry sherbet, soft-
    ened slightly
2 pints orange sherbet,
    softened slightly

Several days ahead, or up to 6 hours before serving: Line 15" by 10" jelly-roll pan with waxed paper, extending paper about 2 inches beyond each short side of pan. Refrigerate until cold. Spread raspberry sherbet evenly in bottom of chilled pan; freeze until firm—about 3 hours. Then spread orange sherbet evenly over raspberry; freeze until firm, but not solid—about 3 hours. (When frozen solid, sherbet does not roll well.)

To roll: With spatula, loosen long sides of sherbet from waxed paper. Working quickly, start with narrow side of paper and roll sherbet tightly, "jelly-roll" fashion. Discard paper. Place roll, seam side down, on freezer-proof platter. Return to freezer until serving time. Makes 10 servings.

## APRICOT RICE PUDDING (negligible fat per serving)

1 16-ounce can peeled apricots
⅔ cup packaged precooked
    rice
¼ teaspoon salt
2 tablespoons lemon juice
cinnamon and nutmeg

About 45 minutes before serving: Preheat oven to 350°F. Pit, then quarter apricots. In 1-quart casserole, combine rice, salt, lemon juice and apricot pieces and syrup. Sprinkle with cinnamon and nutmeg. Bake 20 to 25 minutes, or until rice is tender. Serve warm. Makes 4 servings.

PINEAPPLE RICE PUDDING: Prepare as directed, but substitute 1 15¾-ounce can pineapple chunks packed in pineapple juice for apricots.

## FRUIT-MERINGUE SURPRISE (negligible fat per serving)

1 large apple, thinly sliced
1 to 2 tablespoons lemon juice
1 16-ounce can freestone
  peach halves (8 halves),
  drained
1 13½-ounce can pineapple
  chunks, drained
2 tablespoons cornstarch
¼ teaspoon cinnamon
dash nutmeg
2 cups orange juice
3 egg whites
6 tablespoons granulated sugar
¼ teaspoon salt

About 20 minutes before serving: Toss apple slices with lemon juice; spread in bottom of cake pan. Preheat oven to 450°F. Place 6 peach halves, cut side down, in pan; distribute pineapple around peach halves.

In medium saucepan, mix cornstarch, cinnamon and nutmeg; stir in orange juice until smooth. Stirring constantly, simmer until juice thickens slightly. Pour over fruit.

In medium bowl, beat egg whites until frothy; beating constantly, gradually add sugar and salt until stiff peaks form. Spread meringue on top of fruit, taking care to seal it all around edges of pan. Bake 4 minutes, or until golden-brown. Serve warm or cold. Makes 6 servings.

## BUTTERMILK WAFFLES (10 grams fat per 4-inch waffle)

1½ cups sifted all-purpose
  flour
3 teaspoons double-acting baking powder
2 tablespoons granulated sugar
½ teaspoon salt
1 cup buttermilk
3 egg whites
½ cup salad oil

About 30 minutes before serving: Preheat waffle iron if manufacturer directs. In medium bowl, sift together flour, baking powder, sugar and salt. In small bowl, beat buttermilk with egg whites and oil. Add to flour mixture, beating until flour is almost smooth. Bake as usual. Serve with syrup or jelly. Makes about twelve 4-inch waffles.

## BANANA TEA BREAD (5 grams fat per serving)

1¾ cups sifted all-purpose
  flour
3 teaspoons double-acting
  baking powder
½ teaspoon salt
3 egg whites
⅔ cup granulated sugar
⅓ cup salad oil
1 cup mashed ripe bananas (2
  to 3 medium bananas)

About 6 hours before serving: Preheat oven to 350°F. Grease and flour 9" by 5" by 3" loaf pan. On sheet of waxed paper, stir together flour, baking powder and salt. In medium bowl, beat egg whites until soft peaks form. Beating continually, slowly add ⅓ cup sugar; beat until stiff peaks form. In medium bowl, blend salad oil and remaining ⅓ cup sugar. With mixer at low speed, beat half the dry ingredients into oil-sugar mixture. Beat in half the crushed bananas. Repeat; then beat batter at medium speed one minute. Pour batter over meringue; fold two together until smooth. Pour into prepared loaf pan; smooth surface. Bake 55 minutes, or until bread comes away from edge of pan. Cool 10 minutes on rack, then turn out of pan. Cool thoroughly before cutting. Makes 16 slices—bread will have compact texture.

## SEEDED HERB TOAST (5 grams fat per serving)

1 slice day-old bread
1 teaspoon special margarine
½ teaspoon sesame seed, ½
  teaspoon poppy seed, ¼ teaspoon celery seed; onion salt

About 5 minutes before serving: Spread bread with margarine. Then sprinkle evenly with sesame, poppy and celery seed; sprinkle with onion salt. Heat under broiler until edges of bread are golden. Serve warm or cold.

## EASY STIR-AND-ROLL BUTTERMILK BISCUITS (5 grams fat per biscuit)

2 cups sifted all-purpose flour
2 teaspoons double-acting baking powder
¼ teaspoon baking soda
1 teaspoon salt
⅓ cup salad oil
⅔ cup buttermilk

About 30 minutes before serving: Preheat oven to 475°F. Sift together flour, baking powder, baking soda and salt. Measure salad oil, then buttermilk into measuring cup (don't stir together). Pour, all at once, over flour mixture. With fork, mix to form soft dough that rounds up into a ball. Turn dough onto sheet of waxed paper; knead lightly, without additional flour, 10 times, or until smooth. Between 2 sheets of waxed paper, pat or roll dough ¼-inch thick. Remove top sheet of paper. Cut with unfloured biscuit cutter. Bake on ungreased cookie sheet 10 to 12 minutes, or until golden brown. Makes about 12 biscuits.

## GRANNY'S FAVORITES (2 grams fat per cookie)

Flaky Piecrust (page 292)
¼ cup granulated sugar
¼ teaspoon cinnamon
⅛ teaspoon nutmeg

About 2 hours before serving: Preheat oven to 450°F. Prepare Flaky Piecrust as directed; roll between two sheets of waxed paper to form rectangle about 12″ by 15″ by ⅛″. With 2-inch cookie cutter, cut out and transfer to ungreased cookie sheets. Starting with fresh sheets of waxed paper, reroll scraps and cut as above.

In small bowl, mix sugar, cinnamon and nutmeg. Sprinkle each cookie with ⅛ teaspoon of mixture; spread smoothly over surface. Bake 12 to 15 minutes, or until golden-brown around edges. Remove from cookie sheets; cool; store in airtight container. Makes about 4 dozen.

## LACY ALMOND ROLLS (5 grams fat per cookie)

⅔ cup canned blanched almonds, finely ground
½ cup special margarine
½ cup granulated sugar
2 tablespoons water
1 tablespoon flour
confectioners' sugar

About 1 hour before serving: Preheat oven to 350°F. Grease and flour several cookie sheets. In large skillet, blend almonds, margarine, sugar, water, flour. Heat over low heat, stirring, until margarine is melted and mixture just boils. On prepared cookie sheets, drop batter, by teaspoonfuls, 3 inches apart. Bake, one sheet at a time, 5 to 6 minutes, or until golden. Let cool slightly; then remove cookies, one at a time, from cookie sheet. Quickly roll around handle of wooden spoon; cool. (If cookies become too hard, warm in oven a minute or so, then roll.)

To serve: Dust lightly with confectioners' sugar. Store tightly covered. Makes about 2½ dozen.

## "BUTTER" DIPS (2 grams fat per "dip")

⅓ cup special margarine
2¼ cups sifted all-purpose flour
1 tablespoon granulated sugar
3½ teaspoons double-acting baking powder
1½ teaspoons salt
1 cup skimmed milk or re-liquefied nonfat dry milk

About 35 minutes before serving: Preheat oven to 450°F. Heat margarine in 13″ by 9″ by 2″ baking pan, in oven, until just melted. Sift together flour, sugar, baking powder and salt. Add milk; stir with fork until dough just clings together —about 30 strokes. Turn onto well-floured board. Roll over to coat with flour. Knead lightly about 10 times. Roll out ½-inch thick into rectangle 12″ by 8″. With floured knife, cut dough in half lengthwise, then crosswise into 16 strips. Dip each strip into melted margarine, then lay, close together, in 2 rows in pan. Bake 15 to 20 minutes, or until golden. Makes 32.

## VANILLA COOKIES (2 grams fat per cookie)

2½ cups sifted all-purpose
   flour
1½ teaspoons double-acting
   baking powder
¾ teaspoon salt
¾ cup salad oil
1 cup granulated sugar
3 egg whites
1 teaspoon vanilla etxract

Early in day: Preheat oven to 375°F. Grease cookie sheets. Sift together flour, baking powder, salt. In large mixing bowl, with electric mixer at medium speed, beat oil and sugar until blended. Add whites, one at a time, beating well after each addition. Gradually beat in vanilla and dry ingredients until smooth. With lightly floured hands, roll dough into balls, using a rounded measuring teaspoonful for each; place 2 inches apart on cookie sheets. Bake 10 to 12 minutes. Makes about 5 dozen.

## RAISIN-GINGER BARS (1 gram fat per bar)

2¼ cups all-purpose flour
½ teaspoon baking soda
¼ teaspoon salt
1¼ teaspoons pumpkin-pie
   spice
⅓ cup special margarine
⅔ cup brown sugar, packed
½ cup dark molasses
½ cup raisins

At least 1 hour before serving: Preheat oven to 375°F. Grease a 15½" by 10½" jelly-roll pan. Sift together flour, baking soda, salt, pumpkin-pie spice; set aside. In large bowl, with electric mixer at medium speed, cream margarine and brown sugar until light and fluffy. Beat in molasses. Divide dry ingredients in half and beat in alternately with ½ cup water until blended. Food in raisins. Spread dough evenly in pan. Bake 15 to 20 minutes. Cool in pan. Cut into 2½" by 1¼" bars. Makes 4 dozen.

## FRUIT FRENCH DRESSING (10 grams fat per tablespoon)

½ teaspoon salt
1 teaspoon granulated sugar
dashes pepper and paprika
⅓ cup salad oil
2 tablespoons mild vinegar
2 teaspoons honey
2 teaspoons lemon juice
¼ teaspoon grated lemon peel

About 2 hours before serving: In small jar, shake together all ingredients. Refrigerate until serving time. Makes about ½ cup.

## SIMPLE FRENCH DRESSING (10 grams fat per tablespoon)

¾ teaspoon salt
dash pepper
¼ teaspoon granulated sugar
¼ cup lemon juice or vinegar
¾ cup salad oil
1 garlic clove, minced
½ teaspoon caraway seed
   (optional)

About 2 hours before serving: In pint jar, combine all ingredients. Shake well; cover; refrigerate until serving time. Makes about 1 cup.

## EGGLESS MAYONNAISE (10 grams fat per tablespoon)

½ teaspoon salt
½ teaspoon dry mustard
¼ teaspoon paprika
1 teaspoon granulated sugar
dash cayenne
¼ cup nonfat dry-milk powder
2 tablespoons ice water
¾ cup salad oil
3 tablespoons lemon juice or 2
   tablespoons wine vinegar

About 1 hour before serving: Refrigerate deep medium bowl and electric-mixer beaters. In chilled bowl, mix salt, mustard, paprika, sugar, cayenne, dry-milk powder and water. With mixer at highest speed, add oil, drop by drop, until 2 tablespoons have been used. Still beating, continue to add oil, by half-teaspoonfuls, until 2 more tablespoons have been added. Still beating, add remaining oil by the teaspoonful. Reduce mixer speed; slowly beat in lemon juice or vinegar. Continue to beat until mayonnaise is thick and smooth. Makes about 1 cup.

# LOW-PURINE DIET

A low-purine diet is used to treat both acute and chronic gout, which results when the body is unable to metabolize uric acid properly. Instead of being excreted through the kidneys, uric acid accumulates in the blood stream, forming sodium urate crystals in the joints—particularly in the fingers and toes.

Gout is primarily a disease of older adults—men more frequently than women. During the acute stages it is extremely painful; left untreated, it can cause changes in bone structure that lead to permanent crippling. Medical treatment attempts to accelerate the rate the urate crystals dissolve; dietary treatment attempts to eliminate those foods that are sources of uric acid, plus fats. The latter have a tendency to slow down the rate of excretion of uric acid through the kidneys.

Although the body manufactures its own supply of uric acid, the uric-acid level in the blood can be decreased significantly by eliminating purine-containing food from your diet. The cellular structure of meat, fish, poultry and some vegetables and legumes contain nucleo-proteins. These are broken down in the body to purines, which, in turn, form uric acid. Therefore, all protein-rich foods, except eggs, milk and cheese (which do not produce purines) are severely restricted on a low-purine diet. Some doctors also restrict the use of coffee, tea, chocolate, carbonated beverages, herbs and spices because they believe that these foods can also be converted to purine. (However, now that acute attacks of gout are more frequently controlled with medication, diets are usually more liberal.) Since the stress on the joints produced by gout is greater and more painful for anyone who is overweight, the diet of such a patient is also restricted in calories.

## MODERATE PURINE RESTRICTION

An outline for "Moderate Purine Restriction" follows; it is typical of the diet most often prescribed for chronic gout, and should be more restricted during acute attacks. As always, check with your doctor before using this diet.

**ALLOWED**

**SOUPS**
All except those containing forbidden foods

**MEAT, FISH AND POULTRY**
2-ounce servings 2 to 4 times a week

**EGGS AND CHEESE**
Use as desired but cook with minimum of added fat. Cottage cheese is particularly recommended

**FORBIDDEN**

**SOUPS**
Avoid all broths, consommés, gravies made from meat drippings

**MEAT, FISH AND POULTRY**
Avoid liver, sweetbreads, brains and kidney completely

**EGGS AND CHEESE**
None

**ALLOWED**

**MILK**

Skimmed milk; buttermilk; yogurt; evaporated skimmed milk. Whole milk and evaporated milk as allowed by physician

**VEGETABLES**

As desired except those forbidden

**FRUITS**

As desired

**BREADS, CEREALS AND PASTAS**

Enriched breads, cereals and pastas

**DESSERTS**

Any made with allowed foods

**MISCELLANEOUS**

Nuts; herbs and spices; condiments; sugar; gelatin

**FORBIDDEN**

**MILK**

Whole milk if fat is restricted

**VEGETABLES**

Dried beans and peas; lentils; asparagus; cauliflower; spinach; mushrooms

**FRUITS**

No restrictions

**BREADS, CEREALS AND PASTAS**

Whole-grain breads and cereals. Quick breads high in fat

**DESSERTS**

Cakes, pastries, frozen desserts etc. high in fat; chocolate may be forbidden—discuss with physician

**MISCELLANEOUS**

Alcoholic beverages. Coffee and tea if forbidden by physician. Gravies containing meat drippings, broth or bouillon

The limitation on the sources of protein to primarily eggs, milk and cheese, plus the limitation on fats, makes this a difficult diet to maintain. The cooking and planning aids that follow should be helpful:

- Break away from the habit of meat, potato and vegetable meals; try soup and sandwiches, casserole dishes, salads. (Main-dish salads fit fairly easily into a low-purine diet plan.)
- When possible, serve five or six "snacks" a day instead of three large meals. You'll find the lack of meat won't be quite so obvious. When meat is allowed, slice it thin to make the serving look more generous.
- Mix cottage cheese with apricots, peaches or pineapple for an appetizing off-beat breakfast.
- Try instant breakfast made with skimmed milk; crackers and a salad for lunch or dinner.
- For homemade fried rice: Stir and cook rice in a little butter until brown; add

onion, celery, soy sauce and water; cook until fluffy. Stir in one or two scrambled eggs.
- Check the infinite variety of cheese flavors and textures available at cheese shops; start to accumulate recipes. Avoid cream cheese—it's too high in fat and too low in protein to be a good choice.
- Learn how to incorporate "milk-without-fat" into your diet: Substitute cottage cheese or yogurt for sour cream in baked potatoes; try diet margarine, and make the fat allowance go farther; dilute canned or frozen cream-of-potato soup with half the usual skimmed milk for a hearty main-dish soup; use Mozzarella cheese made from partially skimmed milk.
- For those important snacks: A milkshake made in a blender with ice milk, nonfat dry-milk powder and fruit flavorings; "sour cream dips" made with yogurt (or blend cottage cheese until smooth)—use vegetables as "dippers;" apple slices and cheese; flavored yogurts.

## LOW-PURINE DIETS: 25 Recipes

### YANKEE PASTA (15 grams fat per serving)

1 8-ounce package thin spaghetti
1 15½-ounce jar meatless spaghetti sauce
1 cup grated mild Cheddar cheese (or 1 4-ounce package shredded mild Cheddar cheese)
chopped parsley for garnish

About 30 minutes before serving: Cook spaghetti as label directs; drain. Meanwhile, heat spaghetti sauce to boiling. Toss hot spaghetti with cheese until cheese melts.

To serve: Pile spaghetti in center of serving dish; surround with sauce; top with parsley. Makes 3 servings.

### PINEAPPLE-CHEESE SPREAD (5 grams fat per serving)

1 8½-ounce can crushed pineapple, thoroughly drained
1 8-ounce container small-curd creamed cottage cheese
dash salt
8 slices toast

About 10 minutes before serving: Stir together pineapple, cottage cheese and salt. Use as filling for 4 sandwiches.

### WHITE-CAP STUFFED TOMATOES (10 grams fat per serving)

4 large tomatoes
salt
2 8-ounce containers small-curd, creamed cottage cheese
¾ cup packaged bread-stuffing mix
2 hard-cooked eggs, finely chopped
1 tablespoon butter or margarine
½ tablespoon flour
dash onion powder
½ cup skimmed milk or reliquefied nonfat dry milk
chopped parsley for garnish

About 45 minutes before serving: Preheat oven to 350°F. Wash tomatoes, then cut thin slice from stem end of each. Scoop out seeds and pulp, reserving pulp. Sprinkle insides with salt. Sieve ½ cup of the cottage cheese.

Chop ½ cup tomato pulp; mix with stuffing mix, eggs and unsieved cottage cheese. Use mixture to stuff tomatoes. Place in shallow baking dish; bake 30 minutes.

About 10 minutes before tomatoes are done: In small saucepan, melt butter; add flour and onion powder; stir until smooth and bubbly. Add milk; heat, stirring constantly, until smooth and thickened; stir in sieved cottage cheese; heat to boiling.

To serve: Top each tomato with cottage-cheese sauce; sprinkle with parsley. Makes 4 servings.

### CHEDDAR-STUFFED POTATOES (10 grams fat per serving)

4 large baking potatoes
½ to ¾ cup milk or skimmed milk
1 4-ounce package shredded mild Cheddar cheese (or 1 cup grated mild Cheddar cheese)
2 tablespoons chopped parsley

About 1 hour and 20 minutes before serving: Preheat oven to 450°F. Prick skins of potatoes with fork. Bake 45 to 55 minutes, or until fork-tender. Turn oven to 325°F.

Cut thin slice from each potato and hollow out, leaving shell intact. In medium bowl, with electric mixer at high speed, mash potatoes. Beat in enough milk to make them creamy. Beat in cheese and parsley until cheese is melted. Refill potato shells, heaping them high. Bake, on cookie sheet, 30 minutes, or until potatoes are lightly browned. Makes 4 servings.

## STUFFED TOMATOES PROVENÇALE (10 grams fat per serving)

4 large ripe tomatoes
salt
1 tablespoon butter or margarine
1 small onion, finely chopped
1½ cups cooked rice
1 cup grated mild Cheddar or Swiss cheese

About 30 minutes before serving: Preheat oven to 350°F. Cut thin slice from stem end of each tomato. Scoop out seeds and pulp, reserving pulp. Sprinkle insides with salt. Chop tomato pulp into small pieces.

In medium skillet over medium heat, in butter, sauté onion until golden. Add rice and tomato pulp; heat, stirring constantly, just to boiling. Remove from heat, then stir in cheese. Use mixture to fill tomato shells. Place in baking dish; bake 15 minutes, or until tomatoes are tender. Makes 4 servings.

## OPEN-FACED TOAST AND EGGS (15 grams fat per serving)

4 slices bread
4 1-ounce slices Provolone cheese
4 poached eggs

About 15 minutes before serving: Preheat oven to 350°F. Toast bread, then top each with slice of cheese. Place on cookie sheet and heat in oven until cheese is just melted—about 3 minutes. Top each slice with poached egg. Makes 4 servings.

## BLUE CHEESE AND MACARONI (15 grams fat per serving)

1 8-ounce package elbow macaroni
2 cups skimmed milk or reliquefied nonfat dry milk
1 teaspoon salt
3 ounces blue cheese, crumbled
1 cup grated process Gruyère cheese
2 slices bread, cubed

About 1½ hours before serving: Cook macaroni as label directs but use minimum cooking time; drain. Preheat oven to 350°F. Scald milk; stir in salt. In 1½-quart casserole, layer one-third of hot drained macaroni; top with crumbled blue cheese. Repeat, using macaroni and Gruyère. Top with remaining macaroni; then pour on hot milk. Top macaroni with bread cubes. Bake, covered, 20 minutes; uncover and bake 15 minutes more, or until cubes brown. Makes 4 servings.

## BAKED EGGS ON TOAST (10 grams fat per serving)

butter or margarine
4 slices white bread
4 eggs, separated
salt or seasoned salt

About 20 minutes before serving: Preheat oven to 350°F. Lightly butter each slice of bread; place on cookie sheet. In medium bowl, beat egg whites until stiff peaks form. Heap beaten egg whites on slices of bread; make slight hollow in center of each; fill with yolk; sprinkle entire egg with bit of salt. Bake about 15 minutes, or until yolk is almost set and white is lightly browned. Makes 4 servings.

## FAR-WEST FRIED RICE (20 grams fat per serving)

2 tablespoons butter or margarine
1 stalk green celery, finely chopped
¼ cup finely chopped onion
½ cup chopped walnuts
1 1½-ounce box (⅓ cup) raisins
3 cups cold cooked rice
1 to 2 tablespoons soy sauce
4 poached eggs

About 20 minutes before serving: In large skillet, in butter, sauté celery, onion, walnuts and raisins until onion is golden. Stir in rice; stirring constantly, cook until it begins to brown very lightly. Stir in soy sauce to taste.

To serve: Divide rice among 4 plates, then top each serving with poached egg. Makes 4 servings.

## CHEESE-AND-POTATO SOUP (25 grams fat per serving)

1 10¼-ounce can frozen condensed cream-of-potato soup
1 soup-can skimmed milk or reliquefied nonfat dry milk
1 4-ounce package shredded Cheddar cheese (or 1 cup grated Cheddar cheese)
1 carrot, grated
2 slices dry toast, quartered

About 20 minutes before serving: In medium saucepan, heat soup and milk until soup melts and mixture just boils. If desired, blend soup in electric blender or sieve to make a smooth puree. Add cheese; stir over low heat until melted. Serve, topped with grated carrot and accompanied by toast quarters. Makes two 1¼-cup servings.

## ELEVEN-LAYERED CASSEROLE (15 grams fat per serving)

1 8-ounce package elbow macaroni
2 large tomatoes, sliced
2 cups grated process Cheddar cheese
1 teaspoon salt
¼ teaspoon oregano leaves
2 onions, thinly sliced
1 14½-ounce can evaporated skimmed milk
2 tablespoons shredded Parmesan cheese (optional)

About 1 hour before serving: Cook macaroni as label directs but use shortest recommended cooking time; drain. Butter 2-quart casserole; line sides with tomato slices. Preheat oven to 350°F.

Place half of macaroni in bottom of casserole; top with 1 cup cheese. Combine salt and oregano; sprinkle half of it over cheese. Sprinkle with half of onion slices. Repeat this layering, then pour evaporated skimmed milk over mixture. Sprinkle with Parmesan cheese. Bake 30 minutes, or until lightly browned. Makes 6 servings.

## CURRIED EGGS (15 grams fat per serving)

6 hard-cooked eggs
2 tablespoons butter or margarine
1 medium onion, finely chopped
1 large stalk green celery, finely chopped
3 tablespoons flour
1 teaspoon salt
1 to 2 teaspoons curry
2 cups skimmed milk or reliquefied nonfat dry milk
4 slices toast

About 30 minutes before serving: Shell and thinly slice or chop eggs. In skillet over medium heat, in butter, sauté onion and celery until onion is golden. Stir in flour, salt and curry. Slowly stir in milk; cook, stirring constantly, until thickened and smooth. Stir in chopped eggs; heat just to boiling.

To serve: Top toast with curried eggs. Makes 4 servings.

## CALICO MACARONI AND CHEESE (20 grams fat per serving)

1 8-ounce package elbow macaroni
⅔ cup nonfat dry-milk powder
½ teaspoon dry mustard
1 teaspoon salt
2⅓ cups (1 13¾-ounce can plus 1 6-ounce can) evaporated milk, undiluted
1½ teaspoons Worcestershire
¼ cup minced canned pimento
⅓ cup minced green pepper
½ pound sharp Cheddar cheese, grated

About 1 hour and 10 minutes before serving: Cook macaroni as label directs, but use shortest recommended cooking time. Meanwhile, preheat oven to 350°F. In 2-quart casserole, mix dry-milk powder, mustard and salt; slowly stir in evaporated milk to form a smooth paste. Stir in Worcestershire, pimento and green pepper.

Thoroughly drain cooked macaroni; mix it and grated cheese with milk mixture in casserole. Bake 25 to 30 minutes, or until lightly browned on top. Let stand 10 minutes before serving. Makes 6 generous servings.

## MOLDED COTTAGE-CHEESE SALAD (15 grams fat per serving)

1 8½-ounce can crushed pineapple, drained
1 16-ounce container creamed
   cottage cheese
1 cup grated mild Cheddar
   cheese
4 individual lettuce cups

At least 4 hours before serving: In medium bowl, stir together pineapple, cottage cheese and grated cheese. Pour into
a rinsed 9" by 5" by 3" loaf pan. Refrigerate at least 3 hours.
To serve: Spoon into lettuce cups. Makes 4 servings.

## CORN FRITTERS (10 grams fat per serving)

3 eggs, separated
¼ cup flour
1 teaspoon salt
1 16-ounce can whole-kernel
   corn, thoroughly drained
3 tablespoons salad oil

About 30 minutes before serving: In medium bowl, beat egg
whites until stiff peaks form. In small bowl, beat egg yolks
well; stir in flour and salt, then corn. Fold mixture into
beaten egg whites.

In large skillet over medium heat, in oil, cook batter in
¼-cup dollops until dark-golden brown; turn; brown on other
side. Drain on paper toweling. Makes 4 servings of 3 fritters each.

## HOT EGG-SALAD SANDWICH (10 grams fat per serving)

1 12-ounce loaf French bread
6 hard-cooked eggs, finely
   chopped
1½ cups chopped celery
¼ cup minced onion
1 garlic clove, minced
¾ teaspoon salt
⅓ cup low-calorie (imitation)
   mayonnaise
1 to 2 tablespoons prepared
   mustard
raw vegetable garnishes

About 50 minutes before serving: Preheat oven to 375°F.
Cut bread in half horizontally. Remove most of soft part
from center, leaving shell about ½-inch thick. Prepare one
cup of crumbs from soft part.

In large bowl, toss together 1 cup soft bread crumbs,
chopped eggs, celery, onion, garlic, salt, mayonnaise and
mustard. Use to fill bottom half of bread shell; cover with
top. Using double folds, wrap bread in wide foil. Bake 30
to 40 minutes.

To serve: Cut into quarters; garnish platter with raw vegetables. Makes 4 servings.

## FRIDAY'S LASAGNA (20 grams fat per serving)

1 tablespoon olive oil
1 cup minced onion
1 cup chopped green pepper
1½ teaspoons salt
½ teaspoon oregano leaves
2 tablespoons chopped parsley
1 16-ounce can tomatoes
2 8-ounce cans tomato sauce
1 tablespoon granulated sugar
9 wide lasagna noodles
3 8-ounce containers creamed
   cottage cheese
¾ pound grated Swiss cheese
½ cup grated Edam or Gouda
   cheese

About 1 hour and 45 minutes before serving: In large skillet,
in olice oil, sauté onion and green pepper until onion is
golden. Add salt, oregano, parsley, tomatoes, tomato sauce
and sugar; simmer, uncovered, 30 minutes.

Meanwhile, cook noodles as label directs; drain. Preheat
oven to 350°F. In bottom of 12" by 8" by 2" shallow baking
dish, spread one-quarter of hot tomato sauce. Cover with
three wide noodles, one container of cottage cheese, one-
third of grated Swiss cheese in that order; top with one-
quarter of hot tomato sauce.

Repeat two more times. Top tomato sauce with Edam
cheese. Bake 35 minutes; let stand 15 minutes before
serving. Makes 8 servings.

## ALICE'S HOT-EGG PATTIES (20 grams fat per serving)

butter or margarine
1 tablespoon chopped onion
1 tablespoon chopped parsley
¼ cup flour
1 cup skimmed milk or reliquefied nonfat dry milk
1 teaspoon salt
6 hard-cooked eggs
1 egg
packaged dried bread crumbs
Crushed-Pineapple Relish (optional), see recipe at right, below

About 4 hours before serving: In medium saucepan, in 2 tablespoons butter, sauté onion and parsley until onion is golden. Stir in flour and cook about one minute. Stirring constantly, add milk and salt; heat until thickened and smooth. In medium bowl, finely chop eggs. Stir in hot white sauce; cover; refrigerate.

About 20 minutes before serving: In shallow bowl, beat egg with a bit of water. Pour about ¾ cup bread crumbs onto sheet of waxed paper. Stir cold egg mixture until smooth. Drop a dollop onto bread crumbs; turn over, dip other side, then flatten slightly with spatula. Dip patty into beaten egg; then again into bread crumbs. Repeat, making 8 patties.

In large skillet over medium heat, in 2 tablespoons butter, cook patties until brown—about 5 minutes on each side. Serve with Crushed-Pineapple Relish. Makes 4 servings.

CRUSHED-PINEAPPLE RELISH: In medium saucepan, place 1 8½-ounce can crushed pineapple, drained; mix with 3 tablespoons brown sugar, 1 tablespoon vinegar and 1 tablespoon butter or margarine. Cook, stirring occasionally, 5 to 10 minutes. Makes about 1 cup.

## EGGPLANT STEAKS À LA HOLSTEIN (25 grams fat per serving)

5 eggs
1 tablespoon milk
½ cup packaged dried bread crumbs
⅓ cup grated Parmesan cheese
1 medium eggplant
2 tablespoons butter or margarine
1 cup grated Edam or Cheddar cheese
seasoned salt

About 40 minutes before serving: Preheat oven to 350°F. In flat dish, beat together 1 egg and milk until smooth. On piece of waxed paper, stir together bread crumbs and Parmesan cheese. Cut stem from eggplant, then cut 4 lengthwise slices, ½- to ¾-inch thick, from center of eggplant; pare slices. Taking care to completely coat both sides, dip slices, first into egg-milk mixture, then into crumb-cheese mixture. In large skillet, in butter, brown slices slowly until browned and almost tender; turn; brown other side. Place on cookie sheet; sprinkle with Edam cheese. Bake 10 to 15 minutes, or until cheese melts and eggplant is tender. Meanwhile, poach 4 eggs; sprinkle lightly with seasoned salt. Top each eggplant slice with an egg. Makes 4 servings.

## CHEESE ONION SOUFFLÉ (20 grams fat per serving)

1 medium onion
1 tablespoon butter or margarine
2 tablespoons finely minced onion
¼ cup flour
1 cup skimmed milk or reliquefied nonfat dry milk
½ teaspoon salt
1 cup grated sharp Cheddar cheese (or 1 4-ounce package shredded sharp Cheddar cheese)
4 eggs, separated
seasoned pepper

About 1 hour before serving: Preheat oven to 350°F. Lightly butter 2-quart casserole. Cut onion into very thin slices, then separate rings.

In small saucepan over medium heat, in butter, sauté minced onion until golden. Mix in flour; stirring constantly, slowly add milk and salt until smooth. Cook, continuing to stir, until thickened and smooth. Remove from heat. Stir in cheese until melted, then egg yolks.

In medium bowl, beat egg whites until stiff peaks form. Carefully fold cheese mixture into whites. Turn into casserole; smooth surface. Arrange onion rings in attractive pattern on top; sprinkle to taste with seasoned pepper. Bake 45 minutes, or until a rich brown. Serve immediately. Makes 4 servings.

## BROCCOLI IN CHEESE CUSTARD (20 grams fat per serving)

1 10-ounce package frozen
  chopped broccoli
¾ cup nonfat dry-milk powder
½ cup grated Swiss cheese
2 eggs
2 tablespoons lemon juice
2 tablespoons butter or margarine, melted
1 teaspoon salt

About 1 hour before serving: Preheat oven to 350°F. Cook broccoli as label directs; drain thoroughly. Meanwhile, in large bowl, beat remaining ingredients with 1¼ cups hot water until combined. Place broccoli in 1½-quart casserole; pour in custard mixture. Set casserole in shallow pan on oven rack; add enough hot water to pan to come up an inch around casserole. Bake 40 minutes or until knife inserted in center comes out clean. Makes 4 servings.

## OEUFS À LA BERNADETTE (20 grams fat per serving) ·

butter or margarine
½ tablespoon flour
½ cup milk
½ cup grated Edam or Cheddar cheese
4 slices bread
1 large tomato
salt
4 eggs
paprika and chopped parsley for
  garnish

About 25 minutes before serving: Preheat broiler 10 minutes if manufacturer directs. In small saucepan, melt 1 tablespoon butter or margarine; stir in flour. Add milk; stirring constantly, heat until smooth and thickened; stir in grated cheese.

Lightly butter bread; cut tomato into 4 slices; place bread on cookie sheet; top each slice with tomato slice; sprinkle lightly with salt. Broil until edge of bread toasts lightly and tomato slices are hot.

Meanwhile, poach eggs to desired doneness. Top each tomato slice with poached egg; sprinkle with more salt; add dab of cheese sauce and sprinkle with paprika and parsley. Makes 4 servings.

## GRANDMA'S VEGETABLE CUTLETS (15 grams fat per serving)

butter or margarine
1 cup chopped onion
1 cup grated carrots
½ cup chopped celery
1 8-ounce can cut green beans,
  drained
2 eggs
1 teaspoon salt
¼ cup matzoh meal
chopped parsley for garnish

About 4 hours before serving: In large skillet over medium heat, in 2 tablespoons butter, sauté chopped onion, grated carrots and chopped celery until onion is golden; add green beans. Cool; grind mixture with food chopper. Mix ground vegetables, eggs, salt and matzo meal; cover; refrigerate.

About 30 minutes before serving: In large skillet, heat 2 tablespoons butter or margarine until bubbling. Drop vegetable mixture, by large dollops, into hot pan; spread until about ½- to ¾-inch thick; cook, over medium heat 5 minutes on each side, or until browned. Serve, topped with sprinkling of parsley. Makes 4 servings.

## CHEESY SPAGHETTI OMELET (15 grams fat per serving)

3 eggs, separated
¼ teaspoon salt
1 10¼-ounce can spaghetti in
  tomato sauce with cheese
2 tablespoons salad oil
¾ cup grated process sharp
  Cheddar cheese

About 30 minutes before serving: Mix egg yolks with salt and canned spaghetti in tomato sauce. Beat 3 egg whites until stiff peaks form, then fold spaghetti mixture into whites.

Preheat oven to 375°F. In large skillet, heat oil; pour in spaghetti mixture and cook, over medium heat, 10 minutes, or until omelet is brown on the bottom.

Sprinkle omelet with cheese; bake 10 to 15 minutes, or until cheese is melted and top of omelet light brown and firm. Makes 4 servings.

## MILANESE MINESTRONE (10 grams fat per serving)

2 tablespoons olive oil
1 medium onion, minced
1 teaspoon thyme leaves
2 tablespoons canned Italian
  tomato paste
2 16-ounce cans tomatoes
3 stalks celery, sliced
2 carrots, scraped and thinly
  sliced
2 small zucchini, sliced
2 medium potatoes, cut into
  3/4-inch cubes
1 very small head cabbage, cut
  into 8 wedges
1 tablespoon salt
2 tablespoons chopped parsley
1/3 cup uncooked long-grain rice
1 cup grated Parmesan cheese

About 1 hour and 15 minutes before serving: In large Dutch oven, in olive oil, sauté onion and thyme until onion is golden. Add tomato paste and 1/2 cup water; simmer gently for 10 minutes. Add 4 cups water and remaining ingredients except rice; simmer gently, covered, 20 minutes. Stir in rice; simmer 25 minutes longer. Serve with grated Parmesan cheese. Makes 6 servings.

# LOW-SODIUM DIETS

Salt-free diet is the less accurate, but more descriptive, name for a low-sodium diet. Sodium is a chemical element that forms part of the compound sodium chloride—table salt. It also occurs naturally in other forms, such as monosodium glutamate (a seasoning used as a flavor enhancer which also occurs naturally in foods), sodium caseinate (a protein fraction of milk) and sodium sulfite (used to prevent dried fruit from turning black).

Sodium is an essential nutrient which functions in the body primarily to maintain proper water balance. With too little sodium the body becomes dehydrated; with too much, swelling (edema) occurs. Under normal circumstances the body can handle large quantities of sodium by excreting the excesses through the kidneys. However, in cases of high blood pressure, often in pregnancy and in some kidney diseases, the body is unable to excrete the extra sodium. Edema occurs and high-blood pressure is aggravated.

Treatment is two-fold—medications called diuretics which accelerate the excretion of sodium are given, and the levels of sodium in the diet are restricted. Normal diets vary greatly in sodium content—5 to 10 grams a day is common. Sodium-restricted diets limit this intake to from 2000 (2 grams) to as little as 200 milligrams daily. As the diet becomes more restricted, the need to limit the choice of foods and to depend on home-prepared foods increases. The outlines on pages 307–309 delineate the general restrictions for 2000-, 1000-, 500-, and 250-milligram sodium diets.

If a low-sodium diet is used in treatment of high-blood pressure, it is usually combined with a low-fat, low-cholesterol diet. If used in pregnancy, emphasis is given to providing all the vitamins and minerals needed at that time, but within the 2000 to 2600 calories a day usually recommended. When used to treat kidney conditions such as glomerulo-nephritis and nephrosis, the protein content of the diet may be normal *or* severely restricted. Because of the specialized nature of the low-sodium diet when combined with a low-protein diet, that particular problem is not treated in this book. Restrict sodium in the diet only with a physician's specific instructions.

# 500-MILLIGRAM LOW-SODIUM DIET

Select foods from the following:

## ALLOWED

### MEAT, FISH AND POULTRY

Up to 5 ounces cooked lean meat a day
Unsalted fresh, frozen or canned meat,
    fish or poultry
See exceptions to right

### EGGS AND CHEESE

Eggs are limited to one a day
Unsalted cottage or pot cheese may be
    used in place of meat—$\frac{1}{4}$ cup = 1
    ounce meat

### MILK

Up to 2 cups whole milk, skimmed milk
    or cream a day

### VEGETABLES

All but exceptions listed at right

### FRUITS

All but crystallized or glazed fruit and
    maraschino cherries

### BREADS, CEREALS AND PASTAS

Breads and rolls made without salt
Quick breads made with low-sodium bak-
    ing powder (see page 310)
Low-sodium crackers
Farina, grits, oatmeal and rolled wheat
    cooked without salt
Puffed rice, puffed wheat and shredded
    wheat
Noodles, macaroni, spaghetti and rice
    cooked without added salt

### FATS

Unsalted (sweet) butter or margarine
Salad oil and cooking fat
Low-sodium salad dressings
Unsalted nuts and avocado

## FORBIDDEN

### MEAT, FISH AND POULTRY

Omit all salted, smoked, corned or
    koshered meat, fish or poultry
Organ meats except liver and heart
Frozen fish fillets
Shellfish: clams, crab, lobster, scallops,
    shrimp, etc.

### EGGS AND CHEESE

All cheeses except unsalted cottage or pot
    cheese

### MILK

Buttermilk
Yogurt

### VEGETABLES

Canned vegetables except low-sodium
    packed
Frozen vegetables processed with salt—
    particularly lima beans and peas
These vegetables in any form: artichokes,
    beet greens, beets, carrots, celery,
    chard, dandelion greens, kale, mustard
    greens, sauerkraut, spinach, white tur-
    nips

### FRUITS

Crystallized or glazed fruit and maraschino
    cherries

### BREADS, CEREALS AND PASTAS

Regular homemade and commercial yeast
    breads
Regular commercial and homemade quick
    breads
Self-rising flour
Regular commercial crackers
Quick-cooking and enriched cereals con-
    taining sodium compounds
All other dry cereals except special low-
    sodium packs
Potato chips and pretzels

### FATS

Salted butter or margarine
Bacon fat
Commercial and homemade dressings
Salted nuts

**ALLOWED**

**DESSERTS**

Fruit
Baked goods made without salt and with low-sodium baking powder
Homemade puddings made with allowed milk and no salt
Italian ices
Gelatin dessert made with unflavored gelatin, sugar and fruit juices

**BEVERAGES**

Coffee, tea, decaffeinated coffee, cocoa (see right), carbonated beverages

**CONDIMENTS**

Herbs and spices
Vanilla and other extracts
Vinegar and lemon
Dry mustard

**MISCELLANEOUS**

Sugar, hard candy, honey, jams and jellies (not containing sodium benzoate), maple syrup
Low-sodium peanut butter (make your own in blender with roasted peanuts)

**FORBIDDEN**

**DESSERTS**

Regular commercial and homemade baked goods
Puddings made from mixes
Ice cream and sherbets
Gelatin desserts made from mixes

**BEVERAGES**

Dutch-process cocoa and instant cocoa mixes

**CONDIMENTS**

Salt; celery, onion and garlic salt; monosodium glutamate
Catchup; chili and barbecue sauces
Soy sauce
Prepared mustard and horseradish
Worcestershire, A-1 and Tabasco
Bouillon cubes and canned broth

**MISCELLANEOUS**

Baking powder and soda
Pickles, olives and relishes
Molasses
Canned and frozen soups
Regular peanut butter

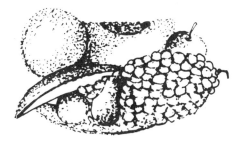

## 250-MILLIGRAM LOW-SODIUM DIET

Follow the 500 milligram diet, but substitute low-sodium milk for regular.

## 1000-MILLIGRAM LOW-SODIUM DIET

Follow the 500-milligram diet, but use up to ¼ teaspoon salt each day to season food. Or substitute 4 slices regular salted bread for unsalted. Add carrots, celery, spinach in moderation.

## 2000-MILLIGRAM LOW-SODIUM DIET

Follow the 500-milligram diet, but add the following: fresh (instead of frozen or canned) shellfish; regular breads, quick breads and crackers (except those with salted tops); salted butter or margarine; all cooked and ready-to-eat cereals; all vegetables except those prepared with brine, such as sauerkraut.

*Sodium Content in Food*

If only the food itself is considered, and it is assumed that no sodium is added during processing, meat and milk are the highest natural source of sodium, fruits and vegetables the lowest. Breads are relatively high because they contain salt. If calories need not be restricted, the emphasis in a low-sodium diet, is placed on limiting the meat, fish and poultry intake to 5 ounces a day, milk to 2 glasses. Both the sodium and calorie levels can be adjusted by varying the amount of breads (regular or salt-free), butter (again regular or salt-free) and fruits and vegetables eaten.

The most important rule to follow in planning a low-sodium diet (and any of the other special diets) is to read labels. Foods which list salt, sodium (as in monosodium glutamate, sodium propionate or sodium alginate), brine, baking powder, or soda (as in bicarbonate of soda or baking soda) in ingredients are forbidden.

There is, however, a variety of low-sodium (unsalted) products on the market. Some are more widely distributed than others. If the items listed below are not available in your local supermarket, try gourmet shops or health-food stores.

| | |
|---|---|
| tomatoes | bouillon cubes |
| tuna | meat tenderizers |
| curry | salad dressings (or make your own |
| chili powder | —see page 317) |
| soups | prepared mustards |
| catchup | unsalted butter or margarine |
| | unsalted melba toast—plain and rye |

On a low-sodium diet, you may have to leave out salt, but there are other ways to add flavor and character to your cooking. Here are a few alternatives:

1. Add wine to sauces and use in gravies. (Do not use "cooking wines"—they contain salt.)
2. Experiment with fruit sauces and sweet-and-sour sauces for pork, chicken and fish.
3. Save cooking liquid from vegetables to substitute for broths as a base for sauces and gravies.
4. Use a wide variety of herbs and spices in your cooking as a substitute for salt. See chart on page 318.
5. Lemon juice is the best all-purpose seasoning on a low-sodium diet. It can add tang to meat, vegetables, fruit and salads.
6. Make homemade seasoned rice mixes, using herbs and spices, dried onion (not containing sodium compounds), curry or garlic or onion powder.

If sodium is restricted in the diet, it is also important to avoid medicines and dentrifices containing it. Alkalizers for indigestion, laxatives, pain relievers, sedatives and cough medicines often contain sodium so don't take even nonprescription medications without your physician's approval. Also, some toothpastes and mouth washes contain sodium. As a precaution, don't swallow toothpaste, and rinse your mouth well after using mouth wash.

Water for drinking is another possible source of sodium. Do not drink water that has been softened by an ion exchange (zeolite) system. Ask your physician about the sodium content of local water—does it contain high amounts of sodium? If there is any doubt, the Department of Health can provide you with the necessary information. If local water can't be used, you will have to drink and cook with distilled water.

---

*Low-sodium baking powder*

Commercial low-sodium baking-powder mixes are available in many drug stores or health-food stores. Follow the label instructions for using each brand. Or ask your druggist to prepare low-sodium baking powder using this formula:

| | |
|---|---:|
| potassium bicarbonate | 79.5 grams |
| cornstarch | 56.0 grams |
| tartaric acid | 15.0 grams |
| potassium bitartrate | 112.3 grams |

Use 1½ teaspoons of this baking powder for each teaspoon of regular baking powder called for in a recipe. (This adjustment has already been made in the special low-sodium recipes that follow.)

LOW-SODIUM DIET: 25 Recipes (also to be used in Low-Fat, Low-Cholesterol Diet, where indicated)

## BREAD OR ROLLS (5 milligrams sodium per slice or per roll)

1 teaspoon active dry yeast
1 cup minus 2 tablespoons warm water
2 tablespoons granulated sugar
1 tablespoon salad oil
2¾ cups sifted all-purpose flour
3 tablespoons wheat germ (optional)
¼ cup skimmed milk or reliquefied nonfat dry milk
unsalted butter or margarine, melted (optional)*

At least 4 hours before serving: In large bowl, dissolve yeast in warm water. Add sugar, salad oil, flour, wheat germ and milk. Mix until dough comes away from bowl; turn out onto generously floured board; knead until smooth and satiny. Place in lightly oiled bowl; cover with damp towel, then let rise in warm place (about 85°F.) for 1 hour, or until double in bulk.

Return to floured board; knead 5 minutes, then form into loaf. Place in lightly oiled 8" by 4" by 3" loaf pan. Spread surface of loaf with butter, if desired.

Preheat oven to 400°F. Let bread rise in warm place until double in bulk—about 30 to 40 minutes. Bake 30 to 40 minutes, or until bread has hollow sound when top is tapped. Immediately remove from pan and cool, right side up, on cake rack. Makes 1 loaf.

**For rolls:** Mix, then let dough rise as directed; after second kneading, treat in one of ways below.

**For crescents:** Divide dough into 2 equal portions. Using pie plate as guide, roll dough into circle 10 to 11 inches in diameter; cut into 10 wedge-shaped sections; lightly brush surface with melted butter; roll each section into crescent, then place on greased cookie sheet. Repeat with remaining half of dough.

**For pan rolls:** Divide batter into 5 equal portions, then divide each portion into 4 equal parts. Roll each into ball; dip into butter and place, almost touching, in 2 greased 8-inch layer-cake pans.

**For Vienna rolls:** Divide dough as for pan rolls. With fingers, flatten each ball until it is a rectangle about 2½" by 1", then taper ends. Place on greased cookie sheet about 2 inches apart; brush each with mixture of egg white and 1 tablespoon water; sprinkle with sesame, caraway or poppy seed, if desired.

Preheat oven to 350°F. Let rolls rise until double in bulk—about 30 to 40 minutes; bake 12 to 15 minutes, or until golden-brown; remove from pan immediately. Serve warm or reheat to serve. Makes 20 rolls.

* For low-fat, low-cholesterol diet use unsalted special margarine.

## MUFFINS (15 milligrams sodium per muffin)

1 cup sifted all-purpose flour
2 teaspoons low-sodium baking powder
1 tablespoon granulated sugar
½ cup milk*
1 egg*
2 tablespoons salad oil*

About 30 minutes before serving: Preheat oven to 400°F. Lightly grease 9 medium cups of muffin pans. In medium bowl, sift together flour, baking powder and sugar. Mix together milk, egg and oil; stir into dry ingredients until latter are just dampened. Fill each muffin cup about half full. Bake 18 to 22 minutes, or until muffins are light golden-brown. Makes 9.

* For low-fat, low-cholesterol diet use skimmed milk and only white of egg; increase salad oil to 3 tablespoons.

## BAKING-POWDER BISCUITS (5 milligrams sodium per biscuit)

1 cup sifted all-purpose flour
2 teaspoons low-sodium baking
powder
1 teaspoon sugar
2 tablespoons unsalted butter
or margarine*
½ cup milk*

About 25 minutes before serving: Preheat oven to 450°F. In medium bowl, sift together flour, baking powder and sugar; cut butter into dry ingredients until mixture is like coarse cornmeal. Stir in milk; beat mixture until smooth. Drop, by rounded tablespoonfuls, onto greased cookie sheet. Bake 12 to 15 minutes, or until surface rebounds when touched; biscuits will be only very lightly browned. Serve warm. Makes 10.
Variations:
• Before baking, sprinkle each biscuit with about ¼ teaspoon grated lemon or orange peel.
• Mix 2 tablespoons fresh chopped chives into batter.
• Before baking, sprinkle each biscuit with about ¼ teaspoon sesame or ⅛ teaspoon poppy seed.
• Mix in ½ cup thoroughly drained, crushed pineapple and decrease milk to ⅓ cup.

* For low-fat, low-cholesterol diet use 3 tablespoons unsalted special margarine and skimmed milk in place of regular.

## CORNBREAD (15 milligrams sodium per serving)

¼ cup unsalted butter or margarine*
¼ cup granulated sugar
1 egg*
1 cup milk*
1⅓ cups sifted all-purpose flour
⅔ cup white or yellow cornmeal
4 teaspoons low-sodium baking powder

About 35 minutes before serving: Preheat oven to 400°F. Grease and lightly flour 9-inch square cake pan. In medium bowl, cream butter and sugar until light and fluffy; stir in egg, then milk. Sift together flour, cornmeal and baking powder; add to butter mixture, then beat until just moistened. Turn into baking pan; smooth surface; bake 20 to 25 minutes, or until bread pulls away from sides of pan. Serve warm, cool, or split and toast until brown. Makes 16 servings.

* For low-fat, low-cholesterol diet use 1/3 cup unsalted special margarine; use only white of egg; substitute skimmed milk for whole.

## LEMON CRISPIES (1 milligram sodium per cookie)

1 cup unsalted butter or margarine*
1 cup granulated sugar
1 egg*
1½ teaspoons lemon extract
1½ cups sifted all-purpose flour

At least 1 hour before serving: Preheat oven to 375°F. In medium bowl, with electric mixer at medium speed, cream butter with sugar, then beat in egg and lemon extract until light and fluffy. At low speed, beat in flour until smooth. Drop batter, by level tablespoonfuls and at least 2 inches apart, onto an ungreased cookie sheet. Bake 10 minutes, or until golden-brown around edges. Let cool a minute or two, then remove from cookie sheet. Makes about 5 dozen.

* For low-fat, low-cholesterol diet use unsalted special margarine and only white of egg.

## CARROT-POTATO PANCAKES (35 milligrams sodium per serving)

1 large or 2 small carrots,
grated
2 medium potatoes, grated
1 medium onion, minced
⅓ cup flour
2 eggs*
dash cayenne

About 45 minutes before serving time: Spread griddle with a bit of oil. Heat until drop of water "dances" on griddle. In large bowl, toss together grated carrots, potatoes and onion. Mix in flour; then add eggs and cayenne. Drop batter, by rounded tablespoonfuls, on griddle; brown on one side at least 5 minutes, then turn. Flatten each pancake with spatula; cook 5 minutes more. Makes 5 servings.

* For low-fat, low-cholesterol diet use only whites of eggs.

## PANCAKES (15 milligrams sodium per pancake)

¾ cup skimmed milk or re-
liquefied nonfat dry milk
1 tablespoon unsalted butter or
margarine, melted*
1 egg, separated*
1 tablespoon sugar
1 cup sifted all-purpose flour
1½ teaspoons low-sodium
baking powder
1 tablespoon wheat germ (optional)

About 30 minutes before serving: Heat griddle until drop of water "dances" on it. In medium bowl, beat milk, melted butter and egg yolk until smooth. Add sugar, flour, baking powder and wheat germ; beat until just mixed. Pour batter, a scant ¼ cup at a time, on heated griddle. When bubbles form on top, turn pancakes; brown on second side. Keep warm until serving time. Makes ten 4-inch pancakes.

* For low-fat, low-cholesterol diet use unsalted special margarine and only white of egg.

## WAFFLES (25 milligrams sodium per waffle)

1½ cups sifted all-purpose
flour
4½ teaspoons low-sodium baking powder
1 tablespoon granulated sugar
2 eggs*
1 cup plus 2 tablespoons
skimmed milk or reliquefied
nonfat dry milk
¼ cup melted unsalted butter
or margarine or salad oil*

About 30 minutes before serving: Preheat waffle iron as manufacturer directs. In medium bowl, sift together flour, baking powder and sugar. In small bowl, beat eggs; add milk and butter, then beat until smooth. Add to flour mixture; beat with egg beater until all the flour is wet and batter is smooth. Using a scant ¼ cup of batter for each 4-inch waffle, cook as directed by manufacturer. Makes about twelve 4-inch waffles.

* For low-fat, low-cholesterol diet use only whites of eggs; use special margarine or oil (not butter); increase margarine to 5 tablespoons.

## WONDERFUL WHITE CAKE (25 milligrams sodium per serving)

2½ cups sifted cake flour
3 teaspoons low-sodium baking
powder
4 egg whites
1½ cups granulated sugar
½ cup unsalted butter or margarine*
1 cup plus 2 tablespoons
skimmed milk or reliquefied
nonfat dry milk
1 teaspoon vanilla extract
¼ teaspoon almond extract
(optional)
low-sodium frosting, if desired

At least 4 hours before serving: Preheat oven to 375°F. Grease, then line with waxed paper, bottoms of two 8-inch layer-cake pans. Sift flour with low-sodium baking powder 3 times.

In small bowl, with electric mixer at high speed, beat egg whites until foamy. Gradually add ½ cup sugar, beating only until mixture holds soft peaks. Set aside.

In large bowl, with mixer at medium speed, cream butter with 1 cup sugar until very light and fluffy—about 2 minutes altogether.

Next, at low speed, beat in alternately, just until smooth, flour mixture by fourths and milk and extracts by thirds. Then thoroughly beat egg-white mixture into batter. Turn into pans. Bake 25 minutes, or until cake tester, inserted in center, comes out clean. Cool 20 minutes on rack, then turn out of pans; peel off waxed paper. Cool thoroughly, then ice with your favorite low-sodium frosting. Makes 16 servings.

* For low-fat, low-cholesterol diet use unsalted special margarine.

## SPONGECAKE (25 milligrams sodium per serving)

3 eggs
1 cup sifted cake flour
1½ teaspoons low-sodium baking powder
1 cup granulated sugar
½ teaspoon grated lemon peel
2 teaspoons lemon juice
6 tablespoons hot milk
confectioners' sugar

At least 6 hours before serving: Set out eggs to warm to room temperature. When ready to make cake, preheat oven to 350°F. In large bowl, with electric mixer at high speed, beat eggs until very thick and light—about 5 minutes. Sift together flour and baking powder. Gradually add sugar to eggs, beating constantly, then beat in lemon peel and juice. Fold flour mixture into egg mixture. Stir in hot milk. Immediately turn batter into ungreased 9" by 5" by 3" loaf pan. Bake 35 minutes, or until cake tester, inserted in center, comes out clean. To cool cake, invert pan and let hang for 1 hour. Remove from pan and serve sprinkled with powdered sugar. Makes 10 servings.

## COD FILLETS WITH CUCUMBER SAUCE (120 milligrams sodium per serving)

3 fresh small cod fillets (about 1 pound)
2 tablespoons melted unsalted butter or margarine*
⅛ teaspoon pepper
2 tablespoons unsalted butter or margarine*
1 teaspoon vinegar
dash cayenne
⅓ cup pared, seeded and grated cucumber
1 tablespoon chopped parsley

About 35 minutes before serving: Preheat broiler 10 minutes if manufacturer directs. Arrange fillets in large shallow pan. Brush with melted butter, then sprinkle with pepper. Broil 5 to 8 minutes, or until fillets flake easily when tested with fork.

Meanwhile, in small saucepan, combine remaining ingredients; cook, over medium heat, until just boiling.

To serve: Transfer fillets to platter; pour cucumber sauce over them. Makes 3 servings.

*For low-fat, low-cholesterol diet use unsalted special margarine.

## CURRIED HADDOCK FILLETS (130 milligrams sodium per serving)

2 tablespoons salad oil
½ cup sliced celery
2 medium onions, thinly sliced
4 small fresh haddock fillets (about 1¼ pounds)
dash pepper
1 teaspoon curry*
1 cup milk†

About 45 minutes before serving: Preheat oven to 350°F. In medium skillet, in oil, sauté celery and onions until golden —do not brown. Place fillets in large (about 13" by 9" by 2") baking dish. Top with sautéed celery and onions. Mix pepper, curry and milk and pour over fillets. Bake 20 to 30 minutes, or until fish flakes easily when tested with fork. Makes 4 servings.

* Use curry not containing salt—check label.
† For low-fat, low-cholesterol diet use skimmed milk.

## HALIBUT STEAK HAWAIIAN (85 milligrams sodium per serving)

2 cups unsalted cooked rice
4 teaspoons lemon juice
¼ cup melted unsalted butter or margarine*
½ teaspoon curry†
1 8-ounce can pineapple tidbits, drained
2 1-pound fresh halibut steaks
1 lemon, cut into wedges for garnish

About 1 hour before serving: Preheat oven to 350°F. In medium bowl, combine rice with 3 teaspoons lemon juice, 2 tablespoons melted butter, curry and all but 10 pineapple tidbits (reserve these for garnish).

Sprinkle each halibut steak with 1 teaspoon lemon juice. Place one steak in large shallow open baking pan; brush with 1 tablespoon melted butter. Press rice filling on top. (Spoon any extra filling alongside.) Top with other halibut steak; brush with remaining butter. Secure in place with metal skewers. Bake 40 minutes, or until fish flakes easily with fork. Remove skewers; garnish with reserved pineapple tidbits and lemon wedges. Makes 6 servings.

* For low-fat, low-cholesterol diet use unsalted special margarine.
† Use curry not containing salt—check label.

## PINEAPPLE-MEAT LOAF (120 milligrams sodium per serving)

1 pound ground round steak
1 8½-ounce can crushed pineapple, undrained
2 slices unsalted bread, finely cubed*
1 egg†
¼ cup finely chopped onion
¼ teaspoon dry mustard
⅛ teaspoon pepper

About 1 hour and 15 minutes before serving: Preheat oven to 350°F. In medium baking pan, mix all ingredients; shape into loaf. Bake 60 minutes, or to desired doneness. Makes 4 servings.

\* If regular bread is used, count meat loaf at 170 milligrams sodium per serving.
† For low-fat, low-cholesterol diet use 2 egg whites in place of whole egg.

## SWISS STEAK (100 milligrams sodium per serving)

1½ pounds rump beef, cut about 1-inch thick
¼ cup flour
⅛ teaspoon pepper
1 tablespoon parsley flakes
2 tablespoons salad oil
1 16-ounce can low-sodium-pack tomatoes*
3 large onions, thinly sliced
1 stalk green celery, sliced
1 garlic clove, minced
1 1½-ounce package (⅓ cup) raisins

About 1½ hours before serving: Trim fat from meat, then cut into serving pieces. Toss together flour, pepper and parsley flakes. Use to coat meat. In large skillet, in oil, brown meat thoroughly on both sides. Pour off oil. Add remaining ingredients. Cover; simmer 1 hour and 15 minutes (adding some water, if needed), or until meat is tender and gravy thickens slightly. Makes 6 servings.

\* Or substitute 6 peeled fresh medium tomatoes and ½ cup water. Fine for low-fat, low-cholesterol diets.

## RHINE CARAWAY MEATBALLS (95 milligrams sodium per serving)

1 cup coarsely grated raw potato
1 pound ground round steak
¼ teaspoon pepper
1 tablespoon parsley flakes
1 small onion, finely grated
lemon peel
1 egg*
4 low-sodium beef-bouillon cubes (optional)
½ teaspoon caraway seed
2 teaspoons cornstarch
chopped parsley for garnish

About 1 hour before serving: In medium bowl, mix potato, meat, pepper, parsley flakes, onion, lemon peel and egg; form into 12 meatballs.

In medium skillet, heat 2½ cups water and bouillon cubes to boiling; add meatballs; cover; simmer 30 minutes. Remove meatballs to warm platter. Add caraway seed and cornstarch dissolved in 1 tablespoon water; stir until thickened and smooth. Pour a bit of the gravy over meatballs; garnish with chopped parsley. Pass remaining gravy. Makes 4 servings.

\* For low-fat, low-cholesterol diet use only egg white.

## TANGY POTTED BEEF (90 milligrams sodium per serving)

1½ pounds rump beef, cut about 1-inch thick
¼ cup flour
½ teaspoon onion powder
½ teaspoon garlic powder
½ teaspoon celery seed
¼ teaspoon pepper
2 tablespoons salad oil
4 thin lemon slices
2 low-sodium beef-bouillon cubes (optional)
1 tablespoon cornstarch (optional)

About 2 hours before serving: Trim fat from meat, then cut into serving pieces. Toss together flour, onion powder, garlic powder, celery seed and pepper. Use to coat meat. In large skillet, in oil, brown meat on both sides. Add lemon slices, bouillon cubes and 1 cup water; cover; simmer 1½ hours, or until meat is tender. If desired, mix enough water with cornstarch to form a smooth paste; stir into hot gravy; cook until slightly thickened. Makes 6 servings.

Fine for low-fat, low-cholesterol diets.

## HAMBURGER PLUS (90 milligrams sodium per serving)

**1 pound ground round steak**
**⅛ teaspoon pepper**
**¼ cup chopped parsley**
**¼ cup finely chopped onion**
**1 egg\***
**1 tablespoon salad oil**

About 30 minutes before serving: Thoroughly mix beef, pepper, parsley, onion and egg. Form into 4 patties. In skillet, in oil, cook patties until done as you like. Makes 4 servings.

\* For low-fat, low-cholesterol diet use only white of egg.

## MEAL-IN-A-DISH CHICKEN (100 milligrams sodium per serving)

**¼ cup flour**
**½ teaspoon onion powder**
**1 teaspoon curry\***
**1 teaspoon tarragon or parsley flakes**
**2 whole chicken breasts (about 1½ pounds), split and skinned**
**2 tablespoons salad oil**
**1 cup pineapple juice**
**2 tablespoons brown sugar**
**2 tablespoons vinegar**
**1 teaspoon chopped chives**
**8 small new potatoes**
**8 carrots, cut into 1-inch slices**

About 1 hour before serving: Mix flour, onion powder, curry and tarragon; use to coat chicken completely. In large skillet, in oil, brown chicken thoroughly. Add pineapple juice, brown sugar, vinegar, chives, potatoes and carrots. Cover; simmer 45 minutes (adding water, if needed), or until vegetables are tender and chicken done. Makes 4 servings.

\* Use curry not containing salt—check label.

Fine for low-fat, low-cholesterol diet.

## CHICKEN MARENGO (90 milligrams sodium per serving)

**¼ cup flour**
**½ teaspoon garlic powder**
**½ teaspoon onion powder**
**½ teaspoon celery seed**
**¼ teaspoon pepper**
**2 whole chicken breasts (about 1½ pounds), split and skinned)**
**2 tablespoons salad oil**
**12 small white onions**
**½ pound fresh mushrooms**
**2 garlic cloves, minced**
**1 16-ounce can low-sodium-pack canned tomatoes\***
**½ cup dry sherry (optional)**

About 1 hour before serving: Mix flour, garlic powder, onion powder, celery seed and pepper. Use to coat chicken. In skillet, in oil, brown chicken thoroughly. Remove chicken, then quickly sauté onions, mushrooms and garlic until golden. Add tomatoes, sherry and chicken. Cover; simmer 40 minutes, or until onions are tender. Makes 4 servings.

\* Or substitute 6 peeled fresh medium tomatoes and ½ cup water.

Fine for low-fat, low-cholesterol diet.

## APPLE-ACORN SQUASH (5 milligrams sodium per serving)

**2 small acorn squash, halved and seeded**
**1 cup canned applesauce**
**¼ teaspoon nutmeg**

About 1 hour before serving: Preheat oven to 425°F. Lightly oil large baking dish. Place squash, cut side down, in baking dish; bake 30 minutes; turn right side up. Meanwhile, mix applesauce and nutmeg. Use to fill squash. Return to oven and bake 20 minutes more, or until tender. Makes 4 servings.

Fine for low-fat, low-cholesterol diet.

## CREAMED CAULIFLOWER (20 milligrams sodium per serving)

1 small to medium head cauliflower
1 low-sodium chicken-bouillon
cube (optional)*
milk (to make 1 cup)†
1 tablespoon unsalted butter
or margarine†
1 tablespoon plus 2 teaspoons
flour
1 teaspoon parsley flakes
generous dash nutmeg
paprika

About 25 minutes before serving: Separate cauliflower into small flowerets; wash; drain. In medium saucepan, bring 1 cup water to boiling; in it dissolve bouillon cube. Add cauliflower; cover; simmer 10 minutes, or until just tender-crisp. Drain cauliflower, reserving cooking liquid. Keep cauliflower warm. Add enough milk to reserved liquid to make 1 cup. In saucepan, melt butter, then stir in flour, parsley flakes and nutmeg. Stirring constantly, slowly add water-milk mixture; cook until thickened.

To serve: Top cauliflower with sauce; sprinkle with paprika. Makes 6 servings.

* Available in many specialty-food stores.
† For low-fat, low-cholesterol diet use skimmed milk and unsalted special margarine.

## POTATOES ROSEMARY (5 milligrams sodium per serving)

1 16-ounce can whole
potatoes*
1 medium onion, thinly sliced
1/2 teaspoon rosemary, crushed
2 teaspoons salad oil

About 25 minutes before serving: In medium saucepan over medium heat, simmer potatoes, onion and rosemary 10 minutes, or until onion is tender; drain off water. In medium skillet, in salad oil, sauté potatoes and onion, stirring occasionally, about 10 minutes until potatoes are golden. Makes 4 servings.

* Use potatoes not containing added salt—check label.

Fine for low-fat, low-cholesterol diet.

## MAYONNAISE (3 milligrams sodium per tablespoon)

1 cup salad oil
1 egg
1 teaspoon granulated sugar
1/2 teaspoon dry mustard
1 1/2 teaspoons lemon juice
1/2 to 1 tablespoon vinegar, as
desired
pepper to taste

At least 2 hours before serving: Refrigerate oil, deep medium bowl and electric-mixer beaters. When bowl is chilled, break egg into it; add sugar, mustard and 1/2 teaspoon lemon juice; beat until well blended and egg is beginning to thicken. With mixer at highest speed, add oil, drop by drop, until 2 tablespoons have been used. Beat in 1/2 teaspoon lemon juice; still beating, continue to add oil by half teaspoonfuls until 2 more tablespoons have been added. Still beating, add 1/2 teaspoon lemon juice and vinegar; then add remaining oil by teaspoonfuls. If desired, beat in additional 1/2 tablespoon vinegar and pepper to taste. Continue to beat until mayonnaise has thickened. Store in warmest part of refrigerator. Makes 1 1/3 cups.

## PIQUANT SALAD DRESSING (3 milligrams sodium per tablespoon)

1 1/2 teaspoons unflavored gelatin
2 cups low-sodium-pack
canned tomato juice
2 tablespoons vinegar
1/4 teaspoon onion powder
1/4 teaspoon garlic powder
1/2 teaspoon pepper
2 tablespoons salad oil

At least 2 hours before serving: In medium saucepan, soften gelatin on 2 tablespoons water; heat to dissolve gelatin. Stir in remaining ingredients. Refrigerate, covered, until serving time.

To serve: Stir until smooth. Makes 2 1/2 cups.

Fine for low-fat, low-cholesterol diet.

## HOW TO USE HERBS AND SPICES ON A LOW-SODIUM DIET

When salt is missing, add flavor with herbs and spices. The chart below gives some favorite combinations.

| Herb/Spice | Use it in | Herb/Spice | Use it in |
|---|---|---|---|
| Allspice | gravies, meat and fish dishes, cakes, puddings, tomato sauces | Nutmeg | cakes, breads, green beans, custard, sauces |
| Basil | green beans, lamb, peas, potatoes, soups, tomato dishes | Oregano | hamburger, omelet, stews, vegetables |
| Bay Leaf | fish, sauces and gravies, stews and soups | Paprika | fish, gravies, meats, salad dressings, vegetables |
| Caraway seed | asparagus, noodles, soups, cookies, breads and rolls, liver, meat loaf | Pepper | soups, vegetables, meat, eggs |
| | | Poppy seed | breads, rolls, cookies, noodles, salad dressings |
| Chervil | fish and poultry dishes, salad dressings, sauces, stews | Poultry seasoning | biscuit dough, poultry dishes |
| Chili powder* | chili con carne, gravies, fish, stew | Rosemary | biscuit dough, potatoes, roasts, sauce for meat and poultry, orange or pear salad |
| Cinnamon | fruits, mashed sweet potatoes, toast, cookies, cakes, biscuits | Sage | fish, pork, veal and poultry, tomato dishes |
| Cloves | pork, peaches, stews, puddings, broiled grapefruit | Saffron | baked goods, rice |
| Curry* | sauce for eggs, fish, meat, poultry, vegetables | Savory | vegetable soup, mushrooms, peas, poultry and tomato dishes |
| Ginger | stewed fruit, applesauce, gingerbread, pumpkin pie, melon | Tarragon | salads, sauces, seafood, tomato dishes |
| Mace | cherries, jellies, canned fruit, gingerbread, fish sauces | Thyme | veal, pork, eggplant, peas, tomatoes, chowders, fish dishes |
| Marjoram | lamb, meat pies, stews, stuffings, asparagus, squash, fish sauces | Turmeric | curries, chicken, eggs, fish |

* Use a brand not containing salt.

# *Appendix*

## APPROXIMATE DAILY CALORIE REQUIREMENTS

| Men (154 lbs.) | Calories | Children up to 10 Years | | Calories |
|---|---|---|---|---|
| 25 yrs. | 2,800 | 1 to 3 | (26–31 lbs.) | 1,100–1,250 |
| 45 yrs. | 2,600 | 3 to 6 | (35–42 lbs.) | 1,400–1,600 |
| 65 yrs. | 2,400 | 6 to 10 | (51–62 lbs.) | 2,000–2,200 |
| | | Children over 10 Years | | |
| Women (128 lbs.) | | Girls: 10 to 14 | (77–97 lbs.) | 2,250–2,300 |
| 25 yrs. | 2,000 | 14 to 18 | (114–119 lbs.) | 2,400–2,300 |
| 45 yrs. | 1,850 | 18 to 22 | (128 lbs.) | 2,000 |
| 65 yrs. | 1,700 | Boys: 10 to 14 | (77–95 lbs.) | 2,500–2,700 |
| | | 14 to 18 | (130 lbs.) | 3,000 |
| | | 18 to 22 | (147 lbs.) | 2,800 |

## MINIMUM DAILY REQUIREMENTS

The term "Minimum Daily Requirements" (MDR) refers to the minimum standard levels established by the Food and Drug Administration for certain essential vitamins and minerals. References to MDR for adults are found on labels of everyday products in terms of percentages of nutrients contained.

| nutrient | infants | children 1–5 years inclusive | children 6 years and over | adults | pregnancy or lactation |
|---|---|---|---|---|---|
| A, U.S.P. units | 1,500 | 3,000 | 3,000 | 4,000 | —— |
| B₁, mg (thiamine) | 0.25 | 0.50 | 0.75 | 1.00 | —— |
| B₂, mg. (riboflavin) | 0.60 | 0.90 | 0.90 | 1.20 | —— |
| Niacin, mg. | —— | 5 | 7.5 | 10 | —— |
| C, mg. | 10 | 20 | 20 | 30 | —— |
| D, U.S.P. units | 400 | 400 | 400 | 400 | —— |
| Calcium, gm. | —— | 0.75 | 0.75 | 0.75 | 1.50 |
| Phosphorus, gm. | —— | 0.75 | 0.75 | 0.75 | 1.50 |
| Iron, mg. | —— | 7.5 | 10 | 10 | 15 |
| Iodine, mg. | —— | 0.1 | 0.1 | 0.1 | 0.1 |

## RECOMMENDED DAILY DIETARY ALLOWANCES

The Recommended Daily Dietary Allowances (RDA) were set up by the Food and Nutrition Board of the National Research Council at the time of World War II. The RDA is an estimate of the levels of important vitamins and minerals, calories and protein needed by men, women and children to assure a nutritionally adequate diet. The allowances are high levels and give a "cushion" of vitamins and minerals, allowing for variation in individual needs. They are reviewed every five years and adjusted to take into consideration changing styles of life in the United States and new nutrition research. A diet containing only the minimum servings of the Basic Four foods will provide the full RDA with the exception of the iron level for women and calories.

## 1968 RECOMMENDED DAILY DIETARY ALLOWANCES[1]

| | Age[2] Years | Weight kg | Weight lbs | Height cm | Height in | K Calories | Protein gm | Vitamin A Activity I.U. | Vitamin D I.U. | Vitamin E Activity I.U. | Ascorbic Acid mg | Folacin[4] mg | Niacin mg. equiv.[5] | Riboflavin mg | Thiamine mg | Vitamin $B_6$ mg | Vitamin $B_{12}$ µg | Calcium gm | Phosphorus gm | Iodine µg | Iron mg | Magnesium mg |
|---|---|---|---|---|---|---|---|---|---|---|---|---|---|---|---|---|---|---|---|---|---|---|
| | | | | | | | | Fat Soluble Vitamins | | | Water Soluble Vitamins | | | | | | | Minerals | | | | |
| **Infants** | 0-1/6 | 4 | 9 | 55 | 22 | $kg \times 120$ | $kg \times 2.2$[3] | 1500 | 400 | 5 | 35 | 0.05 | 5 | 0.4 | 0.2 | 0.2 | 1.0 | 0.4 | 0.2 | 25 | 6 | 40 |
| | 1/6-1/2 | 7 | 15 | 63 | 25 | $kg \times 110$ | $kg \times 2.0$[3] | 1500 | 400 | 5 | 35 | 0.05 | 7 | 0.5 | 0.4 | 0.3 | 1.5 | 0.5 | 0.4 | 40 | 10 | 60 |
| | 1/2-1 | 9 | 20 | 72 | 28 | $kg \times 100$ | $kg \times 1.8$[3] | 1500 | 400 | 5 | 35 | 0.1 | 8 | 0.6 | 0.5 | 0.4 | 2.0 | 0.6 | 0.5 | 45 | 15 | 70 |
| **Children** | 1-2 | 12 | 26 | 81 | 32 | 1100 | 25 | 2000 | 400 | 10 | 40 | 0.1 | 8 | 0.6 | 0.6 | 0.5 | 2.0 | 0.7 | 0.7 | 55 | 15 | 100 |
| | 2-3 | 14 | 31 | 91 | 36 | 1250 | 25 | 2000 | 400 | 10 | 40 | 0.2 | 8 | 0.7 | 0.6 | 0.6 | 2.5 | 0.8 | 0.8 | 60 | 15 | 150 |
| | 3-4 | 16 | 35 | 100 | 39 | 1400 | 30 | 2500 | 400 | 10 | 40 | 0.2 | 9 | 0.8 | 0.7 | 0.7 | 3 | 0.8 | 0.8 | 70 | 10 | 200 |
| | 4-6 | 19 | 42 | 110 | 43 | 1600 | 30 | 2500 | 400 | 10 | 40 | 0.2 | 11 | 0.9 | 0.8 | 0.9 | 4 | 0.8 | 0.8 | 80 | 10 | 200 |
| | 6-8 | 23 | 51 | 121 | 48 | 2000 | 35 | 3500 | 400 | 15 | 40 | 0.2 | 13 | 1.1 | 1.0 | 1.0 | 4 | 0.9 | 0.9 | 100 | 10 | 250 |
| | 8-10 | 28 | 62 | 131 | 52 | 2200 | 40 | 3500 | 400 | 15 | 40 | 0.3 | 15 | 1.2 | 1.1 | 1.2 | 5 | 1.0 | 1.0 | 110 | 10 | 250 |
| **Males** | 10-12 | 35 | 77 | 140 | 55 | 2500 | 45 | 4500 | 400 | 20 | 40 | 0.4 | 17 | 1.3 | 1.3 | 1.4 | 5 | 1.2 | 1.2 | 125 | 10 | 300 |
| | 12-14 | 43 | 95 | 151 | 59 | 2700 | 50 | 5000 | 400 | 20 | 45 | 0.4 | 18 | 1.4 | 1.4 | 1.6 | 5 | 1.4 | 1.4 | 135 | 18 | 350 |
| | 14-18 | 59 | 130 | 170 | 67 | 3000 | 60 | 5000 | 400 | 25 | 55 | 0.4 | 20 | 1.5 | 1.5 | 1.8 | 5 | 1.4 | 1.4 | 150 | 18 | 400 |
| | 18-22 | 67 | 147 | 175 | 69 | 2800 | 60 | 5000 | 400 | 30 | 60 | 0.4 | 18 | 1.6 | 1.4 | 2.0 | 5 | 0.8 | 0.8 | 140 | 10 | 400 |
| | 22-35 | 70 | 154 | 175 | 69 | 2800 | 65 | 5000 | — | 30 | 60 | 0.4 | 18 | 1.7 | 1.4 | 2.0 | 5 | 0.8 | 0.8 | 140 | 10 | 350 |
| | 35-55 | 70 | 154 | 173 | 68 | 2600 | 65 | 5000 | — | 30 | 60 | 0.4 | 17 | 1.7 | 1.3 | 2.0 | 5 | 0.8 | 0.8 | 125 | 10 | 350 |
| | 55-75+ | 70 | 154 | 171 | 67 | 2400 | 65 | 5000 | — | 30 | 60 | 0.4 | 14 | 1.7 | 1.2 | 2.0 | 6 | 0.8 | 0.8 | 110 | 10 | 350 |
| **Females** | 10-12 | 35 | 77 | 142 | 56 | 2250 | 50 | 4500 | 400 | 20 | 40 | 0.4 | 15 | 1.3 | 1.1 | 1.4 | 5 | 1.2 | 1.2 | 110 | 18 | 300 |
| | 12-14 | 44 | 97 | 154 | 61 | 2300 | 50 | 5000 | 400 | 20 | 45 | 0.4 | 15 | 1.4 | 1.2 | 1.6 | 5 | 1.3 | 1.3 | 115 | 18 | 350 |
| | 14-16 | 52 | 114 | 157 | 62 | 2400 | 55 | 5000 | 400 | 25 | 50 | 0.4 | 16 | 1.4 | 1.2 | 1.8 | 5 | 1.3 | 1.3 | 120 | 18 | 350 |
| | 16-18 | 54 | 119 | 160 | 63 | 2300 | 55 | 5000 | 400 | 25 | 50 | 0.4 | 15 | 1.5 | 1.2 | 2.0 | 5 | 1.3 | 1.3 | 115 | 18 | 350 |
| | 18-22 | 58 | 128 | 163 | 64 | 2000 | 55 | 5000 | 400 | 25 | 55 | 0.4 | 13 | 1.5 | 1.0 | 2.0 | 5 | 0.8 | 0.8 | 100 | 18 | 350 |
| | 22-35 | 58 | 128 | 163 | 64 | 2000 | 55 | 5000 | — | 25 | 55 | 0.4 | 13 | 1.5 | 1.0 | 2.0 | 5 | 0.8 | 0.8 | 100 | 18 | 300 |
| | 35-55 | 58 | 128 | 160 | 63 | 1850 | 55 | 5000 | — | 25 | 55 | 0.4 | 13 | 1.5 | 1.0 | 2.0 | 5 | 0.8 | 0.8 | 90 | 18 | 300 |
| | 55-75+ | 58 | 128 | 157 | 62 | 1700 | 55 | 5000 | — | 25 | 60 | 0.4 | 13 | 1.5 | 1.0 | 2.0 | 6 | 0.8 | 0.8 | 80 | 10 | 300 |
| **Pregnancy** | | | | | | +200 | 65 | 6000 | 400 | 30 | 60 | 0.8 | 15 | 1.8 | +0.1 | 2.5 | 8 | +0.4 | +0.4 | 125 | 18 | 450 |
| **Lactation** | | | | | | +1000 | 75 | 8000 | 400 | 30 | 60 | 0.5 | 20 | 2.0 | +0.5 | 2.5 | 6 | +0.5 | +0.5 | 150 | 18 | 450 |

[1] The allowance levels are intended to cover individual variations among most normal persons as they live in the United States under usual environmental stresses. The recommended allowances can be attained with a variety of common foods, providing other nutrients for which human requirements have been less well defined.

[2] Entries on lines for age range 22-35 years represent the reference man and woman at age 22. All other entries represent allowances for the mid-point of the specified age range.

[3] Assumes protein equivalent to human milk. For proteins not 100 percent utilized, factors should be increased proportionately.

[4] The folacin allowances refer to dietary sources as determined by **Lactobacillus casei** assay. Pure forms of folacin may be effective in doses less than ¼ of the RDA.

[5] Niacin equivalents include dietary sources of the vitamin itself plus 1 mg equivalent for each 60 mg of dietary tryptophan.

## DESIRABLE WEIGHTS:
## MEN, AGES 25 AND OVER

| Height (with shoes) | | Weight in Pounds (as ordinarily dressed) | | |
|---|---|---|---|---|
| Feet | Inches | Small Frame | Medium Frame | Large Frame |
| 5 | 2 | 112–120 | 118–129 | 126–141 |
| 5 | 3 | 115–123 | 121–133 | 129–144 |
| 5 | 4 | 118–126 | 124–136 | 132–148 |
| 5 | 5 | 121–129 | 127–139 | 135–152 |
| 5 | 6 | 124–133 | 130–143 | 138–156 |
| 5 | 7 | 128–137 | 134–147 | 142–161 |
| 5 | 8 | 132–141 | 138–152 | 147–166 |
| 5 | 9 | 136–145 | 142–156 | 151–170 |
| 5 | 10 | 140–150 | 146–160 | 155–174 |
| 5 | 11 | 144–154 | 150–165 | 159–179 |
| 6 | 0 | 148–158 | 154–170 | 164–184 |
| 6 | 1 | 152–162 | 158–175 | 168–189 |
| 6 | 2 | 156–167 | 162–180 | 173–194 |
| 6 | 3 | 160–171 | 167–185 | 178–199 |
| 6 | 4 | 164–175 | 172–190 | 182–204 |

## DESIRABLE WEIGHTS:
## WOMEN, AGES 25 AND OVER*

| Height (with shoes) | | Weight in Pounds (as ordinarily dressed) | | |
|---|---|---|---|---|
| Feet | Inches | Small Frame | Medium Frame | Large Frame |
| 4 | 10 | 92– 98 | 96–107 | 104–119 |
| 4 | 11 | 94–101 | 98–110 | 106–122 |
| 5 | 0 | 96–104 | 101–113 | 109–125 |
| 5 | 1 | 99–107 | 104–116 | 112–128 |
| 5 | 2 | 102–110 | 107–119 | 115–131 |
| 5 | 3 | 105–113 | 110–122 | 118–134 |
| 5 | 4 | 108–116 | 113–126 | 121–138 |
| 5 | 5 | 111–119 | 116–130 | 125–142 |
| 5 | 6 | 114–123 | 120–135 | 129–146 |
| 5 | 7 | 118–127 | 124–139 | 133–150 |
| 5 | 8 | 122–131 | 128–143 | 137–154 |
| 5 | 9 | 126–135 | 132–147 | 141–158 |
| 5 | 10 | 130–140 | 136–151 | 145–163 |
| 5 | 11 | 134–144 | 140–155 | 149–168 |
| 6 | 0 | 138–148 | 144–159 | 153–173 |

* From Tables Metropolitan Life Insurance Co.

# CALORIE, PROTEIN, FAT AND CARBOHYDRATE VALUES OF FOODS

The following table lists calorie, protein, fat and carbohydrate values by common serving sizes. All calorie values have been rounded to the nearest five calories. Values for the remaining nutrients are rounded to the nearest gram. Values of 0.5 or less are listed as zero. A dash (—) means no values are available. This table has been abstracted from *Composition of Foods—Raw, Processed, Prepared* and the *Home and Gardens Bulletin Number 72*, both available from the Superintendent of Documents, U.S. Government Printing Office, Washington, D.C. 20402.

| Food | Amount | Calories | Protein | Fat | Carbohydrate |
|---|---|---|---|---|---|
| **Alcoholic Beverages*** | | | | | |
| ale | 1 bottle (12 ounces) | 160 | 1 | 0 | 13 |
| beer | 1 bottle (12 ounces) | 160 | 1 | 0 | 13 |
| bourbon (100-proof) | 1 jigger (1½ ounces) | 125 | 0 | 0 | 0 |
| brandy | 1 jigger (1½ ounces) | 75 | 0 | 0 | 0 |
| champagne | 1 glass (4 ounces) | 85 | 0 | 0 | 5 |
| daiquiri | 1 average | 120 | 0 | 0 | 9 |
| gin (90-proof) | 1 jigger (1½ ounces) | 110 | 0 | 0 | 0 |
| Manhattan | 1 average | 130 | 0 | 0 | 7 |
| old-fashioned | 1 average | 130 | 0 | 0 | 7 |
| rum (80-proof) | 1 jigger (1½ ounces) | 100 | 0 | 0 | 0 |
| rye (90-proof) | 1 jigger (1½ ounces) | 110 | 0 | 0 | 0 |
| Scotch (86-proof) | 1 jigger (1½ ounces) | 105 | 0 | 0 | 0 |
| vodka (86-proof) | 1 jigger (1½ ounces) | 105 | 0 | 0 | 0 |
| wine, dry | 1 wineglass (3½ ounces) | 85 | 0 | 0 | 4 |
| sweet | 1 wineglass (3½ ounces) | 140 | 0 | 0 | 8 |
| **Almonds,** unsalted | 12 to 14 | 85 | 3 | 8 | 3 |
| **Apple** | 1 medium (2½-inch diameter) | 70 | 0 | 0 | 18 |
| **Apple,** baked | 1 medium | 130 | 0 | 0 | 34 |
| **Apple Brown Betty** | ½ cup | 175 | 2 | 4 | 34 |
| **Apple Butter** | 1 tablespoon | 35 | 0 | 0 | 8 |
| **Apple Juice** (Cider) | ½ cup | 60 | 0 | 0 | 15 |
| **Applesauce:** | | | | | |
| sweetened | ½ cup | 115 | 0 | 0 | 30 |
| unsweetened | ½ cup | 50 | 0 | 0 | 13 |
| **Apricot Nectar** | ½ cup | 70 | 0 | 0 | 18 |
| **Apricots:** | | | | | |
| canned in syrup | 4 medium halves, 2 tablespoons syrup | 110 | 1 | 0 | 29 |
| dried | 5 halves | 50 | 1 | 0 | 13 |
| fresh | 3 medium | 55 | 1 | 0 | 14 |
| stewed and sweetened | ½ cup | 200 | 2 | 0 | 51 |
| **Asparagus,** canned/fresh | 4 medium stalks | 10 | 1 | 0 | 2 |
| **Avocado** | ½ 10-ounce avocado | 185 | 2 | 18 | 6 |
| **Bacon:** | | | | | |
| crisp, fried | 2 slices | 90 | 5 | 8 | 1 |
| Canadian, uncooked | 3 ounces | 185 | 17 | 12 | 0 |

* Except as noted, alcoholic beverages do not contain protein, fat or carbohydrate. The calories come directly from the alcohol.

| Food | Amount | Calories | Protein | Fat | Carbohydrate |
|---|---|---|---|---|---|
| **Banana** | 1 medium (6-inches long) | 100 | 1 | 0 | 26 |
| **Bagel** | 1 large (1¾ ounces) | 165 | 6 | 2 | 28 |
| **Barley,** pearl | 1 cup, raw | 700 | 16 | 2 | 158 |
| **Bass,** striped, uncooked | 3 ounces | 90 | 16 | 2 | 0 |
| **Beans:** | | | | | |
| baked, canned, with pork and tomato sauce | 1 cup | 320 | 16 | 7 | 50 |
| green, fresh | 1 cup (1-inch pieces) | 30 | 2 | 0 | 7 |
| kidney, canned | 1 cup | 230 | 15 | 0 | 42 |
| limas, fresh | ½ cup | 95 | 6 | 0 | 17 |
| wax, canned | 1 cup | 45 | 2 | 1 | 10 |
| **Beef:** | | | | | |
| chuck, uncooked, lean meat only | 4 ounces† | 180 | 24 | 8 | 0 |
| uncooked, as purchased, with bone | 1 pound | 985 | 72 | 75 | 0 |
| flank, uncooked, lean meat only | 4 ounces† | 165 | 24 | 6 | 0 |
| uncooked, as purchased | 1 pound | 655 | 98 | 26 | 0 |
| porterhouse, uncooked, lean meat only | 4 ounces† | 185 | 24 | 9 | 0 |
| uncooked, as purchased | 1 pound | 1,605 | 61 | 149 | 0 |
| rib roast, uncooked, lean meat only | 4 ounces† | 220 | 23 | 13 | 0 |
| uncooked, as purchased, no bone | 1 pound | 1,820 | 67 | 170 | 0 |
| round, uncooked, lean meat only | 4 ounces† | 150 | 24 | 5 | 0 |
| uncooked, as purchased, no bone | 1 pound | 895 | 92 | 56 | 0 |
| rump, uncooked, lean meat only | 4 ounces† | 180 | 24 | 9 | 0 |
| uncooked, as purchased, no bone | 1 pound | 1,375 | 79 | 115 | 0 |
| sirloin, uncooked, lean meat only | 4 ounces† | 160 | 24 | 6 | 0 |
| uncooked, as purchased, no bone | 1 pound | 1,510 | 74 | 132 | 0 |
| **Beef,** dried | 2 ounces | 115 | 19 | 4 | 0 |
| **Beef Stew,** canned | 1 serving (1 cup) | 210 | 15 | 10 | 15 |
| **Beet Greens,** cooked | ½ cup | 15 | 1 | 0 | 2 |
| **Beets** | 2 (½ cup, diced) | 25 | 1 | 0 | 6 |

† 4 ounces raw meat will make 3 ounces cooked.

| Food | Amount | Calories | Protein | Fat | Carbohydrate |
|---|---|---|---|---|---|
| **Biscuit Mix,** enriched flour | 1 cup | 530 | 10 | 16 | 86 |
| **Biscuits:** | | | | | |
| baking powder, enriched flour | 1 (2-inch diameter) | 90 | 2 | 3 | 15 |
| refrigerated | 1 biscuit | 60 to 80 (varies according to brand) | | | |
| **Blackberries,** fresh | ½ cup | 40 | 1 | 0 | 9 |
| **Blueberries,** fresh or frozen, unsweetened | ½ cup | 40 | 0 | 0 | 10 |
| **Bluefish:** | | | | | |
| cooked, baked | 4 ounces | 180 | 29 | 6 | 0 |
| uncooked fillets | 1 pound | 530 | 93 | 15 | 0 |
| **Bologna** (all meat) | 1 ounce | 80 | 3 | 7 | 0 |
| **Bouillon cubes** (all types) | 1 cube | 5 | 1 | 0 | 0 |
| **Brains,** uncooked | 3 ounces | 105 | 9 | 7 | 1 |
| **Brazil Nuts** | 2 medium | 55 | 1 | 6 | 1 |
| **Breads,** fresh or toasted: | | | | | |
| Boston brown | 1 slice | 100 | 3 | 1 | 22 |
| cornbread, enriched | 1 slice | 190 | 6 | 4 | 32 |
| cracked wheat | 1 slice | 65 | 2 | 1 | 13 |
| French or Italian, unenriched | 1 slice | 65 | 2 | 0 | 13 |
| Melba toast | 1 slice | 15 | – | – | – |
| rye, light | 1 slice | 60 | 2 | 0 | 13 |
| white, enriched | 1 slice | 70 | 2 | 1 | 13 |
| white, raisin, unenriched | 1 slice | 65 | 2 | 1 | 13 |
| whole wheat | 1 slice | 65 | 3 | 1 | 14 |
| **Bread Crumbs:** | | | | | |
| fresh, unbuttered | 2 slices (1 cup) | 140 | 4 | 2 | 26 |
| packaged dry | ¼ cup | 100 | 3 | 1 | 18 |
| **Broccoli,** cooked | ½ cup | 20 | 2 | – | 4 |
| **Brownies,** with nuts | 1 square from mix | 85 | 1 | 4 | 13 |
| **Brussels Sprouts** | 1 cup | 55 | 7 | 1 | 10 |
| **Butter or Margarine** | 1 tablespoon | 100 | 0 | 12 | 0 |
| | 1 cup | 1,630 | 1 | 184 | 2 |
| **Buttermilk** | 1 cup (8 ounces) | 90 | 9 | 0 | 12 |
| **Cabbage:** | | | | | |
| boiled | ½ cup | 15 | 1 | 0 | 3 |
| raw | ½ cup shredded | 10 | 1 | 0 | 2 |
| | 1 pound | 100 | 5 | 1 | 22 |
| **Cakes:** | | | | | |
| angel-food | 1/12 of 10-inch cake | 135 | 3 | 0 | 32 |
| cheesecake (cream-cheese base) | 1 slice (⅛ of cake) | 450 | 5 | 32 | 40 |
| chiffon | 10-inch cake (1/16 of cake) | 215 | 4 | 9 | 31 |

| Food | Amount | Cal-ories | Pro-tein | Fat | Carbo-hydrate |
|------|--------|-----------|----------|-----|---------------|
| chocolate cake, fudge frosting | 2 9-inch layers (1/16 of cake) | 235 | 3 | 9 | 40 |
| cupcake, unfrosted | 1 medium | 90 | 1 | 3 | 14 |
| fruitcake | 1/30 of 8-inch loaf | 55 | 1 | 2 | 9 |
| poundcake | ½-inch slice | 140 | 2 | 9 | 14 |
| spongecake | 10-inch tube cake (1/12 of cake) | 195 | 5 | 4 | 36 |
| yellow cake, chocolate frosting | 2 9-inch layers (1/16 of cake | 275 | 3 | 10 | 45 |
| **Candy:** | | | | | |
| caramel, plain | 1 small piece | 40 | 0 | 1 | 8 |
| chocolate cream | 1 medium piece | 50 | – | – | – |
| chocolate, milk | 1 ounce | 145 | 2 | 9 | 16 |
| fondant | 1 ounce | 105 | 0 | 1 | 25 |
| fudge | 1 ounce | 115 | 1 | 4 | 21 |
| gum drops | 1 small | 10 | 0 | 0 | 2 |
| hard candy | 1 large sour ball | 35 | 0 | 0 | 9 |
| life savers | 1 | 10 | 0 | 0 | 2 |
| peanut brittle | 1 ounce | 120 | 2 | 3 | 23 |
| **Cantaloupe** | ½ (5-inch diameter) | 60 | 1 | 0 | 14 |
| **Carrots:** | | | | | |
| cooked | ½ cup, diced | 20 | 0 | 0 | 5 |
| raw | 1 cup (½ cup grated) | 20 | 0 | 0 | 5 |
| | 1 pound (tops trimmed) | 155 | 4 | 1 | 36 |
| **Catchup, Chili Sauce** | 1 tablespoon | 15 | 0 | 0 | 4 |
| **Catfish,** uncooked | 4 ounces | 115 | 20 | 4 | 0 |
| **Cauliflower:** | | | | | |
| cooked | 1 cup | 25 | 3 | 0 | 5 |
| raw | 1 pound (fully trimmed) | 50 | 5 | 0 | 9 |
| **Caviar,** pressed | 1 ounce | 90 | 10 | 5 | 1 |
| **Celery,** raw | 1 cup, diced | 15 | 1 | 0 | 4 |
| | 1 pound | 60 | 3 | 0 | 13 |
| **Cereals,** cooked: | | | | | |
| cornmeal, enriched grits | 1 cup | 120 | 3 | 1 | 26 |
| farina, enriched | 1 cup | 105 | 3 | 0 | 22 |
| rolled oats | 1 cup | 130 | 5 | 2 | 23 |
| **Cereals,** ready-to-eat: | | | | | |
| bran flakes | 1 cup | 105 | 4 | 1 | 28 |
| corn flakes | 1 cup (about 1 ounce) | 100 | 2 | 0 | 21 |
| oat cereal | 1 cup (⅔ ounce) | 100 | 3 | 1 | 19 |
| puffed rice, wheat | 1 cup (about ½ ounce) | 55 | 1 | 0 | 13 |
| rice krispies | 1 cup (1 ounce) | 105 | 2 | 0 | 25 |
| shredded wheat | 1 medium biscuit | 90 | 2 | 1 | 20 |
| **Cheese:** | | | | | |
| American, processed or natural | 1 slice (1 ounce) | 105 | 7 | 9 | 1 |
| Camembert | 1 ounce | 85 | 5 | 7 | 1 |
| Cheddar | 1 slice (1 ounce) | 115 | 7 | 9 | 1 |

| Food | Amount | Cal-ories | Pro-tein | Fat | Carbo-hydrate |
|---|---|---|---|---|---|
| cheese spread | 1 ounce | 80 | 5 | 6 | 2 |
| cottage, creamed | ⅓ cup | 85 | 11 | 3 | 2 |
| plain | ⅓ cup | 60 | 11 | – | 2 |
| cream | 2 tablespoons (1 ounce) | 105 | 2 | 11 | 1 |
| Mozzarella, whole milk | 1 ounce | 90 | – | – | – |
| Neufchâtel | 1 ounce | 70 | 3 | 7 | 1 |
| Parmesan or Romano, grated | 2 tablespoons (⅓ ounce) | 50 | 4 | 4 | 0 |
| Ricotta, partially skimmed milk | ⅓ cup | 85 | 9 | 5 | 2 |
| whole milk | ⅓ cup | 120 | 9 | 10 | 2 |
| Roquefort or blue | 1 ounce | 105 | 6 | 9 | 1 |
| Swiss, processed or natural | 1 slice (1 ounce) | 105 | 7 | 9 | 1 |
| **Cheese Soufflé** | 1 serving (about 1½ cups) | 320 | 13 | 25 | 9 |
| **Cherries** | | | | | |
| canned in syrup | ½ cup, 3 tablespoons syrup | 115 | 1 | 0 | 30 |
| canned, red sour pitted | 1 cup | 105 | 2 | 0 | 26 |
| fresh, sweet | 1 cup | 80 | 2 | 0 | 20 |
| **Chewing Gum** | 1 stick | 10 | 0 | 0 | 3 |
| **Chicken,** fryers, uncooked | | | | | |
| breast | 1 whole, small (¾ pound) | 295 | 56 | 6 | 0 |
| leg and thigh | 1 small (½ pound) | 190 | 28 | 7 | 0 |
| roasted, no bone | average serving (4 ounces) | 205 | 33 | 7 | 0 |
| | 5 ounces (1 cup diced) | 225 | 41 | 9 | 0 |
| **Chicken à la King** | 1-cup serving, no biscuit | 410 | 23 | 12 | 5 |
| **Chicken Pot Pie** | 1 4-inch pie | 535 | 23 | 31 | 42 |
| **Chili Con Carne,** canned | 1 cup | 335 | 19 | 15 | 30 |
| **Chocolate:** | | | | | |
| milk | 1 ounce | 145 | 2 | 9 | 16 |
| semi-sweet | 1 ounce | 145 | 1 | 10 | 16 |
| unsweetened (baking) | 1 ounce | 145 | 3 | 15 | 8 |
| **Chocolate Milk Drink** (skim milk) | 1 glass (8 ounces) | 190 | 8 | 6 | 27 |
| **Chocolate Syrup** | 1 tablespoon | 50 | 0 | 1 | 10 |
| **Chop Suey,** canned | 1-cup serving | 145 | 10 | 7 | 10 |
| **Clams,** uncooked | 6 (4 ounces, meat only) | 85 | 14 | 2 | 2 |
| canned | 3 ounces | 45 | 7 | 1 | 2 |
| **Cocoa** | 1 tablespoon | 20 | 1 | 2 | 3 |
| **Cocoa,** prepared with milk | 1 cup | 245 | 10 | 12 | 27 |
| **Coconut,** fresh, shredded | ½ cup | 225 | 3 | 23 | 6 |
| **Cod,** uncooked | 4 ounces | 90 | 20 | 1 | 0 |

| Food | Amount | Calories | Protein | Fat | Carbohydrate |
|---|---|---|---|---|---|
| **Coffee,** without sugar and cream | 1 cup | 0 | 0 | 0 | 0 |
| **Coffee lighteners** | 1 tablespoon | 20 to 30 (varies according to brand) | | | |
| **Cola Drinks** | 6-ounce bottle | 70 | 0 | 0 | 18 |
| **Collards,** cooked | ½ cup | 25 | 2 | 0 | 5 |
| **Cookies:** | | | | | |
| chocolate chip | 1 (1-inch diameter) | 50 | 1 | 3 | 6 |
| fig bar | 1 square | 50 | 1 | 1 | 11 |
| gingersnap | 1 small (2-inch diameter) | 30 | 0 | 1 | 5 |
| macaroon | 1 (2½-inch diameter) | 85 | 1 | 4 | 13 |
| oatmeal | 1 large (3-inch diameter) | 65 | 1 | 2 | 11 |
| sandwich-type | 1 cookie | 50 | 1 | 2 | 7 |
| sugar | 1 medium (3-inch diameter | 80 | 1 | 2 | 12 |
| sugar wafer | 1 2½" x ¾" rectangle | 25 | 0 | 1 | 4 |
| **Corn** | | | | | |
| canned, whole kernel | ½ cup | 85 | 3 | 1 | 20 |
| | 1 pound | 300 | 9 | 3 | 71 |
| fresh | 1 ear (5-inches long) | 70 | 3 | 1 | 16 |
| **Corned-Beef Hash,** canned | 3 ounces | 155 | 7 | 10 | 9 |
| **Cornmeal,** uncooked, enriched | 1 cup | 500 | 11 | 2 | 108 |
| **Cornstarch** | 1 tablespoon | 30 | 0 | 0 | 7 |
| **Cornstarch pudding** | ½ cup | 140 | 4 | 5 | 19 |
| **Crab,** cooked | 4 ounces | 105 | 20 | 2 | 1 |
| **Crackers:** | | | | | |
| graham | 4 (2½-inch diameter) | 110 | 2 | 3 | 21 |
| oyster | 10 crackers | 45 | 1 | 1 | 7 |
| saltine | 4 squares | 50 | 1 | 1 | 8 |
| soda | 2 (2½-inch square) | 50 | 1 | 1 | 8 |
| whole rye | 1 double cracker | 20 | – | – | – |
| **Cranberries,** raw | 1 cup | 45 | 0 | 1 | 11 |
| **Cranberry Juice** | ½ cup | 80 | 0 | 0 | 21 |
| **Cranberry Sauce,** canned | 1 tablespoon | 20 | 0 | 0 | 5 |
| | ½ pound | 330 | 0 | 0 | 85 |
| **Cream:** | | | | | |
| half-and-half | 1 tablespoon | 20 | 1 | 2 | 1 |
| heavy | 1 tablespoon | 55 | 0 | 6 | 1 |
| | 1 cup | 840 | 5 | 90 | 7 |
| light | 1 tablespoon | 30 | 1 | 3 | 1 |
| | 1 cup | 505 | 7 | 49 | 10 |
| sour, commercial | 1 tablespoon | 25 | 0 | 2 | 1 |
| **Cucumbers,** raw | 6 slices (⅛-inch thick) | 5 | 0 | 0 | 2 |
| | 1 pound | 65 | 4 | 0 | 15 |
| **Custard,** baked | ½ cup | 150 | 7 | 7 | 14 |
| **Dandelion Greens,** cooked | ½ cup | 30 | 2 | 0 | 6 |
| **Danish Pastry,** plain | 4½-inch piece | 275 | 5 | 15 | 30 |

| Food | Amount | Cal-<br>ories | Pro-<br>tein | Fat | Carbo-<br>hydrate |
|---|---|---|---|---|---|
| **Dates,** dried and pitted | ¼ cup | 125 | 1 | 0 | 32 |
| **Dessert Topping** | 1 tablespoon | 10 to 25 (varies according to brand) | | | |
| **Doughnuts** (cake type) | 1 medium | 125 | 1 | 6 | 16 |
| **Duck,** uncooked | 1 average serving (4 ounces) | 185 | 24 | 9 | 0 |
| **Eggs:** | | | | | |
| fried | 1 egg, 1 teaspoon butter | 110 | 6 | 10 | 0 |
| omelet | 2 eggs, 2 teaspoons butter, milk | 215 | 14 | 16 | 3 |
| raw: | 1 large | 80 | 6 | 6 | 0 |
| white | 1 large | 15 | 4 | 0 | 0 |
| yolk | 1 large | 60 | 3 | 5 | 0 |
| scrambled | 1 egg, milk and butter | 110 | 7 | 8 | 1 |
| shirred or poached | 1 large | 80 | 6 | 6 | 0 |
| **Eggplant,** raw | 1 slice (5-inch diameter) | 20 | 1 | 0 | 5 |
| | 1 pound | 90 | 4 | 1 | 21 |
| **Escarole,** raw | 4 leaves | 5 | 0 | 0 | 1 |
| **Figs,** dried | 1 large | 60 | 1 | 0 | 15 |
| **Finnan Haddie** | 4 ounces | 120 | 25 | 0 | 0 |
| **Fish Sticks** | 1 breaded stick | 40 | 4 | 2 | 2 |
| **Flounder,** uncooked fillets | 4 ounces | 90 | 19 | 1 | 0 |
| **Flour:** | | | | | |
| all-purpose, enriched | 1 cup, sifted | 420 | 12 | 1 | 88 |
| cake, unenriched | 1 cup, sifted | 350 | 7 | 1 | 76 |
| whole wheat | 1 cup, sifted | 400 | 16 | 2 | 85 |
| **Frankfurters** | 1 medium (8 per pound) | 170 | 7 | 15 | 1 |
| **French Toast** | 1 slice (no syrup) | 140 | 5 | 7 | 12 |
| **Frozen Custard** | ½ cup | 200 (varies according to brand) | | | |
| **Fruit Cocktail,** canned | ½ cup fruit and syrup | 95 | 1 | 0 | 25 |
| **Gelatin Dessert** | ½ cup prepared | 70 | 2 | 0 | 17 |
| **Gelatin,** unflavored, dry | 1 envelope (1 scant tablespoon) | 25 | 6 | 0 | 0 |
| **Ginger Ale** | 1 glass (8 ounces) | 85 | 0 | 0 | 21 |
| **Gingerbread** | 2-inch square (unfrosted) | 175 | 2 | 6 | 29 |
| **Goose,** cooked | 4 ounces | 260 | 38 | 11 | 0 |
| **Grapefruit** | ½ medium | 45 | 1 | 0 | 12 |
| **Grapefruit Juice:** | | | | | |
| sweetened, canned | ½ cup | 65 | 1 | 0 | 16 |
| unsweetened | ½ cup | 50 | 1 | 0 | 12 |
| **Grapefruit Sections** | ½ cup, 1 tablespoon syrup | 90 | 1 | 0 | 22 |
| **Grape Juice** | ½ cup | 85 | 1 | 0 | 21 |
| **Grapes** | 1 cup | 65 | 1 | 1 | 15 |
| **Gravy:** | | | | | |
| canned beef | 2 tablespoons | 15 | 1 | 1 | 1 |
| homemade (from drippings) | 2 tablespoons | 30 | 0 | 3 | 1 |
| **Griddlecakes** | 2 (4-inch diameter, no syrup) | 120 | 4 | 4 | 18 |

| Food | Amount | Calories | Protein | Fat | Carbohydrate |
|------|--------|----------|---------|-----|--------------|
| Guavas | 1 medium | 50 | 1 | 0 | 12 |
| Haddock: | | | | | |
|   pan fried | 1 fillet (3 ounces) | 140 | 17 | 5 | 5 |
|   uncooked fillets | 1 pound | 360 | 83 | 1 | 0 |
| Halibut: | | | | | |
|   broiled | 1 steak (4½ ounces) | 240 | 36 | 10 | 0 |
|   uncooked fillets | 1 pound | 455 | 95 | 5 | 0 |
| Herring: | | | | | |
|   pickled | 3 ounces | 185 | 16 | 13 | 0 |
|   smoked kippered | 3 ounces | 180 | 18 | 11 | 0 |
| Honey | 1 tablespoon | 65 | 0 | 0 | 17 |
| Honeydew Melon | 2-inch wedge from 6½" x 7" melon | 50 | 1 | 0 | 13 |
| Ice Cream, vanilla | 1 cup (10 percent butterfat) | 255 | 6 | 14 | 28 |
| | 1 cup (16 percent butterfat) | 330 | 4 | 24 | 27 |
| Ice-Cream Soda, vanilla | 1 regular | 270 | – | – | – |
| Ice Milk | 1 cup | 200 | 6 | 7 | 29 |
| Jam | 1 tablespoon | 55 | 0 | 0 | 14 |
| Jelly | 1 tablespoon | 50 | 0 | 0 | 13 |
| Junket | ½ cup | 105 | 4 | 4 | 14 |
| Kale, cooked | ½ cup | 15 | 2 | 0 | 2 |
| Kidneys, Beef, uncooked | 3 ounces | 110 | 13 | 5 | 1 |
| Kohlrabi, cooked | ½ cup | 25 | 2 | 0 | 6 |
| Lamb: | | | | | |
|   chop, with bone, lean only | 4 ounces, cooked | 140 | 21 | 6 | 0 |
|   leg, lean meat only | 1 pound, uncooked | 610 | 90 | 25 | 0 |
|   roast, no bone, lean only | 3 ounces, cooked | 155 | 24 | 6 | 0 |
| Lard | 1 tablespoon | 115 | 0 | 13 | 0 |
| Lemon or Lime Juice | ¼ cup (4 tablespoons) | 15 | 0 | 0 | 5 |
| Lemonade, concentrated, frozen | 1 cup, prepared as directed | 110 | 0 | 0 | 28 |
| Lentils, dried, raw | 2½ tablespoons | 85 | – | – | – |
| Lettuce, raw | 2 large leaves | 10 | 1 | 0 | 2 |
| | 1 pound | 55 | 4 | 0 | 13 |
| Liver: | | | | | |
|   beef, uncooked | 4 ounces | 155 | 22 | 4 | 6 |
|   calf, uncooked | 4 ounces | 155 | 22 | 5 | 5 |
|   chicken, uncooked | 4 ounces | 145 | 22 | 4 | 3 |
| Liverwurst | 2 ounces | 175 | 9 | 15 | 1 |
| Lobster, cooked meat | ½ cup (3 ounces) | 80 | 16 | 1 | – |
| Loganberries | ½ cup | 45 | 1 | 0 | 11 |
| Macaroni and Cheese | 1 serving (about 1 cup) | 430 | 17 | 22 | 40 |

| Food | Amount | Cal-ories | Pro-tein | Fat | Carbo-hydrate |
|---|---|---|---|---|---|
| **Macaroni:** | | | | | |
| cooked, enriched | ½ cup | 95 | 3 | 0 | 20 |
| uncooked, enriched | 1 pound | 1,675 | 57 | 5 | 341 |
| **Mackerel,** uncooked | | | | | |
| fillets | 4 ounces | 215 | 21 | 14 | 0 |
| **Mangos** | 1 medium | 85 | 1 | 0 | 23 |
| **Margarine** | 1 tablespoon | 100 | 0 | 12 | 0 |
| | 1 cup | 1,630 | 2 | 184 | 2 |
| **Marmalade, Jam** | 1 tablespoon | 55 | 0 | 0 | 14 |
| **Marshmallows,** plain | 1 average | 25 | 0 | 0 | 6 |
| **Matzoh:** | | | | | |
| egg | 1 regular | 135 | – | – | – |
| plain | 1 regular | 120 | – | – | – |
| **Meat Loaf** | 1 serving (1-inch slice) | 370 | 24 | 27 | 8 |
| **Milk:** | | | | | |
| buttermilk, cultured | 1 glass (8 ounces) | 90 | 9 | 0 | 12 |
| condensed, sweetened | ½ cup | 490 | 12 | 13 | 83 |
| evaporated | ½ cup, undiluted | 175 | 9 | 10 | 12 |
| half-and-half | ½ cup | 165 | 4 | 14 | 6 |
| liquid, skimmed | 1 glass (8 ounces) | 90 | 9 | 0 | 12 |
| liquid, 98% fat-free | 1 glass (8 ounces) | 145 | 10 | 5 | 15 |
| liquid, whole | 1 glass (8 ounces) | 160 | 9 | 9 | 12 |
| malted, dry powder | 3 tablespoons (1 ounce) | 115 | 4 | 2 | 20 |
| milk shake | 1 glass (8 ounces) | 400 | – | – | – |
| nonfat dry milk, in-stant (dry powder) | ⅓ cup | 85 | 8 | 0 | 12 |
| yogurt (made with partially skimmed milk): | | | | | |
| plain | 1 cup (8 ounces) | 120 to 150 (varies according to brand) | | | |
| coffee, vanilla | 1 cup (8 ounces) | 200 to 250 (varies according to brand) | | | |
| fruit flavored | 1 cup (8 ounces) | 230 to 290 (varies according to brand and flavor) | | | |
| **Molasses,** light | 1 tablespoon | 50 | 0 | 0 | 13 |
| **Muffins:** | | | | | |
| blueberry | 1 2½-inch diameter | 140 | 3 | 7 | 32 |
| bran | 1 2½-inch diameter | 100 | 4 | 4 | 14 |
| corn | 1 2⅜-inch diameter | 125 | 3 | 4 | 19 |
| English | 1 3½-inch diameter | 145 | – | – | – |
| plain | 1 3-inch diameter | 120 | 3 | 4 | 17 |
| **Mushrooms:** | | | | | |
| canned | 1 cup (solids and liquid) | 40 | 5 | 0 | 6 |
| fresh | 1 pound | 125 | 12 | 1 | 19 |
| fresh | 4 large | 10 | 1 | 0 | 2 |
| **Noodles:** | | | | | |
| cooked, enriched | ½ cup | 100 | 3 | 1 | 18 |
| Chow-Mein, canned | 1 cup | 240 | 6 | 10 | 26 |
| uncooked, enriched | ½ pound | 880 | 29 | 10 | 163 |
| **Oatmeal,** uncooked | 1 cup | 310 | 11 | 6 | 54 |

| Food | Amount | Cal-ories | Pro-tein | Fat | Carbo-hydrate |
|---|---|---|---|---|---|
| **Oils:** | | | | | |
| corn, cottonseed, olive, peanut, | 1 tablespoon | 125 | 0 | 14 | 0 |
| soybean | ½ cup | 975 | 0 | 110 | 0 |
| **Okra,** cooked | 8 pods | 25 | 2 | 0 | 5 |
| **Olives:** | | | | | |
| green, unstoned | 4 medium | 15 | 0 | 2 | 0 |
| ripe, unstoned | 3 small | 15 | 0 | 2 | 0 |
| **Onion,** raw | 1 medium | 40 | 2 | 0 | 10 |
| | 1 pound | 157 | 6 | 0 | 36 |
| **Orange** | 1 medium (2⅝-inch diameter) | 65 | 1 | 0 | 16 |
| **Orange Juice,** fresh, frozen or canned | ½ cup | 55 | 1 | 0 | 13 |
| **Orange Sections** | ½ cup | 45 | 1 | 0 | 11 |
| **Oysters, Eastern,** uncooked | 6 to 8 medium (4 ounces, meat only) | 75 | 9 | 2 | 4 |
| **Pancakes,** from mix | 2 (4-inch diameter) | 120 | 4 | 4 | 18 |
| **Parsley,** raw | 5 tablespoons, chopped | 5 | 0 | 0 | 1 |
| **Parsnips,** cooked | ½ cup | 50 | 1 | 0 | 11 |
| **Peach Nectar** | ½ cup | 60 | 0 | 0 | 15 |
| **Peaches:** | | | | | |
| canned, syrup pack | ½ cup halves with syrup | 100 | 0 | 0 | 27 |
| | 1 pound, undrained | 355 | 2 | 0 | 91 |
| fresh, uncooked | 1 medium | 35 | 1 | 0 | 10 |
| | 1 pound | 150 | 2 | 0 | 38 |
| frozen, sweetened | ½ cup | 100 | 1 | 0 | 26 |
| **Peanuts,** roasted | 8 to 10 | 55 | 2 | 4 | 2 |
| | ½ pound, shelled | 1,320 | 59 | 110 | 46 |
| **Peanut Butter** | 1 tablespoon | 95 | 4 | 8 | 3 |
| **Pear Nectar** | ½ cup | 65 | 0 | 0 | 16 |
| **Pears:** | | | | | |
| canned, syrup pack | ½ cup halves with syrup | 100 | 0 | 0 | 26 |
| | 1 pound, undrained | 345 | 1 | 1 | 89 |
| fresh, uncooked | 1 medium | 100 | 1 | 1 | 25 |
| | 1 pound | 250 | 3 | 2 | 63 |
| **Peas:** | | | | | |
| green, canned | ½ cup | 80 | 4 | 0 | 15 |
| | 1 pound | 300 | 16 | 1 | 57 |
| fresh, cooked | ½ cup | 60 | 4 | 0 | 10 |
| fresh, shelled | 1 pound, uncooked | 380 | 29 | 2 | 65 |
| split, dried, raw | ½ cup | 345 | 24 | 1 | 62 |
| **Pecans** | 9 medium nuts | 70 | 1 | 8 | 2 |
| | 1 cup, halves | 740 | 10 | 77 | 16 |
| **Peppers,** green, raw | 1 medium | 15 | 1 | 0 | 4 |
| **Perch** (ocean), uncooked | 4 ounces | 105 | 21 | 2 | 0 |
| **Pickles:** | | | | | |
| dill | 1 medium | 10 | 1 | 0 | 1 |

| Food | Amount | Cal-ories | Pro-tein | Fat | Carbo-hydrate |
|---|---|---|---|---|---|
| sour | 1 large | 15 | 1 | 0 | 3 |
| sweet | 1 small | 20 | 0 | 0 | 6 |
| **Pie Crust:** | | | | | |
| homemade, double-crust | 1 9-inch shell | 1,800 | 22 | 120 | 158 |
| homemade, single-crust | 1 9-inch shell | 900 | 11 | 60 | 79 |
| packaged mix, double crust | 1 (8- or 9-inch shell) | 1,480 | 20 | 93 | 141 |
| **Pies:** | | | | | |
| apple, double crust | 4-inch wedge (1/7 of 9-inch pie) | 350 | 3 | 15 | 51 |
| butterscotch | 4-inch wedge (1/7 of 9-inch pie) | 350 | 6 | 14 | 50 |
| cherry, double crust | 4-inch wedge (1/7 of 9-inch pie) | 350 | 4 | 15 | 52 |
| custard | 4-inch wedge (1/7 of 9-inch pie) | 285 | 8 | 14 | 30 |
| lemon meringue | 4-inch wedge (1/7 of 9-inch pie) | 305 | 4 | 12 | 45 |
| mince | 4-inch wedge (1/7 of 9-inch pie) | 365 | 3 | 16 | 56 |
| pecan | 4-inch wedge (1/7 of 9-inch pie) | 490 | 6 | 27 | 60 |
| pumpkin | 4-inch wedge (1/7 of 9-inch pie) | 275 | 5 | 15 | 32 |
| **Pineapple:** | | | | | |
| canned, crushed | ½ cup | 100 | 1 | 0 | 25 |
| | 1 pound | 335 | 1 | 0 | 88 |
| juice | ½ cup | 65 | 1 | 0 | 17 |
| sliced | 1 large or 2 small slices | 90 | 0 | 0 | 24 |
| fresh, sliced | 1 cup, chopped | 75 | 1 | 0 | 19 |
| | 1 pound, untrimmed | 123 | 1 | 0 | 32 |
| **Pizza,** cheese | ⅛ of 14-inch pie | 185 | 7 | 6 | 27 |
| **Plums:** | | | | | |
| canned, syrup pack | ½ cup plums with syrup | 100 | 0 | 0 | 26 |
| | 1 pound (undrained) | 360 | 2 | 0 | 94 |
| fresh | 1 (2-inch diameter) | 25 | 0 | 0 | 7 |
| **Popcorn,** popped, with oil | 1 cup | 40 | 1 | 2 | 5 |
| **Popover** | 1 medium | 120 | 4 | 7 | 10 |
| **Pork:** | | | | | |
| ham, boiled | 1 slice (1 ounce) | 70 | 5 | 5 | 0 |
| ham, cured, uncooked | 3 ounces (lean meat only) | 140 | 18 | 7 | 0 |
| ham, fresh, uncooked | 3 ounces (lean meat only) | 130 | 17 | 7 | 0 |
| loin chop, uncooked | 4 ounces (lean meat only) | 210 | 22 | 13 | 0 |
| **Potatoes:** | | | | | |
| baked or boiled | 1 medium (1 cup, diced) | 90 | 3 | 0 | 21 |
| French-fried | 10 pieces (2" x ½" x ½") | 155 | 2 | 7 | 20 |

| Food | Amount | Cal-ories | Pro-tein | Fat | Carbo-hydrate |
|---|---|---|---|---|---|
| mashed | ½ cup, milk and butter added | 95 | 2 | 4 | 12 |
| scalloped | ½ cup | 120 | – | – | – |
| sweet, baked or boiled | 1 medium (5″ x 2″) | 155 | 2 | 1 | 36 |
| sweet, candied | 1 small (3½″ x 2¼″) | 295 | 2 | 6 | 60 |
| **Potato Chips** | 10 medium (2-inch diameter) | 115 | 1 | 8 | 10 |
| **Poultry Stuffing** | 1 cup | 195 | – | – | – |
| **Pretzels** | 5 3⅛-inch-long sticks | 10 | 0 | 0 | 2 |
| **Prune Juice,** canned | ½ cup | 100 | 0 | 0 | 25 |
| **Prunes,** uncooked | 4 medium | 70 | 1 | 0 | 18 |
| **Pudding:** | | | | | |
| chocolate | ½ cup | 175 | 5 | 6 | 32 |
| cornstarch | ½ cup | 140 | 4 | 5 | 19 |
| **Pumpkin,** canned | ½ cup | 40 | 1 | 1 | 9 |
| **Pumpkin Seeds:** | | | | | |
| shelled | 1 tablespoon | 60 | 3 | 5 | 1 |
| unshelled | ¼ cup | 60 | 3 | 5 | 1 |
| **Rabbit,** uncooked, no bones | 4 ounces | 180 | 24 | 9 | 0 |
| **Radishes,** raw | 4 small | 5 | 0 | 0 | 1 |
| **Raisins,** seedless | ¼ cup | 120 | 1 | 0 | 32 |
| **Raspberries,** red fresh | ½ cup | 35 | 0 | 0 | 9 |
| **Rhubarb:** | | | | | |
| stewed and sweetened | ½ cup | 190 | 0 | 0 | 49 |
| uncooked | 1 pound | 55 | 2 | 0 | 13 |
| **Rice:** | | | | | |
| brown, uncooked | ½ cup (1½ cups cooked) | 300 | 6 | 2 | 63 |
| precooked | 1 cup cooked | 180 | 4 | 0 | 40 |
| white, enriched | | | | | |
| uncooked | ½ cup | 335 | 6 | 0 | 75 |
| | 1 pound | 1,645 | 30 | 2 | 365 |
| cooked | ½ cup | 110 | 2 | 0 | 25 |
| wild, uncooked | ½ cup | 295 | 12 | 1 | 61 |
| **Rice Pudding** | 1 serving (¾ cup) | 225 | 6 | 9 | 32 |
| **Rolls,** plain | 1 small (16 per pound) | 85 | 2 | 2 | 15 |
| | 1 medium (12 per pound) | 115 | 3 | 2 | 20 |
| | 1 large (8 per pound) | 175 | 4 | 4 | 30 |
| **Rye Wafers** | 2 wafers | 45 | 2 | 0 | 10 |
| **Salad Dressings:** | | | | | |
| blue or Roquefort | 1 tablespoon | 75 | 1 | 8 | 1 |
| French | 1 tablespoon | 65 | 0 | 6 | 3 |
| Italian | 1 tablespoon | 80 | 0 | 9 | 0 |
| mayonnaise | 1 tablespoon | 100 | 0 | 11 | 0 |
| salad, cooked type | 1 tablespoon | 65 | 0 | 6 | 2 |
| Thousand Island | 1 tablespoon | 80 | 0 | 8 | 3 |
| **Salmon:** | | | | | |
| baked | 1 steak (4 ounces) | 210 | 30 | 8 | 0 |
| canned (sockeye or red) | ½ cup, flaked (3 ounces) | 120 | 17 | 5 | 0 |

| Food | Amount | Cal-ories | Pro-tein | Fat | Carbo-hydrate |
|---|---|---|---|---|---|
| **Sardines,** canned in oil | 4 medium (1½ ounces) | 85 | 10 | 5 | 0 |
| **Sauces:** | | | | | |
| barbecue | ¼ cup | 80 | 1 | 0 | 16 |
| chocolate syrup | 2 tablespoons | 100 | 0 | 1 | 26 |
| hard | 2 tablespoons | 140 | 0 | 7 | 16 |
| Hollandaise | 2 tablespoons | 175 | 0 | 17 | 0 |
| spaghetti, canned | | | | | |
|   meat sauce | ½ cup | 100 | 5 | 5 | 8 |
| tomato puree, canned | ½ cup | 45 | 2 | 0 | 10 |
| white, medium | ½ cup | 210 | 4 | 6 | 9 |
| **Sauerkraut** | ½ cup | 20 | 1 | 0 | 4 |
| **Sausage,** cooked | 2 links (16 per pound) | 125 | 5 | 11 | 0 |
| brown and serve | 4 ounces (before brown-ing) | 445 | 15 | 41 | 3 |
| **Scallops,** uncooked | 8 medium (4 ounces) | 90 | 17 | 0 | 5 |
| **Sherbet** | ½ cup | 130 | 1 | 1 | 30 |
| **Shortening,** solid | 1 tablespoon | 110 | 0 | 13 | 0 |
| | 1 cup | 1,770 | 0 | 200 | 0 |
| **Shrimp,** shelled, | | | | | |
| uncooked | 12 to 14 medium (3½ ounces) | 90 | 18 | 1 | 1 |
| unshelled | 1 pound | 285 | 57 | 3 | 5 |
| canned | 3 ounces | 100 | 21 | 1 | 1 |
| **Shrimp Creole** | 1 serving (½ cup rice, ¾ cup sauce) | 300 | 18 | 12 | 29 |
| **Soups** (canned soups are prepared according to label directions): | | | | | |
| bean, black | scant cup (⅓ can) | 80 | 5 | 1 | 12 |
| beef broth | scant cup | 20 | 4 | 0 | 2 |
| beef-noodle | scant cup | 60 | 3 | 2 | 7 |
| chicken broth | scant cup | 20 | 2 | 0 | 2 |
| chicken, cream of | | | | | |
|   (with milk) | scant cup | 135 | 5 | 8 | 11 |
| chicken-gumbo | scant cup | 50 | 2 | 1 | 7 |
| chicken-noodle | scant cup | 55 | 3 | 2 | 7 |
| chicken with rice | scant cup | 45 | 3 | 1 | 5 |
| clam chowder: | | | | | |
|   Manhattan | scant cup | 65 | 2 | 2 | 9 |
|   New England | | | | | |
|     (frozen) | scant cup | 145 | 7 | 6 | 14 |
| consommé | scant cup | 30 | 5 | 0 | 2 |
| minestrone | scant cup | 85 | 5 | 3 | 9 |
| mushroom, cream of | scant cup | 185 | 5 | 13 | 12 |
| onion | scant cup | 30 | 3 | 0 | 3 |
| pea, green | scant cup | 115 | 7 | 2 | 19 |
| potato, cream of | | | | | |
|   (frozen) | scant cup | 160 | 6 | 8 | 15 |
| tomato: clear | scant cup | 70 | 1 | 2 | 12 |
|   cream of | scant cup | 140 | 5 | 6 | 17 |
| turkey noodle | scant cup | 65 | 3 | 3 | 7 |
| vegetable | scant cup | 60 | 3 | 2 | 9 |

| Food | Amount | Cal-ories | Pro-tein | Fat | Carbo-hydrate |
|---|---|---|---|---|---|
| **Spaghetti,** cooked | 1 cup | 155 | 5 | 1 | 32 |
| **Spaghetti Sauce:** | | | | | |
| canned mushroom | 1 cup | 155 | 3 | 6 | 22 |
| canned with cheese | 1 cup | 190 | 6 | 2 | 38 |
| **Spinach or other greens,** | | | | | |
| cooked | ½ cup | 20 | 3 | 1 | 3 |
| **Squash:** | | | | | |
| summer, cooked | ½ cup | 15 | 1 | 0 | 3 |
| winter, cooked | ½ cup | 65 | 2 | 0 | 16 |
| **Starch** (arrowroot, corn, | | | | | |
| etc.) | 1 tablespoon | 30 | 0 | 0 | 7 |
| **Strawberries,** fresh | ½ cup | 25 | 0 | 0 | 6 |
| **Sugar:** | | | | | |
| brown | 1 tablespoon | 50 | 0 | 0 | 13 |
| | 1 cup | 820 | 0 | 0 | 212 |
| granulated | 1 tablespoon | 40 | 0 | 0 | 11 |
| | 1 cup | 770 | 0 | 0 | 199 |
| powdered | | | | | |
| (confectioners') | 1 tablespoon | 30 | 0 | 0 | 8 |
| | 1 cup | 460 | 0 | 0 | 119 |
| **Sundaes:** | | | | | |
| chocolate ice cream with chocolate sauce and chopped pecans | ½ cup ice cream, 2 tablespoons sauce and 2 tablespoons chopped pecans | 355 to 405 (varies with ice cream) | | | |
| vanilla ice cream with butterscotch sauce | ½ cup ice cream, 2 tablespoons sauce | 250 to 300 (varies with ice cream) | | | |
| **Sunflower Seeds:** | | | | | |
| shelled | 1 tablespoon | 45 | 2 | 4 | 1 |
| unshelled | ¼ cup | 45 | 2 | 4 | 1 |
| **Sweetbreads,** calves, | | | | | |
| cooked | ¾ cup (3½ ounces) | 170 | 33 | 3 | 0 |
| **Sweet Potatoes** | **See** Potatoes | | | | |
| **Swordfish,** cooked | 1 steak (4 ounces) | 195 | 31 | 7 | 0 |
| **Syrup:** | | | | | |
| maple | 1 tablespoon | 50 | 0 | 0 | 13 |
| table (corn) | 1 tablespoon | 60 | 0 | 0 | 15 |
| **Tangerine** | 1 (2½-inch diameter) | 40 | 1 | 0 | 10 |
| **Tapioca,** quick-cooking | ¼ cup (4 tablespoons) | 140 | 0 | 0 | 36 |
| **Tea** without sugar or | | | | | |
| cream | 1 cup | 0 | 0 | 0 | 0 |
| **Tomato Juice** | ½ cup (4 ounces) | 25 | 1 | 0 | 5 |
| **Tomatoes:** | | | | | |
| canned | ½ cup | 25 | 1 | 0 | 5 |
| | 1 pound | 95 | 4 | 1 | 20 |
| fresh | 1 medium | 40 | 2 | 0 | 9 |
| **Tongue,** uncooked | 4 ounces | 180 | 14 | 13 | 0 |
| **Tripe,** cooked | 4 ounces | 115 | 22 | 2 | 0 |
| **Trout** (rainbow) | | | | | |
| uncooked | 4 ounces (fillets) | 220 | 24 | 13 | 0 |

| Food | Amount | Cal-ories | Pro-tein | Fat | Carbo-hydrate |
|---|---|---|---|---|---|
| **Tuna:** | | | | | |
| canned in oil | ⅔ cup, drained (3 ounces) | 170 | 24 | 7 | 0 |
| | 7 ounces (undrained) | 576 | 48 | 41 | 0 |
| canned water pack | ⅔ cup (3 ounces) | 110 | 23 | 1 | 0 |
| **Turkey,** roasted (white and dark meat) | 3 ounces | 160 | 27 | 5 | 0 |
| | 1 pound | 855 | 143 | 28 | 0 |
| **Turnips,** white, cooked | ½ cup | 15 | 1 | 0 | 4 |
| **Veal:** | | | | | |
| cutlet, cooked, no bone | 3 ounces | 185 | 23 | 9 | 0 |
| roast, cooked, no bone | 1 slice (3 ounces) | 180 | 23 | 10 | 0 |
| **Vegetable Juice,** canned | ½ cup (4 ounces) | 20 | 1 | 0 | 4 |
| **Vienna Sausage,** canned | 1 sausage | 40 | 2 | 3 | 0 |
| **Vinegar** | 1 cup | 30 | 0 | 0 | 7 |
| **Waffle** | 1 7-inch waffle | 205 | 7 | 8 | 27 |
| **Walnuts,** chopped | | | | | |
| English or black | 1 tablespoon | 50 | 2 | 5 | 1 |
| | 1 cup halves, chopped | 790 | 26 | 75 | 19 |
| **Watercress,** raw | 1 bunch, 3″ long | 20 | 2 | 0 | 4 |
| **Watermelon** | 1 wedge, 4″ x 8″ | 115 | 2 | 1 | 27 |
| **Wheat Germ** | 1 tablespoon | 15 | 1 | 0 | 2 |
| **Whipped Toppings:** | | | | | |
| aerosol | 1 tablespoon | 10 (varies according to brand) | | | |
| frozen or mix | 1 tablespoon | 10 to 25 (varies according to brand) | | | |
| **Whitefish,** uncooked fillets | 4 ounces | 175 | 21 | 9 | 0 |
| **Yams,** cooked | **See** Potatoes | | | | |
| **Yeast:** | | | | | |
| dried brewer's | 1 package active dry | 25 | 3 | 0 | 3 |
| regular | 1 cake, compressed | 20 | 3 | 0 | 3 |
| **Yogurt** | **See** Milk | | | | |
| **Zwieback** | 1 cracker | 30 | 0 | 0 | 5 |

# SODIUM AND IRON CONTENT OF FOODS

The following table gives the sodium and iron content of foods by common serving sizes. All sodium values are rounded to the nearest five milligrams; foods containing less than 2.5 milligrams are listed as zero; values for cooked food may assume salt has been added during cooking. Iron values are rounded to the nearest tenth of a milligram (0.1 milligrams). A dash (—) means no values are available. All values are taken from *Composition of Foods—Raw, Processed, Prepared,* or *Home and Gardens Bulletin Number 72,* both available from the Superintendent of Documents, U.S. Government Printing Office, Washington, D. C. 20402.

| Food | Amount | Iron mg. | Sodium mg. |
|---|---|---|---|
| Almonds | 12 to 14 | .7 | 0 |
| Apple | 1 medium | .4 | 0 |
| Apple Butter | 1 tablespoon | .1 | 0 |
| Apple Juice (Cider) | ½ cup | .7 | 0 |
| Applesauce | ½ cup | .6 | 0 |
| Apricot Nectar | ½ cup | .2 | 0 |
| Apricots: | | | |
| canned in syrup | 4 halves, 2 tablespoons syrup | .4 | 0 |
| dried | 5 large halves | 1.0 | 10 |
| fresh | 3 medium | .5 | 0 |
| Asparagus: | | | |
| fresh or frozen | 6 medium stalks | .6 | 0 |
| canned | 6 medium stalks | 1.8 | 225 |
| Avocado | ½ medium | .6 | 10 |
| Bacon, crisp fried | 2 strips | .5 | 165 |
| Canadian, uncooked | 3 ounces | 2.2 | 1610 |
| Banana | 1 medium | .8 | 0 |
| Barley, pearl | 1 tablespoon, uncooked | .3 | 0 |
| Beans | | | |
| baked, canned with pork and tomato sauce | 1 cup | 4.6 | 1210 |
| green | 1 cup | .8 | 5 |
| lima, fresh | ½ cup | 2.1 | 0 |
| canned | ½ cup | 2.2 | 220 |
| frozen | ½ cup | 1.7 | 115 |
| kidney, canned | 1 cup | 4.6 | 10 |
| wax, canned | 1 cup | 2.9 | 295 |
| fresh | 1 cup | .8 | 0 |
| frozen | 1 cup | .9 | 0 |
| Beef (uncooked, trimmed, lean meat only): | | | |
| chuck | 4 ounces* | 3.6 | 75 |
| flank steak | 4 ounces | 3.6 | 75 |
| porterhouse | 4 ounces | 3.6 | 75 |
| rib roast | 4 ounces | 3.5 | 75 |
| round | 4 ounces | 3.6 | 75 |
| rump | 4 ounces | 3.6 | 75 |
| sirloin | 4 ounces | 3.6 | 75 |

* 4 ounces uncooked meat will make 3 ounces cooked.

| Food | Amount | Iron mg. | Sodium mg. |
|---|---|---|---|
| Beef, dried | 2 ounces | 2.9 | 2440 |
| Beef Stew, canned | 1 cup | 2.8 | 965 |
| Beet greens, cooked | ½ cup | 1.4 | 55 |
| Beets: | | | |
| canned | ½ cup | .7 | 195 |
| fresh | ½ cup | .4 | 35 |
| Biscuit mix | 1 cup | 3.9 | 1620 |
| Biscuits: | | | |
| baking powder | 1 medium | .6 | 240 |
| refrigerated | 1 biscuit | .4 | 190 |
| Blackberries, fresh | ½ cup | .6 | 0 |
| Blueberries, fresh or frozen, | | | |
| unsweetened | ½ cup | .7 | 0 |
| Bluefish: | | | |
| cooked, baked | 4 ounces | .8 | 120 |
| uncooked fillets | 1 pound | 2.7 | 335 |
| Bouillon cubes (beef, chicken, | | | |
| or vegetable) | 1 cube | 0 | 960 |
| Brazil nuts | 2 medium | .3 | 0 |
| Breads: | | | |
| Boston brown | 1 slice | .9 | 120 |
| cracked wheat | 1 slice | .3 | 120 |
| cornbread | 1 slice | 1.3 | 490 |
| French or Italian | 1 slice | .2 | 135 |
| rye | 1 slice | .4 | 130 |
| white | 1 slice | .6 | 115 |
| white, unsalted | 1 slice | .6 | 5 |
| whole wheat | 1 slice | .8 | 120 |
| Bread crumbs, packaged dry | ¼ cup | .8 | 160 |
| Broccoli: | | | |
| fresh, cooked | ½ cup | .6 | 10 |
| frozen, cooked (chopped), | ½ cup | .9 | 10 |
| Brownies (with nuts) | 1 2-inch square | .4 | — |
| Brussels sprouts: | | | |
| cooked fresh | 1 cup | 1.7 | 15 |
| cooked frozen | 1 cup | 1.7 | 20 |
| Butter or margarine: | | | |
| salted | 1 tablespoon | 0 | 140 |
| unsalted | 1 tablespoon | 0 | 0 |
| Buttermilk | 1 cup (8 ounces) | .1 | 320 |
| Cabbage: | | | |
| raw | ½ cup shredded | .1 | 10 |
| | 1 pound | 1.6 | 80 |
| cooked | ½ cup | .2 | 5 |
| Cakes: | | | |
| angel-food | 1 2-inch wedge | .2 | 115 |
| cheesecake (cream-cheese | | | |
| base) | 1 slice (⅛ of cake) | .9 | — |

| Food | Amount | Iron mg. | Sodium mg. |
|------|--------|----------|------------|
| chocolate layer, fudge frosting | 9-inch layer (1/16 of cake) | .6 | — |
| chiffon | 10-inch cake (1/16 of cake) | .4 | — |
| cupcake, unfrosted | 1 medium | .1 | — |
| fruitcake | 2″ x 2″ x ¼″ piece | .4 | — |
| poundcake | 2¾″ x 3″ x ⅝″ piece | .2 | — |
| spongecake | 10-inch tube cake (1/12 of cake) | .8 | — |
| white cake, chocolate frosting | 9-inch layers (1/16 of cake) | .5 | — |
| Candy: | | | |
| caramel, plain | 1 small piece | .1 | 25 |
| chocolate, milk | 1 ounce | .3 | 25 |
| fondant | 1 ounce | .3 | 60 |
| fudge, with nuts | 1 piece (1-inch square) | .2 | 30 |
| gum drops | 1 small | 0 | 0 |
| hard candy | 1 large sour ball | .2 | 5 |
| peanut brittle | 1 ounce | .7 | 10 |
| Cantaloupe | ½ (5-inch diameter) | .8 | 25 |
| Carrots: | | | |
| fresh, cooked | ½ cup diced | .2 | 25 |
| canned, cooked | ½ cup diced | .1 | 170 |
| raw | 1 medium | .4 | 25 |
| | 1 pound (tops trimmed) | 2.6 | 175 |
| Catchup, chili sauce | 1 tablespoon | .1 | 175 |
| Catfish, uncooked | 4 ounces | .5 | 70 |
| Cauliflower: | | | |
| cooked, fresh | 1 cup | .8 | 10 |
| cooked, frozen | 1 cup | .6 | 10 |
| raw | 1 pound (fully trimmed) | 1.9 | 25 |
| Celery: | | | |
| cooked | 1 cup | .3 | 115 |
| raw | 3 small stalks | .2 | 65 |
| | 1 pound | 1.0 | 430 |
| Cereals, cooked: | | | |
| cornmeal (enriched) | ¾ cup | .5 | — |
| farina (enriched) | ¾ cup | .5 | 255 |
| rolled oats | ¾ cup | 1.1 | 385 |
| Cereals, ready-to-eat: | | | |
| corn, rice, wheat flakes | 1 cup (about 1 ounce) | .4 | 280 |
| oat cereal (enriched) | 1 cup (about ⅔ ounce) | 1.2 | 225 |
| puffed rice or wheat (enriched) | 1 cup (about 1 ounce) | .3 | 0 |
| shredded wheat | 1 large biscuit | .9 | 0 |
| wheat bran (100%) | ½ cup (1 ounce) | 3.0 | 370 |
| Cheese: | | | |
| American | 1 slice (1 ounce) | .3 | 320 |
| Camembert | 1 ounce | .1 | — |
| Cheddar | 1 slice (1 ounce) | .3 | 200 |
| cheese food | 1 ounce | .2 | — |

| Food | Amount | Iron mg. | Sodium mg. |
|---|---|---|---|
| cottage, creamed | ⅓ cup | .2 | 170 |
| unsalted | ⅓ cup | .2 | 15 |
| cream | 2 tablespoons | 0 | 70 |
| Parmesan or Romano | 2 tablespoons | 0 | 105 |
| Roquefort or blue | 1 ounce | .1 | — |
| Swiss | 1 slice (1 ounce) | .3 | 200 |
| Cheese soufflé | 1 serving (about 1½ cups) | 1.6 | — |
| Cherries: | | | |
| canned in syrup | ½ cup, 3 tablespoons syrup | .4 | 0 |
| canned, red sour | 1 cup | .7 | 5 |
| fresh, sweet | 1 cup | .5 | 0 |
| Chicken: | | | |
| fryers, breast | 1 whole small (¾ pound) | 3.2 | — |
| leg and thigh | 1 small (½ pound) | 1.9 | — |
| roasted, no bone | 4 ounces | 1.7 | — |
| | 1 cup diced (5 ounces) | 2.1 | 110 |
| Chocolate: | | | |
| semi-sweet | 1 ounce | .7 | — |
| milk | 1 ounce | .3 | 25 |
| unsweetened | 1 ounce | 1.9 | — |
| Chocolate syrup | 1 tablespoon | .3 | 10 |
| Clams, uncooked | 6 (4 ounces, meat only) | 6.9 | 135 |
| Cocoa | 1 tablespoon | .8 | 50 |
| Cocoa, prepared with milk | 1 cup | 1.0 | — |
| Coconut, dried, shredded | ½ cup | 1.1 | — |
| Cod: | | | |
| fresh, uncooked | 4 ounces | .4 | 80 |
| frozen, uncooked | 4 ounces | .4 | 290 |
| Coffee, black, no sugar | 1 cup | 0 | 0 |
| Collards, cooked | ½ cup | .5 | — |
| Cookies: | | | |
| chocolate chip | 1 1½-inch cookie | .2 | 50 |
| fig bar | 1 1½-inch square bar | .2 | 40 |
| gingersnap | 1 2-inch cookie | .2 | 5 |
| macaroon | 1 2½-inch cookie | .2 | 5 |
| oatmeal | 1 3-inch cookie | .4 | 25 |
| sugar | 1 3-inch cookie | .2 | 55 |
| sugar wafer | 1 2½" x ¾" rectangle | 0 | 10 |
| Corn: | | | |
| cooked, canned | 1 cup | 1.0 | 0 |
| cooked, fresh | 1 cup | 1.0 | 0 |
| cooked, frozen | 1 cup | 1.0 | 0 |
| Cornmeal, uncooked (enriched) | 1 cup | 4.0 | 0 |
| Cornstarch, uncooked | 1 tablespoon | 0 | 0 |
| Cornstarch pudding (from mix) | ½ cup | .1 | 160 |
| Crab, canned | 3 ounces | .7 | 840 |
| Crackers: | | | |
| graham | 4 small sections | .4 | 95 |
| oyster | 10 crackers | .2 | 110 |

| Food | Amount | Iron mg. | Sodium mg. |
|---|---|---|---|
| saltines (enriched) | 4 2-inch squares | .1 | 90 |
| soda | 1 2½-inch square | .1 | 110 |
| Cranberries: | | | |
| raw | 1 cup | .5 | 0 |
| Cranberry juice | ½ cup | .4 | 0 |
| Cranberry sauce, canned | 1 tablespoon | 0 | 0 |
| Cream: | | | |
| half-and-half | 1 tablespoon | 0 | 5 |
| heavy | 1 tablespoon | 0 | 5 |
| light | 1 tablespoon | 0 | 5 |
| sour | 1 tablespoon | 0 | 5 |
| Cucumber | 1 medium | .6 | 17 |
| Custard, baked | ½ cup | .5 | 100 |
| Dandelion greens, cooked | 1 cup | 1.6 | 40 |
| Doughnuts, cake-type | 1 medium | .4 | 165 |
| Duck, uncooked | 4 ounces | 1.5 | 85 |
| Eggs: | | | |
| whole | 1 medium | 1.1 | 60 |
| white | 1 average | 0 | 50 |
| yolk | 1 average | 1.1 | 10 |
| Eggplant, raw | 1 slice | .5 | 0 |
| Escarole, raw | 4 leaves | .5 | 0 |
| Flounder, uncooked | 4 ounces | .9 | 90 |
| Flour: | | | |
| unenriched all-purpose | 1 cup, sifted | 3.3 | 0 |
| cake | 1 cup, sifted | .5 | 0 |
| whole wheat | 1 cup, sifted | 4.0 | 5 |
| Frankfurter | 1 medium | .8 | 550 |
| French toast | 1 slice | .7 | — |
| Fruit cocktail, canned | ½ cup fruit and syrup | .5 | 5 |
| Gelatin dessert | ½ cup | 0 | 55 |
| Gelatin, unflavored | 1 envelope | 0 | 0 |
| Ginger Ale | 1 glass (8 ounces) | 0 | — |
| Gingerbread | 2-inch square | 1.0 | — |
| Goose, cooked | 4 ounces | 1.9 | 140 |
| Grapefruit, fresh | ½ medium | .5 | 5 |
| Grapefruit juice: | | | |
| canned | ½ cup | .5 | 0 |
| frozen | ½ cup | .5 | 0 |
| Grapefruit sections, canned | ½ cup | .4 | 0 |
| Grape juice, canned | ½ cup | .1 | 0 |
| Grapes | 20 medium | .3 | 5 |
| Griddlecakes | 2 4-inch cakes | .8 | 340 |
| Guavas | 1 medium | .5 | 5 |
| Haddock: | | | |
| cooked, fried | 4 ounces | 1.2 | 200 |
| uncooked fillets | 1 pound, fresh only | 3.2 | 275 |

| Food | Amount | Iron mg. | Sodium mg. |
|------|--------|---------|-----------|
| Halibut: | | | |
| cooked | 4 ounces | 1.1 | 150 |
| uncooked fillets | 1 pound, fresh only | 3.2 | 245 |
| Herring, smoked | 3 ounces | 1.2 | — |
| Honey | 1 tablespoon | .1 | 0 |
| Honeydew melon | 2-inch wedge | .6 | 20 |
| Ice cream, vanilla | ½ cup | .1 | 30 |
| Ice milk, vanilla | ½ cup | 0 | 65 |
| Jam or jelly | 1 tablespoon | .2 | 0 |
| Junket, vanilla | ½ cup | 0 | 50 |
| Kale, cooked | 1 cup | .6 | 25 |
| Kohlrabi, cooked | ½ cup | .2 | 10 |
| Lamb: | | | |
| cooked chop | 4 ounces | 1.5 | 80 |
| leg, lean meat only | 1 pound uncooked | 8.2 | 340 |
| roast, no bone | 4 ounces | 1.7 | 80 |
| Lard | 1 tablespoon | 0 | 0 |
| Lemon juice, fresh | ¼ cup | .1 | 0 |
| Lemonade, frozen, diluted | | | |
| as directed | 1 cup (8 ounces) | 0 | 0 |
| Lettuce, raw | 3 large leaves | .4 | 5 |
| Liver: | | | |
| beef, uncooked | 4 ounces | 7.4 | 155 |
| calf, uncooked | 4 ounces | 10.0 | 85 |
| chicken, uncooked | 4 ounces | 8.9 | 80 |
| Liverwurst | 2 ounces | 3.0 | — |
| Lobster, fresh, cooked | 3 ounces | .7 | 175 |
| Macaroni: | | | |
| cooked, enriched | ½ cup | .7 | 0 |
| uncooked, enriched | ½ pound | 6.5 | 5 |
| Mackerel, uncooked | 3 ounces | 1.1 | — |
| Mangos | 1 medium | .3 | 15 |
| Margarine: | | | |
| salted | 1 tablespoon | 0 | 150 |
| unsalted | 1 tablespoon | 0 | 1 |
| Marmalade, Jam | 1 tablespoon | .2 | 5 |
| Marshmallow, plain | 1 average | .1 | 5 |
| Milk: | | | |
| buttermilk | 1 cup (8 ounces) | .1 | 320 |
| condensed, sweetened | ½ cup | .1 | 170 |
| evaporated | ½ cup | .1 | 150 |
| nonfat dry-milk powder | ⅓ cup | .1 | 125 |
| skimmed | 1 cup (8 ounces) | .1 | 125 |
| whole | 1 cup (8 ounces) | .1 | 125 |
| yogurt, plain | 1 cup (8 ounces) | .1 | 125 |
| Molasses: | | | |
| light | 1 tablespoon | .9 | 5 |
| dark | 1 tablespoon | 1.2 | 10 |

| Food | Amount | Iron mg. | Sodium mg. |
|------|--------|----------|------------|
| Muffins: | | | |
| blueberry | 1 average | .4 | — |
| bran | 1 average | .8 | — |
| corn | 1 average | .5 | — |
| plain | 1 average | .6 | — |
| Mushrooms: | | | |
| canned | 1 cup | 1.2 | 975 |
| fresh | ¼ pound | .9 | 15 |
| Noodles: | | | |
| cooked | 1 cup | 1.4 | 0 |
| uncooked | ¼ pound | 3.2 | 5 |
| Oils (corn, cottonseed, olive, peanut, soybean) | 1 tablespoon | 0 | 0 |
| Okra, cooked fresh | ½ cup | .4 | 0 |
| Olives: | | | |
| green | 4 medium | .2 | 435 |
| ripe | 3 small | .1 | 85 |
| Onion, raw | 1 medium | .6 | 10 |
| Orange, fresh | 1 medium | .5 | 0 |
| Orange juice | ½ cup | .1 | 0 |
| Orange sections, canned | ½ cup | .8 | 0 |
| Oysters, uncooked | 6 to 8 (4 ounces meat) | 6.2 | 85 |
| Parsnips, cooked | ½ cup | .4 | 5 |
| Peaches: | | | |
| canned | 2 halves, 2 tablespoons syrup | .4 | 5 |
| fresh | 1 medium | .5 | 0 |
| frozen sweetened | ½ cup | .6 | 5 |
| Peanuts: | | | |
| salted | 8 to 10 | .2 | 40 |
| unsalted | 8 to 10 | .2 | 5 |
| Peanut butter | 1 tablespoon | .3 | 95 |
| Pears: | | | |
| canned | 2 halves, 2 tablespoons syrup | .2 | 0 |
| fresh | 1 medium | .5 | 0 |
| Peas: | | | |
| canned | ½ cup | 2.1 | 295 |
| fresh, cooked | ½ cup | 1.4 | 0 |
| frozen, cooked | ½ cup | 1.4 | 145 |
| Pecans, unsalted | 9 medium | .3 | 0 |
| Peppers, green, raw | 1 medium | .5 | 5 |
| Perch (ocean), uncooked | 4 ounces, fresh only | — | 70 |
| Pickles: | | | |
| dill | 1 large | .7 | 1950 |
| sour | 1 large | .3 | 1850 |
| sweet | 1 medium | .2 | — |
| Pie Crust, homemade double crust | 1 9-inch crust | 3.1 | — |

| Food | Amount | Iron mg. | Sodium mg. |
|---|---|---|---|
| **Pies:** | | | |
| apple | 1/7 of 9-inch pie | .4 | 405 |
| cherry | 1/7 of 9-inch pie | .4 | 405 |
| custard | 1/7 of 9-inch pie | .8 | 375 |
| lemon meringue | 1/7 of 9-inch pie | .6 | 340 |
| mince | 1/7 of 9-inch pie | 1.4 | 615 |
| pumpkin pie | 1/7 of 9-inch pie | .7 | 280 |
| Pineapple, canned | ½ cup | .4 | 0 |
| Pineapple juice | ½ cup | .3 | 0 |
| **Plums:** | | | |
| canned | 3 plums, 2 tablespoon syrup | 1.1 | 0 |
| fresh | 1 2-inch plum | .3 | 0 |
| Popcorn, popped, unsalted | 1 cup | .2 | 0 |
| Popover | 1 medium | .5 | — |
| **Pork:** | | | |
| ham, boiled | 1 slice (1 ounce) | .8 | 345 |
| ham, fresh, uncooked (with fat removed) | 4 ounces | 2.5 | 60 |
| ham, cured | 3 ounces, lean meat only | 2.7 | 925 |
| loin chop, uncooked, with fat removed | 4 ounces | 3.3 | 80 |
| **Potatoes:** | | | |
| baked or boiled | 1 medium | .7 | 5 |
| French-fried, frozen | ½ cup | .5 | 5 |
| mashed (butter, salt added) | ½ cup | .4 | 285 |
| Potato chips | 10 medium | .4 | 200 |
| Pretzels | 1 small, or 5 thin sticks | 0 | 170 |
| Prune juice, canned | ½ cup | 5.3 | 5 |
| **Prunes:** | | | |
| stewed | 4 prunes, 2 tablespoons syrup | 1.1 | 5 |
| uncooked | 4 medium | 1.1 | 5 |
| **Puddings:** | | | |
| vanilla from mix | ½ cup | .1 | 125 |
| chocolate from mix | ½ cup | .6 | 175 |
| Pumpkin, canned | 1 cup | .4 | 0 |
| Radishes, raw | 4 small | .4 | 5 |
| Raisins | 1 tablespoon | .4 | 5 |
| Raspberries, fresh | 1 cup | 1.1 | 0 |
| **Rhubarb:** | | | |
| stewed | ½ cup | .8 | 0 |
| uncooked | 1 pound | 2.7 | 5 |
| **Rice:** | | | |
| brown, uncooked | ½ cup | 1.3 | 5 |
| precooked, dry | ½ cup (1 cup cooked) | 1.3 | 0 |
| white, uncooked | ½ cup | 2.7 | 5 |
| white, cooked, unsalted | ½ cup | .9 | 0 |
| wild, uncooked | ½ cup | 3.4 | 5 |
| Rice Krispies | 1 cup | .5 | 280 |
| Rice pudding | ¾ cup | .5 | — |

| Food | Amount | Iron mg. | Sodium mg. |
|------|--------|--------|--------|
| Rolls, plain (enriched) ........ | 1 small (16 per pound) ........ | .5 | 40 |
| | 1 medium (12 per pound) ........ | .7 | 60 |
| | 1 large (8 per pound) ......... | 1.0 | 80 |
| Salad dressings: | | | |
| blue .................... | 1 tablespoon ............. | 0 | 165 |
| French ................. | 1 tablespoon ............. | .1 | 205 |
| Italian ................. | 1 tablespoon ............. | 0 | 315 |
| mayonnaise ............. | 1 tablespoon ............. | .1 | 90 |
| Salmon, canned ............. | ½ cup flaked ............. | .7 | 445 |
| Sardines, canned in oil ........ | 4 medium ............. | 1.2 | 345 |
| Sauces: | | | |
| barbecue .............. | ¼ cup .............. | .1 | 365 |
| chocolate ............. | 2 tablespoons .............. | .6 | 20 |
| Hollandaise ............. | 2 tablespoons .............. | .8 | — |
| spaghetti, canned .......... | ½ cup .............. | 1.8 | 740 |
| white ................. | ½ cup .............. | .1 | — |
| Sauerkraut, canned .......... | ½ cup .............. | .6 | 875 |
| Sausage, uncooked ...... | 4 ounces .............. | 1.6 | 840 |
| Scallops, uncooked frozen ...... | 8 medium (4 ounces) .......... | 2.0 | 285 |
| Sherbet .................... | ½ cup .............. | 0 | 10 |
| Shortening, hydrogenated ...... | 1 tablespoon .............. | 0 | 0 |
| Shredded wheat ............. | 2 medium biscuits ......... | 1.8 | 0 |
| Shrimp, uncooked, fresh ....... | 8 medium (¼ pound) ......... | 1.8 | 155 |
| Soups (canned soups prepared according to label directions): | | | |
| asparagus, cream of ........ | scant cup .............. | .9 | 940 |
| beef-noodle .............. | scant cup .............. | .8 | 795 |
| black bean ............. | scant cup .............. | 1.9 | 860 |
| beef broth ............. | scant cup .............. | .2 | 710 |
| chicken broth ............. | scant cup .............. | .2 | — |
| chicken, cream of .......... | scant cup .............. | .9 | 910 |
| chicken-gumbo ............. | scant cup .............. | .6 | 900 |
| chicken-noodle ............. | scant cup .............. | .4 | 870 |
| chicken with rice .......... | scant cup .............. | .3 | 755 |
| clam chowder, Manhattan .... | scant cup .............. | 1.1 | 720 |
| New England ........... | scant cup .............. | .9 | 920 |
| minestrone ............. | scant cup .............. | .7 | 790 |
| mushroom, cream of ........ | scant cup .............. | .4 | 845 |
| onion ............. | scant cup .............. | .8 | 810 |
| pea ............. | scant cup .............. | 1.3 | 760 |
| potato, cream of .......... | scant cup .............. | .8 | 995 |
| tomato ............. | scant cup .............. | .9 | 810 |
| turkey-noodle ............. | scant cup .............. | .6 | 760 |
| vegetable ............. | scant cup .............. | .9 | 730 |
| Spaghetti sauce: | | | |
| canned meat ............. | scant cup .............. | 3.6 | 1480 |
| canned mushroom .......... | 1 cup .............. | 1.8 | 1760 |
| Spinach: | | | |
| canned, cooked .......... | ½ cup .............. | 2.3 | 210 |

| Food | Amount | Iron mg. | Sodium mg. |
|---|---|---|---|
| fresh, cooked | ½ cup | 2.0 | 45 |
| cooked, frozen | ½ cup | 2.0 | 300 |
| Squash: | | | |
| cooked, summer | ½ cup | .4 | 0 |
| cooked, winter | ½ cup | .8 | 0 |
| Strawberries, fresh | 1 cup | 1.5 | 0 |
| Sugar: | | | |
| light brown | 1 tablespoon | .5 | 45 |
| granulated | 1 tablespoon | 0 | 0 |
| Swordfish steak, cooked | 4 ounces | 1.5 | — |
| Syrup: | | | |
| maple | 1 tablespoon | .2 | 0 |
| corn | 1 tablespoon | .8 | 15 |
| Tangerine | 1 medium | .3 | 0 |
| Tapioca, uncooked | ¼ cup | .1 | 5 |
| Tomatoes: | | | |
| regular, canned | ½ cup | .6 | 145 |
| low-sodium, canned | ½ cup | .6 | 5 |
| fresh | 1 medium | .9 | 5 |
| Tomato juice: | | | |
| regular | ½ cup | 1.1 | 245 |
| low-sodium | ½ cup | 1.1 | 5 |
| Tuna: | | | |
| regular, canned | 4 ounces, drained | 2.0 | 895 |
| low-sodium, canned | 4 ounces, drained | 2.0 | 45 |
| Turkey, roasted | 4 ounces | 2.0 | 145 |
| Turnips, cooked | ½ cup | .3 | 25 |
| Veal (cooked, trimmed, lean meat): | | | |
| cutlet | 3 ounces | 2.7 | 65 |
| roast | 3 ounces | 2.7 | 65 |
| Vegetable juice | ½ cup | .5 | 225 |
| Vinegar | 1 cup | .7 | 0 |
| Walnuts, chopped | 1 tablespoon | .5 | 0 |
| Watermelon | 1 4″ x 8″ wedge | 2.1 | 10 |
| Wheat germ | 1 tablespoon | .4 | 0 |
| Whitefish, uncooked | 4 ounces | .4 | 60 |
| Yams, cooked | 1 medium | 1.0 | 15 |

# *Index*

*347*

## ALLERGY DIETS

## BLAND, LOW-RESIDUE AND GALL-BLADDER DIETS

## DIABETIC DIET

## HIGH-IRON DIET

## LOW-FAT AND/OR LOW-CHOLESTEROL DIET

## LOW-PURINE DIET

## LOW-SODIUM DIETS